Money, Banking, and Financial Markets

Third Edition

Roger LeRoy Miller
Institute for University Studies
Arlington, Texas

David D. VanHoose
Department of Economics
Baylor University

Australia · Canada · Mexico · Singapore · Spain · United Kingdom · United States

THOMSON

SOUTH-WESTERN

Money, Banking, and Financial Markets, Third Edition
Roger LeRoy Miller and David D. VanHoose

VP/Editorial Director:
Jack W. Calhoun

VP/Editor-in-Chief:
Alex von Rosenberg

Publisher:
Steve Momper

Senior Acquisitions Editor:
Michael W. Worls

Developmental Editor:
Katie Yanos

Senior Marketing Manager:
John Carey

Production Project Manager:
Ann Borman

Manager of Technology, Editorial:
Vicky True

Technology Project Editor:
Dana Cowden

Web Coordinator:
Karen Schaffer

Senior Manufacturing Coordinator:
Sandee Milewski

Printer:
R. R. Donnelly
Crawfordsville, Indiana

Art Director:
Michelle Kunkler

Internal Designer:
Ann Borman

Cover Designer:
Larry Hanes

Cover Image:
© Corbis

Compositor:
Parkwood Composition Service

Library of Congress Control Number:
2005933015

For more information about our products,
contact us at:

Thomson Learning
Academic Resource Center

1-800-423-0563

Thomson Higher Education
5191 Natorp Boulevard
Mason, OH 45040
USA

Contents in Brief

Contents

Chapter 3
Domestic and International Financial Markets   45

Unit II   Financial Markets and Instruments   67

Chapter 4
Interest Rates   68

Chapter 5
Foreign Exchange Markets   91

Chapter 6
Managing Risks in the Global Economy— Derivative Securities   120

Chapter 7

Finding the Best Mix of Financial Instruments—The Theory of Portfolio Choice and Efficient Markets 142

Unit III   Financial Institutions   159

Chapter 8

Financial Institutions—An Overview   160

Chapter 12

Economic Consequences of Depository Institution Regulation 252

Unit IV   Central Banking, Monetary Policy, and the Federal Reserve System 275

Chapter 13

Why Money and Banking Go Together– Depository Institutions and Money 276

Global Focus:
The Bank of Japan Confronts the Quantity Theory of Money   395

What Happens When . . .
Deflation Occurs as a Result of Falling Aggregate Demand rather than Increasing Aggregate Supply?   399

Management Focus:
A Retooled U.S. Economy Becomes More Insulated from Oil Price Shocks   403

What Happens When . . .
Banks Can "Sweep" Deposits to Accounts Not Subject to Reserve Requirements?   417

Global Focus:
Why Japanese Banks Hold So Many Excess Reserves   419

Management Focus:
For a While, a "Curve-Flattening" Strategy Paid Off for Investors   430

Chapter 20

What Should the Fed Do?—Objectives and Targets of Monetary Policy 438

Chapter 21

What the Fed Does—Interest Rate Targeting and Economic Activity 468

Chapter 22

Policymaking in the World Economy— International Dimensions of Monetary Policy 490

To the Instructor

A course in money, banking, and financial markets is challenging for both students and instructors. Our key objective in writing the previous editions of *Money, Banking, and Financial Markets* was to provide the student reader with a sophisticated, yet accessible understanding of the subject matter while simultaneously providing the instructor with an up-to-date and sensibly organized presentation of the full range of topics appropriate for a thoroughly modern course.

In this third edition, we have again made every effort to create the most pedagogically sound text in the field. We have sought to produce a quality text that is also affordable. We are very pleased that our text has been selected as a Thomson Advantage book that is being priced well below the more expensive hardcover options available to money and banking instructors. For instructors new to our text who are looking for a high-quality, more affordable option for their students, we have provided a transition guide at the text's home page (**http://money.swcollege.com**) to assist in switching to our text.

Past users will see that we have further enhanced the entire teaching-learning package available to adopters of *Money, Banking, and Financial Markets:*

- Instructors can download the *Test Bank* via firewalled, password-protected links available at the text's home page.

- In order to keep test questions fresh and relevant, a *Supplemental Test Bank* will be available the year following publication of the text.

- The *Instructor's Manual, Test Bank,* and *Study Guide* have all been updated and enhanced.

- The text's **MoneyXtra!** site (**http://moneyxtra.swcollege.com**) now contains online *Pre-Test Quizzes* modeled on test bank questions, so that students can engage in pre-exam warm-ups.

- The text's macro-policy content is focused on the fundamental concepts that students must learn in order to understand how monetary policies influence economic activity.

- We have developed **80** new learning-motivating *Policy Focus, Global Focus, Cyber Focus,* and *Management Focus* features that illustrate the applicability of text materials to up-to-date topics of current interest in the areas of money, banking, and financial markets.

- New to this edition is a feature appearing in each chapter that explains to students *What Happens When* an event that is relevant to the content of that particular chapter occurs in the real world.

Of course, all the resources available in previous editions are available for use by instructors and students:

- In addition to resources available at the text's home page (**http://money.swcollege.com**), the MoneyXtra! Web site offers *E-Link to Another Perspective* **readings** relevant to each chapter. References to these readings have been placed in the margin beside the relevant text. Accompanying each Internet-based reading are interactive online quizzes that students can use to test their comprehension.

■ Another Web-based feature that is available at the MoneyXtra! Web site is an *Online Case Study* that relates. References to these case studies have been placed in the margin beside the relevant text. Each *Online Case Study* includes interactive online quizzes that help students evaluate their understanding of how material covered in the text addresses the situations outlined in the case studies.

■ Interactive *Review Quizzes* covering the material in each chapter of the text are available for students at the text's home page (**http://money.swcollege.com**).

■ **PowerPoint slides** for all figures and tables are available to instructors.

■ *Economics Application* **margin features** steer students, via the MoneyXtra! site, to *EconData* and *EconDebate* Web pages provided by South-Western that closely relate to concepts discussed in the text.

Within the text, we have addressed several fundamental issues that have emerged in recent years by including the following:

■ Fully integrated coverage of international financial markets and the global economy is a fundamental characteristic of the text.

■ Cutting-edge developments in information technology and their economic and financial implications are examined throughout.

■ Current-interest features underlining the real-world relevance of the study of money, banking, and financial markets appear in each chapter.

■ Frequent margin references to Internet resources are included, along with end-of-chapter *Online Application* questions.

■ The more than 150 graphs for this textbook are arguably the best in any text in this area. All lines and curves are color coded in a consistent manner, and we have provided full explanations underneath or alongside each graph or set of graphs.

Complete Coverage of Money, Banking, and Financial Markets

In this third edition, we have trimmed down the book while continuing to cover all of the essential elements of money, banking, and financial markets. These include:

■ The forms, functions, and evolution of money and the emergence of digital cash

■ Domestic and international financial markets and the role of electronic trading

■ Interest rate risk, foreign exchange risk, and derivative securities

■ Portfolio choice, international interest rate parities, and market efficiency

■ Financial institutions, the economics of banking, and issues in bank management

■ Depository institution regulation in a rapidly changing environment

■ The money supply process and the implications of electronic money

■ The Federal Reserve and its role in U.S. and global payment systems

- The linkage between day-to-day Federal Reserve policymaking and aggregate economic activity

- Intermediate monetary policy targets, rules versus discretion, and policy credibility

- Conducting monetary policy with an interest rate target

- International dimensions of monetary policy

Full Global Integration Throughout

Money, Banking, and Financial Markets is the first text in this field to fully integrate global economics and finance, starting with Chapter 1. The student is introduced to world issues in the field from the outset. Every chapter that follows continues this integration within whatever topic area the chapter addresses.

Of course, some chapters focus exclusive attention on international topics. Examples are Chapter 5: "Foreign Exchange Markets," and Chapter 22: "Policymaking in the World Economy—International Dimensions of Monetary Policy."

The Importance of New Information Technologies

Nearly forty years ago, banks and other financial institutions were among the first to perceive the dramatic cost efficiencies and potential revenue enhancements available from adopting information technologies. The true banking information technology revolution took place largely out of sight to the general public, in the "back offices," as financial institutions increasingly became interconnected through automated clearinghouses, large-value payment systems, and interbank funds markets.

Today, however, the information technologies in financial markets are visible to all. Internet brokers have transformed retail stock trading in the United States, and wireless online banking is now commonplace. Students know these changes are under way, and they want to learn more about their potential effects. Yet competing texts at most provide lip service to all these issues. A fundamental objective of this text is to provide students with the background they need to understand the implications of emerging **cybertechnologies** for money, banking, and financial markets.

Features That Teach and Reinforce

In our view, real-world applications should be a key aspect of a textbook on money, banking, and financial markets. To motivate student learning, in this edition we have included 102 new examples drawn from throughout the world. Five types of features are incorporated and referred to throughout the text:

GLOBAL FOCUS: Money, banking, and financial markets can no longer be considered a closed-economy subject. Events that affect the U.S. economy, banking system, and financial markets affect nations around the globe and vice versa. Global issues in money, banking, and financial markets are not only exciting to read about, but also important to understand. We have included among others the following:

- A Pan-African Stock Exchange Tries to Get Off the Ground

- In India, *Badla* Falls on Bad Times

- The German DAX Market Is Literally an Overnight Sensation

- Can the Japanese Life Insurance Industry Be Salvaged?

- A Lender of Last Resort Forestalls a Russian Banking Crisis

- The People's Bank of China Learns That the Real Interest Rate Is What Matters

CYBER FOCUS: The integration of emerging information technologies into banking and other financial services and the effects on financial markets dominate today's financial news. Understanding how these developments affect institutions and markets is now a central subject of the study of money, banking, and financial markets. A few of the topics covered include:

- Online Conversion of Dollars into African Vouchers

- In E-Gold We Trust

- A "Mini" Error Can Have a Large Impact in Electronic Markets

- FDIC-Insured Stored-Value Cards Generate Novel Ideas for "Insured Deposits"

- Will Image Processing Drive the Fed Out of the Check-Clearing Business?

- Student to Parent, "Instead of Sending a Check, How About an Online Transfer?"

POLICY FOCUS: Because policy is so often in the news, we felt it appropriate to include a special feature concerned with just policy issues. These features cover a wide variety of topics including:

- The U.S. Treasury Kick-Starts the Market for Inflation-Protected Securities

- Will an Options Market Put Some Economic Forecasters Out of Work?

- A Banking Law Clause That Isn't Binding—Yet

- A Bank-Realtor Fight Heats Up

- A More Open Discount Window Fails to Generate Additional Borrowing

- Would Imposing a "Tobin Tax" Reduce Exchange Rate Volatility?

MANAGEMENT FOCUS: Businesspeople and individuals managing their personal finances must keep abreast of the most recent developments in money, banking, and financial markets, which continually present both opportunities and challenges. To acquaint students with the variety of monetary, banking, and financial issues faced by managers, we have included features on topics such as the following:

- A Hard Currency for a Borderless State of Mind

- "Zero Percent Interest for Life!"

- Keeping the Temperature Level in Futures Markets

- Too Much Trading Can Be Bad for Your Wealth

■ One Bank Learns—the Hard Way—That Capital Requirements Are for Real

■ Bond Investors Discover the Downside of Inflation Protection

WHAT HAPPENS WHEN **FEATURES:** New to this edition are these features explaining "What Happens When . . ." a real-world event occurs that is relevant to a topic covered in each chapter. Examples include the following:

■ *WHAT HAPPENS WHEN* Banks Run Out of Coins?

■ *WHAT HAPPENS WHEN* You Swipe Your Debit Card?

■ *WHAT HAPPENS WHEN* People Will Accept Currency, but Machines Will Not?

■ *WHAT HAPPENS WHEN* Interest Rates on Repurchase Agreements Fall Below Zero?

■ *WHAT HAPPENS WHEN* Diversification by Some Amplifies Risks for Others?

■ *WHAT HAPPENS WHEN* Businesses Suddenly Stop Purchasing Computers and Software?

■ *WHAT HAPPENS WHEN* Money Is Made More Colorful?

■ *WHAT HAPPENS WHEN* What the Fed Says Is Almost As Important As What It Does?

Critical-Thinking Exercises

Critical thinking is an important aspect of every college student's education. We make sure that students are introduced to critical-thinking activities by ending each *Focus* and *What Happens When* feature with critical-thinking questions called "For Critical Analysis." The suggested answers to these critical-thinking questions are included in the *Instructor's Manual*.

Internet Resources

Most students, particularly those taking intermediate-level economics courses, are familiar with how to use the Internet. We provide six important features for them:

1. *E-Link to an Alternative Perspective:* Readings on topics covered in each chapter, which are referenced in the margin of the book beside the most relevant text, are available at the MoneyXtra! Web site (**http://moneyxtra.swcollege.com**). Each *E-Link to an Alternative Perspective* reading includes interactive online quizzes covering the reading's key points.

2. *Online Case Study:* Case studies concerning the subject matter of each chapter and referenced in the margin beside the most relevant text are also available at the MoneyXtra! Web site. Each *Online Case Study* has accompanying online quizzes addressing the key issues raised by the case study.

3. **Review Quizzes:** At the text's home page (**http://money.swcollege.com**), students can take interactive quizzes on concepts covered in each chapter of the text.

4. *Economics Application* **Margin Features:** These features appear in the margin alongside related text and direct students to the MoneyXtra! site for links to *EconData* and *EconDebate* sites of South-Western College Publishing that closely relate to concepts discussed in the text.

5. ***On the Web* Margin URLs:** New and updated *On the Web* features appear in the margins throughout the book. Each opens with a question linking the feature to the text material and provides brief guidance for navigating through the Web site.

6. **Chapter-Ending *Online Applications:*** Each *Online Application* problem is an extensive Internet exercise that takes the student to a particular URL and then asks him or her to engage in an application. Every *Online Application* also includes a section entitled "For Group Study and Analysis."

Key Pedagogy

Learning cannot occur in a vacuum. We have made sure that students using this text have an ample number of pedagogical devices that will help them master the material.

Fundamental Issues and Answers within the Text of Each Chapter

A unique feature of *Money, Banking, and Financial Markets* is the inclusion of **five to seven fundamental issues** at the beginning of each chapter. Within the text itself, but offset so as not to be a distraction from a student's reading, the fundamental issues are repeated with the **appropriate answers.** Students will find these questions and answers invaluable when reviewing the readings and studying for quizzes and examinations.

Vocabulary Is Emphasized

Because vocabulary is often a stumbling block, we have **boldfaced** all important vocabulary terms within the text. Immediately in the margin these boldfaced terms are defined. They are further defined in the end-of-text glossary.

Chapter Summary

The chapter summary is a numbered point-by-point formatting that corresponds to the chapter-opening fundamental issues, further reinforcing the full circular nature of the learning process for each chapter.

Questions and Problems

Each chapter ends with at least 10 questions and problems. Suggested answers are provided in the *Instructor's Manual.*

Selected References and Further Reading

Appropriate references for materials in the chapter are given in this section.

The Supplements

Money, Banking, and Financial Markets is supported by the strongest set of supplements currently available.

Study Guide

The *Study Guide,* which was written by Jim Lee of Texas A&M University at Corpus Christi, is designed to facilitate active learning by students. It provides summaries of chapter contents, including an application of a key diagram used in each chapter, along with lists of the key terms for students to look for and define in their own words as they read the text. To assist students in testing their understanding of the material, the *Study Guide* also includes 20 multiple-choice and 10 short-answer questions per chapter.

Instructor's Manual

The *Instructor's Manual,* also written by Jim Lee, is designed to simplify the teaching tasks that instructors face. For each chapter it offers an overview of key concepts and objectives, a detailed outline built upon chapter headings in the text, and answers to end-of-chapter questions.

Test Banks

One of the most challenging aspects of teaching is evaluation of student performance. To assist instructors in this endeavor, a *Test Bank* that includes between 25 and 50 multiple-choice questions per chapter, along with correct answers, is available to all adopters of *Money, Banking, and Financial Markets* via links from the text's home page (**http://money.swcollege.com**). In order to keep test questions fresh and relevant, a *Supplemental Test Bank* will be available the year following publication of the text.

PowerPoint Slides

For many instructors, multimedia presentations have become an indispensable part of the teaching-learning process. A complete set of PowerPoint slides is available for adopters of this text.

Acknowledgments

We benefited from an extremely active and conscientious groups of reviewers of the manuscript for this third edition of *Money, Banking, and Financial Markets.* At times they were tough and demanding, but the rewrites of the manuscript improved accordingly. To the following reviewers, we extend our sincere appreciation for the critical nature of your comments that we think helped make this a better text.

Ranjit S. Dighe, State University of New York at Oswego
Carole R. Endres, Wright State University
R.W. Hafer, Southern Illinois University—Edwardsville
Thomas J. Kopp, Siena College
Jim Lee, Texas A&M University—Corpus Christi
Larry L. Lilley, Liberty University
John Stiver, University of Connecticut
Bill Yang, Georgia Southern University

Of course, no textbook project is done by the authors alone. We wish to thank our editor, Mike Worls, for his excellent guidance. In particular, we owe tremendous gratitude to our developmental editor, Katie Yanos, who has provided invaluable feedback and guidance. Our production team of Bill Stryker and Ann Borman put together an excellent design and never let us fall behind. The best copyeditor in the business, Pat Lewis, worked her magic to make the book read more smoothly. Dana Cowden and Vicky True provided indispensable oversight of the process of developing the Internet resources for the text. The folks at Parkwood Composition continue their long tradition of speedily preparing finished pages for us to proof. We always owe them our sincere gratitude.

We anticipate revising this text for years to come and therefore welcome all comments and criticism from both students and professors alike.

R.L.M.
D.D.V.

Dedications:

To Sabine,

Your courage
continues to
amaze me.

RLM

For Michael.

DDV

Unit I
Introduction

Contents

Money in Today's World—

An Introduction

Each year, the U.S. government produces about 70 new coins for every U.S. resident, or about 20 billion new coins in all. About half of all the new coins produced are pennies. Thus, if we add up the dollar value of all coins—pennies, nickels, dimes, quarters, and golden dollars—introduced into circulation each year, the total sum is only a few billion dollars. This is a tiny fraction of the $400 billion average annual increase in one measure of the U.S. money supply over the past six years. The quantity of paper currency also increases each year, but currency growth explains only a portion of the annual growth in the U.S. money supply. In this chapter, you will learn about other contributors to U.S. money growth, such as increases in certain deposit account balances at banks, savings institutions, and credit unions.

Fundamental Issues

1. How have financial globalization and cybertechnologies acted together to alter the economic roles of banking institutions and money?

2. What functions does money perform?

3. How has money evolved?

4. What are monetary aggregates, and how are they constructed?

5. How do changes in payments technologies affect our definitions of money?

What are alternative measures of the quantity of money in circulation? Why are there multiple measures of money? To consider the answers to these questions, you must first understand the functions of money.

Objectives of This Book and How They Relate to You

Not surprisingly, a key objective of this text is to help you understand the roles that money performs in the U.S. and world economies. To achieve this goal, however, you must also learn a substantial amount about banking and financial markets. As you will discover, these topics are closely related, because banks and other similar financial institutions issue checking deposits that are part of the quantity of money that circulates within the economy. This chapter explains the concept of money and discusses how money is measured in today's economy. Chapter 2 reviews the changes sweeping today's banking system, as banks, businesses, and households adopt sophisticated new information technologies in an increasingly interconnected world economy. Chapter 3 presents an overview of modern financial markets, instruments, and institutions. Together, these chapters provide essential background. By the time you have completed this book, you should have a clear understanding of why money is so important to society.

To be sure, if you continue your studies in the field of economics, you will find that knowledge of money, banking, and financial markets is critical to understanding macroeconomics and international trade and finance, as well as growth and development. If you choose a career in finance, the connection between this course and the rest of your courses is perhaps even more obvious. Indeed, one might say that a beginning course in money, banking, and financial markets is the basis of the field of finance. If you are going on to business and management in general, you will face a variety of problems throughout your studies and your business career, all of which will relate in some way to what you are going to learn in this text. After all, businesspersons must make decisions each day about how best to hold excess cash, how to pay for inventory, whether a potential investment should be undertaken, and so on. Managers everywhere face a dizzying array of choices about what kinds of technologies to apply to such tasks, and increasingly their concerns range beyond the borders of their home countries.

Finally, even students who go into other fields can benefit from a course in money, banking, and financial institutions. Virtually everyone uses a checking account, borrows to pay for a car or house, contemplates whether to allocate pension savings to an international asset portfolio, or evaluates the potential advantages of getting connected to a bank via the Internet. Money, banking, and financial markets affect us all.

The Globalization of Money, Banking, and Financial Markets

In years past, courses in money, banking, and financial markets typically covered U.S. banking, the Federal Reserve System, and the influence that each had—both independently and together—on the U.S. economy. This approach is no longer feasible. The U.S. banking system is now intricately linked to world financial markets. Financial booms and busts in such diverse locations as Mexico, the Philippines, Russia, and Argentina increasingly have direct effects on the bottom lines of major U.S. financial institutions.

One reason for this is that today many U.S. companies are multinational firms. These corporate clients of U.S. financial institutions are as likely to have a market presence in an Asian nation as they are to have business interests in Europe. Thus, when an economic downturn in Asia affects the fortunes of many U.S.-based companies, the performance of those companies' banks is also affected.

Another reason is that nowadays it is harder to determine where domestic U.S. financial markets end and the global marketplace begins. A major U.S. bank that hopes to make a big loan to a U.S.-based multinational construction company may face competition from banks located in Berlin or Hong Kong. The same bank may raise funds by issuing deposits to individuals or firms in Japan or Australia.

At the same time, events in the United States have significant implications for other nations. People around the world scrutinize the nuances of Federal Reserve policy pronouncements for hints of how they may influence such far-flung locales as Hong Kong, Brazil, Croatia, and South Africa. If the Federal Reserve engages in policy actions that raise U.S. interest rates, savers worldwide may be inclined to sell bonds from these and other countries so that they can purchase U.S. Treasury bonds. In contrast, if the Federal Reserve enacts policies that reduce U.S. interest rates, firms and governments in these and other nations may be able to raise funds from around the world at lower interest rates, thereby improving their near-term growth prospects.

MONEYXTRA!
Another Perspective

To read a detailed evaluation of dollarization around the globe and test your understanding of the concept, go to the Chapter 1 reading, entitled "Dollarization: A Scorecard," by Roberto Chang of the Federal Reserve Bank of Atlanta. **http://moneyxtra. swcollege.com**

In the twenty-first century, the subject of money and banking is unavoidably *international.* This does not mean the subject is any harder to learn than it was in years past. Indeed, the globalization of money and banking in many ways makes it an even more diverse and fascinating area of study.

Money and Banking in the Digital Age

In some respects, the globalization of money and banking is a return to the past. Not until the late 1990s did the relative volumes of world trade—worldwide exports and imports in proportion to total production of goods and services—finally regain the levels they had achieved before the outbreak of World War I in 1914. Thus, the international dimension of money, banking, and financial markets is not entirely new. Where there is trade, there are banks and credit, so it is natural that money, banking, and financial market issues now span national borders.

Back to the Future

Undoubtedly, a "back to the future" component distinguishes today's globalization of money and banking from the experience of the late nineteenth and early twentieth centuries. Before cables were laid across the Atlantic Ocean, it took days for news of a European financial collapse to reach U.S. shores. Even after cables were in place, hours or even days might pass before U.S. savers responded to the news. Now, of course, satellites have reduced the informational delays to minutes or even seconds. Millions of people are on the Internet at any given instant, learning about the financial news literally as it happens. At the click of a button, many of these people can now adjust their own financial positions within seconds after they see the news on their screens.

Cybertechnologies

Cybertechnologies: Technologies that connect savers, investors, traders, producers, and governments via computer linkages.

In the area of money and banking, the development of **cybertechnologies,** which are computer-based techniques for linking savers, investors, traders, producers, and governments, has fundamentally altered the landscape. This has occurred most clearly in the international realm. Late-afternoon financial news in Paris is available instantly to those who are trading in the late morning in the New York financial markets. These individuals can react quickly using the same computers that give them the news, so the Paris and New York financial markets are linked more intimately than at any previous time in history. So, too, are the markets in London and Chicago and the markets in Philadelphia and Tokyo. Even in the absence of the boom in world trade in the latter part of the twentieth century, cybertechnologies would surely have produced nearly as much international financial interdependence as we see today. The growth in world trade has simply increased the volumes of financial flows across borders that cybertechnologies have made possible.

IMPLICATIONS FOR BANKS AND THEIR CUSTOMERS As we shall discuss throughout this book, cybertechnologies promise to transform many aspects of the banking business. In fact, in many ways they already have. Most major banks commonly announce annual targets for growth in online accounts alongside traditional targets for asset growth and profitability. Banks and other providers of mortgage funds now post Web sites for Internet mortgage-loan shopping. Consortiums of banks currently are pursuing alternative cybertechnologies of the not-too-distant future. These include voice recognition systems for deposit withdrawals and software that permits borrowers to download consumer loans onto computer chips on their home personal computers. Then the borrowers can transfer the value of these

CYBER
Focus

Online Conversion of Dollars into African Vouchers

How does a Kenyan or Ugandan immigrant to the United States most easily convert hard-earned U.S. cash into groceries, visits to physicians, and other products for family members still living in Africa? One option is available at the Web site of Mama Mike's. This Nairobi-based service allows individuals to purchase vouchers online. Their family members in Africa are then notified that vouchers are available for them to pick up and spend at participating merchants throughout Kenya and Uganda.

FOR CRITICAL ANALYSIS: In what ways are vouchers such as those issued through Mama Mike's service both like and unlike a government's currency?

---

loans to plastic cards to use when they go shopping. Furthermore, these new cybertechnologies provide the capability to purchase items over the Internet using electronic cash or checks. (Nowadays, it is also possible to go online to purchase vouchers that can be exchanged for goods and services, some of which can be used in other countries; see the *Cyber Focus: Online Conversion of Dollars into African Vouchers.*)

IMPLICATIONS FOR POLICYMAKERS   These developments make money and banking one of the most interesting subjects in economics for any student. As you will learn, they also promise to complicate the lives of policymakers. Previously, a policymaker who made a mistake could "weasel out of it" during the following days and weeks. Now, a big policy mistake can cause rapid market swings within hours or even minutes. On net, the new cybertechnologies promise many social gains. At the same time, however, they raise a number of important issues about monetary and financial policymaking. What is money? Should national and even international regulations, and the institutions that design and enforce those regulations, seek to determine what money will be like in the new world of banking? How will these decisions influence the world economy? These are themes that will surface throughout this text.

> **1. How have financial globalization and cybertechnologies acted together to alter the economic roles of banking institutions and money?** Increased financial globalization has been an inevitable by-product of a significant growth in international trade. Nevertheless, the globalization of money and banking has been hastened by the advent of cybertechnologies that link financial institutions and markets without regard to national borders. In this respect, globalization and the development of cybertechnologies have worked hand in hand to bring about sweeping changes in money and banking.

Money: Its Functions, Forms, and Evolution

Any item that people are generally willing to accept in exchange for goods, services, and financial assets such as stocks or bonds is **money.** Many of us naturally think of money as coins or dollar bills. Most of what constitutes today's money, however, is in accounts in institutions such as banks, savings institutions, and credit unions.

Money: Anything that functions as a medium of exchange, store of value, unit of account, and standard of deferred payment.

Money's Functions

Money performs four key functions. It is a medium of exchange, a store of value, a unit of account, and a standard of deferred payment.

Medium of exchange: An attribute of money that permits it to be used as a means of payment.

Barter: The direct exchange of goods, services, and financial assets.

MEDIUM OF EXCHANGE   The fundamental function of money is to serve as a **medium of exchange.** This means that people who trade goods, services, or financial assets are willing to accept money in exchange for these items. By using money, people avoid engaging in **barter,** or the direct exchange of goods, services, and financial assets. Barter is a very costly activity, because it requires finding others willing to exchange items directly. A key reason that people use money is to avoid this cost.

Store of value: An attribute of money that allows it to be held for future use without loss of value in the meantime.

STORE OF VALUE   Nevertheless, money has other important functions. One is its use as a **store of value.** An individual can set money aside today with an intent to purchase items at a later time. Meanwhile, money retains value that the individual can apply to those future purchases. For example, funds that a college student keeps in a checking account during summer months may be used to pay tuition or to purchase textbooks when the fall semester begins.

Unit of account: An attribute of money that permits it to be used as a measure of the value of goods, services, and financial assets.

UNIT OF ACCOUNT   Money also functions as a **unit of account,** which means that people maintain their financial accounts by using money to value goods, services, and financial assets. Households and businesses quote prices of goods, services, and financial assets in terms of money. For instance, retail stores throughout the United States express the prices of their goods in dollars.

Standard of deferred payment: An attribute of money that permits it to be used as a means of valuing future receipts in loan contracts.

STANDARD OF DEFERRED PAYMENT   Finally, money serves as a **standard of deferred payment.** People agree to loan contracts that call for future repayments in terms of money. These contracts defer repayment of a loan until a later date. Parties to the contract agree to meet financial terms specified in units of money.

> **2. What functions does money perform?**   Money is a medium of exchange through which people make payments for goods, services, and financial assets. In addition, money is a store of value; that is, it is a repository of wealth across time. Money is also a unit of account, meaning that sellers quote prices in money terms. Finally, money is a standard of deferred payment, meaning that loans are extended and repaid using money.

Double coincidence of wants: The situation when two individuals are simultaneously willing and able to make a trade; a requirement for barter.

Commodity money: A good with a nonmonetary value that is also used as money.

Commodity standard: A money unit whose value is fully or partially backed by the value of some other physical good such as gold or silver.

Fiat money: A token that has value only because it is accepted as money.

Methods of Exchange and the Evolution of Money

The earliest economies relied on barter. A person who wished to exchange a good or service had to find a second individual willing to purchase that good or service. Yet that second person also had to possess a good or service that the first person desired as well. Thus, barter requires a **double coincidence of wants:** two individuals must simultaneously be willing and able to make a trade.

The history of money began with a movement away from barter to **commodity moneys,** or physical goods with *both* nonmonetary *and* monetary uses. Societies then progressed from commodity moneys to **commodity standards,** or standardized tokens whose value is backed by the value of a physical monetary good, such as gold or silver. They then adopted **fiat moneys,** or forms of money not backed by anything except faith in its universal acceptance in trade. Today we are observing the continuation of this evolution, with the emergence of **electronic money** (or *e-money*), which is money that people can transfer directly via electronic impulses instead of via coins, paper currency, or checks.

Electronic money (e-money): Money that people can transfer directly via electronic impulses.

COMMODITY MONEYS AND THE PURCHASING POWER OF MONEY Today's moneys are not linked to gold or other commodities. Nevertheless, we can learn much about the workings of any monetary economy from studying how a commodity money system functions. Table 1-1 lists some of the different types of commodity moneys that have existed throughout history. Any commodity money, such as tobacco, tortoise shells, goats, or a metal, typically has value in alternative uses. Metals such as gold or silver are especially easy to divide into smaller units, so they ultimately emerged as the most common type of commodity money. Gold and silver were portable, durable, very recognizable, and, most important, valued highly by nearly everyone because of their relative scarcity and intrinsic usefulness.

Since the beginnings of civilization, people have used gold to craft jewelry and other forms of ornamentation. Later, people learned how to use gold in manufacturing, finding it particularly useful for electrical connectors in devices such as stereo components and computer equipment. Whether used for monetary or other purposes, gold has a price. If gold is a commodity money, as it was in years past, then the price of gold is measured in terms of other goods and services that individuals must give up in exchange for gold. (Keep in mind that in a true gold commodity money system, there are no dollars, pesos, yen, and the like to use as units of account for pricing gold or any other goods and services.) Because the price of gold is measured in units of goods and services per unit of gold, it tells us how many units of goods and services a unit of gold can buy. Thus, the market price of gold measures the equilibrium **purchasing power of money,** or gold's value as a monetary good that people can use to purchase other goods and services.

Purchasing power of money: The value of money in terms of the amount of real goods and services it buys.

A COMMODITY STANDARD A major drawback to using gold or silver as money is that lumps of gold or silver may have different market values because the purity or density of the metal in the lumps can vary. Before sellers accepted gold or silver in exchange, they typically had to verify the purity and weight of the metal that the buyer had offered. To avoid this costly and time-consuming process, people began to use *standardized* units of gold and silver. A monetary system in which the value of the medium of exchange depends on the value of gold

Table 1-1   Different Types of Money

Iron	Corn	Whale teeth	Round stones with
Copper	Salt	Boar tusks	centers removed
Brass	Crystal salt bars	Red woodpecker scalps	Knives
Gold	Horses	Feathers	Pots
Silver	Sheep	Leather	Boats
Wine	Goats	Pitch	Slaves
Rum	Cows	Glass	Paper
Molasses	Tortoise shells	Polished beads	Playing cards
Tobacco	Snail shells	(wampum)	Cigarettes
Rice	Porpoise teeth	Agricultural implements	

Gold standard: A monetary system in which the value of money is linked to the value of gold.

Bimetallic standard: A monetary system in which the value of money depends on the values of two precious metals, such as gold and silver.

is a **gold standard.** When silver served as the underlying commodity for the system, a *silver standard* was in force. Some nations have used both gold and silver as the basis for their monetary systems. A system in which the value of money depends on the values of two precious metals is a **bimetallic standard.**

With gold, silver, or bimetallic standards, people took gold or silver dust or nuggets to a goldsmith, who crafted the dust or nuggets into tokens of equal purity and weight. The goldsmith typically stamped the token to verify that this had been done. To make the tokens more portable and recognizable, they were often formed into flat, disk shapes that came to be called *coins.*

PROLIFERATION OF THE USE OF COINS   Ultimately, coins became the main form of money for two reasons. One was that many shopkeepers would accept only coins validated by a goldsmith's stamp. The other was that governments got involved. In the eighth century, King Pepin the Short of France (the father of Charlemagne) introduced the first governmental system of coinage. He decreed that a pound of silver would be divided into 240 "pennies." Twelve pennies were equal to one-twentieth of a pound of silver, which in turn was exchangeable for a "solidus" of gold as defined by the Byzantine Empire during the third and fourth centuries. In England, a solidus was known as a "shilling," so twelve of the French silver coins were equal to an English shilling.

From the eighth century until our own time, commodity standards were the predominant type of monetary system. Governments either regulated or operated mints that produced coins. The rationale for government regulation of the minting process was to maintain public confidence in a nation's money. Many governments, however, got into the business of producing money for a more basic reason: they could profit from it. Mints owned and operated by rulers or their agents would purchase gold or silver in the form of dust or nuggets. Then they would produce coins that were issued at a face value that typically exceeded the value of the gold or silver content of the coins. The treasury would keep the difference, which was known as **seigniorage.** Seigniorage essentially amounted to a tax, because it was a transfer from citizens to the government.

Seigniorage: The difference between the market value of money and the cost of its production, which is gained by the government that produces and issues the money.

THE ECONOMIC WORKINGS OF A COMMODITY STANDARD   For much of the world's financial history, gold was the centerpiece of the international monetary system. Under the gold standard, which functioned off and on from the early 1800s until the 1930s, the underpinning of a nation's monetary system was the quantity of gold. As in a gold commodity system, people used gold for both nonmonetary and monetary purposes. The quantity of gold devoted to monetary use was called **gold bullion.** Gold bullion functioned as the nation's **monetary base,** or the underlying, "base" amount of money that is the foundation for the entire monetary system.

Gold bullion: Within a gold standard, the amount of gold used as money.

Monetary base: A "base" amount of money that serves as the foundation for a nation's monetary system. Under a gold standard, the amount of gold bullion; in today's fiat money system, the sum of currency in circulation plus reserves of banks and other depository institutions.

Under a typical gold commodity standard, people no longer measure prices of goods and services in units of gold. Instead, they quote prices in *currency units* such as dollars per unit of goods and services. Thus, a currency, which may be in the form of coins and/or paper money, functions as the medium of exchange, unit of account, store of value, and standard of deferred payment. The currency's value, however, is linked directly to gold via a *rate of exchange* between the nation's currency and gold. In most historical instances, a "central bank," such as a private bank like the Bank of England (which was privately owned and operated from 1694 to 1946) or a government agency such as the Federal Reserve, has "pegged" the exchange rate of currency (pounds or dollars) for gold. Central banks accomplished this task by standing ready to buy or sell any amount of gold at the fixed rate of exchange, thereby ensuring that no one else would be able to buy gold for less or sell gold for more than that "pegged" currency price of gold. For example, in a situation where the central bank's gold bullion equals 1 million ounces and the governmentally established dollar-gold exchange rate is $30 per ounce of gold, the total *dollar value* of the gold bullion—the dollar value of the nation's monetary base—under the gold standard is equal to $30 per ounce times 1 million ounces of gold, or $30 million.

Once a central bank establishes the currency price of gold, it can influence the quantity of money by regulating the ratio of coins or notes that private mints or banks issue relative to the amounts of gold they hold as assets, or the *gold reserve ratio*. In this way, the central bank can influence the quantities of both coins (and/or notes) and gold bullion. That is, it can influence the total amount of money.

SEIGNIORAGE AND DEBASEMENT UNDER A COMMODITY STANDARD

Because variations in the quantity of money typically affect an economy's price level, governments have had an incentive to become involved in the supervision of national monetary systems. Indeed, in the past many governments have required that their citizens use only government-produced money as the single, legal medium of exchange. If a government assumes this power—perhaps by operating the nation's central bank—it becomes a *monopoly producer* of money. In such an environment, the government is the only entity from which a nation's residents can obtain a legally recognized, widely accepted medium of exchange.

To maintain their positions as the sole producers of money, governments typically would impose stiff penalties for violating laws requiring the use of their coins in all exchanges. Because the governments profited from producing money, they had a clear motive for doing this: to keep up the demand for their coins. If a government were to permit its residents to use other types of money, then the willingness of the nation's citizens to use its coins might decline, reducing the government's seigniorage earnings. As a result, the government would have fewer resources to expend on governmentally sponsored activities, such as construction of plush government offices, maintenance of a national defense, or other endeavors.

For centuries governments implemented commodity standards, including gold standards, almost solely through coinage. The idea was that the coins' metal content gave them inherent value. Eventually, however, governments mastered the trick of coin **debasement;** they reduced the gold base of the coins by mixing in other metals such as bronze or copper, thereby boosting seigniorage.

Debasement: A reduction in the amount of precious metal in a coin that the government issues as money.

Once governments learned how to debase their coins, they quickly discovered other, even cheaper ways to make money production less expensive. After all, debasement effectively broke the link between the value of the money unit (the coin) and the value of the commodity standard (the gold or silver in the coin). To save themselves the trouble of melting down coins and debasing them, governments began such practices as "coin clipping," or physically cutting out a section—say, a fourth—of each coin and declaring that the value of the clipped coin was the same as before. They could then keep the clippings to mint additional coins. On net, coin production costs were reduced further, and governments earned more seigniorage.

The next step was paper money. Although some European nations experimented with paper money from time to time, American colonists were the first to accept the idea of paper-based commodity standards. Because gold and silver were particularly scarce in the first colonies, the colonial governments issued paper money backed by the value of European (typically English or Spanish) coins. Thus, colonial paper money was backed by European coins, which in turn were backed by gold or silver. This allowed the colonies to *indirectly* use a commodity standard. (A Buddhist guru in Iowa recently issued his own paper currency; see the *Management Focus: A Hard Currency for a Borderless State of Mind.*)

FIAT MONEYS   The colonial governments quickly became frustrated with using an indirect approach to creating the money desired by residents of the growing North American economy. Despite efforts by the British Parliament in 1751 and 1764 to stop them, colonies began issuing paper moneys in the form of *bills of credit* that the governments promised to redeem at a future date. The colonial governments used these bills of credit to purchase items or construct public works projects. Those who obtained the bills of credit in exchange used them as media of exchange for other goods. As long as people believed that the governments could raise sufficient tax revenues to redeem the paper bills as promised, the bills circulated as money.

The First Federal Money   Bills of credit were the first American paper moneys. They also were the first step toward today's fiat money system, because the values of the moneys that the colonial governments issued were no longer linked to commodities. Instead, the value of money depended on people's confidence in the taxing authority of the government. This was also true of the "Continentals" issued by the union of colonies during and after the American Revolution. Unfortunately for this paper money, however, people lost confidence in the taxing power of the confederation of colonies. The value of the Continental money plummeted, giving rise to the popular phrase "not worth a Continental."

From a Gold Standard to Fiat Money   Throughout much of its history, the U.S. government sought to maintain a gold standard, although there were experiments with paper bills of credit from time to time. As the nation's banking system grew dramatically, banknotes and checking accounts became more widespread. Nevertheless, until 1971 the U.S. dollar was tied

---

MANAGEMENT

Focus

A Hard Currency for a Borderless State of Mind

Four decades ago, the Maharishi Mahesh Yogi was best known as a guru to the 1960s rock and roll band called the Beatles. Today he is the head of his own "country," which he refers to as a "borderless state of mind" called the Global Country of World Peace. This "country" has its own currency, the Raam Mudra (or simply, *raam*), which has been printed in notes of one-, five-, and ten-raam denominations.

In Vedic City, Iowa, more than 3,000 of the Maharishi's followers consider themselves part of the Global Country of World Peace. Many of them are students at the Maharishi University of Management. The university, which is located in this Iowa town, offers programs of study that include both an accredited MBA degree and a curriculum in a form of levitation known as "yogic flying." The official currency of the university is the raam. Backing the currency's value in the town is another item: $40,000 in U.S. dollars that the Maharishi has on deposit at Iowa State Bank and First National Bank of Fairfield, Iowa. Anyone in Vedic City who receives a raam-denominated payment from a Maharishi University student but would prefer to have dollars to spend elsewhere in the United States can trade 1 raam for $1 at either of these banks.

FOR CRITICAL ANALYSIS: In what way is the raam similar to a commodity money?

to gold in some fashion. In that year the United States renounced its commitment to the gold standard that was in place at the time. Under this gold standard, the U.S. government had formally tied the value of the dollar to a fixed amount of gold, and other nations in turn linked their currencies to the dollar. In 1971 the United States broke the dollar's ties to gold. And in 1973 most other developed nations agreed to allow their own currencies to "float" in value relative to the dollar. Effectively, the United States and other developed nations decided to experiment with a fiat money system. At present we are in the fourth decade of this "experiment." (For many of the world's nations, this experiment has resulted in currency notes in large denominations ending in numerous zeros; see the *Global Focus: Zeroing Out an Excess of Zeros.*)

In a fiat money system, money has value *only* because it is acceptable as a medium of exchange. In the past, governments issued fiat money in the form of paper currency or cheap metal coins. But the only paper money of the federal government (the U.S. Treasury) today consists of U.S. notes called "greenbacks" that were used to finance the Civil War and that technically are still in circulation (but held by collectors). Most paper money today is issued by central banks. For instance, look at the paper currency that you use. It is composed of "Federal Reserve notes" issued by the Federal Reserve System—an agency that functions as the central bank of the United States. In addition, many private financial institutions legally issue fiat money in the form of checkable deposits that we think of as "checking accounts." Banks, savings and loan associations, and credit unions are examples of such institutions. This is a key reason that we devote much discussion to these institutions in subsequent chapters.

E-MONEYS   Depository institutions remain central to the workings of today's fiat money economy. Nevertheless, their role will continue to evolve as a result of the growing use of e-money. A computer scientist calls e-money a form of "cryptographic algorithm," or secure programming placed upon a microchip embedded within a plastic card. This programming enables the microchip to communicate with similar chips located in electronic cash registers at retail outlets and automated teller machines operated by banks. The bearer of an e-money card can use such peripheral devices to authenticate the validity of the value stored on the card, transfer value from the card, or receive and store additional value.

GLOBAL
Focus

Zeroing Out an Excess of Zeros

Until recently, inflation was so rampant in Turkey that individuals routinely held billions of *lire*, the Turkish currency. Banks commonly transmitted large-value payments denominated in trillions or even quadrillions of lire. All these extra zeros complicated the task of Turkish accountants and statisticians, who commonly spent much of their time making sure they had included the correct number of digits in financial statements and data spreadsheets.

In at effort to end the complexities involved in keeping track of such large numbers of lire, on January 1, 2005, the Turkish government stripped six zeros from its currency so that instead of 1,800,000 lire being equal to 1 euro, only 1.8 lire were equal to 1 euro. This action made Turkey the fiftieth nation in recent years to slash excess zeros from its currency. Other recent examples include Romania, which cut four zeros from its currency, and Bulgaria and Afghanistan, each of which eliminated three zeros.

FOR CRITICAL ANALYSIS: What do you suppose happened to the prices of goods and services in Turkey, Romania, Bulgaria, and Afghanistan after each of these nations redefined its currency?

In E-Gold We Trust

At the Web site **http://www. e-gold.com**, an individual can open an account to use an e-money that is a throwback to the days of commodity moneys. This money, called "e-gold," is fully backed by gold bars stored in repositories certified by the London Bullion Market Association. An account

holder purchases an amount of e-gold based on the weight of actual gold backing the e-money.

E-gold.com's online payment system allows individuals to arrange to make a payment equal to, say, 10 troy ounces worth of e-gold to another authorized account holder located anywhere in the world. For those who prefer to keep track of their e-gold in dollars, euros, or

six other national fiat moneys, the system also automatically permits denomination of e-gold payments in these currencies as well.

FOR CRITICAL ANALYSIS: What feature of the e-gold payment system limits the extent to which this form of e-money can function as a medium of exchange?

E-money, therefore, is a new "token" that people today can use to engage in trade. As such, it may emerge as simply a modern elaboration of fiat money via a new technology, with government-issued currency residing primarily on microchips instead of paper printed by the Bureau of Engraving and Printing. As we shall discuss in more detail in the next chapter, however, the advent of e-money has the potential to more dramatically alter the nature of our fiat money system. (One form of e-money, however, has nothing to do with any of the world's government-issued fiat moneys; see the *Cyber Focus: In E-Gold We Trust.*)

3. How has money evolved? The earliest system of exchange was barter, or the direct exchange of goods and services without the use of money. Barter suffers from the problem of double coincidence of wants, which the use of money helps to solve. Initially, people used commodity moneys that they could apply both for making exchanges and for nonmoney purposes. Later they adopted commodity standards by using tokens with values related to the value of a physical good such as gold. At this point governments often became involved in the production of money because they could earn seigniorage by issuing units of money with a value exceeding the per-unit cost of production. Efforts to reduce the cost of producing money helped pave the way for the development of fiat money not backed by the value of any particular commodity and, today, for the potential emergence of e-money.

Defining and Measuring the Amount of Money in Circulation

Students are often surprised to learn that economists have trouble agreeing about how to define and measure the amount of money in circulation. Some economists believe that what we call "money" should be whatever functions solely as an immediately available means of payment, such as paper currency and coins, checking accounts, and traveler's checks. Other economists, however, believe that this approach is too narrow because money is also a store of value. They argue that other accounts, such as savings deposits and other easily redeemable assets, are so easy to convert into a medium of exchange that we should count them, too.

This dispute revolves around the notion of **liquidity,** or the ease with which an asset can be sold or redeemed for a known amount of cash at short notice and at low risk of loss of nominal value. To those who emphasize the medium-of-exchange approach to measuring money, money consists of currency and coins, checking accounts, and traveler's checks because they are the most obviously liquid of assets. They *already* are cash, so there is no "redeeming" to do. But those who emphasize money's function as a store of value point out that many assets in today's world are extremely liquid. Although they technically are not the medium of exchange, their owners can easily convert them for such use.

There is no simple solution to this dispute. Reasonable people on both sides can make good arguments. As we shall see, the Federal Reserve System—our central bank, commonly called "the Fed"—has sought to satisfy both groups by defining and measuring money in more than one way. The measures of money that the Fed reports are sums of various groupings of financial assets. For this reason, the Fed calls them **monetary aggregates.** These monetary aggregates differ according to the liquidity of the assets that are included or excluded.

The Monetary Base

The *monetary base,* which economists sometimes call "high-powered money," is the narrowest measure of money. In today's fiat money system, it is the amount of money produced directly by actions of the government or a central bank that acts on its behalf. The U.S. monetary base is the sum of currency *outside* the government, the Fed, and depository institutions plus reserves of depository institutions.

CURRENCY   In the United States, **currency** has two main components. One is the dollar value of coins (mainly pennies, nickels, dimes, and quarters) minted by the U.S. Treasury and held *outside* the Treasury, the Federal Reserve banks, and depository institutions. The other is the dollar value of Federal Reserve notes issued by Federal Reserve banks. As stated earlier, some currency notes issued in the past by the U.S. Treasury remain in circulation, but they are a very small part of total currency.

DEPOSITORY FINANCIAL INSTITUTION RESERVES   Commercial banks, savings banks, savings and loan associations, and credit unions are **depository financial institutions** or, more simply, *depository institutions.* These institutions issue checking and savings deposits that are key components of broader measures of money. Depository institutions also must hold funds on deposit with Federal Reserve banks. These funds and the cash that the institutions hold in their vaults constitute the institutions' **reserves.** The source of these funds is the Fed itself, as we shall discuss in greater detail in Chapter 13.

Panel (a) of Figure 1-1 on the next page displays the relative sizes of these two components of the monetary base. The percentages shown here are typical figures that we would observe at any time. Currency normally is the bulk of the monetary base.

M1:   A Basic Definition of "Cash"

A broader definition of money, a monetary aggregate called **M1,** is shown in panel (b) of Figure 1-1. This measure of the quantity of money—which the *Wall Street Journal* and other publications often call "the money supply"—has three components: currency, traveler's

Liquidity: The ease with which an asset can be sold or redeemed for a known amount of cash at short notice and at low risk of loss of nominal value.

Monetary aggregate: A grouping of assets sufficiently liquid to be defined as a measure of money.

On the Web
How have depository institution reserves changed in recent months? Find out by viewing the Federal Reserve's H.3 *Statistical Release* at **http://www. federalreserve.gov/releases/**.

Currency: Coins and paper money.

Depository financial institutions: Financial institutions that issue checking and savings deposits that are included in measures of money and that legally must hold reserves on deposit with Federal Reserve banks or in their vaults.

Reserves: Cash held by depository institutions in their vaults or on deposit with the Federal Reserve System.

M1: Currency plus transactions deposits.

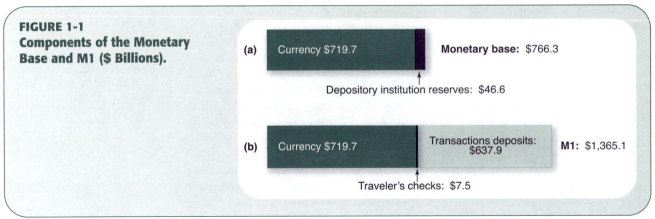

FIGURE 1-1
Components of the Monetary Base and M1 ($ Billions).

(a) Currency $719.7 — **Monetary base:** $766.3

Depository institution reserves: $46.6

(b) Currency $719.7 — Transactions deposits: $637.9 — **M1:** $1,365.1

Traveler's checks: $7.5

SOURCE: Board of Governors of the Federal Reserve System, H.6(508) *Statistical Release,* June 9, 2005.

checks issued by institutions other than depository institutions, and *transactions deposits* held at depository institutions.

CURRENCY AND TRAVELER'S CHECKS   The currency component of M1 is the same as that used to compute the monetary base. (The Federal Reserve is responsible for determining how many coins and currency notes to introduce into circulation; see *What Happens When Banks Run Out of Coins?*) Only traveler's checks issued by nondepository institutions such as American Express and Thomas Cook are included in M1. The reason is that deposi-

What Happens When... Banks Run Out of Coins?

The U.S. Mint produces coins at the Federal Reserve's request and sells them to the Federal Reserve at their face value. Because the coins typically cost much less than their face value to produce, the Mint earns profits, which it transmits to the U.S. Treasury. The coins are placed into circulation, however, by the Federal Reserve, which distributes coins through thirty-seven offices and more than a hundred additional coin terminals operated by armored carriers such as Brinks and Loomis-Fargo. The Federal Reserve pays these private armored carriers to transport coins to commercial banks, savings institutions, and credit unions.

The Federal Reserve makes an effort to anticipate fluctuations in desired coin holdings. Nevertheless, sometimes the Fed errs. The most recent example of a Federal Reserve mistake in estimating the demand for coins occurred after Congress passed a law requiring the Mint to produce commemorative quarters honoring individual U.S. states. When the Fed first began introducing these quarters

into circulation, it severely underestimated the high demand for the new quarters. Within a few days, banks around the nation began reporting quarter shortages. The Fed responded with orders for more quarters from the Mint, where employees worked overtime to produce additional quarters. The Federal Reserve then incurred significant expenses rushing coins to regions experiencing the most severe quarter shortages.

For the Federal Reserve, therefore, the overall quantity of money in circulation is not the only issue of concern. Its policymakers must also consider the *composition* of the quantity of money.

FOR CRITICAL ANALYSIS: If the public's demand for coins were to rise unexpectedly, how could the Federal Reserve place more coins into circulation while simultaneously preventing the monetary base from increasing?

tory institutions place the funds that they use to redeem traveler's checks in special transactions deposit accounts that are already counted among transactions deposits.

TRANSACTIONS DEPOSITS   Deposits at financial institutions from which holders may write checks for purchasing goods, services, or financial assets are **transactions deposits.** There are three types of transactions deposits. One is **demand deposits.** Demand deposits are non-interest-bearing checking deposits. Holders may convert funds in such deposits to currency "on demand" or write a check on these deposits to third parties, who then may access funds from the deposits "on demand." Another type of transactions deposit is a **negotiable-order-of-withdrawal,** or **NOW, account.** NOW accounts are interest-bearing deposits that also offer checking privileges. The third type of transactions deposit is an **automatic-transfer-system,** or **ATS, account.** ATS accounts are combinations of interest-bearing savings accounts and non-interest-bearing demand deposits. Typically, holders of ATS accounts maintain small demand-deposit balances. Yet they may write sizable checks payable from their demand-deposit accounts because funds are transferred automatically from their savings accounts to cover shortfalls.

As panel (b) of Figure 1-1 indicates, currency constitutes over half of M1. Transactions deposits account for most of the rest. Traveler's checks are a relatively insignificant component.

M2: Cash Plus Other Liquid Assets

The monetary base and M1 are alternative definitions of "cash money." The monetary base measures funds made available directly by the U.S. Treasury and the Federal Reserve System, while M1 measures funds more broadly available to the public at large. Both definitions of money include only highly liquid assets.

Yet other financial assets may also be converted very quickly into cash. **M2** is a broader definition of money that includes such assets. The monetary aggregate M2 is equal to M1 *plus* the following:

1. Savings deposits and money market deposit accounts at depository institutions.

2. Small-denomination time deposits at depository institutions.

3. Funds held by individuals, brokers, and dealers in money market mutual funds.

Table 1-2 lists recent dollar amounts of these components of M2.

SAVINGS DEPOSITS AND MONEY MARKET DEPOSIT ACCOUNTS   **Savings deposits** are interest-bearing deposits without set maturities. **Money market deposit accounts** are savings accounts that permit limited checking privileges.

Transactions deposits: Checking accounts.

Demand deposits: Non-interest-bearing checking accounts.

Negotiable-order-of-withdrawal (NOW) accounts: Interest-bearing checking deposits.

Automated-transfer-system (ATS) account: A combined interest-bearing savings account and non-interest-bearing checking account in which the former is drawn on automatically when the latter is overdrawn.

M2: M1 plus savings and small-denomination time deposits and balances of individual and broker-dealer money market mutual funds.

MONEYXTRA!
Economic Applications

How much has M2 grown in recent months? Take a look at EconData Online. **http://moneyxtra.swcollege.com**

Savings deposits: Interest-bearing savings accounts without set maturities.

Money market deposit accounts: Savings accounts with limited checking privileges.

Table 1-2   The Components of M2 ($ Billions)

M1	$1,365.1
Small-denomination time deposits	867.0
Savings deposits and money market deposits	3,574.8
Individual and broker-dealer money market mutual funds	707.8
M2	$6,514.7

SOURCE: Board of Governors of the Federal Reserve System, H.6(508) *Statistical Release,* June 9, 2005.

Small-denomination time deposits: Deposits with set maturities and denominations of less than $100,000.

Money market mutual funds: Pools of funds from savers that managing firms use to purchase short-term financial assets such as Treasury bills and commercial paper.

M3: M2 plus large-denomination time deposits, Eurodollars and repurchase agreements, and institution-only money market mutual funds.

Large-denomination time deposits: Deposits with set maturities and denominations greater than or equal to $100,000.

Repurchase agreement: A contract to sell financial assets with a promise to repurchase them at a later time.

Eurodollars: Dollar-denominated deposits located outside the United States.

SMALL-DENOMINATION TIME DEPOSITS   Time deposits have set maturities, meaning that the holder must keep the funds on deposit for a fixed length of time to be guaranteed a negotiated interest return. **Small-denomination time deposits** have denominations less than $100,000. A variety of small-denomination time deposits are available, including six-month money market certificates of deposit (CDs) and CDs with two to four years maturity.

MONEY MARKET MUTUAL FUNDS   Many financial companies today offer **money market mutual funds,** which are pools of funds from savers that managing firms use to purchase short-term financial assets, such as Treasury bills and large CDs issued by depository financial institutions such as banks. Individuals, brokers, dealers, and larger institutions hold balances at money market mutual funds. The Fed has determined, however, that institutional balances at money market mutual funds typically are not very liquid. Therefore, the Fed includes only individual and broker-dealer holdings in M2. Institutional balances are included in a broader measure of money.

Figure 1-2 compares the monetary base, M1, and M2. Recently, M2 was over eight times larger than the monetary base and more than four times larger than M1. Indeed, savings and money market accounts together were more than twice as large as M1. The sum of small-denomination time deposits and money market funds was almost as large as M1. These comparisons are typical of those we would observe at any given time we might measure these definitions of money.

M3:   The Broadest Monetary Aggregate

The Fed makes greatest use of the monetary base and M1 and M2 measures of money. Nevertheless, it also has a very broad money definition that it calls **M3.** This measure of money adds the following items to M2:

1.   Large-denomination time deposits at depository institutions.

2.   Term repurchase agreements and term Eurodollars.

3.   Repurchase agreements at depository institutions and Eurodollar deposits held by U.S. residents (other than depository institutions) at foreign branches of U.S. depository institutions.

4.   Institution-only money market mutual fund balances.

Table 1-3 lists the amounts of these components of M3.

Large-denomination time deposits are time deposits issued by depository institutions in amounts of $100,000 or more. A **repurchase agreement** is a contract to sell financial assets, such as U.S. Treasury bonds, with a promise to repurchase them at a later time, typically at a slightly higher price. This means that the original holder of financial assets who initiates the repurchase agreement effectively borrows funds for a time. A repurchase agreement permits the original holder to get access to funds for one or more days. Because funds are tied up in overnight repurchase agreements for such a short time, these are relatively liquid assets. For this reason, the Fed includes repurchase agreements in M3.

Eurodollars are dollar-denominated deposits in foreign depository institutions and in foreign branches of U.S. depository institutions. Despite the name "Eurodollar," such deposits might, for instance, be in Japanese or Australian branches of U.S. banks. Given their short, one-day maturities, these dollar funds also are relatively liquid. Finally, *institution-only money market mutual fund balances* include mutual fund balances not held by individuals, brokers, and dealers.

**FIGURE 1-2
Comparing the
Monetary Base, M1,
and M2 ($ Billions).**

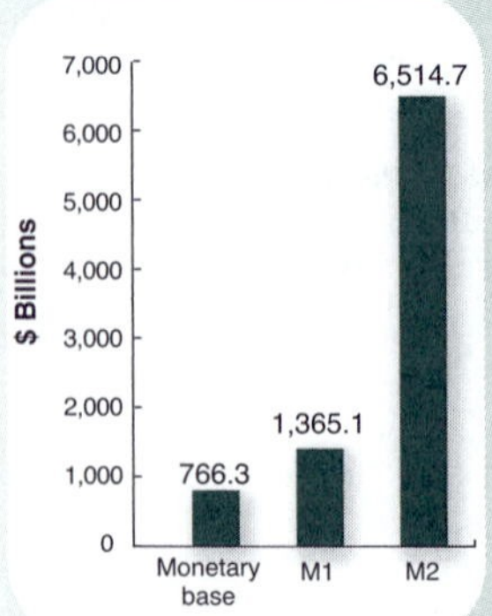

SOURCES: Board of Governors of the Federal Reserve System, H.6(508) *Statistical Release* and H.3(502) *Statistical Release,* June 9, 2005.

Table 1-3 The Components of M3 ($ Billions)

M2	$6,514.7
Large-denomination time deposits	1,203.4
Repurchase agreements and Eurodollar deposits	853.6
Institution-only money market mutual funds	1,039.3
M3	$9,611.0

SOURCE: Board of Governors of the Federal Reserve System, H.6(508) *Statistical Release,* June 9, 2005.

The additional assets that M3 includes—large-denomination time deposits and so on—tend to be much less liquid than those that constitute M2. As a result, the Fed has tended to place less weight on M3 as a reliable measure of money. It also de-emphasizes the monetary base, because checking deposits are such an important means by which households and firms purchase goods, services, and financial assets. Therefore, the Fed has paid most attention to the M1 and M2 monetary aggregates.

Figure 1-3 shows annual percentage growth rates in M1 and M2 since 1970. As the figure indicates, these monetary aggregates have grown at different rates. Sometimes growth of one has declined while the other has grown more quickly. This has complicated the Fed's efforts to decide which of these aggregates is the more useful measure of money.

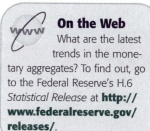

On the Web
What are the latest trends in the monetary aggregates? To find out, go to the Federal Reserve's H.6 *Statistical Release* at **http:// www.federalreserve.gov/ releases/**.

4. What are monetary aggregates, and how are they constructed? Monetary aggregates are groupings of financial assets that are combined based on their degrees of liquidity into overall measures of money. The monetary base, M1, M2, and M3 are today's basic monetary aggregates. Of these, M1 and M2 are the most important to the Federal Reserve.

**FIGURE 1-3
Annual Growth Rates
of M1 and M2.**

The Federal Reserve's two key monetary aggregates often grow at different rates.

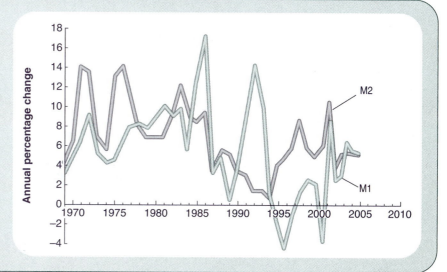

SOURCE: 2005 Economic Report of the President, *Economic Indicators,* various issues.

Can Money Be Defined in a Digital Economy?

History has taught us that money is not immune to technological change. For instance, private banknotes once were the most common form of money. Yet even when such notes were legal currency, technological improvements that made checks simpler and less costly to process gradually led to greater use of checking accounts.

Nonelectronic Payments

Today, currency, checks, and traveler's checks constitute the most widely used media of exchange. Other paper-based means of payment include credit-card transactions and money orders. As panel (a) of Figure 1-4 indicates, about 92 percent of all transactions in the United States for 2006 were made using these nonelectronic means of payment. Electronic means of payment such as **wire transfers**—payments made via telephone lines or through fiber-optic cables—accounted for only about 8 percent of total U.S. transactions (*not* dollar volume, though).

Wire transfers: Payments made via telephone lines or through fiber-optic cables.

Electronic Payments

Ongoing improvements in information-processing technology have the potential to alter our conceptions of feasible means of payment. Panel (b) of Figure 1-4 shows why this is the case. Although nonelectronic means of payment will continue to account for the lion's share of the total number of *exchanges* in the United States, in 2006 about 90 percent of the *dollar value* of such exchanges was made by *electronic* means. Only about 10 percent of the dollar value of 2006 transactions was made with checks, currency, or other physical means of payment.

Direct transfers between parties to exchanges account for the bulk of electronic payments. **Automated clearinghouses** also process payments on behalf of parties to transactions. In addition, **point-of-sale (POS) transfers** are becoming more common than in years past, even though the technology for POS transfers has been available since the 1960s. A POS transfer is an automatic transfer of funds from a deposit account to a retailer that is accomplished electronically from the location where the exchange takes place. For instance, a typical department

Automated clearinghouses: Institutions that process payments electronically on behalf of senders and receivers of those payments.

Point-of-sale (POS) transfer: Electronic transfer of funds from a buyer's account to the firm from which a good or service is purchased at the time the sale is made.

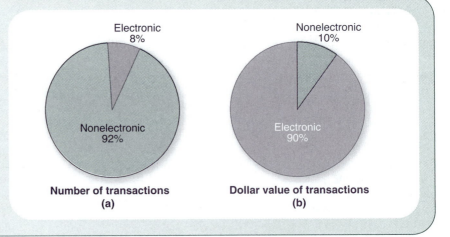

FIGURE 1-4
Electronic versus Nonelectronic Payments.

As panel (a) indicates, nonelectronic transactions account for nearly all payments in the United States. Panel (b), however, shows that the bulk of the dollar value of exchanges is accomplished through electronic means of payment.

Electronic
8%

Nonelectronic
92%

Number of transactions
(a)

Nonelectronic
10%

Electronic
90%

Dollar value of transactions
(b)

SOURCE: Authors' estimates.

store POS cash register is essentially a minicomputer that can communicate with other computers. Once appropriate arrangements have been made with a depository institution, an individual can use a plastic card with magnetically encoded account information to permit the department store POS cash register to transfer funds directly from the individual's deposit account to the account of the retailer.

Payment can also be made electronically through **automated bill payment.** With this payments technology, individuals arrange for depository institutions to pay some of their bills. The depository institutions automatically deduct funds from the individuals' accounts and transfer them electronically.

Automated bill payment: Direct payment of bills by depository institutions on behalf of their customers.

Computer Shopping

A number of firms are selling goods, services, and financial assets over the *Internet*—the electronic information system that links mainframe and personal computers around the United States and the rest of the world. Individuals most commonly use the Internet to send electronic mail or to access information from remote locations. Ever-increasing numbers of people and firms are arranging and executing financial transactions over the Internet, however. As we shall discuss in Chapter 2 and elsewhere in this book, many companies already have set up systems for such exchanges. These and other innovations in electronic payments technology promise to revolutionize the manner in which payments will be made.

Will they also revolutionize the meaning of money? The answer to this question remains unresolved at present. If what matters for measuring money are the items that people use to make the most transactions, then clearly checks and currency remain the key components of any measure of money. Yet it is undeniable that new information-processing technology broadens the liquidity of a number of assets by making them more readily convertible to cash. This indicates that in the future monetary aggregates may include even more items than they do at present.

> **5. How do changes in payments technologies affect our definitions of money?** The more widespread ability to transfer funds electronically makes more assets convertible to money, thereby increasing their liquidity. This may induce central banks to include more assets in the monetary aggregates they use as indicators or targets of their monetary policies.

MONEYXTRA!
Online Case Study

Put yourself in the place of a future Federal Reserve economist trying to evaluate the meaning of money in an economy with digital currency and deposits by going to the Chapter 1 Case Study, entitled "Internet Payments Meet Monetary Aggregates." **http://moneyxtra.swcollege.com**

On the Web
Which banks offer the latest automated bill payment services? One place to check is the search engine offered by Banxquote at **http://www.banx.com**. At the opening page, select "Banking." Then select "Online Banking."

Chapter Summary

1. How Financial Globalization and Cybertechnologies Together Have Altered the Economic Roles of Banking Institutions and Money: Worldwide growth in international trade has contributed to the globalization of financial markets. At the same time, the development of cybertechnologies has linked financial institutions and markets within and across national borders, further enhancing global interdependence. These developments are forcing both financial institutions and monetary and financial policymakers to confront a number of profound issues about their roles in the new world of banking.

2. The Functions of Money: Money has four functions. It is a medium of exchange, which means that people use money to make payments for goods, services, and financial assets. It is also a store of value, so people can hold money for future use in exchange. In addition, money is a unit of account, meaning that prices are quoted in terms of money values. Furthermore, money is a standard of deferred payment, meaning that lenders make loans and buyers repay those loans with money.

3. The Evolution of Money: Early societies relied on barter, or the direct exchange of goods and services without the use of money, but barter poses the problem of double coincidence of wants. To address this problem, people initially facilitated exchanges by using commodity moneys that also had a value for other purposes. Over time, societies established commodity standards involving the use of tokens with values related to the value of a physical good such as gold. Governments often became involved in commodity standards because they could earn seigniorage by issuing units of money with a value exceeding the per-unit cost of production. This practice ultimately provided the impetus for the development of fiat money not backed by the value of any particular commodity. Today society is contemplating the use of e-moneys in the form of cryptographic algorithms transferred in digital form.

4. Monetary Aggregates and Their Construction: Monetary aggregates are groupings of financial assets com-

bined on the basis of their degrees of liquidity in an effort to measure the total quantity of money in circulation. Today's fundamental monetary aggregates are the monetary base, M1, M2, and M3. Of these, M1 and M2 traditionally have been the most important to the Federal Reserve System.

5. Payments Technologies and Definitions of Money: Technological changes in the processes by which payments are made can affect how we define money. Although nonelectronic payments continue to predominate in typical transactions, the bulk of dollars in transactions are transferred electronically. As such electronic transfers become more common, overall asset liquidity may increase, and new assets may gain sufficient liquidity to be classified as money.

Questions and Problems

(Answers to odd-numbered questions and problems may be found on the Web at **http://money.swcollege.com** under "Student Resources.")

1. If a money is a medium of exchange, must it be a store of value? Can you think of any real-world examples in which the two functions might be separated, with one money acting as the exchange medium but the other taking on the role of a store of value?

2. What are some advantages and disadvantages of the alternative forms of money: commodity moneys, commodity standards, and fiat moneys?

3. Based on your answer to question 2, is fiat money necessarily preferable to the other forms of money? Why or why not?

4. In a gold commodity money system, the price of gold recently fell from 2 units of goods and services per unit of gold to 1 unit of goods and services per unit of gold. What has happened to the purchasing power of money?

5. Suppose that a new method of making payments from savings accounts at depository institutions has induced U.S. residents to shift $100 billion from checking accounts to money market deposit accounts. What is the effect, if any, on

   a. the monetary base?

   b. M1?

   c. M2?

6. A new means of drawing on checking accounts electronically to make payments over the Internet has induced U.S. residents to shift

$200 billion from currency holdings to checking accounts. What is the effect, if any, on

   a. the monetary base?

   b. M1?

   c. M2?

7. Using the following data ($ billions), calculate the amount of currency and the value of the M1 monetary aggregate:

Monetary base	500
Traveler's checks	15
Reserves of depository financial institutions	100
Demand deposits	435
Other checkable deposits	550

8. Consider the following data ($ billions), and calculate the monetary base, M1, and M2.

Currency	450
Savings deposits and money market deposit accounts	1,400
Small-denomination time deposits	1,000
Traveler's checks	10
Reserves of depository financial institutions	80
Total money market mutual funds	500
Institution-only money market mutual funds	200
Demand deposits	450
Other checkable deposits	490

9. Suppose that M1 is equal to $1,350 billion. The monetary base is equal to $500 billion, and transactions deposits (both demand deposits and other checkable deposits) and traveler's checks combined amount to $925 billion. What is the amount of reserves at depository financial institutions?

10. Explain in your own words why the growth in electronic means of payment might complicate the task of defining and measuring money.

Before the Test

Test your understanding of the material covered in this chapter by taking the Chapter 1 interactive quiz at **http://money.swcollege.com**.

Online Application

Internet URL: **http://research.stlouis.org/fred2**

Title: FRED (Federal Reserve Economic Data)

Navigation: Go directly to the above URL. Under "Categories," click on "Monetary Aggregates." Next, click on "Demand Deposits at Commercial Banks NOT Seasonally Adjusted (NSA or SA)." In "Chart Range" beneath the figure, click on "Max."

Application: Perform the following operations, and answer the following questions:

1. Select the data series for demand deposits (either seasonally or nonseasonally adjusted). Scan through the data. Do you notice any recent trend? [Hint: Compare the growth in the figures before 1993 with their growth after 1993.]

2. Now go back to the "Monetary Aggregates" page. Click on "M1 Money Stock," and again click on "Max" next to "Chart

Range." Does M1 show any recent trend (pre-1993 versus post-1993)? Based on your answer to question 1, what appears to account for this behavior? [Note: We shall explain this recent behavior of M1 in Chapter 19.]

For Group Study and Analysis: FRED contains considerable financial data series. Assign individual members or groups of the class the task of examining data on assets included in M1, M2, and M3. Have each student or group of students look for big swings in the data. Then ask the groups to report back to the class as a whole. When did clear changes occur in various categories of the monetary aggregates? Were there times when people appeared to shift funds from one aggregate to another? Are there any other noticeable patterns that may have been related to economic events during various periods?

Selected References and Further Reading

Angell, Norman. *The Story of Money.* New York: Frederick A. Stokes Co., 1929.

Antinolfi, Gaetano, and Todd Keister. "Dollarization as a Monetary Arrangement for Emerging Market Economies." Federal Reserve Bank of St. Louis *Review* 83 (November/December 2001): 29–39.

Barro, Robert. "Money and the Price Level under the Gold Standard." *Economic Journal* 89 (March 1979): 13–33.

Clower, Robert. "Introduction." In *Monetary Theory: Selected Readings.* New York: Penguin Books, 1969.

Einzig, Paul. *Primitive Money.* 2d ed. New York: Oxford University Press, 1966.

Gann, William. "How Money Matters." Federal Reserve Bank of St. Louis *Monetary Trends,* June 2004, p. 1.

Walter, John R. "Monetary Aggregates: A User's Guide." Federal Reserve Bank of Richmond *Economic Review* 75 (January/February 1989): 20–28.

MoneyXtra

Log on to the MoneyXtra Web site now (**http://moneyxtra.swcollege.com**) for additional learning resources such as practice quizzes, case studies, readings, and additional economic applications.

Banking in the Digital Age

By the late 1990s, the Federal Reserve was clearing more than 17.1 billion checks per year. There are just over 31.5 million seconds in a year. Thus, by 1999 the Federal Reserve was clearing an average of more than 540 checks per second. Today, however, the Federal Reserve's average check-clearing speed has dropped by nearly 20 percent, to just over 440 checks per second. This drop has not resulted from any Federal Reserve inefficiencies. The Federal Reserve is simply processing fewer checks in the 2000s than it did in the 1990s. Since 1999, the number of checks cleared by the Federal Reserve has decreased at an average annual rate of 3 percent per year. In 2004 alone, the number of checks processed by the Federal Reserve dropped by more than 10 percent.

Fundamental Issues

1. What is the difference between stored-value cards and smart cards?

2. Is digital cash less secure than physical cash?

3. What are the rationales for regulating cyberbanking?

4. Does e-money matter for monetary policy?

Why are U.S. residents writing fewer checks? The answer is that they are making more of their payments using cards that store and transmit encoded data, computers and electronic networks linking retailers and banks, and, increasingly, the Internet. In this chapter, you will learn about how high-speed telecommunications and the Internet are transforming money, banking, and financial markets. You will also learn about the challenges that these and other developments pose for bank regulators.

E-Cash: The Future Is Now

According to the Bank for International Settlements, an institution that coordinates policymaking among the central banks of the world's most developed nations, U.S. residents make more than 300 billion cash transactions every year. Of these, 270 billion are in dollar amounts of less than $2. It is easy to see why people most commonly use paper currency and coins to purchase a soft drink, a candy bar, or a comic book. (If the fast-food retailer McDonald's has its way, however, most of its customers will stop using cash to purchase soft drinks; see the *Management Focus: Why McDonald's Wants Your Card, Not Your Cash.*) Why would people use electronic money, however, instead of currency and coins?

Stored-Value and Debit-Card Systems

To understand the incentives for using e-money instead of real cash, we must first contemplate exactly how e-money transactions take place. First, let's think about the simplest kind of e-money system, which is a **closed stored-value system.** In this type of system, cards containing prestored currency values entitle the bearer to purchase specific goods and services offered by the card issuer. For instance, many university libraries contain copy machines that faculty and students operate after inserting a plastic card that has a magnetic stripe on the back. Each time they make copies, the copy machine automatically deducts the per-copy fee. When the balance on a student's card runs low in the middle of copying an article, the student can replenish the balance by placing the card in a separate machine and inserting real cash. The machine stores the value of the cash on the card. Then the student can go back to the copy machine, reinsert the card, and finish copying the article.

Some closed stored-value cards are disposable, and the card owner throws away the card after spending the value placed on it. Cards with magnetic stripes or other means of electronic-data storage have a broad range of other uses, however. Banks and other issuers now can issue reusable cards for use in **open stored-value systems.** In these systems, there are a number of card issuers, acquirers, and merchants, and the bearer of a card may use it to purchase goods and services offered by any participating merchant.

Another type of card that functions in open systems is the **debit card,** which essentially adapts the technology used by stored-value cards to permit authorization of fund transfers between accounts of consumers and merchants. Figure 2-1 on the next page illustrates a sample transaction flow within a debit-card system. In this example, issuing banks, denoted Bank A and Bank B, provide cards to customers. These cardholders can use the cards to authorize transfers of funds from their checking or savings deposits at the banks so that they can buy goods and services from retailers that participate in the system. At the retail outlets, electronic cash-register terminals record the values of purchases and the routing numbers of issuing banks. The retailers submit the recorded transactions data to the banks where the retailers' own deposit accounts are located, denoted Bank C and Bank D. These banks then forward claims for funds to the system operator, which in turn transmits these claims to the issuing

Closed stored-value system: An e-money system in which consumers use cards containing prestored funds to buy specific goods and services offered by a single issuer of the cards.

Open stored-value system: An e-money system in which consumers buy goods and services using cards containing prestored funds that are offered by multiple card issuers and accepted by multiple retailers.

Debit card: A plastic card that allows the bearer to transfer funds to a merchant's account, provided that the bearer authorizes the transfer by providing personal identification.

MANAGEMENT
Focus

Why McDonald's Wants Your Card, Not Your Cash

Recently, fast-food giant McDonald's initiated a major investment in cashless payments. Virtually every McDonald's restaurant is now equipped to accept credit- and debit-card payments. To make this possible, each restaurant has had to incur a onetime equipment installation cost of about $2,500 and a $100 monthly high-speed telecommunications expense. In addition, to process a bank card transaction, a typical McDonald's restaurant must pay a fee equal to between 1.5 and 2.0 per-

cent of the dollar amount of the transaction. Some McDonald's restaurants have also begun offering radio frequency payment tags, which allow customers to wave a small card across a scanning device instead of having to go to the trouble of swiping a credit or debit card.

For years, McDonald's resisted accepting payment cards, but recent policy changes by bank card issuers tipped the scales in favor of accepting cashless payments. Banks that issue credit and debit cards once required signatures for nearly all transactions, but nowadays they do not. Card issuers also are now willing to process very small-denomination transactions,

such as the purchase of a $1.25 soft drink. Finally, because McDonald's card-processing systems are online, cashless purchases of soft drinks and sandwiches are nearly instantaneous, taking between four and seven seconds to complete. Cashless payments promise to make the process of serving fast food even faster and, consequently, more cost-efficient for McDonald's restaurants.

FOR CRITICAL ANALYSIS: Why might McDonald's anticipate that promoting cashless payments might increase its long-run profitability, even though the company has expended large sums to permit it to process these payments?

FIGURE 2-1
A Debit-Card System.

Holders of cards issued by Bank A and Bank B can arrange for fund transfers from their accounts via card authorizations. Retailers in turn transmit claims to Bank C and Bank D. These banks then transmit their claims for funds to the operator of the system. The system operator transmits the claims to Bank A and Bank B and arranges account settlements among the four banks.

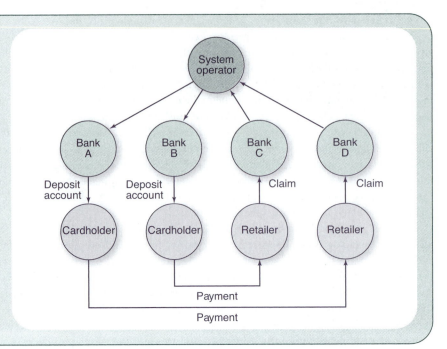

banks, Bank A and Bank B. Once Banks A and B honor their obligations to Banks C and D, the latter banks credit the deposit accounts of the retailers. (Contrary to what many debit-card users believe, most debit-card transactions do not happen instantaneously; see *What Happens When You Swipe Your Debit Card?*)

An important aspect of Figure 2-1 is that it could just as easily illustrate the workings of our current system of paper checks. Instead of using debit cards to buy goods and services from retailers, bank customers could have used checks to make their purchases. Then the retailers would send the checks on to their own banks, which would submit them to a check clearinghouse for payment. The clearinghouse then would process payments among the banks so that the retailers would receive final payment of funds. Thus, a debit-card system effectively amounts to electronic checking. A number of clearinghouse transactions must take place behind the scenes to finalize a transaction much like the clearing of standard paper checks. (A switch is under way to clearing many checks on the Internet; see the *Cyber Focus: Physical Checks Become Digital Images* on page 26.)

Smart Cards and Digital Cash

Smart card: A card containing a microprocessor that permits storage of funds via security programming, that can communicate with other computers, and that does not require online authorization for funds transfer to occur.

A more fundamental innovation has been the development of **smart cards,** which have embedded computer chips that can hold much more information than a magnetic stripe. The microchip on a smart card can do much more than maintain a running cash balance in its memory. These minute silicon chips function as microcomputers that can carry and process security programming.

SMART CARDS   This communications capability of smart cards gives them an advantage over the stored-value card's magnetic stripe that is swiped through a card reader. Magnetic stripe cards have a failure rate—a typical rate of failure to process a transaction correctly—of about 250 per million transactions. For smart cards, the failure rate is less than 100 per mil-

What Happens When... **You Swipe Your Debit Card?**

The majority of debit-card transactions do not occur immediately. When a cardholder swipes a typical debit card, the retailer's electronic cash register automatically routes a request for authorization to the issuing bank. After checking the cardholder's account number against a file of lost or stolen cards and verifying that funds are available in the customer's account, the bank sends confirmation of payment authorization.

Retailers that strive for speed in the delivery of goods and services—such as grocery stores and fast-food restaurants—do not want other customers to stand in line waiting while a customer provides a personal identification number and employees await payment authorization. For this reason, as Figure 2-2 indicates, the majority of debit-card transactions actually take place offline. Many retailers simply store transactions during the day. In some cases retailers store them for a couple of days. Then the retailers transmit requests for payment from banks during off-hours—just as they do with the checks their customers write.

Hence, even though parties to transactions transmit payment authorizations and funds transfers associated with debit cards electronically, only a minority of these transmissions are instantaneous. In contrast to smart-card and other digital-cash transactions, debit-card transactions more often than not entail a delayed exchange of funds to finalize purchases. This exposes firms to delays and costs that are similar to, although typically somewhat lower than, the delays and costs they face when they accept checks from their customers.

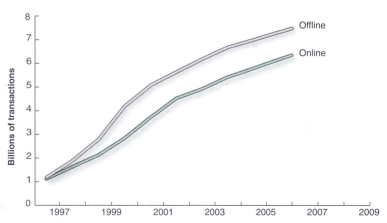

FIGURE 2-2
Total U.S. Debit-Card Transactions.

The use of debit cards has grown at a fast pace in recent years. Nevertheless, the majority of debit-card transactions take place offline instead of online.

SOURCE: Bank for International Settlements and authors' estimates.

FOR CRITICAL ANALYSIS: Who effectively receives a "loan" during the time between the swiping of a debit card and the offline settlement of funds from the cardholder's bank account to the bank account of the retailer?

---

lion transactions. Continuing improvements in microprocessor technology promise to push this failure rate even lower.

The microprocessors on smart cards can also authenticate the validity of transactions. When a cardholder initiates a transaction with a retailer, the chip in the retailer's electronic cash register confirms the authenticity of the smart card by examining a unique "digital signature" stored on the card's microchip. This digital signature is generated by software called a *cryptographic algorithm,* which is a secure program loaded onto the microchip of the card. It guarantees to the retailer's electronic cash register that the smart card's chip is genuine and that it has not been tampered with by another party—such as a thief. Figure 2-3 on the next page illustrates how digital encryption helps to guarantee the security of electronic payments.

Thus, in an **open smart-card system** for e-money transfers, in which there are numerous smart-card issuers, holders, and participating retailers, a cardholder need not provide a personal identification number. Indeed, just as with physical cash, the user of a smart card can

Open smart-card system: An e-money system in which consumers use smart cards with embedded microprocessors, which may be issued by a number of institutions, to purchase goods and services offered by multiple retailers.

Physical Checks Become Digital Images

During the 1990s, the Federal Reserve decided to transfer most of its check-clearing operations to the Federal Reserve Bank of Atlanta. Since then, the Fed's fleet of Lear jets has been flying boxes of checks from the cities of the various Fed district banks to one of the world's busiest airports. There, checks have been loaded onto trucks and driven through some of the busiest city traffic in the nation to a downtown sorting facility. After being sorted and reboxed, they have been driven back through traffic to the Atlanta airport to be flown to their final destinations.

Atlanta traffic notwithstanding, however, the average speed of Fed check clearing has been rising. The reason is that the volume of checks physically circulating through Atlanta has been declining. One factor accounting for this decline is that a growing percentage of physical checks are now cleared online. As authorized by the Check Clearing for the Twenty-First Century, or "Check 21," Act of 2003, both the Fed and private check-clearing services have been using the Internet as a check-processing network. Special machines conduct high-speed scans to create digital images of checks, which are transmitted for final payment clearing via the Web. The checks cleared in this manner require no further transportation beyond the warehouses where they are temporarily stored before being destroyed.

FOR CRITICAL ANALYSIS: What factors do you think motivate people who continue to write checks instead of swiping debit cards?

remain anonymous. There is also no need for online authorization using expensive telecommunication services. Each time a cardholder uses a smart card, the amount of the purchase is deducted automatically and credited to a retailer. The retailer, in turn, can store its electronic cash receipts in specially adapted point-of-sale terminals. The retailer can then transfer the accumulated balances to its bank at the end of the day by means of telephone links. This permits payments to be completed within just a few seconds. (Currently, U.S. residents use only a small percentage of the world's smart cards; see the *Global Focus: Smart Cards Have Caught On in Europe.*)

Digital cash: Funds contained on computer software, in the form of secure algorithms, that is stored on microchips and other computer devices.

DIGITAL CASH What does a smart card have that paper currency and coins do not? The answer is potentially even more convenience. Smart cards permit people to use **digital cash,**

FIGURE 2-3
Digital Encryption and Electronic Payment Security.

An electronic payment instruction starts out in a form readable by a human being, called "plaintext." When this instruction is entered into a computer, it is secured, or encrypted, using an "encryption key," which is a software code. In computer-readable form, the payment instruction is called "ciphertext," which the computer transmits to another location. A computer at the other location uses another software code, called a "decryption key," to read the data and turn the instruction back into a plaintext form that a human operator can read.

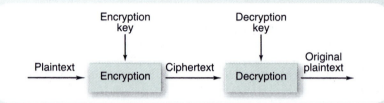

GLOBAL
Focus

Smart Cards Have Caught On in Europe

About 300 million smart cards are in use around the globe. Fewer than 15 million of these are in use in the United States, however. As Figure 2-4 indicates, more than 80 percent of all smart cards are utilized in Europe.

Most of the current growth in smart-card use is also occurring outside the United States. Smart-card distribution is rising, for instance, in Brazil and other South American nations, where use of smart cards is helping banks in those countries cut down on fraudulent transactions.

FOR CRITICAL ANALYSIS: Why do you suppose that U.S. banks' successes in protecting U.S. consumers from payment fraud have contributed to the relatively slow rate of smart-card adoption in the United States?

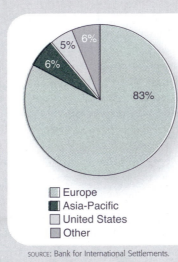

☐ Europe
■ Asia-Pacific
☐ United States
☐ Other

SOURCE: Bank for International Settlements.

FIGURE 2-4
The Distribution of the World's Smart Cards.

The bulk of the world's smart cards are currently held in Europe.

which consists of funds contained on the algorithms stored on microchips and other computer devices. Smart cards' microchips can communicate with any device equipped with appropriate software. In addition to automated teller machines and electronic cash registers, such devices include any computer with sufficient memory and speed to operate the software, such as a personal computer.

This means that unlike paper currency and coins, checks, and stored-value cards, which require physical space to process transactions, digital money stored on smart cards or other devices with smart-card-type microchips can be sent across cyberspace. Thus, an individual can use smart-card technology to purchase a service from an Internet-based retailer. Suppose that a rap-music enthusiast want to hear the latest rendition from a favorite performer. The enthusiast must have a smart-card-reading device connected to his personal computer—or have preloaded digital cash onto a program located on the hard drive of the computer. The performer's recording company must also have the necessary software. If both these conditions are met, then the rap-music enthusiast can enter a designated location on the recording company's Web site, point, click, and download the music as a digital file. His computer automatically sends digital cash as payment for this service. Then the enthusiast can listen to the latest release on his computer's speakers. (This example assumes no fraud.)

On the Web
What are the latest developments in smart-card technology? Learn more about the evolution of and newest innovations in smart-card technology at **http://www. smartcard.co.uk** .

THE ROLE OF PAYMENT INTERMEDIARIES   Just because people have the capability to adopt a technology does not mean that they actually *do* implement it. The basic technology for stored-value cards has been available since the 1970s, but only recently have U.S. residents used the cards to buy such items as telephone calls. In many instances, a chicken-or-the-egg problem has been responsible for the delay. Retailers often do not want to install online systems for processing digital cash until more customers use it. But many customers will not use digital cash until more merchants are online and the customers are convinced that their payments are secure from transmission errors, fraud, and theft.

The breakthrough in matching up retailers and their customers for online trading via smart cards and personal computers came when banks and financial software specialists teamed up to serve as **payment intermediaries,** or institutions that serve as go-betweens in processing the fund transferals that occur during the course of any purchase of goods, services, or financial assets. Banks traditionally have been key payment intermediaries. Since the Middle Ages, banks have served as storehouses for means of payment—gold, other precious metals, checking deposits—that people have accepted as money. The difference today is that banks now offer means of payment via cybertechnologies associated with the provision of digital cash. Banks are providing enhanced access to digital cash for good reason: they think that they can profit from the fees that they anticipate earning once e-money systems are broadly established, with themselves as payment intermediaries.

Payment intermediary: An institution that facilitates the transfer of funds between buyer and seller during the course of any purchase of goods, services, or financial assets.

> ### 1. What is the difference between stored-value cards and smart cards?
> Stored-value cards are capable of storing computer-accessible data, including funds that the bearer of the card typically may spend on a specific good or service. Because they simply store information and do not process the data in any way, stored-value cards are most often used in closed systems operated by a single business or institution. Within open systems, debit cards may be used to transfer funds among accounts as long as the card user can provide authentication of the funds. By way of contrast, smart cards contain microprocessors that, in addition to tabulating data, can process security programs and communicate directly with other computers without need for authentication. This makes smart cards more flexible and secure for online transmission of payments within open systems linking many consumers, businesses, and financial institutions.

Online Banking

Banks everywhere expect to profit in several ways from widespread smart-card adoption. While customers have funds stored on their bank-issued smart cards, technically speaking those funds are still on deposit with their banks. Thus, banks can lend out unused balances on cards to other customers, most likely at a higher interest rate than the rate they pay on smart-card funds. In addition, banks see the promise of fees that they will be able to charge retailers who accept the cards. They also anticipate getting to keep any spare change that customers leave on a card when they decide to throw it away. For instance, suppose that a bank finds that during a given week, a "typical" customer using a disposable smart card leaves 24 cents in "spare change" on the card when throwing it away because the customer does not think spending such a small amount is worth the effort. If 10,000 customers are "typical," then each week the bank will get to keep a total amount of $2,400. Over the course of a year, this "spare change" will accumulate to $124,800!

Many observers, however, feel that before most people become comfortable about cyberspace transmissions of digital cash, they must be certain that online dealings with their own banks are secure. This process is further along than the development of digital cash, so it will not be long before we can evaluate this view.

THE DEVELOPMENT OF ONLINE BANKING Developers of home financial-management software initiated online banking in the United States. Wanting to include as many attractive features in their software packages as they could dream up, they started offering to help software users consolidate bills and initiate payments over the Internet via the software companies. To make this possible, the software companies formed alliances with banks, because bill payments typically had to be issued from bank accounts.

Quickly, banks recognized that they might earn fee income by providing these services themselves. By 2000, 2,000 U.S. banks offered online banking services via the Internet. Today, more than 7,000 U.S. banks have developed some type of online banking, and most of the remainder are planning to offer such services.

Most bank customers who do online banking use three kinds of services. Bill consolidation and payment is one of the most popular. Another is transferring funds among accounts, thereby eliminating the need to make trips to a bank branch or automated teller machine (ATM) to conduct such transfers. The third is making initial applications for loans, which many banks now permit customers to do over the Internet. Although customers typically have to appear in person to finalize the terms of a loan, they can save some time and effort by starting the process at home.

A CHICKEN-OR-THE-EGG PROBLEM? People still cannot engage in two important activities using online banking services: depositing and withdrawing funds. This, of course, is where smart cards should come into the picture. With smart cards, people could upload and download digital cash, thereby transforming their personal computers into home ATMs—which would give them more incentive to bank from home via the Internet. Yet, as noted above, many believe that online banking is the way to introduce people to e-money and thereby induce them to think about using smart cards. This raises the potential for a chicken-or-the-egg problem to develop: bank customers are waiting for widespread acceptability of smart cards before exploring home banking options, while banks are waiting for more customers to choose online banking before making big investments in smart-card technology.

Nevertheless, many bankers have decided that there are two very good reasons to promote online banking irrespective of smart cards. For one thing, once online banking is in place, it is less expensive for the bank because the average cost of performing a transaction is lower. If customers interact directly with automated systems and computers that take only a few people to maintain, then the banks can employ fewer people in traditional branch offices. Although the overall benefits that banks gain from online banking can be difficult to quantify, some banks have reported that customers who use online banking cost as much as 15 percent less to serve than traditional customers. In addition, a typical online banking customer holds about 20 percent more funds on deposit and generates as much as 50 percent more revenues than a traditional customer. (Now that banks have realized the cost savings and revenue gains from online banking, they have reduced the fees they charge their online customers; see on page 30 the *Management Focus: Banks Figure Out How to Induce Customers to Go Online*.)

COMPETITIVE PRESSURES FOR ONLINE BANKING Another key rationale that bankers everywhere have for developing online services is that if they do not, someone else

MONEYXTRA!
Another Perspective

Read a discussion of factors that have motivated the online banking surge in the 2000s by going to the Chapter 2 reading, entitled "'Net Interest' Grows As Banks Rush Online," by Karen Couch and Donna Parker of the Federal Reserve Bank of Dallas. **http://moneyxtra.swcollege.com**

MANAGEMENT
Focus

Banks Figure Out How to Induce Customers to Go Online

Almost every household with Internet access has had the capability to undertake online banking transactions since the late 1990s. Yet, as Figure 2-5 shows, as late as 1998, fewer than 10 percent of households regularly engaged in online banking. Since 1999, in an effort to give more customers a greater incentive to click their way to online deposit transfers, bill payments, loan applications, and the like, banks have sharply reduced the fees they charge for Web access. Indeed, in the 2000s many banks, such as Bank of America and J.P. Mor-gan Chase, have eliminated most online banking fees in an effort to induce their customers to move more transactions to the Internet.

FOR CRITICAL ANALYSIS: How might bank profits increase even if banks do not charge an explicit fee to customers who utilize online banking facilities?

FIGURE 2-5
The Percentage of Households That Bank Online.

Since 1999, banks have sharply reduced or even eliminated the fees charged to customers who bank online. This helps explain why the percentage of households that engage in online banking has increased considerably during the 2000s.

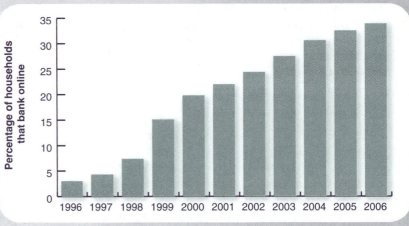

SOURCE: Office of the Comptroller of the Currency.

may beat them to the punch and steal away their customers. Today, a number of banks are already operating exclusively on the Internet. They have no physical branch offices, so they accept deposits through physical delivery systems, such as the U.S. Postal Service or FedEx. This sharply reduces their costs, and these Internet-only banks promise to pass on part of the cost savings to customers in the form of lower fees and higher yields. Some even offer free checking with very low minimum deposits, such as $100, and no-fee money market accounts with average monthly balances of $2,500 or more.

These "virtual banks," as they have come to be known, are not the only potential source of competition faced by traditional banks. Today, there are several Internet loan brokers, such as QuickenMortgage, E-Loan, GetSmart, Lending Tree, and Microsoft's HomeAd-viser. These broker systems use software that matches consumers with loans. The consumer supplies information to the program, which then searches among available loan products for the best fit. The loans are available from lenders with which the broker has a contractual relationship.

Internet loan brokers' biggest forays into banks' turf have been in the credit-card and mortgage markets. In the credit-card business, Internet brokers have been especially successful in providing credit-card debt consolidation services. They do not always compete with banks because often they act as marketers for traditional credit-card-issuing banks. The brokers receive fees for enrolling new customers for the credit-card issuers, which save the cost of developing lists of potential prospects and mailing card offers.

In the mortgage market, however, the competition is more direct. Indeed, Internet loan brokers often take the place of the traditional loan officer at a banking institution that makes mortgage loans. When mortgage rates fell in the late 1990s and again in the early 2000s, people who wished to refinance their houses flooded the telephone lines of traditional banking institutions, only to get lots of busy signals, long waits on hold, and slow responses from loan officers. This led many to turn on their computers and surf the Internet. Some real estate specialists now believe that in a few years at least 10 percent of U.S. mortgage-loan refinancings will be initiated through the Internet.

On the Web
Follow the latest mortgage market developments by visiting HSH Associates at **http://www.hsh.com**, the Microsoft Network at **http://www.moneycentral.msn.com**, the Mortgage Bankers Association at **http://www.mbaa.org**, or Quicken-Mortgage at **http://www.quickenloans.com**.

Regulatory Issues of Electronic Money

E-money makes some people nervous. Some are apprehensive about digital cash for the same kinds of reasons that have slowed adoption of any new technology. Until they have time to evaluate new technologies, people often begin by assuming the worst.

It remains to be seen whether people will find digital cash more convenient than other means of payment. As we have discussed above, there are reasons to think that many people ultimately will desire to use digital cash. The big issue in the minds of most potential users of cybermoney systems such as smart cards or online banking services is the *security* of e-money payments. For those who currently regulate banks, however, the development of a cybereconomy raises two key sets of issues. One involves the security of digital cash. The other relates to the potential for fraudulent banking.

The Security of Digital Cash

Just because smart cards will be equipped with authentication software does not mean they will be 100 percent secure. Ingenious criminals might pilfer digital cash in a number of ways.

DIGITAL COUNTERFEITING One possible way that a crook could steal digital money is very old-fashioned but potentially very lucrative: counterfeiting. The most obvious way to counterfeit would be to produce smart cards that look, feel, and, most importantly, function just like legitimate smart cards.

Potential returns from smart-card counterfeiting might tempt well-trained engineers and computer scientists to form a counterfeiting ring. Such specialists potentially could analyze and "reverse-engineer" smart cards—that is, take apart cards and their software to determine how both are constructed. Then they could experiment with loading value onto fraudulent cards (or trying to fool computers into accepting fake cryptographic algorithms they have placed on the cards' microprocessors). If successful, they could spend the fraudulent digital funds.

Issuers of smart cards already have taken a number of defensive measures to limit the success of such counterfeiting efforts. To make counterfeit smart cards easier to recognize, issuers typically place holographic images on their own legitimate cards, just as credit-card issuers do.

MONEYXTRA!
Online Case Study

To think about whether the social gains from adopting e-money and online banking outweigh the private costs, go to the Chapter 2 Case Study, entitled "Investing in Digital Cash." **http:// moneyxtra.swcollege.com**

Issuers also design the computer code on the microprocessors so that data stored in memory cannot be accessed or changed except through predefined authorization and access software protocols. These software commands in turn are stored in a portion of the microprocessor's memory that can be changed only by altering its internal functions. To help prevent unauthorized reading of any data on the cards, smart cards are equipped with physical barriers intended to inhibit optical or electrical analysis or physical alteration of the microprocessor's memory. Most smart-card chips also are coated with several layers of wiring, installed in such a way that unauthorized removal of the chip is difficult to accomplish without damaging the chip beyond repair.

SWIPING DIGITAL CASH OFFLINE AND ONLINE　　In recent years, a common type of bank robbery has the following *modus operandi:* two or three people drive a pickup truck through the front window of a bank branch or supermarket where an ATM is located, quickly lift the ATM onto the bed of the truck, drive to their hideout, and remove the cash in the ATM. An *offline theft* of digital cash is only slightly more sophisticated: thieves break into a merchant's establishment, physically remove the electronic devices used to store value from customers' smart cards, and download these funds onto their own cards.

More sophisticated thieves might attempt *online theft* by intercepting payment messages as they are transmitted from smart cards and other electronic-funds storage devices to host computers. For instance, if thieves learn the times of day that a large up-scale department store transmits its receipts to a central computer, they could try to tap into the transmission line and steal the funds. These kinds of online theft are most likely to be "inside jobs," in which employees commit *internal theft*—pilfering their own company's funds—using their knowledge of the company's systems for transmitting cybercash.

COULD E-MONEY "CATCH A COLD"?　　Counterfeiting, robbery, and internal theft are old problems. Stealing digital cash requires more technical ability than John Dillinger and Baby Face Nelson needed in the 1930s, but the crime is essentially the same. The dependence of digital cash on correctly functioning microprocessors and software, however, exposes e-money to special dangers.

In the classic James Bond movie *Goldfinger,* a supercriminal plots to blow up a small nuclear device inside Fort Knox, thereby making the gold stored there radioactive and, consequently, worthless. The supercriminal reasons that he will reap huge capital gains on his own hoards of accumulated gold. In a cybereconomy, it would be hard to profit financially from the wholesale destruction of outstanding stocks of digital cash. Not all crimes are committed for financial gain, however. A group of people who are fanatically wedded to some political or personal "cause" and who also happen to possess a talent for creating computer viruses potentially could transform themselves into superterrorists. A virus that damages the input-output mechanisms of smart-card microprocessors and other digital-cash storage and communications devices or that erases data stored on such e-money mechanisms potentially could create financial havoc, thereby attracting considerable attention to the terrorists' cause, whatever it might be.

MALFUNCTIONING MONEY　　Physical cash can wear out, and devices for scanning magnetic ink can misread checks. Nevertheless, people can still exchange physical units of money during electricity outages. Power failures or other equipment breakdowns, by way of contrast, can bring e-money transactions to a grinding halt.

Thus, consumers and retailers may face a trade-off in their use of digital cash. E-money systems are speedier, less costly, and more efficient than currency and checks. Just as air travel is on average the quickest and safest way to traverse a long distance, digital cash is a comparatively effective way to conduct transactions—when it works. Yet, when airplanes fail to operate correctly, the result can be spectacular crashes. Likewise, the gain from using cyberbanking technologies comes at the cost of exposure to new risks of loss.

> **2. Is digital cash less secure than physical cash?** In some respects, the potential security problems of digital cash, such as counterfeiting and outright theft, are simply high-tech versions of security concerns people already experience when they use physical currency and coins. In other ways, however, digital cash has its own special security difficulties. Unlike physical money, digital cash potentially can be infected by computer viruses. In addition, during periods of hardware breakdowns or power failures, digital-cash transactions may be hindered, if not halted.

Bank Fraud: An Old Problem with a New Face

The security issues discussed above highlight potential problems that issuers and users of digital cash can face from external threats. Presumably, all parties normally wish to contain the scope of these problems. What happens, however, if payment intermediaries themselves—that is, bankers that issue smart cards, take in funds, and process payments—try to earn ill-gotten gains?

LESSONS FROM HISTORY: THE FREE-BANKING ERA During much of the nineteenth century, U.S. banks issued their own **banknotes,** which were privately issued paper moneys redeemable in gold. People learned to be wary of so-called wildcat banks, which set up gold-redemption offices in locales where wildcats, not the humans who might wish to redeem the banknotes, were located. Some of these banks were essentially fly-by-night operations that pocketed their customers' deposits of gold and other marketable assets and departed. Evidence now indicates that this practice was not as widespread as many historians initially believed, but there is no doubt that some wildcat banking occurred.

Banknotes: Privately issued paper currency.

What made wildcat banking feasible was the enactment of so-called **free-banking laws** in many U.S. states after 1836. These laws permitted any group to secure a broad corporate charter allowing it to engage in banking practices. Prior to 1836, and in some states even after that date, a bank could be incorporated only if the state legislature gave permission. The requirements for obtaining a free-banking charter varied from state to state; Table 2-1 on the next page lists the states with and without free-banking laws by 1860.

Free-banking laws: Laws in force in many U.S. states between 1837 and 1861 that allowed anyone to obtain a charter authorizing banking operations.

Free banking was not truly "free." Most states required free banks to purchase and deposit state-issued bonds with state banking authorities. This meant that banks in some states were very risky propositions if the bonds issued by their state governments had uncertain prospects for full repayment or if the prices of the bonds fluctuated. Free-banking laws also required banks to pay gold or other specific assets in exchange for the banknotes they issued. Typically, free banks had to restrict their business to a single office; they could not open branches throughout states in which they were incorporated, nor could they branch across state lines.

Nevertheless, in many states free banks faced few other restrictions on their activities. Much recent research has shown that despite this relative lack of state oversight and the considerable latitude for entry into or exit from the industry, the notes of free banks

Table 2-1 States with Free-Banking Laws, 1837–1860

States with Free-Banking Laws	Year Law Passed	States without Free-Banking Laws
Michigan	1837[a]	Arkansas
Georgia	1838[b]	California
New York	1838	Delaware
Alabama	1849[b]	Kentucky
New Jersey	1850	Maine
Illinois	1851	Maryland
Massachusetts	1851[b]	Mississippi
Ohio	1851	Missouri
Vermont	1851[b]	New Hampshire
Connecticut	1852	North Carolina
Indiana	1852	Oregon
Tennessee	1852[b]	Rhode Island
Wisconsin	1852	South Carolina
Florida	1853[b]	Texas
Louisiana	1853	Virginia
Iowa	1858[b]	
Minnesota	1858	
Pennsylvania	1860[b]	

[a]Michigan prohibited free banking in 1840 and allowed it again in 1857.
[b]According to Rockoff, very little free banking was done under the laws in these states.
SOURCE: Reprinted from A. J. Rolnick and W. E. Weber, "Inherent Instability in Banking: The Free Banking Experience," *Cato Journal* 5 (Winter 1986). Their source was Hugh Rockoff, *The Free Banking Era: A Re-Examination* (New York: Arno Press, 1975).

generally were quite safe. Many free banks were long-lived institutions, and very few depositors actually experienced losses as a result of those free banks that closed down their operations at one time or another between 1837 and 1860. In addition, failures of free banks tended to be localized. They rarely led to failures of other banking institutions. Hence, the evidence indicates that most free banks were domesticated, conservative housecats, not fly-by-night wildcats.

In a cybereconomy, in which anyone in principle can post a Web site seeking deposits of funds and offering to pay depositors a rate of return, this nineteenth-century experience with free banking has some modern-day relevance. When contemplating the role of bank regulation in a world of digital cash, a big issue is whether cyberbanks are more likely to turn out to be housecats or wildcats.

WILDCAT BANKING, TWENTY-FIRST-CENTURY STYLE?   In the summer of 1997, a newly formed company, based in a small North Carolina community, announced its intention to provide full-scale banking operations over the Internet. The company proclaimed its right to provide such services under U.S. constitutional law, and its Web site indicated that its deposits were backed by a policy issued by a major insurance company. The company had a "fax-on-demand telephone line" through which prospective customers could order an application to open an account. To attract deposits, the new virtual bank promised to pay annual interest rates up to 20 percent on savings accounts and 10 percent on checking accounts, at a time when most traditional banking institutions were offering deposit rates slightly above 5 percent. The virtual bank also said that it would offer small-business loans, "with no credit checks," at one to two percentage points above the prime rate.

Enforcement Limitations   To the Office of the Comptroller of the Currency (OCC), the federal agency charged with regulating national banks, this essentially was a wildcat bank in the making. This seemed even more probable when it turned out that the "major insurance company" said to back the new bank's deposits announced it had never made such an arrangement. The OCC pointed out to the new company's owners that federal bank laws prevent institutions from accepting deposits without a formal bank charter. Nevertheless, because the OCC has power to enforce actions only against institutions that *do* have federal bank charters, the OCC had to turn to the Federal Trade Commission to enforce the law and stop the new company from opening its banking operations.

Web-Facilitated Risk Taking   Not long after this event, the Federal Deposit Insurance Corporation (FDIC), which administers federal deposit insurance (see Chapter 11) and regulates state-chartered banks, took control of a Kentucky-based banking institution called BestBank. The bank raised many of its deposits on the Internet. By the mid-1990s, its low-cost operations—the bank had only twenty-three employees at a single location—had permitted it to become five times more profitable than the average bank. What it wasn't telling its depositors, however, was that it was lending most of their funds to lower-income individuals via the issuance of a half-million credit cards with $600 borrowing limits. As a precondition for receipt, each cardholder had to join a Florida-based travel company at a fee of $543, which the bank charged to the cardholder's account before sending out the card, leaving only $57 of available credit. Many of the bank's credit-card customers, however, failed to pay off their loan balances. When the FDIC seized the bank, the bulk of the bank's cardholders had defaulted, and the bank was insolvent—its liabilities exceeded its assets by nearly $100 million.

These examples illustrate the dark side of cyberbanking. Certainly, the Internet can be a wonderful way to obtain information about potentially profitable business opportunities, and online banking and digital-cash transmission allow for speedier trading and quicker financial rewards. At the same time, however, these cybertechnologies can serve as a means for unscrupulous people to draw in funds that they plan to use in high-risk, or even fraudulent, ventures.

Regulating Cyberbanking

In light of the new risks—such as the potential for high-tech counterfeiting, system breakdowns or terrorist attacks, or online bank fraud—should governments step in and regulate cyberbanking? Before addressing this question, we first need to think about why governments might wish to regulate banking institutions.

THE RATIONALES FOR BANK REGULATION   Banks have always faced considerable regulation. Since the earliest times, governments have sought to restrain or direct banking activities. The traditional justification for regulating banks has been that if the government were to leave them alone, socially "bad" outcomes might result. In the worst case of a banking panic, many customers might lose their life savings.

Certainly, in the broad sweep of world history many such events have occurred. In the United States between the 1830s and 1930s, national banking panics seemed to occur in nearly regular cycles of fifteen to twenty years, with significant panics taking place in 1837, 1857, 1873, 1893, 1907, and 1929–1933. The severity of the last of these panics motivated much of the federal regulation of depository institutions that exists today. It also lies behind some of the efforts to regulate the application of cyberbanking technologies.

Traditionally, governments have regulated banking institutions in an effort to pursue four essential goals:

1. **Maintaining depository institution liquidity.** A large portion of the liabilities of banking institutions are checking accounts and other types of deposits, which, as we discussed in Chapter 1, customers of the institutions have the legal right to access almost immediately. Any banking institution that finds itself without sufficient cash on hand to meet the needs of its depositors suffers from **illiquidity.** Such illiquidity inconveniences the institution's customers. If a large number of banks are illiquid simultaneously, however, then the result can be a serious disruption in the nation's flow of payments for goods and services, with potentially broader negative effects on the economy.

2. **Assuring bank solvency by limiting failures.** An overriding goal of bank regulation is to reduce the likelihood of widespread bank failures. Any business, including a bank, typically fails and declares bankruptcy when it reaches a point of *insolvency,* at which it is unable to pay debts as they mature. Although an insolvent business may have positive net worth, it is insolvent if it cannot meet its financial obligations. Because many of a bank's assets are financial instruments that are more liquid than most assets of nonfinancial businesses, the terms *bankruptcy* and *insolvency* are generally used synonymously. Consequently, a depository institution generally is considered to have reached a point of **insolvency** when the value of its assets falls below the value of its liabilities, so that the value of its *equity,* or net worth, is negative. A key aspect of the regulation of depository institutions typically is the periodic *examination* of their accounting ledgers to verify that the institutions are solvent. Another aspect normally is the *supervision* of these institutions via the publication and enforcement of rules and standards with which they must comply. A purpose of regulatory supervision is to make insolvency and failure a rare occurrence.

3. **Promoting an efficient financial system.** Another key rationale for bank regulation is to promote an environment in which banking institutions can provide their services at the lowest possible cost. Achieving cost efficiency minimizes the total resources that society expends on the services that banks provide, thereby freeing up the largest possible amount of remaining resources for other social uses.

4. **Protecting consumers.** Throughout history many leading Americans have mistrusted banks. Thomas Jefferson said that they were more dangerous than standing armies. When Andrew Jackson lost considerable personal wealth to banks from foreclosed loans after suffering big losses on land speculation, he made bank bashing a favorite political pastime. Members of Congress have heeded the calls of many of their constituents by passing legislation intended to protect consumers from possible misbehavior by bank managers. Hence, consumer protection is another fundamental goal of bank regulation.

DIFFICULTIES IN ATTAINING ALL REGULATORY GOALS   Regulators of depository institutions struggle to achieve all four goals simultaneously. Typically, achieving one objective may entail sacrificing another. For instance, a problem that regulators often face is distinguishing illiquidity from insolvency. It is possible for a banking institution to be illiquid tem-

Illiquidity: A situation in which a banking institution lacks the cash assets required to meet requests for depositor withdrawals.

Insolvency: A situation in which the value of a bank's assets falls below the value of its liabilities.

porarily yet to be solvent otherwise, just as it is possible for an otherwise wealthy individual to experience temporary "cash flow" difficulties. Bank regulators, and particularly a central bank such as the Federal Reserve, can assist institutions suffering from short-term liquidity problems by extending them credit. The difficulty is that typically illiquidity is one symptom of pending insolvency. Extending such loans can keep otherwise insolvent institutions operating when they really ought to close. Efforts to promote liquidity of banks can thereby permit poorly managed, insolvent banks to run up even more debts, worsening the extent of their insolvency.

In addition, because earning high profits helps banks avoid liquidity and insolvency difficulties, government regulators often are tempted to find ways to protect banks from competition, which might hurt their profitability. At the same time, banks are more likely to operate as efficiently as possible when exposed to considerable rivalry from other financial institutions. Competition, however, drives down bank profitability; if profitability falls too low, unexpected shocks to the economy or financial system can cause banks to operate at significant losses, thereby threatening their liquidity and solvency levels.

INNOVATION MAY BE STIFLED   Furthermore, laws designed to protect bank customers from potentially unscrupulous bank managers can interfere with the development of innovative banking practices that ultimately might improve overall customer service. For example, suppose that a reputable bank develops the ability to post an Internet Web site where a visitor can apply for a loan without having to drive to a bank and conduct a long-winded interview with a bank loan officer. The bank also gains because it reduces the amount of time that loan officers must allocate to such personal interviews. To prevent *un*scrupulous banks from taking advantage of unwary consumers on the Internet, however, government regulators may require this reputable bank to meet a number of standards in posting its Web site. They may also require the bank to file detailed reports about each application it receives. The costs of meeting the government's consumer protection regulations might very well offset the efficiency gains that the bank had hoped to achieve, inducing it to drop its plans to provide the new service. Thus, protecting consumers can reduce bank efficiency.

THE PROS AND CONS OF REGULATING CYBERBANKING   As we shall discuss in more detail in Chapter 11, a key issue of bank regulation is determining how best to trade off progress toward achieving one regulatory goal against sacrificing progress in accomplishing others. Undoubtedly, this will prove to be a challenge as money and banking continue to move across corridors within cyberspace.

On the one hand, for instance, a traditional way to limit banks' potential for insolvency is to require periodic audits of their accounts. To ease the task of auditing banks, regulators typically require them to follow industry and regulatory standards in their business practices. Applying this same approach to cyberbanking would necessitate placing limits on "permissible" cyberbanking business practices. Although such restraints make the regulators' task easier, they would not be consistent with allowing banks to experiment with new ways of operating that might achieve significant cost savings.

On the other hand, permitting unhindered adoption of new ways of banking via cybertechnologies might encourage some bank managers to engage in riskier practices. In addition, entry into banking-related businesses via, say, the Internet could greatly increase the potential for widespread illiquidity, or even insolvencies, if the businesses are based on poorly implemented plans conceived by entrepreneurs unskilled in the arts of banking. Many people could lose their savings as a result, and society as a whole could bear significant costs.

Thus, the decisions about whether or how to regulate cyberbanking technologies involve the same types of trade-offs that bank regulators have always faced. The main difference is that in the new cyberworld, governmental bodies charged with pursuing the traditional goals of bank regulation must keep up with an ever more rapidly changing financial environment.

> **3. What are the rationales for regulating cyberbanking?** The reasons for contemplating regulation of cyberbanking mirror those typically offered for regulating traditional banking activities: preventing illiquidity, limiting insolvencies, promoting efficiency, and protecting consumers. An important issue is whether new cybertechnologies, such as smart cards, digital cash, and online banking, pose unique problems, including greater security concerns and increased potential for bank fraud, that may justify special regulation. Nevertheless, regulators contemplating restrictions on cyberbanking are likely to face trade-offs among their broad regulatory objectives that are similar to those they face in regulating traditional banking activities.

Electronic Money and Monetary Policy

As we shall discuss in detail in Chapter 14, for the past century most nations have entrusted central banking institutions with the task of determining the quantity of money in circulation. By varying the quantity of money, central banks can affect market interest rates, aggregate expenditures, and total income and employment. Thus, central banks can conduct *monetary policy* in an effort to influence overall economic performance. The advent of digital cash, however, raises an important question: Could the widespread use of digital cash complicate central banks' efforts to conduct monetary policy?

Real Money versus Virtual Money—Does It Matter?

Digital cash stored on smart cards and transferred among computers has two characteristics that distinguish it from the currency and coins that people have traditionally used. First, instead of being made of paper and metal, it consists of software stored on microchips. Second, instead of being issued by the government, it is issued by private firms. Consequently, digital cash can have a bearing on the ability of central banks to regulate the total quantity of money only if either or both of these distinguishing features constitute a dramatic departure from the status quo.

Let's begin by contemplating whether the *form* that money takes should make any difference for monetary policy. Consider the $100 bill, which is one of the most popular forms of money in the world. Several weeks each year, the U.S. Bureau of Engraving and Printing prints $100 bills around the clock, bundles them into shrink-wrapped packages containing 4,000 notes each ($400,000 per package), and ships them to Federal Reserve banks for distribution.

In 1991, in the first alteration of U.S. paper currency since 1957, the Bureau of Engraving and Printing began threading metallized plastic strips indicating every bill's official denomination through each bill it printed. This change was intended to stop the practice of bleaching out the printing on $1 bills, then reproducing them as $100 bills on color copiers. The plastic strip does not show up on carbon copies of the bills. (It also glows red under ultraviolet light.) The portrait of Benjamin Franklin that appears on $100 bills was enlarged and moved off-center. There was some concern at the U.S. Treasury that the public might not accept these changes. Nevertheless, even though the plastic strip was clearly visible near the Federal Reserve Board seal printed on each bill and the enlarged Franklin portrait noticeably changed the look of $100 bills, there was no drop in usage of the bills. In fact, worldwide usage of $100 bills increased substantially after 1991.

By the early 2000s, the Treasury had made similar changes in the $5, $10, $20, and $50 bills; in particular, the portraits of Abraham Lincoln, Alexander Hamilton, Andrew Jackson, and Ulysses Grant were enlarged and moved off-center. Even though this and other changes made the bills look much different, people used the bills as before.

This experience provides an important message. Changes in the form of money, in and of themselves, have no implications for monetary policy. As long as there is no change in the purchasing power of the money that people use, they will use whatever money is most convenient, as long as it is widely acceptable in exchange. For example, as long as $20 bills are easy to use and widely accepted by others, people do not particularly care what they look like. Likewise, as long as digital cash is a simple-to-use and generally accepted form of money, the fact that it is an invisible software algorithm is unlikely to make a difference to most people. (Machines have been less forgiving about paper currency redesigns; see the *Policy Focus: What Happens When People Will Accept Currency, but Machines Will Not?*)

The Big Issue: Who Will Issue Digital Cash?

Whether money takes the form of coins, paper, or deposits makes little difference to officials who are charged with conducting monetary policy, as long as it does not interfere with their ability to control the total *quantity* of money in circulation. It is this issue that makes policymakers somewhat nervous about digital cash.

If the Federal Reserve and other central banks desire to control, or at least to influence, the quantity of money in circulation, it is helpful for them to have direct and/or indirect oversight over the process by which money is placed into circulation. Let's begin by thinking about whether current private issuers of money—banks that issue checkable deposits—care about

POLICY
Focus

What Happens When People Will Accept Currency, but Machines Will Not?

On October 9, 2003, the U.S. Treasury Department's Bureau of Engraving and Printing introduced colorful new $20 bills. In a ceremonial introduction of the redesigned currency, Treasury officials put the first bill into circulation by using it to purchase stamps from a vending machine at a Washington, D.C. post office. They did so to prove that the Treasury had made every effort to make certain the new currency would work in vending machines.

Nevertheless, by October 11, 2003, Treasury officials were swamped with calls from owners of grocery stores. When designing the latest $20 bills, the Treasury Department had forgotten to consult with makers of the automated payment machines used at groceries' self-service checkout counters. Grocery managers across the country had to post signs asking customers to exchange new $20 bills for old ones before using the machines to purchase their groceries. The managers then rushed to place orders for software and hardware upgrades for their automated payment machines, often at a cost as high as $40 per machine.

FOR CRITICAL ANALYSIS: Why do you think the Treasury's Bureau of Engraving and Printing introduces new currency gradually, rather than all at once?

the way they "create" money. Then we shall think about why the Federal Reserve might care whether the ability to issue money extends beyond traditional banking institutions.

DIGITAL CASH FROM BANKS' PERSPECTIVE: A TECHNOLOGICAL CHANGE ONLY   To a bank, e-money is just a new way to conduct an old business. This business, which we shall discuss in detail in Chapter 10, is profiting from taking in funds in the form of deposits and lending those funds to others at higher interest rates.

To a traditional banking institution, funds that its customers download onto smart cards are no different than funds they withdraw from ATMs and hold as government-issued paper currency. Otherwise, idle balances in checking accounts—which can also be accessed by smart cards if bank customers use their smart cards as debit cards—are balances that banks can lend to others. Thus, funds that bank customers hold on deposit and access for electronic debiting via their smart-card microprocessors are available for bank lending just as traditional checking funds are. Banks can do this by making traditional loans with terms that loan officers and borrowers negotiate in bank offices. In some cases, however, the entire process might be digital: deposits accessed digitally via smart cards could effectively be "on loan" to bank customers who apply for and receive loans online.

Whether funds held on bank-issued smart cards find their way to bank borrowers through long-established or high-tech lending channels does not matter to banks. All they care about is that they earn maximum profits from undertaking their bread-and-butter business operations. To traditional banking institutions, digital cash simply amounts to a new way of raising funds. Whether those funds come from checking accounts that people can use to buy goods, services, or assets or from balances accessed with smart cards really makes no difference to banks, as long as they profit from either activity.

DIGITAL CASH ISSUED BY NONBANKING INSTITUTIONS: A REVOLUTIONARY CHANGE   It is conceivable, however, that traditional banking institutions, such as commercial banks, savings institutions, and credit unions, will not be the only ones issuing digital cash. To a central bank such as the Federal Reserve, this is the *fundamental* monetary policy issue posed by the development of e-money. Like banks and their customers, the Federal Reserve does not particularly care what form money takes. Nevertheless, it does have some reason to be concerned about who has the power to issue money.

The Entry of Greenbacks   To see why this is so, it is helpful to consider a critical historical period in U.S. monetary history, the Civil War of 1861–1865. Figure 2-6 displays the components of the U.S. money stock in 1861, which totaled $538 million. Demand deposits at banks accounted for well over half of the quantity of money in that year, but nearly all the remainder of the money stock consisted of banknotes issued by state-chartered banks. Only about 3 percent of the quantity of money had been issued by the federal government.

After the formation of the Confederacy, there were two separate moneys: U.S. dollars and Confederate dollars. Both the Union and the Confederate government issued large quantities of paper currency to pay their wartime expenditures. The end of the war left the Confederate currency worthless. The surviving Union was in a quandary about what to do with the paper currency, known as "Greenbacks" because of the distinctive color, that now was a major part of the quantity of money in the United States and was not backed by gold. Determining how to deal with these Greenbacks became a central issue for the next several years. Figure 2-7 displays estimates of the components of the nation's $1.6 billion money stock in 1866. As the fig-

FIGURE 2-6
The Composition of the Quantity of Money in 1861.

At the beginning of the U.S. Civil War, the quantity of money was composed almost solely of privately issued bank deposits and banknotes. Government currency was a very small portion of the total amount of money in circulation in the United States.

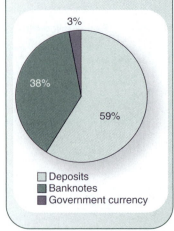

□ Deposits
■ Banknotes
■ Government currency

SOURCE: Richard H. Timberlake, *Monetary Policy in the United States: An Intellectual and Institutional History* (Chicago: University of Chicago Press, 1993).

ure indicates, Greenbacks had replaced banknotes in second place among types of money held by the public and accounted for exactly a third of the quantity of money.

A National Banking System   By the end of the Civil War, another fundamental change had occurred: a significant shift from deposits and notes issued by state-chartered banks to those issued by nationally chartered banks. Naturally, part of this shift resulted from the financial devastation of many state-chartered banks in Confederate states that had been ravaged by war. Another key factor accounting for the change, however, was the passage of the National Banking Act of 1863 and subsequent amendments, which placed a special 10 percent tax on notes issued by state banks. This tax made the issue of state banknotes unprofitable. The federal government had considerable regulatory powers over nationally chartered banks. As Figure 2-8 shows, by the end of 1865 the amount of notes and demand deposits at national banks exceeded the total quantity at state banks. By 1868, in a dramatic example of how war and a policy change can combine to alter fortunes, there were over eighteen times more notes and deposits at national banks than at state banks. Thus, two significant changes occurred between 1861 and 1868: the federal government got into the business of issuing currency, and national banks regulated by the federal government issued most of the rest of the nation's circulating money.

These events set the stage for today's monetary system in the United States, because they laid the foundation for direct government issuance of circulating money and for indirect government control over bank-issued money via a federally regulated banking system. As we shall discuss in greater detail in Chapter 14, the formation of the Federal Reserve System was a natural outgrowth of this development. Since its founding in 1913, the Federal Reserve has had the power to influence the quantity of bank-issued money—demand deposits and other checkable deposits—via its ability to regulate the ability of private banks to issue deposits.

Technology and Accounts That Function as Money   Although, on net, technology has improved the efficiency of the financial system, it has also complicated the Federal Reserve's

FIGURE 2-7
The Composition of the Quantity of Money in 1866.

Following the Civil War, government currency amounted to a third of the quantity of money in the United States.

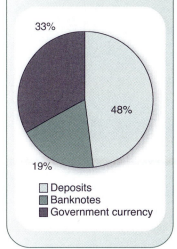

SOURCE: Richard H. Timberlake, *Monetary Policy in the United States: An Intellectual and Institutional History* (Chicago: University of Chicago Press, 1993).

FIGURE 2-8
Notes and Deposits at State and National Banks, 1860–1868.

The state banking system that had existed before the Civil War was largely replaced by a national banking system by the conclusion of the war.

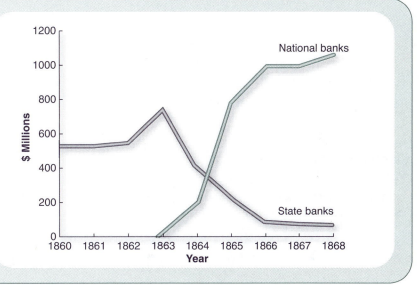

SOURCE: Richard H. Timberlake, *Monetary Policy in the United States: An Intellectual and Institutional History* (Chicago: University of Chicago Press, 1993).

efforts to influence, or perhaps even to try to control, the amount of privately issued money. For instance, the advent of computers and ATMs in the 1970s permitted people to transfer balances from noncheckable savings and time deposits into their checking accounts simply by pushing buttons. The result, as we discussed in Chapter 1, was that savings and time deposit funds came much closer to being "money" than they had been previously.

In principle, anyone can issue digital-cash accounts. Even if the government were to decide that only traditional banking institutions that fall under the Federal Reserve's regulatory umbrella can issue smart cards, what is to stop other firms from setting up e-money accounts over the Internet? That is, what is to stop firms that technically are not "banks" from issuing Internet-based digital "checking accounts" that function as money? Presumably, one answer is that Congress could pass laws prohibiting such accounts, and the Federal Reserve and other bank regulators would police the Internet to ensure that only traditional banks subject to government regulation issue such accounts.

Another possible answer, however, is that ultimately nothing may be able to stop a host of firms from pecking away at legal loopholes and eventually finding a way to essentially enter the banking business by issuing e-money accounts. Balances stored in these digital-cash accounts would be as much a part of the nation's quantity of circulating money as government currency and checkable deposits at traditional banks. As a result, the Federal Reserve's task of measuring and regulating this quantity would become much more complicated. In this way, the new cybereconomy has the potential to profoundly alter monetary affairs in the United States and, indeed, worldwide. We shall return to this theme throughout the remainder of this book because this potential development, more than any other, may be the *truly* fundamental change brought about by the use of digital cash.

---

4. Does e-money matter for monetary policy?   To an individual who uses physical cash, checking deposits, or digital cash, the form of money does not matter as much as its convenience and acceptability in exchange. In addition, a traditional banking institution is more concerned about whether its activity of raising funds and lending them out at higher interest rates is profitable than it is about whether it raises the funds by issuing checking accounts or smart cards. To the Federal Reserve or another central bank, the form that money takes is only a concern if the new form of money, such as digital cash, can be issued by new institutions that are not subject to the rules intended to assist the central bank in controlling the total amount of circulating money.

Chapter Summary

1. The Distinction between Stored-Value Cards and Smart Cards: Consumers can use stored-value cards to maintain balances of electronic money that they can use to purchase specific goods or services. Stored-value cards are most often used in closed systems operated by a single business or institution, but in an open, online system, they can function as debit cards. Smart cards contain computer microchips that permit them to communicate directly with other computers to process software programs containing algorithms that store and transmit cash. In contrast to stored-value cards, smart cards can transfer funds anonymously.

2. The Security of Digital Cash: Counterfeiting and theft are potential problems with digital cash, just as they are for physical currency and coins. Special security problems of digital cash are the threat of infection by computer viruses and the potential for monetary breakdowns caused by power outages or hardware malfunctions.

3. The Rationales for Regulating Cyberbanking: The traditional justifications for regulating traditional banking activities—preventing illiquidity, limiting insolvencies, promoting efficiency, and protecting consumers—are the same rationales commonly offered for restricting cyberbanking. Some observers also argue that unique security concerns and an increased potential for bank fraud justify special regulation of cyberbanking. In any event, however, cyberbanking regulators are likely to face trade-offs among regulatory objectives that are similar to those they experience in traditional regulation of banking institutions.

4. E-Money and Monetary Policy: To private individuals who use money and private institutions that issue it, the form of money does not matter as much as its convenience and general acceptability in exchange. To a central bank such as the Federal Reserve, however, electronic forms of money could complicate its ability to control the amount of money in circulation if they can be issued by institutions not subject to its monetary regulations.

Questions and Problems

(Answers to odd-numbered questions and problems may be found on the Web at **http://money.swcollege.com** under "Student Resources.")

1. The state of New Jersey has what many experts have called the most widely counterfeited driver's license in the world. Partly to combat this problem, recently the state's government contemplated offering a new driver's license called "Access NJ." The proposed plastic card would contain a microprocessor. The programming on the microprocessor would allow the holder to store and transfer funds in payment for public services (such as public transportation), authenticate state certification to bear firearms or to hunt, download public benefits from authorized computer terminals, and obtain entry into public buildings. Based on the discussion of e-money systems in this chapter, what kind of system did the New Jersey government contemplate introducing? Explain your reasoning.

2. Critics of the New Jersey government's proposal discussed in question 1 worry that the Access NJ card might allow the government to create databases of personal information about the state's citizens, which it could then disseminate without their consent. Based on the description of the card in question 1, do you believe this concern might be legitimate? Do you think that "personal privacy" is also likely to be a general concern about smart cards used primarily for storing and transferring digital cash? Why or why not?

3. In what ways is a smart card a "more flexible" payment instrument than a stored-value card? Explain.

4. Most consumers are also taxpayers. To protect honest taxpayers from efforts by others who try to evade taxes, the federal government imposes bank reporting requirements designed to limit *money laundering*, or the funneling of cash into and out of bank accounts for purposes of hiding taxable transactions (as well as otherwise illegal exchanges). For instance, banks have to report to the federal government any funds transfer of $10,000 or more that an individual initiates. A key governmental concern about smart cards is that they may enable tax dodgers to avoid this reporting requirement, thereby inducing a rise in money laundering. Based on what you learned about smart cards in this chapter, does this seem to you to be a legitimate concern? Take a stand, and support your answer.

5. When discussing the pros and cons of e-money systems, a Federal Reserve economist argued that "the current paper-based system doesn't have much to recommend it, other than it works great, is cheap, reliable, and we trust it." Use this statement for evaluating the relative merits of e-money versus the currently dominant system based on using physical currency and checks for retail transactions.

6. In what ways might bank fraud be easier to perpetrate using online banking methods instead of traditional banking practices? Explain.

7. In what ways is digital cash more convenient to use than physical cash? Explain.

8. In what ways is digital cash less secure than physical cash? Explain.

9. How might greater competition in providing means of payment generate efficiency gains for the economy? Be specific.

10. How might greater competition in providing means of payment complicate monetary policy? Be specific.

Before the Test

Test your understanding of the material covered in this chapter by taking the Chapter 2 interactive quiz at **http://money.swcollege.com**.

Online Application

Internet URL: **http://www.firstib.com**

Title: First Internet Bank of Indiana

Navigation: Go directly to the above URL.

Application: Perform the following operations, and answer the following questions:

1. Click on "Contact," then click on "Find Answers." What issues arise with online banking that do not arise at traditional banks? In what ways are these advantages or disadvantages for Internet banks?

2. Back up to the "Personal Accounts" page and review the personal banking services that First Internet Bank provides. Then back up again and click on "Business Accounts" and review those services. Can you think of any basic banking services traditionally available from bricks-and-mortar banks that this Internet bank does not provide?

For Group Study and Analysis: Divide the class into two groups, and have both groups compare the online banking services and interest rates available from First Internet Bank of Indiana and another Internet bank, Nexity Bank of Birmingham, Alabama (**http://www.nexitybank.com**). Reconvene the class, and discuss factors that might contribute to different approaches at these two Internet banks.

Selected References and Further Reading

Committee on Payment and Settlement Systems. "Survey of Electronic Money Developments." Bank for International Settlements, May 2000.

DeYoung, Robert. "The Financial Performance of Pure Play Internet Banks." Federal Reserve Bank of Chicago *Economic Perspectives* (First Quarter 2001): 60–75.

_____. "The Performance of Internet-Based Business Models: Evidence from the Banking Industry." *Journal of Business* 78 (May 2005).

European Central Bank. *Report on Electronic Money*. Frankfurt, Germany: August 1998.

Furst, Karen, William Lang, and Daniel Nolle. "Who Offers Internet Banking?" Special Studies on Technology and Banking, Office of the Comptroller of the Currency, *Quarterly Journal* 19 (June 2000): 27–46.

Humphrey, David, Aris Kaloudis, and Grete Øwre. "The Future of Cash: Falling Legal Use and Implications for Government Policy." *Journal of International Financial Markets, Institutions, and Money* 14 (2004): 221–233.

Mester, Loretta. "Changes in the Use of Electronic Means of Payment." Federal Reserve Bank of Philadelphia *Business Review* (Fourth Quarter 2001): 10–12.

Schreft, Stacey L. "Clicking with Dollars: How Consumers Can Pay for Purchases from E-tailers." Federal Reserve Bank of Kansas City *Economic Review* 87 (First Quarter 2002): 37–64.

_____. "Looking Forward: The Role for Government in Regulating Electronic Cash." Federal Reserve Bank of Kansas City *Economic Review* 82 (Fourth Quarter 1997): 59–84.

Sheehan, Kevin P. "Electronic Cash." *FDIC Banking Review* 11 (1998): 1–8.

Stavins, Joanna, "Who Uses Electronic Check Products? A Look at Depository Institutions." Federal Reserve Bank of Boston *New England Economic Review* (Third Quarter 2002): 3–16.

Stefanadis, Chris. "Why Hasn't Electronic Bill Presentment and Payment Taken Off?" Federal Reserve Bank of New York *Current Issues in Economics and Finance* 8 (July/August 2002).

MoneyXtra

Log on to the MoneyXtra Web site now (**http://moneyxtra.swcollege.com**) for additional learning resources such as practice quizzes, case studies, readings, and additional economic applications.

Domestic and International Financial Markets

It's about 8:00 in the morning in New York City. Two lawyers from a major Wall Street law firm have ordered a taxi to take them to the offices of a well-known investment banker. At the same time, a nervous chief operating officer and chief financial officer are leaving their hotel and taking a taxi to the same investment banking firm. As luck would have it, the four individuals emerge from their taxis in front of the firm simultaneously. They greet each other cordially, but the CEO and CFO still appear nervous. Together, they ride an elevator to the twenty-fifth floor and enter the investment banking firm's trading room, where screens on the wall indicate that activity "on the street" has just begun. All eyes are on the screens, as they track the performance of the initial public offering (IPO) of shares of stock of the company that the CEO and CFO represent. The two lawyers had assisted them with the time-consuming, expensive, and often nerve-racking task of convincing an underwriter to agree to float the company's IPO.

As luck would have it, the newly public company's stock price held firm compared with its offering price and even went up a few dollars that day. The IPO was successful. After paying its lawyers and the underwriter, the company has raised $6 million to finance a planned business expansion.

IPOs are just one aspect of the primary market for securities. Another aspect is the issuance of bonds by the federal government and by private corporations. In this chapter, you will find out about primary and secondary markets for financial instruments as well as more about money and capital markets.

Saving, Investment, and Financial Markets in a Global Economy

As we discuss below, *financial markets* help direct financial resources from the owners of these resources to those who require them to finance productive activities. The owners of financial resources are individuals who accumulate resources rather than consuming them each year. These people are savers of financial resources. When other individuals or businesses use financial resources to finance productive endeavors, they invest these resources. These two groups—those who save and those who invest—interact in financial markets:

Saving and Investment

The key economic function of financial markets is to channel saving to productive investment. **Saving** is forgone consumption. Thus, when an individual does not spend all after-tax income received within a given year, that individual has saved some of her money income.

Savers, however, do not want their savings to sit idly in money balances (currency and non-interest-bearing demand deposits) if there are alternatives that yield positive returns. Typically, such alternatives exist. The reason is that other individuals or firms normally engage in **investment,** or additions to the stock of capital goods. **Capital goods** are goods that may be used to produce other goods or services in the future.

Investment in capital goods can require significant financial resources, so individuals and firms that invest often must borrow funds or sell ownership shares via initial public offerings or issues of new shares. They obtain these funds from savers with a promise to return the borrowed funds on some future date. Those who invest also promise *interest,* or payments for the use of funds borrowed from savers. They finance these interest payments using revenues from the production that their new capital goods make possible.

Savers are the ultimate *lenders* in our economy. Many of the *borrowers* are firms or individuals who wish to undertake investment. Some individuals, of course, borrow to finance current consumption. Nevertheless, the main reasons for lending and borrowing are that savers desire future interest income on the savings that they hold today, while most borrowers desire to finance investment projects that they expect to yield returns in the future.

Financial Markets and Instruments

Financial markets facilitate the lending of funds from saving to those who wish to undertake investments. Those who wish to borrow to finance investment projects sell IOUs to savers, as Figure 3-1 illustrates. Financial markets are markets for these IOUs, which can have many forms. The various forms of IOUs are known as **financial instruments.** Such instruments, which are also called **securities,** are claims that those who lend their savings have on the future incomes of the borrowers who use those funds for investment.

When we think of "instruments," we may think of tools such as a surgeon's scalpel. We refer to financial claims as "instruments" because they also are tools, though they are in the form of paper (or electronic) documents. Yet just as a surgeon's instruments can be used to perform delicate tasks, individuals and firms can use financial instruments to undertake cru-

Saving: Forgone consumption.

Investment: Additions to the stock of capital goods.

Capital goods: Goods that may be used to produce other goods or services in the future.

Financial instruments: Claims that those who lend their savings have on the future incomes of the borrowers who use those funds for investment.

Securities: Financial instruments.

FIGURE 3-1
The Function of Financial Markets.

Financial markets facilitate the transfer of funds from savers to those who wish to invest in capital goods. For instance, companies that wish to

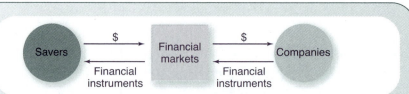

undertake investment projects offer financial instruments to savers in

exchange for funds to finance the projects.

cial exchanges of financial resources. They can also use financial instruments to help reduce risks of financial loss.

> **1. What is the main economic function of financial markets?** The main economic role of financial markets is to direct saving to those who wish to make capital investments, or purchases of capital goods that may be used to produce additional goods and services in the future. Savers provide funds to borrowers by purchasing financial instruments, or claims that savers who lend have on the future incomes of borrowers.

Primary and Secondary Financial Markets

One way of categorizing the many financial markets is to distinguish between primary and secondary financial markets. This approach classifies financial markets according to whether they are markets for newly issued financial instruments.

Primary Markets

A **primary market** is a financial market in which newly issued financial instruments are purchased and sold. For instance, a newly formed business that wishes to sell shares of ownership (commonly called "stocks") offers these shares for sale in a primary financial market. Likewise, when the U.S. Treasury issues new Treasury bonds to fund some of the public debt (which increases when the federal government spends more than its revenues), the Treasury sells these instruments in a primary market.

The first attempt by a business to issue ownership shares to the public in the primary market is called an *initial public offering (IPO).* Although businesses could attempt to manage an IPO on their own, many rely on the assistance of **investment banks.** These institutions specialize in marketing initial ownership shares offered by new businesses. An investment bank typically *underwrites* such issues, meaning that the investment bank guarantees the business's initial fixed share price. Essentially, the investment bank temporarily purchases the shares of the business. Then it attempts to resell them in the primary market at a slightly higher price. The investment bank keeps the difference between the purchase price and the resale price (often 10 percent) as a profit.

Secondary Markets

Most financial instruments sold in primary markets have maturities ranging from several months to many years. The **maturity** of an instrument is the time from the date of issue until final principal and interest payments are due to its holders. Shares of ownership in firms have no set maturities. Firms in principle can last "forever," if they are going concerns. Bonds issued by the U.S. Treasury have fixed maturities in excess of ten years. Yet at some point after the initial purchase of such ownership shares or bonds, but before their maturity dates, the original purchaser may not wish to hold them any longer. Then that original owner may sell them in a **secondary market,** which is simply a market for financial instruments that were issued at some point in the past.

Primary market: A financial market in which newly issued financial instruments are purchased and sold.

> **On the Web**
> What are the prices for the latest IPO filings? To view a directory of the most recent IPOs, visit IPO Central at Hoover's Online at **http://www.hoovers.com**.

Investment banks: Institutions that specialize in marketing and underwriting sales of firm ownership shares.

Maturity: The time until final principal and interest payments are due to the holders of a financial instrument.

Secondary market: A financial market in which financial instruments issued in the past are traded.

Secondary markets contribute to the efficient functioning of primary markets, because the ability to buy or sell previously issued financial instruments makes these instruments much more liquid than they would otherwise be. For instance, persons will be much more likely to buy ownership shares in a fledgling company if they know that there is a readily available market where they can sell the shares if they later wish to access their funds or become dissatisfied with the company's performance.

There are a variety of active secondary markets for financial instruments, including secondary markets for U.S. Treasury securities, shares of ownership in corporations, and state and municipal bonds. Now there are also secondary markets for many consumer credit obligations and for business, mortgage, and consumer loans of financial institutions. For instance, each year banks package billions of dollars of their credit-card loans into separate securities that they sell in secondary markets.

Brokers: Institutions that specialize in matching buyers and sellers of financial instruments in secondary markets.

Much as investment bankers facilitate the functioning of primary markets, **brokers** assist in matching borrowers and lenders in secondary markets. Typically, brokers specialize in a single secondary market and develop expert knowledge of the factors that influence risks, costs, and returns relating to instruments exchanged in that market. Brokers receive fees for the services they provide to secondary market buyers and sellers. For instance, a broker at a firm such as Merrill Lynch earns fee income for attempting to help clients earn the highest possible returns from shares of ownership in corporations.

> **2. What are primary and secondary markets for financial instruments?**
> Primary financial markets are markets in which newly issued financial instruments are offered for sale and purchased by savers. Secondary financial markets are markets in which previously issued financial instruments are traded.

Money Markets and Capital Markets

In addition to classifying financial markets as either primary or secondary markets, we can distinguish between *money* and *capital* markets depending on the maturities of the instruments that are traded in the markets. Although each of the many types of financial instruments has its own special set of characteristics, the most straightforward way of categorizing these instruments is according to their maturities. Maturities of less than a year are **short-term maturities,** maturities in excess of ten years are **long-term maturities,** and maturities ranging from one to ten years are **intermediate-term maturities.** For instance, three-month Treasury bills have short-term maturities, 5-year Treasury notes have intermediate-term maturities, and twenty-year Treasury bonds have long-term maturities. Banks and other depository financial institutions issue six-month certificates of deposit (short term), two-and-one-half-year time deposits (intermediate term), and long-term bonds with varying maturities.

Short-term maturity: Maturity of less than one year.

Long-term maturity: Maturity of more than ten years.

Intermediate-term maturity: Maturity between one year and ten years.

Firms, banks, and individuals trade these and other instruments in many different financial markets. Economists and traders themselves have adopted the convention of classifying markets as money markets, where instruments with short-term maturities are exchanged, or capital markets, where instruments with intermediate- or long-term maturities are exchanged. As we shall discuss in the next chapter, the maturities of financial instruments influence their interest yields. Thus, separating financial markets by maturity is a way of grouping together sets of markets whose interest rates tend to be most closely linked.

Money Markets

The term **money markets** refers to markets for financial instruments with short-term maturities of less than one year. The money markets include markets for short-maturity Treasury securities, including three- and six-month Treasury bills. They also include markets for bank six-month certificates of deposit, which include most of the large certificates of deposit included in the M3 measure of money discussed in Chapter 1.

MONEY MARKET INSTRUMENTS Money market instruments have maturities shorter than one year and typically are very actively traded, with many buyers and sellers entering the market with offers each day. Because there are so many potential buyers, a seller of an instrument in this market can usually find someone who is willing to buy that instrument at a mutually agreeable price. As a result, money market instruments tend to be more liquid than capital market instruments, which generally have fewer buyers and sellers. Most money market instruments also are less risky than capital market instruments because of their shorter terms to maturity. Fewer "bad" things can happen within, say, three months than can occur during a span of twenty years. Thus, market traders usually have fewer risk concerns about a corporation's three-month commercial paper than about a twenty-year corporate bond.

Because of their high liquidity and relatively low risk, money market instruments are widely held and traded by banks and other depository institutions. Large corporations and individuals hold and exchange these instruments as well. Figure 3-2 displays the relative magnitudes of outstanding issues of money market instruments.

Treasury Bills The U.S. government issues financial instruments called *Treasury securities.* These are U.S. government debt obligations that are exchanged in both the money markets and the capital markets. **Treasury bills (T-bills)** are government-issued financial instruments with

Money markets: Markets for financial instruments with maturities of less than one year.

Treasury bills (T-bills): Short-term debt obligations of the federal government issued with maturities of three, six, or twelve months.

**FIGURE 3-2
Money Market
Instruments Outstanding.**

Treasury bills, commercial paper, and certificates of deposit are the predominant instruments traded in the money markets.

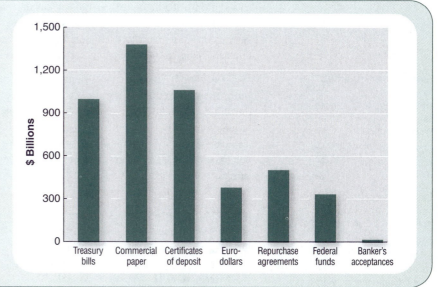

SOURCES: Board of Governors of the Federal Reserve System, *Federal Reserve Bulletin Statistical Supplement,* April 2005.

maturities of less than a year, so they are money market instruments. Traders widely view T-bills as very safe assets. After all, if the government decides that it needs to pay them off, it can always raise taxes. It is this taxing authority of the government that causes most individuals to regard T-bills as having extremely low risk.

Since 1998, the federal government has issued T-bills with minimum denominations of $1,000. Each successive T-bill denomination is in $5,000 increments. T-bills have terms to maturity of 91 days (three months), 182 days (six months), and 52 weeks (twelve months). The government sells T-bills at discounts from the face-value denominations. T-bills are negotiable instruments, which means that the bearer of a T-bill can sell the bill in the secondary market.

Commercial paper: A short-term debt instrument issued by businesses in lieu of borrowing from banks.

Commercial Paper   Banks, corporations, and finance companies often need to obtain short-term funding. One way to obtain such funds is to issue **commercial paper,** which is a short-term debt instrument. For businesses, commercial paper has become an important substitute for borrowing directly from banks.

Issuers typically offer commercial paper in maturities from 2 to 270 days. Most issuers sell commercial paper at a discount, just as the Treasury sells T-bills. Some commercial paper instruments offer coupon returns, however.

Typically, only the most creditworthy banks and corporations are able to sell commercial paper to finance short-term debts. Nevertheless, Moody's and Standard and Poor's assign credit ratings to different issuers. Consequently, commercial paper issues of some companies may have higher market yields than those of others because of differences in risk perceptions.

Certificates of deposit (CDs): Time deposits issued by banks and other depository institutions. Many CDs are negotiable instruments that are traded in secondary markets.

Certificates of Deposit   Banks also raise short-term funds by issuing **certificates of deposit (CDs).** Most CDs are short-term time deposits with maturities of six months, although banks also issue CDs with longer maturities. At one time, CDs were *nonnegotiable,* meaning that the original purchasers could not sell them without incurring interest penalties. Since 1961, however, banks have issued *negotiable CDs.* They now are traded actively in a secondary money market.

Repurchase Agreements   As defined in Chapter 1, a repurchase agreement is a contract to sell a financial asset with the understanding that the seller will buy back the asset at a later date and, typically, at a higher price. This means that effectively the seller of the asset *borrows* from the buyer. Thus, a repurchase agreement amounts to a very short term loan. Most repurchase agreements have maturities ranging between one and fourteen days. Banks and large corporations are active traders in the market for repurchase agreements.

Federal funds market: The money market in which banks borrow from and lend to each other deposits that they hold at Federal Reserve banks.

Federal Funds   Banks lend to each other directly in a money market known as the **federal funds market.** In this private market, banks borrow from and lend to each other deposits that they hold at Federal Reserve banks. This is why it is called a market for "federal" funds, even though the funds actually belong to the lending banks themselves.

Many federal funds loans have maturities of one day, though maturities of a week or two are not uncommon. The interest rate at which federal funds are exchanged is the *federal funds rate.* As you will learn in Chapter 19, the federal funds rate is a closely watched indicator of Federal Reserve monetary policy.

Banker's acceptance: A bank loan typically used by a company to finance storage or shipment of goods.

Capital mobility: The extent to which savers can move funds across national borders for the purpose of buying financial instruments issued in other countries.

Banker's Acceptances   A **banker's acceptance** is a bank loan that typically is used by a company to finance storage or shipment of goods. These instruments commonly arise from international trade arrangements. They are traded in secondary money markets.

INTERNATIONAL MONEY MARKETS   Today, we live in a world with relatively *high capital mobility*. **Capital mobility** refers to the ability to shift funds across borders for the purpose of purchasing financial instruments issued abroad. When capital mobility is high, savers can move funds across borders to aim for the highest available returns in light of the potential risks. Thus, a stock market boom in the United States can induce savers around the world to shift funds from London and Tokyo stock markets to those located in New York. Indeed, this appears to have occurred in recent years. In like manner, a Russian financial market crash can cause savers across the globe to move funds to the "safe haven" of U.S. financial markets, as took place in the late 1990s.

Like domestic markets, international financial markets include both money markets and capital markets. **International money markets** are the markets for cross-border exchanges of financial instruments with maturities of less than one year. Although a number of different types of instruments are traded in international money markets, foreign exchange instruments predominate. The daily activity on the world's foreign exchange markets exceeds $1.5 trillion. Often the daily volume exceeds the amount of total reserves of the world's central banks. In the United States alone, foreign exchange trading averages close to $700 billion per day. This amount is more than 80 percent of the *total assets* of the Federal Reserve System.

Measuring Trading Volumes in International Money Markets   A number of instruments other than foreign exchange instruments are also traded in international money markets. Some economists include *international derivative securities,* or securities whose returns are derived from the returns on other internationally traded instruments, among international money market instruments. There is some debate, however, concerning whether markets for derivatives should be considered alongside traditional money markets. The approach used by most economists, which we shall also adopt in this text, is to treat derivatives markets as separate from both the international money markets and the international capital markets. We shall discuss derivatives in depth in Chapter 6.

Transactions among large banks dominate trading in the international money market. Thus, we can use bank reports of their cross-border asset and liability positions to estimate the size of the market. Table 3-1 on the next page displays data for banks' cross-border positions. Reporting banks had over $20 trillion in both outstanding assets and liabilities. The total change in these positions during a recent year was close to $900 billion.

Table 3-1 also highlights the predominance of the banks in the international money market. Cross-border asset and liability positions of these banks are between $5 trillion and $7 trillion. The importance of the U.S. dollar is also apparent. More than one-third of the outstanding positions are denominated in dollars.

The Eurocurrency Markets   The bulk of the world's money market activity takes place in **Eurocurrency markets,** which are markets for bonds, loans, and deposits denominated in currencies of given nations yet held and traded outside those nations' borders. A Eurocurrency asset or liability is a bank asset or liability denominated in a currency other than that of the nation in which the asset or liability is physically located. For instance, a *Eurodollar deposit* is a bank deposit denominated in U.S. dollars, but located in a bank outside the United States.

The Eurocurrency markets are markets where banks and other institutions borrow and lend Eurocurrency assets or liabilities. These markets permit companies to raise funds in other nations. This is particularly useful for multinational firms. For instance, a German multinational company may issue commercial paper denominated in dollars in London. Thus, the Eurocurrency markets give the German company the capability to borrow from lenders that it would have difficulty connecting with in Germany's domestic financial markets. This is an example of the issuance of **Eurocommercial paper,** which is a short-term debt instrument

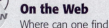

Table 3-1   Cross-Border Positions of Major World Banks (Exchange-Rate-Adjusted Changes)

	Assets ($ Billions)	
	December 2004	Estimated Change in Year 2004
U.S. dollar	$2,614.9	$346.2
Other currencies	4,316.8	546.1
Total	$6,931.7	$892.3
	Liabilities	
U.S. dollar	$2,298.0	$372.7
Other currencies	2,733.5	221.0
Total	$5,031.5	$593.7

SOURCES: Bank for International Settlements, *International Banking Statistics,* June 2005, and authors' estimates.

issued by a firm and denominated in a currency other than that of the country where the firm is located. Each year, firms issue about $100 billion in Eurocommercial paper.

London is the center of trading in the Eurocurrency markets, which are dominated by borrowing and lending activities among the world's largest banks. The most important money market instruments traded in the Eurocurrency market are **Eurocurrency deposits,** which are bank deposits denominated in currencies other than the currency of the nation where the deposits are located. These deposits are a key source of funds for banks heavily involved in multinational lending. (Sometimes Eurocurrency deposits at U.S. banks rise for reasons that have little do with attracting more foreign deposit holders; see *What Happens When Eurocurrency Deposits Encounter Big Exchange Rate Swings?*)

Eurocurrency deposits: Bank deposits denominated in the currency of one nation but located in a different nation.

3. What are money markets, and what are key money market instruments?   Money markets are markets in which financial instruments with maturities of less than one year are traded. Key instruments of the U.S. money markets include U.S. Treasury bills, commercial paper, bank certificates of deposit, repurchase agreements, federal funds, and banker's acceptances. Large volumes of money market instruments also change hands in international money markets. These include Eurocurrency markets, in which money market instruments such as Eurocommercial paper and Eurocurrency deposits are traded across national borders.

Capital Markets

Capital markets: Markets for financial instruments with maturities of one year or more.

Markets for financial instruments with maturities of one year or more are called **capital markets.** The reason for this name is that instruments with such long maturities are likely to be associated directly with funding capital investment projects.

What Happens When... Eurocurrency Deposits Encounter Big Exchange Rate Swings?

Usually, when U.S. banks experience large increases in deposits, it means that they are attracting new customers. Nevertheless, the significant growth of foreign deposits in offices of U.S. banks between 2001 and 2004 depicted in panel (a) of Figure 3-3 probably reflected only a slight increase in new foreign customers of U.S. banks. Because offices of U.S. banks denominate Eurocurrency deposits in the currencies of foreign nations, changes in exchange rates alter the U.S. dollar value of those deposits. As panel (b) of the figure indicates, between 2001 and 2004 the U.S. dollar's value in foreign exchange markets changed dramatically. Instead of the dollar steadily gaining in

value relative to other currencies, as occurred from 1999 to 2001, following 2001 the dollar's value in euros, pounds, and yen began to decline. Consequently, the dollar value of the banks' euro-, pound-, and yen-denominated deposits rose dramatically, even though the actual quantities of euros and pounds held on deposit with U.S. banks had increased only slightly.

FOR CRITICAL ANALYSIS: How can U.S. banks determine whether they have truly succeeded in attracting more foreign-currency-denominated deposits?

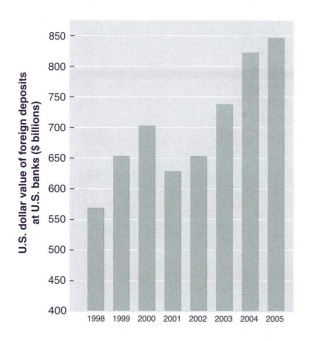

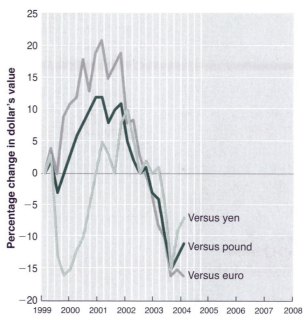

FIGURE 3-3
Foreign Deposits Held at Offices of U.S. Banks.

As shown in panel (a), foreign deposits at U.S. banks increased significantly after 2001. Panel (b) indicates that a key reason behind this increase in deposits was that the falling value of the dollar resulted in a rise in the dollar value of foreign-currency-denominated deposits.

SOURCE: Federal Deposit Insurance Corporation, authors' estimates.

There are several different capital markets. Stock shares of ownership in businesses and bonds issued by corporations are traded in separate capital markets. So are longer-term securities issued by the U.S. Treasury and agencies of the U.S. government, state and local municipal securities, home mortgages, and bank commercial and consumer loans.

Trading in capital markets can be very active, but on a given day relatively fewer buyers and sellers generally interact in these markets than in the money markets. As a consequence, as mentioned earlier, capital market instruments are less liquid than money market instruments.

CAPITAL MARKET INSTRUMENTS   The maturities of capital market instruments exceed one year. Financial instruments with both intermediate-term (one to ten years) maturities and long-term (more than ten years) maturities are included in this category.

As mentioned, capital market instruments are less liquid than money market instruments and generally are regarded as somewhat more risky. Figure 3-4 shows the relative outstanding amounts of various types of capital market instruments.

Equities   Business **equities** are shares of ownership, such as *common stock,* that corporations issue. Owners of equities are *residual claimants* on the income and net worth of a corporation. This means that all other holders of the corporation's debt must be paid before the equity owners. The key advantage of equity ownership, however, is that the rate of return on equities varies with the profitability of the firm. Equities typically offer **dividends,** which are periodic payments to holders that are related to the corporation's profits.

Because corporations are ongoing concerns as long as they remain profitable, the equities that they issue have no stated maturities. Hence, equities are long-term financial instruments and are classified among capital market instruments.

Common Stock   Equity shares most commonly are issued in two forms: common stock and preferred stock. Ownership of **common stock** entitles the shareholder to have some direct say about how the company conducts its business. As a common stock owner, the shareholder is entitled to attend meetings where shareholders can vote in elections for a company's board of

---

MONEYXTRA!
Economic Applications

Have stock prices generally risen or fallen in recent months? Take a look at the recent performance of the S&P stock price index via EconData Online. **http:// moneyxtra.swcollege.com**

Equities: Shares of ownership, such as corporate stock, issued by business firms.

Dividends: Periodic payments to holders of corporate equities.

Common stock: Shares of corporate ownership that entitle the owner to vote on management issues but offer no guarantees of dividends or of market value in the event of corporate bankruptcy.

FIGURE 3-4
Capital Market Instruments Outstanding.

Corporate equities, mortgage instruments, and Treasury notes and bonds are key instruments of the capital markets.

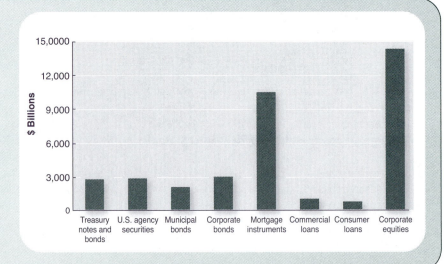

SOURCES: Board of Governors of the Federal Reserve System, *Federal Reserve Bulletin Statistical Supplement,* April 2005; z.1 *Flow of Funds Release,* June 9, 2005.

directors and have some input concerning matters such as management strategy. (Shareholders do not have to attend meetings to vote.)

The fact that owners of common stock are the *residual claimants* means that if a company goes bankrupt, they are the last in line for any remaining assets of the firm. These residual assets could very well have less value than the stated value of the company's stock. Hence, owners of common stock take on more default risk than any other creditors of the company. For this reason they are granted the greatest say in management.

The potential liability of a stockholder, however, is limited to the value of the individual's shareholdings. Hence, if a company goes bankrupt, the most that a stockholder can lose is the funds that he or she has allocated to its shares.

Preferred Stock Holders of **preferred stock** have no voting rights. They sacrifice this power to influence the company's management in exchange for a guarantee that they will receive dividends if any are paid by the company to stockholders. And if the company is forced into bankruptcy, preferred stockholders have first claim on any residual value of the firm after other creditors have been paid.

Preferred stock: Shares of corporate ownership that entail no voting rights but entitle the owner to dividends if any are paid by the corporation and to any residual value of the corporation after other creditors have been paid.

Stock Exchanges Corporate equity shares are traded on **stock exchanges,** which are organized physical locations that function as marketplaces for stocks. Members of stock exchanges function both as brokers and as dealers. As brokers they trade on behalf of others, and as dealers they trade on their own accounts.

Stock exchanges: Organized marketplaces for corporate equities and bonds.

There are several stock exchanges in the United States. The oldest and largest is the New York Stock Exchange (NYSE), which began in 1792. Roughly half of the stock trading in the United States is done on the NYSE. Shares of more than 3,000 companies, including many of the largest U.S. corporations, are traded there. The number of membership positions in the NYSE, called "seats," is fixed at 1,366. Over 500 of these seats are owned by securities firms. About a third of these firms are Exchange *specialists,* which are responsible for laying out and honoring basic ground rules for orderly trading activity in the Exchange. Figure 3-5 on the next page explains how to read NYSE data published in the *Wall Street Journal*.

Over-the-Counter Stocks In recent years a number of corporations have chosen not to be listed on the organized exchanges. Shares in these corporations are **over-the-counter (OTC) stocks** that are traded in decentralized markets. OTC trading volumes have increased in recent years as more OTC stocks are traded on electronic networks that link traders around the world.

Over-the-counter (OTC) stocks: Equity shares offered by companies that do not meet listing requirements for major stock exchanges, or choose not to be listed there, and instead are traded in decentralized markets.

In the United States, most OTC stocks are traded on the **National Association of Securities Dealers Automated Quotation (Nasdaq)** system. In February 1971, Nasdaq was launched as a tiny network of 100 or so securities firms linked by $25 million worth of interconnected "desktop devices" to trade about 2,800 OTC stocks. At that time, trading in the rest of the financial world was done largely through phone calls, and stock prices were often distributed by runners on foot. Indeed, the screens displaying the OTC stock prices on Nasdaq's "desktop devices" were not even known as computer screens—appropriately, because the devices did not actually compute anything. The system simply displayed stock quotes and the phone number of the broker to call to trade. Today, the Nasdaq market links about 500 dealers via true computers, and the market is home to nearly 5,500 stocks, including those of such information technology firms as Microsoft, Intel, and Cisco. (Other nations are hoping that establishing their own versions of the U.S. Nasdaq exchange may serve as a catalyst for the development of their own information technology industries; see on the next page the *Global Focus: Aiming to Duplicate Nasdaq's Successes in China.*)

National Association of Securities Dealers Automated Quotation (Nasdaq): The electronic network over which most over-the-counter stocks are traded.

On the Web
What are the latest innovations at Nasdaq? To find out, visit the National Association of Securities Dealers at **http://www.nasd.com**.
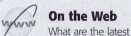

FIGURE 3-5
Reading Stock Quotations.

Each day the *Wall Street Journal* reports New York Stock Exchange and American Stock Exchange stock prices using the format shown here. To understand how to read published stock quotes, consider the information for each column in the quote for the common stock of J. P. Morgan Chase.

YTD % CHG	52-WEEK HI	52-WEEK LO	STOCK (SYM)	DIV	YLD %	PE	VOL 100s	CLOSE	NET CHG
40.1	27.18	12.61 ♣	JLG Ind JGL x	.02	.1	35	40989	27.50	0.38
−8.5	40.45	33.35	JPMorgChas JPM	1.36	3.8	30	90262	35.71	0.11
13.1	29.98	19.18	JabilCircuit JBL		...	32	25194	28.92	−0.35
9.1	41.95	27.06	JackInTheBx JBX		...	17	2033	40.22	−0.26
−7.3	25.50	16.32	JcksnHewitt TaxSvc JTX n	.21e	.9	18	4420	23.41	0.69
14.1	56.80	36.86	JacobEngrg JEC		...	25	1763	54.51	0.03

52 Week Hi: Highest dollar price of a share of J. P. Morgan Chase common stock during the past 52 weeks, which was $40.45.

52 Week Lo: Lowest dollar price of a share of J. P. Morgan Chase common stock during the past 52 weeks, which was $33.35.

Stock: Corporate name of J. P. Morgan Chase.

Sym: Symbol identifying J. P. Morgan Chase, which is JPM.

Div: Annual dollar dividend per share, which was $1.36 per share.

Yld %: Stock yield measured as the annual dividend as a percentage of the closing price for the day, which was $1.36 divided by $35.71 times 100, or approximately 3.8%.

PE: Ratio of stock price to the annual earnings per share, which was equal to 30 for J. P. Morgan Chase.

Vol 100s: Hundreds of J. P. Morgan Chase shares traded this day, or 9,026,200 shares.

Close: Price of J. P. Morgan Chase shares at day's end, or $35.71 per share.

Net Chg: Dollar change in price of J. P. Morgan Chase shares relative to previous day's trading, which was an increase of $0.11.

Corporate bonds: Long-term debt instruments of corporations.

Corporate Bonds Corporations may wish to fund capital expansions by borrowing instead of by issuing stock. One way to borrow is by issuing **corporate bonds,** which are long-term debt instruments of corporations. A typical corporate bond pays a fixed amount of interest twice each year until maturity. Some corporate bonds are *convertible,* meaning that the holder has the right to convert them into a certain number of equity shares prior to maturity. Corpo-

Aiming to Duplicate Nasdaq's Successes in China

Currently, publicly traded stocks of the largest Chinese companies are exchanged on the Shanghai Stock Exchange. Medium-sized and small firms, including new start-up companies, typically must rely on bank loans. Banks, however, are reluctant to lend too heavily to new firms without a proven track record, so smaller firms have difficulty expanding the scale of their operations. In an effort to broaden the sources of funds available to smaller companies, China's State Council recently authorized an existing exchange, the Shenzhen Stock Exchange, to reorient its activities toward stocks of less established Chinese companies. Managers of the Shenzhen Stock Exchange particularly hope to attract shares of new companies specializing in information technologies. Consequently, they are intentionally restructuring the Shenzhen exchange along the pattern established by the U.S. Nasdaq system.

FOR CRITICAL ANALYSIS: Why might those interested in the stocks of information technology companies be particularly attracted to an exchange that functions like the U.S. Nasdaq market?

rations that offer such a convertibility feature usually do so to make the bonds more attractive to potential buyers.

Treasury Notes and Bonds   The U.S. Treasury issues two categories of financial instruments with maturities of more than one year. These are Treasury notes and Treasury bonds. **Treasury notes** have maturities ranging from one to ten years. **Treasury bonds** have maturities of ten years or more. Both notes and bonds have minimum denominations of $1,000. The Treasury sells most notes and bonds at auctions.

Securities of U.S. Government Agencies   These are long-term debt instruments issued by a variety of federal agencies. For instance, one agency called the General National Mortgage Association (GNMA, or "Ginnie Mae") issues securities backed by the value of household mortgages that it holds.

Municipal Bonds   Long-term securities issued by state and local governments are called **municipal bonds.** An attractive feature of these bonds for many holders is that the interest payments the holders receive typically are tax-free. Consequently, the stated interest rates on municipal bonds are lower than the rates on corporate bonds.

Mortgage Loans and Mortgage-Backed Securities   Long-term loans to individual homeowners or to businesses for purchases of land and buildings are **mortgage loans.** Most mortgage loans are made initially by savings banks, savings and loan associations, and commercial banks.

   These depository institutions sell many of the mortgage loans that they initiate to other institutions in a secondary market. The purchasing institutions, which include GNMA and other governmental or quasi-governmental agencies, fund their mortgage purchases by issuing **mortgage-backed securities.** These are financial instruments whose returns are derived from the underlying returns on the mortgage loans held by the issuer, such as GNMA. The existence of secondary markets for mortgage-backed securities makes mortgage loans more liquid than they would otherwise be.

Commercial and Consumer Loans   Long-term loans made by banks to businesses are **commercial loans.** Long-term loans that banks and other institutions, such as finance companies, make to individuals are **consumer loans.** Until recently, there were not many secondary markets for these loans, so they traditionally have been the most illiquid capital market instruments. As we shall discuss in Chapter 10, however, banks have worked in recent years to increase the liquidity of the loans that they make.

INTERNATIONAL CAPITAL MARKETS   Most international bank loans are for terms exceeding a year. Hence, cross-border bank loans are international capital market instruments, as are internationally traded notes and bonds. **International capital markets** are markets where financial instruments with maturities longer than one year are exchanged across national borders. Between 1986 and 2006, total trading activity in international capital markets increased by $1.7 trillion, or more than 3,000 percent. Activity in the international loan market, which accounts for just under a fifth of international capital market trading, has increased by more than 400 percent since the mid-1980s. Growth in international securities activity has been even greater. During the same period, the value of internationally traded securities outstanding has risen by more than 500 percent. (Africa is seeking to internationalize its capital market trading; see the *Global Focus: A Pan-African Stock Exchange Tries to Get Off the Ground* on the next page.)

Treasury notes: Treasury securities with maturities ranging from one to ten years.

Treasury bonds: Treasury securities with maturities of ten years or more.

Municipal bonds: Long-term debt instruments issued by state and local governments.

Mortgage loans: Long-term loans to individual homeowners or to businesses for purchases of land and buildings.

Mortgage-backed securities: Financial instruments whose return is based on the underlying returns on mortgage loans.

Commercial loans: Long-term loans made by banks to businesses.

Consumer loans: Long-term loans made by banks and other institutions to individuals.

International capital markets: Markets for cross-border exchange of financial instruments that have maturities of a year or more.

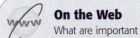

On the Web
What are important issues to keep in mind when building a bond portfolio? Learn more about bond investments at **http://www. investinginbonds.com/**.

GLOBAL
Focus

A Pan-African Stock Exchange Tries to Get Off the Ground

The world's sixteenth-largest stock exchange, located in Johannesburg, South Africa, handles about 75 percent of all African stock trades. Twenty other small stock exchanges across Africa handle the remaining 25 percent of the region's stock transactions. Each of these smaller exchanges lists only about a few dozen stocks, so orders to buy or sell stocks arrive relatively infrequently on days when the exchanges are open. Nevertheless, the smaller exchanges have been attracting some companies' stocks away from the Johannesburg exchange, which has sapped some trading from Johannesburg. As a consequence, someone desiring to sell a share of stock using *any* of the African stock exchanges, including the Johannesburg exchange, often has to wait for days for an interested buyer to place an order.

In an attempt to broaden African stock trading, an effort is under way to combine stock exchanges throughout Africa into one, continent-spanning system. So far, progress toward this goal has been slow. Stock exchanges in developed nations are linked by Internet-based auction systems, but Africa's telecommunications networks lag behind those in the rest of the world. Thus, technological handicaps are hindering efforts to broaden the liquidity of the market for African stocks.

FOR CRITICAL ANALYSIS: Why might infrequent trading in a stock exchange cause prospective investors to regard the stocks traded on that exchange as risky propositions?

Euronotes: Medium-term debt instruments issued in a currency other than that of the country where the instruments are issued.

Eurobonds: Long-term debt instruments issued in a currency other than that of the country where the instruments are issued.

Companies enter the Eurocurrency markets to raise funds in other nations or to issue notes and bonds denominated in other currencies. **Euronotes** are medium-term debt instruments issued in a currency other than that of the country where the notes are issued. These instruments typically have a longer term than Eurocommercial paper and a shorter term than **Eurobonds,** which are long-term debt instruments issued in a currency other than that of the country where the bonds are issued. For instance, if a Canadian business issues Canadian-dollar-denominated twenty-year bonds in London, then it has issued a Eurobond. More than $500 billion in Euronotes and $700 billion in Eurobonds are issued in the international capital markets.

On the Web

www How did the London Stock Exchange evolve from a seventeenth-century joint stock company to one of the world's largest stock exchanges? Read a brief history at **http://www.londonstockexchange.com**. Click on "About the Exchange."

4. What are capital markets, and what are key capital market instruments? Capital markets are markets in which financial instruments with maturities of at least one year are traded. Key instruments of the U.S. capital markets include business equities, corporate bonds, U.S. Treasury notes and bonds, securities of U.S. government agencies, municipal bonds, and mortgage, commercial, and consumer loans. In the international capital markets, important capital market instruments include Euronotes and Eurobonds denominated in currencies other than those of the countries from which they originate.

The Cybertrading Revolution and Its International Ramifications

New technologies have fundamentally altered the way that many people trade financial instruments. The result has been a growing "internationalization" of financial trading.

Electronic Securities Trading

Electronic trading began in the mid-1990s with just a few Internet addresses, such as www.etrade.com, www.schwab.com, and www.lombard.com. These Web sites offered something never before available: the capability to buy shares of stock online.

LOWER FEES   Trading online offers several advantages, including low brokerage fees. For instance, buying 100 shares of stock in International Business Machines (IBM) from a traditional brokerage firm entails fees in the neighborhood of $100, whereas online brokers typically charge $10—or even less—for the transaction. The result has been predictable: online securities trading has taken off. Today, more than a third of all stock trades are processed on *electronic communications networks (ECNs)*, which are Internet-based auction networks linking buyers and sellers of stocks around the world.

SPEED COUNTS   Online trading is faster as well as less expensive. Anyone can reach Internet-based brokerage accounts from any computer with a secure Web browser. Today, literally at one's fingertips are hundreds of sites offering investment research sources and trading capabilities—all of which help make the Web a logical fit with the fast-paced, high-tech world of Wall Street. After a typical Internet trader punches in an ID and account password, she often has access to a package of services that might otherwise be quite costly if purchased separately, such as portfolio tracking and a database containing information about such things as companies' market capitalization and earnings growth. After conducting market research, the Internet trader can scan her portfolio of holdings, search for key information on companies whose stock she owns or is interested in, and send a request to buy or sell stock, all in a few minutes.

SOME BROKERAGE FIRMS BENEFIT   Internet trading also provides payoffs for the brokerage firms that offer it. Most Wall Street discount brokers now accept Internet-generated orders. Internet-based brokerage firms can get by with less printed marketing material to send to clients, smaller customer-service staffs, and fewer physical branches. (Competition among Internet stockbrokers has resulted in many of these cost savings being passed along to customers in the form of lower brokerage commissions and fees; see on the next page the *Management Focus: Pursuit of Frequent Traders Generates an Online Brokerage Price War*.)

DIRECT OFFERING TO SAVERS   Many companies, such as Ford Motor Company and IBM, now issue commercial paper directly to savers through interactive online services. On screen, commercial paper traders can see the issuer, maturity, settlement date, yield, ratings, and trading instructions. Typically, a commercial paper exchange can be completed in as little as eight seconds, although it can take longer if the two sides bargain about the price or yield. If the trader wishes to bargain, the computer program usually gives customers about a half-minute to decide whether to take the yield offered or to counter with a lower yield. At the conclusion of a transaction, the computer automatically thanks the saver and logs the time of the exchange.

Internet trading in commercial paper began in early 1996. By the end of that year, commercial paper trading volumes had surpassed $100 million per day. Current daily volumes average hundreds of millions of dollars.

International Cybertrading

What are CORES, CAES, and CATS? CORES, or the Computer-Assisted Order Routing and Execution System, is a completely automated system based in Tokyo that links buyers and sellers of government securities, corporate bonds, and equity shares. CAES, or the Computer-Assisted

MONEYXTRA!
Another Perspective

For a more detailed discussion of the role of ECNs, see the Chapter 3 reading, entitled "The Emergence of Electronic Communications Networks in the U.S. Equity Markets," by James McAndrews and Chris Stefanadis of the Federal Reserve Bank of New York. **http:// moneyxtra.swcollege.com**

MANAGEMENT
Focus

Pursuit of Frequent Traders Generates an Online Brokerage Price War

The revenues of Internet stockbrokers are generated by commissions and fees earned from executing trades on behalf of their customers. Naturally, this means that the customers who conduct trades most frequently create the most revenues for online brokerages. At the Internet broker Ameritrade, for instance, the 20 percent of its customers who conduct the most trades generate about 80 percent of the firm's revenues. To compete for the business of customers who engage in frequent stock trades, Ameritrade, E*Trade, and other online brokerage firms have been slashing the fees they charge these customers. During the past two years, the average fees that Internet stockbrokers charge to people who trade stocks at least fifty times per month dropped by more than half. In an effort to attract new customers who are most likely to be frequent traders, Ameritrade and E*Trade now offer fifty free trades during the first month of service, and Ameritrade even gives new customers who trade that often a $50 cash rebate.

FOR CRITICAL ANALYSIS: Why do you suppose that online brokerage firms also are competing on the basis of how fast they promise to execute trades on behalf of their customers? (Hint: Many people who trade frequently do so because their strategy for profiting from online trading is to buy stocks and sell them as rapidly as possible at slightly higher prices.)

Execution System, is an analogous system operated by the U.S. National Association of Securities Dealers. CATS, the Toronto-based Computer-Assisted Trading System, performs the same basic functions. These trading systems, plus others in such locales as Denmark, Singapore, Sweden, the United Kingdom, and the United States, share the common feature that they permit traders in financial markets to place orders for purchases and sales of securities via computers.

MECHANICS OF AUTOMATED FINANCIAL TRADING   Each automated trading system has its own unique characteristics, but in general computer-connected traders use system-specific software programs to access information on current market terms on a number of financial instruments. The software displays on the trader's computer screen the best bid and offer with the amounts involved, the most recent sale price and quantity traded, and related spot market prices for reference. The trader may then use the computer's keyboard to interact with the system and make trades via appropriate commands.

Automated trading has made possible nearly seamless, around-the-clock securities trading. When financial markets open in Tokyo, Hong Kong, Australia, and Singapore, it is evening of the previous day in New York and Chicago. At this time, a trader in Tokyo, for instance, may see an acceptable asking price for a financial instrument in New York and initiate a transaction to purchase the instrument. If the instrument is a U.S. Treasury security, then ownership is transferred and payment settled the next business day in the United States. A transaction arranged, for instance, on Wednesday in Tokyo—Tuesday night in New York—would settle on Thursday in New York, about a day and a half later.

POLICY ISSUES OF GLOBALIZED CYBERTRADING   The globalization of financial markets brought about by automated trading has raised three problems for policymakers. One concerns how rules for securities trading on various national trading systems should be adapted to the new global trading environment. Nations with more demanding requirements for trading on their securities exchanges may incur fewer risks to their systems as trading

On the Web
What regulatory issues are currently being pursued by the United Kingdom's Financial Services Authority? You can find out by visiting the FSA at **http://www.fsa.gov.uk/**.

becomes more globalized. At the same time, however, their exchanges may lose business to nations with less stringent rules.

A second concern for policymakers is that automated trading across borders has the potential to exacerbate financial crises. If enough traders react to news of a sudden drop in the price of a financial instrument, market prices of closely related, electronically traded instruments can respond within a very short time. As a consequence, a general fall in market prices can occur very rapidly on electronic networks for trading financial instruments. (Sometimes such rapid price declines can result from an error involving a single trade; see the *Cyber Focus: A "Mini" Error Can Have a Large Impact in Electronic Markets.*)

International cybertrading also increases the speed at which traders can sell one nation's financial instruments and reallocate funds to holdings of instruments issued by another nation. Thus, traders located far from the scene can respond very quickly to financial uncertainties in a country or region. Although this capability is advantageous for individual traders, there may be drawbacks for the countries experiencing such uncertainties. For instance, if many traders respond to greater uncertainty about a country's financial prospects by liquidating their holdings of financial instruments issued by that country, the result can be a collapse in the prices of those instruments. Thus, cybertrading can increase the swiftness with which financial uncertainty gives way to financial crisis. It can also increase the speed with which a financial crisis in one nation or region spills over into another.

CYBER
Focus

A "Mini" Error Can Have a Large Impact in Electronic Markets

To assist in predicting near-term movements of stock prices, economists often consider changes in the prices of *stock index futures contracts,* which yield returns based on the average prices of large groups of stocks. For instance, a rise in the price of futures contracts with returns that depend on the Dow Jones Industrial Average (DJIA), a weighted average of prices of stocks of thirty major U.S. companies, indicates that traders anticipate a general increase in stock prices. An example of a DJIA futures contract is the *e-mini Dow Jones Industrial Average future,* or an "e-mini contract," which traders

exchange solely via an electronic network. Each e-mini contract, which trades on the futures exchange operated by the Chicago Board of Trade (CBOT), is priced at $5 times the value of the DJIA. A DJIA of 10,000, therefore, yields an e-mini contract value of $50,000. If futures traders bid the price of an e-mini down to $45,000, this reflects their anticipation that the DJIA is poised to drop to 9,000.

Recently, however, a sudden drop in the market price of an e-mini contract had nothing to do with traders' anticipation that the DJIA was about to decline. Instead, the drop occurred because a firm erroneously entered an order to sell 10,000 of the contracts, when it intended to sell only 100 contracts. Not knowing this error had occurred, within seconds many traders jumped to the conclusion that the sudden decline in

the price of e-mini contracts might be due to the arrival of news of a terrible event, such as a terrorist incident. Traders began to sell their own e-mini contracts and other futures contracts linked to the DJIA. They also started selling off futures linked to stock indexes such as the Standard & Poor's 500 and the Nasdaq 100 traded on the Chicago Mercantile Exchange (CME). Within minutes, the CBOT and CME halted trading of most stock index futures, and the CBOT canceled many of the trades that took place after the error occurred.

FOR CRITICAL ANALYSIS: Why can a series of very large orders to sell a financial instrument traded electronically cause its market price to drop rapidly?

CAN CAPITAL CONTROLS WORK IN A CYBERWORLD?

A third concern relates to **capital controls,** or limits that countries place on the flows of funds across their borders. Traditionally, national governments impose capital controls in the form of restrictions on their citizenry's holdings of currencies or financial assets issued by other nations. They may also restrict the ability of their nations' residents to move their own currencies or financial assets abroad.

In a world with financial cybertechnologies, imposing capital controls is much more costly than in years past. Indeed, some observers question whether democratic governments can enforce capital controls without fundamental restraints on basic freedoms that are inconsistent with most notions of what "democratic government" is supposed to mean.

Contemplate, for instance, your task if you were charged with enforcing capital controls in today's financial environment. In addition to establishing security details at every major airport, train station, and/or ship harbor, to effectively enforce a typical set of capital controls you would have to train and unleash squads of "cyberpolice" to monitor the computer storage and data interchange systems of every financial firm in the country. Since an intelligent citizenry might find a way around the controls via funds transferals using smart cards or other electronic payments media, you would also have to put the cyberpolice to work monitoring telephone lines and cell phone systems. Of course, once you had gone to the trouble to put this kind of enforcement system into place, you might be tempted to have your cyberpolice eavesdrop on what people were saying about you in their phone calls and e-mail messages.

Thus, effective enforcement of capital controls in a cyberworld would require transforming a nation into something resembling a police state. In fact, most observers believe that not just any police state can enforce capital controls. It would take a *highly efficient* police state—probably one that does intercept and read e-mail messages—to do the job. It seems unlikely that elected governments would be able to justify this type of policing. For this reason, many economists conclude that as cybertechnologies continue to proliferate, capital controls will be increasingly hard for democratic governments to impose.

> **5. Why has automated financial trading grown, and what are its implications for world financial markets?** An increasing number of individuals are trading stocks and bonds via Internet brokers and other automated trading systems because of the convenience and lower costs. Cybertrading across national borders raises three fundamental policy issues. One is the potential mismatch of national regulatory responses to cybertrading. A second issue is the potential for widespread use of automated trading across national borders to heighten national or regional financial uncertainties and to speed the transmission of financial crises from one country or region to another. A third issue is that cybertechnologies may hinder the enforcement of capital controls, or government restrictions on cross-border financial flows.

Vehicle Currencies

If people from around the world continue to interact in increasingly integrated financial markets, what currencies will they use to buy and sell financial instruments? Money market and capital market instruments are denominated in a number of currencies. Most financial instruments, however, are denominated in a few key national currencies, known as **vehicle currencies,** or commonly accepted currencies used worldwide to denominate international financial instruments. For instance, a company in Thailand may issue a bond denominated in U.S. dollars that is subsequently purchased by a European saver. In this instance, the U.S. dollar serves as a vehicle currency. The bond exchange is denominated in U.S. dollars even though no party to the transaction is located in the United States or uses dollars as a medium of exchange.

The Dollar's Traditional Predominance

Just as the automobile is a primary vehicle of transportation, during the initial decades after World War II the dollar was the main "vehicle" for completing international transactions. Even today, almost 70 percent of U.S. paper currency and coins circulate abroad. The dollar serves as a vehicle currency even for relatively small transactions that people use paper currency and coins to finance.

Since the early 1980s, however, there has been a gradual shift toward the use of multiple currencies in international financial transactions. As a result, there have been periods when it appeared that the dollar might lose its dominant position. For example, during the 1960s a succession of "dollar crises" in which the dollar lost considerable value relative to other currencies fueled speculation that it might lose its status as the world's main vehicle currency. Even today, since the full introduction of the euro by nations of the European Monetary Union, experts question whether the U.S. dollar can maintain its position as the world's leading currency. They wonder if the dollar will eventually be replaced by another predominant currency, as Table 3-2 shows has occurred throughout world history.

The Euro's Impact

Table 3-3 on the next page presents data on the use of four leading vehicle currencies—the U.S. dollar, the euro, the Japanese yen, and the British pound. As the data show, the U.S. dollar remains the dominant vehicle currency. It is used to denominate more than 55 percent of banks'

Table 3-2 A Timeline of Vehicle Currencies

The U.S. dollar is the latest in a long line of vehicle currencies.

Period	Nation	Currencies
Pre-600s B.C.	Babylonia	Shekel
600s–500s B.C.	Persia	Daric
400s–200s B.C.	Greece, Macedonia	Drachma, stater
200s B.C.–300s A.D.	Rome	Solidus, denarius, seterce, aureus
300s–1200s	Byzantium	Solidus, besant
600s–1200s	Islamic empire	Dirham, dinar
800s–1200s	China	Tael, chuen
1200s–1500s	Italy	Florin, grosso, sequin, ducat
1500s–1600s	Spain	Real, escudo
1600s–1700s	France	Denier, sol, louis d'or
1700s	India	Rupee, mohur
1800s	France	Franc
1800s–1900s	Britain	Shilling, pound
1900s–2000s	United States	Dollar

SOURCE: Robert Mundell, "The International Impact of the Euro and Its Implications for Transition Economies," in *Central Banking, Monetary Policies, and the Implications for Transition Economies,* ed. Mario Blejer and Marko Skreb (Boston: Kluwer Academic Publishers, 1999), pp. 403–428.

Table 3-3 Leading Vehicle Currencies

	Shares of Market			
	Banks' Cross-Border Positions in Foreign Currencies (Assets)	Banks' Cross-Border Positions in Foreign Currencies (Liabilities)	International Money Market Instruments	International Bonds and Notes
U.S. dollar	56.2%	57.7%	28.4%	46.5%
Euro	24.0	21.1	50.8	37.3
Japenese yen	5.6	4.6	2.4	4.5
British pound	5.2	6.4	13.7	7.0
All other	9.0	10.2	4.7	4.7

SOURCE: Data from Bank for International Settlements, *International Banking Statistics* and *Securities Statistics,* 2005.

cross-border positions, nearly one-third of international money market instruments, and almost 45 percent of notes and bonds traded in international capital markets.

Will the euro ever replace the dollar as the leading vehicle currency? Since its introduction, the euro has made few inroads into the dollar's dominance in banks' cross-border positions, but it has gained a significant share of international money and capital market instruments. Before the euro's introduction, well over half of all international money and capital market instruments were denominated in dollars. Today, the euro has clearly emerged as an important vehicle currency in both sets of international financial markets, where it now accounts for between 37 and 50 percent of instruments outstanding. In these markets, the dollar's traditional preeminence is under challenge.

6. What are vehicle currencies, and what are the predominant vehicle currencies in international financial markets? Vehicle currencies are currencies that individuals and businesses most often use to conduct international transactions. Since the end of World War II, the U.S. dollar has been the primary vehicle currency utilized in the world's financial markets. The euro and the Japanese yen are the next two predominant vehicle currencies. The euro is increasingly being used as a vehicle currency and may eventually rival the dollar's vehicle currency position in international money and capital markets.

Chapter Summary

1. The Main Economic Function of Financial Markets: The fundamental economic role of financial markets is to direct saving to borrowers desiring to finance investments in capital goods, or goods that may be employed to produce additional goods and services in the future. By purchasing financial instruments, or claims on the future incomes of borrowers, savers provide these funds.

2. Primary and Secondary Markets for Financial Instruments: Financial markets in which borrowers offer newly issued financial instruments for sale to savers are primary markets. Financial markets in which financial instruments issued at a previous time are traded are secondary markets.

3. Money Markets and Money Market Instruments: Money markets are financial markets in which instruments with maturities of less than one year are traded. U.S. Treasury bills, commercial paper, certificates of deposit, repurchase agreements, federal funds, and banker's acceptances are important instruments traded in the U.S. money markets. International money market trading involves cross-border exchanges of money market instruments denominated in currencies other than those of the countries from which they originate, such as Eurocommercial paper and Eurocurrency deposits.

4. Capital Markets and Key Capital Market Instruments: Capital markets are financial markets in which instruments with maturities of at least one year are traded. Business equities, corporate bonds, U.S. Treasury notes and bonds, U.S. government agency securities, municipal bonds, and mortgage, commercial, and consumer loans are key instruments of the U.S. capital market. Important instruments traded across national borders via international capital markets include Euronotes and Eurobonds that are issued in one country but denominated in another nation's currency.

5. Automated Trading of Financial Instruments and International Financial Markets: For many traders, cybertrading via Internet brokers and other automated trading systems is more convenient and less costly than using the services of traditional brokers or exchanges. This has contributed to the growth of cybertrading, both within and among nations. Cross-border exchange of financial instruments using automated trading systems has provoked divergent regulatory responses from different nations. International cybertrading also increases the speed at which savers can transfer funds among national markets, which can hasten financial crises and make them more likely to spill over onto other world markets. Cybertechnologies also make it more difficult for governments to impose capital controls.

6. Vehicle Currencies and the Predominant Vehicle Currencies in International Financial Markets: Vehicle currencies are currencies that individuals and businesses most often use to conduct international transactions. Traditionally, the U.S. dollar has been the world's primary vehicle currency. Others are the British pound, the Japanese yen, and, more recently, the European Monetary Union's euro. Although banks continue to use the dollar to denominate most cross-border transactions, the euro has begun to make inroads into the dollar's preeminent position in international money and capital markets.

Questions and Problems

(Answers to odd-numbered questions and problems may be found on the Web at **http://money.swcollege.com** under "Student Resources.")

1. In your view, what are the relative advantages of holding common stock instead of preferred stock? Explain.

2. What are the disadvantages of holding common instead of preferred stock? Explain.

3. How could "impulsive" traders of stocks over the Internet find themselves earning lower net returns on their portfolios of financial instruments, even if on average they hold the same basic portfolios from month to month as more traditional traders? [Hint: Remember that people pay broker's fees when they trade.]

4. During the early years following the formation of the United States, its first Treasury secretary, Alexander Hamilton, worked hard to develop conditions in which secondary financial markets could emerge and grow. Based on this chapter's discussion, can you rationalize Hamilton's actions?

5. In what ways is competition among stock exchanges beneficial for traders and for companies that issue stocks? What gains might emerge if the United States had only one stock exchange? What factors might motivate U.S. stock exchanges to consider merging?

6. Identify each of the following financial instruments as either an international stock share, an international bond, a Eurocurrency deposit, a Euronote, a Eurobond, or Eurocommercial paper.

a. An Argentine company offers a five-year debt instrument for sale to international savers.

b. The government of Russia offers a ten-year debt instrument, denominated in U.S. dollars, for sale in the London securities market.

c. Bank of America lends a pound-denominated deposit to Royal Bank of Canada.

d. A Mexican firm offers shares of its stock for sale to international savers.

e. The government of Australia offers a twenty-year debt instrument, denominated in U.S. dollars, for sale in the French securities market.

7. Why is it easier for funds to flow across national borders via cybertechnologies than with cash or checks? Explain in your own words.

8. In your view, do emerging cybertechnologies make it easier or more difficult, on net, for repressive governments to effectively impose capital controls? Explain your reasoning.

9. Can you think of any ways that the U.S. government benefits from the U.S. dollar's role as the world's predominant vehicle currency? [Hint: Remember that the U.S. Treasury and the Federal Reserve pay no interest on currency.]

10. How might the relative size and openness of a nation's financial markets affect the international circulation of its currency? Why?

Before the Test

Test your understanding of the material covered in this chapter by taking the Chapter 3 interactive quiz at **http://money.swcollege.com**.

Online Application

Internet URL: **http://www.nyse.com/**

Title: The New York Stock Exchange: How the NYSE Operates

Navigation: Begin at the URL listed above. In the left margin, click on "About the NYSE" and then "Education," followed by "Educational Publications." Then click on "Chapter Two: The Trading Floor."

Application: Read the chapter, and answer the following questions:

1. What features distinguish alternative types of orders for purchasing stock?

2. List the key functions of a stock exchange specialist. Why is the cybertechnology called the "Point-of-Sale Display Book" likely to be particularly useful for a specialist?

For Group Study and Analysis: Divide the class into groups, and have each group examine and discuss the description of how NYSE trades are executed. Ask each group to list the various points at which Internet trading may be a more efficient way to execute a trade than trading via a traditional brokerage firm. Then go through these lists as a class, and discuss the following issue: What people in the NYSE cannot be replaced by cybertechnologies?

Selected References and Further Reading

First Boston Corporation. *Handbook of Securities of the United States Government and Federal Agencies.* Published every second year.

Demiralp, Selva, Brian Preslopsky, and William Whitesell. "Overnight Interbank Loan Markets." Board of Governors of the Federal Reserve System, May 2004.

Fleming, Michael. "Measuring Treasury Market Liquidity." Federal Reserve Bank of New York *Economic Policy Review,* September 2003, 83–108.

Fleming, Michael, and Kenneth Garbade. "The Repurchase Agreement Refined: GCF Repo." Federal Reserve Bank of New York *Current Issues in Economics and Finance* 9 (June 2003).

Geisst, Charles. *Wall Street—A History.* New York: Oxford University Press, 1997.

McAndrews, James, and Chris Stefanadis. "The Consolidation of European Stock Exchanges." Federal Reserve Bank of New York *Current Issues in Economics and Finance* 8 (June 2002).

Mundell, Robert. "The International Impact of the Euro and Its Implication for Transition Economics." In *Central Banking, Monetary Policies, and the Implications for Transition Economies,* ed. Mario Blejer and Marko Skreb (Boston: Kluwer Academic Publishers, 1999), pp. 403–428.

Standard and Poors. *Emerging Stock Markets Factbook.* Published annually.

Stigum, Marcia. *The Money Market.* 3d ed. Homewood, Ill.: Dow-Jones-Irwin, 1990.

MoneyXtra

Log on to the MoneyXtra Web site now (**http://moneyxtra.swcollege.com**) for additional learning resources such as practice quizzes, case studies, readings, and additional economic applications.

Unit II
Financial Markets and Instruments

Contents

Interest Rates

On January 2, 2001, television financial news reports showed frantic activity in the bond market. On that day, the Federal Reserve announced that it would reduce its target for a key interest rate, known as the federal funds rate, by one-half of a percentage point, to 6 percent. That decrease in one particular interest rate in the economy sent shock waves through bond markets not only in the United States but around the world. Traders everywhere were shouting orders to buy bonds, whose prices were rising.

On June 29, 2004, for the first time since 2000, just the opposite situation occurred. Television financial news reports showed similar frantic activity in the bond markets. But this time traders were shouting out orders to sell bonds whose prices were falling. Interest rates fall and interest rates rise. So do bond prices. In the late 1970s, interest rates rose by several percentage points, whereas in the early 2000s they fell by several percentage points. The interesting questions are the following: (1) Why do traders behave so frantically when interest rates change, and (2) how are interest rates and bond prices related?

Fundamental Issues

1. Why must we compute different interest yields?

2. How does risk cause market interest rates to differ?

3. Why do market interest rates vary with differences in financial instruments' terms to maturity?

4. What is the real interest rate?

5. What interest rates are the key indicators of financial market conditions?

In this chapter, you will find the answers to these key questions. Along the way you will learn about how inflation affects interest rates. The first order of business, though, is to understand what interest rates are and how to calculate interest yields.

Calculating Interest Yields

By holding financial instruments, such as loans or bonds, savers and financial institutions extend credit to those individuals or firms that issue the instruments. The amount of credit extended is the **principal** amount of the loan or the bond. Those who hold financial instruments do so because they receive payments from the issuers in the form of **interest.** The percentage return earned is the **interest rate.** For a simple-interest, one-year loan, for instance, the interest rate is equal to the ratio of total interest during the year to the principal of the loan. That is, the interest rate is equal to the amount of interest divided by the loan principal.

The interest return from holding a financial instrument is its yield to the owner. Hence, this interest return is often called the *interest yield* of a financial instrument. (Market interest rates are hardly ever negative, but in extremely rare situations, this can happen; see *What Happens When Interest Rates on Repurchase Agreements Fall Below Zero?*)

Interest Rates on Repurchase Agreements Fall Below Zero?

For a time in late 2003, market interest rates on certain repurchase agreements involving U.S. Treasury securities were *negative*. This very rare situation arose in the market for *special collateral repurchase agreements*. These are agreements for a lender of funds to receive securities, such as Treasury notes, as collateral for the loan. The lender agrees to resell the securities to the borrower of funds at a later date—often the following day.

Under normal circumstances, the borrower in a repurchase agreement transaction repays the funds plus interest to the lender. In 2003, however, due to settlement problems in the secondary market for Treasury notes, a number of securities dealers that had agreed to sell the notes found themselves with too few notes on hand to honor their commitments. To obtain more Treasury notes, these dealers entered

the market for special collateral repurchase agreements, where they offered to "lend" funds to holders of Treasury notes and obtain the notes as "collateral" for their loans. In return, the dealers accepted a negative interest rate on their "loans" of funds. Of course, the securities dealers were effectively paying interest to borrow Treasury notes in order to honor their commitments to other parties. Nevertheless, the result was a negative market interest rate on the dealers' "loans" of funds for these special collateral repurchase agreements.

FOR CRITICAL ANALYSIS: Why are negative interest rates hardly ever observed outside of the market for special collateral repurchase agreements?

Different Concepts of Interest Yields

There are different ways to think about the interest yields on financial instruments. The most important are the nominal yield, current yield, and yield to maturity.

NOMINAL YIELD   Suppose that a bond is issued in an amount of $10,000 with an agreement to pay $600 in interest every year. The annual payment of $600 is the bond's annual **coupon return.** This is simply the fixed amount of interest that the bond yields each year. It is called a coupon return because many bonds actually have coupons that represent titles to interest yields.

The **nominal yield** on a bond is equal to

$$r_N = C/F,$$

where r_N is the nominal yield, C is the coupon return, and F is the face amount of the bond. The annual nominal yield of the $10,000 bond with a $600 coupon return is equal to $600/$10,000 = 0.06, or 6 percent.

CURRENT YIELD   The current secondary market price of a bond typically is not the face value of the bond. Bonds often sell in secondary markets at prices that differ from their face values. For this reason, those contemplating a bond purchase often are interested in the **current yield** of a bond. This is equal to

$$r_C = C/P,$$

where r_C denotes the current yield, C is the coupon return, and P is the current market price of the bond.

For instance, the current market price of a bond with a face value of $10,000 might be $9,000. If the coupon return on the bond is $600 per year, then the annual current yield on this bond is equal to $600/$9,000 = 0.067, or 6.7 percent.

Principal: The amount of credit extended when one makes a loan or purchases a bond.

Interest: The payment, or yield, received in exchange for extending credit by holding any financial instrument.

Interest rate: The percentage return, or percentage yield, earned by the holder of a financial instrument.

Coupon return: A fixed interest return that a bond yields each year.

Nominal yield: The coupon return on a bond divided by the bond's face value.

Current yield: The coupon return on a bond divided by the bond's market price.

MONEYXTRA!
Economic Applications

Have Treasury bond yields generally risen or fallen in recent months? Take a look at the recent performance of the yield on ten-year Treasury bonds via EconData Online. **http:// moneyxtra.swcollege.com**

Yield to maturity: The rate of return on a bond if it is held until it matures, which reflects the market price of the bond, the bond's coupon return, and any capital gain from holding the bond to maturity.

Capital gain: An increase in the value of a financial instrument at the time it is sold as compared with its market value at the date it was purchased.

YIELD TO MATURITY   A bond's **yield to maturity** is the rate of return if the bond is held until maturity. Calculating this yield can be complicated, however, because the bond's market price and its face value normally differ.

Typically, bonds are sold at a *discount*, meaning that a bond's selling price is below its face value. Hence, other things being equal, the bondholder receives an automatic capital gain if the bond is held to maturity. A **capital gain** occurs when the value of a financial asset at the time it is redeemed or sold is higher than its market value when it was purchased. At the same time, the bond pays a coupon return. The yield to maturity must account for both the capital gain and the coupon returns that a bond yields to its owner. (In recent years, some credit-card issuers have offered to charge cardholders zero percent interest over the lifetime of specific loans; see the *Management Focus: "Zero Percent Interest for Life!"*)

Calculating Discounted Present Value

To understand the interplay between coupon returns and capital gains in calculating bond yields, consider a specific example—a bond whose maturity is three years. The bond's face value is $10,000. Its annual coupon return is $600. Hence, its nominal yield per year is $600/$10,000 = 0.06, or 6 percent.

DISCOUNTED PRESENT VALUE   To compute the yield to maturity on this bond, we need to determine its market price. Note that the bond's owner receives three payments: $600 after the first year, $600 after the second year, and $10,600 (the principal plus the third year's interest) after the third year. And so the amount that the buyer will be willing to pay for this bond must equal the value of these payments from the buyer's perspective at the time she purchases the bond.

MANAGEMENT

Focus

"Zero Percent Interest for Life!"

Recently, two credit-card issuers, Discover and J.P. Morgan Chase, offered to charge selected consumers zero percent interest on transfers of existing credit-card balances to Discover and J.P. Morgan Chase credit cards. Effectively, therefore, the companies offered to make credit-card loans at zero percent interest. As a further inducement, the companies promised to charge zero percent interest "for life" on the amounts transferred to their credit cards.

The "zero interest for life" offers did not really entail "free" access to credit. Only consumers that the credit-card issuers judged to be highly creditworthy received the offers, and only balances these consumers agreed to transfer to Discover or J.P. Morgan Chase were charged a zero percent rate. Furthermore, consumers who agreed faced unusually stiff penalties for late payments.

Why did Discover and J.P. Morgan Chase extend credit at zero percent interest for the life of these new credit-card loans? The answer was that they desired to attract creditworthy customers who tend to borrow large sums

and maintain high loan balances. The zero-interest promise was intended to dissuade these customers from turning around and transferring their balances to yet another credit-card issuer. The card issuers hoped that these customers would *add* to these balances on their credit-card accounts. Any *additional* borrowing would have been subject to *positive* interest rates charged by the card issuers.

FOR CRITICAL ANALYSIS: Under what circumstances would Discover and J.P. Morgan Chase fail to experience higher revenues as a result of their "zero interest for life" policy?

Today's value of payments to be received at future dates is the **discounted present value** of those payments. Discounted present value is a key financial concept, because it enables us to determine how much a future sum is worth to us from the perspective of today, given current market interest rates. As Table 4-1 shows, the future value of a dollar falls more quickly at higher interest rates. This means that the present value of payments a bond's owner will receive also declines as interest rates increase, thereby reducing the amount that a buyer would be willing to pay for the bond. Consequently, you must understand how to calculate the discounted present value of a future payment before you can understand how to compute bond prices.

In the case of our example of a specific bond with a face value of $10,000 and three annual payments of $600 each, suppose that the prevailing market interest rate is $r = 0.05$, or 5 percent. Consider the first year's return on the bond, which is $600. Note that saving $571.43 for one year at an interest rate of 5 percent would yield an amount of $571.43 (the initial amount) plus 0.05 times $571.43 (the interest), or $571.43 times the factor 1.05. But this works out to be $600. This means that from today's perspective, a $600 payment one year from now at a market interest rate of 5 percent is worth $571.43. Consequently, $571.43 is the discounted present value of $600 a year from now at the interest rate of 5 percent. This amount is equal to the future payment of $600 divided by the sum, $1 + 0.05$, or $600/(1.05) = 571.43. This implies that a formula for calculating the discounted present value of a payment to be received one year from now is

$$\text{Discounted present value} = \text{payment one year from now}/(1 + r).$$

But the bond also pays $600 two years after the time of purchase. Note that at a market rate of interest of 5 percent, holding $544.22 for two years would yield $600. The reason is that if we

Discounted present value: The value today of a payment to be received at a future date.

On the Web
For additional review of present value, go to **http://teachmefinance. com**, and click on "Time Value of Money."

Table 4-1 Present Values of a Future Dollar

This table shows how much a dollar received a given number of years in the future would be worth today at different rates of interest. For instance, at an interest rate of 8 percent, a dollar to be received 25 years from now would have a value of less than 15 cents, and a dollar to be received 50 years from now is worth about 2 cents.

Year	Compounded Annual Interest Rate				
	3%	5%	8%	10%	20%
1	.971	.952	.926	.909	.833
2	.943	.907	.857	.826	.694
3	.915	.864	.794	.751	.578
4	.889	.823	.735	.683	.482
5	.863	.784	.681	.620	.402
6	.838	.746	.630	.564	.335
7	.813	.711	.583	.513	.279
8	.789	.677	.540	.466	.233
9	.766	.645	.500	.424	.194
10	.744	.614	.463	.385	.162
15	.642	.481	.315	.239	.0649
20	.554	.377	.215	.148	.0261
25	.478	.295	.146	.0923	.0105
30	.412	.231	.0994	.0573	.00421
40	.307	.142	.0460	.0221	.000680
50	.228	.087	.0213	.00852	.000109

begin with $544.22 and save it for a year, the accumulated saving after the year will be equal to $544.22 times 1.05, or $571.43. If we save $571.43 for another year, then we end up with $571.43 times 1.05, or $600. This tells us that the discounted present value of $600 to be received two years from now is equal to $600/[(1.05)(1.05)] = $600/(1.05)^2 = $544.22.

From the logic of this calculation, we can see that a general formula for computing the discounted present value of a payment to be received n years in the future is

$$\text{Discounted present value} = \text{payment } n \text{ years from now}/(1 + r)^n.$$

In our two-year example, $n = 2$, $r = 0.05$, and the payment two years from now is $600.

At the end of the third year, the buyer of the three-year bond receives the principal of $10,000 and a final $600 interest payment. We can calculate the discounted present value of this amount using the formula above:

$$\text{Discounted present value of \$10,600 three years hence} = \$10,600/(1.05)^3 = \$9,156.68.$$

Thus, today's value of the $10,600 that the bondholder will receive when the three-year bond matures is $9,156.68. (Some people discount the future at a higher rate than the market interest rate; see the *Management Focus: The Pentagon Learns Just How Much Military Personnel Discount the Future.*)

THE MARKET PRICE OF A BOND   We now can calculate the market value, or price, of this three-year bond. The price is how much the buyer would perceive the bond to be worth at the purchase date, given a market interest rate of 5 percent. (Remember that the bond pays an annual coupon of $600 for three years.) This is the sum of the discounted present values of the payments received in each of the three years. Using the calculations that we have done above, this is

MANAGEMENT
Focus

The Pentagon Learns Just How Much Military Personnel Discount the Future

Suppose that you were offered either a lump-sum payment of $50,000 today or a guaranteed annual $8,000 payment for thirty years. Which would you choose? Recently, the U.S. Department of Defense offered exactly this choice to about 65,000 people leaving posi-

tions in the armed forces. At an annual interest rate of about 5 percent per year, the present value of thirty years of $8,000 annual payments exceeds $150,000, more than triple the $50,000 lump sum. Even at a 10 percent rate of interest, the present value of the annual payments works out to almost $88,000.

In fact, 51 percent of officers and 92 percent of enlisted personnel chose the lump-sum payment. Economists worked out the interest rate that military personnel implicitly used in dis-

counting the thirty years of $8,000 annual payments. It turned out to be in excess of 17 percent! For these individuals, therefore, the personal rate of discount was well above market interest rates.

FOR CRITICAL ANALYSIS: If the average personal rate of discount was equal to 17 percent for the population as a whole, do you think that the market interest rate on risk-free bonds or loans would be above, below, or equal to 17 percent?

Price of three-year bond $= \$600/(1.05) + \$600/(1.05)^2 + \$10,600/(1.05)^3$
$$= \$571.43 + \$544.22 + \$9,156.68$$
$$= \$10,272.33.$$

Thus, $10,272.33 is the market value of the three-year bond with an annual coupon return of $600 and a face value of $10,000 when the market interest rate is 5 percent.

Calculating the Yield to Maturity

So what is the yield to maturity on this bond, if it is purchased for $10,272.33? To figure this out, we could write our formula above in a different way:

$$\$10,272.33 = \$600/(1 + r_m) + \$600/(1 + r_m)^2 + \$10,600/(1 + r_m)^3,$$

where r_m represents the yield to maturity for the bond. We already know that the value for r_m that fits this expression is 0.05. Hence, the yield to maturity for this bond with a price of $10,272.33 is 5 percent (the market interest rate).

It is easy for us to see that 5 percent is the yield to maturity because we constructed the problem with simple numbers. But note that if the market price on the left-hand side of the equation were to rise from $10,272.33 to some larger number, the value for r_m would have to fall somewhat. Calculating r_m requires solving a cubic equation! For this reason, traders use programmed calculators or bond yield tables when evaluating yields to maturity on long-term bonds.

YIELDS ON NONMATURING BONDS   Some financial instruments never mature. For instance, one instrument issued by the British government, a *consol,* pays a fixed coupon return forever. When the bearer dies, she can pass this instrument on to her heir, who receives the coupon return each year during his lifetime.

Such a financial instrument is a perpetual bond, or **perpetuity.** This is simply a bond that never matures. It turns out that the discounted present value of the coupon returns on a perpetuity is easy to calculate. It is equal to the coupon return divided by the market interest rate. For instance, if the annual coupon return is equal to an amount C and the annual interest rate is r, then the price of a perpetuity is

Perpetuity: A bond with an infinite term to maturity.

$$\text{Perpetuity price} = C/r.$$

We let you prove this for yourself in problem 2 at the end of the chapter.

This simple formula illustrates an important fact:

Prices of existing bonds are inversely related to changing market interest rates.

Suppose that the fixed coupon return is $500 per year. If the market interest rate is 5 percent, then the price of the perpetuity is equal to $500/(0.05) = $10,000. But if the interest rate rises to 6 percent, then the perpetuity's price equals $500/(0.06) = $8,333.33. A rise in the interest rate causes the bond's price to decline.

This makes sense. When the market interest rate rises, the discounted present value of each year's coupon return declines. But the bond's price is the sum of the discounted present values of all years' coupon returns. Hence, the bond's price must fall.

Consols are not especially commonplace today. But recall that corporate equities also have no maturity date. Equities, therefore, are a type of perpetuity. Indeed, we might think of the annual dividend on a share of stock as the "coupon return" and the annual rate of return derived from the share as the "interest rate." Then the dividend divided by the stock's annual rate of return will give a rough approximation of the share price. This is only an approximation because stock dividends typically are not constant over time and rates of return on shares typically vary from year to year.

YIELDS ON TREASURY BILLS   Table 4-2 displays interest rates on money market instruments such as federal funds, commercial paper, bank certificates of deposit, and Treasury bills (T-bills).

The published T-bill rates are based on a fictitious 360-day year. They are calculated from the equation

$$r_T = [(F - P)/P](360/n),$$

where r_T is the T-bill rate, F is the face value, P is the price paid, and n is the number of days to maturity.

Consider the 13-week (3-month, or 91-day) T-bill rate of 3.01 percent. The face value of a T-bill is $10,000, so F in the equation is equal to $10,000. The number of days to maturity, n, is equal to 91. The average price at which T-bills sold at this date was $9,924.56. Using the formula then gives us

$$
\begin{aligned}
r_T &= [(F - P)/P](360/n) \\
&= [(\$10{,}000 - \$9{,}924.56)/\$9{,}924.56](360/91) \\
&= (\$75.44/\$9{,}924.56)(3.96) \\
&= 0.0301.
\end{aligned}
$$

Table 4-2 Interest Rates on Money Market Instruments

Federal funds	3.01%
Commercial paper	
Nonfinancial	
1-month	3.05
2-month	3.14
3-month	3.24
Financial	
1-month	3.08
2-month	3.18
3-month	3.25
Certificates of deposit (secondary market)	
1-month	3.17
3-month	3.35
6-month	3.54
Eurodollar deposits (London)	
1-month	3.15
3-month	3.33
6-month	3.52
U.S. Treasury bills (secondary market)	
1-month	2.82
3-month	3.01
6-month	3.14

SOURCE: Board of Governors of the Federal Reserve System, H.15 (519) *Statistical Release,* June 13, 2005.

Thus, the published T-bill yield was 3.01 percent.

Of course, a year really lasts 365 days. A T-bill yield based on the true 365-day year is called the **coupon yield equivalent.** This is an annualized T-bill rate that can be compared with annual yields on other financial instruments. To calculate the coupon yield equivalent, we use the formula

$$r_E = [(F - P)/P](365/n),$$

where r_E is the coupon yield equivalent for the T-bill. Hence, the coupon yield equivalent corresponding to the published yield of 3.01 percent in Table 4-2 would have been

$$
\begin{aligned}
r_E &= [(\$10,000 - \$9,924.56)/\$9,924.56](365/91) \\
&= (\$75.44/\$9,924.56)(4.01) \\
&= 0.0305.
\end{aligned}
$$

The coupon yield equivalent for this T-bill is 3.05 percent. It is higher than the published yield of 3.01 percent because it takes into account the actual number of days in the year.

Traders have a practical use for the formula for the coupon yield equivalent. They use it to determine the yields associated with quoted prices on T-bills being traded in the secondary T-bill market. For instance, suppose that an individual holds a 13-week T-bill for 30 days but then offers to sell it at a price of $9,950. To figure out the yield over the remaining 61 days to maturity, a potential buyer would use the coupon yield equivalent formula. He would set P equal to $9,950 and n equal to 61:

$$
\begin{aligned}
r_E &= [(F - P)/P](365/n) \\
&= [(\$10,000 - \$9,950)/\$9,950](365/61) \\
&= (\$50/\$9,950)(5.98) \\
&= 0.0301.
\end{aligned}
$$

This means that the approximate annual yield on this T-bill at the quoted price would be 3.01 percent. The purchaser can compare this yield with those on other available instruments. Then he can decide if he wishes to pay a price of $9,950.

> **1. Why must we compute different interest yields?** The reason is that interest yields differ depending on the basis of comparison for evaluating the yield and on the period of time that a financial instrument will be held. This leads to a variety of different concepts of interest yields and several different ways to calculate these yields.

The Risk Structure of Interest Rates

Scanning through the interest rates in Table 4-2 indicates that market interest rates differ across financial instruments. Two key factors account for such differences in market rates. One is the term to maturity. The other is risk. Following standard practice, we consider each separately. In reality, however, the two factors together cause market interest rates for different instruments to differ.

The **risk structure of interest rates** refers to the relationship among yields on financial instruments that have the *same maturity* but differ on the basis of default risk, liquidity, and tax considerations.

Coupon yield equivalent: An annualized T-bill rate that can be compared with annual yields on other financial instruments.

On the Web
How can a person keep track of U.S. interest rates from day to day? One way is to view statistics made available by the Federal Reserve at **http://www. federalreserve.gov/releases**. At this site, click on "Selected Interest Rates: H.15 daily."

Risk structure of interest rates: The relationship among yields on financial instruments that have the same maturity but differ because of variations in default risk, liquidity, and tax rates.

Default Risk

There is always a possibility that an individual or a firm that issues a financial instrument may be unable to honor its obligations to pay off the principal and/or interest. This means that any bond is subject to some degree of **default risk.**

The U.S. government has the power to raise taxes to pay off its bonds. If needed, it could even print money to do so. For U.S. Treasury securities, therefore, default risk is very small. The chance of default on a newly issued twenty-year Treasury bond, for instance, is meager, if not virtually zero.

But consider a twenty-year corporate bond. Even if the company that issues it today has a very solid credit rating, there is always a chance that the company's fortunes could change within a few years. Ten or fifteen years from now the company could be near bankruptcy. And so the perceived default risk for the corporate bond is greater than for the twenty-year Treasury bond. As a result, individuals and firms will hold corporate bonds as well as Treasury bonds only if the corporate bond pays a sufficiently higher return to compensate for the greater risk of default.

THE RISK PREMIUM   The amount by which the corporate bond rate exceeds the Treasury bond rate because of greater default risk is the corporate bond's **risk premium.** Suppose that just before the company issues twenty-year bonds, word spreads that prospects for one of its products have worsened. Then those who were contemplating purchasing its bonds will not do so unless the company offers an even higher interest rate relative to the twenty-year Treasury bond rate. The risk premium on the bond will rise because the chance that the company may default is greater than it was before the news.

RATING SECURITIES   Default risk clearly is an important consideration in bond purchases. Two predominant institutions that rate the risks of bonds are Standard and Poor's Corporation and Moody's Investors Service. Just as professors assign students grades for their relative performances, Standard and Poor's and Moody's rate the relative default risks of bonds issued by corporations.

These institutions assign several grades so as to differentiate low, medium, and high risks. Yet both use two broad risk categories. **Investment-grade securities** are those judged to have a fairly low risk of default.

So-called **junk bonds** have significantly greater default risk. Naturally, the risk premiums for junk bonds are larger than those for investment-grade securities. One person's junk, of course, is another's treasure. To an individual who very much dislikes risk, junk bonds truly are "junk"—hence, the name "junk bonds." But to someone who desires high yields and is willing to take on risk, junk bonds are worth holding.

Liquidity

Another reason that corporate bond rates exceed interest rates on U.S. Treasury bonds of identical maturities is that traders regard corporate bonds as less liquid financial instruments. Recall that the secondary market for Treasury securities is well developed and typically has much trading activity. This means that the holder of a Treasury bond knows that the bond will be easy to sell if desired.

The secondary market for corporate bonds, however, is not always so active. Sometimes many who wish to sell corporate bonds enter the secondary market only to find that few stand ready to buy. Hence, a corporate bond may be more difficult to "unload" for cash at a later date. For this reason a corporate bond is less liquid than a U.S. Treasury bond.

Default risk: The chance that an individual or a firm that issues a financial instrument may be unable to honor its obligations to repay the principal and/or to make interest payments.

Risk premium: The amount by which one instrument's yield exceeds the yield of another instrument as a result of the first instrument being riskier and less liquid than the second.

On the Web

What do various bond ratings mean? Learn the answer to this question at Standard & Poor's Web site, **http://www. standardandpoors.com**. In the left-hand margin, under "Credit Ratings," click on "Criteria and Definitions."

Investment-grade securities: Bonds with relatively low default risk.

Junk bonds: Bonds with relatively high default risk.

This means that (all other factors held constant) bondholders typically will require a higher interest rate on corporate bonds, relative to the rate on a Treasury bond of the same maturity. The higher corporate bond rate compensates the bondholders for the chance that they will have more trouble selling the corporate bonds at a future date.

THE LIQUIDITY PREMIUM   Thus, a difference in default risk is not the only reason that bond rates may diverge. There is also a *liquidity premium* that accounts in part for the difference between interest rates on two bonds with identical maturities.

Distinguishing between risk and liquidity premiums would be a difficult proposition, however. For instance, junk bonds are less liquid than investment-grade securities because the secondary market for the latter typically is more active. But a key reason there is less secondary market trading of junk bonds is that fewer individuals are willing to incur risk by holding them. Clearly, default risk and liquidity interact in determining bond interest rate differences.

LIQUIDITY AND RISK   Hence, the term *risk premium* typically is used broadly to characterize interest rate differences resulting from *both* default risk and liquidity considerations. When people refer to a risk premium on one bond relative to another, they really are talking about a difference that arises because one bond has a higher risk of default *and* is less liquid.

Figure 4-1 displays the average annual yields on long-term U.S. Treasury bonds, the highest-rated long-term investment-grade securities (Moody's Aaa), and medium-rated investment-grade securities (Moody's Baa). All three are plotted on a monthly basis since 1984. The interest yields on both classes of corporate bonds always are greater than the yield on Treasury bonds. The reason is that Treasury bonds have much lower default risk and are very liquid. Likewise, the presence of a risk premium is apparent in a comparison of the rates on medium-rated versus highly rated corporate bonds. (Because the overall "risk premium" includes a liquidity premium, changes in the risk premium do not always indicate a perceived reduction in a bond's risk of default; see on the next page the *Management Focus: Explaining a Decline in the Junk-Bond Risk Premium.*)

FIGURE 4-1
Long-Term Bond Yields.

As compared with corporate bonds, Treasury bonds have lower default risk and greater liquidity. Consequently, Treasury bonds consistently have lower yields. Furthermore, the highest-rated investment-grade corporate bonds (Moody's Aaa) have lower default risk, as compared with medium-rated investment-grade corporate bonds (Moody's Baa), and the highest-rated corporate bonds also have lower yields.

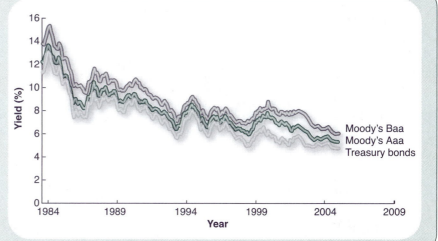

SOURCE: Board of Governors of the Federal Reserve System, *Federal Reserve Bulletin,* various issues.

MANAGEMENT

Focus

Explaining a Decline in the Junk-Bond Risk Premium

Between the fall of 2002 and late 2004, the difference between interest yields on junk bonds and yields on the highest-rated investment-grade bonds fell by about half a percentage point. It is unlikely that junk bonds became any less likely to generate defaults or that investment-grade bonds were at greater risk of default. Instead, trading in junk bonds became much more active during this period, as more investors sought instruments with higher returns as the general level of U.S. interest rates declined. This caused the liquidity premium to fall, which explained much of the reduction in the difference between yields on junk bonds and those on investment-grade bonds.

FOR CRITICAL ANALYSIS: In what sense *did* junk bonds become less risky for investors to hold between 2002 and 2004?

Tax Considerations

A final reason that bonds with identical maturities may have different interest yields is that tax laws treat some bonds differently than others. Individuals typically are not required to pay either federal or state taxes on interest earnings from municipal bonds. This means that the pre-tax and after-tax yields on municipal bonds are identical. But interest earnings on Treasury bonds are subject to federal taxation, which depresses their after-tax yields.

For this reason, higher pre-tax interest rates are required to induce individuals to hold both Treasury bonds and municipal bonds simultaneously. As a result, pre-tax (market) Treasury bond yields tend to exceed yields on municipal bonds, as shown in Figure 4-2.

**FIGURE 4-2
Municipal and Treasury Bond Yields.**

Interest earnings from municipal bonds are exempt from federal taxation, but interest earnings on Treasury bonds are subject to federal taxation. Consequently, Treasury bond yields exceed the yields on municipal bonds.

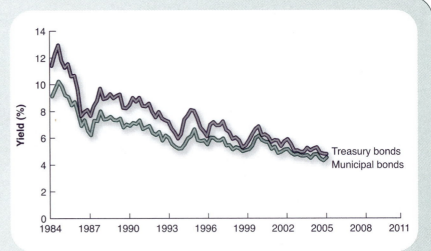

SOURCE: Board of Governors of the Federal Reserve System, *Federal Reserve Bulletin,* various issues.

2. How does risk cause market interest rates to differ? Differences in degrees of default risk and liquidity result in risk premiums that must be present in the yields on financial instruments. Risk premiums differ across instruments, which is one key reason that yields differ. The different rates at which some instruments are taxed also cause their market rates to diverge.

The Term Structure of Interest Rates

The **term structure of interest rates** refers to the relationship among yields on financial instruments that possess the *same risk, liquidity, and tax characteristics* but have differing terms to maturity. Even if bonds with different maturities are identical in every other respect, their yields typically diverge.

Term structure of interest rates: The relationship among yields on financial instruments with identical risk, liquidity, and tax characteristics but differing terms to maturity.

The Yield Curve

This divergence of interest yields across different terms to maturity is easily seen by plotting a **yield curve.** This is a chart that depicts the relationship among yields on similar bonds with different terms to maturity. Figure 4-3 shows a typical yield curve for Treasury securities.

The yield curve in Figure 4-3 slopes upward. This is the normal shape of a yield curve. Interest yields usually are greater as the term to maturity increases. But sometimes yield curves are downward sloping. This happened, for instance, in 2000. When the yield curve slopes downward, it is said to be an **inverted yield curve.** In such a situation, interest yields decline as the term to maturity rises.

Why isn't the yield curve simply horizontal? That is, why do interest yields vary with the term to maturity? Economists have offered three basic theories that seek to address this question. These are the segmented markets theory, the expectations theory, and the preferred habitat theory.

Yield curve: A chart depicting the relationship among yields on bonds that differ only in their terms to maturity.

Inverted yield curve: A downward-sloping yield curve.

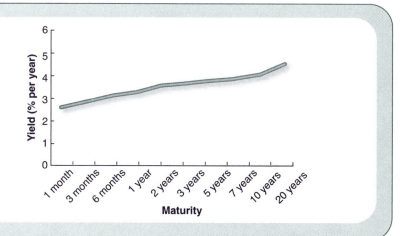

FIGURE 4-3
The Yield Curve.

This is a typical, upward-sloping historical yield curve for U.S. Treasury securities.

source: Board of Governors of the Federal Reserve System, H.15 *Statistical Release,* June 5, 2005.

Segmented Markets Theory

According to the **segmented markets theory** of the term structure of interest rates, bonds with differing terms to maturity are not perfectly substitutable. As a result, they are traded in separate markets. Each market determines its own unique yield.

MATCHING MATURITIES　For instance, depository institutions such as commercial banks issue time deposits with relatively short terms to maturity of one to three years. They often wish to "match" these deposits with assets such as Treasury bonds with similar one- to three-year maturities, so they buy such Treasuries. Pension funds, in contrast, issue pension liabilities with much longer terms to maturity. Consequently, it is natural that they should wish to hold Treasury bonds with ten- to twenty-year maturities. According to the segmented markets theory, bond yields will reflect such differences in trading patterns.

For instance, suppose that initially the yields across Treasury bonds with differing maturities are the same. If banks decide to hold more Treasury bonds with one- to three-year maturities, however, the demand for such bonds will rise, causing an increase in their market price. As a result, the market yield on the Treasury bonds will fall. If all other factors are unchanged, the yields on Treasury bonds with one- to three-year maturities will be lower than those on Treasury bonds with ten- to twenty-year maturities. That is, market yields will differ across terms to maturity, just as we see when we plot yield curves. Indeed, in this example the yield curve slopes upward.

A nice feature of the segmented markets theory is that it can explain why the yield curve is not horizontal. It also provides a ready explanation for an upward- or downward-sloping yield curve: the slope will depend on differences in conditions in markets for shorter- versus longer-term financial instruments.

DRAWBACKS OF THE SEGMENTED MARKETS THEORY　But simplicity is not always a virtue. There are two difficulties with the segmented markets theory. One is that the theory assumes that Treasury bonds with different maturities are not perfect substitutes, yet yields on Treasury bonds tend to move together. This can be seen in Figure 4-4, which depicts

---

FIGURE 4-4
Treasury Security Yields.

The yields on Treasury securities tend to be higher for longer maturities. Nevertheless, the yields on Treasury securities with different maturities tend to move together over time.

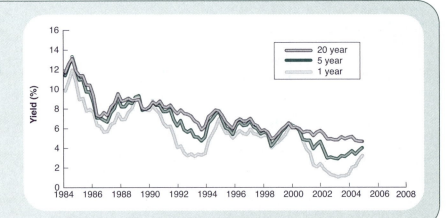

SOURCES: Board of Governors of the Federal Reserve System, *Federal Reserve Bulletin* (various issues) and G.13 (415) *Statistical Release.*

the yields on one-year, five-year, and twenty-year Treasury securities since 1984. If Treasury bonds with different maturities were not substitutable, then there would be no reason that their yields should be related. But they clearly are.

A second problem with the segmented markets theory is that it does not explain why the yield curve should have any natural tendency to slope either upward or downward over its entire range. Yet historically the yield curve typically has sloped upward. Over long periods, downward-sloping yield curves are relatively rare occurrences. But when a yield curve does slope downward, it typically does so over most, if not all, of its range.

Expectations Theory

The **expectations theory** addresses the first difficulty with the segmented markets theory. It explains how expectations about future yields can cause yields on instruments with different maturities to move together. In addition, it can provide insight into why the yield curve may systematically slope upward or downward.

CHOOSING BETWEEN BONDS WITH DIFFERING MATURITIES The essential elements of the expectations theory can be understood by considering a situation in which an individual saver faces a two-year planning horizon. The saver has two alternatives. One is to place funds in a two-year bond for the two years. This bond yields an annual interest rate of R. The other alternative is for the saver to hold one-year bonds for each of the two years. Under this alternative, the saver would place funds in a one-year bond for the first year at an interest rate of r_1. Then, during the second year, the saver would place the principal plus the interest accumulated during the first year in another one-year bond. At the beginning of the two periods, when the saver must make her decision, she expects that the interest rate on the one-year bond during the second year will be r_2^e.

Holding Either Bond This individual will be willing to hold *either* one-year or two-year bonds only if she anticipates that her rate of return across the two years will be the same. This is true if

$$R = (r_1 + r_2^e)/2.$$

That is, the annual interest rate on the two-year bond, R, must equal the average expected annual interest rate from holding one-year bonds, $(r_1 + r_2^e)$. If the two-year bond rate falls below this expected average of one-year rates, then the saver will hold only one-year bonds. But if the two-year bond rate is above this expected average of one-year rates, then the saver will hold only two-year bonds. Consequently, the above condition must be met in the bond markets to induce this saver and others to hold bonds of both maturities.

The Yield Curve's Slope Suppose that the one-year bond pays $r_1 = 0.04$ during the first year and is expected to yield $r_2^e = 0.06$ during the second year. Then the two-year bond rate, R, will be the average of 0.04 and 0.06, which is $(0.04 + 0.06)/2 = 0.05$. Panel (a) of Figure 4-5 on the next page shows the yield curve for this example. The *actual* interest yield for the one-year bond is $r_1 = 0.04$, or 4 percent. For the two-year bond, the interest yield is higher, at $R = 0.05$, or 5 percent. Therefore, the yield curve relating bonds with one- and two-year maturities slopes upward.

Now suppose that for some reason savers anticipate that one-year bond rates will fall sharply. Specifically, suppose that the expectation of the one-year bond rate during the second period falls to $r_2^e = 0.02$ (or 2 percent). If the one-year bond rate is still $r_1 = 0.04$, then the

Expectations theory: A theory of the term structure of interest rates that views bonds with differing maturities as perfect substitutes, so their yields differ only because short-term interest rates are expected to rise or fall.

MONEYXTRA!
Economic Applications

Has the yield curve recently become steeper or more shallow? Take a look at changes in the spread between short- and long-term interest rates via EconData Online. **http://moneyxtra. swcollege.com**

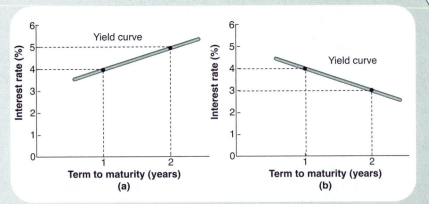

FIGURE 4-5
Sample Yield Curves for the Expectations Theory.

Panel (a) shows an upward-sloping yield curve that arises under the expectations theory of the term structure of interest rates if the one-year bond rate is expected to rise from 4 percent to 6 percent; then the two-year bond rate is the average of the current and expected one-year bond rates, or 5 percent. Panel (b) displays a downward-sloping yield curve that results if the one-year bond rate is expected to   fall from 4 percent to 2 percent; then the two-year bond rate is the average   of the current and expected one-year bond rates, or 3 percent.

two-year bond rate must change to induce savers to be willing to hold either one- or two-year bonds. The new two-year bond rate will have to be

$$R = (r_1 + r_2^e)/2 = (0.04 + 0.02)/2 = 0.03.$$

The two-year bond now will yield 3 percent per year. Panel (b) of Figure 4-5 shows the new yield curve for one- and two-year bonds. It slopes downward.

What has changed to cause the yield curve to be downward sloping, or inverted? Previously, the one-year bond rate was expected to *rise* from 4 percent to 6 percent. This caused the yield curve in panel (a) of Figure 4-5 to slope upward. But now the one-year bond rate is expected to *fall* from 4 percent to 2 percent. This causes the yield curve's slope to be "inverted," as in panel (b). The yield curve now slopes downward.

STRENGTHS AND WEAKNESSES OF THE EXPECTATIONS THEORY   Clearly, the expectations theory is not as simple as the segmented markets theory. Nevertheless, it has a very important virtue: it potentially can explain why yield curves slope upward or downward. An upward-sloping yield curve indicates a general expectation by savers that short-term interest rates will rise. A downward-sloping yield curve indicates a general expectation that short-term interest rates will decline.

There is a problem with the expectations theory, however. Yield curves usually slope upward. According to the expectations theory, this would imply that savers almost *always* expect short-term interest rates to rise. But over long periods interest rates typically are as likely to fall as they are to rise. This means that the expectations theory cannot be a full theory of the term structure of interest rates.

The Preferred Habitat Theory

Preferred habitat theory: A theory of the term structure of interest rates that views bonds as imperfectly substitutable, so yields on longer-term bonds must be greater than those on shorter-term bonds even if short-term interest rates are not expected to rise or fall.

The **preferred habitat theory** combines elements of the segmented markets theory and the expectations theory. According to the segmented markets theory, bonds whose maturities differ are not at all substitutable. The expectations theory, in contrast, assumes that bonds with different maturities are *perfect* substitutes. This is why savers will hold both one- and two-year bonds only if their expected returns are equal.

According to the preferred habitat theory, bonds with different maturities are substitutable, but only imperfectly. Under this theory, savers generally have a slight preference to hold bonds with shorter maturities. Recall from Chapter 3 that money market trading is broader and more active than trading in capital markets. Consequently, money market instruments—bonds with shorter maturities—are more liquid instruments. This greater liquidity of short-term bonds can make them somewhat more attractive to savers than longer-term bonds. Hence, savers can "prefer the habitat" of money markets just as animals prefer their own special habitat, or locations, in the wild.

THE TERM PREMIUM   To induce savers to hold longer-term bonds, the returns on those bonds actually must slightly *exceed* the returns on shorter-term bonds. That is, savers need to earn a **term premium** on longer-term bonds. This compensates savers for holding long-term bonds as well as short-term bonds.

Consequently, the preferred habitat theory modifies the expectations hypothesis by adding a term premium. Using our two-year example, the rate on the two-year bond now would be

$$R = TP + [(r_1 + r_2^e)/2],$$

where TP is the term premium for the two-year bond.

For instance, suppose that $r_1 = r_2^e = 0.04$, so savers expect that the one-year bond rate will remain at 4 percent for both years. Suppose also that savers have a strong preference to hold one-year bonds, so the term premium is $TP = 0.005$, or 0.5 percent. This 0.5 percent premium in the long-term yield is needed to induce savers to hold two-year bonds as well as one-year bonds. The two-year bond rate would be

$$R = TP + [(r_1 + r_2^e)/2]$$
$$= 0.005 + [(0.04 + 0.04)/2]$$
$$= 0.005 + 0.040 = 0.045.$$

So, under these conditions, the two-year bond rate is equal to 4.5 percent even though the one-year bond rate is expected to remain at 4 percent over both years. This implies that the yield curve relating the yields on one- and two-year bonds slopes upward, as shown in panel (a) of Figure 4-6 on the next page. The yield curve slopes upward even though the one-year bond rate is not expected to rise. Hence, over a long period in which interest rates are equally likely to rise or fall, the yield curve typically will have a positive slope.

EXPLAINING CHANGES IN THE SLOPE OF THE YIELD CURVE   Now suppose that all the numbers in our example stay the same except for the expectation of the one-year bond rate for the second year. Let's suppose that savers expect the one-year bond rate to fall from 4 percent in the first year to 3 percent in the second. Then the preferred habitat theory predicts that the two-year bond rate will be

$$R = TP + [(r_1 + r_2^e)/2]$$
$$= 0.005 + [(0.04 + 0.03)/2]$$
$$= 0.005 + 0.035 = 0.040.$$

Hence, the one- and two-year bond rates will be equal. The yield curve will be horizontal, as in panel (b) of Figure 4-6.

Term premium: An amount by which the yield on a long-term bond must exceed the yield on a short-term bond to make individuals willing to hold either bond if they expect short-term bond yields to remain unchanged.

FIGURE 4-6
Sample Yield Curves for the Preferred Habitat Theory.

Panel (a) shows an upward-sloping yield curve that arises under the preferred habitat theory of the term structure of interest rates if there is a 0.5 percent term premium and if the one-year bond rate is expected to remain unchanged at its current level of 4 percent; then the two-year bond rate is the sum of the term premium and the average of the current and expected one-year bond rates, or 0.5 percent + 4 percent = 4.5 percent.

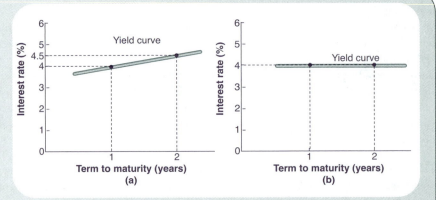

Panel (b) displays a horizontal yield curve that results if the one-year bond rate is expected to fall from 4 percent to 3 percent; then the two-year bond rate is the sum of the term premium and the average of the current and expected one-year bond rates, or 0.5 percent + 3.5 percent = 4 percent.

MONEYXTRA!
Online Case Study

For a practical example contemplating why interest rates on short- and longer-term financial instruments might differ, go to the Chapter 4 Case Study, entitled "Did Mortgage Lenders Make a Killing in 2001 and 2002?"
**http://www.moneyxtra.
swcollege.com**

This means that in our example, the only way that the yield curve could slope downward would be if the one-year bond rate were expected to fall from 4 percent to *below* 3 percent. In contrast, if the one-year bond rate were expected to fall only "a little," say, from 4 percent to 3.75 percent, the yield curve would still slope upward.

The preferred habitat theory predicts that the yield curve will typically slope upward. This squares with the real-world facts. The theory also predicts that the yield curve will slope downward only in situations in which short-term interest rates are expected to decline sharply. Such situations can arise from time to time over long periods, but they nevertheless are relatively rare. Therefore, inverted yield curves should be observed infrequently. This is what we observe.

One feature of the preferred habitat theory is that it enables us to infer general interest rate expectations simply by looking at a yield curve. On the one hand, if we see that a yield curve for Treasury securities is nearly horizontal or inverted, then we can surmise that most savers believe that rates on T-bills are likely to decline. On the other hand, if we observe a very steeply sloped yield curve for Treasury securities, then we can determine that most savers expect that T-bill rates are likely to rise. In the intermediate situation in which most savers do not expect short-term interest rates to change, then, in contrast to the expectations theory's prediction of a horizontal yield curve, the preferred habitat theory indicates that we should observe a Treasury security yield curve with a fairly shallow, upward slope. In fact, this is typically what we see.

3. Why do market interest rates vary with differences in financial instruments' terms to maturity?   Yields across maturities will not be equal for two reasons. One is expectations that short-term rates may rise or fall. Another is that short-term financial instruments generally are more liquid and less risky than longer-term instruments. Hence, a term premium is needed to induce individuals to be indifferent between holding either long-term or short-term instruments.

Nominal versus Real Rates of Interest

To this point, we have discussed interest rates only in *current-dollar* terms. There is a problem with this, however. Inflation can erode the value of interest received when a financial instrument matures. Any individual must take this into account when evaluating how much to save.

For instance, suppose that a saver can earn a stated current-dollar interest rate, or **nominal interest rate,** of $r = 0.06$ (6 percent) on each dollar that he allocates to a one-year bond. Suppose also that the saver expects that prices of goods and services will rise by a factor of $\pi^e = 0.03$ (3 percent) during the coming year, where π^e is the expected rate of inflation. This is the rate of inflation that he expects to face. Such inflation will reduce the amount of goods and services that his interest return will permit him to purchase.

Thus, although the saver earns positive interest on the bond, he anticipates that inflation will eat away at that interest at the rate π^e. Hence, the **real interest rate** that this saver anticipates, or his expected inflation-adjusted interest rate, is *approximately* equal to

$$r^r = r - \pi^e = 0.06 - 0.03 = 0.03,$$

where r^r denotes the real interest rate. In terms of what his savings can buy, this saver actually anticipates earning only 3 percent on his one-year bond.

The real interest rate is crucial for determining *how much* the individual desires to save. The reason is that saving is forgone consumption. This individual is likely to give up more consumption now if the real rate of return on saving is larger. This means that the real interest rate is a crucial determinant of the saving in the nation where this saver is a citizen. Countries with high nominal interest rates often experience very low saving rates because expected inflation is so high. Indeed, U.S. interest rates reached double-digit levels in the 1970s, but expected inflation was also in double digits. During some intervals in that decade, real interest rates were *negative,* which strongly discouraged saving. (Today, investors can purchase inflation-protected Treasury securities and, to a growing extent, a number of privately issued inflation-protected securities; see on the next page the *Policy Focus: The U.S. Treasury Kick-Starts the Market for Inflation-Protected Securities.*)

For purposes of deciding how to allocate saving among alternative financial instruments, however, an individual saver is safe in comparing current-dollar, or nominal, yields. The reason is that to calculate the real yield on each instrument, the saver would subtract the same expected inflation rate π^e from each instrument's annual nominal yield. If the nominal yield on one instrument exceeds the nominal yield on the other, then so will its real yield.

Nominal interest rate: A rate of return in current-dollar terms that does not reflect anticipated inflation.

Real interest rate: The anticipated rate of return from holding a financial instrument after taking into account the extent to which inflation is expected to reduce the amount of goods and services that this return could be used to buy.

> **4. What is the real interest rate?** This is the anticipated inflation-adjusted yield on a financial instrument. The real interest rate is equal to the current-dollar yield less the expected rate of inflation.

Key Interest Rates in the Global Economy

There are many financial markets. Hence, there are many interest rates. Three are especially important as "barometers" of conditions in financial markets.

The Federal Funds Rate

One of these key interest rates is at the shortest end of the maturity spectrum. It is the **federal funds rate,** or the market rate on interbank loans. As you learned in Chapter 3, such loans are known as "federal funds" only because banks make the loans by transferring reserves that they

Federal funds rate: A short-term (usually overnight) interest rate on interbank loans in the United States.

The U.S. Treasury Kick-Starts the Market for Inflation-Protected Securities

On January 29, 1997, the U.S. Department of the Treasury auctioned its first "real interest rate" bonds, or Treasury Inflation-Protected Securities (TIPS). The principal value of a TIPS is adjusted for inflation each day using changes in the consumer price index as a benchmark. Thus, the principal for a TIPS grows at the rate of inflation and maintains its real value. Every six months, the Treasury issues a fixed-rate coupon payment based on the revised principal

amount. Because the fixed-rate coupon rises in proportion to the increase in the principal, the interest rate remains at a constant real level. At maturity, the principal is returned to the investor fully adjusted for inflation.

Until 2002, the volume of TIPS and other inflation-protected securities held by investors worldwide averaged about $250 billion, and traders exchanged about $500 million of such securities each year. By 2004, investor interest in TIPS had increased so much that the U.S. Treasury reintroduced five-year notes and thirty-year bonds with inflation protection.

Now private companies are jumping onto the TIPS bandwagon. Private firms such as Merrill Lynch, Morgan Stanley,

Bear Stearns, and Household International have issued inflation-protected corporate bonds. Since 2003, the outstanding amount of inflation-protected government and corporate securities issued and purchased worldwide has risen to more than $500 billion. Investors now trade an estimated $10 billion of these securities annually in the secondary bond market.

FOR CRITICAL ANALYSIS: How might an investor who holds a regular ten-year Treasury note end up earning higher real interest returns over a decade than someone who holds an inflation-protected ten-year Treasury note for the same period?

hold at Federal Reserve banks. Most of these loans have maturities of one or two days, so these are very short-term loans. Indeed, some federal funds loans have effective maturities of only a few hours.

Because the federal funds rate is a ready measure of the price that banks must pay to raise funds, the Federal Reserve often uses it as a yardstick for gauging the effects of its policies. Consequently, the federal funds rate is a closely watched indicator of the Federal Reserve's intentions.

The "federal funds rate" is really an average of rates across banks. Some banks pay lower interest rates to borrow federal funds than others because they are better credit risks. In addition, some very large banks both borrow and lend federal funds, even during the same day. These banks act as *dealers* in the federal funds market. They profit from lending federal funds at rates that slightly exceed the rates at which they borrow federal funds. Brokers also are active in the federal funds market. They match banks that need to borrow federal funds with other depository institutions that are willing to lend.

The Prime Rate

Prime rate: The interest rate that U.S. banks charge on loans to the most creditworthy business borrowers.

The **prime rate** is the rate that banks charge on short-term loans that they make to many of the most creditworthy business borrowers. These are the borrowers with the lowest perceived risk of default. Many other lending rates are based on the prime rate, so it is a key indicator of conditions in loan markets.

Figure 4-7 displays the behavior of the prime rate since 1940. Note that until the 1970s the prime rate showed little variation. Since then, however, the prime rate has been less rigid.

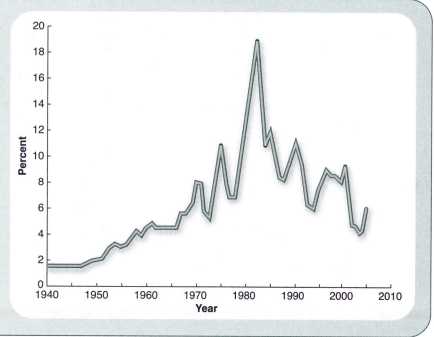

FIGURE 4-7
The Prime Rate.

The prime rate has been more volatile since the 1970s, although it has been less variable in recent years.

SOURCES: *2000 Economic Report of the President* and *Federal Reserve Bulletin,* various issues.

There are two likely explanations for this. One is that interest rates generally have been more volatile since the beginning of the 1970s. Another is that nationwide competition among banks has increased since that time. As a result, banks have adjusted the prime rate more quickly to variations in other market interest rates. In addition, they have also begun to lend to their truly "best" customers at rates below the benchmark prime rate.

The London Interbank Offer Rate (LIBOR)

In international financial markets, bonds and deposits are denominated in a variety of currencies and pay interest yields that apply to these various currency denominations. Comparing interest yields can become complicated for those who trade such instruments. This is particularly true in Eurocurrency markets.

To assist in comparing interest rates in Eurocurrency markets, traders have adopted the convention of quoting rates on such bonds, loans, and deposits using a single interest rate as a benchmark. This benchmark rate is the **London Interbank Offer Rate,** or **LIBOR.** LIBOR is the interest rate at which six large London banks stand willing to lend to or borrow from each other when market trading opens on a given day.

In a sense, LIBOR is the international equivalent of the U.S. federal funds rate. It is a rough measure of the cost of funds to London banks that are especially active in international financial markets. Consequently, it is a useful barometer of conditions in those markets. Rates on Eurocurrency bonds, loans, and deposits therefore are measured as "markups" or "markdowns" from LIBOR. For instance, a Eurocurrency bond rate may be quoted as "LIBOR plus one percent." This indicates that if LIBOR currently is 5 percent, then the Eurocurrency bond rate in question is equal to 6 percent.

 On the Web
What is the current prime rate? View this information, as well as data on many other market interest rates, in the Federal Reserve's H15 *Statistical Release,* at **http://www.federalreserve.gov/releases/H15/update.**

London Interbank Offer Rate (LIBOR): The interest rate on interbank loans traded among six large London banks.

We shall have more to say about these key interest rates and how to interpret their movements in later chapters. In the next chapter, we shall provide background on foreign exchange markets and discussion of how domestic interest rates and foreign interest rates are related. This will set the stage for a fuller analysis of how financial institutions and the economy are affected by variations in the interest yields of domestic and foreign instruments.

> **5. What interest rates are the key indicators of financial market conditions?** The three most widely watched interest rates are the federal funds rate, the prime rate, and the London Interbank Offer Rate (LIBOR).

Chapter Summary

1. Computing Different Interest Yields: Any interest yield must have a basis of comparison, such as the principal of a loan, face value of a bond, or market price of either a loan or a bond. Furthermore, the effective yield on any financial instrument depends on the remaining number of days, weeks, or months until it matures. All these factors affect the calculation of alternative yields on financial instruments. Hence, different yields must be considered.

2. Risk and Market Interest Rates: Risky and fairly illiquid financial instruments will be held when other less risky and more liquid instruments are available only if risk premiums are included in their yields. Therefore, yields on riskier and fairly illiquid instruments typically are higher than the yields of the other instruments.

3. Market Interest Rates and Different Terms to Maturity: Interest yields differ based on term to maturity for two reasons. One is that yields on longer-term financial instruments depend on expectations about yields on shorter-term instruments. Another is that longer-term instruments typically are less liquid and more risky. Consequently, longer-term financial instruments are more likely to be held if they have a somewhat higher yield than shorter-term instruments.

4. The Real Interest Rate: This is the nominal interest rate minus the expected rate of inflation. It provides a measure of the extent to which inflation is anticipated to reduce the purchasing power of interest earnings on financial instruments.

5. Key Interest Rate Indicators of Financial Market Conditions: The federal funds rate is a measure of the immediate cost of funds for U.S. banks and is an important indicator of Federal Reserve monetary policy. The prime rate is a barometer of aggregate loan market conditions and is a base for other lending rates. The London Interbank Offer Rate (LIBOR) is the basis for interest rate quotes on many internationally traded financial instruments.

Questions and Problems

(Answers to odd-numbered questions and problems may be found on the Web at **http://money.swcollege.com** under "Student Resources.")

1. You are scheduled to receive a payment of $104 one year from now. The market interest rate that you use to discount the future is 4 percent. What is the discounted present value of the payment to be received? Suppose that the market interest rate rises to 5 percent. What is now the discounted present value of the future payment?

2. The formula for the price of a consol with an annual coupon return of C is C/r. Note that the discounted present value of C dollars received each year forever is equal to the infinite sum,

$$P = C/(1 + r) + C/(1 + r)^2 + C/(1 + r)^3 + C/(1 + r)^4 + \cdots$$

The amount P should be the price that the bearer of the consol would be willing to pay to hold this instrument. And so P should equal C/r. Prove that this is true. [Hint: Try multiplying the equation above by the factor $1/(1 + r)$. Then subtract the resulting equation from the equation above. Then solve for P.]

3. Explain why bond prices and interest rates are inversely related, holding all other factors unchanged.

4. Suppose that an individual holds a 26-week (182-day) T-bill for 80 days but then offers to sell it to you at a price of $9,850. The face value of the T-bill is $10,000. What is the T-bill's yield over the remaining 102 days before it will mature?

5. Suppose that an individual holds a 13-week (91-day) T-bill for a number of days but then offers to sell it to you at a price of $9,920. The coupon equivalent yield for the T-bill, which has a face value of $10,000, is 5.84 percent. How many days remain before this bill matures?

6. A nation's yield curve slopes downward. Explain what this implies, according to the preferred habitat theory of the term structure of interest rates.

7. Suppose that the three-month T-bill rate is 5.4 percent. The term premium for a six-month T-bill is equal to 0.1 percent, and the current rate on a six-month T-bill is 5.6 percent. According to the basic theory of the term structure of interest rates, what is the expected three-month T-bill rate for three months from now?

8. Most federal funds loans among banks have an overnight maturity. Typically, the overnight federal funds rate exceeds the three-month T-bill rate. Does this mean that the yield curve spanning maturities from one day to three months is normally inverted, or can you think of another possible reason for this observation? [Hint: There is a slight risk that a bank may default, or at least have a liquidity crunch, on any given day.]

9. The real interest rate on a Treasury bond is 3 percent. The anticipated inflation rate is 4.5 percent. What is the Treasury bond's approximate nominal interest rate?

10. Suppose that a market interest rate in Japan is 2 percent, while the comparable rate in the United States is 4 percent. Japan's anticipated rate of inflation is 0.5 percent, and the U.S. anticipated inflation rate is 3 percent. Which nation experiences the higher real interest rate?

Before the Test

Test your understanding of the material covered in this chapter by taking the Chapter 4 interactive quiz at **http://money.swcollege.com**.

Online Application

Internet URL: http://www.federalreserve.gov/

Title: Selected Interest Rates—Board of Governors of the Federal Reserve System

Navigation: Begin at the Federal Reserve Board's home page above. Click on "Economic Research and Data," and then click on "Statistics: Releases and Historical Data."

Application: Follow the remaining instructions, and use data reported about selected interest rates to answer the following questions:

1. Under "Interest Rates," next to "H.15," click on "daily." Does the yield curve for Treasury securities (look at the rates under "Treasury Constant Maturities") have an upward slope? If so, is the slope relatively steep or shallow? Is the yield curve nearly flat or even inverted? Based on your answers to these questions, can you make any rough inferences about general expectations about the future behavior of short-term interest rates on Treasury securities?

2. At the same location, take a look at the yields on corporate bonds, and compare these with longer-term Treasury bond yields. Which rates are higher? Is this because of the term structure of interest rates or the risk structure of interest rates? Explain your reasoning.

For Group Study and Analysis: Go back to the previous screen. Next to "H.15," click on "weekly." Divide into groups, with each group assigned a different monthly release. Have each procure an identical overhead transparency plotting yield against maturity. Have each group plot a yield curve for Treasury securities (using the same "Treasury Constant Maturities" yield data referred to in question 1 above). Then superimpose these transparencies on an overhead projector to get a picture of how the yield curve has shifted and/or twisted over time. Discuss factors that may have led to recent changes in the position and/or shape of the yield curve.

Selected References and Further Reading

Clayton, Gary, and Christopher Spivey. *The Time Value of Money.* Philadelphia: W. B. Saunders, 1978.

Fisher, Irving. *The Theory of Interest.* New York: Augustus M. Kelley, 1965.

Fleming, Michael, and Kenneth Garbade. "Repurchase Agreements with Negative Interest Rates." Federal Reserve Bank of New York *Current Issues in Economics and Finance* 10 (April 2004).

Mehra, Yash. "The Bond Rate and Actual Future Inflation." Federal Reserve Bank of Richmond *Economic Review* 84 (Spring 1998): 27–47.

Sack, Brian, and Robert Elsasser. "Treasury Inflation-Indexed Debt: A Review of the U.S. Experience." Federal Reserve Bank of New York *Economic Policy Review,* May 2004, pp. 47–64.

Wu, Tao. "What Makes the Yield Curve Move?" Federal Reserve Bank of San Francisco *Economic Letter,* No. 2003-15, June 6, 2003.

MoneyXtra

Log on to the MoneyXtra Web site now (**http://moneyxtra.swcollege.com**) for additional learning resources such as practice quizzes, case studies, readings, and additional economic applications.

Foreign Exchange Markets

On this particular day, as on many others in the mid-2000s, the Japanese yen's value was rising relative to the U.S. dollar. Because yen were more expensive to obtain with dollars, U.S. residents faced higher dollar prices when they considered purchasing Japanese-made goods. In an effort to prevent a fall in exports to the United States that would weaken total spending on Japanese goods and services, the Japanese Finance Ministry hurriedly placed a very large order with a private Japanese bank to sell yen for dollars on its behalf.

News of the Finance Ministry's order to sell yen caused many other Japanese banks to anticipate a decline in the currency's value, which encouraged them to buy dollars in hopes of profiting from selling them after the yen's value had declined. When these banks purchased dollars with yen, the yen started to depreciate against the dollar, just as the Finance Ministry desired. In the meantime, as prearranged with the original bank, the Finance Ministry canceled its order for this bank to purchase dollars with yen. The bank was willing to go along because it also would be able to profit from selling dollars for yen after the yen's depreciation. In the end, therefore, the Finance Ministry was not officially involved in efforts to prevent a yen appreciation. Foreign exchange market traders knew better, of course, but as long as private banks could profit from the Finance Ministry's actions, they were willing to participate in its not-so-transparent scheme to hide its activities.

Why did the reactions of Japanese banks in response to the initial sale of yen by the nation's Finance Ministry encourage a fall in the yen's dollar value? In this chapter, you will learn the answer to this question.

> ## Fundamental Issues
>
> 1. What are foreign exchange markets?
>
> 2. What determines exchange rates?
>
> 3. What distinguishes nominal and real exchange rates?
>
> 4. What is purchasing power parity, and is it useful as a guide to movements in exchange rates?
>
> 5. What are the special risks of holding international financial instruments?
>
> 6. In what ways can exchange rates and interest rates be related?

Exchange Rates and the Market for Foreign Exchange

The growth rate in U.S. trading in **foreign exchange,** or exchange of various currencies, has been about 12 percent per year since the early 1990s. By 2005, the average *daily* foreign exchange trading volume in the United States exceeded $650 billion. The large majority of foreign exchange transactions involve the U.S. dollar, but significant volumes of

Foreign exchange: Exchange of currencies issued by different countries.

Foreign exchange market: A system of private banks, foreign exchange brokers and dealers, and central banks through which households, businesses, and governments purchase and sell currencies of various nations.

Exchange rate: The price of one nation's currency in terms of the currency of another country.

Spot market: A market for contracts requiring the immediate sale or purchase of an asset.

Spot exchange rate: The spot-market price of a currency indicating how much of one country's currency must be given up in immediate exchange for a unit of another nation's currency.

trading are devoted to exchanges involving the European Monetary Union's euro, the Japanese yen, the British pound, and the Swiss franc.

Banks are heavily involved in foreign exchange trading. Nearly all banks trade currencies, but the business is largely dominated by U.S. money-center banks, such as Citibank, J. P. Morgan Chase, and Bank of America, and a few European banks such as Deutsche Bank and ABN Amro. These five banks alone typically account for over one-fourth of the transactions in the U.S. **foreign exchange market,** which is a system of private banks, foreign exchange brokers and dealers, and central banks through which households, businesses, and governments buy and sell currencies.

Foreign Exchange Markets and Spot Exchange Rates

Why do banks and other intermediaries, households, firms, governments, and central banks trade such large volumes of foreign exchange? Let's consider an example. A Japanese child greatly enjoys playing with Legos, the classic plastic building-block toys. Therefore, the child's mother decides to buy a large Lego playset for his next birthday. Even though Legos are made in Denmark, at the nearest toy store the price of the playset is posted in yen, the currency that the mother carries in her handbag or holds in her checking account. Thus, her payment to the toy store is denominated in yen, even though the Danish company pays its workers' wages and its owners' dividends in *kroner* (or "crowns"; singular *krone*), the Danish currency.

To make its kroner payments, the Lego company must convert Japanese yen payments for its toys into the Danish currency. It deposits the yen into its bank accounts and has its banks convert the yen into kroner in the foreign exchange market. How many kroner is the yen worth? Said in a different way, what is the value of the yen in terms of kroner? The market **exchange rate,** which expresses the value of one currency in terms of another, gives us the answer to this question.

When most of us think of an institution such as the foreign exchange market, we envision frantic traders on a trading floor. But in the case of Lego's yen-krone transfers, its banks very quietly make its foreign exchange transactions. In addition, these transactions are likely made by the banks with which it does business *within* Japan. Therefore, yen never actually physically flow out of Japan to Lego's headquarters in Denmark. Only Lego toys cross borders.

In fact, the physical flow of currencies among nations is an insignificant portion of total trading in foreign exchange markets. Cross-border movements of physical currencies and coins typically arise from activities such as tourism or illegal exchanges. The instruments most commonly traded in foreign exchange markets are foreign-currency-denominated bonds, stocks, and bank deposits.

Because there are so many different kinds of financial instruments, there are a number of foreign exchange markets. The Lego example above illustrates a *spot-market* currency exchange. Any **spot market** is a market for immediate purchase and delivery of a financial instrument. In the spot foreign exchange market, "immediate delivery" means that transferal occurs within no more than three days.

The **spot exchange rate** is the spot-market price of a currency, measured in the number of units of another currency that must be given up to purchase a unit of that currency. Table 5-1 displays spot exchange rates for foreign exchange transactions at about noon eastern time, which are available each day on the Web site of the Federal Reserve Bank of New York. Thus, the spot exchange rates listed in Table 5-1 apply to large transactions. Those engaging in smaller spot foreign exchange trades, such as tourists, typically face less favorable rates. (Volumes of foreign exchange trading have increased in recent years; see on page 94 the *Global Focus: Just How Much Foreign Exchange Changes Hands Each Day?*)

Table 5-1 Exchange Rates

Country	Monetary Unit	U.S. Dollar Equivalent	Currency per U.S. Dollar
European Monetary Union	Euro	1.2113	0.8256
3-month forward		1.2154	0.8228
6-month forward		1.2208	0.8191
Australia	Dollar	0.7783	1.2849
Brazil	Real	0.4203	2.3790
Canada	Dollar	0.8123	1.2310
China, P.R.	Yuan	0.1208	8.2765
Denmark	Krone	0.1629	6.1370
Hong Kong	Dollar	0.1287	7.7711
India	Rupee	0.0230	43.5000
Japan	Yen	0.0092	108.66
3-month forward		0.0093	107.68
6-month forward		0.0094	106.66
Malaysia	Ringgit	0.2632	3.8000
Mexico	Peso	0.0927	10.7905
New Zealand	Dollar	0.7163	2.1844
Norway	Krone	0.1545	6.4737
Singapore	Dollar	0.5989	1.6698
South Africa	Rand	0.1489	6.7150
South Korea	Won	0.0010	1,008.0000
Sri Lanka	Rupee	0.0100	99.7500
Sweden	Krona	0.1312	7.6210
Switzerland	Franc	0.7873	1.2702
Taiwan	N.T. dollar	0.0319	31.3000
Thailand	Baht	0.0243	41.1400
United Kingdom	Pound	1.8240	0.5482
Venezuela	Bolivar	0.0007	2,144.6000

SOURCE: Federal Reserve Bank of New York, June 21, 2005.

Appreciation versus Depreciation

Table 5-1 displays two versions of the spot exchange rate. The first, the *U.S. dollar equivalent,* tells how many U.S. dollars one must give in exchange for one unit of foreign currency. For instance, Table 5-1 indicates that on June 21, 2005, the U.S. dollar equivalent for the South African rand was 0.1489 dollars per rand. This means that an individual would have to provide 0.1489 U.S. dollars to obtain 1.0 rand in the New York spot foreign exchange market.

It so happens that on June 22, 2005, the U.S. dollar equivalent for the rand fell slightly, to 0.1481 $/rand. Thus, on June 22, a person had to give 0.0008 fewer U.S. dollars in exchange for the South African rand. This decline in the dollar price of the rand indicates that there was a dollar **appreciation** between June 21 and June 22. The dollar gained in value relative to the rand.

Table 5-1 also lists figures for *currency per U.S. dollar.* On June 21, 2005, the spot exchange rate quoted in this unit of measurement was 6.7150 rand per 1.0 U.S. dollar. This amount is the reciprocal of the U.S.-dollar-equivalent rate for the rand: 1/(0.1489 dollars per rand) = 6.7150 rand per dollar. On June 22, the currency-per-U.S.-dollar rate rose to 6.7500

MONEYXTRA!
Economic Applications

What is the current dollar value of another nation's currency? Find out via the Universal Currency Calculator available through Corporate Finance Online.
http://www.moneyxtra. swcollege.com

Appreciation: A rise in the value of one currency relative to another.

GLOBAL
Focus

Just How Much Foreign Exchange Changes Hands Each Day?

Average daily trading volumes in the world's foreign exchange markets since 1989 are displayed in Figure 5-1. Global trading of foreign exchange increased rapidly until 1999, the year that several major European currencies were eliminated by the creation of the euro. Trading activity in the foreign exchange markets took off again beginning in 2001, however. Today, more than $2 trillion worth of foreign exchange changes hands every day that currency markets are open.

FOR CRITICAL ANALYSIS: What could explain why trading in foreign exchange markets has grown at an annual pace much greater than the rate of growth of world trade of goods and services? (Hint: What other items, besides goods and services, do individuals, businesses, and governments desire to buy with foreign currencies?)

FIGURE 5-1
Average Daily Trading in Foreign Exchange Markets.

This figure shows the average daily dollar value of all foreign exchange trading around the world each year since 1989. Although average daily trading dipped between 1999 and 2001, it has risen at a quick pace since 2001.

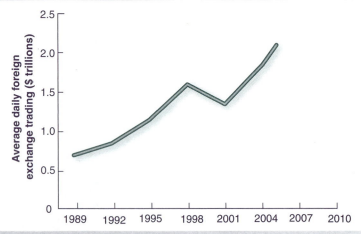

SOURCE: Bank for International Settlements.

rand per dollar, which is the reciprocal of the U.S.-dollar-equivalent rate for that day: 1/(0.1481 dollars per rand) = 6.7500. This rise in the currency-per-U.S.-dollar rate for the rand means that an individual had to give up more rand to obtain dollars on June 22 than on June 21. Hence, there was a rand **depreciation** between June 21 and June 22, meaning that the rand lost value relative to the dollar.

Depreciation: A decline in the value of one currency relative to another.

1. What are foreign exchange markets? Foreign exchange markets are the systems through which people exchange one nation's currency for the currency of another nation. Most transactions in foreign exchange markets entail exchanges of foreign-currency-denominated bonds and deposits. The actual movement of currency from one country to another is a relatively insignificant feature of activity in the foreign exchange market.

The Demand for and Supply of Currencies and the Equilibrium Exchange Rate

The preceding description of foreign exchange markets omitted one important question: What actually determines the exchange rates of the various currencies? As we will see, the interactions between demand and supply in the foreign exchange markets determine the *equilibrium* exchange rates that prevail in those markets.

The Demand for a Currency

The primary international role of a currency is to facilitate trade among nations. Consequently, the demand for a currency is *derived* from the demand for the goods, services, and assets that residents of other countries use the currency to purchase. Let's contemplate two countries, the United Kingdom and the United States. The demand for pounds stems from U.S. residents' demand for British goods, services, and pound-denominated assets. If U.S. consumers' demand for British goods increases, then there is a rise in the demand for pounds to purchase the British goods. The price that U.S. consumers have to pay for the pounds is the prevailing U.S.-dollar-per-pound exchange rate.

THE CURRENCY DEMAND SCHEDULE Figure 5-2 illustrates the demand relationship in the market for British pounds. An appreciation of the dollar relative to the pound leads to a reduction in the U.S.-dollar-per-pound exchange rate because fewer dollars are necessary to purchase each pound. The reasoning behind the downward slope of the demand curve is that as the dollar appreciates relative to the pound, British goods become relatively less expensive for U.S. consumers to purchase. As a result, U.S. consumers choose to buy more British goods and therefore require more British pounds. Thus, there is a negative relationship between the price of the pound—the dollar-pound exchange rate—and the quantity of pounds demanded. This means that a change in the exchange rate brings about a *movement along* the

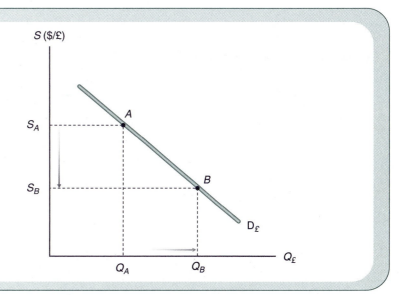

FIGURE 5-2
Demand for the Pound.

The demand schedule for the pound depicts the relationship between the exchange rate and the quantity of pounds demanded. A reduction in the exchange rate from S_A to S_B indicates an appreciation of the U.S. dollar relative to the British pound, which makes British goods and services relatively less expensive for U.S. consumers. As a result, U.S. residents increase the quantity of pounds they wish to purchase with dollars, from Q_A to Q_B.

demand curve. If the dollar appreciates relative to the pound—a fall in the dollar-pound exchange rate—the result is a movement down along the demand curve, as shown by the movement from point *A* to point *B* in Figure 5-2. The appreciation of the dollar relative to the pound brings about an increase in the quantity of pounds demanded.

A CHANGE IN CURRENCY DEMAND   Suppose that U.S. consumers' tastes for goods manufactured in the United Kingdom change so that they demand more British goods at any given exchange rate. This is a *change in the demand* for the pound that, as shown in Figure 5-3, is reflected by a *shift* in the demand schedule. The rightward shift of the demand schedule in Figure 5-3 illustrates an increase in the demand for the pound. A leftward shift would depict a decrease in the demand for the pound.

   The demand for a currency is a derived demand, so the various factors that cause a change in the demand for a currency are the same factors that cause a change in the foreign demand for a country's goods, services, and assets. They include such factors as variations in foreign residents' tastes and preferences, changes in the incomes of foreign residents, and the extent to which other nations restrict imports. Thus, the increase in the demand for the pound illustrated in Figure 5-3 might stem from a shift in U.S. consumers' tastes and preferences for goods produced in Britain, a rise in U.S. incomes, or a relaxation of previously existing restrictions that had limited U.S. imports of British goods, services, or assets.

The Supply of a Currency

Now consider British consumers' demand for U.S. dollars, owing to their demand for U.S. goods, services, and assets. When British consumers purchase U.S. dollars to buy U.S. goods, they exchange pounds for dollars. As a result, there is a rise in the quantity of pounds supplied in the foreign exchange market. Thus, the British demand for dollars also represents the supply of pounds.

FIGURE 5-3
An Increase in Currency Demand.

A rise in the demand for British goods and services by U.S. residents causes an increase in the quantity of pounds demanded at any given exchange rate. Thus, the pound demand schedule shifts rightward, from $D_£$ to $D_£'$.

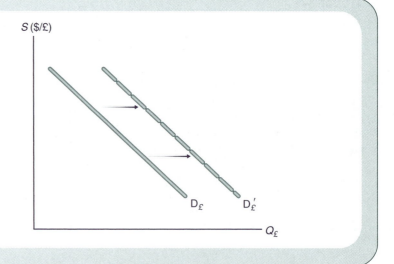

THE CURRENCY SUPPLY SCHEDULE   Figure 5-4 depicts the relationship between the British demand for dollars, shown in panel (a), and the British supply of pounds, illustrated in panel (b). In panel (a), if the pound appreciates (a decrease in the pound-dollar exchange rate), then U.S. goods are relatively less expensive for British consumers to purchase. As a result, British consumers wish to buy more U.S. goods, which requires them to purchase more U.S. dollars. Thus, there is an increase in the quantity of U.S. dollars demanded, shown by the movement from point A to point B in panel (a).

Panel (b) of Figure 5-4 shows an equivalent way to depict this relationship. When the pound appreciates, the dollar-pound exchange rate rises. As British consumers increase the quantity of dollars that they purchase, they exchange their pounds for dollars, so the quantity of pounds supplied increases. Hence, there is a positive relationship between the dollar-pound exchange rate and the quantity of pounds supplied, which is shown as the upward-sloping supply schedule in panel (b). The movement from point A to point B on this currency supply schedule represents an increase in the quantity of pounds supplied in response to an appreciation of the value of the pound relative to the dollar.

A CHANGE IN CURRENCY SUPPLY   If British consumers reduce their desired consumption of U.S. goods at any given exchange rate, then there is a decrease in the demand for the dollar. British consumers cut back on their purchases of dollars used to facilitate their purchases of U.S. goods, thereby reducing the quantity supplied of pounds at any given exchange rate. This constitutes a *fall in the supply* of pounds, which is depicted by a leftward shift of the pound supply schedule in Figure 5-5 on the next page. In contrast, an increase in the supply of pounds would correspond to a rightward shift of the supply schedule.

A change in the supply of a currency is caused by the same factors that induce a change in a country's demand for a foreign country's goods, services, and assets. These include changes

FIGURE 5-4
The Currency Supply Schedule.

Panel (a) shows the demand for U.S. dollars by British residents. A fall in the pound-dollar exchange rate induces an increase in the quantity of dollars demanded, shown by the movement from point A to point B. As British residents use more pounds to purchase dollars, they supply a larger quantity of pounds. Thus, as panel (b) illustrates, the cor-

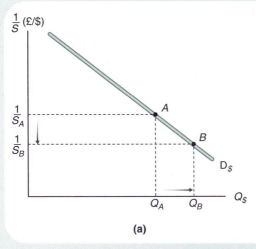

(a)

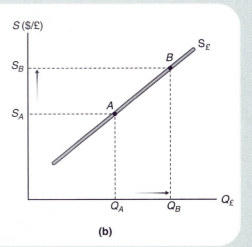

(b)

responding rise in the dollar-pound exchange rate implies an increase in the quantity of pounds supplied for dollars in the foreign exchange market. The pound supply schedule slopes upward.

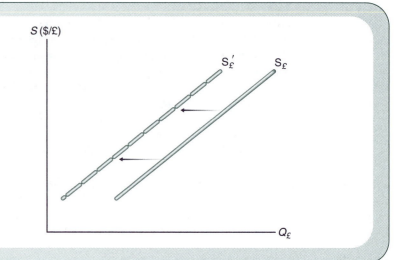

**FIGURE 5-5
A Reduction in Currency Supply.**

If British residents reduce their desired consumption of U.S. goods and services, then they supply fewer pounds in exchange for dollars at any given exchange rate. Thus, the currency supply schedule shifts leftward from $S_£$ to $S_£'$.

in the tastes and preferences of its consumers, changes in its consumers' incomes, and alterations of existing import restrictions. For instance, the fall in the supply of pounds shown in Figure 5-5 might result from a reduced interest in U.S. goods by British consumers, a general decline in British income levels, or stiffened restrictions on British imports from the United States.

The Equilibrium Exchange Rate

In an equilibrium situation in the foreign exchange market, British residents supply an amount of pounds that is equal to the quantity of pounds demanded by U.S. residents. The exchange rate adjusts until this condition is satisfied. Thus, the *equilibrium exchange rate* is the rate at which the quantity of a currency demanded is equal to the quantity supplied. At the equilibrium exchange rate, the foreign exchange market *clears,* meaning that the quantity of the currency demanded is exactly equal to the quantity supplied. (In one currency market, a surprisingly large part of the equilibrium quantity of foreign exchange is traded by a single U.S. company; see the *Management Focus: In This Foreign Exchange Market, One Firm Is a Major Player.*)

FOREIGN EXCHANGE MARKET EQUILIBRIUM   Figure 5-6 shows the point of equilibrium for the foreign exchange market as point E, at which the equilibrium spot exchange rate is S_E, and the equilibrium quantity of pounds exchanged is Q_E. At the exchange rate S_A, the exchange rate is at a level above its equilibrium value, and the quantity of pounds demanded by U.S. residents is equal to Q_1. The quantity of pounds supplied by British residents at the above-equilibrium exchange rate S_A, however, is equal to Q_2. Thus, the quantity of pounds supplied, Q_2, exceeds the quantity demanded, Q_1. The difference $Q_2 - Q_1$ is an excess quantity of pounds supplied in the foreign exchange market. Sellers of pounds will bid down the exchange rate until the pound depreciates to the point at which there is no excess quantity supplied. This is true at point E.

At the below-equilibrium exchange rate S_B, the quantity demanded is Q_2, which exceeds the quantity supplied, Q_1. In this case, the pound's value will appreciate until there is no

MANAGEMENT
Focus

In This Foreign Exchange Market, One Firm Is a Major Player

If Wal-Mart were treated as a separate "country," it would rank as the fifth-largest importer of products manufac-

tured in China, placing it ahead of true nation-state trading partners such as Russia and the United Kingdom. The company accounts for more than 10 percent of all U.S. imports from China. To obtain all the Chinese-made products that it sells in its stores, Wal-Mart enters the foreign exchange market and trades U.S. dollars for the Chinese currency, the yuan. Consequently, Wal-Mart

single-handedly generates a significant fraction of the quantity of dollar-yuan exchanges that take place in the market for this particular currency.

FOR CRITICAL ANALYSIS: When Wal-Mart buys Chinese-manufactured items to sell in its U.S. stores, do its actions affect the demand for or supply of yuan?

excess quantity demanded, once again at point *E*. The foreign exchange market remains in equilibrium at this point unless some factor induces one or both of the schedules to shift.

CHANGES IN THE EQUILIBRIUM EXCHANGE RATE   To see how the exchange rate might rise, consider Figure 5-7 on page 100. In both panel (a) and panel (b), the initial equilibrium is at point *E*, where the equilibrium exchange rate is S_E and the equilibrium quantity of pounds traded is Q_E. Panel (a) illustrates the effects of an increase in the demand for British goods by U.S. consumers. This induces a rise in the demand for pounds, so the currency demand schedule shifts rightward. At the initial equilibrium exchange rate S_E, there is now an excess quantity of pounds demanded. Thus, the exchange rate must rise to a new equilibrium value S_E' at point *E'*, which means that the pound appreciates in value relative to the dollar. Note

---

FIGURE 5-6
Foreign Exchange Market Equilibrium.

At the exchange rate S_E, the quantity of pounds supplied by British residents is equal to the quantity of pounds demanded by U.S. residents. At the above-equilibrium exchange rate S_A, there is an excess quantity of pounds supplied, so the exchange rate will be bid downward toward its equilibrium level (the dollar's value will appreciate relative to the pound). At the below-equilibrium exchange rate S_B, there is an excess quantity of pounds demanded, so the exchange rate will be bid upward toward its equilibrium level (the dollar's value will depreciate relative to the pound).

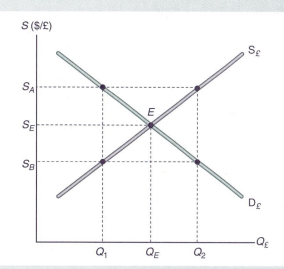

**FIGURE 5-7
An Increase in
the Equilibrium
Exchange Rate.**

In panel (a), an
increase in the
demand for British
goods by U.S. resi-
dents causes the
pound demand
schedule to shift
rightward. At the
initial equilibrium
exchange rate S_E,
there is now an
excess quantity of
pounds demanded, so the exchange
rate is bid upward toward a new equilibrium value equal to S_E'. Panel (b)
illustrates the effect of a reduction in
the British demand for U.S. goods that

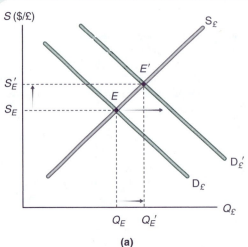
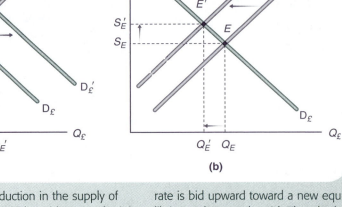

(a) (b)

entails a reduction in the supply of
pounds by British residents. At the initial equilibrium exchange rate S_E,
there is now an excess quantity of
pounds demanded, so the exchange

rate is bid upward toward a new equilibrium value equal to S_E'. Thus, both
examples illustrate a depreciation of
the dollar relative to the pound.

On the Web
Where are data on
the exchange value of
the U.S. dollar relative to the
major currencies of the world?
One place to look is at the
monthly and daily data series
provided by the Federal Reserve
Bank of St. Louis at **http://
www.research.stlouisfed.
org/fred2/categories/15**.

that the appreciation of the pound relative to the dollar makes British goods relatively more
expensive to U.S. consumers, who reduce desired purchases of British goods due to this change
in the exchange rate. As a result, the quantity of pounds demanded declines somewhat, but at
point E' the equilibrium quantity of pounds traded has increased, on net, from Q_E to Q_E'.

Panel (b) of Figure 5-7 illustrates another way that the equilibrium exchange rate can
increase. If British residents cut back on their purchases of U.S. goods, then they supply fewer
pounds in exchange for dollars. As a result, the currency supply schedule shifts leftward. At
the initial equilibrium exchange rate S_E, therefore, there is now an excess quantity of pounds
demanded. To clear the market, the exchange rate must rise to S_E' at point E'. Once again, the
pound appreciates relative to the dollar. This causes a reduction in the equilibrium quantity
of pounds demanded, so the equilibrium volume of pounds traded falls. (An increasing portion of foreign exchange trading takes place on the Internet, but some U.S. state governments
have determined that the risks to individuals of trading currencies online are too high; see the
Cyber Focus: Should Just Anyone Be Able to Trade Foreign Exchange on the Web?)

2. What determines exchange rates? The interaction between the demand for
a currency and the supply of the currency determines the equilibrium exchange rate
for that currency relative to another. The equilibrium exchange rate is the exchange
rate at which the quantity of a currency demanded is equal to the quantity supplied.
Changes in the equilibrium exchange rate occur as a result of variations in the
demand for or the supply of a currency.

Should Just Anyone Be Able to Trade Foreign Exchange on the Web?

Many Web sites offer individuals the opportunity to trade yen, euros, and other currencies on the Internet by setting up currency-trading accounts starting with as little as $500. Nevertheless, many of these sites do not have licenses required by law. In some cases, currency-trading sites have turned out to be fraudulent. Federal law does not

encompass online currency trading, so regulating online currency trading is largely the province of state agencies. Some of these have attempted to completely shut down online trading of foreign exchange. When asked what might be wrong with foreign currency trading on the Internet, an official with the California Department of Corporations, which establishes rules governing financial trading in that state, answered, "That it exists."

A number of foreign-currency-trading sites, however, are legitimate business operations. Owners of these sites argue that like online brokers that allow small

investors to trade stocks and bonds, they provide a service to small currency traders who want to try their hand at profiting from movements in exchange rates. In the site owners' view, efforts by state regulators to halt their operations are really intended to protect banks and other large dealers of foreign exchange from new competition made possible by the Internet.

FOR CRITICAL ANALYSIS: How could widespread fraud at online currency-trading sites bring about a net reduction in equilibrium trading in foreign exchange?

Purchasing Power Parity

From time to time, policymakers and financial media commentators argue that the currency of one nation is "undervalued" or that the currency of some other nation is "overvalued." Unfortunately, it is not always clear what they mean. Often policymakers and commentators do not explain exactly how they reached their conclusions, making it difficult to judge the validity of their claims.

Traditionally, economists have approached the issue of whether a currency's value is "too low" or "too high," meaning that some adjustment is likely to occur in the market, by studying the behavior of *real exchange rates*, which take into account how the exchange rates observed to clear markets today relate to relative differences in nations' overall prices of goods and services. Given a theory of how real exchange rates are determined, economists define an **overvalued currency** as a currency that has a current market value higher than the theory predicts, implying that the currency is likely to experience a depreciation. In contrast, an **undervalued currency** is a currency whose value is weaker than predicted by the theory, indicating that it is likely to appreciate in value.

To judge whether a currency is over- or undervalued, economists often use the theory of *purchasing power parity*. Before we explain this theory, however, you must first understand real exchange rates.

Real Exchange Rates

The exchange rates displayed in Table 5-1 on page 93 are **nominal exchange rates,** which tell us today's market value of our own currency in exchange for a foreign currency. These exchange rates do not reflect changes in price levels in the two nations, however. If we are interested in the amount of foreign goods and services that our currency will buy, then we must take

Overvalued currency: A currency whose present market-determined value is higher than the value predicted by an economic theory or model.

Undervalued currency: A currency whose present market-determined value is lower than that predicted by an economic theory or model.

Nominal exchange rate: An exchange rate that is unadjusted for changes in the two nations' price levels.

Real exchange rate: An exchange rate that has been adjusted for differences between two nations' price levels, thereby yielding the implied rate of exchange of goods and services between those nations.

into account the **real exchange rate,** which adjusts the nominal exchange rate for changes in the nations' price levels and thereby measures the *purchasing power of the domestic goods and services in exchange for foreign goods and services.* To know how much of another country's goods and services we can obtain by trading our own nation's goods and services, using our own currency as a medium of exchange in the transaction, we must know the value of the real exchange rate.

NOMINAL CURRENCY DEPRECIATION   To see why the real exchange rate matters, consider the bilateral exchange relationship between the United States and Canada between 2004 and 2005. In January 2004, the currency-per-U.S.-dollar spot exchange rate for the Canadian dollar (C$) was 1.301 C$/$. By January 2005, the Canadian dollar's value had increased, and the exchange rate was equal to 1.234 C$/$.

Both of these exchange rates are nominal exchange rates. The rate of depreciation of the U.S. dollar relative to the Canadian dollar between January 2004 and January 2005 was equal to [(1.301 − 1.234)/1.301] × 100, which is equal to 5.1 percent. This means that in January 2005 more than 5 percent fewer Canadian dollars—an amount roughly the same as the value of a Canadian nickel—were needed to buy a dollar in the foreign exchange market than had been necessary in January 2004.

THE REAL EXCHANGE RATE AND REAL CURRENCY DEPRECIATION   Clearly, the increase in the value of the Canadian dollar relative to the U.S. dollar had the immediate effects of making Canadian goods and services effectively more expensive for U.S. consumers to purchase and U.S. goods and services cheaper from the perspective of Canadian consumers. Something else also happened between 2004 and 2005. Canada had a lower inflation rate than the United States. The annual rate of consumer price inflation in Canada was only about 2 percent, compared with about 3 percent in the United States.

These relative inflation differences matter because changes in the prices of goods and services alter the effective prices that Canadian residents pay for U.S. goods and services and that U.S. residents pay for Canadian goods and services. To see how, let's take January 2004 as the starting point for comparing the relative purchasing power of the two countries' goods and services. Thus, let's set the consumer price index equal to 100 in both countries at that point in time. This means that by January 2005 the Canadian consumer price index was equal to 102.0, while the U.S. consumer price index was equal to 103.0.

To measure the real exchange rate between Canada and the United States in January 2004, we multiply the nominal exchange rate at that time, 1.301 C$/$, by the ratio of the U.S. consumer price index to the Canadian price index, 100/100, to get 1.301 C$/$. Thus, by choosing January 2004 as our starting point, we have defined the nominal and real exchange rates at that point as being equivalent.

To calculate the real exchange rate for January 2005, we multiply the nominal exchange rate at that time, 1.234 C$/$, by the ratio of the U.S. consumer price index to the Canadian price index, 103.0/102.0, which yields 1.246 C$/$. This implies that the *real rate of depreciation* for the U.S. dollar was equal to [(1.301 − 1.246)/1.301] × 100 = 4.2 percent. This calculated real rate of U.S. dollar depreciation was slightly lower than the nominal depreciation rate of 5.1 percent, because the relatively lower Canadian inflation rate implied somewhat lower prices of Canadian goods and services relative to U.S. goods and services. Thus, the relatively lower inflation in Canada slightly offset the larger nominal depreciation in the U.S. dollar's value that took place in that year.

> **3. What distinguishes nominal and real exchange rates?** A nominal
> exchange rate is the observed rate at which a nation's currency trades in foreign
> exchange markets for units of the currency of another country. Nominal exchange
> rates do not take into account changes in the price levels across nations. A real
> exchange rate adjusts the nominal exchange rate for changes in the nations' price lev-
> els. Hence, real exchange rates measure the purchasing power of a nation's goods
> and services in exchange for the goods and services of other nations.

A Theory of Real and Nominal Exchange Rates: Purchasing Power Parity

The first, and oldest, theory of exchange rates, which many economists still use to gauge whether currencies are over- or undervalued in the marketplace, is the theory of *purchasing power parity*. One reason this theory has proved so popular is that it is easy to understand. Another reason is that it is easy to apply. As you will learn, the simplicity of purchasing power parity may or may not be a virtue. Indeed, generations of economists have literally spent centuries debating the relevance of the theory and its applicability to issues of public policy in the sphere of international economic relations.

In its most basic form, the idea of **purchasing power parity (PPP)** is that, in the absence of factors such as costs of transportation, cross-country tax differentials, and trade restrictions, homogeneous goods and services that are tradable across national borders should have the same price in two countries after converting their prices into a common currency. For this reason, economists often refer to this basic concept of purchasing power parity as the *law of one price*.

Purchasing power parity (PPP): A condition that states that if international arbitrage is unhindered, the price of a good or service in one nation should be the same as the exchange-rate-adjusted price of the same good or service in another nation.

To illustrate the law of one price, suppose that the market price of a high-grade golden delicious apple is US$0.40 in Detroit, Michigan. The market price of the same quality and type of apple in Windsor, Ontario, is C$0.50. This would imply that the dollar-equivalent exchange rate should be US$0.40/C$0.50 = 0.80 U.S. dollar per Canadian dollar. Using this rate, we can convert the Canadian dollar price of the apple in Windsor to a U.S. dollar price of US$0.40 (C$0.50 × 0.80 US$/C$ = US$0.40). Therefore, the apple has the same price in Windsor as it does in Detroit after adjusting for the exchange rate.

ARBITRAGE AND PURCHASING POWER PARITY If, in our apple-exchange example, the exchange rate were not 0.80 US$/C$, then an *arbitrage opportunity* would exist. **Arbitrage** is the process of buying an asset at a given price in one market and profiting by selling it at a higher price in another market. Suppose the exchange rate is equal to 0.85 US$/C$. Then the U.S. dollar price of a golden delicious apple in Windsor would be C$0.50 × 0.85 US$/C$ = US$0.425. A Canadian apple arbitrageur who can buy many apples in Detroit for US$0.40 per apple, place them on a large truck, and drive them a short distance to Windsor to sell for C$0.50 each (US$0.425 in U.S. dollars at the 0.85 US$/C$ exchange rate) will earn a profit of US$0.025 per apple. Thus, if the arbitrageur can move 10,000 apples from Detroit to Windsor to sell in Canada, the profit will be $250, ignoring the relatively small transportation costs.

Arbitrage: Purchasing an asset at the current price in one market and profiting by selling it at a higher price in another market.

If a sufficient number of people engage in this sort of arbitrage activity, then the result will be a flow of apples from Detroit to Windsor. The exchange of Canadian dollars for U.S. dollars on the foreign exchange market thereby will cause an increase in the demand for U.S. dollars relative to Canadian dollars. The three markets (Detroit apple market, Windsor apple market, and foreign exchange market) will experience adjustments. The outflow of apples from Detroit will generate an increase in the price of apples in Detroit. The inflow of apples to Windsor will cause a decrease in the price of apples in Windsor.

If a number of apples and other goods and services are arbitraged in response to the misaligned exchange rate, then the demand for U.S. dollars will increase relative to Canadian dollars. This will cause the value of the U.S. dollar to appreciate relative to the Canadian dollar. All of these adjustments, which result from the arbitrage activity, will tend to equalize the (same currency) prices of traded goods and services, thereby removing any further scope for profiting from cross-border arbitrage.

ABSOLUTE PURCHASING POWER PARITY   This analysis of the relationship between prices and exchange rates implies the condition of *absolute purchasing power parity,* which we can formalize in the following manner. Let's define S to be the U.S.-dollar-equivalent exchange rate of the Canadian dollar, P to be the price of golden delicious apples in the United States, and P^* to be the price of golden delicious apples in Canada. Then we can express absolute PPP as

$$P = S \times P^*.$$

In words, the U.S. price of apples should equal the Canadian price times the spot exchange rate. Thus, in our example, if the U.S. dollar–Canadian dollar exchange rate is 0.80 U.S. dollars per Canadian dollar and the Canadian price of apples is C$0.50 per apple, then the U.S. dollar price of apples should equal US$0.40.

A Theory of the Exchange Rate   If all goods and services are fully and freely tradable across U.S. and Canadian borders, then absolute PPP will hold for all goods. In this instance, we can interpret P as the overall price level of U.S. goods and services and P^* as the overall price level of Canadian goods and services. Note that in this instance, we can rearrange the absolute PPP relationship to solve for the spot exchange rate:

$$S = P/P^*.$$

That is, when absolute PPP holds for all goods and services, the spot exchange rate equals the U.S. price level divided by the Canadian price level. Thus, absolute PPP is a theory of exchange rate determination: if absolute PPP holds, then the spot exchange rate should equal the ratio of the price levels of the two nations. Hence, the demand and supply schedules in foreign exchange markets should move to positions yielding this exchange rate.

Some Limitations   It is a big jump from golden delicious apples to all goods and services, however. To apply the concept of absolute PPP to exchange rate determination, our simplifying assumptions of no transportation costs, no tax differentials, and no trade restrictions that we used in our apple-exchange example must be met in the real world. This is highly unlikely to be true. After all, loading 10,000 or more apples into a truck is a costly endeavor, apple sales might be subject to different tax rates in Canada and the United States, or one of the two nations could have legal restraints on apple trade. Certainly, we might expect transportation expenses, different tax treatment, or trade restrictions to apply for a number of other goods even if they do not have significant effects in the national markets for apples.

Furthermore, even if transportation costs, tax differences, and trade restrictions are insignificant, we still would anticipate problems in applying absolute PPP to all goods and services of two nations. The reason is that people in the two nations may consume different sets of goods and services. As an extreme example, imagine that the typical U.S. consumer buys apples and pears, but the typical Canadian consumer buys apples and oranges. If these are the only goods consumed in each nation, then using overall price levels for the two nations to make a statement about exchange rate determination would be a mistake. The price levels for the two nations would be based on the prices of different goods, meaning that the arbitrage argument that lies behind the absolute PPP condition could not apply. Arbitrage could not really relate the prices of both sets of goods, so we would be mistaken to infer an exchange rate from the absolute PPP relationship.

Absolute PPP and the Real Exchange Rate   Another way to see why absolute PPP is unlikely to hold in the real world is to recall how we calculate a real exchange rate: we multiply the spot exchange rate, S, by the relative price levels for the two countries, P^*/P, so the real exchange rate is equal to

$$S \times (P^*/P).$$

If absolute PPP holds, however, then $S = P/P^*$, so the real exchange rate is equal to

$$S \times (P^*/P) = (P/P^*) \times (P^*/P) = 1.$$

A real exchange rate equal to 1 means that one unit of goods and services in a country, such as the United States, always exchanges one-for-one with a unit of goods and services in another country, such as Canada. Thus, absolute PPP implies that the real exchange rate is always equal to 1. If people in different countries consume goods and services in different proportions, however, it is highly unlikely that this will be so.

RELATIVE PURCHASING POWER PARITY   Not surprisingly, using absolute PPP as a theory of exchange rate determination is not very useful. For this reason, economists often use a different benchmark that is known as *relative purchasing power parity*. Relative PPP relates *proportionate changes* in exchange rates to relative *changes* in countries' price levels.

We can use the expression for absolute PPP to derive the relative version of PPP. Let's denote the percentage change of a variable by placing the characters "%Δ" (percentage change in) in front of the variable. Then, for example, %ΔP would represent the proportionate change in the price level for a period. By calculating the change of each variable in the equation for absolute PPP, we can express relative PPP as

$$\%\Delta S = \%\Delta P - \%\Delta P^*.$$

Thus, relative PPP implies that the percentage change in an exchange rate equals the difference between the percentage changes in the countries' price levels. The percentage changes in the nations' price levels for a given interval are their inflation rates, denoted π and π^*. Thus, we can express relative PPP as

$$\%\Delta S = \pi - \pi^*.$$

According to relative PPP, therefore, the appreciation or depreciation of a currency is equal to the difference between the two nations' inflation rates.

How does relative PPP do as a theoretical predictor of actual exchange rate changes? Most studies indicate that relative PPP performs better than absolute PPP, but relative PPP typically

On the Web
Where can you learn more about recent PPP facts and figures? Try going to **http://pacific.commerce.ubc.ca/xr**. Click on "What Is Purchasing Power Parity?"

is not a very good theory for predicting exchange rate movements over periods of less than a few years. Our earlier example of the 5.1 percent depreciation of the U.S. dollar relative to the Canadian dollar between 2004 and 2005, even though the U.S. inflation rate exceeded the Canadian inflation rate by only 1.0 percentage point, is a case in point.

Relative PPP often does perform better over short-run intervals for countries that experience episodes of very high inflation. This is true because during such episodes, price changes typically are the dominant influence on the value of the domestic currency. Over short-run intervals, however, factors other than relative price levels or inflation rates can have significant effects on exchange rates. Thus, neither version of PPP works particularly well for explaining short-term exchange rate variations.

PURCHASING POWER PARITY AS A LONG-RUN DETERMINANT OF EXCHANGE RATES
Economists have long recognized the factors that limit their ability to use PPP as a complete theory of exchange rate determination. Nevertheless, the logic of the law of one price has led most economists to believe that, given sufficient time, exchange rates should *eventually* adjust to values consistent with PPP, at least in its relative form.

Random-Walk Exchange Rates   In the 1970s and 1980s, however, study after study found that it was difficult to rule out the possibility that real exchange rates follow a "random walk." This meant that if some event, such as an abrupt, temporary change in the price level in one nation, were to occur, the real exchange rate would move to a new level. The real exchange rate would tend to stay at this new level until the next unexpected, short-lived event took place to "bump" it to another level. As we already noted, absolute PPP implies that the real exchange rate should tend toward the value of 1. As we discussed, relative PPP is less restrictive. Nonetheless, if relative PPP holds, it turns out that the real exchange rate should tend toward a *constant* value (but not necessarily a value of 1). If the real exchange rate were to follow a random walk, however, then as time passes it would not necessarily settle down to a constant value. Thus, random-walk behavior of real exchange rates was strong evidence against PPP.

By the mid-1980s, the PPP doctrine was in such doubt that *The Economist* magazine developed an initially satirical measure of PPP called the "Big Mac Index." The idea was that McDonald's Big Mac sandwich has the same basket of ingredients in all world locations, so if the law of one price holds, the exchange-rate-adjusted price of a Big Mac should be the same everywhere. In fact, however, from year to year the Big Mac guide to exchange rates does relatively poorly (see the *Global Focus: PPP Packed into a Sesame Seed Bun*).

Saving PPP?   In the 1990s and 2000s, new rounds of research on real exchange rates evaluated the possibility that earlier studies were biased because they considered only a few countries or relatively short spans of time. Looking at insufficient observations of the real exchange rate might make short-term variations in the real exchange rate look like random-walk movements when in fact they were simply movements of real exchange rates toward levels consistent with PPP. One set of studies, therefore, examined large numbers of countries' real exchange rates simultaneously, thereby evaluating PPP with massive amounts of cross-country data. These studies consistently found little evidence of random-walk behavior of exchange rates. Recently, however, a debate has arisen about whether this "cross-country approach" to evaluating PPP suffers from its own special difficulties.

This has led other researchers to concentrate on real-exchange-rate behavior over long time periods, spanning from six decades to as long as nearly seven centuries. The idea is that if PPP holds, it must hold on average over such long intervals. Indeed, these studies find strong evidence that, given sufficient time, real exchange rates tend to settle down at constant

MONEYXTRA!
Online Case Study

To contemplate the limitations of purchasing power parity for managers, go to the Chapter 5 Case Study, entitled "Purchasing Power Parity as a Business Guide?" **http://moneyxtra. swcollege.com**

PPP Packed into a Sesame Seed Bun

Among businesspeople, the most popular version of PPP is the Big Mac Index from *The Economist* magazine.

The 2005 version of the Big Mac Index appears in Table 5-2.

Table 5-2 shows that the price of a Big Mac in the United States is $3.06, whereas the price of a Big Mac in Japan is ¥250. Using the equation for absolute PPP, $S = P/P*$ ($P* = $ U.S. price), the implied exchange rate is 81.7¥/$, which is shown in the third column. The fourth column gives the actual value of the yen-dollar exchange rate at the time, 106¥/$. The true, market-determined value of the dollar relative to the yen is higher than the value implied by absolute PPP. The Big Mac Index, therefore, indicates that the yen is undervalued relative to the dollar. We can express this undervaluation as the percentage difference between the implied value of the dollar according to the Big Mac PPP measure and the market value. This works out to be 23 percent for the yen. Hence, according to the Big Mac measure of PPP, the yen should appreciate relative to the dollar.

How does the Big Mac perform as a guide to exchange rate movements? In the short run, the index certainly is not an accurate predictor of exchange rates. The index performs better in the long run, but most of the adjustment to PPP occurs through price changes.

FOR CRITICAL ANALYSIS: Studies have found that the Big Mac Index is closely related to several other more elaborate measures of PPP, so some economists have concluded that the Big Mac Index is a surprisingly good longer-term indicator of PPP valuations of exchange rates. What does the predictive performance of the Big Mac Index imply about the likely usefulness of absolute PPP as a shorter-term measure of currency under- or overvaluation?

Table 5-2 The Big Mac Index

	Big Mac prices in local currency	Big Mac prices in dollars	Implied PPP* of the dollar	Actual dollar exchange rate	Under (−)/over (+) valuation against the dollar, %
United States[†]	$3.06	3.06			
Argentina	Peso 4.75	1.64	1.55	2.87	−46
Australia	A$3.25	2.50	1.06	1.29	−18
Brazil	Real 5.90	2.39	1.93	2.47	−22
Britain	£1.88	3.44	1.63	1.83[‡]	+12
Canada	C$3.27	2.63	1.07	1.24	−14
Chile	Peso 1,500	2.53	490	590	−17
China	Yuan 10.50	1.27	3.43	8.28	−59
Czech Rep	Koruna 56.28	2.30	18.4	24.5	−25
Denmark	DKr27.75	4.58	9.07	6.05	+50
Euro area	€3.21	3.58	1.05	1.23[§]	+17
Hong Kong	HK$12.00	1.54	3.92	7.80	−50
Hungary	Forint 529	2.60	173	204	−15
Indonesia	Rupiah 14,600	1.53	4,771	9.540	−50
Japan	¥250	2.34	81.7	106	−23
Malaysia	M$5.26	1.38	1.72	3.8	−55
Mexico	Peso 28.00	2.58	9.15	10.9	−16
New Zealand	NZ$4.44	3.17	1.45	1.51	−4
Peru	New Sol 9.00	2.76	2.94	3.43	−10
Philippines	Peso 79.87	1.47	26.1	54.4	−52
Poland	Zloty 6.49	1.96	2.12	3.12	−36
Russia	Rouble 41.92	1.48	13.7	28.4	−52
Singapore	S$3.61	2.17	1.18	1.66	−29
South Africa	Rand 13.95	2.10	4.56	6.61	−31
South Korea	Won 2,500	2.49	817	1,009	−19
Sweden	SKr30.60	4.17	10.1	7.43	+36
Switzerland	SFr6.30	5.05	2.06	1.25	+65
Taiwan	NT$75.00	2.41	24.5	31.0	−21
Thailand	Baht 60.00	1.48	19.6	40.8	−52
Turkey	Lira 4	2.92	1.31	1.38	−5
Venezuela	Bolivar 5,600	2.13	1,830	2,614	−30

*Purchasing power parity; local price divided by price in the United States.
[†]Average of New York, Chicago, San Francisco, and Atlanta. [‡]Dollars per pound. [§]Dollars per euro.

SOURCES: McDonald's; *The Economist*.

long-term levels predicted by the PPP doctrine. These studies conclude that a reason there is so little evidence in favor of PPP over shorter-term periods is that departures from PPP take so long to disappear. For example, if some temporary factor causes the real exchange rate to move above the level consistent with PPP, these studies of long-run horizons indicate that it typically takes between three and seven years for the real exchange rate to get halfway back to its PPP level. If these more recent studies are correct, PPP is truly a long-run determinant of exchange rates. This may help explain why *The Economist*'s Big Mac Index has performed better when evaluated over intervals of several years, even though it consistently fails to fit exchange rates on a year-to-year basis.

> **4. What is purchasing power parity, and is it useful as a guide to movements in exchange rates?** Purchasing power parity is a theory of the relationship between the prices of traded goods and services and the exchange rate. Economists have used two key versions of PPP to try to understand how exchange rates are determined. Absolute PPP relates price levels to the nominal exchange rate. Relative PPP relates inflation rates to exchange rate appreciation or depreciation. Because people in different countries consume various baskets of goods and services, relative PPP has the greatest potential as an approach to exchange rate determination. Nevertheless, most evidence indicates that even relative PPP is at best a long-run guide to understanding how exchange rates are determined.

Risks of Holding International Financial Instruments

Economics is often called the "dismal science," because a fundamental implication of economic analysis is that every facet of human experience involves trade-offs. This is no less true of trading foreign exchange and holding international financial instruments. Engaging in these activities can generate returns and profits. At the same time, however, holding international financial instruments exposes individuals and businesses to other types of risks known as *foreign exchange risks* and *country risk*.

Foreign Exchange Risks

Foreign exchange risk: The potential for the value of a foreign-currency-denominated financial instrument to vary because of exchange rate fluctuations.

Transaction risk: A foreign exchange risk arising from the possibility that the proceeds from trading a financial instrument may change as a result of exchange rate variations.

Translation risk: A foreign exchange risk resulting from altered home-currency values of foreign-currency-denominated financial instruments caused by fluctuations in exchange rates.

As displayed in Table 5-3, a saver faces three basic types of **foreign exchange risk,** which is the prospect that the value of a foreign-currency-denominated financial instrument will change as a result of exchange rate variations. One type of foreign exchange risk is **transaction risk,** which is the risk that the proceeds from exchanging a financial instrument may change. Typically, transaction risk arises when a saver commits to a foreign-currency-denominated asset exchange at some future date. This exposes the saver to a change in the expected return on the transaction caused by a change in the exchange rate during the intervening period.

Another type of foreign exchange risk is **translation risk.** This risk arises when the values of foreign-currency-denominated financial instruments are converted into a single currency value. To see how translation risk can arise, consider the balance sheet of a multinational corporation based in the United States. Because the company does business in so many locations around the world, its assets and liabilities are denominated in a number of currencies. At the end of the company's fiscal year, when it is time to report the company's net worth to shareholders and regulators, its accountants must express the value of all assets and liabilities in

Table 5-3 Types of Foreign Exchange Risk

Type of Risk	How Risk Exposure Arises
Transaction risk	Commitment to a future transaction denominated in a foreign currency
Translation risk	Conversion of values of foreign-currency-denominated assets and liabilities into home-currency units
Economic risk	Changes in underlying asset returns and, thus, discounted future income streams, resulting from exchange rate variations

terms of U.S. dollars. Fluctuations in the value of the dollar relative to other currencies before the reporting date induce variations in the dollar values of the assets and liabilities outside the United States, thereby influencing the reported net worth of the company.

The third type of foreign exchange risk is **economic risk,** which is the prospect that exchange rate variations can affect the discounted present value of future streams of income. For a saver, economic risk arises when exchange rate changes affect the present value of earnings from financial instrument holdings. For a company, economic risk arises when movements in exchange rates influence the present value of the firm's earnings, thereby affecting the long-term ability of the firm to compete.

Exchange rate variations may have positive or negative effects on the prospects faced by a saver or a company. Nevertheless, risk-averse savers and managers typically wish to avoid foreign exchange risks to the extent possible. International portfolio diversification is one way to try to reduce exposure to foreign exchange risks. By holding a broad portfolio of international financial instruments, for example, a saver is somewhat insulated from foreign exchange risks, because adverse effects of depreciation of one country's currency may be offset somewhat by the implied appreciation of the currency of another country. Likewise, owning plants and offices in various countries can help a firm avoid some of the foreign exchange risks it would face if all its plants and offices were located in a single country. As we shall discuss in Chapter 6, it is also possible to *hedge,* or offset, exposure to many foreign exchange risks by using derivative securities.

Economic risk: A foreign exchange risk that stems from the possibility that exchange rate movements can affect the discounted present value of future streams of income.

Country Risk

In addition to foreign exchange risks, holding international financial instruments exposes savers to **country risk,** which is the prospect of variations in returns generated by uncertainties about the political and economic environments of nations. For instance, governments with considerable amounts of external debt could, when faced with tough economic times, seek to postpone debt payments or possibly even default on some of their foreign debts. In times of economic or political difficulties, governments have been known to take over foreign-owned factories and offices or to outlaw flows of funds across their borders.

Thus, a nation's prospects for economic and political stability influence the perceived riskiness of the securities issued by its government and of the bills, notes, bonds, and stocks of companies that do business in that country. Naturally, country risk is particularly difficult to measure. Determining the degree of country risk of a government bond can entail trying to forecast the outcomes of elections, the potential for internal political turmoil, and the likelihood of border disputes becoming all-out war. The market prices of a nation's financial instruments respond quickly to good or bad news about the country's economic and political prospects, thereby exposing holders of the instruments to risks.

Country risk: The potential for returns on international financial instruments to vary because of uncertainties concerning possible changes in political and economic conditions within a nation.

To a large extent, country risk is idiosyncratic. This means that savers can attempt to reduce the extent of country risk by holding a diversified portfolio containing international assets from a broad range of locations. Thus, the adverse effects of turbulent political times in one part of the world may be counterbalanced by the positive effects of peace and tranquillity in other regions.

> **5. What are the special risks of holding international financial instruments?** One is foreign exchange risk, which arises in three forms: (1) transaction risk, which is the risk that the proceeds from holding a financial instrument may change because of exchange rate variations; (2) translation risk, which is the risk owing to varying home-currency values of foreign-currency-denominated instruments in the presence of exchange rate fluctuations; and (3) economic risk, which is the risk that exchange rate variations may affect the discounted present value of streams of returns from financial instrument holdings. The second type of risk is country risk, which is the risk of variations in returns on financial instruments owing to nation-specific economic and political factors.

Exchange Rates and Interest Rate Parity Conditions

As described earlier, absolute and relative purchasing power parity arise from arbitrage across national markets for goods and services. Arbitrage can also take place across national financial markets, as traders attempt to earn profits by buying and selling financial instruments issued by individuals, companies, or governments of various nations. Engaging in such transactions, however, exposes traders to foreign exchange risks.

The Forward Exchange Market and Covered Interest Parity

Suppose the interest rate on a U.S. financial instrument is 4.1 percent. At the same time, the interest rate on a European Monetary Union (EMU) financial instrument with the same riskiness, liquidity, tax treatment, and term to maturity is 5.6 percent. Could a U.S. saver profit from shifting funds from the United States to the EMU? The answer depends on whether the realized return on the EMU financial instrument is greater than the realized return on the U.S. financial instrument. Comparing the realized returns, in turn, requires taking into account how *covered* interest returns (returns completely insulated against foreign exchange risk) on holdings of the EMU financial instrument depend on exchange rates. Thus, exchange rates and national interest rates ultimately must be taken into account by anyone who seeks arbitrage profits from trading financial instruments internationally.

COVERING A FOREIGN EXCHANGE TRANSACTION WITH A FORWARD CONTRACT Many individuals, firms, and banks can use financial instruments called **forward currency contracts** to protect themselves against foreign exchange risks. These contracts require delivery of foreign currency or a foreign-currency-denominated financial instrument at a specified exchange rate on a particular date.

To see how a forward currency contract can be used to cover foreign exchange risk, think about the situation faced by a multinational firm that has promised, after considerable bargaining, to purchase some equipment from a foreign supplier for delivery three months from

Forward currency contract: A forward contract calling for delivery of foreign currency, or financial instruments denominated in a foreign currency, at a specific exchange rate on a certain date.

now. The multinational firm's managers know that the company will have to make a payment to the supplier that is denominated in the supplier's national currency. In addition, however, the firm's managers realize that there is a possibility that the foreign currency could rise in value during the next three months, which would effectively raise the price the firm would have to pay for the equipment when the payment date arrives. To eliminate the risk of this occurrence, the managers can enter into a forward currency contract in which they agree to purchase the required amount of foreign currency at the currently prevailing three-month *forward exchange rate,* which is the exchange rate on foreign exchange to be delivered three months from now. By doing this, the managers ensure that the firm will pay the agreed price for the equipment, so all its hard bargaining will not have been in vain.

Note that if the forward exchange rate of a currency is greater than the spot exchange rate, the currency is said to trade at a *forward premium.* If the forward exchange rate is less than the spot exchange rate, the currency trades at a *forward discount.* The forward discount or premium is equal to the difference between the forward exchange rate and the spot exchange rate divided by the spot exchange rate.

The market for forward contracts may be limited by two factors: (1) difficulties in setting the terms of the contracts and (2) default risk. Parties to forward contracts must agree to specific contract terms. Sometimes it is hard for two parties to do this. In our example, we simply assumed that the multinational firm could reach mutually satisfying terms with another party. In reality, reaching an agreement on the terms of forward contracts can be a complex undertaking.

Default risk also somewhat deters the use of forward contracts. It is rare for banks to fail to follow through on forward contracts or other interbank financial transactions, but such defaults have been known to occur. This potential for default makes forward currency contracts riskier and less liquid, thereby restraining trading volumes somewhat.

ALTERNATIVE SAVING CHOICES   To consider how the use of forward contracts to cover foreign exchange risks may affect exchange rates and interest rates, let's suppose that a U.S. resident has two alternatives. One is to purchase a one-period, dollar-denominated bond that has a market interest yield of r_{US}. After one year, the U.S. resident will have accumulated $1 + r_{US}$ dollars for each dollar saved.

The other saving option is to use each dollar to buy EMU euros at the spot exchange rate of S dollars per euro, thereby obtaining $1/S$ euros with each dollar. Then the U.S. resident would use the $1/S$ euros to buy a one-year EMU bond that pays the rate r_E. After a year, the person will have accumulated $(1/S)(1 + r_E)$ *euros.* When the U.S. resident buys the EMU bond, however, we assume that at the same time he sells this quantity of euros in the forward market at the forward exchange rate of F dollars per euro. This "covers" him against risk of exchange rate changes by ensuring that the effective gross return on the EMU bond will be $(F/S)(1 + r_E)$.

COVERED INTEREST PARITY   The returns on the two bonds will be the same, so there will be no incentive for U.S. savers to arbitrage across the U.S. and EMU financial markets, if

$$1 + r_{US} = (F/S)(1 + r_E).$$

Now we can use the algebra fact that

$$F/S = (S/S) + (F - S)/S = 1 + (F - S)/S$$

to rewrite the condition as

$$1 + r_{US} = [1 + (F - S)/S](1 + r_E).$$

The term $(F - S)/S$ in this equation is the forward premium or discount mentioned above. If $(F - S)/S$ is positive, it is a forward premium. If negative, it is a forward discount. Now we can cross-multiply the right-hand side to get

$$1 + r_{US} = 1 + (F - S)/S + r_E + [r_E \times (F - S)/S].$$

Because r_E and $(F - S)/S$ are both typically small fractions, their product is approximately equal to zero. [For example, if r_E is 0.056 and $(F - S)/S$ is -0.047, then their product is equal to -0.0026, which is very close to zero.] Making this approximation and subtracting 1 from both sides yields

$$r_{US} = r_E + (F - S)/S.$$

Covered interest parity: A prediction that the interest rate on one nation's financial instrument should approximately equal the interest rate on a similar instrument in another nation plus the forward premium, or the difference between the forward exchange rate and the spot exchange rate divided by the spot exchange rate.

This last equation is called the **covered interest parity** condition, which says that the interest rate on a U.S. bond should approximately equal the interest rate on the foreign EMU bond plus the forward premium or discount.

If this condition failed to hold, then U.S. savers could engage in *covered interest arbitrage* by cashing in U.S. financial instruments and purchasing EMU financial instruments. This activity would tend to push national interest rates toward levels consistent with the covered interest arbitrage condition.

Uncovered Interest Arbitrage and Uncovered Interest Parity

As we have discussed, covered interest arbitrage—covering the foreign exchange risk associated with financial instrument transactions across national borders—leads to the covered interest parity condition. Under covered interest parity, the interest rate on a financial instrument in one nation equals the interest rate on the equivalent instrument in another country plus the forward premium. What happens, however, if people do not cover their exposure to foreign exchange risks?

Someone might choose not to use a forward currency contract to hedge against foreign exchange risks, for instance, because the transaction is too small to warrant the trouble to set up a forward contract. Indeed, a typical forward currency contract has a denomination of at least $1 million. Hence, the individual might decide to use a different instrument (see Chapter 6) or might choose not to cover the transaction at all.

UNCOVERED INTEREST PARITY   In our example, we considered a U.S. saver with a choice between a U.S. financial instrument and an EMU financial instrument with equivalent riskiness, tax treatment, liquidity, and term to maturity. Let's consider the same example, but assume that the U.S. saver does not purchase a forward exchange contract or hedge the foreign exchange risk in any other way, so the transaction is *uncovered*.

In this case, the U.S. saver again anticipates a *dollar*-denominated interest return of r_{US} by holding a U.S. financial instrument to maturity or a *euro*-denominated interest return of r_E by holding an equivalent EMU financial instrument to maturity. To the U.S. saver, however, what matters in choosing between the two instruments is the anticipated *dollar* value of the return on the EMU instrument. This is equal to $r_E + s^e$, where s^e denotes the rate at which the dollar is expected to depreciate (or, if s^e is negative, appreciate) relative to the euro. If s^e is positive, then the U.S. saver anticipates that the dollar will depreciate in value relative to the euro and will wish for the U.S. instrument's interest rate to be higher than the rate on the EMU instrument to compensate for this expected depreciation of the dollar.

Thus, this U.S. saver will be indifferent between holding U.S. or EMU instruments only if the anticipated returns are equal. This will be true when

$$r_{US} = r_E + s^e.$$

If the U.S. interest rate is less than the EMU interest rate plus the expected rate of dollar depreciation, then U.S. savers who do not cover their transactions will allocate more savings to EMU financial instruments. If the U.S. interest rate is greater than the EMU rate plus the anticipated depreciation rate of the dollar, then U.S. savers will allocate fewer savings to EMU financial instruments. In theory, shifts of funds in this pursuit of *uncovered arbitrage* profits will tend to push both interest rates to levels consistent with equality between the U.S. interest rate and the sum of the EMU interest rate and the expected rate of dollar depreciation.

The above equality is called **uncovered interest parity.** It is called "uncovered" interest parity because it does not arise from foreign exchange transactions that cover risks.

RISK AND UNCOVERED INTEREST PARITY   The uncovered purchase of a foreign financial instrument exposes a U.S. saver to foreign exchange risks because the saver's expectation about currency depreciation or appreciation during the term to maturity may turn out to be incorrect. In this instance, the realized return on the foreign financial instrument would differ from the anticipated return.

If the value of a nation's currency is highly variable, then predicting its future value is difficult. This makes allocating a portion of one's wealth to holdings of foreign financial instruments a much riskier proposition. Consequently, borrowers located in nations with volatile currency values may have to offer higher interest returns to induce savers to purchase the financial instruments they issue. In this instance, it may be appropriate to include a risk premium in the uncovered interest parity condition. The risk premium is the increase in the return offered on a financial instrument to compensate individuals for the additional foreign exchange risk they undertake in uncovered transactions.

For instance, if the U.S. dollar's exchange value becomes more volatile and less predictable, then the uncovered interest parity condition may be expressed as

$$r_{US} = r_E + s^e + RP,$$

where *RP* is the risk premium that compensates savers for holding U.S. financial instruments instead of equivalent EMU instruments. In this situation, the differential between the U.S. interest rate and the EMU interest rate should equal the expected depreciation of the dollar relative to the euro plus the risk premium. (Evaluating the uncovered interest parity condition is complicated by the fact that people who hold bonds to maturity receive interest payments only at the times when the bonds mature; see on the next page *What Happens When Opportunities for Uncovered Interest Are Greatest?*)

Uncovered interest parity: A relationship between interest rates on bonds that are similar in all respects other than that they are denominated in different nations' currencies. According to this condition, the yield on the bond denominated in the currency that holders anticipate will depreciate must exceed the yield on the other bond by the rate at which the currency is expected to depreciate.

Simultaneous Interest Parities

Note that the two international interest parity conditions discussed above provide two reasons why the interest rate for a U.S. financial instrument might be higher than the interest rate on an otherwise identical EMU instrument. One reason, provided by the *covered* interest parity condition, is the presence of a forward premium in the forward exchange market, so that the differential between the U.S. interest rate and the EMU interest rate is equal to

$$r_{US} - r_E = (F - S)/S.$$

What Happens When... **Opportunities for Uncovered Interest Are Greatest?**

Uncovered interest parity is one of the most widely studied concepts in economics. So far, however, the only consensus economists have reached is that, more often than not, data from real-world markets do not appear entirely consistent with the uncovered interest parity condition.

Federal Reserve economists Alain Chaboud and Jonathan Wright point out that for most financial instruments, interest payments are made only when an instrument matures. This suggests, they argue, that the uncovered interest parity condition is most likely to be satisfied during a short interval immediately before an instrument matures and interest payments are received by the instrument's holder. Consequently, savers have the greatest incentive to reshuffle their portfolios of home and foreign assets during the final minutes before maturity. Chaboud and Wright propose, therefore, that market exchange rates

should be most likely to be at levels consistent with uncovered interest parity in the last few minutes before savings instruments mature. To test this hypothesis, they have examined ten years of observations of interest rates and exchange rates during the short interval around 5 P.M. eastern time, when many financial instruments reach maturity in New York financial markets. Their conclusion is that, in fact, during this relatively brief period the uncovered interest parity condition is typically satisfied.

FOR CRITICAL ANALYSIS: Why would all the adjustments to attain uncovered interest parity have to take place through changes in market exchange rates during the final minutes before a financial instrument matures?

The other reason is implied by the *uncovered* interest parity condition:

$$r_{US} - r_E = s^e.$$

This condition indicates that, in the absence of a risk premium, the amount by which the U.S. interest rate exceeds the EMU interest rate should be the expected rate of depreciation of the dollar relative to the euro.

The only way that both of these interest parity conditions are satisfied is if the right-hand terms in both are equal, or if

$$(F - S)/S = s^e.$$

This relationship states that the forward premium (or discount) for the euro relative to the dollar is equal to the rate at which the dollar is expected to depreciate (appreciate) relative to the euro in the spot foreign exchange market. Let's denote the expected future spot exchange rate at the time that a forward currency contract settles as S^e. It follows that the expected rate of dollar depreciation during the term of the contract, s^e, is equal to the expected change in the spot exchange rate, $S^e - S$, divided by the current spot exchange rate, S. Thus, $s^e = (S^e - S)/S$. If both covered and uncovered interest parity hold true, then

$$(F - S)/S = (S^e - S)/S.$$

Foreign exchange market efficiency: A situation in which the equilibrium spot and forward exchange rates adjust to reflect all available information, in which case the forward premium is equal to the expected rate of currency depreciation plus any risk premium. This, in turn, implies that the forward exchange rate on average predicts the expected future spot exchange rate.

This yields a condition called **foreign exchange market efficiency,**

$$F = S^e.$$

which indicates that if both interest parity conditions are satisfied in the marketplace, the forward exchange rate is equal to the anticipated spot exchange rate at the time of settlement of the forward currency contract. In this situation, the forward exchange rate is a good predictor—often called an "unbiased predictor"—of the future spot exchange rate, meaning that on average the forward exchange rate turns out to equal the future spot exchange rate.

Real Interest Parity

The covered and uncovered interest parity conditions relate *nominal* interest rate differentials to spot and forward exchange rates and expected spot exchange rates. Over shorter-term horizons, when changes in inflation may be relatively small, the effects of different national inflation rates may have little effect on saving flows. Nevertheless, saving decisions are more likely to respond to overall price changes over longer time horizons. Thus, over longer intervals savers' decisions about financial instrument allocations are likely to be motivated by real interest rate differentials instead of *nominal* differentials.

THE FISHER EQUATION   Recall from Chapter 4 that the real interest rate is approximately equal to the nominal interest rate less the expected inflation rate, or

$$\rho = r - \pi^e$$

where ρ is the real interest rate and π^e is the expected rate of inflation. If we rearrange this expression for the real interest rate, we can write it as

$$r = \rho + \pi^e.$$

This relationship, often called the **Fisher equation** after the famous economist Irving Fisher who used it early in the twentieth century, states that the nominal interest rate equals the real interest rate plus the expected rate of inflation.

> **Fisher equation:** An equation stating that the nominal interest rate equals the sum of the real interest rate and the expected inflation rate.

For example, suppose that the real rate of interest for a one-year period is 2.5 percent. The Fisher equation indicates that if the expected inflation rate is 3 percent, then savers will require a nominal return equal to the sum of these two amounts, or 5.5 percent, to ensure that they earn the market real interest rate.

COMBINING RELATIVE PURCHASING POWER PARITY AND UNCOVERED INTEREST PARITY   Earlier we examined relative purchasing power parity, which relates inflation rates of two nations (denoted π^e and π^{*e}) to the percentage change in the spot exchange rate for their currencies. If savers anticipate that relative purchasing power parity will hold, then that implies that the following condition should be satisfied:

$$\pi^e - \pi^{*e} = s^e.$$

That is, if relative purchasing power parity holds, the expected difference between the two nations' inflation rates will equal the expected rate of currency depreciation.

Recall that if uncovered interest parity holds, and if there is no risk premium, then it will also be the case that

$$r - r^* = s^e,$$

so that the differential between the two nations' interest rates equals the expected rate of currency depreciation. If we put the above equations together, we get

$$\pi^e - \pi^{*e} = r - r^*.$$

Finally, we can rearrange to obtain the following relationship:

$$r - \pi^e = r^* - \pi^{*e}.$$

This says that if both relative purchasing power parity and uncovered interest parity hold true, then the real interest rate in one country, $\rho = r - \pi^e$, equals the real interest rate in the other country, $\rho^* = r^* - \pi^{*e}$.

Real interest parity: An equality between two nations' real interest rates that arises if both uncovered interest parity and relative purchasing power parity are satisfied.

This is called the **real interest parity** condition, under which real interest returns on equivalent financial instruments of two nations are equal. Given the way we have obtained it, real interest parity is a condition that requires both relative purchasing power parity and uncovered interest parity to hold.

REAL INTEREST PARITY AS AN INDICATOR OF THE SCOPE OF INTERNA-TIONAL ARBITRAGE   Recall that uncovered interest parity is more likely to hold if savers can take advantage of opportunities for uncovered interest arbitrage. At the same time, relative purchasing power parity is more likely to hold if markets for goods and services are also more open to arbitrage.

It follows that if real interest parity holds true, then there are considerable opportunities for arbitrage to exist in international financial *and* goods market. Work by Richard Marston of the University of Pennsylvania has shown that real interest differentials tend to be relatively small, particularly among the most developed, open economies. This provides some indication that there is considerable scope for arbitrage in international markets.

> **6. In what ways can exchange rates and interest rates be related?**   A forward premium (discount) exists if the forward exchange rate exceeds (is less than) the spot exchange rate determined in the spot market for the currency. The covered interest parity condition arises if individuals cover risks of future exchange rate changes using forward currency contracts. It states that the interest rate in one nation equals the sum of another nation's interest rate and the forward premium or discount, which is the difference between the forward exchange rate and the spot exchange rate divided by the spot exchange rate. If individuals purchase bonds denominated in different currencies but with identical risks and do not cover their transactions using forward contracts, then uncovered interest parity may apply. Under uncovered interest parity, the interest rate on a bond denominated in a currency that is expected to depreciate must exceed the other bond's interest rate by the rate at which the currency is expected to depreciate. Finally, if the purchasing power parity condition is expected to be satisfied and if the uncovered interest parity condition also holds, then real interest rates are equalized across nations, and real interest parity exists.

Chapter Summary

1. The Foreign Exchange Markets: These markets are systems through which individuals, companies, and governments exchange one nation's currency for the currency of another nation. The spot exchange rate is the rate at which people agree to trade currencies to be delivered immediately, typically in the form of foreign-currency-denominated bonds or bank deposits. Actual trades of currency and coins constitute a very small portion of total activity in foreign exchange markets.

2. Determining the Value of a Currency: The interaction of the forces of supply and demand in the foreign exchange market determines the value of a currency. The equilibrium spot exchange rate is the exchange rate at which the total desired quantity of a currency for immediate delivery is equal to the total quantity of the currency supplied. Variations in the equilibrium exchange rate occur as a result of changes in the demand for or the supply of a currency.

3. Distinguishing Nominal and Real Exchange Rates:
The equilibrium rate of exchange of one nation's currency in the foreign exchange market is the nominal exchange rate. The nominal exchange rate does not take into account changes in the price levels across nations. The real exchange rate adjusts the nominal exchange rate for price-level changes. Consequently, a real exchange rate measures the purchasing power of a nation's goods and services in exchange for the goods and services of another country.

4. Purchasing Power Parity and Its Usefulness for Predicting Exchange Rates:
In its simplest form, known as the law of one price, purchasing power parity implies that the exchange-rate-adjusted price of a tradable good in one nation should equal the price of that good in another nation. There are two versions of PPP as an approach to understanding how exchange rates are determined. Absolute PPP relates the price levels of two countries to the exchange rate. Relative PPP relates two nations' inflation rates to the rate of change in the exchange rate. Most evidence indicates that neither approach is particularly useful as a short-run guide to exchange rate movements. Relative PPP may be a useful guide to exchange rates over long-run horizons, however.

5. Special Risks of Holding International Financial Instruments:
Two categories of risk apply specifically to international financial instruments. One is foreign exchange risk. There are three types of foreign exchange risk: transaction risk, which is the risk that the returns from holding financial instruments may vary because of exchange rate changes; translation risk, which is the risk resulting from fluctuations in home-currency values of foreign-currency-denominated instruments caused by exchange rate movements; and economic risk, which is the risk that exchange rate changes can influence the discounted present value of returns from holding financial instruments. The second category of risks from holding international financial instruments is country risk. This is the risk of varying returns on financial instruments caused by country-specific economic and political factors.

6. Relationships between Exchange Rates and Interest Rates:
The covered interest parity condition holds true if individuals use forward currency contracts to cover risks of exchange rate movements related to international financial transactions. It implies that the interest rate in one nation equals another nation's interest rate plus the difference between the forward exchange rate and the spot exchange rate divided by the spot exchange rate, or the forward premium or discount. If individuals hold bonds denominated in foreign currencies but do not cover the associated risks using forward contracts, then the uncovered interest parity condition may hold. In this situation, the interest rate on a bond denominated in a domestic nation's currency equals the interest rate on a bond denominated in a foreign nation's currency plus the rate by which the domestic currency is expected to depreciate. Finally, if people anticipate that purchasing power parity will hold and if the uncovered interest parity condition is also satisfied, then real interest parity exists, meaning that real interest rates are equalized across nations.

Questions and Problems

(Answers to odd-numbered questions and problems may be found on the Web at **http://money.swcollege.com** under "Student Resources.")

1. Suppose that on Thursday the U.S.-dollar-equivalent exchange rate of the Brazilian real (the name of the Brazilian currency) was 0.3325. On Friday this value fell to 0.3262. Did the Brazilian real appreciate or depreciate relative to the U.S. dollar?

2. In question 1, what was the percentage appreciation/depreciation of the real?

Use the data in the table below to answer questions 3, 4, and 5.

	1996 Spot Exchange Rate	2006 Spot Exchange Rate	1996 Consumer Price Index	2006 Consumer Price Index
Japan	$0.0073/yen	$0.0092/yen	100	105.8
Canada	$0.867/C$	$0.651/C$	100	129.8
U.S.			100	119.0

3. In 1996, what was the nominal spot exchange rate for the Canadian dollar relative to the Japanese yen? What was the nominal exchange rate between these two currencies in 2006?

4. What was the real exchange rate for the U.S. dollar relative to the Japanese yen in 1996? In 2006? Did the U.S. dollar experience a real appreciation or depreciation relative to the yen between 1996 and 2006?

5. What was the real exchange rate for the U.S. dollar relative to the Canadian dollar in 1996? In 2006? Did the U.S. dollar experience a real appreciation or depreciation relative to the Canadian dollar between 1996 and 2006?

6. Suppose that the current U.S.-dollar-equivalent exchange rate between the Hungarian forint and the U.S. dollar is equal to 0.005. A change in the demand for the forint results in a rise in this value to 0.006. Did the demand for the forint rise or fall, assuming that the supply schedule did not shift? Use a diagram of the market for forint to explain your reasoning.

7. Suppose that at present, the U.S.-dollar-equivalent value of the Slovakian koruna is 0.0216. At this exchange rate, however, U.S. residents interested in purchasing koruna with U.S. dollars cannot find a sufficient number of Slovakian residents willing to provide koruna in exchange. What must happen to the exchange rate, and why? Use a diagram to assist in explaining your answer.

8. Initially, the currency-per-U.S.-dollar exchange rate relating the value of the Mexican peso was equal to 13.0. Then there was a sharp drop-off in the U.S. demand for Mexican-produced goods and services. At the same time, residents of Mexico sharply increased their desired consumption of U.S.-manufactured goods. Use a diagram to assist in explaining the likely effects of these events on the value of the peso.

9. Suppose the Swiss franc price of a dollar was 1.6341 Sfr/$ in 1990 and 1.4322 Sfr/$ in 2007. The price index for Switzerland (1990 = 100) is 128.11 in 2007, and the price index for the United States (1990 = 100) is 111.86 in 2007. According to absolute PPP, is the dollar over- or undervalued, relative to the Swiss franc in 2007? Considering this information, would you expect the dollar to appreciate or depreciate? By what percentage?

10. Using the data provided in question 9, was the dollar over- or undervalued in 2007 according to relative PPP? Considering this information, would you expect the dollar to appreciate or depreciate and by how much (in percentage terms)?

11. A large multinational firm has determined that its year-end balance sheet shows a negative net worth in one country but a positive net worth in another country. Explain how this might occur, assuming that the company holds a number of assets and liabilities valued in more than one currency.

12. Suppose that a U.S. Treasury bill has an annualized yield of 6.5 percent. A German government bill with the same maturity and equal risk characteristics has an annualized yield of 5.5 percent. Which country's currency is expected to *depreciate?* What is the expected rate of depreciation of this nation's currency?

13. A Malaysian government bond has an annualized yield of 12.25 percent. A U.S. Treasury bond with the same maturity has a yield of only 5.85 percent, however. Is it necessarily the case that the Malaysian currency (the ringgit) is expected to depreciate, or could there be another possible explanation for the difference in the yields? Justify your answer.

Before the Test

Test your understanding of the material covered in this chapter by taking the Chapter 5 interactive quiz at **http://money.swcollege.com**.

Online Application

Internet URLs: http://www.oecd.org/statistics and **http://www.federalreserve.gov/releases/g5a**

Titles: Purchasing Power Parities and Exchange Rates

Navigation: First go to the home page of OECD statistics (**http://www.oecd.org/statistics**). Click on "Prices and Purchasing Power Parities," and then on "Purchasing Power Parities for OECD Countries." Print this document. Next, go to the Federal Reserve Board's home page (**http://www.federalreserve.gov**), and click on "Economic Research and Data," then click on "Statistics: Releases and Historical Data." Under "Exchange Rates and International Data," click on "G/5 annual."

Application: Use the reports to apply PPP.

1. The OECD table gives the currency-per-U.S.-dollar exchange rates consistent with PPP. The Federal Reserve Board provides data on actual exchange rates. Select a nation in the OECD's PPP table, and compare the exchange rates predicted by PPP for a selected year in the table with *actual* exchange rates. During the year you selected, did PPP indicate that this nation's currency was over- or undervalued?

2. Look over the nation's exchange rates in the Federal Reserve's H.10 release for all five years in the OECD table. Were the actual exchange rates consistent with PPP over this five-year period?

For Group Study and Analysis: Assign questions 1 and 2 to several groups, each of which will examine the data for a different country. Discuss possible reasons why PPP may apply better for some countries than for others.

Selected References and Further Reading

Al-Loughani, Nabeel E., and Imad A. Moosa. "Covered Interest Parity and the Relative Effectiveness of Forward and Money Market Hedging." *Applied Economics Letters* 7 (October 2000): 673–675.

Chaboud, Alain, and Jonathan Wright. "Uncovered Interest Parity: It Works, but Not for Long." Board of Governors of the Federal Reserve System, International Finance Discussion Paper No. 252, January 2003.

Flood, Robert, and Andrew Rose. "Uncovered Interest Parity in Crisis." *IMF Staff Papers* 49 (2002): 252–266.

Frankel, Jeffrey, and Andrew Rose. "A Panel Project on Purchasing Power Parity: Mean Reversion within and between Countries." *Journal of International Economics* 40 (May 1996): 209–224.

Goldberg, Linda. "Industry-Specific Exchange Rates for the United States." Federal Reserve Bank of New York *Economic Policy Review,* May 2004, pp. 1–16.

Lothian, James, and Mark Taylor. "Real Exchange Rate Behavior: The Recent Float from the Perspective of the Past Two Centuries." *Journal of Political Economy* 104 (June 1996): 488–509.

Mansori, Kashif. "Following in Their Footsteps: Comparing Interest Parity Conditions in Central European Countries to the Euro Countries." CES IFO Working Paper No. 1020, August 2003.

O'Connell, Paul. "The Overvaluation of Purchasing Power Parity." *Journal of International Economics* 44 (February 1998): 1–19.

Pakko, Michael, and Patricia Pollard. "For Here or to Go? Purchasing Power Parity and the Big Mac." Federal Reserve Bank of St. Louis *Review* 78 (January/February 1996): 3–22.

Rogoff, Kenneth. "The Purchasing Power Parity Puzzle." *Journal of Economic Literature* 34 (June 1995): 647–668.

Taylor, Mark. "The Economics of Exchange Rates." *Journal of Economic Literature* 33 (March 1995): 13–47.

Wolff, Christian C. P. "Forward Foreign Exchange Rates and Expected Future Spot Rates." *Applied Financial Economics* 10 (August 2000): 371–377.

MoneyXtra

Log on to the MoneyXtra Web site now (**http://moneyxtra.swcollege.com**) for additional learning resources such as practice quizzes, case studies, readings, and additional economic applications.

Managing Risks in the Global Economy—

Derivative Securities

In 2003, a group of analysts at the U.S. Department of Defense proposed a novel approach to predicting when terrorists might strike next. Their idea was for the government to promote the development of a market for financial instruments with returns based on terrorism outcomes. In this proposed market, people would trade terrorism futures contracts *that would provide payoffs only if terrorist events actually took place around specific dates. Traders of the futures contracts would thus have an incentive to make predictions based on the best available information about likely terrorist attacks. Consequently, the defense analysts suggested, prices of these contracts would provide a gauge of the probability of an attack. If the prices rose, government agencies could then respond with appropriate security enhancements.*

The proposal sparked a number of objections, however. One concern was that terrorists might be able to use the prices to gauge when security is weak or even buy or sell the futures contracts themselves in order to spread disinformation. Another objection was that it simply seemed inhumane for anyone to be able to profit from terrorist actions. Indeed, some critics pointed out that terrorists themselves might be able to profit from buying futures contracts and then committing acts that would generate payoffs for themselves. In the end, therefore, the idea for a government-sponsored market for terrorism futures contracts was scuttled.

In this chapter, you will learn about actual futures contracts and other related forms of financial instruments called derivative securities.

Interest Rate Risk, Duration, and Derivative Securities

In Chapter 4 we explained how to compute interest yields and discussed how interest rates and market prices of financial instruments are related. As Figure 6-1 indicates, interest rates can be volatile over time. This means that the market values of financial instruments also can vary considerably. As a result, anyone holding such instruments incurs an inherent risk.

FIGURE 6-1
Selected Interest Rates.

Interest rates can vary considerably over time. This exposes owners of financial instruments to the risk of capital losses.

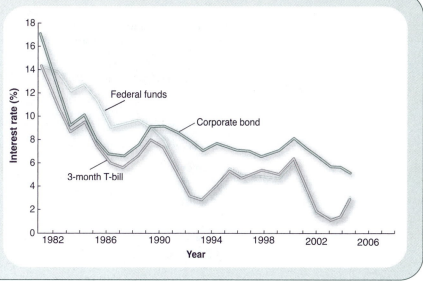

SOURCES: *Economic Report of the President, 2005;* and *Economic Indicators.*

Interest Rate Risk

A key issue that anyone who holds financial instruments must face is that such instruments are risky. One source of risk, of course, is the risk of default. Another, however, is the chance that the market value of an instrument will vary as interest rates change. This type of risk is called **interest rate risk.**

As we discussed in Chapter 4, bond prices and interest yields are interdependent, and the effective yield on an instrument such as a Treasury bill depends on the time remaining until the instrument matures. It follows that how much bond prices vary in response to interest rate changes depends in part on the time remaining until the bond matures. The price of a bond, of course, is the market value of the bond. Hence, the extent to which a bond's value varies as interest rates change depends on the time until the bond matures. This, in turn, implies that the interest rate risk of the bond will depend on how far off the bond's maturity date is.

TERM TO MATURITY AND INTEREST RATE RISK   To better understand why time to maturity matters for interest rate risk, consider an example of two very simple bonds. One pays $10,000 after a single year. The other pays $10,000 after the passage of two years. Such bonds are known as **zero-coupon bonds** because they pay lump-sum amounts at maturity.

Table 6-1 on the next page calculates the prices of the two bonds for market interest rates of 7 percent and 8 percent. A rise in the market interest rate from 7 percent to 8 percent causes the price of each bond to decline. Holders of the bonds would incur **capital losses,** meaning that the market value of their bond holdings will fall.

The calculations in Table 6-1 show that the percentage capital loss on the two-year bond is 1.8 percent, which is twice the 0.9 percent capital loss on the one-year bond. The reason is that the rise in the market interest rate from 7 percent to 8 percent applies across two years for the two-year bond. But the same interest rate rise affects the one-year bond's price just for the bond's one-year lifetime.

Interest rate risk: The possibility that the market value of a financial instrument will change as interest rates vary.

Zero-coupon bonds: Bonds that pay lump-sum amounts at maturity.

Capital loss: A decline in the market value of a financial instrument at the time it is sold as compared with its market value at the time it was purchased.

Table 6-1 Effects of an Interest Rate Increase on the Market Prices of Two Zero-Coupon Bonds

This example illustrates that the prices of bonds with longer maturities fall in greater proportion following an expected rise in the market interest rate. Consequently, bonds with longer lifetimes have greater exposure to interest rate risk.

	One-Year $10,000 Zero-Coupon Bond	Two-Year $10,000 Zero-Coupon Bond
Bond Price at 8% Rate	$10,000/(1.08) = $9,259.26	$10,000/(1.08)^2 = $8,573.39
Bond Price at 7% Rate	$10,000/(1.07) = $9,345.79	$10,000/(1.07)^2 = $8,734.39
Dollar Price Change	−$86.53	−$161.00
Percentage Price Change	(−$86.53/$9,345.79) × 100 = −0.9%	(−$161.00/$8,734.39) × 100 = −1.8%

This simple example illustrates that a bond's *lifetime* plays a key role in determining the proportionate capital loss incurred when market interest rates rise. Bonds with longer terms to maturity are susceptible to greater risk of capital loss. Thus, bonds with longer lifetimes have greater exposure to interest rate risk.

FREQUENCY OF COUPON RETURNS AND INTEREST RATE RISK   Another key factor influencing interest rate risk is how often bonds pay coupon returns. For instance, think about a zero-coupon bond that pays $10,000 to the bearer after two years, as compared with a bond that pays a stream of $10,000 at quarterly intervals ($1,250 per quarter for eight quarters) over two years. The bearer of the latter bond receives returns on the bond much more quickly. Hence, if market interest rates rise, the effective capital loss on the bond that pays out quarterly coupon returns will be lower, even though both bonds have the same two-year maturity.

Interest rate risk poses both rewards and challenges to an individual or firm. The rewards arise if the individual or company finds ways to profit from increases in financial instruments' market values following reductions in market interest rates. The challenges entail balancing the potential for such capital gains against the possibility of *capital losses* that will be incurred if market interest rates rise, thereby reducing the market values of financial instruments.

FINANCIAL INSTRUMENT DURATION   Thus, *two* factors influence interest rate risk. One is term to maturity, or a bond's lifetime. The other is how often a bond pays returns to the holder. To assess interest rate risk, bond traders need to be able to measure these factors together. They do this using a concept called **duration.** This is a measure of the average time required to receive all payments of principal and interest.

Strategies for Limiting Interest Rate Risk

Various strategies can be used to limit exposure to interest rate risk. One approach might be to hold mostly short-term financial instruments. Financial instruments with short-term maturities, as we noted earlier, have lower risk of capital losses when interest rates rise as compared

On the Web
Where on the Web can a person learn how to calculate duration? One place to check is the Financial Pipeline home page, **http://www.finpipe.com**. Click on "Bonds" in the left-hand margin, then click on "Valuing Bonds," and under "Related Articles," click on "Duration."

Duration: A measure of the average time during which all payments of principal and interest on a financial instrument are made.

with instruments of longer maturity. A more sophisticated strategy might be to hold bonds with shorter durations. This takes into account both the maturity of the financial instrument and the frequency of payments received.

There are three problems with both strategies, however. One is that if the yield curve slopes upward, long-duration instruments are more likely to provide greater returns. This is so because if all other factors are unchanged, duration rises with the term to maturity. The longer the term to maturity, the higher the interest yield when the yield curve exhibits its normal shape. Thus, holding only short-duration instruments constitutes a low-return strategy.

Second, continually selling and repurchasing—"rolling over"—short-term instruments can be costly. Traders would incur both opportunity costs of time spent on this activity and direct costs in expending effort. Furthermore, rolling over instruments with short terms to maturity entails potentially significant exposure to **reinvestment risk.** This is the possibility that market yields will decline by the time the short-term instrument matures. In that case, a trader could have earned a higher net yield by holding longer-term instruments instead.

Reinvestment risk: The possibility that available yields on short-term financial instruments may decline, in which case holdings of longer-term instruments might be preferable.

Furthermore, holding only short-maturity instruments sacrifices benefits that traders can gain from *portfolio diversification.* As we shall discuss in greater detail in Chapter 7, diversification entails spreading risks across holdings of financial instruments with different characteristics. Portfolio diversification can also help reduce interest rate risk. For instance, short-term yields may fall at the same time that long-term yields are rising. Thus, placing funds in a portfolio consisting only of short-term instruments could lead to a lower return than one could otherwise earn by holding a broader mix of instruments. If traders allocate their funds to a portfolio including longer-term instruments, then the rise in yields on these instruments helps offset the effect on the total portfolio return from declines in short-term yields. (Sometimes portfolio diversification by some traders can contribute to greater interest rate risks for others; see *What Happens When Diversification by Some Amplifies Risks for Others?*)

Hedging and Derivative Securities

In light of the drawbacks of holding primarily shorter-maturity, low-duration financial instruments, individuals, companies, and banks have developed an alternative strategy for addressing interest rate risk. This is *hedging* against risk. The fundamental instruments for engaging in hedging are *derivative securities.*

What Happens When... **Diversification by Some Amplifies Risks for Others?**

The Federal National Mortgage Association (FNMA or "Fannie Mae") and the Federal Home Loan Mortgage Corporation (FHLMC or "Freddie Mac") are large, government-sponsored institutions that hold large volumes of financial instruments. If interest rates on long-term Treasury bonds rise, Fannie Mae and Freddie Mac typically seek to diversify their portfolios by selling long-term Treasury bonds and purchasing shorter-term Treasury bills and notes. It is not unusual for the quantities of long-term bonds that they offer for sale to be large relative to the total quantities traded in the rest of the market. Consequently, their actions to diversify their bond portfolios place addi-

tional downward pressure on long-term bond prices, thereby placing further upward pressure on long-term market interest yields. Federal Reserve economists Roberto Perli and Brian Sack have found that if long-term interest rates rise by 1 percentage point, portfolio reshuffling by Fannie Mae and Freddie Mac can cause these interest rates to increase by an additional 0.15 to 0.30 percentage point.

FOR CRITICAL ANALYSIS: Why do sales of Treasury bonds by Fannie Mae and Freddie Mac tend to push up market interest rates on these bonds?

Hedge: A financial strategy that reduces the risk of capital losses arising from interest rate or currency risks.

HEDGING   To reduce interest rate risk on a portfolio, it is possible to use other instruments to **hedge,** or engage in a countervailing financial trading strategy that reduces interest rate risk in the underlying portfolio. A *perfect hedge* fully eliminates these risks. Hedging strategies can also help reduce, or even fully offset, the *foreign exchange risks* that we discussed in Chapter 5.

Market interest and exchange rate conditions can vary from one hour to the next. Consequently, holders of financial instruments must meet two key requirements to hedge interest rate risk and foreign exchange risks. One is sufficient *flexibility* to adapt to various situations that one might face. Another is the capability to conduct necessary transactions *rapidly*. The desire to find hedging strategies that combine both flexibility and speed has led to the development of sophisticated instruments called *derivative securities,* or "derivatives."

Derivative securities: Financial instruments whose returns depend on the returns of other financial instruments.

DERIVATIVE SECURITIES   A **derivative security** is any financial instrument whose return is linked to, or derived from, the returns of other financial instruments. Derivatives trading has increased dramatically worldwide since the 1980s. Indeed, between 1995 and 2006 alone, the "notional value" of derivatives (the value based on underlying market values of the financial instruments) held by U.S. banks increased by over 725 percent, to more than $91 trillion, as bank managers found ways to use derivative securities in hedging strategies. By way of contrast, in 1986, banks held less than $1.5 trillion in derivative securities.

A number of banks and other derivatives traders have also found that they can earn significant short-run profits by speculating with derivative securities. Some traders have learned, however, that derivatives speculations can turn out to be wrong. The results have been sizable speculative losses, the most notable of which we tabulate in Table 6-2. Particularly dramatic among these were the 1994 loss of over $1.5 billion by Orange County, California, the 1995 loss of about $1.4 billion by Britain's Barings Bank, and the 1998 loss of about $3.5 billion by Long-Term Capital Management. The broader consequences of these losses were layoffs for Orange County employees and the collapses of Barings Bank and Long-Term Capital Management.

The derivatives-related losses summarized in Table 6-2 captured media attention and caused many to question the trillions of dollars of derivatives trading by individuals, companies, and banks. As we have noted, however, most traders use derivatives to *hedge* against risks. Thus, you may wonder how it is that so many have lost so much by trading these instruments. To understand how this can happen, you must first have a better understanding of what derivative securities are and how people can use them both to hedge *and* to gamble. As you will see, it is derivatives *gambles* that most often lead to big losses—and, for some, to sizable profits.

> **1. What are interest rate risk, financial instrument duration, and derivative securities?**   Interest rate risk is the chance that the prices of financial instruments may vary because of unexpected movements in market interest rates. The two key determinants of interest rate risk are the maturity and frequency of returns on financial instruments. Instruments of longer maturities and with less frequent returns, which therefore have longer durations, or average periods necessary to receive all principal and interest payments, possess greater interest rate risk. Derivative securities are financial instruments whose returns are based on the returns of other financial instruments. Traders may use derivative securities to hedge against interest rate and foreign exchange risks. They may also use derivatives to try to earn profits based on speculations about future movements in interest rates and exchange rates.

Table 6-2 Major Derivatives Losses since 1990

A number of companies and municipalities have experienced multimillion-dollar losses from derivatives.

Estimate of Loss ($ Millions)	Company/Municipality	Primary Derivatives
$3,500	Long-Term Capital Management	Swaps
1,500	Orange County, California	Mortgage derivatives
1,400	Barings Bank, UK	Stock index futures
720	Deutsche Bank	Swaps and options
691	Allied Irish Banks	Currency options
689	United Bank of Switzerland	Stock index futures
260	Volkswagen	Currency futures
195	Wisconsin Investment Funds	Swaps
157	Procter & Gamble	Currency futures
150	Glaxo, Inc.	Mortgage derivatives
149	NatWest Bank	Swaps and options
100	Cargill Fund	Mortgage derivatives
100	Florida State Treasury	Mortgage derivatives
83	Bank of Tokyo-Mitsubishi	Swaps and options
65	PacifiCorp	Currency options
50	Capital Corp. Credit Union	Mortgage derivatives
50	First Boston	Options
35	Dell Computer	Swaps and options
25	Escambia County, Florida	Mortgage derivatives
20	Gibson Greeting Cards	Swaps
20	Paramount Communications	Swaps

Forward and Futures Contracts

There are several categories of derivative securities. The characteristic that they all share is that their returns stem from returns on other financial instruments. In addition, traders may use them for hedging or in speculative strategies.

Forward Contracts

An important example of a derivative security is a **forward contract,** which is a contract requiring delivery of a commodity or a financial instrument at a specific price on a particular date. The delivery price of the financial instrument depends in part on the market value of the financial instrument, which means that the value of the forward contract itself is *derived from* the instrument's market price. This is why a forward contract is a derivative security.

Forward contract: A contract requiring delivery of a financial instrument at a specified price on a certain date.

HEDGING WITH FORWARD CONTRACTS   To hedge against interest rate risk, financial market traders can use a particular type of forward contract. Called an **interest-rate forward contract,** it guarantees the future sale of a financial instrument at a specified interest rate as of a specific date.

To see how an interest-rate forward contract can be a *perfect* hedge for two parties to such a contract, consider an example. Suppose that a Paris bank is sure that next year it will receive 10 million euros in future interest and principal payments from very creditworthy customers

Interest-rate forward contract: A contract committing the issuer to sell a financial instrument at a given interest rate as of a specific date.

who have borrowed from the bank. As part of a new strategy, the bank's managers have decided to reduce the bank's lending next year and to place half that amount, or 5 million euros, in default-risk-free five-year notes issued by the nations within the European Monetary Union (EMU). The bank's managers wish to guarantee that at this time next year the bank will still be earning the current market interest yield on the European government notes, which we shall suppose is equal to 5 percent. At the same time, a Tokyo bank's securities portfolio contains several million euros worth of five-year European government notes that will mature in three years. The Tokyo bank's managers believe that market interest rates may rise above 5 percent during the next three years, which would imply a fall in the prices of the notes, causing the bank to incur a capital loss on its euro-denominated note holdings.

To try to hedge against the risks that they face, the Paris and Tokyo banks negotiate an interest-rate forward contract. The Paris bank agrees to purchase five-year European government notes valued at 5 million euros *one year from now* at a price that would yield the 5 percent interest yield currently in effect for those notes. The Paris bank thereby guarantees that it will earn today's 5 percent market rate a year from now. The Tokyo bank also relieves itself of the risk of capital loss within the next year on a significant portion of its portfolio of five-year European government notes. This is because the contract guarantees the Tokyo bank that the price of the notes will be consistent with a 5 percent yield in the following year.

SPECULATION WITH FORWARD CONTRACTS   In this example, the banks use derivative securities as hedging instruments to protect their portfolios from risks of loss. This does not, however, rule out the possibility that traders may use derivative securities for purposes of risky speculation in the pursuit of profits.

How Attempts to Hedge Can Amount to Risky Speculation

To understand how derivatives transactions may *increase* overall risk, let's slightly change the conditions of the example. Suppose now that the Paris bank's managers believe that the interest cost of their bank's funds, which currently averages 4 percent, is likely to be lower by this time next year. Their belief, however, is not consistent with the widespread views of other financial market participants, who generally expect a significant increase in the average funding costs Paris banks will face during the next year. Nevertheless, the Paris bank's managers are so sure that their expectation will turn out to be correct that they are willing to enter into the interest-rate forward contract with the Tokyo bank that we discussed above.

Recall that this contract commits the Paris bank to buy the European government notes at a price consistent with the *current* market yield of 5 percent. This means that if the expectation that banks' average interest funding costs will rise significantly by the following year is correct, then the net interest profit that the Paris bank will earn on the European government notes will be much lower next year than the bank's managers currently *speculate* that it will be. For example, if banks' average funding costs rise as high as 5 percent or more, then the net profit that the Paris bank will earn on its EMU notes will turn out to be zero or below. Thus, to the extent that the consensus forecast of higher bank funding costs indicates a strong likelihood that this actually will occur, the Paris bank will have negotiated a speculative contract and added to its overall risk.

This example indicates that while financial market traders can use derivative securities to hedge against risks, they also can use them to engage in speculation. If speculations fail to pay off, then parties to derivative contracts can lose. Where did all the "lost" funds tabulated in Table 6-2 end up? The answer is that the funds did not evaporate. Instead, they fell into the possession of individuals, businesses, financial institutions, and government agencies that made the right choices in their own speculative strategies. For instance, in our example if the Paris bank's managers turn out to be incorrect in their anticipation of a fall in average bank funding costs, then the Paris bank will experience losses from the interest-rate forward contract. The "lost" funds will flow to the Tokyo bank, which will be able to remove the EMU notes from its portfolio at a 5 percent yield, and hence at an above-market price, in the following year.

Both a Winner and a Loser   This leads us to the following conclusion about losses in trading forward contracts and other derivatives transactions:

> **For each "loser" in derivatives speculation, there must also be a "winner" on the other side of the transaction.**

From society's perspective, gains and losses from derivatives speculation must, in a purely accounting sense, "cancel out." As we shall discuss below, however, this does not imply that governments have been unconcerned about the potential for broader fallout from large derivatives losses.

SHORT AND LONG POSITIONS IN FORWARD CONTRACTS   In the example of an interest-rate forward contract between Paris and Tokyo banks, the Paris bank agreed to purchase European government notes in the following year at a price consistent with the current market yield. In the terminology of forward contracts, the Paris bank took a **long position,** meaning that the bank is obliged to *purchase* the European government notes next year at a fixed yield. By way of contrast, the Tokyo bank selling the notes took a **short position,** meaning that the bank must *sell* the European government notes the following year at the contracted price. By entering into the forward contract, however, the Tokyo bank's managers were able to remove the European government notes from their portfolio more quickly, thus avoiding incurring a capital loss if market yields were to rise.

Long position: An obligation to purchase a financial instrument at a given price and at a specific time.

Short position: An obligation to sell a financial instrument at a given price and at a specific time.

Futures Contracts

One disadvantage with forward contracts is that they are not "standardized." They tend to share similar features, but parties to a contract must work out the specific terms. This can take much time and effort.

Like a forward contract, a **futures contract** is an agreement by one party to deliver to another a quantity of a commodity or financial instrument at a specific future date. In contrast to forward contracts, however, futures contracts specify *standardized* quantities and terms of exchange. Futures contracts specify in advance the amounts to be traded and the guidelines for transactions. Because futures contracts are standardized, parties do not have to spend time working out the contract terms.

Holders of futures experience profits or losses on the contracts at any time before the contracts expire. This is because futures contracts require daily cash-flow settlements. In contrast, profits or losses occur only at the expiration date of a forward contract, which requires settlement at maturity.

The futures exchange is an organized market that simplifies the task of selling futures contracts, thereby making them highly liquid. Consequently, futures trading has grown much more rapidly than trading in forward contracts. Nevertheless, derivatives trading outside public futures exchanges is hardly "small potatoes"; the estimated annual value of worldwide forward contracts and other derivatives transactions amounts to more than $400 trillion, or nearly forty times the amount of *annual* U.S. nominal national income. (It is possible to

Futures contract: An agreement to deliver to another a given amount of a standardized commodity or financial instrument at a designated future date.

hedge against numerous risks in futures markets, including variations in the weather; see the *Management Focus: Keeping the Temperature Level in Futures Markets.*)

Interest rate future: A contract to buy or sell a standardized denomination of a specific financial instrument at a given price at a certain date in the future.

INTEREST RATE FUTURES   **Interest rate futures** are contracts requiring delivery of standard quantities of a financial instrument at a specified price and rate of return and on a certain date. Traders undertake transactions in these contracts at the Chicago Board of Trade (CBOT) futures exchange and other exchanges around the world. Each exchange establishes requirements that parties to such a transaction must meet. The financial instruments of futures contracts usually are U.S. Treasury bonds and other government bonds. For instance, a trader may enter into a five-year U.S. Treasury note futures contract, which constitutes an agreement to purchase or sell U.S. Treasury notes in standard denominations of $100,000.

Stock index future: An agreement to deliver, on a specified date, a portfolio of stocks represented by a stock price index.

STOCK INDEX FUTURES   **Stock index futures** are standardized agreements to deliver, on a specified date, a portfolio of stocks represented by a stock price index. For example, in the case of Standard and Poor's (S&P) 500 futures traded at the Chicago Mercantile Exchange (CME), the stock portfolio is representative of the market value of the 500 companies listed in the S&P index. Likewise, Nikkei-225 Stock Average futures are based on a portfolio of 225 stocks traded on the Tokyo Stock Exchange. In 1995, a series of bad bets, made by a poorly supervised manager, about Nikkei-225 futures traded in the Singapore International Monetary Exchange (Simex) led to the downfall of Barings Bank, a 233-year-old British institution.

To see how to calculate the value of a futures contract, let's consider an example involving an S&P 500 index futures contract. Computing the dollar value of such a contract requires multiplying the current market price of the futures contract times $500. For instance, if the S&P 500 futures price is 400, then the value of the contract is equal to $200,000. If an individual takes a *short position* with an S&P 500 futures contract, she agrees to deliver a cash amount of $500 times whatever the futures price turns out to be at the date in the contract. The party on the other end of the transaction, in contrast, takes a long position and agrees to pay 400 times $500 for this contract today. Assume that when the date arrives, the market price of the futures contract is equal to 500. Therefore, the contract has a dollar value of $250,000, so the individual in the short position loses $50,000 and the buyer in the long position gains $50,000. The buyer in the long position has paid $200,000 for the $250,000 cash payment that the seller in the short position is obligated to make. (Although Indian financial markets reflect certain Western features adopted during British colonial rule in the nineteenth

MANAGEMENT

Focus

Keeping the Temperature Level in Futures Markets

Unusual swings in temperatures can generate significant changes in the demand for cold drinks, such as soft drinks, juices, and beers. For this rea-

son, companies such as Coca-Cola and Heineken use *weather futures* as hedging instruments to shield their revenues from the effects of extreme variations in weather. Futures contracts relating to North American weather can be traded over-the-counter on the Chicago Mercantile Exchange.

FOR CRITICAL ANALYSIS: Why do you suppose that the generally more moderate climate in Europe is commonly cited as a reason that trading of futures relating to European weather has been slow to take off?

century, traders in India have been reluctant to give up ancient forms of futures contracts; see the *Global Focus: In India,* Badla *Falls on Bad Times.*)

CURRENCY FUTURES   **Currency futures** are futures contracts entailing the future delivery of national currencies. Currency futures contracts, like other futures, entail daily cash-flow settlements, whereas currency forward contracts (discussed in Chapter 5) entail a single settlement only at the date of maturity. As a result, the market prices of forward and futures contracts usually differ. In addition, futures contracts typically involve smaller currency denominations than forward contracts involve. Large banking institutions and corporations that transmit large volumes of foreign currencies in their normal business operations are the primary users of forward contracts. Individuals and smaller firms that wish to undertake hedging or speculative strategies typically trade currency futures instead.

Hedging with Currency Futures   As we discussed in Chapter 5, exchange rate movements cause those who trade in international financial markets to face risks arising from variations in asset prices. They also experience interest rate risks arising from interest rate volatility. Let's consider how traders confront this additional source of risk.

How can currency futures be used to hedge against foreign exchange risk? Suppose that a British firm has a franchise operation in the United States. The firm's managers anticipate that the current year's profits from this operation will be $4 million, which they plan to convert to British pounds. If the dollar depreciates relative to the pound during the year, then the pound-denominated value of the $4 million will be lower at year's end. That is, the British firm's exposure to translation risk would cause it to lose part of its dollar-denominated profits from its U.S. operation. To hedge against this risk, the firm's managers can take a long position via a pound future that expires in December. As the firm's dollar-denominated profit earnings decline in value relative to the British pound, the pound-denominated value of the firm's December future will rise, thereby offsetting, at least partially, the effect of the dollar's depreciation against the pound.

Reducing translation risk requires the firm to establish a margin account with a futures broker. The firm posts an initial margin (sometimes called the *bond performance requirement*) in

Currency future: An agreement to deliver to another a standardized quantity of a specific nation's currency at a designated future date.

GLOBAL
Focus

In India, *Badla* Falls on Bad Times

In India, a traditional form of futures speculation is known as *badla*. It is a method of carrying trades of commodities, stocks, or currencies into future periods without engaging in final settlement—essentially, an informal futures contract. To finance their *badla* positions, traders often borrow large sums by depositing very small sums in margin accounts. After several financial

failures associated with *badla* speculations in the late 1980s and early 1990s, the Indian government's Securities Exchange Board banned the use of *badla* between 1993 and 1995. In 1996, this agency permitted reintroduction of a more regulated version.

Nevertheless, the *badla*'s days may be numbered. In the early 2000s, the Bombay Stock Exchange and the National Stock Exchange of India began offering Western-style futures contracts. Since then commodities and

currency futures have also been introduced to Indian commodities and foreign exchange markets. These less risky forms of futures contracts are already beginning to replace the *badla* in the Indian financial system.

FOR CRITICAL ANALYSIS: Why might futures contracts tend to be favored over *badla* even if they have higher average prices than *badla* contracts?

this account by paying a small portion of the total value of the futures that the broker will purchase on the firm's behalf. Typically, the initial margin is less than 2 percent of the total value of the futures purchased. During the year, the firm must maintain a maintenance margin (sometimes called the *minimum bond performance requirement*), which is a minimum balance that must remain in its account with the futures broker. The broker and the firm also establish a *mark-to-market* procedure for applying the futures contract gains and losses to the firm's account at the close of each trading day.

Consider Figure 6-2, which displays the currency futures price quotes for British pounds that a firm can view at the Web site of the Chicago Mercantile Exchange (**http://www.cme.com**). Suppose that the market price for a December pound future is 1.8100 dollars per pound, as shown in Figure 6-2. The standard size of a pound future is 62,500 pounds. If the current spot exchange rate is 1.8126 dollars per pound, then the firm purchases an amount of pound futures equal to ($4 million/$1.8126 per pound)/62,500 pounds, which is approximately equal to 35. Therefore, purchasing 35 standard pound futures contracts provides the best possible futures hedge for the British firm. Note that with a $2,000 initial margin per contract, the firm's initial margin is 35 × $2,000 = $70,000. Thus, for a $4 million futures account, the firm must post only $70,000 in its margin account with its broker.

Daily Futures Settlement   To illustrate the daily settlement process of a typical futures contract, let's extend our example by supposing that on the first trading day the market closes at a futures price of $1.8120 per pound, so the firm's 35 pound futures appreciate. To keep things simple, let's also assume that the firm pays no brokerage fees. On the first day, the firm earns a profit equal to ($1.8120 per pound − $1.8100 per pound) × 62,500 pounds × 35

FIGURE 6-2
Currency Futures Prices for the British Pound.

The Chicago Mercantile Exchange reports futures prices using the format shown here. To understand how to read published currency futures quotes, consider the information for each column.

MTH/ STRIKE	OPEN	---SESSION--- HIGH	LOW	LAST	SETT	PT CHGE	EST VOL	---PRIOR DAY--- SETT	VOL	INT
SEP05	1.8164	1.8186B	1.8140A	1.8171	1.8172	+87	1471	1.8085	19883	66829
DEC05	- - - -	1.8100B	- - - -	1.8100B	1.8122	+87		1.8035		63
MAR06	- - - -	- - - -	- - - -	- - - -	1.8072	+87		1.7985		3
JUN06	- - - -	- - - -	- - - -	- - - -	1.8022	+87		1.7935		
SEP06	- - - -	- - - -	- - - -	- - - -	1.7972	+87		1.7885		1
DEC06	- - - -	- - - -	- - - -	- - - -	1.7922	+87		1.7835		
TOTAL										
TOTAL							EST. VOL 1471	VOL 19883		OPEN INT. 66896

Mth/Strike:	Maturing month.
Open:	Price of futures contract at the opening of business. On this day, a contract for 62,500 pounds for September 2005 began trading at $1.8164 per pound.
High:	Highest price of the futures contract during the day; $1.8100 per pound on this day for a December contract.
Low:	Lowest price of the futures contract during the day; $1.8140 per pound on this day for a September contract.
Last:	Price of the last futures contract at the close of business; $1.8100 per pound for a December contract.
Pt. Chge:	Change in price during the day.
Est. Vol.:	Approximate number of pound futures transactions during the day.
Prior Day Sett.:	Price of the contract at market close the previous day.
Prior Day Vol.:	Volume of futures contracts traded the previous day.
Prior Day Int.:	Number of contracts outstanding on the previous trading day.

= $4,375. The firm's margin account thereby rises from $70,000 (the initial margin) to $70,000 + $4,375 = $74,375.

If the closing futures price on the second trading day drops to $1.8090 per pound, then the firm experiences a dollar loss on the pound futures equal to ($1.8090 per pound − $1.8120 per pound) × 62,500 pounds × 35 = −$6,562.50. The firm's margin account thereby falls from $74,375 to $74,375 − $6,562.50 = $67,812.50.

Now suppose that the futures price rises to $1.8130 per pound on the third trading day. Then the firm earns a dollar profit equal to ($1.8130 per pound − $1.8090 per pound) × 62,500 pounds × 35 = $8,750, and the firm's margin account thereby rises from $67,812.50 to $67,812.50 + $8,750 = $76,562.50.

Note how the set of 35 futures contracts serves as a hedging instrument for the British firm. If during the course of the year the pound appreciates against the dollar, then the firm's realized pound-denominated value of profits from its U.S. franchise operation declines, so each dollar of profits from those operations has a smaller pound-equivalent value at the end of the year. As the pound appreciates against the dollar, however, the British company's futures margin position improves, thereby offsetting some or all of the firm's translation risk exposure.

> **2. What are forward and futures contracts, and how can they be used to limit risks?** Forward contracts are agreements to provide commodities or financial instruments on future dates and at specific prices. Futures contracts are similar agreements, but the quantities of commodities or financial instruments exchanged via futures contracts are standardized. Individuals, companies, and banks can use forward and futures contracts to ensure interest rate or exchange rate responses of derivatives returns that tend to offset variations of returns on other asset holdings. This reduces net exposures to interest rate risk and to foreign exchange risks.

Options

Another type of derivative instrument is an **option,** which is a financial contract giving the holder the right to purchase or sell an underlying financial instrument at a given price. The holder of this right is not required to buy or sell, but has the *option* to do so. The given price at which the holder of an option can exercise the right to purchase or sell a financial instrument is the option's **exercise price,** which traders also call the *strike price.*

Types of Option Contracts

Call options allow the holder to *purchase* a financial instrument at the exercise price. **Put options** allow the buyer to sell a financial instrument at the exercise price. In addition, traders call an option granting the holder the right to exercise the right of purchase or sale at any time before or including the date at which the contract expires an **American option.** They call an option that allows the holder to exercise the right of purchase or sale *only* on the date that the contract expires a **European option.**

STOCK OPTIONS AND FUTURES OPTIONS Many individuals and firms use options to hedge against risks owing to variations in interest rates or stock prices. To do this, they trade **futures options,** which are options to buy or sell stock index futures or interest rate futures, and **stock options,** which are options to buy or sell shares in corporations.

Option: A financial contract giving the owner the right to buy or sell an underlying financial instrument at a certain price within a specific period of time.

Exercise price: The price at which the holder of an option has the right to buy or sell a financial instrument; also known as the *strike price.*

Call option: An option contract giving the owner the right to purchase a financial instrument at a specific price.

Put option: An option contract giving the owner the right to sell a financial instrument at a specific price.

American option: An option that allows the holder to buy or sell a security at any time before or including the date at which the contract expires.

European option: An option that allows the holder to buy or sell a financial instrument only on the day that the contract expires.

Futures options: Options to buy or sell futures contracts.

Stock options: Options to buy or sell firm equity shares.

Trading volumes in the stock index futures market have risen considerably since the 1980s. Paralleling this growth has been broadened trading in the futures options market. In fact, today more options on stock index futures—essentially derivatives of derivatives—are traded than options based on actual stocks. (There are now even options on economic data; see the *Policy Focus: Will an Options Market Put Some Economic Forecasters Out of Work?*)

Currency option: A contract granting the holder the right to buy or sell a given amount of a nation's currency at a certain price within a specific period of time.

CURRENCY OPTIONS **Currency options** are contracts that give the owner the right to buy or sell a fixed amount of a given currency at a specified exchange rate at a certain time. Currency put options grant the holder the right to sell an amount of currency, while currency call options grant the holder the right to purchase an amount of currency. Multinational corporations can purchase currency options directly from banks via *over-the-counter* contracts and can also purchase them in organized exchanges.

MONEYXTRA!
Another Perspective

Sometimes firms have to adjust their portfolios of underlying assets to hedge against swings in the values of their option contracts. To read about how they do this, go to the Chapter 6 reading, entitled "Issues in Hedging Options Positions," by Saikat Nandi and Daniel Waggoner of the Federal Reserve Bank of Atlanta. **http://moneyxtra. swcollege.com**

Using Option Contracts to Reduce Exposure to Foreign Exchange Risks

The best way to understand how to use options to hedge against foreign exchange risks is by considering an example. Let's evaluate how currency call options help to limit losses and provide profit opportunities for a fictitious U.S. importer.

Let's consider how a U.S. importer buying 2 million euros worth of finished goods for an agreed-upon December payment might hedge against foreign exchange risk using a currency call option. If the current spot rate is $1.340 per euro, then the 2 million euros are equal to $2,680,000. To hedge against an unanticipated change in the exchange rate between now and December, the importer purchases December euro call options.

Figure 6-3 displays currency option quotes that the importer can locate at the Web site of the Chicago Mercantile Exchange (**http://www.cme.com**). At an exercise price of $1.420 in Figure 6-3, the upper limit on the dollar cost of the imported goods is $2,840,000. In Figure 6-3, a

POLICY
Focus

Will an Options Market Put Some Economic Forecasters Out of Work?

Since 2002, Goldman Sachs and Deutsche Bank have been auctioning options on economic news releases, such as government reports on nonfarm payrolls, retail sales, gross domestic product, measures of consumer confidence, and inflation. For instance, a call option on the federal government's

nonfarm payrolls report with an exercise price of 100 garners $1 per thousand jobs created in excess of 100,000. Consequently, if the government reports that nonfarm payroll growth was, say, 125,000 jobs, the buyer of the call options receives $25 for each option purchased.

For the first month that call options on the nonfarm payrolls report were sold, the consensus of forecasts by professional economists was that nonfarm payrolls would *grow* by 20,000 jobs. In contrast, the market price of the option contracts three days before the report

was released implied a prediction that nonfarm payrolls would *shrink* by 38,000 jobs. In fact, the report revealed an actual decline of 43,000 jobs. Traders of economic-data futures who actually had their own funds at stake apparently did a better job of forecasting than professional economic forecasters.

FOR CRITICAL ANALYSIS: What types of companies might be able to use nonfarm payroll options to hedge against risk?

FIGURE 6-3
Currency Options Prices for the Euro.

The Chicago Mercantile Exchange reports currency options prices on the Internet using the format shown here. To understand how to read published currency options quotes, consider the information for each column.

MTH/STRIKE	OPEN	HIGH	LOW	LAST	SETT	PT CHGE	EST VOL	SETT	VOL	INT
ZC DEC05 EURO FX OPTIONS CALL										
1370	----	----	----	----	.00160	+3		.00130		26
1380	----	----	----	----	.00130	+3		.00100		56
1385	----	----	----		.00110	+2		.00090		1
1390	----	----	----	----	.00100	+2		.00080		31
1400	----	----	----	----	.00080	+1		.00070	7	1570
1410	----	----	----	----	.00060	UNCH		.00060		37
1420	.00050	.00050	.00050	.00050	.00045	−.5	5	.00050		8
1440					.00020	UNCH		.00020		224
1450	----	----	----	----	.00010	UNCH		.00010		140
TOTAL							EST. VOL		VOL	OPEN INT.
TOTAL							876		5496	62816
ZC DEC05 EURO FX OPTIONS PUT										
1090	----	----	----	----	.00190	−8		.00270		22
1100	.00320	.00320	.00320	.00320	.00250	−9	5	.00340	26	41
1110	.00400	.00400	.00400	.00400	.00330	−9	5	.00420	40	59
TOTAL							EST. VOL		VOL	OPEN INT.
TOTAL							1565		4231	52374

Mth/Strike: Month of maturity and various exercise (or strike) exchange rates of option contracts on 62,500 euros.

Open: Price of options contract at the opening of business. On this day, a call option contract of 62,500 euros for December 2005 with an exercise exchange rate of 1.420 began trading at $0.0050 per option.

High: Highest price of option contracts reached during the day.

Low: Lowest price of option contracts reached during the day.

Last: Price of the last option contract at the close of business.

Pt. Chge: Change in price during the day.

Est. Vol.: Approximate number of euro options transactions during the day.

Prior Day Sett.: Price of the contract at market close the previous day.

Prior Day Vol.: Volume of options contracts traded the previous day.

Prior Day Int.: Number of contracts outstanding on the previous trading day.

December option with this exercise price has a *premium* of $0.0050 per euro, which is the effective cost of purchasing the contract. Consequently, one contract for the standard amount of 62,500 euros requires an expenditure of $312.50. Covering the 2 million euros in standard allotments of 62,500 euros requires exactly 32 contracts, for a total expenditure, or *total premium,* of 32 × $312.50 = $10,000.

Once the importer purchases the 32 option contracts for $10,000, if the dollar depreciates above $1.420 per euro, and if we ignore exercise fees that the contract might specify, then the importer would choose to exercise the option. For example, if the dollar depreciates to an exchange rate of $1.440 per euro, then it costs the importer $2,880,000 to obtain 2 million euros in the spot market. The exchange rate change increases the importer's costs by $2,880,000 − $2,680,000 = $200,000. Exercising the option and obtaining the 2 million euros at the exercise price of $1.420 per euro, or at a total dollar expenditure of $2,840,000, thereby saves $40,000. Considering the premium that the importer paid for the options, the importer comes out ahead by an amount equal to $40,000 − $10,000 = $30,000.

Note that the firm did not fully hedge against losses if the spot exchange rate turns out to be $1.440 per euro, because the firm pays a total of $2,840,000 + $10,000 = $2,850,000 using its option contracts. This is $170,000 more than the $2,680,000 that the firm would have had to pay if the exchange rate had remained at its initial value of $1.340

per euro. Hence, the firm still incurs a net loss of $170,000 as a result of a rise in the exchange rate from $1.340 per euro to $1.440 per euro. Nevertheless, this is better than the $200,000 loss it would otherwise have incurred without the currency options.

A spot exchange rate of $1.440 per euro is just one possible outcome, however. Figure 6-4 illustrates the limited loss and potential profit resulting from the importer's call options for a range of values of the spot exchange rate. The maximum net loss that the importer can experience is the total premium of $10,000 for the 32 option contracts. Below the strike exchange rate of $1.420 per euro, the importer is "out of the money," meaning that the firm cannot exercise the options. If the spot exchange rate rises to $1.420 per euro, however, then the importer can exercise the options. At this strike exchange rate, the importer is "at the money." Above the strike exchange rate, the firm is "in the money," meaning that it earns gross receipts that begin to offset the premium it paid for the options.

If the spot exchange rate rises to $1.425 per euro, then the gross earnings from exercising the option increase to $10,000, which exactly recoups the total premium of $10,000. Hence, the spot exchange rate of $1.425 per euro is the *break-even point* for the importer's option contracts. If the spot exchange rate rises above $1.425 per euro, then the importer earns net profits from its options; that is, its gross earnings exceed the total premium paid for the option contracts. Note that if the spot exchange rate turns out to be $1.440 per euro in Figure 6-4, then the importer's net gain from the option contracts is equal to ($1.440 per euro − $1.425 per euro) × 2,000,000 euros = $30,000, which is the amount we calculated previously.

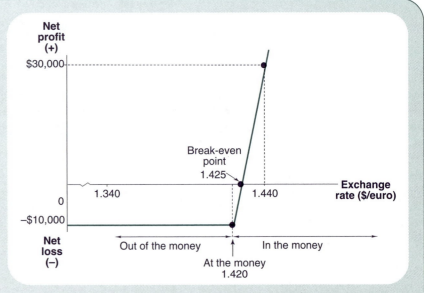

FIGURE 6-4
Potential Profit and Limited Loss from a Call Option.

At a per-contract premium of $0.0050 per euro, each 62,500-euro contract entails a premium expenditure of $312.50, so the holder of the options pays the total premium of 32 × $312.50 = $10,000. The maximum loss that the holder can incur on the options is limited to this amount. At or above the exercise exchange rate of $1.420 per euro, the holder may exercise the options and recoup at least a portion of the premiums paid for the options. At the spot exchange rate of $1.425 per euro, the holder's earnings from exercising the options just cover the total premiums paid. At a higher spot exchange rate, the holder earns a net profit. For example, at the spot exchange rate of $1.440 per euro, the holder earns a net profit of $30,000.

> **3. What are options, and how can they be used to reduce foreign exchange risk exposure?** Options are contracts that permit the owner to buy or sell a financial instrument at a certain price within a specific interval. Traders and all participants in foreign-currency-denominated contracts can use currency options to respond to a currency appreciation or depreciation by buying or selling the currency and earning net returns that are higher than those they would otherwise have achieved.

Swaps

Swaps are financial contracts in which parties to the transactions exchange *flows* of payments. Typically, these are flows of interest payments or payments denominated in foreign currencies.

Swap: A contract entailing an exchange of payment flows between two parties.

Interest Rate Swaps

An **interest rate swap** is an important type of swap in international financial markets. Under this contract, one party commits itself to exchange a set of interest payments that it is scheduled to receive for a different set of interest payments owed to another party.

Interest rate swap: A contractual exchange of one set of interest payments for another.

Financial market traders can use interest rate swaps to reduce their exposure to interest rate risk. For instance, a company holding a portfolio consisting primarily of long-duration financial instruments might engage in an interest rate swap for a stream of interest returns on a portfolio consisting mainly of shorter-duration instruments. This strategy could reduce the overall interest rate risk that the company faces.

Currency Swaps

Another key swap contract is a **currency swap,** which is an exchange of payment flows denominated in different currencies. Figure 6-5 on the next page illustrates a currency swap, in which we suppose that Ford Motor Company earns a flow of Japanese-yen-denominated revenues from auto sales in Japan, while Honda earns dollar revenues from selling autos in the United States. Ford pays dollar dividends and interest to its owners and bondholders, and Honda pays yen-denominated dividends and interest to its owners and bondholders. Therefore, Ford and Honda could, in principle, use a currency swap as a mechanism for trading their yen and dollar earnings for the purpose of paying income streams to their stockholders and bondholders.

Currency swap: An exchange of payment flows denominated in different currencies.

There are various types of interest rate and currency swaps. The most common swap is the *plain vanilla swap* (sometimes called a *bullet swap*), in which two parties to the swap arrangement agree simply to trade streams of payments to which each is entitled. Other swap contracts are more sophisticated. For instance, a *forward swap* delays the actual swap transaction for a period ranging from a few days to a few years. A *swap option* (sometimes called a *swaption*) grants the owner the right to enter into a swap when the swap's market price reaches an exercise or strike price. Determining the effective returns on these and other derivatives of swaps can be fairly complicated. This has led to the emergence of a group of financial economists who call themselves "financial engineers" and who seek to develop methods for computing the appropriate market prices of these derivative securities.

FIGURE 6-5
A Sample Currency Swap.

Ford Motor Company receives yen-denominated earnings from selling automobiles in Japan, and Honda receives dollar-denominated earnings from selling autos in the United States. The two companies could use a currency swap contract to trade their yen- and dollar-denominated earnings to make payments to holders of their stocks and bonds.

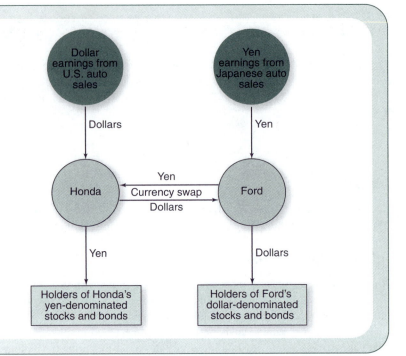

4. What are swaps, and how are they used to hedge against risks? A swap is an exchange of payment flows between two parties. Traders typically engage in swaps of promised streams of interest payments or of flows of payments denominated in foreign currencies. Trading flows of payments derived from portfolios with differing maturities can help reduce interest rate risk, and trading foreign-currency-denominated payment flows can reduce foreign exchange risk exposures.

Derivative Risk and Regulation

Table 6-2 on page 125 shows that those who trade derivatives can incur big, and sometimes even huge, losses. Clearly, trading in derivative securities is not a risk-free endeavor.

Derivatives Risk

Financial engineers also seek to identify and measure the risks that traders incur by speculating with derivatives. This is a challenging task, partly because simply determining the dollar amounts of derivatives trading can be difficult.

MEASURING DERIVATIVES RISKS A widely used measure of aggregate derivatives volume, which some use as a rough measure of exposure to derivatives risk, is the *notional value* of derivatives, or the amount of principal that serves as a basis for computing streams of payments. The estimated notional value of derivative contracts worldwide in 2006 exceeded $400 trillion, up from just over $43.2 trillion in 1996.

Replacement cost exposure is another popular measure of derivatives-related risk. This is the cost that a party to a derivatives contract faces at current market prices if the other party in the derivative contract defaults before contract settlement. In 1992, the total derivatives replacement cost exposure of U.S. commercial banks amounted to 4 percent of their assets. By 1997, this figure had risen to 8 percent. Today, it exceeds 11 percent.

TYPES OF DERIVATIVES RISKS By holding derivatives, firms expose themselves to three basic types of risk. One type is **derivative credit risk.** This is the risk associated with potential default by a contract party or an unexpected change in credit exposure resulting from changes in the market prices of the underlying instruments on which derivative yields depend. The replacement-cost-exposure measure focuses on this form of derivatives risk.

Another type of risk is **derivative market risk,** which is the risk of potential losses stemming from unexpected glitches in the payments system or unusual price changes at the time of settlement. Such events can cause derivative traders' liquidity levels to drop and can slow their normal efforts to adjust their derivatives holdings, thereby exposing them to risks of loss. For instance, a multinational firm may decide to execute a currency option before an anticipated unfavorable price movement, but when it tries to do so, it finds that a critical computer link is temporarily "down," thereby causing it to experience a loss when the price changes. In like manner, the price of an underlying asset in a derivatives transaction might fluctuate unexpectedly at the last moment before settlement, also causing the holder to incur a loss.

Finally, derivatives traders must confront **derivative operating risk,** or the risk of loss owing to unwise management. Many of the notable derivatives losses summarized in Table 6-2 on page 125 resulted from situations in which firm managers incorrectly valued derivatives and discovered their errors only at settlement. Institutions such as Bankers Trust, which settled several lawsuits concerning derivatives trading that it performed on behalf of client firms, had problems due to inadequate internal controls. These resulted in poorly supervised trading by mid-level managers, who were accused of mispricing derivatives and of misleading the bank's clients about the risk exposures they faced by holding derivatives.

As individuals, banks, and companies have become more adept at finding ways to use various derivatives for both hedging and speculation, the markets for these instruments have continued to grow around the world. So have some of the losses that have arisen when institutions have done a poor job of managing their risks. This potential for loss has begun to capture the attention of the world's financial regulators. Many regulators have been endeavoring for the past several years to do a better job of assessing both the benefits and the costs associated with derivatives. (Risks of loss are spread across a wide variety of types of derivative securities; see on page 138 the *Management Focus: What Are the Most Commonly Traded Derivatives?*)

Derivative credit risk: Risk stemming from the potential default by a party in a derivative contract or from unexpected changes in credit exposure because of changes in the market yields of instruments on which derivative yields depend.

Derivative market risk: Risk arising from unanticipated changes in derivatives market liquidity or from failures in payments systems.

Derivative operating risk: Risk owing to a lack of adequate management controls or from managerial inexperience with derivative securities.

Should Derivatives Trading Be Subjected to Greater Regulation?

Recall from Chapter 2 that bank regulators seek to attain four fundamental goals:

1. Increased bank efficiency

2. Limited risk of bank illiquidity

MANAGEMENT
Focus

What Are the Most Commonly Traded Derivatives?

When most people think of derivative securities, they tend to focus on *exchange-traded derivative instruments,* which include futures and options traded in organized exchanges. Perhaps this is because, as panel (a) of Figure 6-6 indicates, the value of derivatives traded in organized exchanges has grown considerably in recent years. Despite this growth, however, exchange-traded derivatives transactions are dwarfed by trades of *over-the-counter (OTC) derivatives instruments,* which are contractual arrangements negotiated between parties without the use of organized exchanges.

Panel (b) of Figure 6-6 displays worldwide allocations of derivative securities, including both exchange-traded derivatives and OTC derivatives. Today, interest rate swaps account for almost 60 percent of the total value of all derivative securities. The next most commonly used derivative securities are interest rate option contracts, which also are OTC derivatives and which account for about 9 percent of total derivatives.

FOR CRITICAL ANALYSIS: What factors influence whether a firm hedges risks using a forward contract, a swap, a future, or an option?

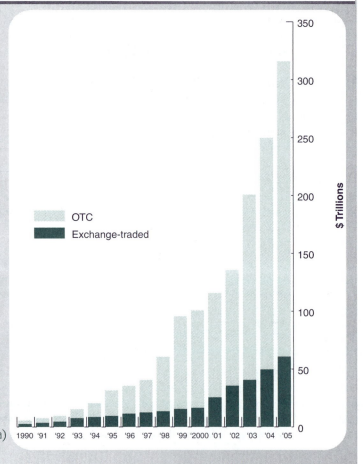

(a)

FIGURE 6-6
Values of Derivatives Traded in Organized Exchanges and Over-the-Counter.

Panel (a) shows that total derivatives trading has soared in recent years, with most of the growth occurring in trading of OTC derivatives. Panel (b) displays the overall distribution of derivative securities traded on both organized exchanges and over-the-counter.

SOURCES: Donald Mathieson and Garry Schinasi *et al., International Capital Markets: Developments, Prospects, and Policy Issues,* August 2001, International Monetary Fund; BIS Global OTC Derivatives Market Semi-Annual Reports; BIS International Banking and Financial Market Developments.

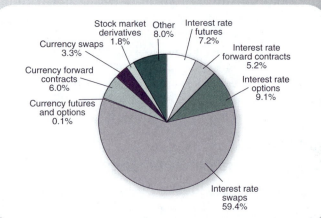

(b)

3. Reduced potential for bank insolvency

4. Protection of consumers of banking services

So far, bank regulators and other financial regulators have concluded that derivatives trading makes banks and financial markets more efficient. In addition, they have noted that the multimillion-dollar losses that have captured so much media attention over the years pale in significance next to the tens of trillions of dollars of worldwide derivatives trading that takes place each year.

To this point, therefore, most financial regulators have been hesitant to impose direct restrictions on derivatives trading by banks and others. Instead, as you will learn in Chapter 12, they have tried to induce individuals, companies, and banks to fully report their derivatives activities. For instance, in 1998 the U.S. Securities and Exchange Commission began requiring most large banks and about 500 other publicly traded companies to disclose estimates of their derivatives risks. The idea behind this requirement was that public information about high derivatives risks would reduce the affected firms' market values, giving them an incentive to reduce their derivatives risks voluntarily.

Another major effort to regulate derivatives has come from the U.S. Financial Accounting Standards Board (FASB—pronounced "fazbee"). In 1998, this regulatory body decided to change U.S. accounting standards to require banks and companies to report on how the market values of their derivatives holdings affect the net-worth positions that they report to shareholders. Today, financial and nonfinancial firms must attempt to provide regular assessments of their derivatives risk exposure in their financial reports.

---

5. What are the key risks of derivative securities, and what regulations govern derivatives trading? Derivatives credit risk is the potential for default or unanticipated changes in the prices of securities from which derivatives' returns are derived. Derivatives market risk is the possibility of losses caused by payment-system breakdowns or unusual price changes at settlement. Derivatives operating risks are the potential losses caused by poor management of trading positions. At present, derivatives are subject to limited regulation in the United States, most of which is confined to reporting requirements that exceed those of most other locales.

Chapter Summary

1. Interest Rate Risk, Financial Instrument Duration, and Derivatives: Interest rate risk is the potential for prices of financial instruments to vary because of unanticipated changes in interest rates. The two key factors influencing interest rate risk are the maturity and frequency of returns on financial instruments. Instruments of shorter maturities and with more frequent returns have shorter durations, or average periods necessary to receive all principal and interest payments. Such shorter-duration instruments possess lower interest rate risk. Derivative securities are financial instruments with returns derived from the returns of other financial instruments. Traders can use derivative securities to hedge against interest rate and foreign exchange risks. They can also employ derivatives to engage in profitable or unprofitable speculations about future movements in interest rates and exchange rates.

2. Forward and Futures Contracts, and How They Can Be Used to Limit Risks: A forward contract is a commitment to provide commodities or financial instruments on a future date and at a specified price. A futures contract is a similar instrument, but futures contracts specify standardized quantities of commodities or instruments. Traders can use forward and futures contracts to establish flows of returns based on interest rate or exchange rate movements that tend to counter variations of returns on other asset holdings. The result is a net reduction in exposure to interest rate risk or to foreign exchange risks.

3. Options and How They Can Be Used to Reduce Foreign Exchange Risk Exposure: Options are financial contracts granting the owner the right to purchase or sell a financial instrument at a certain price within a specific period. Traders can use currency options to respond to a currency appreciation or depreciation by buying or selling the currency at a prearranged exchange rate. This can allow them to earn higher net returns.

4. Swaps and How They Are Used to Hedge against Risks: A swap is an agreement between two parties to exchange payment flows, such as streams of promised

interest payments or flows of foreign-currency-denominated payments. Exchanging flows of payments derived from portfolios with differing maturities can help reduce interest rate risk, and trading payment flows denominated in different currencies can reduce foreign exchange risk exposure.

5. Key Risks of Derivative Securities and Derivatives-Trading Regulations: Derivatives credit risk is the possibility of default or of unanticipated changes in the prices of securities from which derivatives' returns are derived. Derivatives market risk is the potential for losses stemming from payment-system glitches or unusual price changes at settlement. Derivatives operating risks are the risks of losses resulting from bad management of trading positions. Most derivatives regulation takes place in the United States, where banks and corporations face stiffer reporting requirements than in other nations.

Questions and Problems

(Answers to odd-numbered questions and problems may be found on the Web at **http://money.swcollege.com** under "Student Resources.")

1. What is interest rate risk?

2. Explain why a financial instrument's duration influences the degree of interest rate risk incurred by holding the instrument.

3. Explain why the losses displayed in Table 6-2 on page 125 are private losses and not social losses.

4. How does a currency futures contract differ from a forward currency contract?

5. Banks make heavy use of forward contracts, while individual and corporate traders tend to use futures contracts. Can you think of a reason why this is the case? [Hint: Think about the drawbacks of forward contracts as compared with futures contracts and why these might pose less of a problem for banks.]

6. Why is a stock futures option a "derivative of a derivative"? Explain briefly.

7. Suppose that a bank has flows of future payments and receipts denominated in foreign currencies. Evaluate the pros and cons of using currency options or currency swaps to reduce foreign exchange risks associated with these forthcoming payments and receipts. [Hint: Think about the relative costs of the two hedging instruments, and contemplate the problems of finding a partner in a swap arrangement.]

8. Banks are heavily involved in trading currency swaps. In light of your answer to question 7, explain why this makes sense.

9. Evaluate the usefulness of the notional value of derivatives as compared with their replacement cost exposure as measures of overall risk exposure to derivatives.

10. Of the three types of derivatives risks, which would you expect to be most common? Least common? Why?

Before the Test

Test your understanding of the material covered in this chapter by taking the Chapter 6 interactive quiz at **http://money.swcollege.com**.

Online Application

Internet URL: http://asx.com.au

Title: Australian Stock Exchange Derivatives

Navigation: Begin at the above Web site.

Application: Follow the directions below, and answer the related questions:

1. Go to "About ASX," choose "Publications," and download the booklet entitled "What Is a Derivative?" Read the text. What is a warrant? What makes a warrant different from a basic option contract?

2. Back up to the opening page. Then click on "Understanding Margin Obligations" and download the booklet. Based on the dis-

cussion in the booklet, explain in your own words, without any equations or formulas, what a margin is and how it generally is calculated. How do people typically meet margin requirements?

For Group Study and Analysis: The second page of the booklet entitled "What Is a Derivative?" describes "covered call writing" as a simple and common strategy for earning extra income from existing holdings of stock. Split the class into four groups that are assigned to examine how this strategy is likely to pan out under the following scenarios: bull market, steady market, bear market, market collapse. Have each group determine whether covered call writing functions as a hedging or a speculative strategy in each scenario.

Selected References and Further Reading

Abken, Peter, and Milind Shrikhande. "The Role of Currency Derivatives in Internationally Diversified Portfolios." Federal Reserve Bank of Atlanta *Economic Review* 82 (Third Quarter 1997): 34–59.

Bartolini, Leonardo. "Foreign Exchange Swaps." Federal Reserve Bank of Boston *New England Economic Review* (Second Quarter 2002): 11–12.

Brewer, Elijah, III, William Jackson III, and James Moser. "The Value of Using Interest Rate Derivatives to Manage Risk of U.S. Banking Organizations." Federal Reserve Bank of Chicago *Economic Perspectives* (Third Quarter 2005): 49–66.

Craig, Ben. "Options and the Future: What Do Markets Think?" Federal Reserve Bank of Cleveland *Economic Commentary*, October 1, 2002.

Gunther, Jeffery, and Thomas Siems. "Debunking Derivatives Delirium." Federal Reserve Bank of Dalles *Southwest Economy* 2 (March/April 2003): 1–9.

Haubrich, Joseph. "Swaps and the Swaps Yield Curve." Federal Reserve Bank of Cleveland *Economic Commentary*, December 2001.

Kawaller, Ira G., Paul D. Koch, and Timothy W. Koch. "The Relationship between the S&P 500 Index and S&P 500 Index

Futures Prices." Federal Reserve Bank of Atlanta, *Financial Derivatives: New Instruments and Their Uses,* December 1993, pp. 40–48.

Klitgaard, Thomas, and Laura Weir. "Exchange Rate Changes and Net Positions of Speculators in the Futures Market." Federal Reserve Bank of New York *Economic Policy Review,* May 2004, pp. 17–28.

Koprianov, Anatoli. "Derivatives Debacles: Case Studies of Large Losses in Derivatives Markets." Federal Reserve Bank of Richmond *Economic Quarterly,* Fall 1995, pp. 1–40.

Lopez, Jose. "Financial Instruments for Mitigating Credit Risk." Federal Reserve Bank of San Francisco *Economic* Letter, No. 2001-34, November 23, 2001.

Nandi, Saikat, and Daniel Waggoner. "Issues in Hedging Options." Federal Reserve Bank of Atlanta *Economic Review* (First Quarter 2000): 24–39.

Sierra, Gregory, and Timothy Yeager. "What Does the Federal Reserve's Economic Value Model Tell Us about Interest Rate Risk at U.S. Community Banks?" Federal Reserve Bank of St. Louis *Review* 86 (November/December 2004): 46–60.

MoneyXtra

Log on to the MoneyXtra Web site now (**http://moneyxtra.swcollege.com**) for additional learning resources such as practice quizzes, case studies, readings, and additional economic applications.

Finding the Best Mix of Financial Instruments—

The Theory of Portfolio Choice and Efficient Markets

The combined net worth, or wealth, of all U.S. households—the total amount of resources that they owe to no one else—is fast approaching $45 trillion. One out of every 125 U.S. residents is now a "millionaire," meaning that they possess at least $1 million in financial or other liquid assets. Of these roughly 2.4 million U.S. millionaires, about 30,000 are classified as "ultra-rich" individuals who have more than $30 million of financial or other liquid assets. Nonmillionaires, millionaires, and the ultra-rich share one thing in common: they must decide how to allocate their wealth among myriad alternative assets.

What determines how households allocate their total financial assets? To answer this question, you must learn about the theory of portfolio choice.

Financial Instrument Portfolios

In the preceding chapters, you have learned about various types of financial instruments, about the ways in which market interest rates are related, about international connections among financial markets, and about how exchange rates are determined. In this chapter, we shall combine these concepts to contemplate how savers allocate their wealth among the broad array of financial instruments available in today's world.

Saving and Wealth

When people add to their holdings of financial instruments, they *save*. All their holdings of financial instruments are part of their total *wealth*. Before we proceed further, it is important to understand the distinction between these two concepts.

SAVING   As we discussed in Chapter 3, saving is the act of forgoing consumption. Setting aside a portion of income earned during the most recent week or month can permit an individual to expand his or her capability to consume in the future—provided that the amount the individual saves retains or, better yet, increases in value over time.

Saving is a *flow*. That is, it is an amount that a person *adds* to savings accumulated in previous weeks and months. Thus, economists measure saving as the amount added to an individual's total accumulated savings from one point in time to another.

WEALTH A person's **wealth** consists of all the resources owned by that individual. An individual who saves a portion of her or his income each month adds to *accumulated savings* at the end of each month. For most people, accumulated savings constitute a large portion of total wealth. Economists often broaden the definition of wealth to include nonfinancial resources, such as durable goods that have a current market value. They also often include *human capital,* which is the amount of knowledge and training possessed by an individual. People can transform their human capital into income and thereby can use human capital to accumulate more financial wealth. Certainly, bankers recognize this when they contemplate making loans. They are more likely to make a loan to a college graduate who is in every other way identical to a person without a college degree, because they realize that the college graduate possesses additional human capital.

Nevertheless, a person cannot trade durable goods or human capital directly for stocks, corporate bonds, or Treasury securities. In this chapter, we shall focus our attention on the part of wealth that people hold as financial instruments. This is their *financial wealth,* or their accumulated financial savings. Financial wealth is a *stock,* meaning that we measure a person's wealth at a point in time. Wealth is a snapshot at a specific point in time. It is the amount of total savings the person has accumulated as of a particular date.

Wealth: An individual's total resources.

Financial Portfolios

A key reason that most people forgo consumption is so that they can expand their capability to consume in the future. At some later time in their lives, they hope to be able to direct accumulated savings to future expenditures on items such as a bigger or better home for themselves and their families, higher education for their children, or perhaps more "frivolous" expenditures such as a European vacation or an Alaskan cruise.

To be able to make the greatest possible future expenditures, however, people must find ways to retain the value of their financial wealth. Indeed, they must find ways to expand their financial wealth as much as possible given the circumstances that they face. As you learned in Chapter 4, holdings of financial instruments yield rates of return. Thus, directing saving to purchases of interest-bearing financial instruments is a fundamental saving allocation for most individuals who wish to increase their future spending potential as much as they can.

The set of financial instruments that an individual possesses at a given point in time is his financial **portfolio.** These holdings constitute the individual's allocation of his financial wealth. Given that an individual's objective is to be able to use this portfolio to finance future consumption, choosing the "best" mix of financial instruments is a fundamental issue for any saver. The *theory of portfolio choice* provides insights into the manner in which savers identify the financial instruments that they should hold in their portfolios.

Portfolio: The group of financial instruments held by an individual, which together make up the individual's financial wealth.

> **1. What is a financial portfolio?** A financial portfolio is the set of financial instruments currently owned by an individual. This combined portfolio is the individual's financial wealth, and one key way that an individual saves is by adding to an existing financial portfolio, thereby expanding financial wealth.

Fundamental Determinants of Portfolio Choice

Figure 7-1 displays the aggregate portfolio allocations of U.S. households. As you can see, U.S. households hold a number of different types of assets in their portfolios. The percentage allocations to various assets in Figure 7-1 tell us something about the average portfolio of a typical U.S. household. The portfolios of individual households vary widely, however. Why is this so? To answer this question, let's begin by thinking about the factors that influence portfolio choice.

Wealth

Naturally, a key determinant of any individual's portfolio of financial assets is the person's total wealth. To understand why this is so, imagine two different college students. Both are females, have similar intellectual capabilities, maintain the same grade point average, live in the same apartment complex, and major in the same subject. They have nearly identical course schedules, and they even have similar tastes in music, movies, and sports. The main way they differ, however, is their wealth. After paying tuition and fees for the current semester, one student has $1,500 in financial wealth. The other has financial wealth equal to $150,000.

At the end of last week, the less wealthy student had $750 in a checking account at a bank and $750 in a savings account. The wealthier student had $25,000 in a checking account with the same bank. In addition, she had $125,000 in savings deposits.

Now think about each student's reaction to receiving identical cash windfalls of $1,500 this week. Both students, we shall assume, are thrifty individuals who want to save these windfalls. Undoubtedly, they will allocate the new funds differently, however, because their total wealth and current portfolio allocations are significantly different. Let's suppose that the less wealthy student chooses to place $500 in her bank checking account and the remaining $1,000 in her bank savings account. In contrast, the wealthier student adds $100 to her checking deposits

FIGURE 7-1
**Aggregate Portfolio
Allocations of U.S. Households.**

The majority of U.S. household wealth is allocated to pension funds and equity holdings.

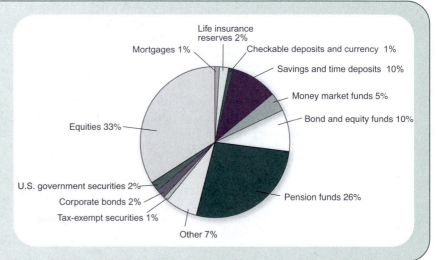

SOURCE: *Flow-of-Funds Accounts,* Board of Governors of the Federal Reserve System, June 30, 2005.

and $1,400 to her savings deposits. (To simplify, we assume that these are the only savings options either student considers in the near term.)

THE WEALTH ELASTICITY OF ASSET DEMAND In our example, the less wealthy student experienced a doubling of her financial wealth. That is, her financial wealth increased by 100 percent. She responded by increasing the size of her checking account holdings by 67 percent (the $500 addition to her initial $750 checking balance) and by raising her savings account balance by 133 percent (the $1,000 addition to her initial $750 savings balance). These figures tell us something about the *sensitivity* of each desired asset allocation to the change in wealth that she experienced. Economists call this sensitivity the **wealth elasticity of demand,** which is the percentage change in the quantity of an asset demanded divided by a given percentage change in wealth. Thus, the less wealthy individual's wealth elasticity of demand for bank checking deposits is equal to 67 percent divided by 100 percent, or 0.67. Her wealth elasticity of demand for savings deposits is equal to 133 percent divided by 100 percent, or 1.33.

The wealthier student experienced a much smaller percentage increase in wealth equal to 1 percent ($1,500 is 1 percent of $150,000). She increased her checking account balance by 0.4 percent ($100 is 0.4 percent of $25,000), so her wealth elasticity of demand for checking deposits is equal to 0.4 (0.4 percent divided by 1 percent). Her savings deposits rose by 1.12 percent ($1,400 is 1.12 percent of $125,000), so her wealth elasticity of demand for savings deposits is equal to 1.12 (1.12 percent divided by 1 percent).

As we might expect, the students responded to their $1,500 windfalls by making very different *absolute* dollar allocations between the two types of bank accounts. The sensitivities of their demands for assets also differ, with the less wealthy student showing greater sensitivity in her demand for both checking and savings deposits in response to a proportionate increase in her wealth. This is a normal observation. Wealth elasticities of demand for any asset tend to be larger for less wealthy individuals. Because they have less wealth to begin with, they tend to allocate relatively higher shares of wealth increases to all their asset holdings, as compared with the way wealthier individuals would allocate an identical wealth increase.

NECESSITY ASSETS VERSUS LUXURY ASSETS For both students, however, the wealth elasticity of demand for checking deposits is less than 1. This indicates that the students regard checking deposits as a **necessity asset,** meaning that they feel they must have a checking account on hand (for buying groceries, paying rent, and so on), but will increase their holdings of this asset less than proportionately as their wealth increases. Furthermore, at sufficiently high levels of wealth people typically reach a point at which they add proportionately little to their holdings of necessity assets, as is the case for the wealthier of the two students in our example.

An asset is a **luxury asset** when people respond to a rise in their wealth by increasing their demand for the asset more than proportionately. The wealth elasticity of demand for savings deposits is greater than 1 for both students, indicating that both regard savings accounts as luxury assets.

This example illustrates two important facts about portfolio choice. First, greater wealth tends to lead an individual to increase her holdings of any financial asset. Second, the proportionate increase in the quantity of a financial instrument that a person holds following an increase in her wealth depends on her wealth elasticity of demand for the instrument. Her wealth elasticity of demand, in turn, depends both on her total wealth and on whether she regards the asset as a necessity asset or a luxury asset.

Wealth elasticity of demand: The percentage change in the quantity of an asset demanded by an individual divided by a given percentage change in the individual's wealth.

Necessity asset: An asset with a wealth elasticity of demand less than 1, which implies that an individual increases holdings of the asset less than proportionately in response to a given proportionate increase in wealth.

Luxury asset: An asset with a wealth elasticity of demand greater than 1, which indicates that an individual raises holdings of the asset more than proportionately in response to a given proportionate increase in wealth.

Expected Asset Returns

Suppose that someone offers to sell you two financial instruments. Both are equally suscepti-ble to variations in their market values, and both are equally likely to be salable in secondary markets if you should desire to convert them into cash in a hurry. They differ in only one respect: one asset has a higher expected return than the other.

Our guess is that you would find this choice to be a "no-brainer." Why? The reason is that the asset with the higher expected return will permit you to engage in higher expected con-sumption of goods and services in the future. (Sometimes people decline to hold certain assets even when they have higher expected returns than alternative assets; see the *Management Focus: Forgoing the "Vice Premium."*)

A number of factors influence the expected return on a financial instrument. As you learned in Chapter 4, one is the instrument's anticipated nominal yield. Another is the extent to which governments tax the nominal returns on the instrument. Furthermore, the antici-pated inflation rate affects the real yield that one anticipates earning by holding the instrument to maturity. In addition, if the financial instrument is denominated in a foreign currency, then the expected rate of appreciation or depreciation affects the expected return.

Asset Liquidity

In fact, financial instruments have a number of characteristics that typically distinguish them. For example, suppose that two financial instruments have the same expected return. Indeed, they are identical in all other respects as well, except for one. This one distinguishing feature is that market trading volumes for one instrument usually are higher than for the second instrument.

This means that if the person who owns the second instrument wishes to exchange it for cash, perhaps because of a family emergency that requires a significant expenditure of funds, he has a lower chance of getting an offer to buy the instrument. Hence, the second instrument has less *liquidity*. As a result, holding it instead of the first instrument that is exchanged in a market with greater trading volumes is less desirable.

On the Web

How can a trader assess expected returns on financial assets? Use The Hedgehog's financial calcu-lators to answer this question at **http://hedge-hog.com**.

MANAGEMENT

Focus

Forgoing the "Vice Premium"

In recent years, an increasing number of people have chosen to place sav-ings in mutual funds or pension funds that purchase only financial instru-ments issued by companies deemed to be "socially responsible." In most cases, selecting this option precludes holding assets of companies involved in alcohol, military armaments and

hardware, gambling, and tobacco prod-ucts. Since the late 1990s, portfolios consisting solely of assets issued by these companies, such as the portfolio of a Dallas-based mutual fund called Vice Fund, have outperformed most other portfolios. The rate of return to shareholders in the Vice Fund has per-sistently been several percentage points higher than the rate of return of stocks in the Dow Jones Industrial Average and Standard & Poor's 500.

Thus, choosing to invest only in "socially responsible" companies has entailed forgoing a "vice premium."

FOR CRITICAL ANALYSIS: Is it possible that being deemed by many people to be "socially irresponsible" may require certain companies, such as gambling and tobacco firms, to pay higher rates of return on their financial instruments?

Of course, as we discussed in Chapter 4, it is unlikely that the two instruments would have the same expected returns for very long. People would opt to purchase the more liquid instrument, thereby increasing the demand for that instrument and pushing up its market price. This would tend to reduce its yield relative to that of the less liquid instrument. Indeed, this happened in the market for U.S. Treasury securities in the fall of 1998, when trading volumes for Treasury bonds with 28 and 29 years remaining to maturity fell off sharply relative to volumes of trading for 30-year-maturity Treasury bonds. As a result, people who previously had actively traded Treasury bonds maturing in 28 and 29 years became skittish about continuing to hold the bonds. Market demand for the bonds dropped off, and the yield on 30-year bonds dropped below the yields on bonds maturing in 28 and 29 years. (As discussed in Chapter 4, longer bonds normally carry greater yields.) This is a real-world example of how liquidity is an important determinant of portfolio choice—and market yields.

Information Costs

Another key factor influencing portfolio choice is asymmetric information—information possessed by those who issue financial instruments that is not available to those who buy them. As Chapter 8 will explain in more detail, it is costly for buyers of financial instruments to try to overcome informational asymmetries. Doing so requires obtaining reports about the prospects of issuers, spending time evaluating those reports, and reaching conclusions about the trustworthiness of the information they contain. All these activities entail both explicit and opportunity costs.

Thus, financial instruments for which information is more readily available are, holding all other factors equal, more desirable for inclusion in a portfolio. Holding such instruments reduces the costs of managing the portfolio, thereby raising the overall expected net return on the portfolio as a whole.

Asset Risk

Another crucial factor influencing portfolio choice is the relative riskiness of alternative financial instruments. Most savers are **risk-averse,** meaning that if all other characteristics of financial instruments are the same, savers prefer to hold the financial instrument with the least potential for swings in its yield and, consequently, its price. Of course, some people enjoy taking risks. Nevertheless, most people prefer to reduce their risks of loss whenever possible.

Risk aversion: The preference, other things being equal, to hold assets whose returns exhibit less variability.

ASSET RETURN RISKS   To see how risk can influence a person's choice between competing financial instruments, consider a situation in which a new company has an initial public offering. Stock market analysts have determined that there is a 50 percent chance that the company's shares will yield a 5 percent annual return and a 50 percent chance that they will yield a 7 percent annual return. Therefore, the expected annual return from purchasing the new company's shares is the average of the two returns, or 6 percent.

At the same time, another new company is also issuing shares for the first time. Analysts forecast that there is a 50 percent chance that its shares will yield an annual return of 12 percent. There is also a 50 percent chance that the annual return will turn out to be 0 percent. Consequently, the expected annual return from purchasing this company's shares is also the average of these returns, or 6 percent.

Given this choice, a risk-averse saver will prefer to buy shares issued by the first company, because there is less potential deviation of actual returns from the expected returns of its

On the Web
How can an investor keep up with scheduled initial public offerings and news of mergers and acquisitions? One approach is to visit The Online Investor at **http:// theonlineinvestor.com**.

shares compared with the second company. Even though the expected returns for both companies are the same, the return offered by the first company's shares tends to exhibit greater *stability*. This makes its shares less risky financial instruments. (Arguably, for some individuals, some asset return risks arise from their own tendencies to trade financial instruments too often; see the *Management Focus: Too Much Trading Can Be Bad for Your Wealth.*)

MEASURING RISK   Table 7-1 summarizes the various factors that can affect the choice of which financial instruments to hold. Savers know their own financial wealth and can make forecasts of average returns. In addition, savers know the information costs that they face, and data about trading volumes are readily available in financial publications. But how can savers measure the riskiness of financial instruments?

Because assets that have returns with greater potential deviations from expected returns are riskier, a natural measure of asset risk is the *statistical variance*. This is a summary statistic that

MANAGEMENT
Focus

Too Much Trading Can Be Bad for Your Wealth

Brad Barber and Terrance Odean of the University of California at Davis have studied the relationship between how often people buy and sell assets and the net returns they earn on their overall asset portfolios. Barber and

Odean classified people as more active traders if their portfolios had very high rates of turnover—that is, active traders frequently added to and subtracted from their portfolios by buying and selling assets. As Figure 7-2 shows, the most active traders experienced the lowest net returns on their portfolios. One factor reducing the net returns of particularly active traders was that trading entailed broker's fees and other

trading costs. Another was that the average portfolios of more active traders typically ended up including financial instruments yielding lower average returns.

FOR CRITICAL ANALYSIS: How could more active traders earn lower net returns than less active traders even if the more active traders always succeed in their efforts to "buy low and sell high"?

FIGURE 7-2
Net Portfolio Returns and Trading Turnover Rates.

Traders who have the highest monthly rates of asset turnover—purchases and sales—in their portfolios also earn the lowest net portfolio returns.

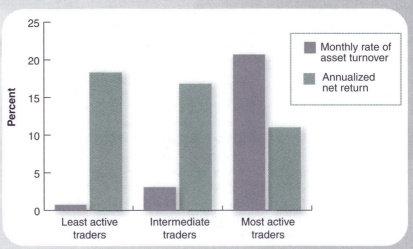

SOURCE: Brad Barber and Terrance Odean, "Trading Is Hazardous to Your Wealth: The Common Stock Investment Performance of Individual Investors," *Journal of Finance* 55 (April 2000): 773–806.

Table 7-1 Factors That Influence Portfolio Choice

Factor	Effect of an Increase in Factor on Desired Asset Holdings
Wealth	Increase
Expected asset return	Increase
Asset liquidity	Increase
Information costs	Decrease
Asset risk	Decrease

indicates how widely actual values of an asset's return tend to vary relative to the expected return. Thus, a financial instrument whose return has a larger statistical variance is judged to be riskier than one that has the same expected return but with a smaller statistical variance. (Trading in a particular German futures market has generated both significant mean returns and a high variance of returns; see the *Global Focus: The German DAX Market Is Literally an Overnight Sensation*.)

As we discuss below, this approach to measuring risk leads naturally to the application of *mean-variance analysis,* or the evaluation of trade-offs between financial assets' expected returns and variances of returns, to the portfolio-choice problem. First, however, let's consider how savers' concern about risk can induce them to hold a *mix* of different kinds of financial instruments.

On the Web
What are the basic issues concerning personal investment choices? Contemplate this question further at **http://www.maxinvest.com**.

2. What are the key determinants of portfolio choice? Other things being equal, savers will prefer to hold more of a given financial instrument (1) if they experience an increase in their wealth, (2) if the instrument's expected return rises, (3) if the savers are risk-averse and the riskiness of the instrument's return declines, (4) if the instrument's market liquidity increases, and (5) if the costs of acquiring information about the instrument fall.

GLOBAL

Focus

The German DAX Market Is Literally an Overnight Sensation

In recent years, trading volumes have jumped in the German DAX market, in which futures on stocks of top German companies are exchanged. The DAX market has three characteristics that have attracted U.S. traders. First, the minimum trading-account balance required for U.S. residents to participate in the market is lower than the balances typically required by many other exchanges. Second, the DAX market is open when it is nighttime in the United States, so U.S. residents with full-time day jobs can trade the German futures in the wee hours of the morning and still hope to catch a nap before time to leave for work. Third, DAX contracts tend to exhibit rapid and volatile price swings that offer higher expected profits to those who hope to reap gains from buying low and selling high. Just a few years ago, U.S. traders accounted for only about 5 percent of the total volume of DAX contracts traded. Today, more than 25 percent of all trading in this German futures market is generated by individuals and firms located in the United States.

FOR CRITICAL ANALYSIS: Why do high mean returns and a high variance of returns naturally go together for U.S. residents who desire to profit from trading in the German DAX market?

The Gains from Domestic and International Diversification

Figure 7-1 on page 144 shows that U.S. households possess a wide array of financial instruments. Some of these instruments have higher expected returns than others, and some are riskier. Indeed, it is possible that some instruments have lower expected returns and greater risk than others. How could this be true if risk-averse individuals prefer to hold financial instruments with higher expected returns and lower riskiness? The answer is that savers can benefit from *diversifying* their portfolios, thereby reducing their *overall* portfolio risk. Sometimes achieving such overall risk reduction can require holding financial instruments that individually have lower expected returns and greater inherent riskiness.

Idiosyncratic Risk versus Market Risk

There is risk in holding any financial instrument. The bottom could drop out from under stock prices on any given day. A hedge fund collapse could take down a closely linked corporation, making its commercial paper worthless. In 1996, a political stalemate led to a perception that the U.S. government might suspend payments on its debts, so for a time traders perceived even Treasury securities as somewhat risky.

Financial economists view the risk of any financial instrument as separable into two components: *idiosyncratic risk* and *market risk*. Holding a mix of financial assets can help reduce the first type of risk but cannot offset the second type.

Idiosyncratic risk: Risk that is unique to a particular financial instrument; also known as *nonsystematic risk.*

IDIOSYNCRATIC RISK   The first form of risk, **idiosyncratic risk** (sometimes called *nonsystematic risk*), is risk that is unique to a specific financial instrument. For example, shares of stock issued by a new company that specializes in security encryption for e-money trades are subject to very special risks. For instance, there is always the possibility that the encryption codes, which are crucial to the company's future performance, have an undetected flaw that a capable computer hacker will discover in the near future. Or it may be that a key individual involved in developing the encryption software is a disgruntled employee who may leave for another job. Perhaps the company's encryption software will turn out to be particularly susceptible to a new computer virus. Perhaps the company's prospectus provides misleading information that has not yet been discovered by the Securities and Exchange Commission.

These and a number of other factors specific to this e-money security company could cause the value of its shares to fall in the marketplace at some future date. The risk of such company-specific events occurring is the idiosyncratic risk associated with shares of stock issued by the company.

Idiosyncratic risk is not necessarily company specific. It could apply to all e-money security companies. For example, it is possible that all such companies, including this specific firm, have jumped the gun, entering the e-money encryption market before people are ready to buy e-money security services. As a result, near-term performances of such companies could turn out to be very poor. As a result, the returns on shares in these companies might be much lower than expected.

Even though each of these scenarios is possible, and even though this makes holding shares of stock in the e-money security company risky, a saver can offset the risk through **diversification,** or holding a mix of financial instruments that have returns that typically do not move in the same direction simultaneously. As a result, the saver can reduce overall portfolio risk even though the financial instruments of specific issuers are individually risky.

On the Web
How does the Securities and Exchange Commission seek to limit the risks faced by individual investors? Explore this issue at the SEC's Web site, **http://www.sec.gov/investor/alerts.shtml**.

Diversification: Holding a mix of financial instruments with returns that normally do not move together.

To see how a saver can do this, note that a person who wishes to hold shares in the specific e-money security company could opt to hold shares in several other e-money security firms as well. Then, if the encryption software of an individual company turns out to be easy for a hacker to decrypt, if a key employee leaves a firm, if software is susceptible to a virus, or if a firm's managers commit fraud, solid performances by other e-money security firms will generate strong returns that will offset this one weak performance.

In addition, the saver could hold financial instruments issued by providers of traditional payment technologies, such as makers of automated teller machines, producers of check-processing technology, or even private firms that make coins for the Treasury Department. Then, if e-money security technology turns out to be an idea ahead of its time as far as market performance is concerned, continued solid performances by producers of traditional payment systems will yield returns that will compensate for low returns from the shares issued by the e-money security companies.

MARKET RISK   The other component of the risk of any financial instrument is **market risk** (also called *systematic risk*), or risk coming from the entire system. This is risk that all financial assets in a portfolio share in common, perhaps because of general variations in common economic conditions that influence all issuers of financial instruments.

Because market risk is common to all financial instruments within a portfolio, diversification cannot reduce the overall market risk of the portfolio. Hence, savers cannot reduce market risk by altering the mix of financial instruments that they hold. Savers can, however, try to avoid holding financial instruments with returns that largely move with returns of other instruments in their portfolios, thereby allowing them to reap the fullest possible benefits of diversification.

For instance, banking tends to be a cyclical business. When economic performance is weak, the returns on bank shares tend to fall, and when the economy is doing well, the returns on bank shares tend to rise. (A desire to combine sources of revenues with different cycles motivated one of the largest bank mergers in U.S. history; see on page 152 *What Happens When Banking Opposites Attract?*) This is true of many other businesses, such as the automobile industry. Thus, the returns on stocks of banks, automobile manufacturers, and many other companies tend to move together during the course of economic cycles. A saver may wish to hold shares in stocks that move *countercyclically,* such as shares of companies that specialize in retraining unemployed workers, to help insulate the overall portfolio return from the market risk of economic fluctuations.

Market risk: Risk that is common to all financial assets within a portfolio; also called *systematic risk.*

MONEYXTRA!
Another Perspective

Read about the special problems that financial institutions face in managing their portfolio risks in the Chapter 7 reading, entitled "The Challenges of Risk Management in Diversified Financial Companies," by Christine Cumming and Beverly Hirtle of the Federal Reserve Bank of New York. **http://moneyxtra. swcollege.com**

3. What is the distinction between idiosyncratic risk and market risk?
Idiosyncratic risk is risk that is specific to a financial instrument. Market risk, in contrast, is risk that stems from general factors affecting the returns of all financial instruments. Holding a diversified portfolio of financial instruments with counterbalancing idiosyncratic risk characteristics reduces the overall portfolio risk because their returns tend to move in offsetting directions.

Portfolio Diversification within and across Borders

Market risk is not equal across financial instruments. The returns from holding some financial instruments may be more susceptible to nondiversifiable market risk than are the returns of other instruments. A natural question then is how a saver can identify financial instruments with mostly idiosyncratic risks that can be offset via portfolio diversification.

What Happens When... **Banking Opposites Attract?**

In 2004, two unlikely banking partners-to-be, New York–based J.P. Morgan Chase and Chicago-based Bank One, surprised many people by announcing that they had decided to combine their operations. This $60 billion banking merger entailed a union of two companies that seemed to have very little in common. In contrast to J.P. Morgan Chase's relatively small network of branches limited mainly to New York and parts of Texas, Bank One possessed a sprawling system of branch banks stretching from West Virginia to Oregon. J.P. Morgan Chase's lending expertise was focused on large corporate accounts, while Bank One held a large portfolio of mortgage, consumer, and credit-card loans. After the merger was announced, however, the banks' share prices experienced big jumps, indicating that stockholders anticipated that the merger would create significant diversification benefits.

FOR CRITICAL ANALYSIS: Why do you suppose that many banks have recently sought to establish footholds in businesses tangentially related to banking, such as the provision of realtor services?

Beta: A measure of the sensitivity of a financial instrument's expected return to changes in the value of all financial instruments in a market portfolio; calculated as the percentage change in the value of a financial instrument resulting from a 1 percent change in the value of all financial instruments in the portfolio.

MONEYXTRA!
Online Case Study

For a concrete application of the concepts of market risk and idiosyncratic risk, go to the Chapter 7 Case Study, entitled "Portfolio Diversification via Bank Branching or a Merger?" **http://moneyxtra.swcollege.com**

IDENTIFYING ASSETS WITH DIVERSIFIABLE RISKS   Savers will shy away from a financial instrument whose risk stems primarily from market risk, because they cannot mitigate that risk through diversification. Financial economists try to judge a financial instrument's market risk via a measure called **beta** (the Greek symbol ß), which is the sensitivity of the financial instrument's expected return to changes in the complete set of financial instruments. For instance, the beta value for a share of stock in an e-money security company measures the percentage increase in the value of the stock generated by a 1 percent rise in the value of all shares in the stock market as a whole. For example, if a 1 percent increase in the value of all shares traded in the stock market is accompanied by a 2 percent rise in the value of the shares of the e-money security company, then the value of beta for that company's stock is equal to 2. If the result is only a 1 percent rise in the value of the company's shares, then the value of beta is equal to 1, indicating half as much systematic risk as a beta of 2.

Savers prefer financial instruments with lower values of beta, because these instruments possess more *diversifiable* risk that the savers can reduce by holding diversified portfolios. Thus, if confronted with a choice between two financial instruments with equal expected returns, liquidity, and information costs, savers will choose the financial instrument with the lower beta value.

INTERNATIONAL PORTFOLIO DIVERSIFICATION   Although financial instruments from other nations may be held for various reasons including the pursuit of arbitrage profits, a fundamental rationale for holding internationally issued financial instruments is *international portfolio diversification*. Recall that market risk arises from common factors influencing the returns of financial instruments in a saver's portfolio. A key common factor is overall economic performance. A nationwide U.S. recession, for instance, tends to reduce the returns of most U.S. financial instruments, which makes aggregate economic performance an important source of market risk for a U.S. saver's portfolio.

In today's more financially integrated world, however, savers can regard even the risk of an overall U.S. economic downturn as somewhat diversifiable. Certainly, the United States is the world's largest economy, so a U.S. recession potentially can slow the economic growth rates of its major world trading partners. Nevertheless, it is not uncommon for an Asian economic expansion to take place in the midst of a U.S. recession, as occurred in the early 1990s. Indeed, U.S. savers who held financial instruments issued by companies and governments of many Asian nations during the early 1990s earned less volatile overall portfolio returns than U.S. savers who held only U.S. financial instruments. Likewise, Asian savers who held European and U.S. financial instruments in the later 1990s insulated themselves somewhat against the considerable variability of returns on Asian financial instruments during the sharp Asian downturn during this period.

Thus, in a truly integrated world financial system, the scope for market risk would be limited to broad global risk factors. Savers in an integrated system could regard even national economic variability as a form of idiosyncratic risk. Thus, savers around the globe can increasingly diversify against country-specific risks.

MONEYXTRA!
Economic Applications

Are stock returns in different countries diverging or converging? For links to the stock markets of various nations, go to Corporate Finance Online.
http://moneyxtra. swcollege.com

> **4. How does holding international financial instruments make a portfolio more diversified?** If national financial markets were completely unrelated, then a key source of nondiversifiable market risk would be national economic factors that influence financial instrument returns. If savers can purchase financial instruments of other nations, however, then national sources of risk become more idiosyncratic and, consequently, diversifiable. In a completely integrated world financial system, market risk would arise only from common global factors that affect the returns of all financial instruments.

Efficient Markets

You learned in Chapter 4 that bond prices are inversely related to interest rates. To demonstrate this inverse relationship, we considered perpetual bonds that pay an infinite stream of coupon returns. To calculate the price that someone would be willing to pay for such a bond, we summed up the discounted present value of the stream of coupon returns. To compute the discounted present value of each year's coupon return, we used the current market interest rate. But what if the market interest rate might vary from year to year? Then the price of the bond would actually equal the *expected* discounted present value of the stream of coupon returns, based on people's *expectations* of future market interest rates.

This reasoning forms the basis for the **efficient-markets hypothesis,** which states that prices of financial assets should reflect all available information, including traders' understanding of how financial markets determine asset prices. As applied to the perpetual bond we studied in Chapter 4, the theory indicates that the current price of a bond should be equal to traders' forecast of the discounted value of the sum of coupon returns yielded by the bond.

More generally, the efficient-markets theory says that the price of *any* asset should reflect traders' forecast of the asset's returns. Consequently, the market price of any financial instrument, whether it is a share of stock, a corporate bond, or a derivative security, should reflect a recognition of all available information by those who trade the instrument. If the market price of the financial instrument were to fail to reflect all such information, that would imply that the market for that instrument functions inefficiently, because traders could earn higher returns if they accounted for the unused information.

The efficient-markets hypothesis has three key implications. First, it indicates that there should be a definite relationship between the market price or the return on a financial instrument and traders' expectation of the market price or return. Second, it implies that some factors are likely to cause greater movements in prices or returns than others. Finally, the hypothesis has an important prediction about efforts by traders to earn higher-than-average rates of return.

Efficient-markets hypothesis: A theory that states that equilibrium prices of and returns on financial instruments should reflect all past and current information plus traders' understanding of how market prices and returns are determined.

The Expected Price of a Financial Instrument

The efficient-markets hypothesis implies that a person's best guess of the price of an asset should take into account everything that people know about factors that influence the asset's price.

INDIVIDUAL FORECASTS AND AVERAGE PRICES OF FINANCIAL INSTRU-MENTS   The factors that determine the price of a financial instrument are all those that traders know will affect the demand for and supply of that instrument. They likely will include such factors as the wealth and income levels of all traders, changes in the riskiness, liquidity, and tax treatment of the instrument, and so on. Of course, those who buy and sell financial instruments cannot perfectly predict future values of all these factors.

Nevertheless, to make the best decisions about the quantities of a financial instrument to buy or sell, each trader must form his or her own best estimates of these factors. This allows each trader to make his or her own *individual forecast* of the market price of a financial instrument. Let's call this individual price forecast P^f. This is the individual forecast of the market price of the financial instrument based on a typical trader's information about current and past market prices and understanding of how the market determines the instrument's price.

Now let's think about the average, or *mean,* market price of the instrument, which is also the *expected* market price, denoted P^e. This is the *true* average price of the financial instrument, taking into account the way that random factors can influence the market demand for and market supply of the instrument. The behavior of these random factors depends on the true *distributions of probabilities* for what these factors will turn out to be in the future. Because the average market price P^e reflects these distributions of probabilities for the market as a whole, economists call the true average price the *market expectation* of the financial instrument's price.

Under the efficient-markets hypothesis, each trader does her or his best to form an individual forecast of the market price, P^f, taking into account all relevant information. In turn, "all relevant information" includes the factors that ultimately affect the market price, *including* the scope for random factors to affect the market demand for and market supply of the financial instrument. This means that the forecast of any particular trader should typically be as good, on average, as the market price expectation, P^e. If an individual trader's forecast of the market price were consistently worse than the true average price, then the trader would seek better information and improve her or his forecasting performance.

Hence, when all traders form their individual forecasts in this way, their forecasts typically will correspond to the average market price. That is, it will be true that $P^f = P^e$. The best individual forecast will equal the expected, or average, market price of the financial asset.

ACTUAL AND FORECAST PRICES OF FINANCIAL INSTRUMENTS   Of course, it is a rare event for any forecast to be exactly on the mark. Thus, the *actual* price of a financial instrument, denoted P, usually will reflect random factors that cause market demand and supply to change in ways that traders could not have completely anticipated in advance. Thus, the market price will turn out to equal its average price, P^e, plus an unpredictable random component, which we shall call ϵ. That is, the market price is equal to

$$P = P^e + \epsilon.$$

Thus, the difference between the actual market price of a financial instrument and its average value, $P - P^e$, arises from the unpredictable random component, ϵ, which in turn stems from random factors influencing the demand for and supply of the financial instrument.

MONEYXTRA!
Economic Applications

How does market efficiency create an environment for stock markets to thrive? Find out via Corporate Finance Online.
http://moneyxtra. swcollege.com

As noted above, if individuals use all available information and their understanding of how financial instruments' prices are determined, their forecast of a financial instrument's price will equal the market expectation of the price, or the average price, so that $P^f = P^e$. This means that another way to express the true market price of a financial instrument is

$$P = P^f + \epsilon.$$

Thus, the market price is equal to the typical *trader's* price forecast plus an unpredictable random element that the trader lacks information to forecast.

Implications for Variations in Financial Instrument Prices

The final expression for a financial instrument's price under the efficient-markets hypothesis is very simple, but it has two important implications. The first is that the market price of a financial instrument reflects traders' best forecasts of the instrument's price given the information available to them. In other words, the actual market price can differ from a typical trader's forecast only because of factors that traders cannot systematically predict.

Thus, the efficient-markets hypothesis indicates that there are two reasons that prices of financial instruments might change. One is that unpredictable, random events can occur. These can cause the demand for or supply of financial instruments to vary unexpectedly, inducing an unanticipated change in the price.

Such unanticipated price variations are likely to be short term in nature, however. The reason is that if they resulted from factors that caused *persistent* changes in the demand for or supply of financial instruments, traders would be able to forecast these factors. Thus, another way that financial instrument prices can change is because of *predictable* changes in the underlying demand for and supply of the instruments. These predictable factors, which financial economists often call the *fundamental* determinants of the market price, or simply the *fundamentals,* are the factors that traders incorporate into their individual forecasts of the market price, P^f. Fundamental, predictable determinants of the market price also determine the average price, P^e.

In the absence of short-term, unpredictable variations in the price of a financial instrument—that is, if ϵ has a value of zero—the price of a financial instrument will vary only because of variations in the fundamentals, so that $P = P^e = P^f$. In an efficient market, the true market price will equal the expected market price that people can forecast given the information available to them. If this condition did not hold, then traders would fail to take into account all available information about the fundamental determinants of variations in the market prices of financial instruments. As a result, they would earn lower returns than they would earn if they used all information in their possession.

Can People Beat the Market?

Recognition that failure to use all available information about factors that cause market prices to vary would result in lower returns than traders could otherwise earn leads to another key implication of the efficient-markets hypothesis:

> **In an efficient financial market, there should be no unexploited opportunities for traders to earn higher returns.**

If such opportunities existed, then a number of traders would seek to profit from buying or selling greater quantities of a given financial instrument. This would cause the market price of the instrument to change.

What direction would the instrument's price move? The answer is that it would adjust to its efficient-market price, which would reflect the forecasts of individual traders. Market expectations would induce trading that would yield this efficient-market price.

Does this mean that no trader could ever earn profits from trading bonds? The answer clearly must be no—otherwise people would not earn their livelihoods by speculating in financial markets. Nevertheless, the efficient-markets hypothesis does indicate that speculators should not be able to earn profits from taking advantage of unused information for very long. Any unexploited information will be quickly recognized by a sufficient number of traders that market prices and returns will adjust quickly. Profits from such trades may be significant, but they will also be fleeting.

According to the efficient-markets hypothesis, therefore, people cannot "beat the market." They cannot consistently earn above-average returns from holding either stocks or bonds issued by companies or governments, either domestically or internationally.

---

5. How are the prices of financial instruments determined in efficient markets? According to the efficient-markets hypothesis, the market price of a financial asset should reflect all available information in that market. This is so because the demand for and supply of an asset, such as a bond, will take into account expectations of future prices of the asset that traders form in light of all information in their possession. The efficient-markets hypothesis implies that individual forecasts of the market price of a financial instrument should be the same as the average price of the instrument, because otherwise individual traders would not efficiently use all information in their possession. Furthermore, the actual market price of an instrument will equal its average price plus an unpredictable component, which will be the same as a typical trader's individual forecast of the market price plus the unpredictable component of the price. This means that on average no individual trader should be able to do a better job of predicting an instrument's actual price than any other trader. Thus, in an efficient market no single trader should systematically be able to earn higher returns than other traders.

Chapter Summary

1. Financial Portfolios: A financial portfolio is the complete group of financial instruments that an individual holds at a point in time. These holdings constitute the individual's financial wealth, which the individual can increase by allocating saving to purchases of additional financial instruments.

2. The Key Determinants of Portfolio Choice: One key factor that influences portfolio decisions of savers is their wealth. Another is the expected return from holding the instrument. A third is the riskiness of the instrument's return, and a fourth is the market liquidity of the instrument. Finally, the costs of acquiring information influence

savers' choices of financial instruments to hold in their portfolios.

3. The Distinction between Idiosyncratic Risk and Market Risk: Idiosyncratic risk is risk that is specific to a given financial instrument, whereas market risk arises from factors that influence the returns of all financial instruments. A saver can reduce the overall riskiness of a portfolio by holding a diversified portfolio of instruments with offsetting idiosyncratic risk characteristics, so that their returns tend to move in opposite directions.

4. How Holding International Financial Instruments Makes a Portfolio More Diversified: If international financial markets were completely separate, then a key source of nondiversifiable market risk would be national economic factors that influence financial instrument returns. If savers can purchase financial instruments of other nations, however, then national sources of risk become more idiosyncratic and, consequently, diversifiable. In a completely integrated world financial system, market risk would arise only from common global factors that affect the returns of all financial instruments.

5. Financial Instrument Prices in an Efficient Market: The efficient-markets hypothesis indicates that the market price of a financial asset should reflect all available information in that market. It should also reflect the expectations about the price of the asset on the part of those who wish to buy and sell the asset. Under the efficient-markets hypothesis, the realized market price of a financial instrument will equal its average price plus an unpredictable component. Thus, on average no individual trader should be better able to predict an instrument's actual price than any other trader. It follows that in an efficient market no single trader can systematically earn higher returns than other traders.

Questions and Problems

(Answers to odd-numbered questions and problems may be found on the Web at **http://money.swcollege.com** under "Student Resources.")

1. Suppose that an individual's wealth increases by 2 percent. Listed below are the individual's percentage increases in holdings of certain financial instruments. Calculate this individual's wealth elasticity of demand for each instrument and identify the instrument as either a necessity asset or a luxury asset for this individual.

   a. Treasury bills: +1.4 percent

   b. Treasury bonds: +3.0 percent

   c. Corporate stock: +1.8 percent

2. Even though asset risk and market liquidity are separate determinants of portfolio choice, in actual practice it can sometimes be very difficult to disentangle the separate effects of these factors on household portfolio allocations. Explain why this is so. [Hint: As an example, consider the fact that trading of high-risk, so-called junk bonds dropped off considerably in the late 1990s at the same time that the perceived riskiness of those bonds increased sharply.]

3. Explain why a saver can diversify against idiosyncratic risks. Then explain why market risks are nondiversifiable.

4. In your view, which of the following risks is nondiversifiable in today's financial system? For those that you believe to be diversifiable, give an example of how you might diversify against this risk in your own portfolio (assuming you have the resources to do so).

   a. The risk that a sharp downturn in the wool industry will cause a drop in the share prices of major wool producers.

   b. The risk that a political revolution will topple the leader of an African nation, causing the nation to default on its bonds.

   c. The risk that a sharp rise in world energy prices will cause a global economic downturn.

5. In 1998, the Federal Reserve helped arrange a privately funded bailout of Long-Term Capital Management, a large hedge fund based in Connecticut. Many market participants interpreted this as a signal that the Federal Reserve considered such hedge funds "too big to fail." If you had been considering holding shares in a large hedge fund, how would this action have influenced your decision about whether to hold hedge fund shares instead of alternative financial instruments? Explain your reasoning.

6. Bonds A and B have equal maturities and expected returns, and both have similar daily market trading volumes. Savers have identical information about both bonds. The variance of bond A's return is higher than the variance of the return on bond B. Bond B, however, has a higher beta value than bond A. For a risk-averse saver, is holding one bond preferable to holding the other, if all other factors are the same? Explain.

7. Stock X has a lower risk premium, measured against a risk-free rate, and a lower beta than stock Y. Both have the same expected return, and the costs of acquiring information about the two stocks are not significantly different. Other things also being equal, and assuming that savers are risk-averse, is holding one stock preferable to holding the other? Explain.

8. You have been made chief financial officer for an equities fund that has significant holdings in winter sportswear companies. Provide some suggestions for how the equities fund might diversify its risks by using new funds it has raised to add to its existing stock holdings. Justify your choices.

9. As part of a strategy to diversify internationally, a U.S. money market fund holds a number of stocks and bonds denominated in various other currencies. Periodically, it also adjusts its international asset holdings by purchasing and selling international financial instruments. Discuss the pros and cons of this strategy.

10. Explain the distinction between the fundamental determinants of a financial instrument's price and factors that are not "fundamental" but can still induce short-term price variations.

11. In your view, would the efficient-market hypothesis be valid if illegal insider trading were widespread? Explain.

Before the Test

Test your understanding of the material covered in this chapter by taking the Chapter 7 interactive quiz at **http://money.swcollege.com**.

Online Application

Internet URL: http://cme.com

Title: The Chicago Mercantile Exchange (CME)

Navigation: Begin with the CME home page (**http://cme.com**). Click on "About CME," and then, from the left-hand menu, click on "Sharehold/Member."

Application: Read the discussion, and then answer the following questions:

> **1.** Click on "Membership Prices." What was the last price at which a full CME membership traded? Why would someone be willing to pay that much to have the right to execute a trade on the CME?

2. Based on what you have learned about prices of financial instruments, if you were contemplating allocating some of your wealth to purchasing a CME membership—which you would regard as an asset within your overall portfolio of assets—what factors do you think might determine the price of a membership? [Hint: Imagine holding this membership for a number of years and earning an annual return each year, and then think about how to price the anticipated stream of returns from a CME membership.]

For Group Study and Analysis: Divide into groups, and discuss what factors might cause the price of a CME membership to *vary*. After the class reassembles, discuss the various factors that groups have identified as likely determinants of the riskiness of owning a CME membership.

Selected References and Further Reading

Aitcorbe, Ana, Arthur Kennickell, and Kevin Moore. "Recent Changes in U.S. Family Finances: Evidence from the 1998 and 2001 Survey of Consumer Finances." *Federal Reserve Bulletin* 89 (January 2003): 1–32.

Elton, Edwin, and Martin Gruber. "Modern Portfolio Theory, 1950 to Date." *Journal of Banking and Finance* 21 (December 1997): 1743–1759.

Fama, Eugene. "Multifactor Portfolio Efficiency and Multifactor Asset Pricing." *Journal of Financial and Quantitative Analysis* 31 (1996): 441–465.

Markowitz, Harry. *Portfolio Selection.* New Haven: Yale University Press, 1959.

Sarkar, Asani, and Kai Li. "Should U.S. Investors Hold Foreign Stocks?" Federal Reserve Bank of New York *Current Issues in Economics and Finance* 6 (March 2000).

Szego, Giorgio. *Portfolio Theory with Application to Bank Asset Management.* New York: Academic Press, 1980.

Tracy, Joseph, and Henry Schneider. "Stocks in the Household Portfolio: A Look Back at the 1990s." Federal Reserve Bank of New York *Current Issues in Economics and Finance* 7 (April 2001).

Wei, K. C. John. "An Asset-Pricing Theory Unifying the CAPM and APT." *Journal of Finance* 43 (September 1988): 881–892.

MoneyXtra

Log on to the MoneyXtra Web site now (**http://moneyxtra.swcollege.com**) for additional learning resources such as practice quizzes, case studies, readings, and additional economic applications.

Unit III
Financial Institutions

Contents

Financial Institutions—

An Overview

Fundamental Issues

1. Why do financial intermediaries exist, and what accounts for international financial intermediation?

2. What do securities market institutions do, and how does the government regulate these institutions?

3. What do insurance companies do, and who regulates their activities?

4. How are pension funds structured, and why have they grown?

5. How do mutual funds and hedge funds differ?

6. What financial institutions specialize in lending directly to individuals and businesses?

In Russia, the current male life expectancy of fifty-nine years is lower than the official retirement age of sixty-five, and the average monthly pension payment to a retiree is only $63. Nevertheless, the Russian pension system is in trouble. The problem is that the system, which for years has been operated by the Russian government, is run on a pay-as-you-go basis in which current workers finance payments to retirees. Russia's population has decreased by more than 2 million since 1990, so today there are only about 1.7 workers per retiree, down from about 2.3 workers per retiree just over a decade ago. If the nation's population continues to shrink at this rate, by 2020 each worker will have to provide sufficient funds to cover one retiree's pension.

In an effort to save the nation's pension system, the Russian government has opened it to private pension companies. These companies will provide benefits based solely on accumulated contributions saved by people during their working years. For the next several decades, therefore, Russian retirees will receive pensions split between payouts from the government-operated system and private pension plans. The share of payouts provided privately will steadily increase over time, as the government's pay-as-you-go arrangement becomes a smaller part of the nation's pension system.

By providing a national payment system, the Russian government acted as a *financial intermediary* known as a pension fund. In this chapter, you will learn about the important functions that financial intermediaries perform.

Domestic and International Financial Intermediation

When a saver allocates funds to a company by purchasing a newly issued corporate bond, she effectively lends directly to the company. That is, she takes part in *directly financing* the capital investment that the company wishes to undertake.

But the process of financing business investment is not always so direct. Consider, for instance, a situation in which the saver also holds a long-term time deposit with a bank. The bank can use these funds, together with those of other depositors, to purchase the same company's corporate bonds. In this instance, the saver has *indirectly financed* business capital investment. The bank, in turn, has *intermediated* the financing of the investment.

Figure 8-1 illustrates the distinction between direct and indirect finance. In the case of direct finance, the process does not involve a financial intermediary such as a bank. A saver lends directly to parties who invest. In the case of indirect finance, however, some other institution allocates the funds of savers to those who wish to invest in capital.

This latter process of indirect finance, in which an institution stands between savers and ultimate borrowers, is **financial intermediation.** The institutions that serve as the "middlemen" in this process are *financial intermediaries.* They exist solely to channel the funds of savers to ultimate borrowers. (The extent to which capital investment takes place through financial intermediaries differs considerably across countries; see on the next page the *Global Focus: The Varying Importance of Financial Intermediation across Nations.*)

> **Financial intermediation:** Indirect finance through the services of an institutional "middleman" that channels funds from savers to those who ultimately make capital investments.

Asymmetric Information

Why do many savers choose to hold their funds at a financial intermediary instead of lending them directly? Most economists agree that one key reason is *asymmetric information* in financial markets.

Suppose, for instance, that a resident of Seattle, Washington, has an opportunity to purchase a relatively high-yield municipal bond issued by a town in New Jersey. One reason that the municipal bond may have a relatively high yield is that the town issuing the bond intends to direct the funds it raises to a risky investment project. For instance, the town may be planning to use the funds to build a convention-center hotel and auditorium complex that has uncertain financial prospects. Unless the Seattle resident happens to be an expert on the economics of municipal convention centers, he likely will find it difficult to evaluate the true riskiness of the municipal bond. This makes it hard for him to compare the yield on this bond with yields on alternative financial instruments.

FIGURE 8-1
Indirect Finance through Financial Intermediaries.

Those savers who exchange funds for the financial instruments of companies in financial markets undertake *direct finance* of the capital investments of those companies. Financial intermediaries make *indirect finance* possible by issuing their own financial instruments and using the funds that they obtain from savers to finance capital investments of businesses.

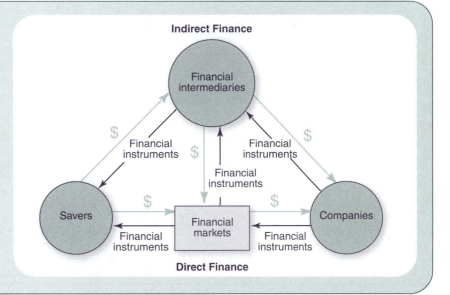

The Varying Importance of Financial Intermediation across Nations

To measure the relative importance of financial intermediaries within a coun-try's overall financial markets, econo-mists usually examine the share of the nation's total financial assets held by financial intermediaries. Figure 8-2 shows that financial intermediaries' shares of assets differ noticeably from country to country. For instance, in Egypt the share of the country's finan-cial assets held by financial intermedi-aries is nearly twice the share of financial assets held by financial inter-mediaries in Singapore.

FOR CRITICAL ANALYSIS: What factors could help to explain why financial intermediation might be relatively more important in one nation than in another?

FIGURE 8-2
Financial Intermediaries' Share of Total Financial Assets in Selected Nations.

The percentage of total financial assets held by financial intermediaries varies considerably across countries.

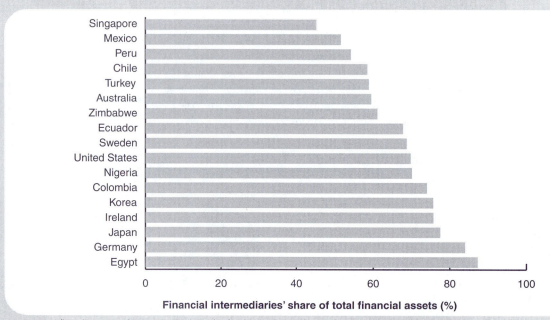

Financial intermediaries' share of total financial assets (%)

SOURCE: Asli Demirguc-Kunt and Ross Levine, "Bank-Based and Market-Based Financial Systems: Cross-Country Comparisons," World Bank and University of Minnesota, 2003.

In contrast, the New Jersey town issuing the municipal bond likely has considerable infor-mation about the prospects for its convention center. On the one hand, the prospects may be very good for its long-term financial success. Perhaps the city has hard evidence that it can expect significant earnings from the project. On the other hand, the program may have been launched primarily for the short-term political gains that the mayor and town council expect to reap from pleasing owners of construction companies and other local businesses. Either way, the town issuing the municipal bond has information about its risk that the Seattle resident does not possess. Whenever one party in a financial transaction has information not possessed by the other party, **asymmetric information** exists.

ADVERSE SELECTION   In the situation just described, the New Jersey town has information that the Seattle resident will not have when contemplating whether to purchase the town's municipal bond. Suppose the town's leaders know at the outset that the long-term prospects for the convention center are poor, but they think voters like the idea. In this circumstance, the town's leaders know that their bond may have *adverse,* or unfavorable, implications for those who purchase it. This aspect of asymmetric information is called **adverse selection;** it refers to the potential for those who desire funds for undeserving projects to be the most likely to wish to borrow funds or to issue debt instruments. Because people such as the Seattle resident know that the adverse-selection problem exists, they may be less willing to lend to or hold debt instruments issued by those seeking to finance otherwise high-quality projects.

MORAL HAZARD   Now suppose that the leaders of the town issuing the municipal bond have every reason to believe the convention center they have planned will be a long-term financial success. After the town sells the bonds, however, an electoral turnover takes place, and the new town leaders double the size of the convention center, almost ensuring that it will fail to be profitable over the long run. This action increases the risk that bondholders will not receive the promised yields on the town's municipal bond. This possibility that a borrower may behave in a way that increases risk after a loan has been made or a debt instrument has been purchased is **moral hazard.** In other words, after a financial transaction has taken place, a borrower may undertake actions that raise the riskiness of the financial instrument that the borrower has already issued, thereby acting "immorally" from the perspective of the lender.

One way for the Seattle resident to deal with the adverse-selection and moral-hazard problems he faces is to make several trips to assess and then to monitor the New Jersey town's convention-center project. By acquiring as much hands-on information as possible, the Seattle bondholder could reduce the informational asymmetry he experiences concerning the municipal bond's prospects. This endeavor would be very costly, however. The Seattle bondholder would have to pay the direct costs of making the trips and would also incur opportunity costs, because all the time he devoted to information collecting could be used in other ways.

Benefits of Financial Intermediation

A fundamental reason for the existence of financial intermediaries is to collect information on behalf of savers so that they will not have to incur these direct and opportunity costs. Financial intermediaries cannot completely eliminate the adverse-selection and moral-hazard problems resulting from asymmetric information. Nevertheless, they can reduce these problems by specializing in gathering information about the likely prospects of financial instruments and monitoring the performance of those who issue such instruments.

Economies of Scale

Another key reason for the existence of financial intermediaries is **economies of scale,** or the reduction in average operating costs that can be achieved as a financial trader's scale of operations increases. Some financial intermediaries assist people in pooling their funds, thereby increasing the amount of funds that are saved. Pooling allows an intermediary to manage a

Asymmetric information: Information possessed by one party to a financial transaction but not by the other party.

Adverse selection: The problem that those who desire to issue financial instruments are most likely to use the funds they receive for unworthy, high-risk projects.

Moral hazard: The possibility that a borrower may engage in more risky behavior after a loan has been made.

MONEYXTRA!
Online Case Study

To test your understanding of asymmetric-information concepts, contemplate the problems that a government faces when it acts as a financial intermediary by providing deposit insurance to banks. Go to the Chapter 8 Case Study, entitled "Asymmetric Information and Deposit Insurance." **http://moneyxtra. swcollege.com**

Economies of scale: The reduction in the average cost of fund management that can be achieved by pooling savings together and spreading management costs across many people.

larger amount of funds, thereby reducing average fund management costs below those that people would incur if they managed their savings individually. If intermediaries can manage funds for many savers at a lower average cost than all the savers would face if they managed their funds alone, then financial economies of scale exist. Several financial institutions, such as mutual funds and pension funds, owe their existence in large part to their ability to realize such cost reductions on behalf of individual savers.

Financial Intermediation across National Boundaries

Instead of buying a bond issued by a New Jersey municipality, the Seattle resident in our example might contemplate purchasing a bond issued by a municipality located across the border in Canada. The U.S. saver might wish to hold bonds issued by a Canadian city for several reasons. One reason might be to earn an anticipated higher return.

Another reason might be to avoid risks specific to the United States by allocating a portion of savings to Canadian municipal bonds. More broadly, as you learned in Chapter 7, the saver's goal might be to achieve overall risk reductions via international financial diversification, or holding bonds issued in various nations and thereby spreading portfolio risks across both U.S.-issued *and* foreign-issued financial instruments.

INTERNATIONAL FINANCIAL INTERMEDIATION   Rather than buying U.S. and Canadian municipal bonds, our Seattle resident might decide to allocate part of his savings to a global bond mutual fund, thereby becoming a participant in the process of *international financial intermediation.* This is the indirect finance of capital investment across national borders by financial intermediaries such as banks, investment companies, and pension funds.

The rationales for international financial intermediation are the same as for domestic intermediation. For the Seattle-based U.S. saver, for example, evaluating the riskiness of Canadian bonds presents asymmetric-information problems that are probably at least as severe as those associated with assessing the riskiness of U.S. bonds. By allocating a portion of his total savings to a global bond mutual fund operated, say, by an investment company, the saver assigns that company the task of judging and tracking the prospects and performances of bond issuers around the world. In exchange for this service, the saver pays the investment company management fees.

ECONOMIES OF SCALE AND GLOBAL FINANCIAL INTERMEDIATION   The Eurocurrency markets are at the center of international financial intermediation. Very few nations' capital investment projects are purely domestically financed. Even in the United States, non-U.S. intermediaries finance a portion of investment. Today, the largest U.S.-based multinational corporations on average have accounts with more foreign banking institutions than with U.S. banks.

Furthermore, as Table 8-1 indicates, the world's largest banking institutions are not necessarily located in the United States. Most of the largest institutions, sometimes called *megabanks,* are based in Europe and Japan. These megabanks take in deposits and lend throughout the world. They report their profits and pay taxes in their home nations, but otherwise they are truly international banking institutions.

One possible reason that megabanks exist is economies of scale. Some economists argue that a particular form of economies of scale may help explain the megabank phenomenon: *economies of scale in information processing.* According to these economists, because many companies now have operations that span the globe, banking institutions must also have world-

Table 8-1 The World's Largest Banking Institutions

Bank	Country	Assets ($ Billions)
Mizuho Financial Group	Japan	$1,285
Citigroup, Inc.	United States	1,264
UBS AG	Switzerland	1,121
Credit Agricole Groups	France	1,105
HSBC Holdings PLC	United Kingdom	1,034
Deutsche Bank	Germany	1,015
BNP Paribas Group	France	989
Mitsubishi Tokyo Financial Group	Japan	975
Sumitomo Mitsui Bank	Japan	950
Royal Bank of Scotland	Scotland	806

SOURCE: *The Banker,* July 2004.

wide offices to assess and monitor the creditworthiness of these companies. Having an international presence, they argue, allows banking institutions to address asymmetric-information problems at lower average cost than they could if they were purely domestic intermediaries. Thus, this explanation of the megabank phenomenon hinges on the existence of *both* asymmetric information *and* economies of scale in international intermediation operations.

> **1. Why do financial intermediaries exist, and what accounts for international financial intermediation?** A key reason that financial intermediaries exist is to address problems arising from asymmetric information. One such problem is adverse selection, or the potential for the least creditworthy borrowers to be the most likely to seek to issue financial instruments. Another is moral hazard, or the possibility that an initially creditworthy borrower may undertake actions that reduce its creditworthiness after receiving funds from a lender. A further reason for the existence of financial intermediaries is the existence of economies of scale, or the ability to spread costs of managing funds across large numbers of savers. A potential justification for international financial intermediation by global banking enterprises is that they may experience economies of scale in information processing by spreading their credit evaluation and monitoring operations across the world.

Securities Market Institutions

When business firms issue new shares of stock or offer to sell new bonds, these firms and those who contemplate buying their securities face two asymmetric-information problems. One stems from adverse selection. Some firms that issue new securities may have an incentive to do so because they are strapped for cash and teetering on the edge of financial disaster. Those considering buying new stock or bonds recognize this possibility and need to be able to identify creditworthy firms. The firms themselves recognize this and need a way to signal their creditworthiness to potential purchasers of their securities. Securities market institutions such as investment banks and securities brokers and dealers help provide this signal by intermediating firms' securities.

Securities market institutions also assist in minimizing moral-hazard problems that arise when firms that are successful in raising funds via security issues might have an incentive to misuse those funds. By monitoring the performances of issuing firms, these institutions assure stock- and bondholders that the firms maintain their creditworthiness. This ensures that the shares of stock or the bonds of issuing firms remain liquid instruments that retain the risk characteristics that they possessed when the firms first issued them.

Investment Banks

Investment banks are financial institutions that serve as intermediaries between businesses that issue stocks and bonds and those that purchase those securities. Typically, investment banks specialize in **securities underwriting,** which means that they guarantee that the issuing firm will receive a specified minimum price per share of stock or per bond.

Under **firm commitment underwriting,** an investment bank actually purchases the new securities offered by a business and then distributes them to dealers and other buyers. The investment bank seeks to profit from the spread between the price it pays the issuing firm and the actual price that others pay for the securities. In contrast, under **standby commitment underwriting** an investment bank earns commissions for helping the issuing firm sell its securities and agrees only to purchase any securities that remain unsold after the initial sale. It then seeks to find buyers for those remaining securities.

Another possible arrangement is for the investment bank to act solely as an *agent* for the issuing firm. The firm then pays the investment bank commissions for its marketing services. Under such an arrangement, which is called a **best efforts deal,** the investment bank usually has an option to buy a portion of the issuing firm's securities, but it is not obligated to exercise that option. Best efforts deals were much more common in the nineteenth and early twentieth centuries than they have been in recent decades. Nowadays these arrangements tend to arise when the securities of the issuing firms are regarded as highly risky instruments. (Some have suggested that investment banking might become an anachronism in the age of Internet auctions, but Google's recent experience failed to support that view; see the *Cyber Focus: Google's Untraditional Initial Public Offering.*)

Securities Brokers and Dealers

Although some financial firms are either brokers or dealers, in many cases a firm that acts as a broker is also a dealer. As discussed in Chapter 3, a *broker* specializes in matching buyers and sellers in secondary financial markets. Brokers receive commissions and fees as payment for their services. A *dealer,* in contrast, sells securities from its own portfolio and seeks to profit by buying low and selling high. *Broker-dealers* engage in both businesses. Most major Wall Street brokerage firms are broker-dealers, trading both on behalf of customers and on their own accounts.

TYPES OF BROKERS   When any broker makes securities trades on a customer's behalf, it acts as the customer's *agent.* This means that the broker makes the trade in place of the customer but must act as the customer wishes. A *full-service broker* offers a range of other financial services, including consultations about what financial instruments to buy or sell and other financial planning advice. The only service that a *discount broker* offers is making securities trades for clients.

Securities underwriting: A guarantee by an investment bank that a firm that issues new stocks or bonds will receive a specified minimum price per share of stock or per bond.

Firm commitment underwriting: An investment banking arrangement in which the investment bank purchases and distributes to dealers and other purchasers all securities offered by a business.

Standby commitment underwriting: An investment banking arrangement in which the investment bank earns commissions for helping the issuing firm sell its securities under the guarantee that the investment bank will purchase for resale any initially unsold securities.

Best efforts deal: An investment banking arrangement in which the investment bank has an option to buy a portion of the issuing firm's securities but is not required to do so.

MONEYXTRA!
Economic Applications
What are useful links to major securities market and banking institutions? Take a look at FinanceLinks Online. **http:// moneyxtra.swcollege.com**

CYBER
Focus

Google's Untraditional Initial Public Offering

If Google, the Internet search engine company, had conducted a traditional initial public offering (IPO) of ownership shares, it would have hired a group of investment banks to oversee the process. These banks would have choreographed a series of high-profile stories about the IPO in top financial media outlets and released a formal document describing Google's business. To start the IPO rolling, the banks would have bought a portion of the company's shares. They would have established an initial share price anticipated to be

somewhat below the market price at which shares would actually trade following the IPO. Hopes of profiting from a post-IPO price increase would have induced more investors to consider purchasing the stock—and would have generated profits for the investment banks.

Instead, Google decided to offer its shares in an auction conducted partly on the Web and intended to ensure sales at the highest possible price. The company initially determined that this price would be in a range of $108 to $135 per share. Google's owners stated in a magazine interview that at a price within this range, they expected to sell 25 million shares and obtain between $2.7 billion and $3.4 billion. From this point onward, the IPO started going

downhill for Google. First, the Securities and Exchange Commission expressed concerns that the magazine interview might be interpreted as an illegal solicitation. Furthermore, many investors decided that they would not participate in the auction if the price was likely to be above $100. In the end, Google lowered its asking price to $85 per share and raised $1.7 billion. Investment bankers also breathed a sigh of relief that Google's unconventional IPO had faltered, thereby demonstrating the value of the IPO services they traditionally provide.

FOR CRITICAL ANALYSIS: Why might the experience of investment bankers have value to a firm considering an IPO?

One type of discount broker is a *share broker,* which bases its commission charges on the volume of shares that it trades on a customer's behalf. In contrast, a *value broker* charges commissions that are a percentage of the dollar value of each transaction. For those who wish to trade sizable volumes of securities, a share broker's services entail lower cost. Those who typically trade small numbers of shares gain from using the services of a value broker.

As we noted in Chapter 3, Internet brokers have made major inroads in the brokerage business. This has increased competition among both new Internet brokers and more established brokerage firms that have also sought to stake a claim to the growing Internet stock trading. Many brokers have responded by setting fixed fees for customers who desire only that brokers execute trades on their behalf. Commission charges increasingly apply only to traditional broker-client relationships in which the broker also offers stock information and trading advice to a client.

OVER-THE-COUNTER (OTC) BROKER-DEALERS Another type of broker, an **over-the-counter (OTC) broker-dealer,** specializes in trading shares of stock that are not listed on organized stock exchanges. Such OTC stocks are traded in decentralized markets linking OTC broker-dealers. As noted earlier, OTC stocks typically are those of smaller companies that do not meet listing requirements for the New York Stock Exchange.

Although OTC stock trading falls outside the rules of the centralized exchanges, it still must meet standards set by the *National Association of Securities Dealers (NASD).* This self-regulating group of OTC broker-dealers also operates the *NASD Automated Quotation (Nasdaq)* system. As noted in Chapter 3, Nasdaq began as a national market system of computer and

Over-the-counter (OTC) broker-dealer: A broker-dealer that trades shares of stock that are not listed on organized stock exchanges.

telephone links between OTC broker-dealers. Today, it also connects traditional stock exchanges such as the American Stock Exchange, which merged with Nasdaq in 1998.

SPECIALISTS Some broker-dealers perform special roles in securities markets. These **specialists** are members of stock exchanges that are responsible for preventing wide swings in stock prices. They do this by adding to or reducing their own holdings of stock to counteract major changes in demand or supply conditions.

Specialists are responsible for executing specific trades called **limit orders.** These are instructions from other stock exchange members to execute trades when stock prices reach certain levels. For instance, when a share price is equal to $25, a specialist might receive a limit order to sell a given amount of shares on the ordering broker's behalf if the share price slips to $23. Only if the share price reaches $23 would the specialist make the trade. But if the share price does hit $23, the specialist is bound by the rules of the exchange to do so. In return for this service, the specialist receives a commission from the ordering broker.

As brokers place limit orders, specialists list them in ledgers called *specialist's books.* A given specialist's ledger details the specialist's own holdings of securities and the sequence of limit orders received from other brokers. If the specialist's book contains an unexecuted limit order, then the specialist cannot trade securities on its own account at the limit order price *until* it executes the limit order first. From time to time this restriction can force the specialist to forgo earnings. The limit order commissions compensate the specialist for this sacrifice.

Regulation of Securities Market Institutions

All securities market institutions must meet regulations established by the **Securities and Exchange Commission (SEC).** Congress created the SEC in the *Securities Exchange Act of 1934.* The SEC is composed of five commissioners appointed by the president of the United States on a rotating basis to five-year terms. The president names one of these individuals as chair of the SEC.

The SEC's mandate is to enforce both the 1934 act and the *Securities Act of 1933.* The 1933 act requires that all securities for sale be registered and that detailed information about each security be disclosed in a **prospectus,** or formal written offer to sell securities. The 1934 act requires securities market institutions to refrain from manipulating stock and bond prices. In light of these requirements, the SEC establishes and enforces a number of rules that govern securities trading. It also oversees and approves rules established by groups such as the NASD.

> **2. What do securities market institutions do, and how does the government regulate these institutions?** Investment banks underwrite and market new stock and bonds that corporations issue. Brokers trade securities on behalf of clients, and dealers trade on their own accounts. The Securities and Exchange Commission regulates the activities of these firms.

Insurance Institutions

Insurance companies are financial institutions that specialize in trying to limit the adverse-selection and moral-hazard problems unique to efforts to insure against possible future risks of loss. They issue *policies,* which are promises to reimburse the holder for damages suffered as the result of a

---

Specialists: Stock exchange members that are charged with trading on their own accounts to prevent dramatic movements in stock prices.

Limit orders: Instructions from other stock exchange members to specialists to execute stock trades at specific prices.

Securities and Exchange Commission (SEC): A group of five presidentially appointed members whose mandate is to enforce rules governing securities trading.

Prospectus: A formal written offer to sell securities.

On the Web
What has been the recent financial performance of property-casualty insurers? Find out by visiting the Insurance Information Institute at **http://www.iii.org**.

"bad" event, such as an auto accident. Certainly, individuals could insure others. But such direct insurance usually is limited to informal agreements. For instance, parents often stand ready to lend financial assistance to their young-adult children who experience "bad" events, so in a sense they offer insurance. But parents also have a lot of information about their children's behavior that others do not have. Most of us, therefore, ultimately turn to insurance companies that specialize in dealing with the asymmetric-information problems associated with insuring risks.

There are two basic kinds of insurance companies. *Life insurance companies* charge premiums for policies that insure people against the financial consequences associated with death. They also offer specialized policies called **annuities,** which are financial instruments that guarantee the holder fixed or variable payments at some future date. *Property and casualty insurers* insure risks relating to property damage and liabilities arising from injuries or deaths caused by accidents or adverse natural events. Property and casualty insurance companies offer policies that insure individuals and businesses against possible property damages or other financial losses resulting from injuries or deaths sustained as a result of accidents, adverse weather, earthquakes, and the like.

Annuities: Financial instruments that guarantee the holder fixed or variable payments at some future date.

Dealing with Asymmetric-Information Problems in Insurance

Most insurance policies have a number of common features. Companies design these features to reduce the extent of the problems that they face in light of asymmetric information. After all, those who apply for insurance know much more about their risks of loss than do the insurance companies, and those who receive insurance can do the most to limit the risks of such losses.

LIMITING ADVERSE SELECTION   One way that insurance companies seek to reduce the adverse-selection problem is by restricting the availability of insurance. Insurance companies will not sell every available policy to every individual. For instance, suppose that an individual has a spouse and four children but no life insurance. This person then learns of impending death from an illness for which there is no cure. If the individual cares about the spouse and children, then the person has every incentive after learning of the illness to purchase a life insurance policy. If the insurer would permit a person in such a situation to buy such a policy, then the insurer also would be taking on a 100 percent probability of a claim that would amount to more than the premiums it would collect from that individual. No insurance company could stay in business for very long if it made its policies available to all who might like to buy them.

Insurers also deal with the adverse-selection problem by limiting how much insurance any one individual or firm can buy. To reduce their exposure to losses from policies taken out by applicants who may know that they have life-shortening conditions, insurers typically place limits on the dollar amount of coverage that individuals may purchase. In addition, insurance companies typically require policyholders who purchase large life insurance policies or who decide to increase their current policy coverages significantly to undergo blood tests or other physical examinations, such as a heart treadmill stress test.

LIMITING MORAL HAZARD IN INSURANCE   Another feature of insurance policies is that they contain provisions that restrict the behavior of policyholders. These provisions are intended to reduce the extent of the moral-hazard problem that insurers also face.

As noted above, limiting the amount of insurance can counter the adverse-selection problem. It can also reduce the extent of some moral-hazard problems. For example, if a company that operates agricultural grain elevators could insure them for more than they are worth, then it would have little incentive to operate the elevators safely by keeping flammable liquids or spark-producing equipment away from them. Consequently, the risk of an explosion would increase—and so would the insurer's chances of making payments on losses. Hence, insurers typically limit policy coverages to the maximum possible losses that policyholders could incur.

One key weapon against moral-hazard problems is an insurance company's ability to cancel insurance because of "bad behavior" by a policyholder. Most insurance policies include a clause threatening cancellation if the policyholder develops a record of reckless behavior after the policy has been issued.

Insurance companies also combat the moral-hazard problem by offering policies with *deductible* and *coinsurance* features. A **deductible** is a fixed amount of a loss that a policyholder must pay before the insurance company must provide promised payments. For example, if a homeowner's child throws a rock through a $400 picture window in the insured house and the homeowner's policy has a $200 deductible against such a loss, then the homeowner is required to pay $200 of the cost of replacing the window. The insurance company pays the remaining $200. The presence of the deductible feature gives the homeowner an incentive to lecture the child about throwing rocks, thereby reducing the risk that the homeowner and the insurer will incur such a loss. This feature of the policy also gives the homeowner a reason to monitor the child's behavior.

Coinsurance is a feature that requires the policyholder to pay a fixed percentage of any loss above the specified deductible. In the example of the broken picture window, a policy with a coinsurance feature might require that the policyholder pay 10 percent of the loss over the $200 deductible. In this case, the homeowner's total loss would be $220—the $200 deductible plus 10 percent of the additional $200 loss ($20). This coinsurance feature gives the homeowner an added incentive to keep rocks from flying from the child's hands.

DETERMINING POLICY PREMIUMS   The essential principle of insurance is the pooling of risks of loss that might be incurred by individual members of a large group. Even though all members of the group might experience a loss at any time, only a small number will actually incur a loss. For example, suppose that over any one-year period, on average, two of every 10,000 retail businesses experience a major fire that destroys a retail outlet. The risk of fire damage, however, may be distributed across all 10,000 businesses, so that each pays 1/10,000 of the annual loss expected to be incurred by two of them. When the actual losses occur, sufficient funds will be on hand to reimburse the two businesses that, on average, experience fires.

Insurance companies use this type of statistical approach to computing policy premiums. They rely on **actuaries,** who specialize in using statistical and mathematical principles to calculate premiums sufficient to cover expected losses to policyholders. The premiums that are just sufficient to cover expected insured losses are called *actuarially fair* insurance premiums. Actuaries also assist in estimating the value of the insurance company, which is never known for certain because the company's losses—and consequently its liabilities—are subject to risk.

Premiums on insurance policies actually are somewhat higher than the actuarially fair premiums. As with any market price, the market premium for an insurance policy is influenced by revenue and cost conditions faced by insurers. For instance, in times when interest rates are low, insurance premiums tend to rise. The reason is that companies' loss reserves earn interest, so if market rates are low, the companies must bolster reserves and maintain profits by raising premiums.

Life Insurance

Usually, in any given year, about 400 million life insurance policies are in effect in the United States. (Some people carry multiple policies.) Life insurance companies typically classify policies into separate categories. *Ordinary* life policies in amounts of $1,000 or more and *industrial*

Deductible: A fixed amount of an insured loss that a policyholder must pay before the insurer is obliged to make payments.

Coinsurance: An insurance policy feature that requires a policyholder to pay a fixed percentage of a loss above a deductible.

Actuary: An individual who specializes in using mathematical and statistical principles to calculate insurance premiums and to estimate an insurance company's net worth.

Whole life policy: A life insurance policy whose benefits are payable to a beneficiary whenever the insured person's death occurs and that accumulates a cash value that the policyholder may acquire prior to his or her death.

Level premium policy: A whole life insurance policy under which an insurance company charges fixed premium payments throughout the life of the insured individual.

life policies in amounts less than $1,000 cover individuals. *Group* life policies cover a number of people under terms specified by a master contract that applies to all who are covered. Finally, *credit* life policies insure a borrower against loan foreclosure in the event of death before full payment of the loan. Figure 8-3 shows the distribution of these policies.

Most policies that life insurance companies issue guarantee payments to a designated beneficiary, such as a spouse or child, when the insured individual dies. Actuaries determine the actuarially fair premiums for life insurance policies using historical experience on probabilities of death at various ages. Because life expectancies across many policyholders are predictable, life insurance companies have a good idea how many benefits they will need to pay out in future years. Thus, the companies typically feel secure holding relatively illiquid long-term corporate bonds and stocks as sizable components of their portfolio of financial instruments.

WHOLE VERSUS TERM LIFE INSURANCE   There are two basic types of life insurance policies. Under a **whole life policy,** a benefit is payable at the death of the insured, and the policy has an accumulated cash value that the policyholder may acquire before death. Whole life policies come in two forms: a **level premium policy,** in which the insurance company charges fixed premium payments throughout the life of the insured individual, and a **limited payment policy,** in which the insured individual pays premiums only for a fixed number of years and is insured during and after each payment period. Both kinds of whole life policies typically have a *cash surrender value,* meaning that after a specific date the policyholder can exchange the policy for a lump-sum amount. Hence, for some people whole life policies are saving instruments.

The other basic type of life insurance policy is a **term life policy.** Under this kind of policy, an individual is insured only during a limited period that the policy is in effect. Premiums for term life policies depend on the age of the insured person and typically increase each year that the policy renews because as the individual ages, the chance of death increases. Nevertheless, term life policies typically have lower premiums over an average life span than whole life policies. The reason is that a term life policy has no cash surrender value and thus no additional savings component. The premium therefore reflects only the risks that the insurer takes on by providing the policy.

ANNUITIES   Life insurers may guarantee payments to beneficiaries in the form of a lump sum or an annuity, which is a stream of payments over a period or perhaps until the death of the beneficiary. There are two types of annuities. A **fixed annuity** makes payments to the holder in regular installments of constant-dollar amounts beginning at a specific future time. With a **variable annuity,** the payouts that the holder receives depend on the value of the underlying portfolio of assets that the insurance company uses to fund the payouts. (Recently, the Japanese parliament passed a law that prevented widespread failures among the nation's insurance companies but potentially weakened the industry's long-term prospects nonetheless; see on page 172 the *Global Focus: Can the Japanese Life Insurance Industry Be Salvaged?*)

Property-Casualty Insurance

Insurance against property and casualty losses covers a variety of contingencies. Property-casualty companies issue property policies covering losses stemming from accidental or fire damage to autos, buildings, boats, ships, crops, furnaces, factory equipment, and other property. Policies also cover losses resulting from injuries or deaths due to accidents. Businesses cover their employees through policies offered in the form of workers' compensation insurance. Finally, property-casualty companies also offer policies covering liabilities stemming

FIGURE 8-3
The Distribution of Life Insurance Policies.

Ordinary and group insurance policies account for the bulk of life insurance policies in the United States.

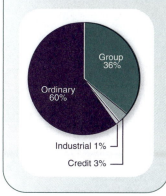

Percentages are rounded to the nearest whole percent.
SOURCE: A. M. Best, 2005.

Limited payment policy: A whole life insurance policy under which an insured individual pays premiums only for a fixed number of years and is insured during and after the payment period.

Term life policy: A life insurance policy under which an individual is insured only during a limited period that the policy is in effect.

Fixed annuity: A financial instrument, typically issued by an insurance company, that pays regular, constant installments to the owner beginning at a specific future date.

Variable annuity: A financial instrument, typically issued by an insurance company, that beginning on a specific future date pays the owner a stream of returns that depends on the value of an underlying portfolio of assets.

GLOBAL
Focus

Can the Japanese Life Insurance Industry Be Salvaged?

With policies outstanding valued at more than $10.5 trillion, Japan's insurance industry is the world's second largest, behind only the U.S. industry. Since the early 1990s, Japanese insurers have seen the returns on their portfolios of stocks and bonds deteriorate as a result of declining stock prices and market bond yields that have hovered close to 0 percent. In recent years, insurance companies have paid out at least $5 billion more per year to policyholders than the companies earned in revenues. Several major insurers have failed in the past few years, and many others have contemplated declaring bankruptcy. To stave off massive insurance failures, the Japanese parliament has made it legal for troubled insurers to break whole life and annuity contracts offering guaranteed annual rates of return to policyholders.

Naturally, this measure has kept many insurers in business at the expense of existing policyholders. To the longer-term detriment of the industry, however, it has also induced younger people to avoid life insurance policies and annuities in favor of alternative means of saving. Many Japanese insurers now worry that their companies will eventually die off along with their aging policyholders.

FOR CRITICAL ANALYSIS: How did Japan's legal change affect the perceived value of whole life policies and annuities to potential new customers of insurance companies?

FIGURE 8-4
The Distribution of Property-Casualty Premiums by Line of Business.

Premiums for policies covering autos account for nearly half of the total premium volumes of property-casualty insurers.

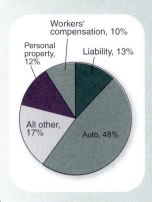

Percentages are rounded to the nearest whole percent.

SOURCE: Insurance Information Institute, 2005.

from automobile accidents, poorly designed or produced products, or medical malpractice. Figure 8-4 shows the percentage of premiums by line of business for all property-casualty insurance companies.

Because property-casualty companies insure against such a variety of types of losses, actuaries for these companies treat each line of business separately for premium calculations. Furthermore, the varied nature of these lines of business makes it more difficult for property-casualty insurers to be certain of likely payouts to insured individuals and firms. For this reason, property-casualty insurance companies usually hold much more diversified portfolios of financial instruments than the portfolios of life insurance companies.

Regulation of Insurance Companies

Although insurance companies must meet the terms of a number of federal laws and regulations, the primary supervisory authorities for life insurance companies are in each of the fifty states. Insurers must meet not only the minimal standards established by the state where they are incorporated but also the standards set by states where they sell policies. This means that companies doing business in all states must meet the minimal standards specified by the toughest state regulator.

---

3. What do insurance companies do, and who regulates their activities?
Insurance companies offer policies that are financial guarantees to cover losses of life and property. They use a variety of techniques to minimize significant adverse-selection and moral-hazard problems inherent in insurance. Individual states regulate insurance companies, so the toughest state regulators can affect nationwide industry standards.

Pension Funds

Pension funds are institutions that specialize in managing funds that individuals put away as a "nest egg" for when they retire from their jobs and careers. Part of the compensation of many workers is in the form of employer contributions to such funds.

The key specialty of pension funds is creating financial instruments called *pension annuities,* which are similar to the annuities offered by life insurance companies. But life insurance annuities usually are intended as supplements to a person's income at some fixed point in the future, whether or not the person is working at the time. In contrast, pension annuities apply only to the future event of retirement. Most people regard pension annuities as their main sources of income after retirement.

Growth of Pension Funds

As Figure 8-5 indicates, the share of financial institution assets held in pension funds has grown steadily since the 1950s. There are two likely reasons for this relative growth of pension funds. One is the gradual aging of the baby boom generation. Most "baby boomers" began working in the 1960s and 1970s. As they have aged, their incomes and, consequently, their contributions to pension funds have risen. Another reason is that pension funds have become more popular savings vehicles for many people. This has occurred both because pension funds have made pension arrangements more flexible over time and because most pension income is tax-deferred, meaning that contributions and earnings are not taxable until individuals begin drawing on accumulated pension savings.

Why do people use the services of pension funds instead of saving on their own? One reason certainly is asymmetric information: those who operate pension funds may be better informed about financial instruments and markets than individual savers. But the existence of economies of scale is probably a more important reason. Many people would find it very costly to monitor the instruments that they hold on a day-by-day basis throughout their lives. Pension funds do this for many people at the same time, thereby spreading the costs across large numbers of individuals.

MONEYXTRA!
Online Case Study

To evaluate a major challenge facing property-casualty insurance companies today, go to the Chapter 8 Case Study, entitled "Insurers Face Facts as Customers Self-Insure More of Their Risks." **http://moneyxtra. swcollege.com**

Pension funds: Institutions that specialize in managing funds that individuals save for retirement.

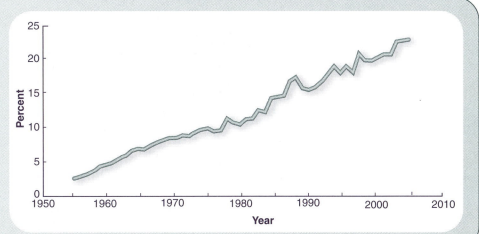

**FIGURE 8-5
Pension Funds'
Share of Financial
Institution Assets.**

The share of total assets of all financial institutions held by pension funds has increased steadily since the 1950s.

SOURCE: *Flow-of-Funds Accounts,* Board of Governors of the Federal Reserve System, various issues.

Types of Pensions

Any pension is an arrangement in which an employer agrees to provide benefits to retired employees, usually in the form of annuities. Pensions may be **contributory pensions,** meaning that both the employer and the employee contribute to the pension fund, or **noncontributory pensions,** meaning that only the employer contributes.

Contributory pensions: Pensions funded by both employer and employee contributions.

Noncontributory pensions: Pensions funded solely by employers.

ALTERNATIVE PENSION BENEFIT ARRANGEMENTS   There are two basic types of pension plans. With a *defined-contribution plan,* a person receives pension benefits that are based on total pension contributions during working years. With a *defined-benefits plan,* future benefits are set in advance. Thus, for defined-benefits plans a key issue is determining whether benefits will be completely funded at retirement.

ALTERNATIVE PENSION FUNDING ARRANGEMENTS   There are also two essential approaches to funding pensions. **Terminally funded pensions** are fully funded for the payment of benefits to an employee beginning at the employee's retirement date. When an employee covered by such a pension will receive retirement benefits from his employer even if he leaves the employer prior to the retirement date, the employee is said to be *vested.* For instance, a teacher who is vested in a state teachers' pension fund will receive benefits upon retirement even if he leaves the public school system and teaches at a private school before retirement.

Terminally funded pensions: Pensions that must be fully funded by the date that an employee retires.

Some employers offer **pay-as-you-go pensions,** in which pensions are not fully funded when employees retire. Instead, the employer funds pension benefits for current retirees out of current earnings produced by current (nonretired) workers. Some employers operate pension plans that combine terminal funding with pay-as-you-go funding provisions.

Pay-as-you-go pensions: Pensions that are not fully funded when employees retire.

TRANSFERABILITY OF PENSION FUNDS   **Single-employer pensions** are established by an employer only for its own employees. Funding and benefits for such pensions are nontransferable. When an employee leaves to take another job, accumulated pension funds cannot be shifted into the new employer's pension plan.

Single-employer pensions: Pensions that are established by an employer only for its own employees and are nontransferable to other employers.

In contrast, under **multi-employer pensions** employees may transfer accumulated funds and benefit rights when they change jobs. (This is called pension *portability*.) Multi-employer pensions typically apply to a specific industry, however. For instance, many colleges and professors contribute to TIAA-CREF, which is a multi-employer pension fund for colleges and universities. But accumulations and benefit rights from that plan generally are not transferable if a professor leaves a college to enter private industry or government service. (Yet all accumulations up to that point are fully vested and available as annuities.)

Multi-employer pensions: Pensions whose accumulations and benefit rights may be transferred from one employer to another.

Pension Fund Insurance and Regulation

Many pension funds have insurance to cover the contingency that they will be unable to honor their obligations to make future payments to retirees. Such funds operate under legal contracts that are mutually binding on both the pension fund and the insurer. Other pension funds that are not insured typically fund their benefits under a *trust* agreement, in which a neutral party, called the *trustee,* administers the distribution of benefits to retirees.

On the Web
How did the federal government get involved in guaranteeing defined-benefits pension plans? To learn more about the history of the Pension Benefit Guaranty Corporation, go to **http://www.pbgc.gov**, and click on "About PBGC."

In 1974, concerns about the solvency of some pension funds led Congress to pass the *Employment Retirement Income Security Act (ERISA).* This act and subsequent amendments set out federal rules for disclosure of pension information, funding arrangements, and vesting provisions. It also created the *Pension Benefit Guaranty Corporation (PBGC),* which provides federal insurance for all pensions with tax-deferred benefits, which are the bulk of pensions in the United States. (This federal pension insurance program faces looming financial troubles, however; see *What Happens When Companies Fail to Honor Their Pension Obligations?*)

What Happens When... **Companies Fail to Honor Their Pension Obligations?**

By law, the Pension Benefit Guaranty Corporation (PBGC) cannot deny insurance to most pension funds and can impose only limited restrictions on underfunded pension plans. The PBGC provides federal insurance for a number of major U.S. companies, including airlines, steelmakers, and auto manufacturers. As Figure 8-6 shows, the financial positions of the pension plans of these and other companies in the Standard & Poor's 500 improved considerably during the late 1990s. A key factor accounting for this improvement was a significant run-up in stock prices. By 1999, pensions of these companies were overfunded by close to $250 billion. Consequently, many companies reduced or halted contributions to their pension funds, thereby freeing up funds for other uses, such as business investment.

In the early 2000s, however, stock prices declined considerably, and a business downturn occurred. A number of firms responded by continuing to cut back on their pension contributions. In some cases, companies declared bankruptcy and defaulted on their pensions—leaving the PBGC to cover the pension obligations to their employees. Currently, U.S. pensions are underfunded by more than $350 billion. Of this amount, at least $90 billion is insured by the PBGC. At present, the PBGC's liabilities officially exceed its assets by more than $12 billion, but its actual financial situation may be much worse.

FOR CRITICAL ANALYSIS: If the federal government were to "bail out" the PBGC by providing extra funding, who effectively would pay for the pension benefits of many U.S. retirees?

FIGURE 8-6
Pension Funding at Standard & Poor's 500 Companies.

This figure displays the projected pension benefit obligations of companies included in the Standard & Poor's 500.

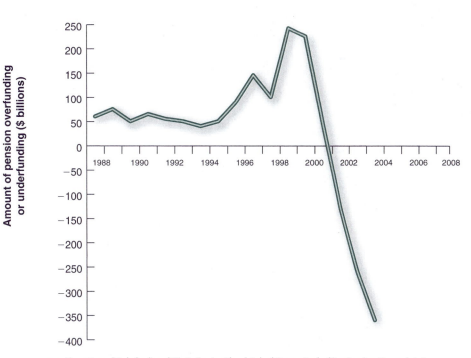

SOURCES: Simon Kwan, "Underfunding of Private Pension Plans," Federal Reserve Bank of San Francisco *Economic Letter,* No. 2003-16, June 13, 2003; Congressional Budget Office.

4. How are pension funds structured, and why have they grown? Non-contributory pension funds accumulate via funding provided solely by employers, whereas contributory pension funds also are funded by employees. Some pensions have terminal funding, which requires that they be fully funded by the time the employees retire, while pay-as-you-go pensions are funded out of the firm's current earnings. Pension funds have grown significantly because of the aging of the baby boom generation, the growing flexibility of the funds, and the tax deferments permitted by law.

Mutual fund: A mix of financial instruments managed on behalf of shareholders by investment companies that charge fees for their services.

On the Web
How can one choose from among the many mutual funds? Learn more about how investors make this decision by clicking on "Other Investments" in the right-hand margin and selecting "Mutual Funds" at **http://www.investorguide.com**.

Mutual Funds and Hedge Funds

A **mutual fund** is a mix of redeemable instruments, called "shares" in the fund. These shares are claims on the returns on financial instruments held by the fund, which typically include equities, bonds, government securities, and mortgage-backed securities.

Like pension funds, mutual funds take advantage of financial economies of scale. Mutual fund shareholders typically pay lower fees to investment companies than they might have to pay brokers to handle their funds on a personal basis. The reason is that mutual fund managers can spread the costs of managing shareholders' funds across all the shareholders.

Mutual funds are usually operated by investment companies, which charge shareholders fees to manage the funds. The popularity of mutual funds increased considerably during and after the 1970s. Figure 8-7 depicts the growing relative importance of stock and bond and money market mutual funds since the middle of the twentieth century. Today, more than 7,000 mutual funds are in operation.

FIGURE 8-7
Mutual Fund Growth.

The relative shares of total assets of all financial institutions held by stock and bond and money market mutual funds have risen rapidly since the 1970s.

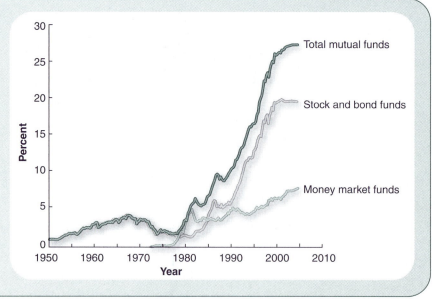

Types of Mutual Funds

Mutual funds can be categorized along two dimensions. **Load funds** are mutual funds that generally are marketed by brokers. Returns on such funds are reduced by commission rates paid to the brokers. Investment companies market **no-load funds** directly to the public, so there are no commission charges on such funds, which charge annual management fees to shareholders (as do load funds).

Some mutual funds are **closed-end funds,** which sell shares in an initial offering. The shares in closed-end funds cannot be redeemed but may be sold to others much like stocks. The shares' market values vary with the market values of the pools of financial instruments held by the mutual funds. In contrast, shares of an **open-end fund** are redeemable at any time at a price based on the market value of the mix of financial instruments held by the fund. Because shares of open-end funds are redeemable, they are more liquid than those offered by closed-end funds.

Nearly all mutual funds are public companies. Consequently, they must register with the SEC, which requires mutual funds to issue prospectuses and performance reports. Making performance information public helps prospective shareholders compare rates of return and risk of the myriad mutual funds available.

Hedge Funds

On September 23, 1998, the world learned that on the previous evening, the Federal Reserve Bank of New York had helped arrange a privately funded, $3.5 billion "bailout" of Long-Term Capital Management (LTCM). LTCM was a *hedge fund* with twenty-five financial economists with Ph.D.'s on its payroll, including two who had received the Nobel Prize in economics. The leading firms in the bailout were Goldman Sachs, Merrill Lynch, J.P. Morgan, and United Bank of Switzerland. These institutions and several others effectively took over the operations of LTCM.

Among the several remarkable aspects of this event was that many people had little idea what a hedge fund was, let alone how it could lose so much money so fast. In a sense, hedge funds are a type of mutual fund. Indeed, some observers call hedge funds "unregulated mutual funds for the affluent." The key distinction is that a **hedge fund** typically is established as a limited partnership, rather than a public company; thus, these financial intermediaries avoid being regulated by the SEC. Hedge funds also charge higher fees, often 20 percent of the profits they make for investors, than mutual funds. They also typically offer higher average returns. At the same time, hedge funds tend to take on greater portfolio risk, so their returns often are more variable. Consequently, the term *hedge fund* often is something of a misnomer because some hedge funds actually offer relatively risky, unhedged returns.

Hedge funds have been in existence since the 1940s. Today, there are about 3,000 hedge funds holding more than $300 billion in total assets. Between 1994 and 2006, hedge fund assets more than doubled.

One reason that classifying hedge funds can be difficult is that their management strategies vary widely. Some call themselves *macro funds;* they earn profits by speculating within particular bond markets or making bets on changes in exchange rates. Other hedge funds specialize in speculating about events such as mergers or bankruptcies. Others simply make bets in stock markets. (Some hedge funds are known as "funds of funds"; see on the next page the *Management Focus: Looking to Diversify at Hedge Funds?*)

Load funds: Mutual funds marketed by brokers who receive commissions based on the return of the funds.

No-load funds: Mutual funds that investment companies market directly to the public and that charge management fees instead of brokerage commissions.

Closed-end funds: Mutual funds that sell nonredeemable shares whose market values vary with the market values of the underlying mix of financial instruments held by the mutual funds.

Open-end funds: Mutual funds whose shares are redeemable at any time at prices based on the market values of the mix of financial instruments held by such funds.

Hedge funds: Limited partnerships that, like mutual funds, manage portfolios of assets on behalf of savers, but with very limited governmental oversight as compared with mutual funds.

MONEYXTRA!
Another Perspective

For a more detailed discussion of hedge funds, use the Chapter 8 reading entitled "The Truth about Hedge Funds," by William Osterberg and James Thomson of the Federal Reserve Bank of Cleveland. **http://moneyxtra. swcollege.com**

Looking to Diversify at Hedge Funds?

In years past, most investors regarded hedge funds as relatively high-risk choices that offered potentially high rates of return. During the early 2000s, however, a number of hedge funds earned significantly negative rates of return. This gave investors an incentive to try to diversify their hedge fund holdings. New hedge funds sprang up to meet the growing demand for hedge fund diversification. These hedge funds, called *funds of funds,* operate like mutual funds, except their portfolios consist entirely of shares in other hedge funds.

FOR CRITICAL ANALYSIS: What are likely to be the possible diversification benefits and costs of holding shares in a fund of funds instead of a single hedge fund?

On the Web

What financial strategies do hedge funds pursue? To find out, visit the Hedge Fund Association at **http://thehfa.org**, click on "About Hedge Funds," and then scroll down to "Hedge Fund Strategies."

5. How do mutual funds and hedge funds differ?   Mutual funds are public companies that differ across two dimensions. One is whether they entail commission payments to those who market the funds (load funds) or simply require management fees (no-load funds). The other is whether the shares of the funds are redeemable upon demand (open-end funds) or are nonredeemable and can be sold only in secondary markets (closed-end funds). Most hedge funds are private companies that typically are operated as limited partnerships subject to little or no government regulation.

Financial Institutions Specializing in Direct Lending

Have you ever sought a loan to help finance the purchase of a vehicle, such as a motorcycle or an automobile? If you have, or whenever you do in some future year, you probably will not apply for credit from any of the financial institutions discussed to this point. The reason is that special asymmetric-information problems are associated with making loans directly to individuals and businesses. Three basic types of institutions commonly specialize in this form of financial intermediation: depository institutions, finance companies, and various government-sponsored credit agencies.

Depository Financial Institutions

The most important financial institutions that extend credit directly to individuals and firms are *depository financial institutions* or, for short, *depository institutions*. As we discussed in Chapter 1, one key characteristic of depository institutions is that their liabilities include various deposits, such as time, savings, or checking accounts. But most depository institutions also deal with asymmetric-information problems specific to loan markets.

Commercial banks: Depository financial institutions that issue checking deposits and specialize in making commercial loans.

COMMERCIAL BANKS   Financial firms known as **commercial banks** are depository financial institutions that specialize in sizing up the risk characteristics of loan applicants. To limit their exposure to adverse-selection difficulties, these institutions collect information about the creditworthiness of individuals and businesses that desire loans. In addition, commercial banks keep tabs on the customers to which they lend, thereby limiting the risks arising from moral hazard.

SAVINGS BANKS AND SAVINGS AND LOAN ASSOCIATIONS   Residential housing accounts for a large portion of capital investment in the United States. **Savings and loan associations** and **savings banks** are depository institutions that traditionally have specialized in extending mortgage loans to individuals who wish to purchase homes. These institutions also face asymmetric-information difficulties. A person who wants a mortgage loan may or may not be a good risk for a loan. That person also may or may not be tempted to become a bad risk after receiving the loan. Thus, there are adverse-selection and moral-hazard problems specific to mortgage lending.

CREDIT UNIONS   A **credit union** is a depository institution that accepts deposits from and makes loans to only a closed group of individuals. In the past, a credit union's services were usually available only to people employed by a business with which the credit union was affiliated. As we shall discuss in Chapter 9, however, in recent years credit unions have significantly expanded the "closed groups" eligible for membership. Credit unions typically have specialized in making consumer loans, though some have branched into the mortgage-loan business.

We shall have considerably more to say about depository institutions in Chapter 9, which focuses exclusively on these important financial intermediaries.

Finance Companies

A **finance company** also specializes in making loans. Finance companies, however, do not offer deposits. Instead, they use the funds invested by their owners or raised through issuing other instruments to finance loans to individuals and small businesses. Finance companies traditionally have specialized in lending to businesses and individuals that are of insufficient size or creditworthiness to issue financial instruments in the money or capital markets or to borrow from other lenders such as commercial banks. (For many individuals, another way to borrow is to place collateral equal to the amount of the loan with a pawnbroker; see on the next page the *Global Focus: U.S. Pawnshops Move South of the Border.*) **Business finance companies** typically make loans to small businesses. In many instances they extend credit by saving the small businesses the trouble of collecting accounts that have not yet been paid. A business finance company often purchases accounts receivable, or receivables, owed to a small firm at a discount below the face value. For example, suppose that a small business has $51,000 in receivables. Of these, the business reasonably expects to collect $50,000. One way to finance continued operations might be for the business to sell the $51,000 in receivables to a finance company at a price of $46,000. The finance company makes a profit on this arrangement when it collects the $4,000 in easily collectible debts and some of the $1,000 in debts that the small business has already written off.

Other finance companies specialize in offering financial services to individuals. **Consumer finance companies** make loans enabling individuals to purchase durable goods such as home appliances or furniture or to make improvements to existing homes. **Sales finance companies** make loans to individuals planning to purchase items from specific retailers or manufacturers, such as Sears or Ford Motor Company. (For one automaker that operates a finance company, earnings from its financial operations often dwarf its revenues from vehicle sales; see on page 181 the *Management Focus: For General Motors, Selling Cars Looks like a Sideline.*)

Government-Sponsored Credit Agencies and Institutions

The federal government also operates or subsidizes some of the largest financial institutions in the United States. Among these are the Federal Financing Bank, which coordinates federal and federally assisted borrowing, and the Banks for Cooperatives, Federal Intermediate Credit

---

Savings and loan association: A type of depository institution that has traditionally specialized in mortgage lending.

Savings bank: Another type of depository institution that has specialized in mortgage lending.

Credit union: A type of depository institution that accepts deposits from and makes loans to only a group of individuals who are eligible for membership.

Finance company: A financial institution that specializes in making loans to relatively high-risk individuals and businesses.

Business finance companies: Finance companies that typically specialize in making loans to small businesses.

Consumer finance companies: Finance companies that specialize in making loans to individuals for the purchase of durable goods or for home improvements.

Sales finance companies: Finance companies that specialize in making loans to individuals for the purchase of items from specific retailers or manufacturers.

U.S. Pawnshops Move South of the Border

Pawnshops, or *pawnbrokers,* are financial institutions that extend very small loans (usually in the range of $100 to $150) with very short maturities. These loans are collateralized by the borrower's personal property, such as watches, jewelry, televisions, stereos, musical instruments, cameras, and firearms. Pawnbrokers typically make loans at annualized interest rates much higher than those of other financial institutions—often anywhere from 30 to 240 percent. Pawnshops have been in existence for centuries. They take their name from *pawn,* an old British term meaning a pledge for payment of a debt.

Most U.S. states regulate the activities of pawnshops by limiting the number of shops that a pawnbroker chain can open within a given area and requiring expensive checks to make certain pawned items have not been stolen. The costs of meeting these regulations have induced pawnbroker chains based in Texas and other U.S. states bordering Mexico to move many of their pawnshops to Mexico. Another incentive is that an estimated 90 percent of Mexican residents have done business with pawnshops.

FOR CRITICAL ANALYSIS: Why do you suppose that the interest rates charged by pawnshops are so high?

Banks, and Federal Land Banks, which are supervised directly or indirectly by the Farm Credit Administration.

The government also sponsors four institutions that support housing markets: the Federal National Mortgage Association (FNMA, or "Fannie Mae"), the General National Mortgage Association (GNMA, or "Ginnie Mae"), the Federal Home Loan Banks (FHLBs), and the Federal Home Loan Mortgage Corporation (FHLMC, or "Freddie Mac"). These agencies make mortgage markets more liquid by buying mortgages with funds that they raise by selling mortgage-backed securities. The twelve FHLBs, which are governed by the Federal Housing Finance Board, also provide government-subsidized financing of loans for residential housing and community development. The Federal Housing Administration (FHA), the Department of Housing and Urban Development (HUD), and the Veterans Administration (VA) also support the housing market by making mortgage loans directly to eligible individuals or by subsidizing and guaranteeing loans that they receive from private lenders.

In addition, the federal government operates the Farm Credit System, which makes loans to farmers. Such loans are guaranteed by the Farmer's Home Administration. The Student Loan Marketing Association is a government-assisted agency that purchases student loans that are guaranteed by the Department of Education.

> **6. What financial institutions specialize in lending directly to individuals and businesses?** The most important financial institutions that extend credit directly are depository institutions, which use the funds they raise from deposits and other sources to extend loans to individuals and firms. Finance companies also lend funds directly, but these institutions raise their funds from nondeposit sources and specialize in making loans to less creditworthy individuals and firms. A number of lending institutions, in particular institutions that operate in mortgage markets, receive government sponsorship.

MANAGEMENT
Focus

For General Motors, Selling Cars Looks like a Sideline

GMAC, the finance company owned by General Motors, was originally created to help the company's customers finance their purchases of its vehicles. A few years ago, the company branched out into the mortgage business by creating a mortgage-originating subsidiary called Ditech.com. Increasingly, GMAC's business activities are accounting for a significant portion of the company's profitability. During some intervals in recent years, GMAC generated as much as 90 percent of General Motors' profits.

FOR CRITICAL ANALYSIS: In what important way is General Motors' GMAC division different from a depository institution that makes mortgage loans?

Chapter Summary

1. Financial Intermediaries: Financial intermediaries help to reduce problems stemming from the existence of asymmetric information in financial transactions. Asymmetric information can lead to adverse-selection and moral-hazard problems. Financial intermediaries may also permit savers to benefit from economies of scale, which is the ability to reduce the average costs of managing funds by pooling the funds and spreading the costs across many savers.

2. Securities Market Institutions: These are investment banks, brokers, and dealers. Investment banks help to guarantee securities offerings of firms by underwriting those securities, meaning that they buy or have options to buy those securities. Brokers make securities market trades for their customers, and dealers seek to profit from buying instruments at low prices and selling them at higher prices. Most of the largest brokerage firms are also dealers. The main government agency that regulates these institutions is the Securities and Exchange Commission, which requires them to register with the government, disclose information about their activities, and follow prescribed trading rules.

3. Insurance Companies: These financial institutions intermediate significant asymmetric-information problems associated with providing financial guarantees against possible future contingencies. Insurance companies tend to specialize either in life insurance or in property-casualty insurance. States are the chief regulators of these companies' activities.

4. Pension Funds: These institutions manage the retirement savings of many employed U.S. residents. The accumulations in noncontributory pension funds come only from employers, but in contributory pension funds, employees also can add to their pension savings. Terminally funded pensions have sufficient savings accumulated to fully pay benefits to employees when they retire, whereas pay-as-you-go pension funds depend on current earnings of employers to fund benefit payments to current retirees. As the baby boom generation has matured, pension funds have grown dramatically. Also contributing to this growth have been the growing flexibility of pension plans and the deferment of taxes on current allocations.

5. Mutual Funds and Hedge Funds: Mutual funds, which are public companies that pool savings of shareholders for the purchase of a mix of financial instruments, differ across two dimensions. Commission payments to marketers of load funds reduce shareholders' returns, whereas those who hold shares in no-load funds simply pay fixed management fees. Closed-end funds do not permit shareholders to redeem their shares at current market values, while open-end funds do permit such redemptions. Hedge funds are limited partnerships that are not public companies and hence are relatively unregulated institutions, despite their propensity to experience significant losses in recent years.

6. Financial Institutions That Specialize in Direct Lending: The key financial institutions that make loans directly to individuals and businesses are depository institutions, including commercial banks, savings banks and savings and loan associations, and credit unions. In addition, finance companies have found their niche in lending to borrowers that are either too small or too uncreditworthy to issue their own debt instruments or to borrow from depository institutions. Furthermore, the federal government sponsors a number of direct-credit-granting institutions.

Questions and Problems

(Answers to odd-numbered questions and problems may be found on the Web at **http://money.swcollege.com** under "Student Resources.")

1. Explain why best efforts deals in investment banking now apply primarily for firms whose creditworthiness has not yet been proved, whereas firm commitment underwriting is common for firms with proven track records. In light of your explanation, can you also hypothesize why best efforts deals are much less common today than they were in the past?

2. What is the difference between a broker and a dealer? Why do you suppose that firms commonly do both kinds of business?

3. What would a broker-dealer give up to be a specialist? What would such a firm gain? In light of your answers, can you surmise why firms that trade large volumes of securities each day are especially likely to be specialists?

4. Although both life insurance companies and pension plans issue annuities, they generally are regarded as fundamentally different types of financial intermediaries. Can you explain why?

5. Many insurance companies will not extend life insurance to individuals who have received treatment for depression. Why do you suppose that companies have this restriction in their life insurance policies?

6. Contrast the pros and cons, from a consumer's standpoint, of term versus whole life insurance.

7. As we discussed, the Pension Benefit Guaranty Corporation (PBGC) insures all pensions with tax-deferred contributions. Some critics believe that the creation of the PBGC helped encourage the growth of pensions and, more specifically, growth in the share of pay-as-you-go pensions. Does this argument make sense to you? Explain your reasoning.

8. Evaluate the various factors that an individual saver must take into account when choosing among mutual funds. In light of the discussions of mutual funds in this chapter and of portfolio management in Chapter 7, should a wealthy saver hold shares in more than one mutual fund? Explain your reasoning.

9. Some hedge funds are officially based outside the United States, in locales such as the Caribbean islands. This has led many to question whether expanding federal regulations to include the activities of hedge funds would have much effect because many funds based in the United States could respond by simply moving their operations offshore. In light of this argument, do you believe hedge funds should nonetheless be subjected to greater governmental oversight? Why or why not?

10. Commercial banks make various loans, such as loans to businesses, but they also issue a variety of deposits, such as checking accounts. Do you believe that, in the absence of asymmetric-information problems in lending, commercial banks might cease to exist? Or would there still be a place for commercial banks? Explain your reasoning.

11. Commercial and savings banks issue loans and hold other financial instruments that yield interest returns. These banks pass some of this interest income on to their depositors through the interest rates that they pay on deposits that they issue. Bank deposits also are federally insured. Mutual fund shares, in contrast, are not federally insured. Would you expect that mutual fund shares would pay higher or lower returns to shareholders, as compared with rates of return on bank deposits? Explain your reasoning.

12. A number of small-town banks in rural areas complain that they are at a competitive disadvantage when farmers consider borrowing from them or from the government-supported Farm Credit System. In your view, does this argument have any merit? Explain.

13. In years past, investors have often viewed Fannie Mae (FNMA) debt securities as virtually "risk-free." A number of economists have predicted that after the bulk of the baby boomers retire and begin drawing on pensions, there will be a big wave of sell-offs of financial assets as pension funds convert assets to cash to fund pension payouts to retirees. Included would be sales of mortgage-backed securities issued by government-backed agencies. These economists think that the likely result will be a big decline in the market value of these securities. Assuming that this prediction turns out to be true, are Fannie Mae securities truly "risk-free" for those who hold them? [Hint: Consider who bears the risk of Fannie Mae securities.]

Before the Test

Test your understanding of the material covered in this chapter by taking the Chapter 8 interactive quiz at **http://money.swcollege.com**.

Online Application

Internet URL: http://www.mfea.com

Title: Mutual Fund Investor's Center: Education Alliance

Navigation: Begin at the home page of the Mutual Fund Investor's Center (**http://www.mfea.com**). Select "Investment Strategies," and from the drop-down menu click on "Asset Allocation." Then click on "Model Portfolios."

Application: Read the article, and then answer the following questions:

1. Based on the discussion of "Aggressive Growth Funds," would you anticipate that the returns earned by these mutual funds are typically more or less variable than the returns on most other mutual funds? Why?

2. Based on the discussion of "Money Market Mutual Funds," would you anticipate that the returns earned by these mutual funds are typically higher or lower than the returns on most other mutual funds? Why?

For Group Study and Analysis: Separate into groups, and ask each group to rate the relative expected return and risk that it would anticipate for each type of mutual fund discussed in the article. Compare the groups' ratings. Then compare them with those provided in the table at the conclusion of the article.

Selected References and Further Reading

Ackert, Lucy, and Bryan Church. "Competitiveness and Price Setting in Dealer Markets." Federal Reserve Bank of Atlanta *Economic Review,* Third Quarter 1998, pp. 4–11.

American Council of Life Insurance. *Life Insurance Fact Book.* Published annually.

Anderson, Richard. "The Nationalization of Housing Finance." Federal Reserve Bank of St. Louis *Monetary Trends,* November 2004, p. 1.

Frame, W. Scott, and Lawrence J. White. "Emerging Competition and Risk-Taking Incentives at Fannie Mae and Freddie Mac." Federal Reserve Bank of Atlanta *Working Paper* No. 2004-4, February 2004.

Guzman, Mark, and Fiona Sigalla. "Is the Pension System a Liability?" Federal Reserve Bank of Dallas *Southwest Economy,* September/October 2004, pp. 1–12.

Insurance Information Institute. *The Fact Book.* Published annually.

Kwan, Simon. "Underfunding of Private Pension Plans." Federal Reserve Bank of San Francisco *Economic Letter,* No. 2003-16, June 13, 2003.

Marquis, Milton. "What's Different about Banks—Still?" Federal Reserve Bank of San Francisco *Economic Letter,* No. 2001-09, April 6, 2001.

Sigalla, Fiona. "Insurance: A Risk to the Economy?" Federal Reserve Bank of Dallas *Southwest Economy,* July/August 2002, pp. 1–6.

Simons, Katerina. "Risk-Adjusted Performance of Mutual Funds." Federal Reserve Bank of Boston *New England Economic Review,* September/October 1998, pp. 33–48.

MoneyXtra

Log on to the MoneyXtra Web site now (**http://moneyxtra.swcollege.com**) for additional learning resources such as practice quizzes, case studies, readings, and additional economic applications.

Depository Financial Institutions

Once upon a time, banks used to give new customers free toasters or dinnerware for opening deposit accounts. Today, banks are offering bigger-ticket items, such as DVD players, flat-screen televisions, personal paper shredders, and Sony Playstations.

Recently, a New York bank even handed out free cars to people willing to place at least $100,000 into a five-year term deposit account paying 1 percent interest annually. In exchange for a $100,000 deposit, a new customer received a Pontiac Sunfire. Opening a $400,000 deposit account qualified a new customer to receive a Cadillac SRX.

Clearly, banks regard deposits as a crucial element of their business. What types of deposits do banks and other depository institutions offer their customers? Toward what purposes do these institutions direct the funds of their depositors? In this chapter, you will learn the answers to these questions.

The Origins and Global Development of Depository Institutions

Depository financial institutions have existed since the days of the earliest human civilizations. Consequently, their evolution has spanned the time that organized societies have inhabited the earth.

Goldsmith Bankers

As discussed in Chapter 1, inconveniences associated with barter ultimately led people to use commodities, particularly gold and silver, as money. Both metals were relatively scarce and highly valued. Both were easy to divide into units of various sizes so that people could make change.

GOLDSMITHS AND BULLION　In the earliest times, people used uncoined gold and silver, known as **bullion,** to make transactions, but the purity of bullion often is not readily discernible, so its users were exposed to asymmetric-information problems. Goldsmiths specialized in reducing the extent of these asymmetric-information problems. Parties to a transaction would pay a goldsmith to weigh bullion and to assess its purity. Many goldsmiths would issue the holder of bullion a certificate attesting to the bullion's weight and gold or silver content. Other goldsmiths went a step further. To provide the holder of bullion with ready proof of the bullion's weight and purity, they produced standardized weights of gold or silver that they imprinted with a seal of authenticity. These standardized units were the earliest *coins*.

BULLION DEPOSITS AND FRACTIONAL-RESERVE BANKING   Eventually, some goldsmiths simplified the process further by issuing paper notes indicating that the bearers held gold or silver of given weights and purities on deposit with the goldsmiths. Then the bearers of these notes could transfer the notes to others in exchange for goods and services. These notes were the first *paper money*. The gold and silver held on deposit with goldsmiths were the first *bank deposits*. Indeed, by providing depository services, these goldsmiths became the first bankers.

Once goldsmiths became depository institutions, it was only a matter of time before they took the final step toward modern banking by becoming lenders. Goldsmiths began to notice that withdrawals of bullion relative to new bullion deposits were fairly predictable. Therefore, as long as the goldsmiths held *reserves* of gold and silver to cover expected bullion withdrawals, they could lend paper notes in excess of the amounts of bullion that they actually kept on hand. They could charge interest on the loans by requiring repayment in bullion in excess of the value of the notes that they issued.

By lending funds in excess of the reserves of money (gold and silver bullion) that they actually possessed, these goldsmith-bankers developed the earliest form of **fractional-reserve banking.** As long as economic conditions were stable and the goldsmiths managed their accounts wisely, those who held the goldsmiths' notes would be satisfied with this arrangement. But in bad times or in instances when a few goldsmiths overextended themselves, many noteholders might show up at the same time demanding the gold or silver bullion. These were the earliest "bank runs," and if too many noteholders demanded bullion at the same time, the businesses of the goldsmith-bankers failed. Bearers of the notes would discover the notes were nearly worthless pieces of paper.

The Roots of Modern Banking

The first goldsmith-bankers cannot be traced with certainty to any specific time or place. There is evidence that such activities took place in Mesopotamia sometime during the first millennium B.C. In ancient Greece goldsmith operations existed in Delphi, Didyma, and Olympia at least as early as the seventh century B.C. By the sixth century B.C., banking was a well-developed feature of the economy of Athens.

Banking also arose elsewhere in the Mediterranean world, in cities such as Jerusalem, and further east in Persia. Banking facilitated trade because merchants who shipped goods to faraway locations typically needed loans to fund their operations. After receiving payment from the purchasers of their goods, the merchants then would repay those who had provided loan financing. These lenders became known as *merchant bankers*. Merchant banking ultimately became a linchpin of the trade linking the principalities of the Roman Empire.

THE ITALIAN MERCHANT BANKERS   The modern term *bank* derives from the merchants' bench, or *banco,* on which money changed hands in the marketplaces of medieval Italy. The term *bankruptcy* refers to the "breaking of the bench" that occurred when an Italian merchant banker overextended, then experienced a run on his notes, and failed. Most Italian merchant bankers avoided this fate, however. Indeed, during the medieval period of the twelfth and thirteenth centuries A.D. merchant bankers flourished throughout Italy.

Bullion: Uncoined gold or silver used as money.

Fractional-reserve banking: A system in which banks hold reserves equal to less than the amount of total deposits.

By the time of the Italian Renaissance during the fifteenth and sixteenth centuries, merchant bankers such as the Medici family of Florence had accumulated enormous wealth and political power. Although these Italian merchant bankers directed some of their wealth to financing the fabulous art of masters such as Michelangelo and Leonardo da Vinci, ultimately they squandered much of it by building armies and conducting wars over territory and riches.

THE ADVENT OF MODERN BANKING   While most of the Italian merchant bankers quarreled, those originally from the Lombardy region of Italy worked to maintain their merchant banking operations in other European locales, such as London and Berlin. In London, the Italian merchant bankers became such an important fixture that the city's financial dealings were centered around Lombard Street, which remains the financial heart of the city today. The German central bank, the Deutsche Bundesbank, called one interest rate at which it lent funds to private banks the *Lombard rate*. Even after the Italian city-states fell into political disarray, Italian merchant bankers hailing from Genoa financed the activities of the rising Hapsburg Empire of seventeenth- and eighteenth-century Europe.

Others in Europe eventually copied the banking practices of the Italian merchant bankers, however. The banking business took on three key features. First, as in the days of the earliest goldsmiths, banks took deposits from customers and maintained accounts on their behalf. Second, banks managed payments on behalf of customers by collecting and paying checks, notes, and other "banking currency." Finally, like the merchant banks of old, these modern banks provided advances to customers in the form of loans. The interest on these loans and the fees that banks charged for accounting and deposit services were the banks' sources of revenues and, ultimately, profits.

> **1. What are the historical origins of modern banking institutions?**   Banks originated in the earliest civilizations as depositories for gold and silver. They evolved into merchant banking firms in medieval Italy. These firms, like modern banks, maintained deposit accounts for, processed payments on behalf of, and made loans to their customers.

Early American Banking

Naturally, before the American Revolution (1775–1783), British banking firms financed most trading between the American colonies and Britain. When the rebellion against British rule cut the ties to British banking firms, the former colonies were left in a financial bind. Although a few finance companies operated by Americans existed when the Revolution began in 1775, there were no independent banks on American soil. This complicated wartime financing, and the Continental Congress had to borrow from governments and bankers in France, Holland, and Spain and to issue currency in the form of Continental dollars, or *Continentals*. By the end of the war in 1783, the Continental Congress had printed so many Continentals that each was worth one five-hundredth (1/500th) of its face value.

PRIVATE VERSUS PUBLIC BANKING IN THE NEW REPUBLIC   In 1781 Robert Morris, a Philadelphia financier, spearheaded the establishment of the Bank of North America. This bank was chartered by the Continental Congress and was the first nationally chartered bank on the North American continent. After 1783, however, the Philadelphia-based bank operated under a Pennsylvania charter, though for a time other states, including New York and Massachusetts, granted it charters as well. The national government's role in banking expanded after the individual states formally joined the United States of America. Alexander Hamilton, the first secretary of the Treasury of the new federal republic, looked to the Bank of North America as an example of how to establish a federally chartered bank, which he proposed as the First Bank of the United States. President George Washington sided with his Treasury secretary and permitted the bill authorizing a twenty-year charter for the First Bank to become law. Washington's action set the precedent for a **dual banking system,** in which U.S. banks could receive either federal or state charters.

Dual banking system: A regulatory structure in which either states or the federal government can grant bank charters.

THE SECOND BANK OF THE UNITED STATES   When the charter of the First Bank of the United States expired in 1811, Congress did not renew the charter. This arguably was not a good decision. Congress declared war on Britain the next year and found itself without a ready means of financing the war effort. This experience convinced Congress to issue a twenty-year federal charter for the Second Bank of the United States in 1816.

A dual banking system with one large national bank and many smaller state banks continued through 1836. But in 1819 many people in emerging states such as Kentucky and Tennessee blamed the Second Bank for a financial panic that brought ruin to many farmers and landholders. Among those who developed a deep distrust of the Second Bank was President Andrew Jackson, who vetoed an 1832 bill authorizing recharter of the Second Bank. After winning reelection in that year, Jackson removed all federal government deposits from the Second Bank and placed them with state banks. The Second Bank ceased to exist four years later. For twenty-six years, the federal government's direct involvement in banking was suspended.

The Free-Banking Period

From 1837 until 1863, there were two types of banks. One group consisted of banks operated by or on behalf of the state governments. As we noted in Chapter 2, the other group consisted of private banks incorporated under free-banking laws enacted in a number of states, including New York, Michigan, Wisconsin, and Alabama. Historians and economists now call this the *free-banking era* of U.S. history.

Traditional historical accounts of the free-banking era focused on the so-called wildcat banks—unscrupulous operations that printed notes that they never intended to redeem (see Chapter 2)—and on the prevalence of counterfeiting. Indeed, by the end of the 1860s, more than 5,000 separate types of counterfeit notes were in circulation.

In recent decades, however, many historians and economists have reexamined the free-banking period in light of hard evidence that they have unearthed from the accounting ledgers of free banks and state examiners. This evidence indicates that in many states, "free banks" were not very free. Several states required banks to hold risky bonds that the states themselves issued. They also enacted laws prohibiting banks from branching within states or across state lines.

In states that subjected free banks to fewer restrictions of this type, instability was less pronounced. Some states, and notably New York, subjected free banks to state audits to assure depositors that the banks were soundly managed. In such states the notes of free banks were quite safe, and very few depositors experienced losses. Furthermore, bank failures and closings in other states with less soundly structured arrangements typically did not cause difficulties for free banks in states with better designed free-banking laws.

Consequently, the mainstream view among today's economic historians is that free banking ultimately might have been a more successful experiment if events had followed a different course. But the Civil War permanently altered the course of U.S. banking, much as it forever changed the political landscape.

The Two-Tiered Banking System

In 1863 Congress passed the National Banking Act, which granted federal charters to a number of banks (all within the Union states) and, as amended in 1864, imposed a federal tax on all notes issued by state banks (mostly based in Confederate states). This act also imposed reserve requirements on the deposits of banks and prohibited state-chartered banks from engaging in **branch banking,** in which a depository institution operates offices in more than one geographic location. It also required national banks to back their notes by posting government bonds with the Comptroller of the Currency, a U.S. Treasury official who was designated the chief supervisor of national banks.

Branch banking: A depository institution organizational structure in which institutions operate offices at a number of geographic locations.

The National Banking Act had far-reaching consequences for U.S. banking. First, it ended the free-banking experiment. Second, for the first time in the nation's history, the federal government became directly involved in the affairs of most of the nation's banks. Third, the act laid the groundwork for today's *two-tiered* system of both state and nationally chartered banks. Dual banking became a permanent feature of the U.S. scene.

The Rise of Thrift Institutions

In the fifth century B.C., Xenophon, a Greek soldier and historian, proposed the formation of a publicly owned goldsmith institution for the city-state of Athens. He envisioned the mutual sharing of interest returns by all citizens of the city. Xenophon's dream was not realized, but it foreshadowed the development of **mutual ownership** of savings institutions, or the ownership of such institutions by all depositors. In an echo of Xenophon's idea, in 1697 Daniel Defoe, the author of *Robinson Crusoe,* proposed the formation of mutually owned institutions to promote saving among working-class and poor individuals in England. A number of years later, in 1765, the first institution of this type was established in England. By the early 1800s, such institutions had spread to Scotland and the United States, where they became known as *savings banks.* These were the first so-called *thrift institutions.*

Mutual ownership: A depository institution organizational structure in which depositors own the institution.

A related type of savings institution also arose in England. This was the "building society," in which individuals pooled their savings to make loans to society members, who then used the funds to finance the construction of new homes. In 1831 a Philadelphia group formed the first U.S. building society, which was called a *savings and loan association.* Within a couple of decades, most savings and loan associations were accepting deposits from the general public, and the number of such associations expanded dramatically throughout the remainder of the nineteenth century. By the 1930s both savings banks and savings and loan associations had become the mainstay lenders in the market for residential mortgages. Today, we refer to savings and loan associations and savings banks collectively as *savings institutions.*

Credit unions began in Germany and Italy in the mid-nineteenth century. They were cooperative institutions serving closed memberships of individuals with common interests. Some credit unions were associated with churches, while others had memberships drawn from fraternal orders. Most, however, drew their members from employees of specific firms. Credit unions first appeared in Canada at the start of the twentieth century, and the first U.S. credit union was set up in 1909.

Until the late 1980s, savings institutions and credit unions were commonly grouped together in the broad category of *thrift institutions.* By the early 1990s, however, many savings institutions in the United States had failed, while most credit unions remained solvent. Because of their differing performances and prospects, the collective term *thrift institutions* is not used as widely as in the past to refer to these two groups of institutions. (Thrift institutions have been around only a little over half a century in Mexico, but they now serve a significant portion of the nation's residents; see the *Global Focus: Mexico's Social-Banking System.*)

Segmented Banking in the Twentieth Century

Like the Civil War, the Great Depression of the 1930s was a defining period for U.S. depository institutions. Congress responded to the events of the Great Depression by involving the federal government even more directly in the affairs of commercial banks, savings institutions, and credit unions.

BANK RUNS   One key event associated with the Great Depression was a series of bank failures and **bank runs,** or widespread deposit withdrawals at banks that often induced their failure, throughout much of the United States. Congress responded with legislation intended to sharply restrict the ability of banks to undertake risky activities. In 1933 Congress passed the Glass-Steagall Act, which separated commercial and investment banking. This legislation, which was significantly scaled back in 1999 (see Chapters 11 and 12), also prohibited commercial banks from paying interest on checking deposits, authorized the regulation of interest on bank savings deposits, and enacted an elaborate system of federal insurance of bank deposits under the administration of the Federal Deposit Insurance Corporation.

Bank run: An unexpected series of cash withdrawals at a depository institution that can induce its failure.

EXTENSIVE FEDERAL REGULATION   Another problem during the Great Depression was that real estate values fell sharply as many people halted their mortgage payments. This led to widespread foreclosures on mortgage loans by savings institutions and of consumer loans by credit unions. But such foreclosures left the thrift institutions holding properties with depressed values, causing many savings institutions to declare bankruptcy. Congress responded with a series of laws intended to shore up the shaky thrift industry; this legislation included the Home Owners Loan Act of 1933, which established a federal charter for savings institutions, and the National Housing Act of 1934, which created a system of deposit insurance for savings institutions. In 1934 Congress also enacted the Federal Credit Union Act, which authorized federal charters for credit unions.

GLOBAL
Focus

Mexico's Social-Banking System

In 1951, two brothers, both Catholic priests, introduced the first *cajac,* or cooperative bank, to Mexico. Today, a typical *cajac* still has no checkbooks or automated teller machines, but a customer needs only 100 pesos (less than $10) to open a savings account. In some locations, a *cajac* is the only financial institution available to people who wish to accumulate savings and interest. Now there are 600 of these institutions. Together with credit unions, they provide a social-banking system that serves almost 30 percent of Mexico's residents.

FOR CRITICAL ANALYSIS: How do you suppose that the estimated 35 percent of Mexico's residents without access to financial services store their savings?

Consequently, within a very short interval in the 1930s, the U.S. government became closely involved in the business practices of all depository financial institutions. The government regulated interest rates, restricted banking practices, and insured bank and thrift institution deposits. Federal laws also formally segmented depository institutions into formal categories: commercial banks, savings institutions, and credit unions. Essentially, these congressional actions solidified the separate categories of depository institutions that remain with us today.

> ### 2. How did today's segmented groupings of depository institutions arise?
> The dual, or combined state and federal, structure of U.S. banking has its roots in decisions that the first Congress and President Washington made in the first years of the republic. After later experiments with free banking at the state level, Congress reinstituted dual banking during the Civil War. Savings institutions and credit unions have always had specialized niches, but Congress solidified the distinctions among commercial banks, savings institutions, and credit unions in a series of laws passed in the 1930s.

Commercial Banks

A commercial bank is a depository institution that faces few legal restrictions on its powers to lend to businesses and can legally issue checking deposits from which holders may write unlimited numbers of checks. There currently are nearly 8,000 commercial banks in the United States, and they are the predominant depository financial institutions in the country.

Commercial Bank Assets

Asset: Anything owned by a person or business that has a market value.

For any individual or firm, including a banking firm, an **asset** is any item legally owned by that person or business that has a market value. For instance, when a commercial bank makes a loan to a business, that loan represents a legal obligation of the business to repay the loan principal and interest to the lending bank within a specified period. Consequently, the loan is an asset of the bank.

Table 9-1 lists the *combined* total assets of *all* domestically chartered commercial banks in the United States. Three important classifications of assets are listed in Table 9-1. We consider each in turn.

LOANS   A key reason for the existence of banks is that they specialize in handling asymmetric-information problems in lending markets. Because lending is the bread-and-butter business of commercial banks, loans compose the predominant category of assets held by commercial banks. There are four important loan categories.

Commercial and industrial (C&I) loans: Loans that commercial banks and other depository institutions make to businesses.

Collateral: Assets that a borrower pledges as security in case it should fail to repay the principal or interest on a loan.

Commercial and Industrial Loans   Those loans that commercial banks and other depository institutions make to businesses are **commercial and industrial (C&I) loans.** Businesses use funding from C&I loans to meet day-to-day cash needs or to finance purchases of plants and equipment. Businesses typically must secure C&I loans with **collateral,** or assets that a borrower pledges as security in the event it fails to fulfill its obligation to repay the principal and interest on a loan. A lending bank may seize the collateral, or a portion of it, in the event

Table 9-1 Commercial Bank Assets ($ Billions), May 31, 2005

Commercial & industrial loans	$ 985.4	11.8%
Consumer loans	704.7	8.4%
Real estate loans	2,684.3	32.0%
Interbank loans	285.6	3.4%
Other loans	422.0	5.0%
Total loans	$5,082.0	60.6%
U.S. government securities	$1,202.2	14.4%
Other securities	862.8	10.3%
Total securities	$2,065.0	24.7%
Cash assets	$ 340.2	4.1%
Other assets	$ 891.3	10.6%
Total assets	**$8,378.5**	**100.0%**

SOURCE: Board of Governors of the Federal Reserve System, H.8(510) *Statistical Release.*

of nonpayment. Though many C&I loans require collateral, it is not uncommon for some C&I loans to extremely creditworthy borrowers to be uncollateralized.

All told, C&I loans account for almost 12 percent of total bank assets. Such loans have varying degrees of default risk and liquidity. In recent years banks have worked hard to increase the liquidity of their C&I loan holdings, as we shall discuss in greater detail in Chapter 10.

Consumer Loans Commercial banks also extend credit to individuals. These loans are *consumer loans.* About a third of such loans typically finance purchases of automobiles. Many individuals also obtain consumer loans for the purchase of mobile homes, durable consumer goods such as household appliances, or materials for home improvements.

Banks typically issue consumer loans for the purchase of autos or mobile homes in the form of **installment credit.** Under an installment credit agreement, the individual borrower agrees to repay the principal and interest in equal periodic payments. Payment schedules for consumer loans typically span one to five years. Interest rates on these loans usually are fixed and initially are set relative to the prime rate or an index of capital market rates, such as an index of Treasury rates. Some consumer loans, however, have adjustable interest rates.

Installment credit: Loans to individual consumers that entail periodic repayments of principal and interest.

Included among consumer loans is **revolving credit,** which refers to bank lending to individuals up to some preset limit, or ceiling. Under a revolving credit agreement, consumers have automatic approval to borrow as long as they do not exceed their specified credit ceilings. They also may pay off their loan balance at any time. Credit cards are the most widely used form of consumer revolving credit.

Revolving credit: Loans to individuals that permit them to borrow automatically up to specified limits and to repay the balance of the loan at any time.

Real Estate Loans A third major type of bank lending consists of *real estate loans,* which are loans that banks make to finance purchases of real property, buildings, and fixtures (items permanently attached to real estate) by businesses and individuals. Banks make the bulk of their real estate loans to businesses. In the 1980s and 1990s, real estate lending became a relatively more important business for commercial banks. The share of total commercial bank assets held as real estate loans rose from around 17 percent in 1985 to the 32 percent figure in Table 9-1. Much of the growth in real estate lending has been fueled by increases in *home* *equity loans,* which are loans to individual property owners that are secured by the owners' shares of title to real estate. (Extending credit at interest is forbidden to practitioners of the Islamic faith, but U.S. and European banks are learning to adapt to Muslim financial rules; see *What Happens When Islamic Finance Moves Westward?*)

Interbank (Federal Funds) Loans   As discussed earlier, banks extend interbank loans in the federal funds market. Most federal funds loans have one-day maturities, but some, called **term federal funds,** have maturities exceeding one day. Banks typically lend these funds in large-denomination units ranging from $200,000 to well over $1 million per loan. Although large banks both lend and borrow federal funds, smaller banks are predominantly federal funds lenders.

SECURITIES   *U.S. government securities,* including Treasury bills, notes, and bonds, are a key type of security held by commercial banks. Commercial bank holdings of these securities account for more than 14 percent of all assets. The other group of securities is *state and municipal bonds.* These make up the bulk of the "other securities" category in Table 9-1 on page 191, or just over 10 percent of bank assets.

CASH ASSETS   The most liquid assets that banks hold are **cash assets,** which are the bank assets that function as media of exchange. One component of cash assets is **vault cash,** which is currency that commercial banks hold at their offices to meet depositors' needs for cash withdrawals on a day-to-day basis. Vault cash typically accounts for about 2 percent of total bank assets.

A second type of cash asset is **reserve deposits** at Federal Reserve banks. These are checking accounts that commercial banks hold with the Federal Reserve bank in their geographic district. Reserve deposits usually account for about 1 percent of total bank assets. Banks write checks out of or wire-transfer funds from these reserve deposit accounts when they make federal funds loans, purchase repurchase agreements, or buy securities. Funds held as reserve deposits also count toward meeting the Federal Reserve's legal reserve requirements.

A third form of cash asset is **correspondent balances,** which normally account for just under 1 percent of bank assets. These are funds that banks hold on deposit with other private commercial banks called *correspondents.*

Term federal funds: Interbank loans with maturities exceeding one day.

Cash assets: Depository institution assets that function as media of exchange.

Vault cash: Currency that a depository institution holds on location to honor cash withdrawals by depositors.

Reserve deposits: Deposit accounts that depository institutions maintain at Federal Reserve banks.

Correspondent balances: Deposit accounts that banks hold with other banks.

What Happens When... **Islamic Finance Moves Westward?**

The world's 1.3 billion Muslims are bound by Islamic law, called *sharia.* Among other things, this system of rules bars involvement in *riba,* or the payment of or receipt of interest. It also cautions against *gharar,* or excessive risk taking. Over the years, *sharia* has given rise to a broad set of precedents governing allowable financial transactions by a practicing Muslim. In an effort to serve the large body of Muslims who now live in Western nations, several large international banks have set up Islamic-finance subsidiaries. Examples include Citibank's Citi Islamic Bank and United Bank of Switzerland's Noriba Bank. These institutions offer "investment accounts" that pay

shares of profit, rather than interest, to a Muslim saver. Instead of lending funds at interest to a Muslim who wishes to purchase an automobile, an Islamic bank purchases the vehicle for the customer and then sells it to the customer at a profit. To finance the purchase of a house, an Islamic bank likewise purchases the residence and then charges a set of steadily increasing monthly rents. When the rents are fully paid, ownership is transferred to the bank's customer.

FOR CRITICAL ANALYSIS: What is the incentive for banks in the Western world to operate Islamic subsidiaries?

The final type of cash asset is **cash items in process of collection** or, more simply, "cash items." These are checks or other cash drafts that the bank lists as deposited for immediate credit but that the bank may need to cancel if payment on the items is not received. Whenever you deposit or cash a personal or payroll check at a bank, the bank lists that check as a cash item until it "clears" and the bank has received payment on the check from the issuer's financial institution. Cash items in process of collection usually amount to about 0.5 percent of total commercial bank assets.

Cash items in process of collection: Checks deposited with a bank for immediate credit but not yet cleared for final payment to the bank; usually referred to simply as "cash items."

> **3. What are the key assets of commercial banks?** Bank assets fall into three main categories: loans, securities, and cash assets. Loans include commercial and industrial loans, real estate loans, consumer loans, and very short-term loans that banks make in the federal funds market or through purchases of repurchase agreements. Securities include U.S. government securities and municipal and state bonds. Cash assets include vault cash, reserve deposits at Federal Reserve banks, correspondent balances, and cash items in the process of collection.

TRENDS IN BANK ASSET ALLOCATIONS Figure 9-1 plots the shares of bank assets allocated to cash assets, securities, and all other assets (loans and miscellaneous other assets) at various intervals since 1961. As the figure indicates, there has been a general downward trend in relative holdings of cash assets.

A similar downward trend also existed for bank security holdings until the latter 1980s. The portion of bank assets held as securities began to drift upward in 1986 and then rose sharply in early 1991. The reason was that between 1990 and 1992 banks curtailed lending fairly dramatically. As you can see in Figure 9-1, "other assets," nearly all of which were loans, declined during this period as the portion of assets allocated to securities increased. Many economists have classified this period as a *credit crunch*, in which banks are willing to lend

On the Web
Do you want to keep up on the latest news about events affecting the banking industry? If so, read the "Daily Newsbytes" at the American Bankers Association home page, **http://www.aba.com**.

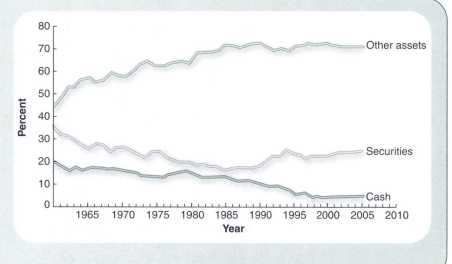

**FIGURE 9-1
Commercial Bank
Asset Allocations.**

During the past four and a half decades, there has been a general downward trend in commercial banks' holdings of cash assets relative to total assets. Over the same period, there has been a general upward trend in proportionate holdings of loans and other assets. The portion of assets held as securities increased in the early 1990s, when banks noticeably reduced lending in favor of security holdings.

SOURCES: *Federal Reserve Bulletin* and H.8(510) *Statistical Release,* Board of Governors of the Federal Reserve System, various issues.

only to their most creditworthy customers (we shall have more to say about the causes of this crunch in Chapter 11).

Commercial Bank Liabilities and Equity Capital

Liability: A legally enforceable claim on the assets of a business or individual.

Any **liability** is the dollar value of a legal claim on the assets of an individual or business at a given point in time. In the case of a bank loan to a business, the business legally owes funds to the bank, so the loan is a liability of the business. But banks have liabilities as well. For instance, if you have a checking or savings deposit at a bank, then the bank owes you the funds in the account. While you regard the deposit as an asset, the bank views it as a liability.

Net worth: The excess of assets over liabilities, or equity capital.

Equity capital: The excess of assets over liabilities, or net worth.

If you were to add up estimates of your own assets and liabilities and subtract liabilities from assets, you would come up with an estimate of your **net worth,** or the net amount of total funds that you owe to no one. A synonym for net worth is **equity capital.** A commercial bank's equity capital is its net worth, or the amount by which its assets exceed its liabilities.

Table 9-2 lists the *combined* total liabilities and equity capital of *all* domestically chartered commercial banks in the United States. Note that the dollar amount of total liabilities and equity capital in Table 9-2 is exactly equal to the dollar amount of total assets in Table 9-1 on page 191. This illustrates an important accounting definition: total bank assets must always equal the sum of total liabilities and equity capital.

Noncontrollable liabilities: Liabilities whose dollar amounts bank customers largely determine once banks have issued the liabilities to them.

NONCONTROLLABLE LIABILITIES Bankers typically classify their liabilities into two categories: noncontrollable and controllable. The term **noncontrollable liabilities** is something of a misnomer in that a bank certainly could decide not to issue any particular liability. The idea behind this term, however, is that once a bank issues one of these liabilities to a customer, the *customer,* and not the bank, has considerable discretion concerning how large the customer's deposit holdings will be. It is in this sense that a bank regards such a liability as "noncontrollable."

There are four key types of noncontrollable liabilities. One is *transactions deposits,* which, as discussed in Chapter 1, include demand deposits and other checkable deposits such as

Table 9-2 Commercial Bank Liabilities and Equity Capital ($ Billions), June 30, 2005

Transactions deposits	$ 678.8	8.1%
Small time and savings deposits	1,293.6	15.4%
Large time deposits	2,853.0	34.1%
Total deposits	**$4,825.4**	57.6%
Borrowings from banks	$ 362.6	4.3%
Other borrowings	1,245.4	14.9%
Total borrowings	**$1,608.0**	19.2%
Other liabilities	**$1,266.4**	15.1%
Equity capital*	$ 678.7	8.1%*
Total liabilities & equity	**$8,378.5**	**100.0%**

*Authors' estimate.
SOURCE: Board of Governors of the Federal Reserve System, H.8(510) *Statistical Release.*

NOW (negotiable order of withdrawal) accounts. Demand deposits are non-interest-bearing accounts, whereas banks pay market interest rates on other checkable deposits. Transactions deposits account for just over 8 percent of total bank liabilities and equity capital.

Two other noncontrollable liabilities are *savings deposits* and *small-denomination time deposits*. Savings deposits account for more than 15 percent of total bank liabilities and equity capital. Included among savings deposits are passbook and statement savings accounts typically held by small savers and money market deposit accounts usually held in somewhat larger denominations. Savings deposits have no set maturities. In contrast, small-denomination time deposits have fixed maturities. They have denominations under $100,000. (At one time, when you obtained a loan, there was a good chance that your neighbors' deposits provided the funding, but this is increasingly unlikely; see the *Management Focus: A Deposit at Your Local Bank Isn't Necessarily "Local."*)

The last noncontrollable liability is *deferred availability cash items*. These represent payments by banks to other parties that the banks have not yet made but have promised to make or that the banks have made but which have not yet "cleared." Deferred availability cash items are included among the "other liabilities" in Table 9-2.

CONTROLLABLE LIABILITIES AND EQUITY CAPITAL Bankers refer to the remaining liabilities that they issue as **controllable liabilities.** These are liabilities whose amounts the bankers themselves can more readily determine on a monthly, weekly, or even daily basis.

Controllable liabilities: Liabilities whose dollar amounts banks can directly manage.

MANAGEMENT
Focus

A Deposit at Your Local Bank Isn't Necessarily "Local"

The ten banks with the most deposits in the United States are listed in Table 9-3. Together, these ten banks account for about 48 percent of all U.S. deposits at commercial banks, and more than a third of U.S. bank deposits are held at the top five banks listed in Table 9-3.

Four of these banks—Bank of America, J.P. Morgan Chase, Wells Fargo, and U.S. Bankcorp—have branches in at least half of all U.S. states. One of the top ten banks based on U.S. deposits, HSBC Holdings of London, is not even a U.S. bank. Increasingly, funds that individuals and firms deposits with their local banks are pooled together for banks to allocate to assets held across wide geographic areas.

FOR CRITICAL ANALYSIS: If you apply for a loan from a Bank of America branch, would the funds for that loan necessarily come from deposits held by customers of that branch?

Table 9-3 The Top Ten Banks Based on Deposits in the United States

Together, the ten banks with the most deposits in the United States account for more than $2.4 trillion in deposits, or nearly half of all the deposits held at U.S. commercial banks.

Bank	Deposits ($ Billions)
Bank of America	$575.5
Citigroup	524.4
J.P. Morgan Chase	346.5
Wells Fargo	268.1
Wachovia	245.6
Washington Mutual	126.6
U.S. Bankcorp	119.9
SunTrust	85.5
HSBC Holdings	75.4
National City	73.0

SOURCES: *American Banker,* October 19, 2004; *Federal Reserve Bulletin.*

Large-Denomination Time Deposits   Banks raise a significant amount of funds by issuing *large-denomination time deposits.* Many of these are *large-denomination certificates of deposit (CDs)* issued as controllable liabilities. These CDs have denominations above $100,000 and typically fund a significant amount of banks' short-term lending operations. Large CDs pay market interest rates, and many are negotiable. Banks and other depository institutions issue large CDs in a variety of maturities, but most large negotiable CDs have six-month terms and trade actively in the money markets. Banks issue CDs in groups when they feel the timing is best, and banks also determine the denominations of the CDs. All told, large CDs and other large-denomination time deposits account for over 34 percent of bank liabilities and equity capital. (To encourage depositors to purchase their certificates of deposit, banks have unveiled a wide variety of CD products in recent years; see the *Management Focus: The New CD Menagerie.*)

Purchased funds: Very short-term bank borrowings in the money market.

Purchased Funds   Bankers often refer to another set of controllable liabilities as **purchased funds.** These are very short-term borrowings in the money market. The most important type of purchased funds is *interbank (federal funds) borrowings,* or commercial bank borrowings from other banks in the federal funds market, which typically account for about 4 percent of total bank liabilities and equity capital.

Other Borrowings   Three other kinds of purchased funds are included in the "other borrowings" category in Table 9-2 on page 194. These are *sales of repurchase agreements, borrowings from the Federal Reserve,* and *Eurodollar liabilities.* When a bank sells securities under an agreement to repurchase them later and to pay an interest yield on the transaction, it borrows for the length of the agreement. Consequently, sales of repurchase agreements are liabilities. Likewise, banks that borrow federal funds thereby issue new controllable liabilities.

All federally insured commercial banks have the privilege of applying for loans from the Federal Reserve bank in their geographic district. The Federal Reserve permits banks to borrow to meet seasonal fluctuations resulting from agricultural or construction cycles, and it lends to banks during times of acute financial distress that have made the banks illiquid but not bankrupt.

MANAGEMENT
Focus

The New CD Menagerie

When U.S. market interest rates began gradually rising after 2003, banks responded by rolling out new certificates of deposits for their customers to consider. "Opt-Up" and "Convertible" CDs permit depositors to shift funds from existing lower-rate CDs at no penalty but typically lock customers into terms ranging between twelve and thirty months. At some banks, depositors can purchase "Indexed" CDs with yields that adjust quarterly based on changes in yields on three-month Treasury bills. For depositors worried about inflation, there are now "Floating-Rate" CDs with money coupon payments that automatically vary with the year-to-year percentage change in the consumer price index. Some banks offer CDs with features similar to option contracts, such as the "No-Regrets" CD, which allows savers to adjust the CD's interest rate one time during its term without penalty, as long as they maintain the CD until its maturity. Others provide CDs with features similar to money market funds, such as the "Ready Access" CD that allows depositors to withdraw funds without penalties beginning seven days after purchasing the CD.

FOR CRITICAL ANALYSIS: Given that large-denomination CDs account for only about 15 percent of total liabilities and equity capital, what motivates banks to offer so many inducements for depositors to hold these deposits?

Many large CDs and repurchase agreement sales are dollar-denominated liabilities that banks issue outside U.S. borders. Consequently, these are Eurodollar liabilities of banks, which we discussed earlier in Chapter 3. Eurodollar liabilities are also included in the "other borrowings" category in Table 9-2.

The final kinds of controllable liabilities that banks issue are **subordinated notes and debentures.** These are capital market instruments with maturities in excess of one year. Many are similar to corporate bonds. But all banks issue subordinated notes and debentures with the understanding that those who hold them will have *subordinated claims* in the event of bank failures. This means that if a bank fails, holders of its subordinated notes and debentures will receive no payments until all depositors at the bank have received the funds from their accounts. These commercial bank liabilities are a portion of the "other liabilities" category in Table 9-2.

The equity capital of a bank is the excess of total assets over total liabilities. For the banking system as a whole, we estimate that equity capital amounts to about 8 percent of all bank liabilities and capital. The Federal Reserve reports equity capital infrequently, so we must rely on estimates for this figure.

> **4. What are the key liabilities of commercial banks?** Noncontrollable bank liabilities are demand deposits, other checkable deposits, savings deposits, and small-denomination time deposits. Controllable bank liabilities are large-denomination time deposits such as large CDs, purchased funds including sales of repurchase agreements, federal funds borrowings, borrowings from the Federal Reserve, and subordinated notes and debentures. The excess of assets over liabilities is a bank's equity capital, or net worth.

TRENDS IN BANK LIABILITIES AND EQUITY CAPITAL Figure 9-2 on the next page depicts the shares of total bank liabilities and equity capital accounted for by total deposits, other liabilities, and equity capital at various dates since 1961. "Other liabilities" include both purchased funds and subordinated notes and debentures.

As the figure makes clear, the general trend has been toward reduced dependence by banks on deposit funding. There has also been a slight upward trend in equity capital. The use of purchased funds and subordinated notes and debentures increased gradually through the 1960s, 1970s, and early 1980s, rose considerably during the 1990s, dropped slightly in the early 2000s, and then turned upward again.

Savings Institutions

Like commercial banks, savings institutions issue transactions deposits. Savings institutions differ from commercial banks mainly in the way they allocate their assets. Traditionally, these institutions have also faced a number of regulations designed especially for them.

A Diminished Industry

Over the last decades, savings institutions have experienced serious problems. Between 1986 and 1991, savings institutions as a whole failed to earn a net profit. The scope of the problems of the savings institution industry is displayed in Figure 9-3 on page 198, which plots the total

Subordinated notes and debentures: Capital market instruments with maturities in excess of one year that banks issue with the provision that depositors have primary claim to bank assets in the event of failure.

MONEYXTRA!
Online Case Study

To contemplate the kinds of management issues that banks face as they allocate their assets and liabilities, use the Chapter 9 Case Study, entitled "Getting Control of the Balance Sheet." **http://moneyxtra. swcollege.com**

On the Web
Where can one find the quickest links to banks on the Internet? The answer is AAAdir, located at **http://www.aaadir.com**. This site has links to more than 3,500 banking institutions and over 1,000 credit unions.

FIGURE 9-2
Commercial Bank Liabilities and Equity Capital.

Since the 1960s, there has been an overall decline in commercial banks' reliance on deposit funds. During the 1990s, banks increasingly funded their operations with purchased funds and other liabilities. After a slight dropoff, this trend has continued in recent years. They have also gradually increased their equity positions.

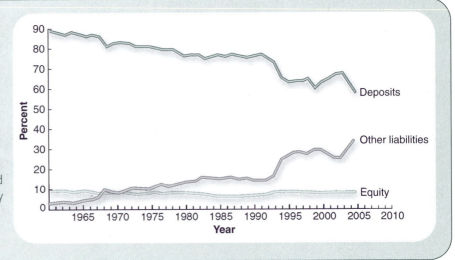

SOURCES: *Federal Reserve Bulletin* and H.8(510) *Statistical Release,* Board of Governors of the Federal Reserve System, various issues.

deposits at these institutions since early 1988. Total deposits at savings institutions have declined from nearly $1 trillion in the spring of 1988 to today's level of just under $800 billion, which nonetheless marks a recovery from the levels in the 1990s. Furthermore, even though the general savings institution collapse had ended by the beginning of 1993, these institutions continued to lose deposits at an average rate of nearly $3 billion each month. If this pace had continued, savings institutions would have ceased to exist by the second decade of this century.

What happened? There is no single answer to this question. Some savings institutions failed because of fraudulent business practices. Some failed because of economic circumstances beyond their control. Nevertheless, as we shall discuss in Chapter 11, most economists concur that the main reason that so many savings institutions disappeared was that

FIGURE 9-3
Deposits at Federally Insured Savings Institutions.

In spite of a recent recovery, deposits at savings institutions are more than 20 percent lower than at the end of the 1980s.

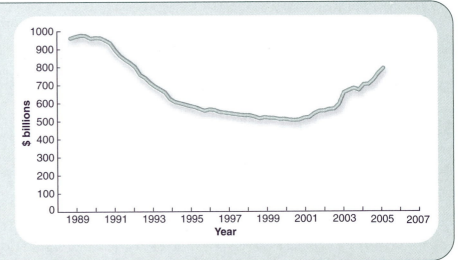

SOURCES: *Federal Reserve Bulletin,* Board of Governors of the Federal Reserve System; and *Quarterly Financial Results and Conditions of the Thrift Industry,* Office of Thrift Supervision, various issues.

federal regulations and deposit insurance combined to produce a significant moral-hazard problem. Their exposure to interest rate risk had already made savings institutions very fragile by the end of the 1970s, and then regulatory changes in the 1980s encouraged savings institution managers to undertake riskier activities. Their customers' deposits were federally insured, yet the premiums that savings institutions paid on their deposits were unrelated to the risks that they incurred. The result was a crisis that engulfed a very large number of savings banks and savings and loan associations. In the end, federal regulators seized and sold over $400 billion in savings institution assets. The ultimate loss to taxpayers in funding insured deposits lost by these institutions amounted to over $200 billion, or enough to fund much of the federal government's deficit for any year in the 1980s and early 1990s. As a consequence of these problems, the savings institution industry today is much smaller than it once was.

Assets and Liabilities of Savings Institutions

Table 9-4 lists the *combined* assets and liabilities of all of the nearly 900 federally insured savings institutions. Comparison of these institutions' assets and liabilities with those of commercial banks in Tables 9-1 and 9-2 shows some vague similarities. Both types of depository institutions issue deposits and depend on deposit funds in similar proportion to finance their activities. From Table 9-2, nearly 58 percent of commercial banks' liabilities and net worth is in deposit liabilities; Table 9-4 shows a 58.5 percent figure for savings institutions. Both kinds of institutions also make loans and hold securities and cash assets. There are dramatic differences, however, in the institutions' *asset allocations*.

MORTGAGE LOANS   From Table 9-4, we can see that the clearly dominant asset category for savings institutions is mortgage lending, which accounts for more than 62 percent of total savings institution assets.

A mortgage loan finances a purchase of real estate such as a tract of land or a structure such as a house. The borrower of a mortgage loan has the right to use the property while the mortgage is in effect. In return, the borrower must make regular payments of principal and interest.

Savings banks and savings and loan associations have always specialized in mortgage lending. Traditionally, this specialty has been their strength as well as their great weakness. It has been a strength because savings institutions have developed techniques for dealing with adverse-selection and moral-hazard problems that are endemic to mortgage lending. Savings institutions thereby have a managerial advantage over other potential competitors in this business.

Table 9-4 Assets and Liabilities of Savings Institutions ($ Billions)

Cash and securities	$ 74.0	5.5%	Total deposits	$784.6	58.5%
Mortgage loans	838.3	62.5%	Government borrowings	241.6	18.0%
Mortgage-backed securities	159.2	11.9%	Other borrowings	166.1	12.4%
Commercial loans	40.6	3.0%	Other liabilities	25.4	1.9%
Consumer loans	77.6	5.8%	Equity capital	123.1	9.2%
Other assets	151.1	11.3%			
Total assets	**$1,340.8**	**100.0%**	**Total equity & liabilities**	**$1,340.8**	**100.0%**

SOURCE: *Quarterly Financial Results and Conditions of the Thrift Industry,* Office of Thrift Supervision, May 2005.

The mortgage lending specialty of savings institutions has been a weakness because of the *interest rate risk* inherent in mortgage lending. Home mortgage loans typically have terms to maturity ranging from fifteen to thirty years. This means that when a savings institution grants a thirty-year mortgage loan at a fixed rate of 6 percent, it takes a chance that the rates that it must pay on its deposits and other liabilities will stay sufficiently below 6 percent to permit a long-term profit on the mortgage. Many savings institutions made exactly this bet in the early 1970s before adjustable-rate mortgages had become common. Then they watched in the late 1970s as market interest rates on deposits rose above the rates they were earning on their fixed-rate mortgage loans!

MORTGAGE-BACKED SECURITIES   As discussed in Chapter 3, a mortgage-backed security is a title to a share in the principal and interest earnings from a group of mortgages with similar characteristics, such as nearly identical default risks and the same terms to maturity. Many mortgage-backed securities are issued by government-sponsored agencies, such as the General National Mortgage Association (GNMA or "Ginnie Mae") or the Federal National Mortgage Association (FNMA or "Fannie Mae").

An institution such as the FNMA usually purchases mortgage loans from the savings institutions that initiated the loans. Typically, it pays the initiating institution fees to continue to collect principal and interest payments on its behalf. It *pools,* or segregates, the mortgage loans that it owns into groupings with like characteristics. It then sells mortgage-backed securities with yields based on the principal and interest payments derived from the underlying pools of loans.

Savings institutions themselves usually buy large numbers of mortgage-backed securities. As Table 9-4 indicates, savings institutions' holdings of mortgage-backed securities amount to almost 12 percent of their total assets. Consequently, these institutions allocate a total of 74 percent of their assets to mortgage-related activities.

OTHER LOANS AND ASSETS   Legislation passed by Congress in the early 1980s gave savings institutions the legal power to make commercial and consumer loans within specified limits. Most savings institutions have not reached those limits, however. Together, commercial and consumer loans amount to just over 14 percent of their assets.

Like commercial banks, savings institutions hold cash assets. They also hold U.S. government securities and state and municipal bonds. Together these assets amount to about 5.8 percent of the total assets of savings institutions.

> **On the Web**
> How does a credit union get started? To learn more about how to form a credit union, go to the home page of the National Credit Union Administration at **http://ncua.gov**. Under "General Information," click on "Guides, Manuals, and Forms." Then click on "Express Chartering Procedure."

> **5. How do savings institutions differ from commercial banks?**   The fundamental difference between savings institutions and commercial banks is that savings institutions are much more specialized in mortgage-related lending, and a much larger portion of their security holdings is devoted to mortgage-backed securities.

Credit Unions

There are almost 9,000 federally insured credit unions in the United States, serving over 70 million members. Table 9-5 shows the combined assets and liabilities of all federally insured credit unions, which make up 97 percent of the total number of these depository institutions.

Credit unions normally are relatively uncomplicated institutions. Share deposits of members account for more than 86 percent of liabilities and net worth of these institutions, and loans to members compose almost two-thirds of all credit union assets. Unlike commercial banks, credit unions are nonprofit institutions. Credit unions also differ from other depository institutions in that they take in deposits from members only and lend only to members. Most surveys show that credit unions charge 10 to 25 percent less than banks for car loans, credit cards, and unsecured personal loans and pay one-half to one percentage point higher yields on deposits.

Defining the Limits of Credit Union Membership

The Federal Credit Union Act of 1934 limited membership in these depository institutions to "groups having a common bond of occupation or association, or to groups within a well-defined neighborhood, community, or rural district." Congress designed this Depression-era law to ensure that low-income customers shunned by banks would nonetheless be able to obtain bank-like services at reasonable rates. Qualifying for membership in a credit union required an individual to meet legal criteria specific to that credit union. Credit union membership rules typically required an individual to be associated with a particular business or occupation.

Two benefits were associated with membership restrictions. One was that they usually limited the credit unions' clienteles to people who had steady incomes. Thus, credit unions had access to thrifty savers who provided funds that credit unions could then lend to other members who were more creditworthy than the average personal-loan customer of a commercial bank. Because the loans required less monitoring, credit unions could keep costs low. The reduced risks and lower costs that credit unions faced enabled them to pay higher rates on deposits and charge lower rates on loans.

Second, when Congress established membership rules for credit unions, it "compensated" credit unions for the restriction by exempting them from most types of taxation faced by commercial banks. This tax exemption is another factor that gave credit unions a significant cost advantage over commercial banks and many savings institutions.

Conservative No Longer?

In July 1998, Congress changed the definition of a credit union to "a viable alternative retail bank." It directed the National Credit Union Administration (NCUA), the chief federal regulator, to define a "local, well-defined community" for credit union membership. The NCUA

MONEYXTRA!
Another Perspective

To learn more about the issues posed by recent changes in credit union membership rules, see the Chapter 9 reading, entitled "Credit Unions and the Common Bond," by William Emmons and Frank Schmid of the Federal Reserve Bank of St. Louis.
**http://moneyxtra.
swcollege.com**

Table 9-5 Assets and Liabilities and Equity at Federally Insured Credit Unions ($ Billions)

Loans	$419.0	63.3%	Share deposits	$570.2	86.1%
Securities	163.7	24.7%	Other liabilities & equity	92.2	13.9%
Cash assets	53.6	8.1%			
Other assets	26.1	3.9%			
Total assets	**$662.4**	**100.0%**	**Total liabilities & equity**	**$662.4**	**100.0%**

SOURCE: *Statistics for Federally Insured Credit Unions,* National Credit Union Administration, May 2005.

Just How Large Is an Appropriate "Field of Membership" for a Credit Union?

In March 2003, the National Credit Union Administration (NCUA) issued new "field-of-membership" regulations aimed at clarifying the "common interests" required to define a target community for a credit union. A month later, a credit union in Utah expanded its "field of membership" beyond a single county. According to the credit union, under the new rules its legally permissible field of membership included seven counties, which together encompassed a geographic area larger than the state of Maryland. Currently, the American Bankers Association is testing the legal limits of the NCUA's new field-of-membership rules in U.S. federal court.

FOR CRITICAL ANALYSIS: Why do you suppose that commercial banks contend that current laws and court interpretations of those laws give credit unions an "unfair" competitive advantage?

responded by developing criteria that directed any credit union seeking to serve a county of less than 300,000 people to cite evidence of "interaction" or "common interests" in the target community, such as the existence of local festivals or area newspapers. (Credit unions are viewing "common interests" as encompassing ever-larger geographic regions; see the *Policy Focus: Just How Large Is an Appropriate "Field of Membership" for a Credit Union?*)

Under these new definitions, credit unions are beginning to serve members who look more like the traditional household customers of commercial banks. As a result, credit unions have begun to grapple with problems faced by banks. For instance, credit unions have faced important risk issues in recent years. Some credit unions have run into significant difficulties as they have sought to increase their returns through derivatives speculation. At various times in the past, this has led regulators to contemplate significant changes in the structure of the federal insurance for credit unions.

6. How do credit unions raise and allocate their funds? Nearly all the funds raised by credit unions come from share deposits that they issue to members. They allocate the majority of their funds to loans and the remainder to securities and cash. Until fairly recently, credit union deposit-taking and lending activities were restricted to narrowly defined memberships. Today, however, the criteria for credit union membership are so broadly defined that credit unions are likely to more closely resemble commercial banks in the future.

Chapter Summary

1. The Historical Origins of Modern Banking Institutions: Deposit-taking, lending institutions have existed since the earliest human civilizations. Modern versions of these institutions originated with the merchant bankers of medieval Italy. Since that time, depository institutions have specialized in maintaining deposit accounts for, processing payments on behalf of, and making loans to their customers.

2. Why Depository Institutions Are Segmented: Commercial banks, savings institutions, and credit unions have always specialized. In the 1930s, however, Congress enacted legislation that strengthened the distinctions among these institutions.

3. The Key Assets of Commercial Banks: These include loans such as commercial and industrial, real estate, and consumer loans; securities such as U.S. government bonds; and cash assets such as vault cash and reserve deposits held at the Federal Reserve.

4. The Key Liabilities of Commercial Banks: These include so-called noncontrollable liabilities such as checking, savings, and small-denomination time deposits and controllable liabilities such as certificates of deposit and federal funds borrowings.

5. How Savings Institutions Differ from Commercial Banks: The key difference is that savings institutions have specialized much more narrowly in mortgage-related activities. Key activities include mortgage lending and holding mortgage-backed securities.

6. How Credit Unions Raise and Allocate Their Funds: Almost all of credit union funds come from share deposits of members. Credit unions lend the majority of these funds to members. In the past, credit union membership was limited to specific occupations, but legislation enacted in the 1990s significantly broadened the scope of eligible credit union members. Thus, in the future credit unions undoubtedly will come to look more like commercial banks.

Questions and Problems

(Answers to odd-numbered questions and problems may be found on the Web at **http://money.swcollege.com** under "Student Resources.")

1. Explain why it was natural in early times for goldsmiths to become bankers.

2. Which types of modern bank assets do you think might be similar to those on the balance sheets of Italian merchant bankers? What bank assets might truly be "new"?

3. Explain the difference between an asset and a liability.

4. Based on the data in Tables 9-1 on page 191, and 9-2 on page 194, would you expect that bank assets or bank liabilities would tend to have longer maturities, on average? Do you think that this could pose any problems for bank managers?

5. Based on the data in Table 9-4 on page 199, would you expect that savings institution assets or liabilities would have longer average maturities? Explain your reasoning. Discuss the enhanced problems that this maturity "mismatch" poses for managers of savings institutions. How do these problems compare with those faced by commercial banks (see question 4)?

6. Derivative instruments (covered in Chapter 6) do not appear anywhere in the balance sheets discussed in this chapter. Yet many depository institutions are active derivatives traders. Explain why derivatives are absent from depository institution balance sheets.

7. In light of your answers to questions 4 and 5, why do you suppose that depository institutions use derivatives? In answering this question, draw from what you also learned in Chapter 6 about the uses of derivative securities.

8. Based on the total asset figures in Tables 9-1 on page 191, 9-2 on page 194, and 9-4 on page 199, how much larger (in percentage terms) is the commercial banking industry as compared with savings institutions? As compared with credit unions?

9. What are fundamental differences between savings institutions and commercial banks? What are key similarities between the two types of depository institutions?

10. Commercial banks have contended that the broadened membership criteria for credit unions are "unfair." Do you agree? Why?

Before the Test

Test your understanding of the material covered in this chapter by taking the Chapter 9 interactive quiz at **http://money.swcollege.com**.

Online Application

Internet URL: **http://www.ots.treas.gov**

Title: Office of Thrift Supervision (OTS)

Navigation: Go to the OTS home page at the above Web site. Click on "Applications." Then click on "Application Status Reports," and then "Applications in Process Data Base."

Application: Under "Date," select "Filed Date," and within the field for the period, type in a recent period spanning at least several months. Under "Application Type," select "New Institution." Leave institution and location boxes blank, and leave all other boxes set on "All." Then click on "Search."

1. How many applications for *new* savings institutions did the OTS receive during the period you selected?

2. Now go back to the Applications page, reset the "Application Type" field to "Subsidiary," and redo the search leaving all other fields the same. Were there more or fewer applications for new subsidiaries? What can you conclude about the main way that applicants seek to enlarge their presence in the savings institution industry? Is this experience consistent with the discussion in this chapter?

For Group Study and Analysis: Assign groups to use the search technique above to track applications for new savings institution charters and subsidiaries by state or region. Have the groups report back to the class. Are there any clear geographic trends in the savings institution industry?

Selected References and Further Reading

Ashcraft, Adam. "Are Banks Really Special? New Evidence from the FDIC-Induced Failure of Healthy Banks." Federal Reserve Bank of New York Staff Report No. 176, December 2003.

Dwyer, Gerald. "Wildcat Banking, Banking Panics, and Free Banking in the United States." Federal Reserve Bank of Atlanta *Economic Review* 81 (December 1996): 1–20.

Emmons, William, and Frank Schmid. "Membership Structure, Competition, and Occupational Credit Union Deposit Rates." Federal Reserve Bank of St. Louis *Review* 83 (January/February 2001): 41–50.

Hammond, Bray. *Banks and Politics in America.* Princeton: Princeton University Press, 1985.

Laderman, Elizabeth, and Wayne Passmore. "Is Mortgage Lending by Savings Associations Special?" Federal Reserve Bank of San Francisco *Economic Review* (no. 2, 1998): 30–45.

Srinivasan, Aruna, and B. Frank King. "Credit Union Issues." Federal Reserve Bank of Atlanta *Economic Review* 83 (1998): 32–41.

White, Eugene. *The Regulation and Reform of the American Banking System, 1900–1929.* Princeton: Princeton University Press, 1983.

Wicker, Elmus. *The Banking Panics of the Great Depression.* Cambridge: Cambridge University Press, 1996.

MoneyXtra

Log on to the MoneyXtra Web site now (**http://moneyxtra.swcollege.com**) for additional learning resources such as practice quizzes, case studies, readings, and additional economic applications.

The Business of Banking—

Depository Institution Management and Performance

The latest big trend at U.S. banks is to find as many new ways as possible to make their wealthy customers feel as though they are VIPs. A growing number of banks have created special divisions that cater to the rich, the richer, and the richest. The superwealthy qualify for services and products that banks reserve for only the most important VIPs, such as week-long seminars on inheritance law and currency trading for the children of multimillionaires. At the same time, banks are also finding new ways to cater to the "mass affluent"—people who aren't quite "rich" but still have at least $100,000 in total assets. Without giving the "mass affluent" true VIP treatment, banks are offering this group preferred terms on loans and bonus services, such as extra help on planning for retirement and developing college savings plans.

Banks outside the United States are also making efforts to cater to their rich customers. HSBC, a large bank based in London, provides its own special set of services to wealthy people all over the world. For example, the bank offers special etiquette classes for self-made Asian entrepreneurs who want to learn how to mingle properly with others in their income group. In addition, if a wealthy Pakistani customer cannot decide who should take over the family business, the bank will fly a top psychologist to Karachi to offer advice about which family member's personality is best suited to the job.

> ## Fundamental Issues
>
> 1. What are the key sources of depository institution revenues and costs?
>
> 2. What are common measures of depository institution profitability?
>
> 3. How has the philosophy of depository institution management evolved?
>
> 4. What are key elements of the modern asset-liability approach to managing risks at depository institutions?
>
> 5. What is the main determinant of depository institutions' performance?

Although every bank has its own way of attracting and trying to keep wide varieties of customers, it is not unusual for certain general management philosophies to become predominant across nearly all banks. In this chapter, you will learn about alternative bank management approaches. In addition, you will consider the sources of depository institution profitability and evaluate the recent performance of these financial institutions.

Basic Issues in Depository Institution Management

As we discussed in Chapter 9, banks, savings institutions, and credit unions specialize in various ways. Nevertheless, the fundamental economics of these depository institutions is very similar. All depository institutions incur the same basic kinds of expenses, and all derive earnings from similar, if not always identical, types of operations. The profits that they earn, of course, are the excess of revenues over costs. We begin our discussion of the economics of depository institutions by evaluating how to judge their performances in the marketplace.

Sources of Depository Institution Revenues

Interest income: Interest revenues that depository institutions derive from their holdings of loans and securities.

Noninterest income: Revenues that depository institutions earn from sources other than interest income, such as trading profits or fees that they charge for services that they provide their customers.

Banks measure their *revenues,* or incomes, as *flows* over time. For instance, a depository institution can track its interest income from loans and securities over a month, a quarter, or a year. Most depository institutions report quarterly and annual income flows.

INTEREST INCOME   Interest earnings on assets such as commercial and industrial loans are a key factor influencing the economic behavior of banks. The interest earnings that depository institutions derive from their loans and securities are the institutions' **interest income.** To see how interest income is a *flow* of earnings over time, consider an example in which a bank makes a $15,000 loan to an individual to help finance the purchase of a new car. The loan is a $15,000 asset for the bank at the moment it is made. If the auto loan is a typical installment loan, then the borrower will make monthly payments of principal and interest. This interest income is part of the bank's total revenues.

As Figure 10-1 shows, interest income accounts for about 64 percent of the revenues of commercial banks. It also represents the bulk of income to savings institutions and credit unions.

NONINTEREST INCOME   As Figure 10-1 indicates, commercial banks earn about 36 percent of their revenues as **noninterest income.** Noninterest income includes all income from sources other than interest income and is generated in several ways. One way that many depository institutions generate noninterest income is by selling some of the loans that they have made to other financial institutions—often at a higher market value. In addition, such loan sales commonly include an arrangement in which the depository institution selling the loans continues to maintain the loan accounts on behalf of the purchaser. That is, it continues to manage and process payments and expenses relating to the loans even though those loans are off its books. In return for such services, the depository institution charges fees to the loan purchaser. These loan management fees are a source of noninterest income.

TRADING INCOME   Depository institutions also generate noninterest income from trading in derivative instruments such as futures, options, or swaps. As discussed in Chapter 6, derivatives trading is often intended to *hedge* against risks. Such trading typically generates few revenues because depository institutions design hedges to avoid capital losses, thereby eliminating profit opportunities as well. Nevertheless, depository institutions also engage in speculative derivatives trading that can generate income (and losses!).

INCOME FROM CUSTOMER FEES   *Deposit fee income,* the income that depository institutions earn by charging fees for their depository services, has been a growing source of noninterest income. Many depository institutions now charge many of their customers

---

FIGURE 10-1
Sources of Commercial Bank Revenues.

Noninterest income has become a more important source of bank revenues in recent years, although banks continue to derive the majority of their revenues from their interest earnings.

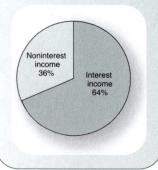

SOURCE: Federal Deposit Insurance Corporation.

fees for printing checks, clearing checks, making cash withdrawals above a certain number per month, and making transfers between accounts. Today, most commercial banks charge a fee to use automated teller machines (ATMs), whereas in 1989 only a fifth of banks charged such a fee.

Some banks have even experimented with charging fees when customers with small accounts do business with human tellers at their branches. For example, in the mid-1990s First Chicago Bank began charging a $3 teller fee to account holders with checking balances under $2,500 or a combined checking/saving balance less than $15,000. As justification, the bank pointed out that, in a given year, a $500 checking account would usually yield $25 in interest income and $100 in fee income to the bank. But if the account holder were to make eight ATM transactions and four teller transactions per month, maintaining the account would cost the bank $216. Hence, the bank claimed it would lose $91 per year on such an account. For a checking account with a balance of over $5,000, the bank would earn a net profit of $314.

Naturally, account holders do not like deposit fees, and their complaints get a lot of media attention. But in the big picture of depository institution revenues, deposit fees are small potatoes. Such fees account for only about 4½ to 5 percent of the total revenues of commercial banks. Nevertheless, fees typically account for 15 to 25 percent of total noninterest income. The total estimated deposit fee income earned by commercial banks in 2006 was more than $40 billion—more than six times the amount of fee income that banks earned in 1985. Deposit fees promise to continue to rise as a share of the noninterest income that banks and other depository institutions earn.

Costs of Depository Institution Operations

The costs that depository institutions incur include interest expenses, expenses for loan loss provisions, and real resource expenses.

INTEREST EXPENSES   Depository institution managers issue deposits and other liabilities to raise the funds that they allocate to income-generating assets. To attract funds, depository institutions must pay interest on these liabilities, and this **interest expense** is a major component of depository institution costs. As shown in Figure 10-2, interest expense accounts for 31 percent of the total costs incurred by commercial banks. Typically, this percentage is approximately the same for savings institutions and credit unions as well.

EXPENSES FOR LOAN LOSS PROVISIONS   Banking is a risky business because borrowers default on their loans from time to time. Consequently, depository institutions earmark part of their cash assets as **loan loss reserves.** This portion of their cash assets is held as available liquidity that the banks will recognize as depleted in the event that loan defaults actually occur. (Establishing appropriate loan loss reserves is one of the most challenging day-to-day management tasks at depository institutions; see on the next page *What Happens When the Art of Setting Loan Loss Reserves Is Subjected to Harsh Criticism?*)

From year to year, depository institutions must add to their loan loss reserves as loan defaults cause them to decline. These additions are **loan loss provisions,** and they constitute an expense for depository institutions. That is, they are funds that depository institutions must spend to make up for loan defaults that are an unavoidable part of their lending operations. Figure 10-2 shows that loan loss provisions account for about 12 percent of expenses by commercial banks.

Interest expense: The portion of depository institution costs incurred through payments of interest to holders of the institutions' liabilities.

Loan loss reserves: An amount of cash assets that depository institutions hold as liquidity that they expect to be depleted as a result of loan defaults.

Loan loss provisions: An expense that depository institutions incur when they allocate funds to loan loss reserves.

**FIGURE 10-2
Commercial
Bank Expenses.**

Over half of the expenses of commercial banks are noninterest expenses on real resources such as labor and capital goods. Interest expenses on deposit funds and purchased funds account for nearly all remaining expenses, although expenses on loan loss provisions typically account for a portion of total bank costs.

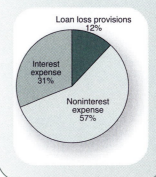

SOURCE: Federal Deposit Insurance Corporation.

The Art of Setting Loan Loss Reserves Is Subjected to Harsh Criticism?

Accountants at depository institutions like to say that determining the "best" level of loan loss reserves at a depository institution is an art, not a science. In recent years, depository institutions have confronted a number of critics of their "artistic" ability in performing this fundamental management task.

Traditionally, depository institution managers have prided themselves on being conservative by setting aside potentially more-than-sufficient loan loss reserves. In 1998, however, the Securities and Exchange Commission claimed that SunTrust Bank had overstated its loan loss reserves in an effort to manipulate its earnings reports. In the early 2000s, the Federal Accounting Standards Board also began

criticizing all depository institutions for being too conservative in their loan loss provisions. During the same period, however, depository institution regulators such as the Federal Deposit Insurance Corporation and the Office of Thrift Supervision penalized several depository institutions for failing to set aside *enough* loan loss reserves. Not surprisingly, many depository institution managers have come to dread meetings to establish loan loss reserves.

FOR CRITICAL ANALYSIS: How could depository institution managers "manipulate earnings" by varying loan loss reserves?

REAL RESOURCE EXPENSES Like any other kind of firm, a depository institution must use traditional factors of production—labor, capital, and land—in its operations. It must pay wages and salaries to its employees, purchase or lease capital goods such as bank branch buildings and computer equipment, and pay rental fees for the use of land on which its offices and branches are situated.

Figure 10-2 indicates that expenses on real resources amount to over half of total costs for commercial banks. Clearly, real resource expenditures are not a trivial portion of total depository institution costs. In recent years, even though many depository institutions have sought to cut these expenses by reducing their employment of human resources, total employment in banking has increased. (Indeed, banking employment has grown relative to other jobs in the economy; see the *Policy Focus: Is Banking a New Engine for U.S. Employment Growth?*)

> **1. What are the key sources of depository institution revenues and costs?**
> The predominant source of revenues for a typical depository institution is interest income. A secondary source is noninterest income, of which a growing portion is deposit fee income. The two main types of costs that depository institutions incur are interest expenses and real resource expenses. A third key cost is expenses arising from provisions for loan loss reserves.

Measuring Depository Institution Profitability

A depository institution's *profit,* or net income, is the dollar amount by which its combined interest and noninterest income exceeds its total costs. The dollar amount of profit by itself does not always tell us much, however. To see this, suppose that you are told that an unnamed bank earned $10 million in profit last year. This seems like a lot. And it would be if the bank had only $100 million in assets, because then the bank would have earned an average *rate* of profit of 10 percent relative to its base of assets. But if the bank had *$10 billion* in assets, a dollar profit of $10 million would be minuscule; its rate of profit relative to its assets would be

Is Banking a New Engine for U.S. Employment Growth?

In the early to middle 2000s, the media focused considerable attention on the slow pace of U.S. job creation. As Figure 10-3 indicates, during this period employment at commercial banks, savings institutions, and credit unions increased as a share of total employment. Indeed between 1995 and 2005, depository institutions created more than 1 million new jobs for the U.S. economy.

FOR CRITICAL ANALYSIS: How might greater U.S. exports of financial services to other nations have contributed to more hiring at U.S. depository institutions?

FIGURE 10-3
Employment at Depository Institutions as a Share of Total U.S. Employment.

Employment increased at depository institutions in the 2000s even as overall U.S. job growth lagged.

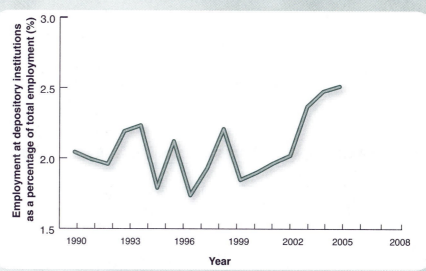

SOURCES: *American Banker; Economic Indicators;* authors' estimates.

---

only 0.1 percent. Consequently, to make better judgments about how to rate a depository institution's profitability relative to others, we need to compare its absolute profit with some measure of the depository institution's size.

RETURN ON ASSETS   There are two key measures of depository institution profitability that permit such comparisons. One is **return on assets,** which is absolute dollar profit as a percentage of the dollar value of the depository institution's assets. We can compute return on assets using the following formula:

$$\begin{array}{c} \text{Percentage} \\ \text{return} \\ \text{on assets} \end{array} = \frac{\text{absolute profit}}{\text{total assets}} \times 100.$$

Return on assets: A depository institution's profit as a percentage of its total assets.

For the case of a bank with $1 billion ($1,000 million) in assets earning an annual profit of $10 million, the return on assets is equal to the ratio $10 million/$1,000 million multiplied by a factor of 100, or 1 percent. For the bank with assets of $10 billion ($10,000 million) and an annual profit of $10 million, the return on assets is equal to the ratio $10 million/$10,000 million multiplied by 100, or 0.1 percent. The return-on-assets measure of profitability makes clear that in this example the smaller bank is much more profitable than the larger bank.

RETURN ON EQUITY   Another common measure of depository institution profitability is **return on equity.** This is the absolute profit of a depository institution as a percentage of the depository institution's equity capital. To compute return on equity, we use the following formula:

$$\text{Percentage return on equity} = \frac{\text{absolute profit}}{\text{equity capital}} \times 100.$$

Suppose that a small bank has $70 million in equity capital and earns a profit of $10 million during a given year. Then its return on equity for the year is equal to the ratio $10 million/$70 million multiplied by 100, or about 14.3 percent. During the same year, a larger bank with $800 million in equity capital earns a profit of $130 million, so its return on equity is equal to the ratio $130 million/$800 million multiplied by 100, or 16.3 percent. Based on this return-on-equity measure, the larger bank has outperformed the smaller bank.

Figure 10-4 shows how commercial banks have performed since 1990 based on both their average return on assets and their average return on equity. Banks' returns on assets and equity rose in the early 1990s and leveled off thereafter.

NET INTEREST MARGIN   Return on assets and return on equity are *retrospective* measures of profitability, meaning that we can calculate them after the fact. Once we know a depository institution's profit and the amount of its assets or equity capital for a recent period, we can compute either profitability measure. Then we can try to judge how well the institution has performed in the near past.

But suppose that we are trying to gauge a depository institution's *current* or likely *future* profitability performance. Although recent figures on return on assets and return on equity might give us some basis for estimating the institution's present or future profitability, it would be nice to have a more *prospective,* or forward-looking, indicator of profitability. This would be especially true for a bank stockholder who is trying to assess the current performance of the bank's managers.

The most common prospective indicator of a depository institution's profitability is called the **net interest margin.** This is the difference between a depository institution's interest income and interest expenses as a percentage of total assets. We can calculate net interest margin as follows:

$$\text{Net interest margin} = \frac{\text{interest income} - \text{interest expenses}}{\text{total assets}} \times 100.$$

Because interest income is such a large portion of depository institution revenues while interest expenses represent a significant portion of costs, net interest margin is an indicator of current and future performance. A depository institution's exact net interest margin can be computed retrospectively by looking at past interest income, interest expenses, and assets. But the future net interest margin for a depository institution can also be approximated using current data.

To see how this may be done, consider an example. During the year just past, a bank's net interest margin, calculated by computing the difference between interest income and expenses

---

Return on equity: A depository institution's profit as a percentage of its equity capital.

On the Web
How are U.S. banks performing? Keep tabs on various banking performance measures at the Web site of the Federal Deposit Insurance Corporation, **http://www.fdic.gov**. Click on "Industry Analysis," and then on "Bank Data and Statistics." Then click on "Statistics on Banking" to review the latest quarter's bank performance data.

Net interest margin: The difference between a depository institution's interest income and interest expenses as a percentage of total assets.

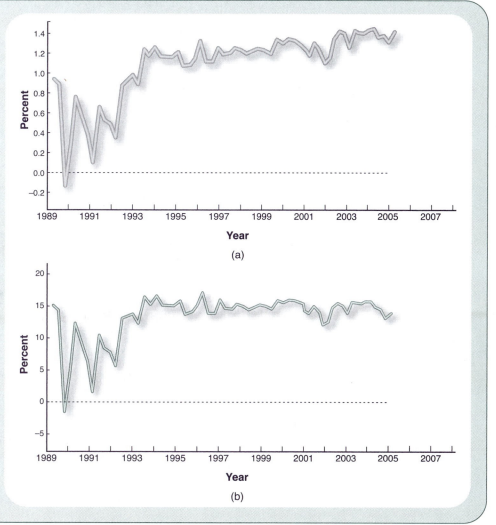

FIGURE 10-4
Commercial Banks' Average Returns on Assets and Equity.

Panel (a) shows that the average return on assets of commercial banks rose in the early 1990s and then leveled off, and panel (b) shows that this was also true of the average return on equity. Both measures of bank profitability were much more volatile in the early 1990s than they have been since.

SOURCE: Federal Deposit Insurance Corporation.

as a percentage of the bank's total assets, was 3.3 percent. During the most recent quarter, however, the bank's average interest earned on loans and securities was 8.2 percent, while the average interest rate that it paid to borrow funds and issue deposit liabilities and raise equity funds was 5.4 percent. Assuming that the bank can maintain this most recent level of performance across all assets and liabilities, then the *prospective* net interest margin is simply the difference between 8.2 percent and 5.4 percent, or 2.8 percent. This would indicate that, relative to last year, this bank's performance for the current year is deteriorating.

To see how the net interest margin often proves to be a useful indicator of depository institution profitability in the near future, consider the following figures for the 1990s and 2000s. The average net interest margin at commercial banks gradually increased during the early 1990s by nearly one-half of a percentage point. This rise in the net interest margin preceded the sharp increase in return on equity shown for that time in Figure 10-4. By 2000 the net

MONEYXTRA!
Online Case Study

To contemplate an example of a situation in which it is important to understand the various measures of bank performance, go to the Chapter 10 Case Study, entitled "Market Share versus Profits in Banking." **http:// moneyxtra.swcollege.com** interest margin had leveled off and begun to decline, as had the returns on assets and equity shown in Figure 10-4 before a sustained recovery beginning in 2001.

> **2. What are common measures of depository institution profitability?** One typical profitability measure is return on assets, which is profit as a percentage of total assets. Another is return on equity, or profit as a percentage of equity capital. A profitability measure that people often use to assess the current and future prospects of a depository institution is its net interest margin, which is the difference between the depository institution's interest income and interest expenses as a percentage of total assets.

Theories of Bank Management

Certainly, the state of the economy, the stability of financial markets and interest rates, and other factors affecting depository institution costs and revenues can have significant effects on depository institution profitability. For reasons that we discuss later in the chapter, however, many economists believe the quality of any given depository institution's management is the most crucial factor influencing the institution's performance.

The Evolution of Depository Institution Management Philosophy

There is no single "right" way to operate a commercial bank or other depository financial institution. Indeed, there are several competing theories of depository institution management.

THE REAL BILLS DOCTRINE   The Italian merchant bankers discussed in Chapter 9 found that they faced a fundamental trade-off between earnings and liquidity. If a merchant bank made loans to Mediterranean traders who could repay the loans very quickly, then the bank could feel secure that it would maintain a ready stock of cash assets. Such loans would not only make the bank more liquid but would also reduce the riskiness of its portfolio of loans. The problem was that high-liquidity, low-risk loans also yielded low returns to the bank. The Italian merchant bankers tried to balance liquidity, risk, and return by making short-term loans to traders who needed them to finance transporting goods to another location for sale. There were risks of damage or loss in Mediterranean storms, but if the traders could offer proof of insurance and of ready buyers at the goods' destinations, then the banks could feel fairly confident of repayment of such loans.

Real bills doctrine: A bank management philosophy that calls for lending primarily to borrowers who will use the funds to finance production or shipping of physical goods, thereby ensuring speedy repayment of the loans.

Self-Liquidating Loans   Banks also began to make loans to finance the production of goods, knowing that they would receive payment when the goods were produced and sold. Loans to finance the transportation or production of goods came to be called self-liquidating loans, because the likelihood of repayment was so high that the banks could regard them as highly liquid. (For several key Chinese banks, loans have been far from "self-liquidating"; see the *Global Focus: Reforming China's Banking System*.)

Later, as other banks across Europe adopted this approach to lending, the term *real bills* came to be used for these loans, because banks viewed the loans as bills of credit that were claims on the resources whose transit the loans were used to finance. As a result, the bank management philosophy of lending to finance production or shipping of goods came to be known as the **real bills doctrine.**

GLOBAL
Focus

Reforming China's Banking System

China has nearly 1.3 billion residents and is experiencing one of the fastest rates of economic growth in the world. Yet only 1 million Chinese residents, or less than one out of every thousand, possess a credit card. Even though small and medium-sized firms account for nearly half of total annual sales in China, they receive only slightly over 10 percent of total business loans.

The reason Chinese banking is lagging is that 59 percent of all deposits are held at the four largest institutions, all of which are government sponsored. Although these banks recently received $16 billion in additional public funds, each is technically insolvent—the value of the liabilities it owes to others exceeds the value of its assets, or amounts owed to the bank by others. At least 20 percent of each government-sponsored bank's loans are nonperforming, meaning that the bank is unlikely to receive full repayment of interest and principal.

To promote modernization in lending techniques, the Chinese government recently opened banking markets to entry by both newly chartered private Chinese banks and more than 200 foreign banks. It has also reduced certain regulatory constraints on the large banks it sponsors, in the hope that eventually those banks will become more like private banks in other nations—particularly in terms of pursuing profitable but high-quality loan customers.

FOR CRITICAL ANALYSIS: Why might government sponsorship have contributed to less innovation and slower development of Chinese banking?

A Self-Defeating Approach There are two difficulties with the real bills doctrine. First, if banks restrict themselves to the most short-term, highly liquid loans, then they also must accept lower returns on their lending, because more liquid loans normally carry lower risk. The second difficulty arises if all banks follow the real bills doctrine simultaneously and an economic downturn occurs. If producers and traders who otherwise would like to borrow find that the demand for their goods has fallen, then they will be unable to convince banks to lend to them. After all, such loans will not appear to banks to be self-liquidating. But if banks follow the real bills doctrine and choose not to lend, their borrowers' businesses most likely will fail, reinforcing the economic—and banking—downturn.

One way to try to salvage the real bills doctrine is to create a *central bank* that would stand ready to lend to banks when economic downturns reduce the liquidity of bank loans. Thus, the central bank would act as a *lender of last resort* during bad times. It would ensure liquidity of the banking system as a whole and thereby permit banks to follow the real bills doctrine. Although we shall see in Chapter 14 that today many economists question whether this is the fundamental rationale for central banking, it was in the minds of many who designed the Federal Reserve System in the early 1900s.

THE SHIFTABILITY THEORY In light of the problems that the real bills doctrine posed for earnings and for liquidity during economic downturns, many banks adopted a compromise position. They still made self-liquidating loans when feasible, but they also began to make longer-term loans with higher default risk. To balance the liquidity loss and greater risk, banks used some of their available funds to acquire low-risk securities such as government securities and commercial paper. Banks regarded these securities as **secondary reserves** that could easily be converted into cash if some borrowers defaulted as depositors sought to withdraw some of their funds. These secondary reserves of securities supplemented the traditional **primary reserves** of cash assets that the banks held.

This approach to "shifting" bank asset allocations to attain a different balance among earnings, liquidity, and risk became known as the **shiftability theory** of bank management. It was

Secondary reserves: Securities that depository institutions can easily convert to cash in the event that such a need arises.

Primary reserves: Cash assets.

Shiftability theory: A management approach in which depository institutions hold a mix of illiquid loans and more liquid securities that act as a secondary reserve held as a contingency against potential liquidity problems.

the original justification for the modern management strategy in which depository institutions hold a mix of long-term loans, short-term loans, and liquid securities.

Many U.S. depository institutions had adopted the shiftability theory by the end of the 1920s. But the stock market crash of 1929 and the subsequent years of the Great Depression exposed a fundamental difficulty with this approach. The problem was that even high-liquidity securities with low default risk were subject to significant interest rate risks. Securities prices plummeted at the outset of the Great Depression, so securities did not turn out to be such an effective counterbalance to longer-term, higher-risk lending after all. A number of banks (over one-third of those then in existence) failed during the Great Depression years.

Anticipated-income approach: A depository institution management philosophy that calls for depository institutions to make loans more liquid by issuing them as installment loans that generate income in the form of periodic payments of interest and principal.

THE ANTICIPATED-INCOME APPROACH   After World War II, depository institution managers developed a way to make their loans more liquid. Adopting the **anticipated-income approach** to depository institution management, they made a larger number of loans as installment loans. As we discussed in Chapter 9, with these loans borrowers repay the principal and interest in installments.

This approach to loan management automatically made the loan portfolios of depository institutions more liquid. Because depository institutions receive continuous streams of payments from borrowers, the anticipated-income approach effectively made many more loans "self-liquidating" in a manner that the Italian merchant bankers of old could not have imagined. Even long-term installment loans now could generate month-to-month cash liquidity.

Conversion-of-funds approach: A depository institution management philosophy under which managers try to fund assets of specific maturities by issuing liabilities with like maturities.

THE CONVERSION-OF-FUNDS APPROACH   The anticipated-income approach was a breakthrough in depository institution management and continues to be widely used today. But, in the 1960s and 1970s, depository institutions sought to find ways to better manage all items on their balance sheets. This led to the **conversion-of-funds approach** to management, in which depository institution managers tried to fund assets of given maturities with sources of funds with maturities of similar length.

For example, under this approach a commercial bank manager contemplating an expansion of short-term business lending would fund new loans by issuing short-term deposits. This would ensure that the bank's net interest margin would be fixed over the short end of the maturity spectrum, thereby protecting the profitability of its short-term loan portfolio from interest rate risk.

> **3. How has the philosophy of depository institution management evolved?**   The fundamental trade-off that depository institutions face is between earnings and liquidity. The real bills doctrine sought to achieve both higher earnings and higher liquidity by lending only for projects that would yield quick and sure returns. Because relatively few such lending opportunities are available, over the years depository institution managers have developed a number of competing approaches to the earnings-liquidity trade-off. These include the shiftability theory, the anticipated-income approach, and the conversion-of-funds approach.

Asset-liability management approach: A depository institution management philosophy that emphasizes the simultaneous determination of both the asset and the liability sides of the institution's balance sheet.

Modern Asset-Liability Management

The conversion-of-funds approach to depository institution management was the last step to the modern approach. Today, depository institution managers actively follow an **asset-liability management approach,** which entails the coordination of all balance-sheet items so as to maximize the profitability of the depository institution. The problem, however, is figuring out how to coordinate asset-liability choices. How should a depository institution decide which short-term or long-term loans to make, which securities to hold and at what maturities, how much cash to keep on hand, how many certificates of deposit (CDs) to issue and at what maturities, how much overnight or term federal funds borrowing to do, and so on? The modern answer to this question is for depository institution managers to try to mix and match maturities while simultaneously choosing which assets to hold and which liabilities to issue in light of the interest rate risks that they face.

GAP MANAGEMENT One technique that many depository institution managers have developed to help them manage both sides of their balance sheets simultaneously is **gap management.** This asset-liability management technique focuses on the difference, or "gap," between the amount of assets subject to significant interest rate risk ("rate-sensitive" assets such as federal funds loans and money market securities) and the quantity of liabilities subject to such risk ("rate-sensitive" liabilities such as sales of repurchase agreements or short-maturity CDs). If the gap is positive, then rate-sensitive assets exceed rate-sensitive liabilities. In this case a rise in market interest rates will tend to raise the depository institution's net interest margin, because its earnings from its rate-sensitive asset holdings will rise by more than its expenses on the smaller quantity of rate-sensitive liabilities. In contrast, a negative gap will have the opposite effect on the institution's net interest margin if interest rates rise.

It follows that a depository institution manager who expects market interest rates to rise will prefer to maintain a positive gap. In contrast, a manager who anticipates a decline in interest rates will want a negative gap. Alternatively, either manager could attempt to insulate the institution's income from the effects of market interest rate changes by maintaining a "zero gap" by matching the institution's amount of rate-sensitive assets with an equal quantity of rate-sensitive liabilities.

Many depository institution managers today do not look just at the overall gap for their institution. They also compute gaps at various maturities. For instance, depository institutions typically have negative gaps at short maturities of three months or less, because they issue checking and other deposits, to which customers have immediate access, but use those liabilities to fund longer-term assets. At maturities longer than three months, most depository institutions have positive gaps between rate-sensitive assets and liabilities. By monitoring gaps at different maturities, a manager can better gauge the institution's exposures to interest rate risk across the term structure of its assets and liabilities.

DURATION GAP ANALYSIS A more sophisticated gap-management method, which many banks have adopted in recent years, is to apply the concept of *duration* when conducting gap management. As you learned in Chapter 6, the duration of a financial instrument within a bank's portfolio of assets is a measure of the average time during which the bank receives all payments of principal and interest on the instrument. Likewise, the duration of a financial instrument, such as a deposit, that the bank issues as a liability is a measure of the average interval within which the bank makes payments on its liabilities.

To assess a bank's overall exposure to interest rate risk, its managers can use *duration gap analysis.* They do this by calculating an average duration for *all* of the bank's assets and an average duration for *all* of its liabilities. The difference between the average asset duration and the average liability duration is the bank's **duration gap.** If the bank's duration gap is positive and its managers anticipate a rise in market interest rates, then the managers can seek a higher net interest return by trying to reconfigure the bank's mix of terms to maturity for its assets and liabilities to achieve a negative duration gap. By way of contrast, if managers anticipate a decline in market interest rates, then a positive duration gap is an appropriate asset-liability structure.

Gap management: A technique of depository institution asset-liability management that focuses on the difference ("gap") between the quantity of assets subject to significant interest rate risk and the amount of liabilities subject to such risk.

Duration gap: The average duration of a depository institution's assets minus the average duration of its liabilities.

Other Methods of Managing Risk

In addition to coordinating balance-sheet items to limit risk and increase profitability, depository institutions today use a variety of other methods to manage risks. These range from sharing risks with other banks through syndicated loans to using models to measure credit risks and reducing exposure to those risks by using credit derivatives.

WHAT IF INDIVIDUAL BORROWERS ARE TOO BIG FOR ONE BANK? Even though 95 percent of the U.S. banking industry's business is within U.S. borders, many U.S. companies are now multinational conglomerates with globe-spanning operations. We observe similar situations in Europe and Japan. Some companies are so large that their credit needs dwarf the capability of any bank to serve as sole lender.

Syndicated loan: A loan arranged by one or two banks but funded by these and other banks.

Banks have responded to this situation by developing a market in **syndicated loans,** which are loans pieced together by groups of banks. Typically, one or two banks arrange a syndicated loan in return for syndication-management fees. These lead banks line up a group, or *syndicate,* of banks that fund portions of the total amount of the loan, earning interest just as they would on any other loan they extend. In addition, banks' shares of many syndicated loans are marketable instruments, meaning that participating banks under some circumstances can sell their shares of the loan to other banks.

Panel (a) of Figure 10-5 shows the worldwide amounts of syndicated lending in recent years. Comparing panel (b) of the figure with panel (c), you can see that the relative role of syn-

FIGURE 10-5
Bank Syndicated Lending in Total and As a Share of Total Corporate Financing.

As shown in panel (a), global syndicated lending by banks has jumped in the 2000s. A comparison of panels (b) and (c) indicates that the relative role of syndicated loans in corporate financing has increased significantly.

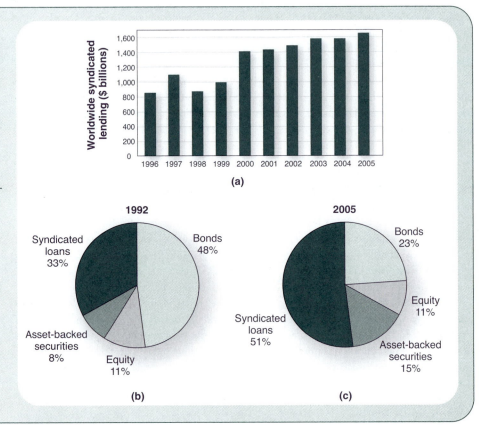

SOURCE: Bank for International Settlements, *Quarterly Banking Profile,* various issues.

dicated loans in worldwide financing of corporation operations has increased dramatically. The share of total new corporate financing accounted for by syndicated loans rose from about 33 percent in 1992 to 51 percent in 2005.

THE MODEL-BASED APPROACH TO CREDIT-RISK MANAGEMENT   In the late 1990s, J.P. Morgan (now part of J.P. Morgan Chase) announced that Standard & Poor's, Moody's Investors Service, Price Waterhouse, and several other credit-rating institutions would cosponsor the bank's new credit-risk management system, called *CreditMetrics*. (J.P. Morgan Bank may have been the last of a dying breed of depository institutions; see the *Management Focus: Where, Oh Where, Did the "Money Centers" Go?*) The model, which now is marketed by a company called RiskMetrics, is one of several *value-at-risk models* that depository institution managers began to use in the 1990s. A **value-at-risk model** is a statistical framework for evaluating how changes in interest rates and financial instrument prices are likely to affect the overall value of a portfolio of financial assets.

The CreditMetrics value-at-risk model allows banks to measure credit risks with portfolio-analysis techniques used to evaluate the risks of stocks, bonds, commodities, and currencies. CreditMetrics includes a historical database that indicates the statistical likelihood of credit-rating changes and loan defaults, as well as default recovery rates, among different types of loans.

UNLOADING LENDING RISKS: CREDIT DERIVATIVES   Since the 1990s, an increasing number of depository institutions have been addressing their exposure to credit risks in an entirely different way. They are using **credit derivatives,** which are financial instruments whose returns depend on the underlying credit risks of loans. Under the terms of a credit derivative contract, the failure of a borrower to pay off a loan is a "credit event" that requires the contract counterparties to cover the risk.

As Figure 10-6 on page 218 shows, since the mid-1990s the funds that U.S. banks have allocated to credit derivatives have increased significantly. U.S. banks' holdings of credit derivatives accounted for about half of the worldwide total of nearly $6.4 trillion in 2005.

The most popular credit derivative is a **default swap,** in which the seller of the swap, sometimes called a *credit protection seller*, agrees to take over the face value of a debt if the borrower

Value-at-risk model: A statistical framework for evaluating how changes in interest rates and financial instrument prices are likely to affect the overall value of a portfolio of financial assets.

On the Web
To contemplate special risk-management issues faced by depository institutions that offer online banking services, go to **http://www. bis.org/publ/bcbs98.htm**, where you can read a Bank for International Settlements report on this topic.

Credit derivatives: Financial instruments that have returns based on loan credit risks.

Default swap: A credit derivative that requires the seller to assume the face value of a debt in the event of default.

MANAGEMENT

Focus

Where, Oh Where, Did the "Money Centers" Go?

For years, the largest U.S. commercial banks were classified into two categories: "regional banks" and "money center banks." Regional banks, such as Bank One and NationsBank, possessed large branch networks and specialized in collecting deposits from wide ranges of individuals and firms. Money center

banks, such as J.P. Morgan, Chase Manhattan, First Chicago, and Bank of America, emphasized deposit accounts with large corporate customers and specialized in loans to the largest national and international companies.

By 2000, however, most money center banks had merged with major regional banks. Bank of America, for instance, merged with NationsBank, and First Chicago merged with Bank One. In an effort to keep the money center banking model alive, in September

2000 J.P. Morgan merged with Chase Manhattan to become J.P. Morgan Chase. By 2004, however, this last true money center bank had merged with Bank One's sprawling branch network, and "money center bank" became a term that had lost its meaning.

FOR CRITICAL ANALYSIS: How do you suppose that the gradual breakdown of regulations restricting interstate banking may have contributed to the demise of money center banks?

FIGURE 10-6
Notional Value of
Credit Derivatives Held
by U.S. Commercial Banks.

The notional value of U.S. commercial banks' credit derivatives has risen considerably since 1997.

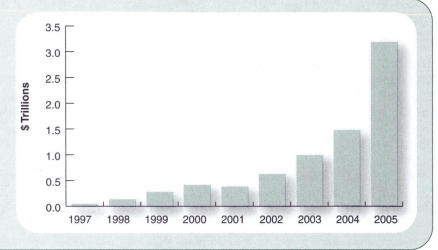

SOURCES: Office of the Comptroller of the Currency, *Bank Derivatives Report,* various issues; authors' estimates.

defaults. In return, the seller collects a fee from the counterparty, called a *credit protection buyer.* Thus, if a bank's managers think that the bank has taken on too much risk of default in a big loan to a single client, they can buy credit protection by using a default swap to reduce the bank's risk exposure. The credit protection seller in the transaction takes on this risk in exchange for payment of a regular fee from the bank. In the event of a default, the credit protection seller reimburses the bank for its losses. Such an arrangement does not hurt the bank's standing with its clients because borrowers are not even informed of the existence of most credit derivative contracts.

Panels (a) and (b) of Figure 10-7 show the distribution of credit protection sellers and buyers in the market for credit derivatives. Although banks account for 47 percent of credit pro-

FIGURE 10-7
Global
Distribution of the
Notional Value of
Credit Derivatives
among Contract
Counterparties.

Various types of financial institutions both sell and buy risk protection via credit derivatives. Panel (a) shows the distribution of credit protection sold by financial institutions using credit derivatives, and

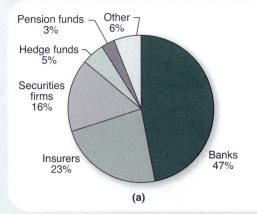

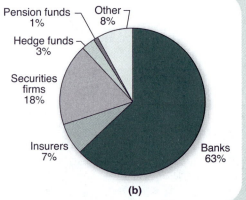

panel (b) displays the distribution of purchases of credit protection. Pension funds, hedge funds, and insurers tend to be net sellers of credit protection.

SOURCE: Bank for International Settlements.

tection sales, they are the predominant buyers of credit protection, accounting for about 63 percent of total purchases of credit protection via derivatives. In principle, this has enabled banks to shift significant amounts of their lending risks to other sellers of credit protection, such as insurance companies, which account for only about 7 percent of the total credit protection purchased in the market for credit derivatives but account for 23 percent of the total credit protection sold.

> **4. What are key elements of the modern asset-liability approach to managing risks at depository institutions?** In recent years, depository institutions have widely adopted the asset-liability management approach, which uses gap-management techniques to address interest rate risk while striving for high earnings and liquidity. In addition, depository institutions have used value-at-risk models to manage their risks. Furthermore, a growing number of depository institutions seek to reduce their exposure to lending risks through the use of credit derivatives.

An Evolving Depository Institution Market Structure

As noted earlier, interest income constitutes a large portion of depository institutions' revenues. How are market interest rates determined for bank loans and deposits? The answer to this question depends on depository institution **market structure,** or the organization of the markets in which depository institutions interact. Because the market structure affects the interest rates that depository institutions receive on their loans and pay on their deposits, it ultimately is a key determinant of the institutions' profitability.

A traditional issue has been how and why the degree of **market concentration**—the extent to which the few largest depository institutions dominate loan and deposit markets—affects the behavior of depository institutions. Market concentration can be measured in several ways, but the most straightforward is to look at the market shares of the largest few depository institutions. Typically, if the three or four largest institutions together have a large fraction of total loans or deposits, say, 70 percent or more, then the market is said to be relatively concentrated. But if the three or four largest institutions have a combined market share that is much smaller, then the degree of competition is likely much greater.

Perfect Competition

One possible type of depository institution market structure is **perfect competition.** Under perfect competition, no single depository institution can influence loan or deposit interest rates. Unrestricted rivalry among depository institutions drives loan and deposit rates to levels that just cover the costs that the institutions incur in making loans and issuing and servicing deposits.

Economists typically regard perfect competition as the optimal market structure. The reason is that if rivalry among depository institutions pushes loan and deposit rates closely in line with the costs of providing loans and issuing deposits, consumers pay and receive interest rates just sufficient to cover those costs. As a result, they are not in any way forced to pay loan rates that are "too high" or to earn deposit rates that are "too low," given the actual costs that depository institutions incur in providing financial intermediation services. In fact, under perfect competition depository institutions earn no more than a **normal profit,** or a profit just

Market structure: The organization of the loan and deposit markets in which depository institutions interact.

Market concentration: The degree to which the few largest depository institutions dominate loan and deposit markets.

Perfect competition: A market structure in which no single depository institution can influence loan or deposit interest rates. Hence, rivalry among institutions yields market loan and deposit interest rates that just cover the costs that the institutions incur in making loans and issuing and servicing deposits.

Normal profit: A profit level just sufficient to compensate depository institution owners for holding equity shares in the depository institution instead of purchasing ownership shares of other enterprises.

sufficient to compensate owners for holding equity shares in depository institutions instead of directing their funds to other enterprises.

Imperfect Competition and Market Power

Pure monopoly: The dominance of a loan or deposit market by a single depository institution or by a small group of institutions that work together to maximize their profits.

At the opposite extreme from perfect competition is a depository institution market structure called **pure monopoly.** This occurs when a loan or deposit market is dominated by a single depository institution or by a *cartel*, or small group of institutions that effectively coordinate their actions so that they jointly maximize their profits.

Although situations close to pure monopoly certainly have existed in loan and deposit markets in local areas, pure monopoly has not been a very common type of depository institution market structure in the United States. Nevertheless, there is evidence that in some locations and during some periods, depository institutions have possessed **market power.** This refers to the ability of one or a few depository institutions to set loan rates higher than they would have been under perfect competition in lending, or to set deposit rates lower than they would have been under perfect competition in issuing and servicing deposits. As a result of the higher loan rates and lower deposit rates, both lending and holdings of deposits are less than they would be under perfect competition. Depository institution customers pay more interest for fewer loans and receive less interest for fewer deposits.

Market power: The ability of one or a few depository institutions to dominate loan and deposit markets sufficiently to set higher loan rates and lower deposit rates as compared with purely competitive market interest rates.

Supranormal profits: Levels of profit above those required to induce depository institution owners to hold shares of ownership in those institutions instead of shares of other businesses.

If depository institutions have market power, then their ability to set loan rates "too high" or deposit rates "too low" relative to perfectly competitive levels means that they can earn **supranormal profits.** These are levels of profit that are above the normal profits necessary simply to induce depository institution owners to direct their funds to the banking business instead of to some other endeavor. If depository institution owners earn supranormal profits because market power exists, then they effectively have "gouged" consumers of the services of these institutions because the institutions are able to charge higher prices for fewer services.

Back in 1982, Stephen Rhoades, an economist at the Federal Reserve Board in Washington, attempted to measure the effects of market power among commercial banks in loan markets in 1978. He found that market power caused total bank lending to be 14 percent lower than it otherwise would have been under perfect competition. Rhoades also estimated that banks earned supranormal profits. He concluded that bank profit levels in 1978 were over $1 billion, or about 13 percent, more than they otherwise would have been in perfectly competitive banking markets.

Does Market Concentration Matter?

As we shall discuss in Chapters 11 and 12, many barriers to greater rivalry in banking markets have fallen in recent years, so a lot has changed since 1978. Yet some economists argue that unrestricted rivalry among depository institutions ultimately can lead to too much *market concentration*, a situation in which only a few depository institutions compete to lend and issue deposits and related services. Such concentration, they contend, feeds on itself and leads to anticompetitive behavior by commercial banks and other financial institutions. Thus, there is a natural tendency for unrestricted rivalry among depository institutions to lead to less, rather than more, competition.

Structure-conduct-performance (SCP) model: A theory of depository institution market structure in which the structure of loan and deposit markets influences the behavior (conduct) of depository institutions in those markets, thereby affecting their performance.

THE STRUCTURE-CONDUCT-PERFORMANCE MODEL   Those who subscribe to this view base their evaluation on the **structure-conduct-performance (SCP) model** of depository institution market structure. Figure 10-8 illustrates the basic reasoning of this theory. According

FIGURE 10-8
The Structure-Conduct-Performance Model.

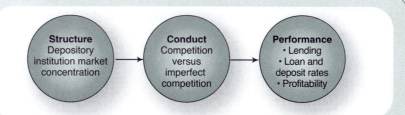

According to the structure-conduct-performance model, depository institution market structure can be measured by the concentration of banking markets (for instance, the combined market share of the few largest banks in a market). Depository institution market structure, in turn, determines whether the institutions conduct themselves competitively or imperfectly competitively. Depository institution market conduct then determines the performance of banks, as measured, for instance, by the amount of lending, loan and deposit rates, and profitability.

to the SCP model, the *structure* of a financial market influences the *conduct* of the institutions in the market. Their conduct, in turn, determines the *performance* of those institutions.

The basic prediction of the SCP theory is that more concentrated loan and deposit markets lead to market power, which as a result yields higher loan rates, lower deposit rates, and supranormal depository institution profits. This prediction causes proponents of the SCP model to prescribe an active role for governmental oversight of depository institution markets. According to SCP proponents, government regulators need to ensure that greater rivalry in banking markets does not lead to the gobbling up of small competitors by larger institutions.

THE EFFICIENT STRUCTURE THEORY   On the other side are economists who promote the **efficient structure theory** of depository institution market structure. Figure 10-9 depicts their line of reasoning. According to this view, greater market concentration arises from the fact that a few depository institutions can operate more efficiently in loan and deposit

Efficient structure theory: A theory of depository institution market structure in which greater market concentration and higher depository institution profits arise from the fact that a few depository institutions can operate more efficiently in loan and deposit markets than a large number of institutions.

FIGURE 10-9
The Efficient Structure Theory.

According to the efficient structure theory, any banking organization grows only as long as it remains cost-efficient. Furthermore, depository institutions that can provide their services at lower cost are more profitable institutions and naturally gain market share as a result. Consequently, the structure of loan and deposit markets and the performance of depository institutions in those markets depend on cost efficiencies that institutions can achieve.

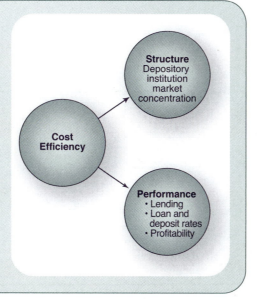

markets than a large number of institutions. They can do so because they can spread their costs over large computer, branching, and managerial networks.

In the past, this argument has been based in part on the idea of *economies of scale*. As discussed in Chapter 8, economies of scale refer to the ability to reduce average costs by pooling together financial resources. By pooling together ever-larger amounts of resources, efficient structure theorists argue, larger institutions can provide their services at lower costs than their competitors. The result is lower lending rates and higher deposit rates, so consumers are better off. But the reward to the more efficient institutions is *higher* profits. Consequently, the efficient structure theory, like the SCP model, predicts that greater concentration should yield greater profitability. But according to some who promote the efficient structure view, these higher profits stem from the greater efficiency of larger firms that dominate financial markets. (The predominance of larger banks is growing; see the *Management Focus: Small Banks Are Capturing a Smaller Share of the Market.*)

Recent Evidence on the Market Structure Debate

So who is correct about the effects of unrestricted rivalry on depository institution market structure and performance? Recent work looking at the relationship between commercial bank market concentration and profitability has cast a little more light on the broader debate between SCP proponents and efficient structure theorists.

In a recent study, Allen Berger of the Federal Reserve Board's economic staff analyzed extensive data on 4,800 commercial banks for each year of the 1980s. Berger defined local loan and deposit markets based on Metropolitan Statistical Areas (MSAs) defined by the U.S. Census Bureau and on non-MSA counties. He used batteries of statistical tests to determine how market concentration related to bank profits and used a variety of tests to try to determine which theory received more support from the data. Berger reached the conclusion that there is little evidence that the SCP model fits the real world, except perhaps in a much more limited form. There is evidence that large commercial banks earn higher profits because they are successful in gaining sufficient market shares to differentiate themselves from rivals. This, he

MANAGEMENT

Focus

Small Banks Are Capturing a Smaller Share of the Market

Since 1984, the share of total commercial bank assets held by small banks—commercial banks with less than $1 billion in assets—has nearly been cut in half, from 23 percent to 13 percent. The reason that smaller banks are a shrinking part of the commercial banking industry is simple: being small has come to mean being less profitable. Between the mid-1980s and the mid-1990s, small banks earned an average return on assets at least a third higher than the average return on assets earned by large banks—those with assets exceeding $25 billion. Since the mid-1990s, however, large banks have earned a higher average return on assets. The differential between the average returns on assets has been increasing and is now about 40 percentage points. This has provided a strong incentive for small banks to merge, which is why small banks account for a declining portion of the U.S. banking industry.

FOR CRITICAL ANALYSIS: What might account for the fact that larger banks are currently more profitable than smaller banks?

concludes, gives them some market power. They are able to use this market power to earn some supranormal profits.

The efficient structure theory's emphasis on economies of scale also did not hold up to the statistical tests that Berger conducted. What Berger found was that a somewhat altered version of the efficient structure theory seemed to explain banks' performances into the 1990s. According to this variation on the efficient structure hypothesis, what really counts is the efficiency of the management of a commercial bank, irrespective of the bank's absolute size or its market share. Well-run banks earn higher profits. Banks whose managers do not do a good job of controlling costs can sometimes still become large banks, but these banks tend to earn lower profits. In general, however, more efficiently operated banks do capture larger market shares. As the efficient structure theory predicts, this is because they are better at what they do.

Surely, this conclusion would not surprise too many depository institution managers. These people must confront the real world of business decisions about lending operations and the provision of deposit services that economic theorists do not see. At this point, however, a consensus seems to be emerging among *both* economists *and* bankers: what really matters most for the performance of depository institutions, from the perspectives of their owners, managers, *and* customers, is how well they are operated.

> **MONEYXTRA!**
> **Another Perspective**
> Consider why some economists have recently proposed that some social gains may be associated with market power in banking by going to the Chapter 10 reading, entitled "Competition among Banks: Good or Bad," by Nicola Cetorelli of the Federal Reserve Bank of Chicago. **http://moneyxtra.swcollege.com**

---

5. What is the main determinant of depository institutions' performance?
Although there is limited evidence that loan and deposit market concentration influences depository institution profitability by affecting the degrees of competition and market power, recent evidence indicates that the overriding factor determining profitability is the capability of a depository institution's managers.

Chapter Summary

1. Key Sources of Depository Institution Revenues and Costs: The main source of revenues for depository institutions is interest income derived from interest that they earn on loans and securities. The other revenue source is noninterest income, which includes fee income and trading profits. The two main sources of costs incurred by depository institutions are interest expenses on liabilities that they issue and real resource expenses for the use of productive factors such as labor, capital, and land. A third expenditure is provisions for loan loss reserves.

2. Common Measures of Depository Institution Profitability: Two commonly used measures are return on assets, or profit as a percentage of total assets, and return on equity, which is profit as a percentage of equity capital. Another measure that analysts often use to assess the near-term and future profitability of a depository institution is its net interest margin, which is the difference between interest income and interest expense as a percentage of total assets.

3. The Evolution of the Philosophy of Depository Institution Management: Under the real bills doctrine that was popular until the end of the nineteenth century, depository institutions tried to make only the most liquid loans. The shiftability theory dictated achieving more liquidity by holding securities, thereby allowing institutions to make less liquid loans. The anticipated-income approach led to the growth of installment loans as a means of generating liquidity via periodic payments of principal and interest. Under the conversion-of-funds approach, depository institution managers sought to fund assets with liabilities with similar maturities.

4. Key Elements of the Modern Asset-Liability Approach to Managing Risks at Depository Institutions: Today, most depository institutions utilize the asset-liability approach to bank management. This method entails applying gap-management techniques to minimize interest rate risks in an effort to maintain high earnings and liquidity simultaneously. Depository institutions have also used value-at-risk models to manage their risks. By applying these statistical models, institutions can evaluate the exposures of their portfolios to interest rate risk. Increasingly, depository institutions seek to transfer a portion of their exposure to lending risks to other parties by using credit derivatives.

5. The Main Determinant of a Depository Institution's Profitability: At present, most evidence indicates that the key factor determining a given institution's profit performance is the quality of its management. In addition, short-term factors such as changes in the overall economic climate can have large effects on profitability, as can the structure of the market in which a depository institution operates.

Questions and Problems

(Answers to odd-numbered questions and problems may be found on the Web at **http://money.swcollege.com** under "Student Resources.")

1. In 2005, the aggregate return on assets for all commercial banks in the United States was just below 1.4 percent, and the return on equity was nearly 14 percent. Explain why the return on equity typically is so much greater than the return on assets.

2. In recent years, noninterest income has become a more important source of revenues for depository institutions. Discuss how this may affect the usefulness of net interest margin as an indicator of depository institution profitability.

3. Some have argued that if depository institutions had not given up their strict adherence to the real bills doctrine, they would ultimately have ceased to exist. Evaluate this argument.

4. In your view, what is the biggest drawback of the shiftability theory of bank management?

5. Explain why it makes sense that the fee income of banks has increased substantially in recent years.

6. Suppose that a commercial bank has a negative gap at maturities of twelve months or less but a positive gap at maturities exceeding twelve months. If the yield curve (recall this concept from Chapter 4) *rotates* in such a way that short-term interest rates rise while longer-term interest rates fall, what is likely to happen to the bank's profitability? Explain your reasoning.

7. How does derivatives trading complicate the evaluation of the overall performance of, and the prospects for, depository institutions?

8. Why do you suppose that some banking specialists worry that relying solely on value-at-risk models could actually expose some depository institutions to *greater* risks of loss?

9. Are society's overall credit risks reduced by the increasing use of credit derivatives by depository institutions? Explain.

10. Profitability sometimes is greater at the larger institutions in specific loan and deposit markets. Discuss alternative ways that structure-conduct-performance model proponents and efficient structure theorists would probably explain such observations.

Before the Test

Test your understanding of the material covered in this chapter by taking the Chapter 10 interactive quiz at **http://money.swcollege.com**.

Online Application

Internet URL: http://www.fdic.gov

Title: Historical Statistics on Banking

Navigation: Begin at the FDIC's Web site at the above address. Click on "Industry Analysis" and then click on "Bank Data and Statistics." Next, click on "Historical Statistics on Banking." Finally, click on "Commercial Bank Reports."

Application: Follow the instructions, and answer the questions.

1. Under "Geographical Area," select "United States (50 states and DC)." Click on "CB04: Net Income." Beginning with the most recent year, and at ten-year intervals going back to 1966, calculate the ratio of noninterest income to total income (which you can calculate by adding together interest income and noninterest income). Do you see a trend? If so, discuss why it may exist.

2. Go back to the "Select Report" section, and click on "CB07: Noninterest Income and Noninterest Expense." Beginning with the most recent year. and at ten-year intervals going back to 1966, calculate the ratio of fee income to noninterest income. Do you see a trend? If so, discuss why it may exist.

For Group Study and Analysis: Form groups, and have each group examine the report entitled "Interest Income of Insured Commercial Banks" in the "Select Report." In the "State" box, click on "United States." Have each group make a determination about the most notable recent change in the various sources of commercial bank interest income. In addition, have each group examine the loan interest income from foreign sources relative to loan interest income from domestic sources and then report about whether they see any evidence that the U.S. banking industry as a whole is significantly more involved in international lending than in past years.

Selected References and Further Reading

Berger, Allen. "The Profit-Structure Relationship in Banking—Tests of Market-Power and Efficient-Structure Hypotheses." *Journal of Money, Credit, and Banking* 27 (May 1995): 404–431.

Berger, Allen, and Timothy Hannan. "The Efficiency Cost of Market Power in the Banking Industry: A Test of the 'Quiet Life' and Related Hypotheses." *Review of Economics and Statistics* 80 (August 1998): 454–465.

Cetorelli, Nicola, and Phillip Strahan. "Finance as a Barrier to Entry: Bank Competition and Industry Structure in Local U.S. Markets." Federal Reserve Bank of Chicago Working Paper No. 2004-04.

Dick, Astrid. "Nationwide Branching and Its Impact on Market Structure, Quality, and Bank Performance." *Journal of Business,* April 2006.

Emmons, William, and Frank Schmid. "Bank Competition and Concentration: Do Credit Unions Matter?" Federal Reserve Bank of St. Louis *Review* 82 (May/June 2000): 29–42.

Gunther, Jeffrey, and Robert Moore. "Small Banks' Competitors Loom Large." Federal Reserve Bank of Dallas *Southwest Economy,* January/February 2004, pp. 1–13.

Guzman, Mark. "Bank Competition in the New Economy." Federal Reserve Bank of Dallas *Southwest Economy,* March/April 2001, pp. 1–9.

Kimball, Ralph. "Economic Profit and Performance Measurement in Banking." Federal Reserve Bank of Boston *New England Economic Review,* July/August 1998, pp. 35–53.

_____. "Innovations in Performance Measurement in Banking." Federal Reserve Bank of Boston *New England Economic Review,* May/June 1997, pp. 3–22.

Rhoades, Stephen. "Welfare Loss, Redistribution Effect, and Restriction of Output due to Monopoly in Banking." *Journal of Monetary Economics* 9 (January 1982): 375–387.

Schuermann, Til. "Why Were Banks Better Off in the 2001 Recession?" Federal Reserve Bank of New York *Current Issues in Economics and Finance* 10 (January 2004).

Simons, Katerina. "Value at Risk—New Approaches to Risk Management." Federal Reserve Bank of Boston *New England Economic Review,* September/October 1996, pp. 3–14.

Stiroh, Kevin, and Jennifer Poole. "Explaining the Rising Concentration of Banking Assets in the 1990s." Federal Reserve Bank of New York *Current Issues in Economics and Finance* 6 (August 2000).

Wall, Larry, and Timothy Koch. "Bank Loan-Loss Accounting: A Review of Theoretical and Empirical Evidence." Federal Reserve Bank of Atlanta *Economic Review,* Second Quarter 2000, pp. 1–19.

MoneyXtra

Log on to the MoneyXtra Web site now (**http://moneyxtra.swcollege.com**) for additional learning resources such as practice quizzes, case studies, readings, and additional economic applications.

Foundations of Depository Institution Regulation

When a regulatory agency examines a depository institution, it dispatches a group of examiners to the institution's location. The examiners look over accounting data, interview managers, and evaluate the institution's performance to develop a "CAMEL" (an acronym for capital-assets-management-earnings-liquidity) rating for the bank. A CAMEL rating of 1 or 2 indicates that the examiners regard the institution as healthy. A rating of 3 causes the agency to place the institution on its "watch list," and a rating of 4 or 5 indicates that the examiners consider the institution to be in serious trouble.

Conducting an examination requires allocating full-time use of examiners' expertise and time, transporting the examiners to the institution's location, and housing them during the period of the examination. Somehow regulatory agencies must generate revenues to cover these costs. To do so, regulatory agencies subject depository institutions to "assessments." The Office of Thrift Supervision, for instance, charges holding companies that own savings banks and savings and loan associations $6,000 per year, plus additional fees based on the company's size and complexity. The Office of the Comptroller of the Currency (OCC) also imposes assessments that vary with the sizes of the national banks it regulates. The smallest banks with no more than $2 million in assets pay the OCC about $15,000 per year, and larger banks pay progressively higher assessments. All told, the assessments collected by U.S. agencies that regulate depository institutions exceed $2 billion per year.

Why does the federal government require depository institutions to submit to such detailed and costly examinations of their operations? In what ways does the government regulate these institutions? This chapter addresses these and other questions regarding the current regulatory environment faced by depository institutions.

The Evolution of U.S. Depository Institution Regulation

We discussed the traditional rationales for government regulation of depository financial institutions in Chapter 2. They are as follows:

Fundamental Issues

1. In what ways did laws adopted in the 1930s exert long-term effects on the U.S. banking industry?

2. How did deposit interest rate ceilings ultimately help to spur depository institution deregulation in the 1980s?

3. Why does the provision of federal deposit insurance help to justify federal regulation of depository institutions?

4. How has the federal government sought to reduce the FDIC's exposure to losses?

5. How did the Financial Services Modernization Act of 1999 alter the structure of U.S. bank regulation and supervision?

6. Do national bank regulators coordinate their policies?

1. **Maintaining depository institution liquidity.** Any depository institution without sufficient cash on hand to meet the needs of its depositors suffers from *illiquidity* that inconveniences its customers. Illiquidity throughout the banking system threatens the smooth flow of payments for goods and services and can have negative consequences for the broader economy.

2. **Assuring bank solvency by limiting failures.** A depository institution is *insolvent* if the value of its assets falls below the value of its liabilities so that the value of its *equity,* or net worth, is negative. A fundamental purpose of regulatory supervision of depository institutions is to reduce the likelihood of insolvency and the resulting failure of a depository institution to remain a going concern.

3. **Promoting an efficient financial system.** A banking system that is most cost-efficient economizes on the real resources that a nation commits to the services that banking institutions provide, thereby freeing up the largest possible amount of remaining resources for other social uses. Thus, another key goal of depository institution regulation is to promote an environment in which these institutions can provide their services at the lowest possible cost.

4. **Protecting consumers.** *Asymmetric information* can make it difficult for consumers to make informed choices in their dealings with depository institutions. In some instances, unscrupulous depository institution managers might be able to use asymmetric information to their advantage, thereby subjecting consumers to contract terms that some might regard as "unfair." For this reason, in most countries consumer protection is another fundamental goal of bank regulation.

As also noted in Chapter 2, one of the great challenges of regulating depository institutions is balancing these goals. The evolution of U.S. depository institution regulation reflects the government's "balancing act" in the face of potentially conflicting objectives. Complicating the U.S. regulatory effort have been programs that the federal government itself has adopted, including the public insurance of most deposits issued by private depository institutions.

Federal Regulation: 1933–1970

The federal government's involvement in banking dates to the earliest days of the United States. Nevertheless, the federal government's role was relatively limited until the twentieth century. In response to the economic hardships of the Great Depression, in the 1930s Congress initiated a series of measures that dramatically increased the federal government's role in the affairs of depository financial institutions. The *McFadden Act* of 1927, which restricted nationally chartered banks to branching only according to state laws, already had done much to limit the scope for competition among banks. Nevertheless, many in Congress blamed the large number of bank failures of the early 1930s—about 2,000 per year between 1929 and 1933—on "destructive competition" in banking. Congress therefore set out to reduce the scope for competition and to make the federal government a "traffic cop" overseeing the nation's channels of financial commerce.

The Banking Act of 1933, otherwise known as the *Glass-Steagall Act,* created the Federal Deposit Insurance Corporation (FDIC), which supervises the nation's taxpayer-guaranteed deposit insurance system for commercial banks and savings institutions. (Federal deposit insurance is also provided to a special category of financial institution that exists only in two western U.S. states; see the *Policy Focus: Not Only Depository Institutions Receive FDIC*

POLICY

Focus

Not Only Depository Institutions Receive FDIC Coverage

Since 1995, assets held by various forms of financial intermediaries in the states of Utah and Nevada have multiplied by a factor of almost 100. What lies behind this development is a special kind of "nonbank bank" unique to these states, called an *industrial loan corporation,* or *ILC.* These institutions first arose in the 1920s in Utah, where they specialized in lending to fledgling companies trying to establish niches in then-unproven western U.S. markets.

When some of those markets boomed, so did the fortunes of many of the western ILCs. Today, ILCs are not all home-grown institutions. The two largest ILCs are operated by Merrill Lynch and American Express, and others are owned by companies such as General Electric, BMW, and Toyota.

The federal government's insurance program protects the first $100,000 of each checking and savings account held at ILCs, just as it insures deposits at more traditional banking institutions. Nevertheless, federal laws exempt ILCs from many of the regulatory burdens faced by commercial banks, savings institutions, and credit unions. Although ILCs must submit to basic safety and

soundness examinations to maintain their access to federal deposit insurance, they are able to avoid a number of other forms of federal regulatory oversight. As a consequence, ILCs can engage in certain types of businesses that are out of bounds for traditional depository institutions, even though ILCs offer the same basic depository and lending services.

FOR CRITICAL ANALYSIS: How might exemptions from certain forms of federal regulation assist ILCs in attracting customers from traditional depository institutions located in other parts of the United States?

Coverage.) The Glass-Steagall Act also separated commercial and investment banking and placed interest rate ceilings on checking deposits of commercial banks. In short, this legislation formally made the federal government the legal supervisor of the activities undertaken by depository institutions.

FEDERAL DEPOSIT INSURANCE Under the terms of the Glass-Steagall Act, the FDIC initially supervised a "Temporary Deposit Insurance Fund." Both the FDIC and its fund became more permanent fixtures of the nation's banking system in early 1935.

As part of the *National Housing Act* of 1934, Congress also set up a separate system of federal deposit insurance for savings institutions under the supervision of a Federal Home Loan Bank System that Congress had created in the *Federal Home Loan Bank Act* of 1932. The Federal Home Loan Bank Board governed the Federal Home Loan Bank System.

Credit unions also have federal deposit insurance. The National Credit Union Administration (NCUA), which Congress established in 1970, supervises this deposit insurance system. Instead of paying annual premiums to the NCUA's National Credit Union Share Insurance Fund, credit unions deposit 1 percent of their deposits with the NCUA fund. (Note that this 1 percent is a total stock of deposits, not to be confused with an annual *flow* assessment such as the FDIC's annual risk-based bank and savings institution insurance fees.)

THE SEPARATION OF COMMERCIAL AND INVESTMENT BANKING Some commercial banks that failed at the outset of the Great Depression were also heavily involved in securities underwriting. To many observers at that time, it appeared that such activities had entailed significant risk for those banks and had contributed to highly visible failures that had reduced the public's confidence in the banking system. This lack of confidence, many argued, helped to fuel the banking panics that followed. Consequently, a key provision of the 1933 Glass-Steagall Act was the prohibition of securities underwriting by commercial banks or any other depository institutions.

BRANCHING RESTRICTIONS   The Glass-Steagall Act also amended the 1927 McFadden Act in ways that further discouraged nationally chartered banks from attempting to open branch offices in states other than those in which their home offices were located. This made nationwide or even regional branching impossible without the explicit permission of both the state of a bank's origin and the state in which the bank wished to branch. For a number of years, very few states were willing to allow such arrangements. Consequently, **interstate branching,** or the opening of banking offices in more than one state, effectively was illegal.

Indeed, until the 1970s many states made branching a difficult proposition even *within* their boundaries. These states restricted even **intrastate branching,** permitting banks to open branch offices only within their home counties, or perhaps in adjacent counties. Some *unit banking* states went even further, preventing banks from operating any branch offices whatsoever. Only recently have most U.S. states permitted unlimited branching within their borders.

In spite of the various state regulations inhibiting branching, banks found ways to expand their branch networks considerably over the years. Indeed, the number of bank branches in the United States grew significantly during past decades even as the number of banks remained steady and, in recent years, began to decline.

Interstate branching: The operation of banking offices in more than one state.

Intrastate branching: The operation of banking offices anywhere within a state.

INTEREST RATE REGULATION   The Glass-Steagall Act of 1933 also prohibited the payment of interest on demand deposits at commercial banks, which until the 1970s were the only form of checking deposits in the United States. The rationale for this provision was that if banks had to pay market interest rates on demand deposits when economic times were good, then they would be forced to search for high-interest assets that also entailed significant risks. Following an economic downturn, such risky assets would lose their market values. Then banks would lose liquidity and be unable to honor depositors' requests for funds. The result would be banking panics, such as those the country had experienced between 1929 and 1933. Those who framed the 1933 legislation sought to eliminate interest on checking deposits as a means of inhibiting such "destructive competition."

In addition, the Glass-Steagall Act authorized the Federal Reserve to place interest rate ceilings on bank savings and time deposits. The Federal Reserve imposed such ceilings through a rule it called Regulation Q. These "Reg-Q" ceilings, as they were called, remained in place until the 1980s. One Glass-Steagall interest ceiling, a zero-interest restriction on business demand deposits, remains in effect today.

Until the 1960s such interest rate ceilings applied only to commercial bank deposits. But under the terms of the Interest Rate Adjustment Act of 1966, similar ceilings constrained interest rates on savings and time deposits at savings institutions. The result of the imposition of these ceilings was the "Credit Crunch of 1966." When market interest rates rose well above the deposit rate ceilings at banks and savings institutions, depositors removed many of their funds from these institutions and used those funds to purchase alternative financial instruments, such as Treasury bills. This left depository institutions with fewer funds to lend. They responded by cutting back on loans, so otherwise creditworthy individuals and businesses were unable to obtain loans. Congress responded by raising the minimum T-bill denomination from $1,000 to $10,000, thereby inhibiting the ability of small savers to shift their funds in this manner. This action was not reversed until 1998.

> **1. In what ways did laws adopted in the 1930s exert long-term effects on the U.S. banking industry?** The Glass-Steagall Act of 1933 had far-reaching effects on the depository institution industry. It strengthened interstate-branching restrictions and established the first federal deposit insurance fund, which laid the foundation for the establishment of the Federal Deposit Insurance Corporation. In addition, the legislation authorized ceilings on bank interest rates, including the zero-interest restriction on business demand deposits still in force today.

The Experiment with Partial Deregulation: 1971–1989

Disintermediation: A situation in which customers of depository institutions withdraw funds from their deposit accounts and use these funds to purchase financial instruments directly.

By the end of the 1960s, it had become apparent that interest rate regulations were likely to cause periodic **disintermediation.** During these intervals, other market interest rates rose sufficiently to induce savers to withdraw their funds from depository institutions and other financial intermediaries and use them to purchase financial instruments with higher, unregulated yields. The problem for depository institutions was that even when other market interest rates fell back to previous levels, former customers did not necessarily redeposit their funds. Rather than return to depository institutions to intermediate the savings-investment process, these former customers purchased financial instruments directly—hence the term *disintermediation.* The problems of the depository institutions were worsened by technological advances in information processing that had made it easier for other institutions to offer depository services.

THE DEPOSITORY INSTITUTIONS DEREGULATION AND MONETARY CONTROL ACT OF 1980 In 1980, Congress took steps to improve the ability of depository institutions to compete for funds. It reduced some of the regulatory constraints on banks, savings institutions, and credit unions by enacting the *Depository Institutions Deregulation and Monetary Control Act (DIDMCA).* The act contained three provisions that greatly improved the competitive position of all depository institutions. First, it set up a six-year phaseout of all interest rate ceilings that these institutions faced. Second, beginning in 1981, it permitted all depository institutions nationwide to offer negotiable-order-of-withdrawal (NOW) accounts, which essentially were interest-bearing checking deposits. Third, the DIDMCA increased federal deposit insurance coverage from $40,000 per deposit account to $100,000. Notably, *Congress raised this limit without increasing the insurance premiums that depository institutions had to pay to the FDIC.* (Even though the FDIC currently insures deposits up to a limit of $100,000 per depositor per institution, depositors can achieve additional federal coverage by spreading their funds across institutions; see the *Management Focus: Helping Depositors Federally Insure All Their Funds.*)

The DIDMCA also had some special benefits for savings institutions and credit unions. Savings institutions were allowed to make consumer loans, purchase commercial paper up to a limit of 20 percent of total assets, and issue credit cards. Credit unions could now make residential and real estate loans. These changes permitted more direct competition among savings institutions, credit unions, and commercial banks.

The DIDMCA of 1980 was a complicated piece of legislation. Although in the above respects it deregulated depository institutions, in other ways it increased their federal regula-

On the Web
How is federal deposit insurance administered? To find out, go to **http://www.fdic.gov**.

MANAGEMENT
Focus

Helping Depositors Federally Insure All Their Funds

Each customer's deposits at a depository institution are federally insured up to a limit of $100,000. This limit has been in place since 1980. Since then, inflation has nearly doubled the nominal value of deposits, thereby pushing more customers' total deposit holdings above the limit. For a private company called Promontory Interfinancial Network, this situation has created a business opportunity. Promontory operates a deposit-placement service. The firm breaks up customers' large deposits into smaller amounts of less than $100,000 and places those deposits within a network of more than 600 banks that participate in its Certificate of Deposit Account Registry Service. Promontory arranges for customers to receive one interest rate, one consolidated bank statement, and one 1099 tax form for reporting their taxable interest earnings. Using this service, depositors can ensure that up to $20 million of their funds receive federal deposit insurance.

FOR CRITICAL ANALYSIS: How do the activities of companies such as Promontory Interfinancial Network expand the overall coverage of federal deposit insurance?

tory burdens. For instance, it required all federally insured depository institutions to meet reserve requirements established and maintained by the Federal Reserve on transactions deposits (demand deposits and NOW account deposits). It also required depository institutions to pay the Federal Reserve for check-clearing and wire-transfer services that they chose to use. Before the DIDMCA, only commercial banks that were members of the Federal Reserve System had to hold reserves with Federal Reserve banks, and these institutions had received Fed services without charge. The advantage of the DIDMCA for Fed member banks was that it effectively reduced their reserve requirements. For institutions that previously had not been required to hold reserves with the Fed, the advantages were access to Fed services (albeit at a cost) and the authorization to apply to Federal Reserve banks for loans when they faced liquidity difficulties.

On net, therefore, the DIDMCA did two things. Without doubt, it significantly deregulated depository institutions. Yet, at the same time, by placing all these institutions under the regulatory umbrella of the Federal Reserve System, a quasi agency of the U.S. government, and dramatically raising federal deposit insurance coverage, the DIDMCA effectively *increased* the federal government's stake in these institutions. Consequently, the DIDMCA only *partially* deregulated depository institutions. In several ways it enlarged the federal government's role in the industry.

THE GARN–ST GERMAIN ACT OF 1982 In 1982, Congress passed another important piece of legislation that became known as the *Garn–St Germain Act.* One feature of this act was the authorization of *money market deposit accounts.* As noted in Chapter 1, these are savings deposits that offer market interest rates and a limited number of transfers each year. Within two years after their mid-1982 introduction, these accounts accumulated to almost $400 billion at all depository institutions. Undoubtedly, depository institutions won back some of their previous depositors, because shares in investment companies' money market mutual funds, which had grown at the depository institutions' expense during the 1970s, declined by nearly $50 billion during the same period. But most of the funds were deposited by people who already had savings accounts at depository institutions. These individuals simply moved their funds to money market deposit accounts to earn higher yields. As a result, many depository institutions found themselves incurring significantly greater interest expenses for only slightly larger volumes of deposits.

The other key elements of the Garn–St Germain Act attempted to address a festering problem. Since the 1970s the combined net worth of all savings institutions had declined precipitously. Some economists, such as Edward Kane of Boston College, used market value measures that indicated that much of the industry was technically bankrupt by the early 1970s. Even without taking into account the market values of their assets, by the middle of 1980 one-third of all savings institutions, with over a third of the total assets of such institutions, were operating at losses. To try to help savings institutions compete more effectively with other depository institutions, the Garn–St Germain Act increased the DIDMCA limit on consumer loans and commercial paper, authorized savings institutions to make commercial real estate loans, and gave these institutions the power to purchase "unsecured loans," including low-rated, "junk" bonds, discussed in Chapter 4.

Finally, to further the process of closing troubled banks and savings institutions, the Garn–St Germain Act gave the FDIC broad powers to permit such institutions to merge with healthier partners, even across state lines. In retrospect, this provision of the legislation may have been the most successful. Many blame the Garn–St Germain Act for spurring the savings institution crisis that mushroomed a few years hence. Nevertheless, in later years the FDIC found itself putting its expanded powers to much greater use than Congress could have imagined when it passed the 1982 law.

> **2. How did deposit interest rate ceilings ultimately help to spur depository institution deregulation in the 1980s?** Legal ceilings on deposit interest rates placed depository institutions at a competitive disadvantage whenever other market interest rates rose well above the ceilings, inducing depositors to withdraw their funds in search of higher yields. This so soured the fortunes of banks and savings institutions that Congress felt obliged to reduce the regulatory burdens that they faced in the laws that it passed in 1980 and 1982.

Deposit Insurance: The Big Regulatory Complication

In the United States, depository institution regulators face a major complication: the bulk of the deposits of nearly all depository institutions are insured by the federal government.

Deposit Insurance and Moral Hazard

Until recently, a key feature of the U.S. deposit insurance system was that depository institutions paid flat amounts for federal deposit insurance irrespective of their risks. In addition, all depository institutions are eligible for such insurance as long as they meet certain minimal standards.

THE MORAL-HAZARD PROBLEM OF DEPOSIT INSURANCE   Recall from Chapter 8 that private insurance companies use a number of techniques to protect themselves from the fundamental *moral-hazard* problem of insurance. The difficulty is that once an individual or business receives insurance coverage, the covered person or firm may be tempted to behave more recklessly. After all, once one is insured, the expected personal cost arising from losses that might result from reckless behavior will be lower.

The existence of federal deposit insurance likewise can lead depository institution managers to make riskier choices than they might otherwise. This means that federal deposit insurance can expose the entire depository institution industry to significant moral-hazard problems.

REGULATION AS A PARTIAL SOLUTION   The potential solution to the moral-hazard problem that arises from federal deposit insurance is depository institution regulation. By conducting periodic examinations of insured institutions and by issuing and enforcing rules for prudent management, depository institution regulators can reduce the scope for widespread moral-hazard difficulties. (Nevertheless, an FDIC proposal regarding the insurability of amounts held on stored-value cards may have induced efforts by depository institutions to expand the scope of federal deposit insurance; see the *Cyber Focus: FDIC-Insured Stored-Value Cards Generate Novel Ideas for "Insured Deposits."*)

As we have seen, deposits at U.S. depository institutions have not always been federally insured. Once the U.S. government extended such insurance, however, the extent of federal regulation of depository institutions increased markedly.

TOO BIG TO FAIL?   Deposit insurance covers deposits only up to certain limits, but what happens when deposits exceed those limits? The answer may depend on the size of the depository institution. In 1982, a large bank named Penn Square failed because declining energy prices had caused the market values of energy-related loans that the bank had extended to fall dramatically. Penn Square had close financial dealings with a number of other institutions, including Continental Illinois Bank, which was based in Chicago and at the time was the nation's seventh largest commercial bank. Continental Illinois had purchased over $1 billion of Penn Square's energy loans and soon found itself on the same slippery slope toward bankruptcy.

CYBER

Focus

FDIC-Insured Stored-Value Cards Generate Novel Ideas for "Insured Deposits"

In 1996, the Federal Deposit Insurance Corporation proposed extending federal insurance to funds that depositors hold on stored-value cards issued by commercial banks, savings institutions, and credit unions. Since then the agency has been developing rules for determin- ing which types of cards are covered by federal deposit insurance. Just as the agency was finally about to issue cover- age to stored-value cards in the mid-2000s, some depository institutions announced preliminary plans to adver- tise new card products as "FDIC insured." Among these new products were payroll cards, which are stored-value cards that some employers use to transmit wages to workers instead of old-fashioned paychecks. Others included various bank-intermediated cards that state governments issue for unemployment and public assistance payments and that retailers sell to cus- tomers to give away as gifts. Soon the FDIC postponed a decision about whether it would in fact insure stored-value cards under the rules it had just finished composing, which appeared to extend insurance to all these bank-intermediated cards.

FOR CRITICAL ANALYSIS: Would insuring bank-intermediated stored-value cards issued by governments and retailers in any way "insure" these entities as well as depository institutions?

It is difficult for a large bank to keep such problems secret. When word of Continental Illinois's problems began to spread, it became the victim of an electronic bank run. Depositors whose account balances exceeded the $100,000 limit for deposit insurance coverage made wire transfers out of their accounts at the bank, causing it to lose over $10 billion in deposits within a two-month period in the spring of 1984. The bank offered above-market interest rates in an effort to induce individuals and firms to purchase its certificates of deposit, and it sold billions of dollars of its assets, but to little avail. By May of 1984, the FDIC decided to bail out Continental Illinois by purchasing over $2 billion in subordinated notes from the bank. In addition, the Federal Reserve Bank of Chicago extended long-term credit to the bank.

These actions by the FDIC and the Federal Reserve to keep the bank from failing were unprecedented in that they protected uninsured depositors of the bank as well as those whose funds were covered by federal guarantees. In September of 1984, the comptroller of the currency, the chief regulator of national banks, announced to Congress that he and his staff had decided that the eleven largest national banks in the United States were "too big to fail." This **too-big-to-fail policy** had its intended effect of shoring up public confidence in the nation's banking system. Ultimately, the other federal banking regulators, the Federal Reserve and the FDIC, implicitly adopted the same policy. (Since 2002, federal banking regulators have adopted a more direct approach to examining the activities of the largest U.S. banks; see *What Happens When the Greatest Regulatory Risks Are Concentrated among the Largest Banks?*)

Too-big-to-fail policy: A regulatory policy that protects the largest depository institutions from failure solely because regulators believe that such failure could undermine the public's confidence in the financial system.

THE SAVINGS INSTITUTION CRISIS   In the late 1980s and early 1990s, banking regulators sought to shore up the position of commercial banks for two reasons. One reason was that bank ratios of equity to assets had sunk to low levels in any event. A second reason, however, was that regulators wanted to avoid a commercial banking collapse analogous to the one that had just engulfed many U.S. savings institutions. The latter collapse was staggering in its own right: between the mid-1980s and 1990, more than half of all savings institutions—almost 1,500 institutions—failed outright or were closed by regulators. A similar collapse of the commercial banking industry would have been a real catastrophe.

What caused the savings institution crisis? Certainly, the cumulative effects of high and variable interest rates during the 1970s had driven up interest expenses at savings institutions

---

What Happens When... **The Greatest Regulatory Risks Are Concentrated among the Largest Banks?**

Six U.S. banks—J.P. Morgan Chase, Bank of America, Citigroup, Wachovia, Washington Mutual, and Wells Fargo—together account for about 40 percent of the assets of all banks. From the perspective of federal banking regulators, therefore, about 40 percent of the risks that taxpayers face in providing bank deposit insurance are concentrated among these few institutions.

Since 2002, the Federal Deposit Insurance Corporation has given six of its banking examiners unique assignments: constant surveillance of these banks. An examiner is based in an office located on the premises of each bank. These on-site examiners collect real-time information about the largest banks' activities and specialize in evalu-

ating the internal workings of their organizations. The examiners work together to produce weekly, quarterly, and annual reports on the six banks they examine. Twice each week they participate in conference calls with other FDIC officials to discuss developing trends. In this way, the FDIC keeps constantly abreast of the banks' activities that pose the greatest potential risk of loss to the government's deposit insurance system.

FOR CRITICAL ANALYSIS: Who do you suppose covers regulatory costs not fully funded by fees that depository institutions pay their regulators?

even as their interest incomes remained relatively fixed. This exposure to interest rate risks had already pushed many savings institutions to the brink of insolvency by the end of the 1970s. In addition, increased competition stemming from deregulation in the early 1980s compressed the profit margins at many institutions that already were trying to overcome managerial inexperience with new lines of business permitted under the Garn–St Germain Act. Furthermore, a major decline in oil prices slashed real estate prices and mortgage values in the southwestern United States, where livelihoods depended heavily on energy-related industries. Finally, there was outright fraud at some institutions.

Most economists agree, however, that the crisis was really caused by two related factors: *moral hazard* and *regulatory failure.* By insuring the deposits of savings institutions, the government gave the managers of these institutions an incentive to undertake riskier activities. The deregulation provisions of the 1980 DIDMCA and 1982 Garn–St Germain Act added to these incentives. As discussed earlier in this chapter, a key rationale for regulation is to minimize this moral-hazard problem. In the case of savings institutions in the 1980s, regulation failed to perform this function. Indeed, otherwise well-meaning congressional actions largely induced the great savings institution debacle of the 1980s and 1990s.

> **3. Why does the provision of federal deposit insurance help to justify federal regulation of depository institutions?** Providing deposit insurance exposes the federal government to the moral-hazard problem that managers of depository institutions will respond by making riskier decisions. A way to try to prevent more reckless behavior by depository institution managers is to subject them to regulatory examination and supervision.

Reregulation versus Deregulation in the Late 1980s and Early 1990s

By early 1987 the savings institution deposit insurance fund was technically insolvent. Yet not until 1989 did Congress pass legislation to deal with the savings institution crisis.

THE FINANCIAL INSTITUTIONS REFORM, RECOVERY, AND ENFORCEMENT ACT OF 1989   The 1989 legislation specified means of enforcing broad governmental mandates to accomplish the recovery objective. Consequently, Congress called the legislation the *Financial Institutions Reform, Recovery, and Enforcement Act (FIRREA).*

Although the FIRREA left the Federal Home Loan Bank System largely intact, it dismantled the Federal Home Loan Bank Board. As a new regulator for savings institutions, the FIRREA created the Office of Thrift Supervision (OTS) within the Treasury Department. The legislation also created the Federal Housing Finance Board to supervise the operations of the Federal Home Loan Bank System but gave this board meager regulatory responsibilities. The FIRREA reassigned the supervision of the savings institution deposit fund to the FDIC; it continued the traditional separation of bank and savings institution deposit funds, however. One FDIC fund, the **Bank Insurance Fund (BIF),** covers commercial banks; another, the **Savings Association Insurance Fund (SAIF),** provides federal deposit insurance to savings institutions.

To shore up the SAIF, the FIRREA gave the FDIC broadened authority to try to recover asset values of insolvent savings institutions, and it authorized tax-financed funding of savings institution "resolutions," which Congress found to be a nicer word than "closings." The

Bank Insurance Fund (BIF): The FDIC's fund that covers insured deposits of commercial banks.

Savings Association Insurance Fund (SAIF): The FDIC's fund that covers insured deposits of savings institutions.

FIRREA specified that funding for such resolutions was to be handled through the Treasury Department and another new agency, the Resolution Finance Corporation (RFC). Yet another agency, the Resolution Trust Corporation (RTC), handled the day-to-day aspects of closing down insolvent savings institutions. The FIRREA set 1992 as a target date for the completion of the duties of the RFC and RTC, but these agencies did not go out of business until 1994.

Another set of provisions in the FIRREA reversed the deregulation thrust of the DIDMCA and the Garn–St Germain Act. The FIRREA prohibited savings institutions from holding junk bonds (high-interest, high-risk bonds), and it toughened the limitations on commercial real estate lending.

THE FDIC IMPROVEMENT ACT OF 1991   The FIRREA basically was a stopgap effort to deal with old problems. In contrast, the *FDIC Improvement Act (FDICIA)* of 1991 represented a forward-looking effort. By passing this legislation, Congress sought to reform various aspects of depository institution regulation and to revamp specific elements of federal deposit insurance. The FDICIA of 1991 did a number of things:

1. Established regulatory responses to banks failing to meet capital standards.

2. Established a regulatory system of **structured early intervention and resolution (SEIR),** under which the FDIC has authority to intervene much more quickly in the affairs of a depository institution that may generate losses for either the BIF or the SAIF.

3. Required the FDIC to set up a clear set of rules for determining when a depository institution's net worth reaches a sufficiently low level that it must be closed.

4. Authorized the FDIC to shore up both the BIF and the SAIF by setting **deposit insurance premiums,** or annual charges to depository institutions for depository insurance, high enough to increase both insurance funds.

5. Restricted the extent to which the Federal Reserve can lend to undercapitalized depository institutions.

6. Required bank regulators to treat troubled large banks under the same timetables and procedures that they apply to small banks that are failing.

7. Mandated a system of **risk-based deposit insurance premiums,** under which the premiums that depository institutions pay the FDIC to fund the BIF and the SAIF depend on the institutions' degrees of capitalization.

(Since 1997, however, very few banks have been paying any deposit insurance premiums at all; see the *Policy Focus: A Never-Ending "Premium Holiday" for Nearly All U.S. Banks.*)

The Great Regulatory Experiment: Capital Requirements

At the same time that the federal government sought to bolster the FDIC's deposit insurance funds, it developed a new framework aimed at reducing the potential for failure of individual depository institutions. This new approach focused attention on depository institutions' equity capital positions.

Structured early intervention and resolution (SEIR): A regulatory system, established by the FDIC Improvement Act of 1991, that authorizes the FDIC to intervene quickly in the management of a depository institution that threatens to cause losses for the federal deposit insurance funds.

Deposit insurance premium: The price that depository institutions pay to the FDIC's insurance fund in exchange for a guarantee of federal insurance of covered deposits that they issue.

Risk-based deposit insurance premiums: Premiums that depository institutions pay the FDIC based on the varying degrees to which they are capitalized and on the differing risk factors that they exhibit.

A Never-Ending "Premium Holiday" for Nearly All U.S. Banks

In early 1993, the Federal Deposit Insurance Corporation implemented risk-based deposit insurance under the terms of the 1991 FDIC Improvement Act. The FDIC established three broad categories based on depository institutions' capital ratios and defined them as "highly capitalized," "adequately capitalized," and "under-capitalized." Within

each of these three categories were three additional classifications, labeled A, B, and C, that the FDIC determined based on aspects of the institutions' risk positions that are unrelated to their levels of capitalization. The riskiest institutions that the FDIC placed in classification C paid a rate of 0.31 percent, whereas those viewed as least risky that fell into classification A were subject to the lowest insurance premium rate of 0.23 percent.

In 1997, however, the FDIC insurance fund reached its minimum legal level of 1.25 percent of all insured deposits. At that time, the FDIC decided

to grant a "premium holiday" to all institutions in classification A and reduce their deposit insurance premium rates to 0 percent. Originally, the FDIC expected this "holiday" to be temporary, but it is still in effect today. Thus, since 1997 the base insurance premium for more than 92 percent of U.S. depository institutions has been zero.

FOR CRITICAL ANALYSIS: Does a premium rate of 0 percent for most institutions increase or reduce the scope of the moral-hazard problem of federal deposit insurance?

Capital Requirements

A depository institution's equity capital represents a "cushion" against losses to depositors, who have the first crack at getting back their funds if an institution should fail. Holders of equity shares, in contrast, are the last in line for funds in such an event. For this reason, depository institution regulators—and in particular the FDIC as the supervisor of federal deposit insurance—regard capital as the first line of defense against depositor losses in the event of a failure. In recent years this has led regulators to impose **capital requirements,** or enforced minimum standards for depository institution equity capital.

Although various requirements on depository institution equity capital positions had existed prior to the 1980s, it was not until Congress passed the *International Lending Supervision Act* of 1983 that regulators began efforts to impose relatively uniform standards for depository institutions. A provision of this legislation authorized the Federal Reserve, the Office of the Comptroller of the Currency (OCC), and the FDIC to determine and supervise capital requirements for commercial banks. In 1985, these three regulators set up a system of capital requirements using two measures of capital. The narrower measure essentially included most equity shares and loan loss reserves (see Chapter 10), and the broader measure added remaining equity shares and subordinated debt—long-term bond issues by depository institutions. The regulators then required banks to meet a two-tiered requirement involving ratios of the capital measures to assets.

The imposition of these capital standards helped end a gradual decline in bank capitalization that had begun in the 1960s (see Figure 9-2 in Chapter 9). Nevertheless, a commonly recognized problem with simple ratios of capital to assets was that they treated any two banks with the same dollar-denominated capital and asset positions as identical. In fact, however, one bank might have made huge loans to a developing country on the verge of default while the other might have maintained a well-diversified portfolio of high-quality loans and safe

Capital requirements: Minimum equity capital standards that regulators impose upon depository institutions.

On the Web
What types of regulatory issues are attracting the attention of international banking supervisors today? To stay up-to-date, go to the home page of the Bank for International Settlements (**http://www.bis.org**), and click on "Basel Committee, publications" to view a listing of the committee's recent reports on issues in bank regulation.

securities. Consequently, simple ratios mainly affect the mix of liabilities and equity capital of depository institutions. Influencing this mix might make sense if regulators care only about *liquidity risks,* or risks associated with loss of liquidity resulting from unexpected deposit withdrawals. Using simple capital ratios alone, however, would fail to account for differences in *credit risks,* or risks relating to the quality of assets, among depository institutions.

ESTABLISHING RISK-BASED CAPITAL REQUIREMENTS

In 1988, the Basel Committee on Banking Supervision—senior representatives of bank supervisory authorities of the United States and eleven other industrialized nations whose activities are based at the Bank for International Settlements in Basel, Switzerland—announced a system of **risk-based capital requirements.** This system was intended to factor risk characteristics into the computation of required capital standards. Under this system, which applies to most banks in the developed world, institutions compute ratios of capital in relation to **risk-adjusted assets.** This figure is a weighted average of all the bank's assets, in which the weights account for risk differences across types of assets.

The safest assets, which regulators traditionally have perceived to be cash assets, U.S. Treasury securities, and fully government-guaranteed GNMA ("Ginnie Mae") mortgage-backed securities, receive a zero weight and hence do not count at all in the computation of risk-adjusted assets. Assets that regulators view as having a slight possibility of default, such as interbank deposits, municipal bonds, and partially government-guaranteed FNMA ("Fannie Mae") mortgage-backed securities, receive a weight of 20 percent. Riskier assets such as first home mortgages receive a weight of 50 percent. All other loans and securities receive a 100 percent weight. In addition, regulators compute "credit exposure dollar equivalents" for banking activities such as derivatives trading that do not appear as assets or liabilities on banks' balance sheets. These typically also receive a 100 percent weight. Then regulators add up all the weighted dollar amounts to get a bank's total risk-adjusted asset figure. This amount is the denominator of the capital ratios that banks have to compute.

Under the Basel capital standards, banks calculate two ratios of capital relative to risk-adjusted assets, based on separate "tiers" of bank capital. The first, "Tier 1 capital," or **core capital,** consists of common shareholders' equity plus retained earnings (income not paid out to shareholders). Regulators have defined a bank's **total capital** as core capital plus "Tier 2 capital," or **supplementary capital.** This latter measure includes some types of preferred stock and most types of subordinated debt.

Since 1989, the regulations have called for the ratio of core capital to risk-adjusted assets to exceed 4 percent and the ratio of total capital to risk-adjusted assets to be greater than 8 percent. In addition, the regulators imposed a simple-ratio standard in which the ratio of total capital to *unadjusted total assets* must exceed 4 percent. Thus, this structure of capital requirements sought to address both liquidity risk and credit risk.

CALCULATING RISK-BASED CAPITAL REQUIREMENTS

To see how these original capital requirements worked, consider a very simple example of two banks. One has $1 million in cash, $2 million in U.S. Treasury securities, and $10 million in commercial loans, so its total assets equal $13 million. It has $0.5 million in common stockholders' equity and retained earnings and $0.5 million in subordinated debt. Hence, its core capital is $0.5 million, and its total capital is $1 million. The $3 million in cash and Treasury securities do not count toward the bank's risk-adjusted assets. Its $10 million in commercial loans count 100 percent, so its total risk-adjusted assets equal $10 million. Consequently, its ratio of core capital to risk-adjusted assets is equal to $0.5 million/$10 million, or 5 percent. Its ratio of total capital to

Risk-based capital requirements: Regulatory capital standards that account for risk factors that distinguish different depository institutions.

Risk-adjusted assets: A weighted average of bank assets that regulators compute to account for risk differences across types of assets.

Core capital: Defined by current capital requirements as shareholders' equity plus retained earnings.

Total capital: Under current bank capital requirements, the sum of core capital and supplementary capital.

Supplementary capital: Under current standards used to calculate required capital, a measure that includes certain preferred stock and most subordinated debt.

MONEYXTRA!
Another Perspective

Evaluate the details of a proposal for using subordinated debt as a key component of market-oriented bank regulation by going to the Chapter 11 reading from the Federal Reserve Bank of Chicago, entitled "Subordinated Debt as Bank Capital: A Proposal for Regulatory Reform," by Douglas Evanoff and Larry Wall. **http://moneyxtra.swcollege.com**

risk-adjusted assets is equal to $1 million/$10 million, or 10 percent. Its unadjusted capital ratio is $1 million/$13 million, or about 7.7 percent. Thus, this bank meets all required capital standards.

Now consider a bank with $0.5 million in cash, $0.5 million in securities, and $12 million in commercial loans. Like the first bank, this one has $13 million in assets on its balance sheet. In contrast, however, it has sufficient off-balance-sheet activities to merit a "credit exposure dollar equivalent" rating of $3 million. Like the first bank, this bank also has $0.5 million in core capital and $0.5 million in supplementary capital. Consequently, the second bank's unadjusted capital ratio, like that of the first bank, is equal to 7.7 percent. Yet the second bank clearly is riskier because it has more loans and undertakes off-balance-sheet activities. This shows up in the current capital requirement calculations. The second bank's $1 million in cash and securities do not count toward its risk-adjusted assets, but its $12 million in commercial loans and $3 million in "credit exposure dollar equivalents" from its off-balance-sheet activities count fully, giving it a risk-adjusted asset total of $15 million. This bank's ratio of core capital to risk-adjusted assets then is $0.5 million/$15 million, or 3.3 percent. Its ratio of total capital to risk-adjusted assets is $1 million/$15 million, or 6.7 percent. Thus, even though it has the same actual assets and capital as the first bank, the second bank fails both the 4 percent and the 8 percent capital standards that apply to core capital and total capital, respectively. (A bank that merely meets all minimum requirements achieves only an "adequately capitalized" rating. It often pays for depository institutions to achieve higher capital ratios; see the *Management Focus: One Bank Learns—the Hard Way—That Capital Requirements Are for Real*.)

The Effects of Capital Requirements

After announcing the new capital standards, banking regulators phased them in gradually through the end of 1992. A number of banks failed to meet the three ratio requirements. In particular, banks often failed the 4 percent simple-ratio requirement even when they met the risk-adjusted ratio standards. To adjust to the requirements, banks could have issued new stock or cut back on lending. Banks' stock prices tend to decline sharply, however, whenever

MANAGEMENT
Focus

One Bank Learns—the Hard Way—That Capital Requirements Are for Real

In the summer of 2004, one of the nation's largest and most respected banks, J.P. Morgan Chase, allowed the unthinkable to happen. It let its ratio of capital to risk-based assets sink to 9.79 percent. This was less than a fourth of

a percentage point below the 10 percent ratio the bank had to maintain to be classified as a "highly capitalized, well-managed" institution and avoid paying deposit insurance premiums. At a ratio 0.21 percentage point below the 10 percent standard, J.P. Morgan Chase became only an "adequately capitalized, well-managed" institution and therefore was assessed a deposit insurance premium equal to 1.5 cents for every $100 of its $210.2 billion of insured deposits. As a result, the bank

had to hand over about $31.5 million to the Federal Deposit Insurance Corporation.

FOR CRITICAL ANALYSIS: Why do you suppose that in 2004 banking analysts criticized J.P. Morgan's managers for making too many loans that turned out to be unprofitable even though they were fully repaid?

they announce that they plan to issue new shares. This tendency may have discouraged many banks from issuing new stock and induced them to cut back on issuing new loans instead. Refer back to Figure 9-1 on page 193, and you will see that commercial bank lending did indeed fall off noticeably in the early 1990s.

In the longer run, however, as Figure 11-1 shows, the adoption of the risk-based capital standards also had the effect on aggregate equity positions of U.S. commercial banks that regulators had hoped to achieve. For the first time in almost fifty years, the ratio of equity to assets rose, beginning in 1990. Figure 11-1 shows that the adoption of the new capital standards may have ended a 150-year downward trend in the overall equity ratio at commercial banks. Furthermore, as market interest rates declined in the late 1990s, the cost of meeting capital requirements declined at banks, inducing a recovery in lending.

New Capital Requirements for the 2000s?

When the Basel Committee on Banking Supervision first proposed and implemented risk-based capital requirements in 1989, some bankers complained that the risk weights were arbitrary. The bankers contended that banks with balance sheets that were treated identically for the purpose of the 1989 capital requirements could actually have very different degrees of risk. One bank, for instance, might make loans only to the most creditworthy businesses, while another might lend to highly risky enterprises, yet for purposes of calculating capital ratios under the 1989 standards the banks' loan portfolios were to be treated the same.

To address these and other issues associated with capital requirements, in June 2004 the Basel Committee approved an expanded system of capital and regulatory supervision, known as Basel II, that is scheduled to be fully in place by 2008. The Basel II system, which some U.S. banks are already beginning to implement, is based on three key points, called "pillars."

FIGURE 11-1
Equity as a Percentage of Bank Assets in the United States, 1940–Present.

U.S. bank equity ratios fell considerably between the mid-nineteenth and the mid-twentieth century. More recently, they have risen slightly.

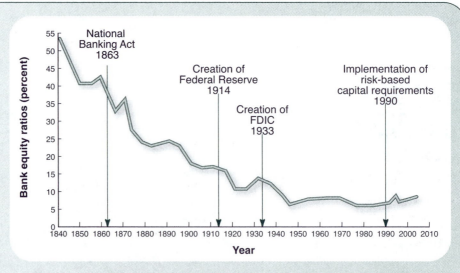

SOURCES: Allen N. Berger, Richard J. Herring, and Giorgio P. Szego, "The Role of Capital in Financial Institutions," *Journal of Banking and Finance* 19 (June 1995); and Federal Deposit Insurance Corporation.

Pillar 1: Modified risk-based capital requirements. Pillar 1 is a slightly modified version of the current rules governing capital requirements. This pillar includes a greater-than-100 percent risk weighting for particularly low-quality loans. It also adds a special capital requirement for institutions judged to have high *operational risks,* such as risks arising from potential computer failures, poor management documentation, or weak antifraud efforts.

Pillar 2: Greater supervisory discretion. Pillar 2 of the new Basel system grants national banking supervisors the power to increase regulatory capital requirements at their own discretion. Regulators can also require certain banks to protect against operational and credit risks by using advanced systems, some of which require sophisticated computer technologies that cost as much as $100 million to put into place.

Pillar 3: Increased disclosure of information to markets. Pillar 3 supplements the capital requirements with rules requiring institutions to disclose more about their business performances. It also allows for regulatory actions in response to market reactions to these disclosures. We shall explore the possible role of market-based risk assessments in bank regulation in Chapter 12.

So far, U.S. regulators have chosen to apply all three pillars of the Basel II system to only a handful of the nation's largest banks. Nevertheless, several other large banks have indicated that they plan to participate voluntarily. Some banking analysts anticipate that as many as fifty of the largest U.S. banks eventually may *choose* to operate under the Basel II regulatory system.

---

4. How has the federal government sought to reduce the FDIC's exposure to losses? Legislation enacted in 1989 and in 1991 established clear rules that the FDIC must follow to identify potential risks to the federal deposit insurance funds. These laws also specify actions that the FDIC can take to enforce its efforts to limit the risk of depository institution failures, including closure of weak institutions. An additional feature of the legislation was the authorization of risk-based deposit insurance premiums. To induce banks to restrain their risk of loss and failure, regulators have developed narrow and broad measures of bank capital and a measure of assets that adjusts for differences in risk across groups of assets. The regulators have set mimimum requirements for the ratios of the two capital measures relative to the measure of risk-adjusted assets. Banks must meet these capital standards or face greater supervision or perhaps even closure.

The Current Regulatory Framework

Of the various banking laws reviewed in this chapter, the most far-reaching was the Glass-Steagall Act of 1933. For sixty-seven years, this legislation provided the structure for U.S. financial intermediation. Nevertheless, within a few years of its passage, bills were introduced in nearly every Congress to amend or even to repeal various aspects of the act. Senator Carter Glass himself decided that the law was overly restrictive and introduced bills aimed at modifying it. Year after year, however, efforts to loosen some of the restraints of the act failed to advance to law. Finally, in 1999, Congress reached a consensus that the Glass-Steagall Act had outlived its usefulness.

The Financial Services Modernization Act of 1999

The law that Congress passed, the *Financial Services Modernization Act* of 1999, also called the *Gramm-Leach-Bliley Act,* swept away a number of Glass-Steagall's provisions. The two key provisions of the new law were the following:

1. Securities firms and insurance companies are permitted to own commercial banks.

2. Banks are empowered to underwrite insurance and securities, including shares of stock.

Thus, securities brokers and dealers, investment banks, and insurance companies can now compete directly with commercial banks. In addition, commercial banks can compete directly with traditional insurers, brokers and dealers, and investment banks. They do so by establishing *financial holding companies,* which are umbrella organizations, regulated by the Federal Reserve, that can own multiple types of financial institutions.

   The Gramm-Leach-Bliley Act has paved the way for major changes in U.S. financial intermediation. Commercial banks, securities firms, and insurers increasingly are forming financial conglomerates. Some financial firms have retained their individual identities but now work more closely together. For instance, some insurers package and manage insurance products that banks market to their customers, and the two types of institutions share the revenues from these activities. We shall explore more fully the ramifications that the Gramm-Leach-Bliley Act has had for commercial banks in Chapter 12. The law also has important implications for how U.S. banking regulation and supervision are likely to be conducted in the future.

Effect of the 1999 Law on the Regulation and Supervision of Commercial Banks

The present regulatory structure for commercial banks stems in part from the dual banking system that emerged after the Civil War. The Office of the Comptroller of the Currency (OCC) has always been the primary regulator of national (federally chartered) banks, and the OCC continues in this capacity today. Under the Banking Act of 1935, which you will learn in Chapter 14 significantly restructured the Federal Reserve, by 1937 all federally insured state banks either had to join the Federal Reserve System and be regulated and supervised by the Fed or had to subject themselves to regulatory supervision from the FDIC. This produced a trilateral federal regulatory structure. The OCC regulates national banks, the Federal Reserve regulates state banks that are members of the Federal Reserve System, and the FDIC regulates state banks that do not opt to be members of the Federal Reserve System.

THE BASIC BANK REGULATORY STRUCTURE

This commercial bank regulatory structure, therefore, has existed for over sixty years. The only "wrinkle" was the establishment of the Federal Reserve as the chief regulator of *bank holding companies,* some of which own national banks or state banks that are not Federal Reserve member banks. But the three regulatory bodies have worked out lines of authority that apply to such situations.

   Each of the three commercial bank regulators retains staff accountants, statisticians, and economists. These individuals examine and audit the books of the banks that they regulate,

MONEYXTRA!
Economic Applications

Was the Gramm-Leach-Bliley Act a good idea, or was it bad public policy? To review alternative perspectives on this debate and make your own judgment, go to EconDebate Online. **http:// moneyxtra.swcollege.com**

On the Web
   How many types of regulations do banks face? For an A to Z listing of Federal Reserve regulations, go to the home page of the Federal Reserve Bank of New York (**http://www.ny.frb.org**), and click on "Banking" and then "Supervision and Regulation." Finally, click on "Regulations" (**http://www.ny.frb.org/ banking/regulations.html**).

collect and analyze data from specific institutions and for all institutions combined, and evaluate the effectiveness of current or proposed regulatory policies. Of the nearly 8,000 commercial banks, about 2,000 are national banks that the OCC regulates. Of the 6,000 or so state-chartered banks, about 900 are Federal Reserve members and thereby fall under the Fed's regulatory umbrella. At present, the FDIC has oversight responsibilities for over 5,000 commercial banks.

BANKING REGULATION AND SUPERVISION UNDER THE GRAMM-LEACH-BLILEY ACT From the perspective of individual banks, the Gramm-Leach-Bliley Act did not alter the basic trilateral structure of banking regulation. In one respect, however, the act split supervisory authority between the Federal Reserve and the OCC. In a compromise worked out with the two regulators, Congress gave the Fed and the OCC the authority to veto each other's decisions to grant new powers to commercial banks under their respective regulatory jurisdictions. This means that these two bank regulators will be forced to cooperate in determining whether commercial banks may create subsidiaries that act as investment banks, brokers, or insurers.

Nevertheless, the Gramm-Leach-Bliley Act left the Fed solely in charge of supervising bank holding companies. This means that the Fed is the ultimate regulator of multiservice, financial-holding-company conglomerates such as Citigroup. In an important sense, therefore, the Gramm-Leach-Bliley Act made the Fed the preeminent banking regulator. The Fed has the authority to permit bank holding companies to branch out into various lines of business—securities underwriting, insurance, and the like—without any input from other banking regulators.

Regulation and Supervision of Savings Institutions

The Gramm-Leach-Bliley Act had fewer implications for the regulation and supervision of savings institutions. Under a provision of the 1989 Financial Institutions Reform, Recovery, and Enforcement Act, the main federal regulator of savings institutions remains the Office of Thrift Supervision (OTS). The OTS is a bureau within the Treasury Department, and its relationship to nationally chartered savings institutions mirrors the OCC's relationship to nationally chartered commercial banks in many respects.

Nevertheless, in some ways the authority of the OTS is limited. Feeling somewhat "burned" by the regulatory breakdowns that occurred during the savings institution crisis of the 1980s, in 1989 Congress gave the FDIC the power to overrule the OTS in some instances. For instance, the FDIC can close OTS-regulated institutions or withdraw federal deposit insurance from such institutions even in the face of OTS objections. At the same time, Congress reduced the likelihood of such squabbles by also making the heads of the OCC and OTS members of the five-person board of directors of the FDIC.

Under the Gramm-Leach-Bliley Act, state authorities continue to regulate state-chartered savings institutions. Nevertheless, nearly all such institutions are federally insured. The OTS does not have supervisory authority over state-chartered savings institutions, but these institutions must meet standards established by the FDIC. Consequently, state-chartered savings institutions ultimately must meet federally mandated standards and effectively must satisfy FDIC regulations. (Sometimes financial institutions obtain federal thrift charters to avoid cumbersome state regulations; see on the next page the *Cyber Focus: Quicken Loans Decides It Wants Federal Regulation.*)

On the Web
How do bank examiners at various U.S. regulatory agencies coordinate their activities? To find out, visit the Web site of the Federal Financial Institutions Examination Council, **http://www. ffiec.gov**.

MONEYXTRA!
Online Case Study

To contemplate the pros and cons of a recent proposal to consolidate the U.S. Treasury's regulation of banks and savings institutions, see the Chapter 11 Case Study, entitled "Time to Combine the OCC and the OTS?" **http://moneyxtra. swcollege.com**

Quicken Loans Decides It Wants Federal Regulation

Quicken Loans is one of the top online mortgage lenders in the United States. The company also has long owned a savings bank in the Detroit, Michigan area, which has a state charter to make mortgage loans and to operate three physical branches. Because its online operations are open to anyone, however, Quicken Loans extends credit throughout the fifty U.S. states, where it increasingly faced a complicated patchwork of state and local laws prohibiting "predatory" lending.

In 2004, the Office of Thrift Supervision declared that all institutions it regulates are exempt from such state laws. This policy change induced Quicken Loans to formally consolidate all its operations within a single savings bank with an OTS charter. By choosing to be regulated by this federal agency, Quicken Loans obtained greater flexibility in its business, thereby reducing its costs and potentially entering lines of business that state and local laws might have prohibited.

FOR CRITICAL ANALYSIS: Why do you suppose that other online mortgage lenders are also considering obtaining federal charters?

Regulation and Supervision of Credit Unions

The Gramm-Leach-Bliley Act had very little to say about the structure of federal regulation and supervision of credit unions. Under the terms of earlier laws, the key federal regulator of credit unions is the National Credit Union Administration (NCUA). A board of three individuals governs this government agency, which has sole responsibility for chartering, insuring, supervising, and examining federally chartered credit unions. The NCUA administers the National Credit Union Share Insurance Fund, and most state-chartered credit unions contribute to and are covered by this insurance fund. Although state regulatory bodies have immediate supervisory responsibilities for such state-chartered institutions, those covered by the NCUA's insurance program must meet the standards that it sets for coverage. Because the NCUA's fund covers all federally insured credit unions, the FDIC plays no role in the supervision or regulation of credit unions.

Indeed, those who have advocated streamlining the regulatory environment faced by commercial banks often point to the NCUA as a possible model for a simplified bank regulatory structure. Those who favor maintaining the status quo for commercial bank regulation respond that even though there are more credit unions than commercial banks, the amount of dollars involved in the two industries differs dramatically. After all, the assets of all credit unions combined amount to less than one-tenth of the assets of commercial banks, and the latter institutions have played more dominant and varied roles in the nation's financial system. This, goes the counterargument, helps to justify the more complex web of regulators and regulations that commercial banks face. We should note, however, that this counterargument may lose some of its force in the future, because the NCUA is contemplating the imposition of capital requirements, as well as other bank-type regulations, on the credit unions that it regulates.

5. How did the Financial Services Modernization Act of 1999 alter the structure of U.S. bank regulation and supervision? Since the 1930s, commercial banks have had three regulators: (1) the Office of the Comptroller of the Currency (OCC), which supervises nationally chartered banks, (2) the Federal Reserve, which supervises state-chartered banks that are members of the Federal Reserve System (Fed), and (3) the Federal Deposit Insurance Corporation (FDIC), which supervises the remaining state-chartered banks. The Financial Services Modernization Act, or Gramm-Leach-Bliley Act, of 1999 altered the U.S. financial landscape by allowing direct ties between and rivalry among commercial banks, securities firms, and insurance companies. This required modifying the structure of federal banking supervision, and Congress gave the Fed primary authority over umbrella, financial-holding-company conglomerates that own both banks and other financial firms. The Fed and the OCC share authority to determine what types of financial firms individual banks may own. The Gramm-Leach-Bliley Act did little to alter the basic structure of federal regulation of savings institutions, which are supervised by the Office of Thrift Supervision (OTS), or of credit unions, which are supervised by the National Credit Union Administration (NCUA).

International Dimensions of Bank Regulation

Countries do not always share the same cultures, languages, or political systems. One thing that countries all over the world do have in common, however, is their recent propensity to experience major banking catastrophes.

The Global Epidemic of Bank Failures

In the United States, the final bill for the government-arranged bailout of the nation's savings and loan industry during the early 1990s totaled at least $200 billion, or just over 2 percent of the total national output for a single year. But this is a drop in the bucket compared with the banking problems that other countries have faced in recent years. For example, efforts by Argentina's government to recover from a banking crisis in the early 1980s probably cost more than half of that country's single-year gross domestic product. Today, the country is again struggling with banking instability.

BANK TROUBLES IN THE WEST . . . As banking systems in some locales such as the United States rebounded in the 1990s, conditions worsened in many other regions of the Western world, including Scandinavia. Between 1992 and 1993, Norway's government effectively purchased over half of the nation's banking system to keep it financially afloat, and in 1992 the government of Sweden took control of two of the country's four largest banking institutions. Eastern Europe experienced even worse problems. In 1996, Bulgaria's banking system imploded and had to be rescued by the country's government. Today, nearly a third of the loans issued by banks in the Czech Republic and in Slovakia are "nonperforming," meaning that the banks will be unlikely to recover significant portions of the principal amounts of the loans.

Other parts of the Western world also slid into crisis. Since 1994, Venezuela has spent over 25 percent of its national output for one year repairing its banking system. The cost of

Mexico's 1995 banking collapse, which the Mexican government is still dealing with today, has been estimated at nearly 15 percent of that country's output for a given year.

On the Web

How is South Korea's financial system structured? Learn more about South Korean banking by visiting the home page of the Bank of Korea at **http://www.bok. or.kr**. First, select the English-language version at the upper right. Then click on "Financial System."

. . . AND MAJOR BANKING PROBLEMS IN THE EAST   The biggest problems, however, have arisen in East Asia. By 1997, South Korea's banking system teetered on bankruptcy, as more than 10 percent of all loans by that country's banks—nearly $25 billion, or the combined market value of all South Korean banks—were nonperforming. In that same year, banking systems collapsed in Indonesia, Malaysia, and Thailand.

Today, banking conditions have improved somewhat in these Southeast Asian nations. Nevertheless, national banking systems throughout Asia continue to be troubled. In India, nearly a fifth of the loans extended by twenty-seven government-owned banks are nonperforming. The Bank of China estimates that about the same portion of Chinese bank loans also are nonperforming.

Even in Japan, more than $250 billion in bank loans soured in 1995 alone when home mortgage companies known as *jusen* went bankrupt following a collapse in Japanese real estate prices. Within just a few years, the Japanese banking system was reeling, as banks faced a cumulative total of more than *$600 billion* in bad loans to clean up. One bit of market "fallout" from these problems has been the *Japan premium*. Since the late 1990s, Japanese banks have had to pay 0.20 to 0.25 percentage points more for interbank loans than U.S., British, German, and other Western banks must pay. A little over two-tenths of a percentage point may not seem like much until one takes into account the hundreds of billions of dollars of worldwide money market funds that Japanese banks must raise. For each billion-dollar increment of fund-raising in global money markets, a 0.20 percent "Japan premium" translates into an additional $2 million that Japanese banks must pay for funds. This extra funding cost, of course, has placed Japanese banks at a considerable competitive disadvantage in international lending markets.

A BIG WORLD WITH RELATIVELY FEW HEALTHY BANKS   Recently, the International Monetary Fund (IMF) estimated that since 1980, 133 of 181 IMF member nations have suffered banking problems that it judged to be "significant." Moody's Investors Service, which rates the riskiness of banks in 61 nations on a scale ranging from A (best risk) to E (worst risk), has determined that more than thirty countries have "average banks" that rate D or E. Banks in the A and B categories are concentrated in countries within the European Monetary Union, the United States, and the United Kingdom.

Why have so many countries' banking systems faltered in recent decades? There are two basic viewpoints on this issue. One is that banking is an inherently unstable business whose fortunes ebb and flow with the performances of national economies. From this perspective, government regulation and "safety nets," such as deposit insurance or "last-resort" governmental lending agencies, must be put in place to prevent periodic banking collapses from taking place.

Another argument, however, is that governmental safety nets themselves may be responsible for recent banking crises. According to this view, if bankers know that governments stand ready to bail them out if their "bets" turn sour, then they have every incentive to make highly profitable loans whose yields include hefty risk premiums. Thus, goes this argument, banking safety nets create moral-hazard problems for taxpayers, who ultimately must back up governmental guarantees.

International Linkages and Bank Regulation

The declining strength of banking and other financial markets around the world in recent years has had significant implications for banking policies in the United States and elsewhere.

LIMITING REGULATORY ARBITRAGE   One special area of concern for banking regulators has been the potential for banks to engage in **regulatory arbitrage.** Through this process, banks try to escape the effects of regulations imposed by authorities in their home nations by shifting operations and funds to offices in locales where regulatory constraints are less substantial.

Regulatory arbitrage: The act of trying to avoid regulations imposed by banking authorities in one's home country by moving offices and funds to countries with less constraining regulations.

To avoid the potential for regulatory arbitrage by U.S. banks, U.S. banking regulators have sought to coordinate their policies with those of banking regulators in other developed nations. For instance, in 1988 the Federal Reserve, the FDIC, and the OCC joined with banking regulators of most major nations to develop and implement the risk-based capital requirements described earlier in the chapter. The idea behind this internationally coordinated policymaking was that if all banks in such nations as Germany, Japan, the United Kingdom, and the United States had to meet the same basic capital requirements, then the banks would face similar constraints. In addition to limiting the scope for regulatory arbitrage, therefore, this coordinated action was intended to ensure that major banks would not face competitive advantages or disadvantages in international competition for loans and deposits.

THE LIMITATIONS OF INTERNATIONAL COORDINATION   When the banking regulators gathered at the Bank for International Settlements in Basel, Switzerland, to announce the coordinated system of risk-based capital requirements, they viewed the event as a watershed in international coordination of banking policies. Ultimately, nearly forty nations signed on to what became known as the "Basel Accord" on risk-based capital standards. In the end, however, national enforcement of the standards has varied so widely that "coordination" has never been achieved.

Undeniably, the Basel capital standards had a significant effect on international banking. Consider, for instance, their initial impact on Japanese banking. During the 1980s, Japanese banks had emerged as global powerhouses, establishing major presences as lenders in Africa, Asia, Europe, the Middle East, South America, Mexico, and even the United States. In 1995, most of the top ten banks in the world were based in Japan.

Since the late 1990s, however, a number of large Japanese banks have barely held sufficient capital to meet the risk-adjusted capital ratio requirement of 8 percent. Because their share values also have declined in the Japanese stock market, capital ratios of Japanese banks have been squeezed from both directions: rising values of yen assets and declining values of yen-denominated capital measures. They have had no choice but to reduce their presence in global lending markets. Indeed, a few large banks have sold some of their loans, in what some analysts call an ongoing "fire sale." Over time, a number of these banks have merged to form new Japanese megabanks that are less internationally active than Japanese banks were in the 1980s. (Indeed, Japan's bank regulators have recently given the nation's banks a greater incentive to operate only domestically; see on the next page the *Global Focus: Japan Largely Opts Out of "Pillar 2."*)

6. Do national bank regulators coordinate their policies?   The Basel capital standards were determined after considerable consultation among banking regulators of major industrialized nations. In this sense they reflected international coordination of regulatory policies. In recent years, however, national regulators have differed in their interpretation and enforcement of the Basel capital requirements.

Japan Largely Opts Out of Pillar 2

Pillar 2 of the Basel II capital adequacy standards, scheduled to go into effect in many parts of the world by 2008, provides several options for regulators desiring to impose tougher standards on "internationally active" banks. For instance, one element of the Pillar 2 standards includes a so-called scaling factor—a multiplier that a regulator can apply at its discretion to increase a bank's required capital. At present, the Basel II scaling factor is 1.06. Thus, if a

banking regulator determines that a bank has too little capital in light of its risks, the regulator can multiply its normal capital requirement by 1.06 to obtain a higher level of required capital.

When Japanese bank regulators began implementing the Basel II agreement, however, they largely ignored the Pillar 2 standards. As long as a Japanese bank is primarily involved in domestic markets, it must satisfy only the minimum Pillar 1 capital requirements. The official Japanese capital requirements do not mention a

scaling factor, and the tough discretionary standards set forth in Pillar 2 are absent. Many economists have concluded that Japan's primarily domestic banks now face the weakest capital standards of any developed nation. They also predict that even more Japanese banks are likely to reduce their international operations.

FOR CRITICAL ANALYSIS: Why do you suppose that the Basel II agreement gives national banking regulators considerable discretion regarding how to implement rules for their own banking systems?

Chapter Summary

1. The Long-Term Effects of Banking Laws Adopted in the 1930s: The Glass-Steagall Act of 1933 toughened interstate-branching restrictions and put limits on linkages between banking and other financial services. The act also laid the foundation for the establishment of the Federal Deposit Insurance Corporation and authorized ceilings on bank interest rates, including today's zero-interest restriction on business demand deposits.

2. How Deposit Interest Rate Ceilings Spurred Deregulation: During periods when other market interest rates rose well above the legal ceiling rates on deposits, disintermediation occurred as depositors withdrew funds to place them in instruments with higher yields. Ultimately, in the 1980s the threat that disintermediation posed to depository institutions led Congress to pass laws that significantly deregulated depository institutions.

3. Deposit Insurance as a Justification for Federal Regulation: Because a large portion of the deposits at depository institutions receives federal insurance guarantees, depository institution managers may be induced to make riskier asset and liability choices. Hence, federal deposit insurance exposes the government (taxpayers) to

a significant moral-hazard problem. Monitoring insured institutions via periodic examinations and providing enforceable supervisory rules that managers must follow are means that governmental regulators can use to reduce the magnitude of the moral-hazard problem.

4. How the Federal Government Has Sought to Reduce the FDIC's Exposure to Losses: In 1989 and in 1991, Congress passed laws that set out strict procedures that the FDIC must follow to identify potential risks to the federal deposit insurance funds. The laws authorize the FDIC to enforce its efforts to limit the risk of depository institution failures by closing particularly troubled institutions. The legislation also authorized risk-based deposit insurance premiums. In an effort to directly constrain the riskiness of banks, regulators have defined two measures of bank capital. Then they examine ratios of these measures relative to a risk-adjusted measure of a bank's assets. Failure of a bank to maintain ratios that regulators deem sufficient can result in more regulatory supervision or possibly even closure of the bank.

5. The Financial Services Modernization Act of 1999 and the Structure of U.S. Bank Regulation and Supervision: Supervision of the activities of commercial banks is split among three regulators. The Office of the Comptroller of the Currency (OCC) supervises nationally chartered banks, while the Federal Reserve supervises state-chartered banks that are members of the Federal Reserve System (Fed). The Federal Deposit Insurance Corporation (FDIC) supervises state-chartered banks that are not members of the Federal Reserve System. The Financial Services Modernization Act, or Gramm-Leach-Bliley Act, of 1999 permits direct linkages between banks and other financial firms. Thus, the Gramm-Leach-Bliley Act changed the structure of federal banking supervision. It requires the Fed and the OCC to jointly decide what types of financial firms individual banks may own. Nevertheless, it made the Fed the primary regulator of financial holding companies that own both banks and other financial firms, thereby centralizing considerable regulatory authority with the Fed. The Gramm-Leach-Bliley Act did not fundamentally change the basic structure of federal regulation of savings institutions, which are supervised by the Office of Thrift Supervision (OTS), or of credit unions, which are supervised by the National Credit Union Administration (NCUA).

6. International Coordination of Bank Regulatory Policies: Bank regulators of major developed economies established the Basel capital standards following considerable consultation. Thus, the implementation of bank capital requirements reflected international policy coordination. During the past several years, however, national regulators have interpreted and enforced the Basel capital requirements differently.

Questions and Problems

(Answers to odd-numbered questions and problems may be found on the Web at **http://money.swcollege.com** under "Student Resources.")

1. Many economists believe that markets should be as free and unregulated as possible. Yet a number of these same economists have been critical of federal depository institution regulations that they perceive as having been too "lax" in past years. What might account for these apparently contradictory positions?

2. Disintermediation has commonly occurred during intervals when many individuals and firms that in the past had been able to get bank loans found that banks no longer were willing to lend. Explain why this makes sense.

3. Economists have found that banks that were judged too big to fail in the late 1980s sometimes could pay lower interest rates on their large certificates of deposit. Explain why this might have happened.

4. Because the FDIC's insurance funds are judged to be "fully capitalized," nearly all depository institutions pay no deposit insurance premiums. In your view, is this a desirable situation, given that regulatory supervision continues and capital requirements remain in force? Take a stand, and support your answer.

5. Suppose that a depository institution has $20 million in cash assets and U.S. Treasury securities. It also has $5 million in GNMA mortgage-backed securities and $10 million in FNMA mortgage-backed securities. It has $48 million in mortgage loans outstanding. It is not involved in any off-balance-sheet activities. If its core capital is $2 million and its total capital is $3 million, would this depository institution meet the capital requirements established in 1989? Show your work and explain.

6. In 2006, a Danish bank has total assets of 1,000 million kroner. Of these assets, 80 percent are loans to businesses, and the remainder are holdings of cash assets and government securities. The bank engages in derivatives trading that Danish regulators, who strictly follow the 1989 Basel capital standards, assign a credit equivalence exposure value of 400 million kroner. The bank's equity capital amounts to 100 million kroner, and the bank has no subordinated debt. Does the bank meet current capital requirements? Show your work and explain.

7. Economists usually use the term *regulatory arbitrage* to refer to international banking activities. Given the current structure of depository institution regulation in the United States, could U.S. depository institutions potentially engage in regulatory arbitrage within U.S. borders? Explain. [Hint: There are three federal commercial banking regulators and federal and state regulators of savings institutions and credit unions.]

8. Explain why purely domestic considerations can make it difficult for national banking regulators to abide by international agreements to coordinate regulatory policies.

9. Shortly after the Gramm-Leach-Bliley Act passed, a number of financial institutions rushed to establish financial holding companies merging banking, insurance, mutual funds, and securities firms under a single corporate structure. By 2002, however, several of the new corporations were already "spinning off" some of these lines of business into separate firms specializing in particular activities. Does this imply that the legislation was misguided? Take a stand, and explain your reasoning.

10. As noted in this chapter, the new Basel capital requirements that will be fully in effect by 2008 attempt to account for operational risks relating to equipment failures and managerial errors or fraud.

Bankers have complained that attempts to "quantify" these risks will be so judgmental that capital ratios will become too subjective to provide meaningful ratings of a bank's capital adequacy. Evaluate this argument.

Before the Test

Test your understanding of the material covered in this chapter by taking the Chapter 11 interactive quiz at **http://money.swcollege.com**.

Online Application

Internet URL: http://www.fdic.gov

Title: FDIC Rules and Regulations

Navigation: Begin at the home page of the FDIC given above, and click on "Regulations & Examinations." In the left margin, click on "Laws & Regs." Then click on "FDIC Law, Regulations, and Related Acts." Next, click on "6000 Bank Holding Company Act."

Application: Follow the instructions, and answer the corresponding questions.

1. Under "Sec. 2: Definitions," click on "(c) Bank Definition." According to the Bank Holding Company Act, what is a "bank"? Does this definition correspond to the definition provided in Chapter 9? In what ways is it more specific or more general? Explain.

2. Back up to the table of contents, and under "Sec. 3: Acquisition of Bank Shares and Assets," click on "(d) Interstate Banking." Under the original Bank Holding Company Act, are federal or state laws binding on the permitted extent of interstate branching?

For Group Study and Analysis: Divide into groups, and have each group assign its members to review various sections of the Bank Holding Company Act and determine what types of institutions a bank holding company may own. In class, have each group report back its findings about allowable activities of bank holding companies. Based on these findings, to what extent can banking and various financial services be combined under this law?

Selected References and Further Reading

Barth, James. *The Great Savings and Loan Debacle.* Washington, D.C.: American Enterprise Institute Press, 1991.

Berger, Allen, Richard Herring, and Giorgio Szego. "The Role of Capital in Financial Institutions." *Journal of Banking and Finance* 19 (June 1995): 393–430.

Gup, Benton. *The New Basel Capital Accord.* New York: Thomson, 2004.

Kane, Edward, and Asli Demirgue-Kunt. "Deposit Insurance around the Globe: Where Does It Work?" National Bureau of Economic Research Working Paper No. 8493, September 2001.

Kopecky, Kenneth, and David VanHoose. "Capital Regulation, Heterogeneous Monitoring Costs, and Aggregate Loan Quality." *Journal of Banking and Finance* 30 (Forthcoming 2006).

_____ . "A Model of the Monetary Sector with and without Binding Capital Requirements." *Journal of Banking and Finance* 28 (March 2004): 633–646.

Laevon, Luc. "The Political Economy of Deposit Insurance." World Bank Policy Research Working Paper No. 3247, March 2004.

Lopez, José. "Off-Site Monitoring of Bank Holding Companies." Federal Reserve Bank of San Francisco *Economic Letter,* No. 2002-15, May 17, 2002.

_____ . "Supervising Interest Rate Risk Management." Federal Reserve Bank of San Francisco *Economic Letter,* No. 2004-26, September 17, 2004.

_____ . "What Is Operational Risk?" Federal Reserve Bank of San Francisco *Economic Letter,* No. 2002-2, January 25, 2002.

Martin, Antoine. "A Guide to Deposit Insurance Reform." Federal Reserve Bank of Kansas City *Economic Review,* First Quarter 2003, pp. 29–54.

O'Hara, Maureen, and Wayne Shaw. "Deposit Insurance and Wealth Effects: The Value of Being 'Too Big to Fail.'" *Journal of Finance* 45 (December 1990): 1587–1600.

Thomson, James. "Who Benefits from Increasing the Federal Deposit Insurance Limit?" Federal Reserve Bank of Cleveland *Economic Commentary,* September 15, 2001.

Weinberger, John. "Competition among Bank Regulators." Federal Reserve Bank of Richmond *Economic Quarterly* 88 (Fall 2002): 19–36.

MoneyXtra

Log on to the MoneyXtra Web site now (**http://moneyxtra.swcollege.com**) for additional learning resources such as practice quizzes, case studies, readings, and additional economic applications.

Economic Consequences of Depository Institution Regulation

*Since 2000, more than 600 banks have elected to become financial holding compa-
nies under the terms of the Gramm-Leach-Bliley Act, thereby gaining the authority
to offer a variety of additional financial services. All these banks aimed to profit
from taking this step, and many perceived that the key to increased profits would be
"relationship banking." The idea was that banks could cash in on existing relationships by persuading their depositors and loan customers to engage in one-stop
shopping for mutual funds, insurance policies, and various other services. Toward
this end, the newly formed financial holding companies began launching a variety
of relationship-banking products. For instance, some banks offered packages of low-
interest mortgage loans and credit life insurance policies, and others granted special access to low-priced services to customers who also opened mutual fund
accounts.*

    *By the mid-2000s, however, Federal Reserve officials charged with regulating
financial holding companies had begun to regard many forms of "relationship
banking" as illegal tying arrangements. Under a tying arrangement, a company
requires a consumer to purchase one of its products as a precondition to buying
another. In late 2004, the Fed began to take action. It slapped a bank with a $3
million fine for requiring some corporate borrowers to allow it to act as their
investment bank in exchange for its commercial lending services. More broadly, the
Fed began to develop more stringent antitying regulations. By 2005, the Fed was
unveiling tough restrictions on relationship banking, thereby transforming banks'
dreams of unhindered profits into a more regulated, less profitable reality.*

The Fed's antitying efforts are just one example of how regulatory actions can significantly
constrain depository institutions. In this chapter, you will learn about key economic consequences of depository institution regulation.

Fundamental Issues

1. Has interstate banking made depository institutions more cost-efficient?

2. What are the pros and cons of depository institution mergers and universal banking?

3. How has off-balance-sheet banking complicated the task of regulating depository institutions?

4. What are the benefits and costs of financial consumer protection laws?

5. How might depository institution regulators use financial markets to help guide their supervisory activities?

Economies of Scale and Scope: Does Bank Size Matter?

In recent years, the number of commercial bank branches in the United States has increased even as the total number of banks has declined. All told, depository financial institutions (including both banks and savings institutions) insured by the Federal Deposit Insurance Corporation (FDIC) operate more than 90,000 branches in the United States. Prior to 1996 only about 50 of these were interstate branches, and they existed only as a result of specific historical exceptions to the general prohibitions on interstate banking discussed in Chapter 11. A few had existed before the passage of laws restricting interstate branching arrangements. Others served military installations and received special exemptions as a result. In other cases, regulators had permitted interstate branches to facilitate the mergers of failing depository institutions with healthier institutions located in different states.

The Current Status of Interstate Banking

During the 1970s and 1980s, various constituencies began to argue in favor of lifting the ban on interstate branching. They included some states, which believed interstate branching would lead to capital inflows for their states; people living in metropolitan areas spanning more than one state, who felt it would add convenience and flexibility; and many depository institutions, which argued that it would enable them to achieve more geographic diversification and take advantage of technological developments to market their products nationwide.

LEGAL CONSIDERATIONS   Standing in the way of interstate banking were two key pieces of legislation left over from the early part of the twentieth century. The 1927 McFadden Act left it to the states to determine whether national banks could branch across state lines. The 1933 Glass-Steagall Act had toughened this restriction, effectively making interstate branching illegal unless states voluntarily opened themselves to branching by banks based in other states. This effectively meant that all fifty states would have to coordinate if full interstate banking were to become feasible throughout the nation.

It took several decades, but by the early 1990s the states had made significant progress in this direction largely by permitting banking corporations to acquire banks across state lines. Initially, many states required *reciprocity* from other states. For instance, Missouri would agree to let a bank based in Illinois acquire a Missouri-based bank only if Illinois would allow Missouri banks to acquire Illinois banks. By the mid-1990s, roughly half of all states had worked out such reciprocity arrangements with other states. Several of the remaining states permitted acquisitions under an open invitation for reciprocity from any other state. A number had no reciprocity requirement. Consequently, the nation entered the 1990s with a crazy quilt of interstate banking arrangements stemming from laws enacted several decades before.

This situation began to change in 1997 as a result of the *Interstate Banking and Branching Efficiency Act of 1994.* Under this legislation, an umbrella banking corporation can own a depository institution anywhere in the United States. The legislation allows holding companies to consolidate into a single, multistate bank, thereby saving the companies the expense of setting up legally distinct institutions with separate boards of directors and officers in each state where they have branches.

CONSOLIDATION OF DEPOSITORY INSTITUTIONS   Many commentators hailed the 1994 legislation as a precursor to truly sweeping changes in the structure of U.S. banking. Several observers predicted that within a few years the number of commercial banks would fall from about 10,000 to fewer than 4,000 or 5,000. They also predicted that large depository institutions would become even larger as they swallowed up smaller banking organizations around the country, thereby consolidating existing banking operations among fewer institutions. There is now some evidence supporting these predictions. Most noticeably, the number of U.S. banks has declined by more than 20 percent since the Interstate Banking Act's passage.

Cross-Border Deposits   In states that have opened their borders to interstate acquisitions of banking offices, the shares of deposits held by out-of-state depository institutions have increased considerably in recent years. By the early 2000s, citizens of the "average" state who owned deposits at commercial banks held one-fourth of their deposits in depository institutions based in states outside their own. In extreme cases, such as Arizona, Washington, and Nevada, residents with commercial bank deposits held over 80 percent of their deposits with banks headquartered in other states.

Furthermore, the largest banks really have been getting bigger. Before 1960, the largest 50 banks in the United States issued fewer than 40 percent of all bank deposits, and the largest 100 banks issued less than half of all deposits. Today, the largest 100 banks together account for about 80 percent of all bank deposits. The largest 50 banks issue more than 70 percent of all deposits.

Limits on Consolidation   Nevertheless, there are also good reasons to question just how dramatic banking consolidation may be as interstate banking restrictions wither away. One point that is easy to overlook is just how effectively depository institutions already had sidestepped the McFadden Act and Glass-Steagall Act by forming multistate umbrella banking corporations. Furthermore, as discussed in Chapter 10, it pays for banks to get bigger and bigger only if there are unlimited economies of scale so that larger banks experience lower average operating expenses. Yet most studies have found that economies of scale are not particularly significant in banking. Certainly, the absolute number of depository institutions will decline dramatically in coming years. Much of this decline, however, will likely occur simply because multistate umbrella companies can drop the names of all the separate institutions that laws have required that they incorporate. How much further these holding companies may expand their acquisitions of existing depository institutions remains to be seen. A key issue will be whether further acquisitions make the holding companies and their subsidiaries more cost-efficient. (Another factor that may ultimately limit consolidation in the U.S. banking industry is a legal clause; see the *Policy Focus: A Banking Law Clause That Isn't Binding—Yet.*)

Cost Efficiencies from Interstate Mergers

Recall from Chapter 10 that one perspective on depository institution market structure and its implications is offered by *efficient structure theory*. It indicates that the consolidation of banking resources that may result from interstate banking could generate more cost efficiency. If true, this might be a significant benefit from interstate banking arrangements.

As discussed in Chapter 10 and noted above, however, the efficient structure theory's earlier reliance on economies of scale as the source of cost savings from mergers is not supported by real-world data. In recent years, most proponents of the efficient structure theory—and, indeed, depository institution owners and managers themselves—have contended that the

POLICY

Focus

A Banking Law Clause That Isn't Binding—Yet

The Interstate Banking and Branching Efficiency Act contains a provision that is now beginning to loom as a potential constraint on banking consolidation. This legal clause prevents a single bank- ing company from expanding beyond the point at which it has more than 10 percent of the nation's total deposits. Bank of America and Citigroup already have greater than 10 percent shares of total deposits at U.S. commercial banks, although each bank remains well below a 10 percent share of *all* deposits held at the nation's commercial banks, sav- ings banks, savings and loan associa- tions, and credit unions. Nevertheless, if consolidation among depository institu- tions continues at a pace close to that of the previous decade, sometime within the next ten years at least one depository institution may be con- strained by the overall 10 percent limit.

FOR CRITICAL ANALYSIS: Why do you suppose that Congress decided to limit individual banks to no more than 10 percent of the nation's total deposits?

main cost savings from mergers should arise from greater managerial efficiency. According to this argument, interstate consolidations of depository institutions should help cut the size of administrative bureaucracies by eliminating duplicative layers of management.

Before interstate banking was legalized, studies by Aruna Srinivasan of the Federal Reserve Bank of Atlanta, both alone and with Larry Wall of the same bank, cast doubt on how big such cost savings were likely to be. In their joint work, Srinivasan and Wall found little evidence that mergers significantly reduced banks' expenses. In her separate study, Srinivasan found some evidence that larger banks created by mergers were able to reduce salary expenses by elimi- nating redundant management and staff positions, as predicted by efficient structure theorists. But she also found that these savings were typically offset by increased expenses on other aspects of the banks' operations, such as information systems and marketing.

Of course, to get around past interstate banking restrictions, multistate umbrella corpora- tions had to incur significant expenses in setting up organizational structures to meet the requirements of various state laws. Under interstate banking, many of these artificial structures are not needed. Consequently, a movement toward interstate banking undoubtedly must save on some expenses. Studies of bank mergers in the late 1990s and into the mid-2000s, after interstate banking was legalized, support this conclusion. They find that the cost savings from more recent bank mergers were more than double those realized from mergers in the 1980s. Mergers occurring after the early 1990s reduced the merging banks' expenses by more than 30 percent, whereas mergers during the earlier interval resulted in cost reductions of only 15 percent on average.

> **1. Has interstate banking made depository institutions more cost-efficient?**   A large number of bank mergers have taken place since the 1980s. Many merging institutions claimed that they would realize significant cost savings. The evidence is that efficiency gains from bank mergers were relatively modest during the 1980s and early 1990s. The 1994 federal legislation legalizing interstate banking beginning in 1997 set off a wave of merger activity, and the cost savings from these mergers have been relatively higher.

Depository Institution Market Concentration and Performance

From the late 1990s onward, so much bank merger activity occurred that some people began to joke that eventually there would be just one commercial bank for the Fed, the FDIC, and the Office of the Comptroller of the Currency to regulate. The only issue, they opined, was what name the surviving bank would go by.

Without exception, merging banks mentioned potential cost-efficiency gains as a key justification for combining their operations. As noted above, however, studies of earlier mergers indicated that merger-related reductions in average operating costs may have been small for a number of banks. As the merger wave progressed, therefore, a number of merging banks began to mention another potential advantage of banking consolidation, which they often referred to as "revenue enhancement." That is, another rationale for bank mergers is that they may lead to higher average earnings.

Concentration and Performance

Customers of depository institutions are directly concerned with the prices they must pay for services, the interest rates they must pay on loans, and the interest yields they receive on deposits. As we discussed in Chapter 10, a theory that competes with the efficient structure theory is the traditional *structure-conduct-performance (SCP) model* of depository institution markets. This model predicts that more heavily concentrated market structures lead to higher loan interest rates and lower deposit rates. The SCP model also indicates that customers of depository institutions in more concentrated markets usually must pay higher fees for the services provided by these institutions. Thus, the SCP model implies that bank mergers yield "revenue enhancements" for merging banks.

HIGHER LOAN RATES AND LOWER DEPOSIT RATES   As we also noted in Chapter 10, recent studies have provided at best very limited real-world support for the SCP model's prediction that greater loan and deposit market concentration leads to higher depository institution profits. Research by Allen Berger and Timothy Hannan, both on the Federal Reserve Board staff, indicates that the SCP model's prediction about the effects of concentration on interest rates and fees may be more relevant. The reduced rivalry among institutions caused by increased concentration in loan and deposit markets apparently does give those institutions greater market power. Outcomes of market power are higher loan rates, higher fees for banking services, and lower deposit rates.

HELPING OUT RIVALS?   Interestingly, Katerina Simons and Joanna Stavins of the Federal Reserve Bank of Boston have provided evidence that the banks that experience the greatest revenue enhancements from mergers are the rivals of the merging banks. These researchers hypothesize that the greater market concentration resulting from mergers typically has two immediate effects. The first is increased market power for the fewer rivals in the affected market. The second effect, however, typically is a reduction in service quality on the part of the merged institutions. Quality of customer service often declines as managers struggle to develop new operational procedures that may conflict with those previously used at one or both of the merged institutions. Managers of merged banks typically try to reap cost-efficiency gains by firing or laying off employees, but this hurts employee morale. Another common managerial aim is to adopt a common "corporate culture," even though the cultures of the merged institutions may differ dramatically. In the midst of this short-term internal turmoil, Simons and Stavins conclude, service quality of the merged institutions suffers, making it difficult for the institution created by the merger to cut deposit rates. In contrast, quality of service at rival institutions is unaffected by the merger, so these rivals can take full advantage of reduced competition to pay lower rates to their deposit customers.

Defining Depository Institution Markets

As discussed above, the top 50 and top 100 depository institutions have become larger, and interstate banking has increased the trend toward more consolidation of banking resources. In light of the evidence we have reviewed, does this mean that because of increased interstate banking, consumers must pay more for loans and services while receiving less for their deposits?

IDENTIFYING "LOCAL MARKETS"   To answer this question, the first thing to recognize is that what matters to an individual consumer—such as you—is not whether the top 50 or top 100 banks are getting larger, or even smaller. The SCP model indicates that a key factor affecting the market interest rate that you might have to pay on an auto loan in your location, or perhaps the market interest rate that you might receive on a deposit account at a depository institution in your area, is the extent of loan and deposit market concentration in your *local market*. Indeed, when depository institution regulators and the antitrust authorities review plans for mergers among institutions, they consider the effects that such mergers might have on local rivalry.

Unfortunately, there is no good way to define geographic loan and deposit markets for purposes of measuring the extent of market rivalry. Depository institution regulators define such markets on a case-by-case basis when institutions apply for permission to merge. Most economists—including those who assist regulators in evaluating the likely effects of mergers—approximate local banking markets in towns and cities using *metropolitan statistical areas* as defined by the government for census purposes. For rural areas economists typically assume that *nonmetropolitan counties* are the relevant geographic markets.

LOCAL CONCENTRATION—LITTLE CHANGED   Interestingly, although large banks have generally become bigger on a national basis, at these local levels the concentration of banking resources has varied extremely little during the past thirty years. For instance, in 1976 the three largest banking organizations in a typical U.S. metropolitan statistical area issued a little over 68 percent of deposits, compared with just under 67 percent of deposits today. In nonmetropolitan counties, the extent of concentration was—and is—much higher: in 1976, the three largest depository institutions in a typical nonmetropolitan county issued about 90 percent of the deposits; at present, this figure hovers around 89 percent.

It is not apparent from these figures that changes in interstate—or intrastate—competition have had much influence on the average extent of depository institution rivalry in local banking markets. Most economists interpret this evidence as an indication that interstate banking has likely had little effect on consumer interest rates and fees. For whatever reason, this and other changes in banking arrangements during past years do not seem to have much effect on local market conditions. It may be that there is some "natural" level of rivalry that loan and deposit markets can support at local levels.

Universal Banking and the Separation of Depository Institutions from Other Businesses

Universal banking: A banking environment in which banks face few, if any, restrictions on their powers to offer a full range of financial services and to own shares of stock in corporations.

In recent years, U.S. regulators and owners of U.S. depository institutions have been contemplating the pros and cons of **universal banking,** under which depository institutions would face few, if any, limits on their power to offer wide ranges of financial services and to own corporate stock. As discussed in Chapter 11, the Glass-Steagall Act prohibited all forms of U.S. universal banking from 1933 until 1999, when the Gramm-Leach-Bliley Act broadened the allowable activities of U.S. banks. In Europe, in contrast, universal banking has long been the norm.

Should U.S. depository institutions be permitted to expand into ever-wider ranges of financial services? Should they even be able to purchase shares of ownership in nonfinancial businesses? Should nonfinancial firms, such as automakers or computer software companies, be permitted to own depository institutions? Increasingly, these questions are likely to surface in regulatory discussions of the appropriate scale and scope of the operations of depository institutions.

Cost-Based Justifications for Universal Banking

Economies of scope: The ability to produce a mix of products at a lower cost than the overall cost of producing each product separately.

Some who favor universal banking suggest that the business of banking may involve **economies of scope.** This term refers to the capability of a single firm to produce several types of financial services at a lower cost than separate firms could otherwise provide those same services.

Over the years, economists have conducted numerous studies aimed at determining whether depository institutions experience economies of scope, but they have failed to reach unambiguous conclusions. Some evidence suggests that depository institutions may be able to produce certain mixes of financial services at lower costs than if the same sets of services were provided by separate firms. For instance, some studies indicate that commercial banks are particularly efficient at extending loans. As a consequence, they may be able to extend this efficiency to sales of insurance and mutual funds. (In a few European nations, government labor-market regulations may have contributed to bank efforts to break into the insurance business; see the *Global Focus: Keeping Bank Employees Occupied in Southern Europe.*)

Risk-Based Arguments for and against Universal Banking

Insider information: Information that is not available to the public.

Those who favor universal banking argue that holding shares of ownership in commercial firms gives depository institutions **insider information,** or knowledge about the internal operations of firms normally available to inside directors and officers but not widely available to the general public. Having such knowledge could make it easier for depository institutions to evaluate and monitor these firms' creditworthiness, thereby reducing bank costs. Depository institutions also might be less likely to force companies having difficulties into bankruptcy because banks with insider information would be able to distinguish near-term liquidity shortfalls from longer-term solvency threats. Some favoring universal banking contend that it could limit market expectations of bankruptcies, thereby lowering firms' borrowing costs.

A fundamental justification for the Glass-Steagall Act's original prohibition of universal banking was that shares of stock typically are riskier financial instruments than government securities and municipal bonds. The objective of the Glass-Steagall Act was to establish a "firewall" between commercial and investment banking, thereby insulating commercial banks from risks generated by stock market volatility. Nevertheless, a recent argument for universal banking is that holding individually risky shares of stock may, in fact, *help* a depository institution to *reduce* its overall risk of loss. For example, during a period when stock returns rise

GLOBAL
Focus

Keeping Bank Employees Occupied in Southern Europe

Since the early 1990s, depository institutions in Italy, Portugal, and Spain have faced increased competition from abroad, which has reduced the profits they earn from providing traditional banking services. During the same period, however, the governments of these nations have adopted labor-market rules making it very difficult to shed workers. Southern European depository institutions, therefore, found themselves with more employees than they needed to serve dwindling numbers of borrowers and depositors. Several of these banks discovered a profitable solution to their overstaffing problem: the insurance business. Training bank employees to sell insurance policies could be done at relatively little expense, and banks found that customers were very open to buying insurance from local bank branches. Today, southern European banks function as insurance distribution centers and account for more than half of insurance sales in Italy, Portugal, and Spain.

FOR CRITICAL ANALYSIS: What characteristics of depository institutions do you think might enable them to succeed in marketing nontraditional products such as insurance?

but many bond yields or returns on loans are falling, holding shares of stock could reduce the riskiness of a depository insitution's overall asset portfolio.

Arguments against Eliminating the Barriers between Banking and Other Businesses

A traditional concern about universal banking has been that it might promote conflicts of interest. The conflicts could take different forms depending on whether a bank owns shares in another company or is owned by another company. For example, a bank that purchases a stake in a new cybertrading firm would prefer for that firm's share price to remain high. Accordingly, the bank might try to induce its customers to purchase the company's shares, or it might buy shares in the company to add to portfolios that it manages on behalf of clients, even though owning the shares might not be in the customers' best interests. The bank might even cut back on its lending to a rival Internet company.

Allowing businesses to own depository institutions presents other potential problems. The most obvious is that a business might pressure the banks that it owns to extend it credit. If the business needs additional credit because it is taking on too many risks, extending the credit would increase the possibility that the depository institutions would become insolvent. Depositors and other creditors of the depository institutions then would suffer. So would taxpayers, given the existence of federal deposit insurance.

A related problem is that the ownership of depository institutions by commercial firms could further expose depository institutions to the ill effects of economic downturns. Consider, for instance, what could happen if an auto manufacturer owned a large bank and a sharp recession hit. Such a recession usually causes immediate reductions in sales of new cars. Not uncommonly, the share prices of automakers plummet, and the ratings of their debt issues are downgraded. If an automaker also owned a bank, then a particularly sharp recession could cause the public to lose confidence in that bank when the fortunes of its owner soured. The result could be a run on that bank. At a minimum, it would experience liquidity problems.

Finally, the lines of authority of banking regulators and the Federal Reserve System potentially would be broadened if commercial firms could own banks. If a company owned a bank,

MONEYXTRA!
Another Perspective

To learn more about the issues associated with mergers between banks and nonfinancial firms, go to the Chapter 12 reading, entitled "The Separation of Banking and Commerce," by John Krainer of the Federal Reserve Bank of San Francisco. **http:// moneyxtra.swcollege.com** then it would be a bank holding company and would be subject to Federal Reserve oversight. As a result, the Federal Reserve might have to examine all the books of a company such as General Motors or Microsoft.

So far, these concerns have led U.S. regulators to adopt a go-slow approach to universal banking. When Congress passed the Gramm-Leach-Bliley Act in 1999, it decided in favor of moving toward more nearly universal banking. It explicitly ruled out permitting nonfinancial firms to own banks, however. (Nevertheless, the legislation may allow banks to own companies specializing in sales of residential housing and office buildings; see the *Policy Focus: A Bank-Realtor Fight Heats Up.*)

2. What are the pros and cons of depository institution mergers and universal banking? Mergers between or among depository institutions that compete within the same local market make the market more concentrated, which can lead to higher loan rates and fees and lower deposit rates for depository institution customers in that market. Mergers that take place across markets, however, such as mergers involving depository institutions in different geographic regions, could actually generate greater rivalry in some banking markets. Under universal banking, mergers between depository institutions and a wide variety of companies could also be contemplated. Key rationales favoring universal banking include potential diversification gains and lower monitoring costs. These advantages of universal banking are at least partly counterbalanced by the higher volatility of equity share values relative to values of traditional banks and the potential for conflicts of interest. Full-fledged universal banking also would entail ownership of depository institutions by commercial firms, leading to additional potential for conflicts of interest, greater exposure of depository institutions to the ill effects of economic downturns, and regulatory complications.

POLICY

Focus

A Bank-Realtor Fight Heats Up

To sell real estate, one must typically obtain a realtor's license granted by a state or municipality. If some commercial banks have their way, however, they someday will be able to compete with realtors in buying, selling, and brokering real estate deals without obtaining such licenses. In 2000, both the Federal Reserve and the U.S. Treasury Department suggested that the Gramm-Leach-Bliley Act allows financial services companies to own both banks and realtors. Three years later, the Office of the Comptroller of the Currency began shielding federally chartered banks from various state laws, which in principle could include state realtor-licensing requirements.

Although no federal regulator has yet granted any institution the power to act as a realtor or to own any real estate businesses, the National Association of Realtors has begun a quiet war to keep depository institutions out of its markets. Throughout the 2000s, the realtor group has successfully lobbied Congress not to fund further study of the Federal Reserve–Treasury banking-realtor proposal. Recently, the group has also indicated a willingness to bring suits in both state and federal courts to fight efforts by banks to infringe on its turf. So far, these actions have stymied bank designs on real estate markets. Nevertheless, most banking analysts think it is only a matter of time before the separation between financial services and real estate brokering begins to erode.

FOR CRITICAL ANALYSIS: Why might banks feel that they might gain from potential economies of scope in offering realtor services and mortgage loans as a combined product?

Regulating Off-Balance-Sheet Banking

One of the most important modern developments at depository institutions has been their growing reliance on **off-balance-sheet banking,** which involves activities that generate income outside the institutions' balance sheets. The growth in these activities has prompted regulators to reconsider many long-standing approaches to examining and supervising depository institutions.

Securitization and Loan Commitments

Two key off-balance-sheet activities of depository institutions are *securitization* and *loan commitments.* **Securitization** is the pooling of loans into groups that share similar characteristics and risks for sale as asset-backed securities. A **loan commitment** is a depository institution's promise to make a loan up to some specified limit under a contracted interest rate and within a given interval.

Neither of these activities appears on a depository institution's balance sheet. When an institution securitizes a loan, by definition it has sold the loan and removed it from its asset portfolio. Likewise, a loan commitment is not a loan until the depository institution must honor the commitment. Nevertheless, these off-balance-sheet activities yield income to depository institutions. They can also complicate the tasks that regulators face. In the case of securitization, there can also be some benefits for regulators.

SECURITIZATION AND "MARKING TO MARKET"   Securitization has made it feasible for depository institutions to earn fee income for originating, servicing, and insuring loans while selling them to others. Depository institutions issue two basic kinds of asset-backed securities. One type, illustrated in Figure 12-1 on the next page, is a *pass-through security.* When a depository institution issues this type of asset-backed security, it passes interest and principal payments that it receives from borrowers through to holders of securities on a proportionate basis. For example, holders of a specific asset-backed security collateralized by a depository institution's holdings of credit-card debts might receive 80 percent of the interest and principal payments paid by credit-card customers to the depository institution. To compensate the depository institution for the service it provides in monitoring the underlying pool of loans and making payments to the holders of the pass-through securities, these holders pay fees to the depository institution.

Another type of asset-backed security is called a *pay-through security.* Under this type of securitization arrangement, the interest and principal payments from an underlying pool of loans are held by the depository institution, which reallocates them into two or more separate sets of securities that have different payment and maturity structures.

A *collateralized mortgage obligation (CMO)* is a type of pay-through security. Under a CMO, principal and interest payments from the underlying pool of loans at the depository institution go first to holders of the CMOs with the earliest dates of maturity. Once those payments are "paid through," holders of later maturing CMOs receive their payments from the depository institution, and so on. Holders of the CMOs pay fees to the depository institution for handling the paperwork associated with this arrangement.

Securitization benefits depository institutions by shifting the default risks and interest rate risks of some loans to others. It also generates stable sources of fee income for the institutions. For this reason, depository institution regulators generally have raised few concerns about securitization.

Off-balance-sheet banking: Bank activities that earn income without expanding the assets and liabilities that the banks report on their balance sheets.

Securitization: The process of pooling loans with similar risk characteristics and selling the loan pool in the form of a tradable financial instrument.

Loan commitment: A lending arrangement in which a depository institution promises to extend credit up to some predetermined limit at a contracted interest rate and within a given period of time.

**FIGURE 12-1
Asset Securitization via a
"Pass-Through" Arrangement.**

A depository institution receives interest and principal payments from borrowers of loans that it originates. It then issues securities backed by these loans through a trust department and an underwriter, and investors purchase the securities. The interest and principal payments from the loans are forwarded to a trustee, who passes through to the securities investors a portion of those payments as an interest payment on the asset-backed securities.

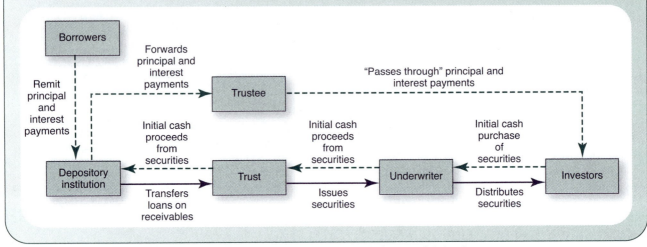

SOURCE: Thomas Boemio and Gerald Edwards, Jr., "Asset Securitization: A Supervisory Perspective," *Federal Reserve Bulletin* (1989).

Market value accounting: An accounting procedure in which a depository institution (or its regulator) values its assets in terms of the approximate market prices at which those assets would sell at present in secondary markets.

Historical value accounting: A traditional accounting procedure in which a depository institution's assets are always valued at their original values.

In fact, a key advantage of securitization for regulators is that it gives them up-to-date information on market values of many types of bank loans. Regulators can determine market prices of loans that depository institutions have recently sold in secondary markets. They can then use these prices as indications of the market values of similar loans that depository institutions do *not* choose to sell in secondary markets. This practice of valuing a depository institution's assets at current market values is known as "marking loans to market," or **market value accounting.** This approach to measuring the values of depository institutions' assets contrasts with traditional **historical value accounting,** in which an institution records the initial value of a loan or security and then carries this value in its books until the loan is repaid or the security is redeemed.

Regulators prefer market value accounting because it provides a more accurate assessment of the solvency of a depository institution. In recent years a number of proposals have surfaced that would authorize the FDIC and other regulators to require depository institutions to switch to market value accounting or at least to report market values of assets alongside historical values on a periodic basis. Most of these proposals have not advanced in the face of the opposition of depository institutions, which argue that market value accounting would be prohibitively expensive. The institutions also typically argue that market values fluctuate so much that they can provide misleading information about the long-term values of assets. Nevertheless, regulators have continued to use prices of securitized assets as important information for assessing the solvency of the institutions that they examine and supervise.

LOAN COMMITMENTS AND RISK   As Figure 12-2 shows, commitment lending grew significantly in the 1980s before leveling off in the 1990s and 2000s. During the 1970s, loans made under commitment accounted for only about 20 percent of total bank loans. Today, more than two-thirds of loans that banks extend are commitment loans.

With a typical loan commitment, a bank and a prospective borrower agree to terms, which specify a limit on how much credit the borrower can get from the bank (the borrower's "line of credit"), what the loan interest rate will be or how it will be determined, and the fee that the borrower must pay for any unused portion of the line of credit. This arrangement yields benefits for both the bank and the borrower. The borrower has a guarantee of credit at a given interest rate whenever it is needed within the specified period. The bank receives interest income on the portion of the credit line that is drawn upon by the borrower and noninterest fee income on the unused portion.

Under a *fixed-rate loan commitment,* the interest rate on any credit that a depository institution extends is set at a predetermined level. In contrast, a *floating-rate loan commitment* ties the loan rate to another market interest rate, such as the prime loan rate or the London Interbank Offer Rate discussed in Chapter 4. Most loan commitments of either type are **revolving credit commitments.** These allow borrowers to borrow and repay as desired, very much like revolving credit agreements for charge cards. Other loan commitments are **confirmed credit lines,** which normally are agreements for a bank to provide a fixed amount of credit upon demand within some short-term interval.

The growth of loan commitments has raised two types of concerns for bank regulators. One is that some banks might overextend themselves by making too many commitments, thereby creating liquidity problems. A related concern is that a few banks might extend commitment loans to overly risky borrowers, thereby placing themselves at risk. So far commitment lending does not appear to have caused many difficulties of this type. Nevertheless, the

Revolving credit commitments: Loan commitments that permit borrowers to borrow and repay as often as they wish within an interval in which the commitment is binding on a depository institution.

Confirmed credit lines: Depository institution commitments to provide an individual or a business with a fixed amount of credit upon demand within some short-term interval.

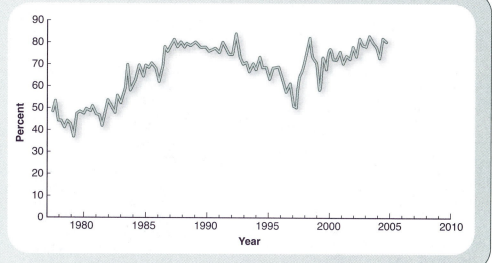

FIGURE 12-2
Growth in the Share of Commitment Lending.

This chart shows the portion of total commercial and industrial loans with maturities of less than a year that commercial banks made under commitment. The loan-commitment share of bank lending increased considerably during the 1980s before leveling off in recent years.

SOURCES: John Duca and David VanHoose, "Loan Commitments and Optimal Monetary Policy," *Journal of Money, Credit, and Banking* 22 (May 1990): 178–194; and Board of Governors of the Federal Reserve System, *Federal Reserve Bulletin* and *Statistical Supplement,* various issues.

inclusion of loan commitments in the computation of risk-adjusted assets in capital ratio calculations reflects regulators' concerns about such risks.

Derivatives

Recall from Chapter 6 that derivatives are financial instruments whose returns are derived from the yields on other securities. Examples of derivatives include forward, futures, option, and swap contracts. As discussed in Chapter 10, depository institutions have made greater use of derivative instruments in recent years. A few have tried to establish derivatives trading and management as a major line of business.

Because the values of derivative instruments stem from the values of other assets, measuring depository institutions' participation in the markets for derivatives is a difficult proposition. One possible measure, called the *notional value* of derivatives, is the total amount of principal upon which interest payments stemming from derivatives are based. The notional value of commercial bank derivatives holdings grew from $1.4 trillion to $8.6 trillion between 1986 and 1992. By 2006 this figure had risen to more than $75 trillion.

Another measure of bank involvement with derivatives—the *replacement cost exposure*—is the cost that a party to a derivatives contract would face at current market prices if the counterparty to the contract were to default before settlement of the contract. In 1992, the total derivatives replacement cost credit exposure of commercial banks amounted to about 4 percent of their assets. By 2006 this figure had risen to 17 percent. Clearly, by either measure banks are much more heavily involved in derivatives operations. (In recent years, banks and Wall Street brokers have sought to spread derivatives risks more broadly by securitizing credit derivatives; see the *Management Focus: Securitizing Credit Derivatives.*)

REGULATING DERIVATIVES TRADING As we discussed in Chapter 6, depository institutions expose themselves to three basic types of risks when they hold and trade derivatives:

MANAGEMENT

Focus

Securitizing Credit Derivatives

As you learned in Chapter 10, credit derivatives are financial instruments with returns linked to the underlying credit risks of bank loans. Today, the use of credit derivatives allows banks to transfer some of their loan risks to outside investors. In an effort to broaden the group of investors willing to purchase credit derivatives, a bank, J.P. Morgan Chase, and a securities firm,

Morgan Stanley, recently launched an effort aimed at essentially securitizing these derivatives. These institutions created the "TRAC-X index," a credit derivatives index that is now listed as a Dow Jones index. The banks have introduced separate TRAC-X indexes in U.S., European, and emerging market corporate debt. Institutional investors such as mutual funds and pension funds can, if they wish, trade securities linked to these indexes just as they have traditionally traded securities linked to the Standard & Poor's 500 index.

FOR CRITICAL ANALYSIS: Why do some financial analysts worry that investors who purchase credit-derivatives-backed securities might expose themselves to risks arising from adverse-selection or moral-hazard problems? (Hint: Why might banks that are most willing to make loans to the least creditworthy borrowers or banks that discover the fortunes of existing borrowers have soured have the greatest incentive to hedge their loan risks using credit derivatives?)

1. **Derivative credit risks.** The risks generated by the potential default of a contract coun-terparty or by the possibility of an unanticipated change in credit exposure caused by variations in market prices of underlying instruments on which derivative returns depend.

2. **Derivative market risks.** The risks of potential losses resulting from market liquidity reductions, payment-system breakdowns or unusual price changes at the time of settle-ment, or cross-market spillover effects.

3. **Derivative operating risks.** The risks owing to the possibility of misguided supervision and oversight of derivatives holdings and trading by depository institution managers.

Certainly, depository institutions themselves have strong incentives to keep tight rein on these risks. Nevertheless, the existence of federal deposit insurance weakens managers' and owners' incentives to contain derivatives risks. For this reason, depository institution regulators evalu-ate derivatives risks as part of their supervisory efforts.

Regulators have viewed the growth of derivatives trading by depository institutions as a positive development in some respects but as a real area of concern in other respects. On the one hand, derivatives permit depository institutions to hedge against a variety of interest rate and currency risks. In this regard, regulators have even promoted the use of derivatives by depository institutions.

On the other hand, a number of depository institutions have failed to maintain adequate internal controls over their derivatives operations and to develop appropriate techniques for valuing derivatives contracts. This, in turn, has complicated the task of examining and super-vising depository institutions. Regulators now must be well versed in valuation methods for derivatives, and they must double-check the adequacy of the management methods that the institutions adopt for their derivatives operations. Derivatives are fairly new to most bank examiners just as they are relatively new to bankers, and so regulators themselves have had a lot to learn.

---

3. How has off-balance-sheet banking complicated the task of regulating depository institutions? Although securitization generally reduces depository institutions' exposure to risks and helps regulators evaluate market values of loans, greater commitment lending has the potential to expose institutions to more liquidity and solvency risks. Derivatives trading has its own unique risks, of which perhaps the most important is the risk of inadequate internal management controls.

Consumer Protection Regulations

Throughout history many leading U.S. citizens have mistrusted banks. Thomas Jefferson said that they were more dangerous than standing armies. When Andrew Jackson lost con-siderable personal wealth to banks from foreclosed loans after suffering big losses on land speculation, he made bank-bashing a favorite political pastime. More recently, members of Congress have heeded the calls of many of their constituents by passing legislation intended to protect consumers from possible misbehavior by managers of banks and other depository financial institutions.

There are bad people in all walks of life just as there is a bad apple in every barrel. Certainly, there have been unscrupulous bank managers in the past, and some probably are sitting behind desks around the country as you read these words. Should the government attempt to protect us from such individuals? Can it?

The first of these questions calls for an opinion. Whether or not the government *should* try to protect us from depository institutions, the fact is that political leaders presumably have acted upon the desires of many citizens by attempting to do so. The question of whether the government *can* protect citizens at least has the potential to be answered based on factual evidence. Certainly, if the government expends sufficient resources enforcing efforts to stop unsavory bankers from gouging consumers, such gouging will ultimately decline.

Basic Consumer Protection Regulations

Congress has enacted several consumer protection laws applying to depository institutions, and various governmental agencies seek to enforce them. Before we discuss their provisions, however, let's contemplate why such laws exist.

THE RATIONALE FOR PROTECTING CONSUMERS

Why can't people just protect themselves? After all, rarely has a lender forced a borrower to sign a loan contract. One key rationale for consumer protection laws and regulations relies on the problem of asymmetric information. Just as a lender has trouble identifying a creditworthy borrower, a prospective borrower can struggle to find a dependable and honest lender. Indeed, a borrower faces both adverse-selection and moral-hazard problems. An adverse-selection problem arises because unscrupulous lenders have the greatest incentive to disguise their credit terms to make them look more attractive than the honest terms quoted by more trustworthy lenders. A moral-hazard problem arises because after a lender grants credit, there is always a chance that the lender may attempt to reinterpret the loan contract in ways that are more favorable to the lender than the interpretation offered before the borrower entered into the contract.

THE SCOPE OF CONSUMER PROTECTION VIA REGULATION

The *Consumer Credit Protection Act (CCPA) of 1968* is the foundation for much of the government's effort to protect consumers from costs that they might otherwise incur because of these problems of asymmetric information. This legislation requires that institutions provide every applicant for consumer credit with the specific dollar amount of finance charges and with annual percentage interest rates computed on the unpaid amount of the total quantity of a loan. Under the law, all institutions must make this information available so that consumers can make direct comparisons across institutions as they shop for credit. This provision of the CCPA attempts to reduce the extent of the adverse-selection problem that consumers face with respect to information. Other provisions bind lenders to the terms that they give consumers, thereby addressing the moral-hazard problem.

A difficulty with the CCPA was that it did not anticipate complications that arose when adjustable-rate mortgages became popular in the 1970s. A provision of the Depository Institutions Deregulation and Monetary Control Act of 1980 amended the CCPA to account for variable-rate loans. It requires potential lenders to construct hypothetical fixed- and variable-rate examples that enable prospective borrowers to compare the amounts that they might pay depending upon which type of loan they choose.

The CCPA applies to all financial institutions that extend credit. It also covers all loan applicants irrespective of their race, ethnicity, gender, or age. In recent years, however, these applicant characteristics have been the subject of much interest in the consumer protection area.

Banking Regulation and Race, Ethnicity, Gender, and Age

A major policy issue in recent years has been the extent to which depository institutions may treat customers differently based on their race, gender, ethnicity, or age. Congress has enacted laws addressing this issue. Furthermore, Congress has charged depository institution regulators with monitoring and enforcing these laws.

REDLINING One way that depository institutions allegedly have discriminated against specific groups is by refusing to provide loans to individuals or businesses located in specific geographic areas. Such a practice is called **redlining** because depository institution managers supposedly used red ink to outline certain areas on maps that were ineligible for loans. Managers allegedly would instruct lending officers to deny loans to anyone located in such areas or to applicants for mortgage or real estate loans intended to purchase properties there.

Note that redlining is not necessarily a form of racial, ethnic, or gender discrimination, although it might effectively be used as a means of such discrimination if redlined areas were predominantly occupied, say, by African American or Hispanic households or by female-owned businesses. Nevertheless, the basic allegation is that redlining, if it occurs, discriminates against individuals simply because of where they live or operate their businesses. In the case of mortgage redlining, the depository institutions that redline would effectively discriminate against the owners of properties within redlined regions. Those outside the area who wished to buy the properties would also feel victimized by discrimination because they would experience difficulties obtaining credit to purchase these properties.

Redlining: A practice under which some depository institution managers allegedly have refused to lend to individuals or businesses located in particular geographic areas.

ANTIDISCRIMINATION LAWS Depository institutions must meet requirements established by three key antidiscrimination laws. The first of these is the *Equal Credit Opportunity Act (ECOA) of 1975*. This legislation broadened some of the CCPA's provisions by outlawing retaliation by a lender against a borrower who insists upon rights granted by the CCPA, by applying CCPA provisions to many business and commercial transactions, and by extending consumer lending protections in a variety of ways. But the ECOA's novel feature was its prohibition of lending discrimination on the basis of an applicant's race, color, religion, national origin, gender, age, or marital status.

Because of concerns about widespread allegations of mortgage redlining by some depository institutions, Congress also passed the *Home Mortgage Disclosure Act (HMDA)* in 1975. This legislation requires depository institutions to report information about mortgage loan applications and lending decisions. It also requires depository institution regulators to collect and analyze this information.

Then, in 1977, Congress passed the now-controversial *Community Reinvestment Act (CRA)*, which added considerably to the reporting requirements that the HMDA had imposed on depository institutions. The basic paperwork required from each depository institution under the CRA includes the following:

1. A statement listing the types of loans that the institution is willing to make.

2. Acceptable evidence that the institution's board of directors reviews this statement at least once each year.

3. A map showing the boundaries of the communities in which the institution lends.

4. A visible notice to customers advising them of the CRA.

5. A CRA file open for review by any member of the public who would like to read it.

On the Web
How do banks go about complying with the Home Mortgage Disclosure Act? To find out, take a look at the Federal Financial Institutions Examination Council's "Guide to HMDA Reporting" at **http://www.ffiec.gov/hmda/pdf/guide.pdf**.

6. Implementation of a "CRA planning process" supported by a full analysis of the geographic distributions of the institution's major lines of business.

7. Collection of complete data concerning lending applications, acceptances, and denials.

8. Analysis of how these data relate to the characteristics of the populations in the areas where the institution lends.

Under the CRA, depository institution regulators are to aim to achieve twelve separate objectives relating to redlining and other forms of lending discrimination. For instance, regulators are supposed to use the data that institutions report to evaluate each institution's record of lending to various groups of the populations that it serves. Furthermore, the CRA requires that regulators examine institutions and provide them with ratings of their performances in meeting the credit needs of all groups. All major regulators have attempted to coordinate their CRA ratings schemes so that clearly defined sets of institutions receive roughly similar CRA examinations. (Depository institutions do not have to make loans or even provide any financial services to comply with certain CRA requirements; see the *Management Focus: To Meet CRA Requirements, Banks Sometimes Give Money Away.*)

Benefits and Drawbacks of Consumer Protection Regulations

Presumably, the consumer protection laws that Congress has put in place would not exist if many citizens did not believe that they were beneficial. Nevertheless, any law can produce unexpected complications. Therefore, it is not surprising that consumer protection laws that apply to depository institutions have both benefits and costs for society.

BENEFITS OF CONSUMER PROTECTION REGULATIONS   The most obvious benefits of consumer protection regulations are that they reduce the extent of potential adverse-selection and moral-hazard problems faced by depository institution customers. By requiring institutions to make comparable quotes of loan terms, these laws confound the ability of unsavory managers to mislead loan applicants. The laws also make it more difficult for depository institutions to alter their interpretations of loan terms after customers are bound to agreements.

MANAGEMENT

Focus

To Meet CRA Requirements, Banks Sometimes Give Money Away

Among other things, the CRA requires a depository institution to prove that it has provided "community service." Pittsburgh's PNC Financial Services Group, Inc., recently satisfied this requirement by spending more than $40 million on a program aimed at preparing preschoolers for kindergarten. The bank allocated part of these funds to compensate 4,000 of its employees for about 100,000 hours of time that they spent as volunteers tutoring children. PNC Financial directed the rest of the funds as grants to early childhood development organi-zations based in states where it has branches. The bank recently announced plans to spend a total of at least $100 million on preschool programs over a ten-year period.

FOR CRITICAL ANALYSIS: Who ultimately pays the costs of bank-financed employee volunteerism that helps satisfy CRA requirements? (Hint: Who ultimately receives a bank's profits?)

Consumer protection laws also give customers of depository institutions legal recourse if they are treated unjustly by lenders. In addition, the laws follow in the tradition of many civil rights laws by attempting to assure equal treatment of all loan applicants irrespective of their race, gender, ethnicity, age, or other characteristics.

COSTS OF CONSUMER PROTECTION LAWS Several costs are associated with consumer protection regulations in banking. The most glaring are the explicit costs associated with meeting the reporting requirements of the various laws that Congress has passed. Some of this expense undoubtedly leads to higher loan interest rates and higher fees for consumers.

Enforcing consumer protection laws such as the CRA is also a costly undertaking. Considerable regulatory resources, most of which are taxpayer financed, go into monitoring, analyzing, and investigating possible instances of anticonsumer or discriminatory behavior by depository institutions. Depository institutions also face considerable costs in complying with the provisions of the CRA. Federal banking regulators have calculated that depository institutions together expend 1.25 million hours a year on compliance, which translates into an estimated dollar cost exceeding $35 million a year. Individual institutions with more than $250 million of assets typically spend 500 to 635 hours a year complying with the CRA, and smaller institutions devote 50 to 200 hours a year.

Some critics argue that banking regulators overenforce the CRA. A recent study of the more than 16,000 CRA examinations of small banks and savings institutions during the entire 1990s found that only three institutions failed to comply. This led Congress to push for a reduction in the number of CRA compliance reviews for smaller depository institutions. (Recently, regulatory coordination of CRA examinations for small depository institutions broke down; see *What Happens When One Regulator Unilaterally Decides to Simplify CRA Examinations?*)

What Happens When... **One Regulator Unilaterally Decides to Simplify CRA Examinations?**

For years, regulators have conducted different CRA examinations for "large" banks than for "small" banks. Banks classified as "large" experience very thorough examinations that require them to incur significant resource costs for making advance preparations, addressing examiners' questions, and then following up with postexam management changes. In contrast, small banks face a much more streamlined—and, hence, less costly—CRA examination.

Until recently, regulators of commercial banks, savings banks, and savings and loan associations used the same definition of a small bank. The Federal Reserve, FDIC, Office of the Comptroller of the Currency (OCC), and Office of Thrift Supervision (OTS) agreed that a bank with fewer than $250 million in assets was "small." All banks with more than $250 million in assets were "large." In late 2004, however, the OTS broke ranks with the other bank regulators. It decided that a complete CRA examination imposed too many costly burdens on savings banks and savings and loan associations with less

than $1 billion in assets. The OTS unilaterally defined a new category of "medium-sized institutions" with between $250 million and $1 billion in assets and promised them a CRA examination nearly as streamlined as the exam faced by small banks. Nearly 90 percent of all savings banks and savings and loan associations qualify for the more streamlined CRA supervision. Initially, the other bank regulators said that they would not change their definitions of bank size. Then some medium-sized commercial banks suggested that they might switch to savings bank charters to qualify for less costly CRA examinations. Soon, the other regulators began publicly announcing plans to propose their own "medium-sized institutions" category.

FOR CRITICAL ANALYSIS: Why might a single depository institutions regulator have an easier time sticking with tough regulations than a group of regulators such as the Fed, FDIC, OCC, and OTS?

4. What are the benefits and costs of financial consumer protection laws? Consumer protection laws benefit depository institution customers by reducing the extent to which they face adverse-selection and moral-hazard problems when they apply for and agree to loans. The laws also help ensure that depository institutions treat individuals equally irrespective of their gender, ethnicity, race, age, or other characteristics. These laws can, however, be costly to administer and enforce. They can also generate large paperwork expenses for regulated institutions.

Using Financial Markets to Guide Bank Regulation

Depository institution supervision is a costly activity for society. Considerable social resources are required to employ and transport armies of bank examiners to conduct frequent on-site inspections of income statements and balance sheets. In recent years, regulators themselves have been exploring alternatives to direct examination and supervision.

Market-Based Regulation

Market-based regulation: Regulation that uses observable measures of depository institution risk as guidelines for supervisory enforcement.

An alternative that has received considerable attention is **market-based regulation,** or regulation based in part on market measures of bank risk. One key measure that a number of financial economists have contemplated is the market value of bank debt instruments. As discussed in Chapter 9, *subordinated debt instruments* are an important liability of banks and are included by regulators in one measure of bank capital. These instruments are long-term bonds that banks issue to raise funds in the capital markets. The basic idea of market-based regulation is to use the market prices of depository institutions' subordinated debt as a fundamental indicator of the riskiness of the institutions' activities.

A fundamental assumption of this approach is that private market traders of depository institutions' debt securities have good information about depository institution risks. Another assumption is that the market for depository institution debt instruments is efficient so that the market prices of the securities fully reflect these risks. Thus, financial economists have sought to determine if the yields on depository institution debt securities closely track accounting measures of the issuers' risk characteristics commonly used by bank examiners. A number of studies in the 2000s have found considerable evidence that this was the case for large banks' debt securities, thereby lending credence to the idea of linking regulatory enforcement to movements in market yields on depository institution debt instruments. With this approach, governments could realize significant resource savings by having smaller regulatory staffs track market yields, instead of paying large numbers of examiners to do on-site examinations.

Do Regulators Have an Informational Advantage?

Market-based regulation has some obvious drawbacks. One is that not all depository institutions issue subordinated debt. This is particularly true of smaller depository institutions in the United States and other developed nations. In emerging economies where financial markets are less developed, the lack of bank access to debt markets makes the proposal for market-based regulation a tough sell. Indeed, following the Asian, Russian, and Argentine financial crises in the late 1990s and early 2000s, the International Monetary Fund, central bankers, and private bankers alike called for more U.S.-style, hands-on examination and supervision in many countries that previously had relied on private markets to discipline their banks. The argument was that financial markets in many emerging economies are too inefficient for market yields to fully reflect bank risks.

In addition, many of the debt securities issued by depository institutions are traded relatively infrequently, so even in developed financial systems, markets for these securities typically are relatively less liquid than many other financial markets. Those who promote market-based regulation recognize this point and typically include, as part of their proposals, the requirement that all depository institutions issue debt securities. This requirement would ensure that market participants and regulators alike could track every institution's securities and that the market would be sufficiently liquid that yields would adequately reflect the underlying riskiness of the institutions.

A third, and perhaps most fundamental, difficulty is that the direct examination of depository institutions' income statements and balance sheets may give regulators an informational advantage over private financial market traders. A recent study by Robert DeYoung of the Federal Reserve Bank of Chicago, William Lang of the Office of the Comptroller of the Currency, and Mark Flannery and Sorin Sorescu (the authors of an earlier study that provided some support for market-based regulation) found that government regulatory examinations of large national banks provided significant information about the banks' riskiness that debt yields failed to reflect for periods as long as several months—plenty of time for a bank's fortunes to collapse and induce failure.

Thus, the current research on using depository institution debt yields as guidelines for regulatory enforcement provides only limited support for the idea. Although yields of depository institution debt securities appear to reflect the riskiness of the institutions, they may do so only after relatively lengthy intervals. Of course, regulators themselves could reduce these intervals by immediately publicizing the results of examinations rather than keeping the information private. Nevertheless, large numbers of examiners would still be needed to conduct frequent examinations, thereby weakening a key argument favoring market-based regulation, which is the possibility of reducing or eliminating direct examinations.

> **5. How might depository institution regulators use financial markets to help guide their supervisory activities?** Proponents of market-based regulation, which would involve using yields on depository institution debt securities as measures of the riskiness of those institutions, contend that using such market-based risk measures would save on examination costs and would reduce the need for traditional supervision. This position receives some support from studies indicating that the risks revealed by government examinations of income statements and balance sheets are fully reflected in the yields on depository institution debt securities. Other evidence, however, suggests that depository institution regulators have an informational advantage because frequent examinations can reveal new risks before information about those risks becomes available to traders of debt securities.

Chapter Summary

1. Interstate Banking and Depository Institution Efficiency: Bank mergers became increasingly common in the 1980s and early 1990s, but economists typically found that relatively small cost savings resulted. The Interstate Banking and Branching Efficiency Act of 1994 removed nearly all barriers to interstate banking beginning in 1997. This promised the potential for achieving enhanced efficiencies through mergers, and recent evidence indicates that the cost savings from bank mergers have indeed been more significant.

2. The Pros and Cons of Depository Institution Mergers and Universal Banking:
Depository institution mergers within the same local market make the market more concentrated. Theory indicates that the resulting increase in market power can generate higher loan rates and fees and lower deposit rates for customers of depository institutions. Mergers that make depository institutions more efficient, however, could have the opposite effects. Mergers that allow depository institutions to engage in universal banking may yield diversification gains and lower monitoring costs. Nevertheless, these potential advantages are partly offset by the greater variability of equity returns relative to returns on traditional depository institution assets and possible conflicts of interest. Truly universal banking would also open up ownership of depository institutions to commercial firms. This could lead to additional potential for conflicts of interest, greater exposure of depository institutions to the ill effects of economic downturns, and involvement of bank regulators in the affairs of commercial firms.

3. Regulatory Complications Arising from Off-Balance-Sheet Banking:
Securitization simplifies the task of regulators by removing risky loans from depository institutions' balance sheets. In contrast, loan commitments expose institutions to greater liquidity risks and to potential default risks. In recent years, the rapid growth of derivatives trading by depository institutions has exposed them to new types of risks, and regulators have had to adjust their examination and supervision procedures in light of these risks.

4. The Benefits and Costs of Financial Consumer Protection Laws:
Such laws help reduce the extent of adverse-selection problems that consumers might otherwise face if confronted with loan interest rate calculations that are difficult to compare, and the laws decrease somewhat a moral-hazard problem arising from the possibility that a lender might attempt to reinterpret loan contract terms before the consumer has repaid the loan. These laws are costly for depository institutions to abide by because they require so much paperwork from the institutions. The laws are also costly to enforce.

5. Market-Based Regulation of Depository Institutions:
Some financial economists have proposed using yields on depository institution debt securities as risk indicators, thereby enabling governments to save on examination costs and reducing the need for traditional supervision. On the one hand, some evidence indicates that the risks uncovered by government examinations of depository institutions are fully reflected in the yields on depository institution debt securities. On the other hand, evidence also indicates that frequent government examinations may reveal new risks before information about those risks becomes available to traders of debt securities

Questions and Problems

(Answers to odd-numbered questions and problems may be found on the Web at **http://money.swcollege.com** under "Student Resources.")

1. Explain in your own words why the growth of umbrella corporations owning banks in more than one state during the 1980s may have made the effects of the 1994 law deregulating interstate branching more muted than they might otherwise have been.

2. Why was the number of depository institutions likely to fall after the legalization of interstate banking even if multistate umbrella corporations did not acquire any more institutions based in other states? Explain your reasoning.

3. Discuss circumstances in which widespread depository institution mergers could actually increase rivalry in banking markets.

4. What competitive advantages do you believe a large bank is likely to have over a small bank? What advantages do you think a small bank has over a large bank? Explain your reasoning.

5. In your view, who most likely gains from interstate banking? Support your answer.

6. On net, is universal banking a good or bad idea? Take a stand, and support your answer.

7. Many observers believe that as depository institution managers become more adept with derivatives operations, most risks associated with their involvement in derivatives will dissipate. Do you agree with this assessment?

8. Some depository institution managers have proposed that the federal government should pay the costs that the institutions currently bear in complying with consumer protection laws. Can you see any reasonable economic basis to support such a proposal? Explain.

9. In what ways could a bank loan officer who reviews Internet loan applications continue to practice discrimination against particular groups?

10. Discuss the pros and cons of market-based regulation of depository institutions.

Before the Test

Test your understanding of the material covered in this chapter by taking the Chapter 12 interactive quiz at **http://money.swcollege.com**.

Online Application

Internet URL: http://www.occ.treas.gov

Title: Community Reinvestment Act Regulations

Navigation: Start at the home page of the Office of the Comptroller of the Currency (OCC) given above. In the left margin, click on "CRA Information." Scroll down, and then click on "CRA Regulation."

Application: Follow the instructions, and answer the associated questions.

1. Click on "25.22 Lending Test." Make a list of the criteria that the OCC evaluates in testing whether a national bank has met the CRA's lending standards. In your view, what is the main objective of the OCC's lending test?

2. Go back to the previous page and click on "25.24 Service Test." Make a list of the criteria that the OCC evaluates in testing

whether a national bank has met the CRA's service standards. In your view, what is the main objective of the OCC's service test?

For Group Study and Analysis: Divide the class into groups. Have each group pretend that it is a board of directors for a new bank that is making a proposal for a national charter. To obtain a charter, the new bank must meet CRA standards established by the OCC. Have each group read "25.27 Strategic Plan" at the above Web site, and assign each group to draft its own "strategic plan" for the new bank it is proposing. Reconvene the class, and have each group report on the plan it has drafted. Compare the plans. Which CRA features did each group emphasize? Do the OCC's standards appear to push new banks toward developing similar strategic plans for CRA compliance?

Selected References and Further Reading

Avery, Robert, Raphael Bostic, and Glenn Canner. "The Profitability of CRA–Related Lending." Federal Reserve Bank of Cleveland *Economic Commentary,* November 2000.

Berger, Allen, and Timothy Hannan. "The Price-Concentration Relationship in Banking." *Review of Economics and Statistics* 71 (May 1989): 291–299.

Black, Harold, M. Cary Collins, and Ken Cyree. "Do Black-Owned Banks Discriminate against Black Borrowers?" *Journal of Financial Services Research* 11 (1997): 189–204.

Bliss, Robert. "Market Discipline and Subordinated Debt: A Review of Some Salient Issues." Federal Reserve Bank of Chicago *Economic Perspectives,* First Quarter 2001, pp. 24–45.

Bostic, Raphael, and Glenn Canner. "Do Minority-Owned Banks Treat Minorities Better? An Empirical Test of the Cultural Affinity Hypothesis." Board of Governors of the Federal Reserve System, December 1997.

Contz, Daniel, Diana Hancock, and Myron Kwast. "Market Discipline in Banking Reconsidered: The Roles of Funding Manager Decisions and Deposit Insurance Reform." Finance and Economics Discussion Series No. 2004-53, August 2004.

DeYoung, Robert, Mark Flannery, William Lang, and Sorin Sorescu. "The Information Content of Bank Exam Ratings and Subordinated Debt Prices." *Journal of Money, Credit, and Banking* 33 (November 2001): 900–925.

Ergungor, O. Emre. "Securitization." Federal Reserve Bank of Cleveland *Economic Commentary,* August 15, 2003.

Federal Reserve Bank of New York. "Beyond Pillar 3 in International Banking Regulation: Disclosure and Market Discipline of Financial Firms." *Economic Policy Review* 10 (September 2004).

Flannery, Mark, and Sorin Sorescu. "Evidence of Bank Market Discipline in Subordinated Debenture Yields: 1983–1991." *Journal of Finance* 51 (September 1996): 1347–1377.

Guzman, Mark. "Slow but Steady Progress toward Financial Deregulation." Federal Reserve Bank of Dallas *Southwest Economy,* January/February 2003, pp. 1–12.

Hirtle, Beverly. "What Market Risk Capital Reporting Tells Us about Bank Risk." Federal Reserve Bank of New York *Economic Policy Review,* September 2003, pp. 37–54.

Jagtiani, Julapa, James Kolari, Catherine Lemieux, and Hwan Shin. "Early Warning Models for Bank Supervision: Simpler Could Be Better." Federal Reserve Bank of Chicago *Economic Perspectives,* Third Quarter 2003, pp. 49–60.

Klein, Peter, and Kathrin Zoeller. "Universal Banking and Conflicts of Interests: Evidence from German Initial Public Offerings." University of Missouri CORI Working Paper No. 2003-06, September 2003.

Krainer, John. "The Separation of Banking and Commerce." Federal Reserve Bank of San Francisco *Economic Review,* 2000, pp. 15–25.

Kwan, Simon. "Banking Consolidation." Federal Reserve Bank of San Francisco *Economic Letter,* No. 2004-15, June 18, 2004.

Srinivasan, Aruna. "Are There Cost Savings from Bank Mergers?" Federal Reserve Bank of Atlanta *Economic Review* 77 (March/April 1992): 17–28.

Srinivasan, Aruna, and Larry Wall. "Cost Savings Associated with Bank Mergers." Federal Reserve Bank of Atlanta Working Paper No. 92-2, February 1992.

Walter, John. "Banking and Commerce: Tear Down This Wall?" Federal Reserve Bank of Richmond *Economic Quarterly* 89 (Spring 2003): 7–31.

MoneyXtra

Log on to the MoneyXtra Web site now (**http://moneyxtra.swcollege.com**) for additional learning resources such as practice quizzes, case studies, readings, and additional economic applications.

Unit IV
Central Banking, Monetary Policy, and the Federal Reserve System

Contents

Why Money and Banking Go Together—

Depository Institutions and Money

Fundamental Issues

1. How does a change in total depository institution reserves cause a multiple expansion of the deposit liabilities of these institutions?

2. What are Federal Reserve open market operations?

3. What is the money multiplier, and why is it important?

4. What factors influence the money multiplier?

5. What is the credit multiplier?

6. How will electronic money affect the money supply process?

Between 2001 and 2005, total consumer indebtedness more than doubled. During the same period, more and more individuals indicated in regular surveys that they felt overwhelmed by their debts. Most media analysts blamed consumers themselves for their predicaments. Nevertheless, under headlines such as "As Fed Expands Credit, Consumers Drown in Debt," some media analysts argued that others shared the blame: namely, officials of the Federal Reserve System. Critics complained that during the post-2001 period, the Federal Reserve's willingness to expand the quantity of money in circulation had also induced millions of U.S. households to convert assets into burdensome debts.

Economists are typically less willing to blame the Fed for consumer indebtedness—after all, lenders rarely (if ever) force someone to borrow funds. Nevertheless, economists do agree with the Fed's critics on one point: aggregate expansion of the money supply and increases in total credit do tend to go together.

How does the Federal Reserve generate an increase in the quantity of money in circulation? Why is an increase in the quantity of money usually associated with an expansion of total credit? In this chapter, you will learn the answers to these fundamental questions.

Reserve Requirements and Deposit Expansion

Depository institutions are "special" financial institutions in one key respect: they issue transactions deposits—demand deposits and negotiable-order-of-withdrawal (NOW) accounts. These deposits, as you learned in Chapter 1, are fundamental components of the most common measures of the quantity of money in our economy. Hence, depository institutions represent the crucial link between policies to influence the quantity of money and the actual effects that these policies have on that quantity. Our goal in this chapter is to explain how depository institutions perform this role.

Required Reserves and Depository Institution Balance Sheets

As we discussed in Chapter 9, the main liabilities of depository institutions are deposit accounts, such as transactions deposit (checkable or debitable) accounts. (Many transactions deposit holders who use debit cards are learning that signing a receipt may earn a reward from their bank, whereas keying in a personal identification number can incur a penalty; see the *Cyber Focus: Debiting with a PIN May Further Debit Your Transactions Account.*) Depository institution assets are loans, securities, and cash assets. A portion of cash assets is composed of vault cash and reserve deposits held at Federal Reserve banks, even though neither reserves at the Fed nor vault cash yields interest to depository institutions.

Traditionally, a key reason that depository institutions hold cash in their vaults or on deposit at the Fed is that they are *required* to do so. Recall from Chapter 11, that the Depository Institutions Deregulation and Monetary Control Act of 1980 gave the Federal Reserve the authority to place reserve requirements on all federally insured depository institutions that offer transactions accounts. The Federal Reserve establishes its reserve requirements using **required reserve ratios,** which are fractions of transactions deposit balances that depository institutions legally must maintain either as deposits with Federal Reserve banks or as vault cash. At present the Federal Reserve subjects most transactions deposits to a required reserve ratio of 10 percent. Thus, for every $10 of transactions deposits at a depository institution, the institution must hold $1 on deposit with a Federal Reserve bank and/or in its vault. Ignoring any other complications—and in the real world, as we discuss in Chapter 19, there is an important complication known as *sweep accounts*—if the institution issues $1,000 million ($1 billion) in transactions deposits, then it is obliged to hold total reserves of $100 million. This total amount of legally mandated cash reserve holdings constitutes the institution's **required reserves.**

DEPOSITORY INSTITUTION BALANCE SHEETS AND T-ACCOUNTS The existence of this reserve requirement implies that a single depository institution can use any new transactions deposit funds to make new loans or buy new securities only to the extent that it has cash reserves above the required level. That is, the depository institution can lend or purchase securities only if it possesses **excess reserves,** or reserves in excess of reserves that it must hold to meet reserve requirements.

Required reserve ratios: Fractions of transactions deposit balances that the Federal Reserve mandates that depository institutions maintain either as deposits with Federal Reserve banks or as vault cash.

Required reserves: Legally mandated reserve holdings at depository institutions, which are proportional to the dollar amounts of transactions accounts.

Excess reserves: Depository institutions' cash balances at Federal Reserve banks or in the institutions' vaults that exceed the amount that they must hold to meet legal requirements.

CYBER

Focus

Debiting with a PIN May Further Debit Your Transactions Account

Typically, depository institutions allow holders of transactions deposits to choose whether to sign a receipt or punch in a personal identification number (PIN) when they use a debit card to authorize a funds transfer to a retailer. Under most agreements that depository institutions have with retailers, depository institutions earn higher revenues when debit-card customers sign for their purchases. In contrast, retailers pay lower processing fees to depository institutions when customers key in their PINs. To encourage transactions deposit holders to sign for their purchases, about 14 percent of depository institutions now charge a fee, ranging from as low as 10 cents to as much as $2, each time a debit-card user punches in a PIN. Some banks, such as Wachovia and Bank of America, have even begun to offer rebates to depositors who sign debit-card payment authorizations instead of entering PINs.

FOR CRITICAL ANALYSIS: Why do you suppose that depository institutions require debit-card users to authorize a purchase by signing a receipt or keying in a PIN? (Hint: There are legal and contractual limitations on a customer's liability arising from fraudulent use of a stolen debit card.)

Total reserves: The total balances that depository institutions hold on deposit with Federal Reserve banks or as vault cash.

T-account: A side-by-side listing of the assets and liabilities of a business such as a depository institution.

Consider a depository institution with $1,000 million in transactions deposit liabilities. To make our example a little more concrete, we'll assume that this depository institution is based in Boston. To simplify, however, we assume that the institution has no other liabilities and no equity capital. If it holds all these funds as cash assets, then it has total cash reserves of $1,000 million. For simplicity we shall refer to the institution's total cash reserves as **total reserves.** In Figure 13-1 we display this institution's assets and liabilities inside a **T-account,** which is just a listing of the assets of the depository institution alongside its liabilities. You saw the equivalent of T-accounts in Chapter 9 when we discussed the assets and liabilities of commercial banks, savings institutions, and credit unions. As we discussed in Chapter 9, a depository institution's assets must be matched exactly by the sum of its liabilities and equity capital. Consequently, this depository institution's total reserves of $1,000 million exactly balance with its transactions deposit liabilities of $1,000 million. Because T-accounts display such a balancing of assets and liabilities, they are also often called *balance sheets.*

As Figure 13-1 indicates, this depository institution's required reserves are $100 million, or 10 percent of its transactions deposits of $1,000 million. This means that its excess reserves are $900 million, or the amount by which its total reserves of $1,000 million exceed the institution's legal reserve requirement of $100 million.

A "LOANED-UP" DEPOSITORY INSTITUTION   Excess reserves earn no interest income for the depository institution. Therefore, no profit-maximizing depository institution would permit itself to remain in the situation shown in Figure 13-1 for very long. The Boston institution's managers will allocate the institution's $900 million in excess reserves to alternative uses, such as holdings of loans and securities.

Figure 13-2 shows the result of such a managerial reallocation of the depository institution's assets. Once the managers have used all available excess reserves to make loans or to buy securities, then the institution is said to be fully "loaned up," meaning that it has expanded its loans and other interest-bearing assets as fully as possible in view of the required reserve ratio that it faces. For a fully loaned-up institution, excess reserves are equal to zero, and total reserves equal required reserves, as in Figure 13-2. Once this depository institution's managers have allocated all excess reserves to loans and securities, the institution's excess reserves fall to zero, and its total reserves decline to the level of its required reserves, or $100 million.

The Deposit Expansion Process

The Boston-based depository institution that we have envisioned is only one of thousands of such institutions throughout the United States. To understand how its indirect interactions with these other institutions in the face of transactions by the Federal Reserve can influence the total quantity of deposits in *all* institutions combined, let's expand our example.

FIGURE 13-1
T-Account for the Boston Depository Institution.

Assets		Liabilities	
Total reserves	$1,000 million	Transactions deposits	$1,000 million
Required reserves ($100 million)			
Excess reserves ($900 million)			

FIGURE 13-2	Assets		Liabilities	
T-Account for the Boston Depository Institution When It Is Fully Loaned Up.	Total reserves *Required reserves* *($100 million)* *Excess reserves* *($0)* Loans & securities	$ 100 million $ 900 million	Transactions deposits	$1,000 million
	Total:	$1,000 million	Total:	$1,000 million

HOW A RESERVE INCREASE AFFECTS A SINGLE DEPOSITORY INSTITUTION

Suppose that a New York securities dealer has a transactions deposit account at the Boston-based depository institution that we considered above. Let's suppose that the Federal Reserve Bank of New York buys $100 million in U.S. government securities from the securities dealer. Then the dealer receives $100 million from that Federal Reserve bank, which it places in its transactions account at the depository institution that we considered in Figures 13-1 and 13-2.

As shown in Figure 13-2, before the dealer's transaction with the New York Federal Reserve Bank, the Boston institution had $1,000 million in transactions deposit liabilities, $100 million in total reserves, and $900 million in loans and securities. Figure 13-3 displays the situation faced by this depository institution after the dealer's transaction with the Fed. Because $100 million in new funds have flowed into the dealer's transactions deposit account with the depository institution, the institution now has $100 million in new cash reserves, or total reserves of $200 million. But the depository institution also has $1,100 million in transactions deposit liabilities, so its required reserves have risen from $100 million to $110 million (10 percent of the $1,100 million in total transactions deposits). Because the institution has $200 million in total reserves but faces a reserve requirement of $110 million, it has $90 million in excess reserves. As a result of its customer's transaction with the New York Federal Reserve Bank, the Boston depository institution is no longer fully loaned up.

The managers of this depository institution have an additional $90 million in excess reserves that they may either lend or use to buy securities. Figure 13-4 on the next page shows the T-account for the Boston institution after its managers have reallocated its assets so that the institution once again is fully loaned up. When this position is reattained, the institution's excess reserves again equal zero, and its total reserves equal its required reserves, which now

FIGURE 13-3	Assets		Liabilities	
Boston Depository Institution's T-Account after New York Securities Dealer's Transaction.	Total reserves *Required reserves* *($110 million)* *Excess reserves* *($90 million)* Loans & securities	$ 200 million $ 900 million	Transactions deposits	$1,100 million
	Total:	$1,100 million	Total:	$1,100 million

FIGURE 13-4
Boston Depository Institution's T-Account after It Once Again Is Fully Loaned Up.

Assets		Liabilities	
Total reserves	$ 110 million	Transactions deposits	$1,100 million
Required reserves ($110 million)			
Excess reserves ($0)			
Loans & securities	$ 990 million		
Total:	$1,100 million	Total:	$1,100 million

are equal to $110 million. The amount of loans and securities has expanded to $990 million, so the institution's total assets remain equal to $1,100, which is the same as the amount of its total transactions deposit liabilities.

HOW A RESERVE INCREASE SPILLS FROM ONE INSTITUTION TO OTHERS

Note in Figure 13-4 that for the Boston depository institution, the $100 million transaction between the securities dealer and the Federal Reserve Bank of New York has led to a $10 million expansion of total reserves, from $100 million to $110 million, and a $90 million expansion of loans and securities, from $900 million to $990 million. Yet this cannot be the conclusion of the story for all depository institutions. The reason is that when the Boston institution extends more loans and buys more securities, the recipients of the $90 million in new loans and funds that it pays for securities now have $90 million in funds that *they* may deposit in transactions deposit accounts at the depository institutions where they maintain such accounts. (A number of depository institutions are working hard to make the process of completing checking transfers among deposit accounts more efficient; see the *Cyber Focus: Remote Capture Speeds the Check-Clearing Process.*)

To make this point more concrete, let's suppose that the Boston depository institution expanded its combined loan and security assets simply by buying $90 million in government

CYBER
Focus

Remote Capture Speeds the Check-Clearing Process

Wachovia Corporation, Bank of America, and Bank of New York have joined a movement initially pioneered by Internet-based institutions, such as NetBank and E-Trade, to engage in *remote capture* of paper checks. With remote capture, a business electroni-

cally scans checks received from its customers. The business then transmits a digital image to its bank, which automatically forwards the image either to the Federal Reserve or to a private clearinghouse for processing. The traditional check-clearing process, which requires paper checks to be carried from businesses to a bank's branches and then to the bank's check-clearing offices, typically takes at least one to three days to complete. Remote capture cuts the time to just an hour.

Hence, this innovation promises to dramatically reduce the time required to complete transfers of funds between transactions accounts at depository institutions.

FOR CRITICAL ANALYSIS: It is technologically feasible for businesses to transmit check images directly to the Federal Reserve or a private clearinghouse. Why do businesses use depository institutions as go-betweens in the check-clearing process?

FIGURE 13-5
Chicago Depository Institution's T-Account Changes after Second Security Purchase.

	Assets			Liabilities	
Total reserves		+$90 million	Transactions deposits		+$90 million
Required reserves					
(+$9 million)					
Excess reserves					
(+$81 million)					
Total:		+$90 million	Total:		+$90 million

securities from a securities dealer based in Chicago. Furthermore let's suppose that the Boston depository institution makes payment by transferring the $90 million directly into the Chicago securities dealer's transactions deposit account in a Chicago-based depository institution. Figure 13-5 shows only the *changes* faced by the Chicago institution after this second transaction occurs. Its transactions deposit liabilities have *increased* by $90 million, so its required reserves have *risen* by $9 million (10 percent of the $90 million in new deposits). Hence, the Chicago depository institution now has $81 million in new excess reserves that *its* managers may use to make new loans or to buy new securities.

Suppose that the Chicago-based depository institution makes a loan of $81 million to a Milwaukee-based company. Then, as shown in Figure 13-6, this means that in the end the Chicago institution's total reserves expand by only the required amount, or $9 million. Its total assets rise by $90 million, or the amount of the increase in deposits caused by the security transaction between the Boston-based depository institution and the Chicago securities dealer.

THE ULTIMATE CHAIN REACTION: AGGREGATE DEPOSIT EXPANSION   Yet our story *still* is not finished. When the Milwaukee company spends the $81 million that it borrows to purchase a needed piece of equipment, its payment for this equipment will show up in the account that the equipment manufacturer has at some other depository institution, perhaps in Minneapolis. This causes the reserve requirement at this new institution to rise by 10 percent of $81 million, or $8.1 million, leaving it with $72.9 million in new excess reserves that it can use to make new loans or to purchase new securities.

Indeed, this process of redepositing followed by further lending and security purchases by depository institutions continues through a long line of institutions and their deposit customers. Table 13-1 on the next page shows how our story works out if we continue it to its

FIGURE 13-6
Chicago Depository Institution's T-Account Changes after It Once Again Is Fully Loaned Up.

	Assets			Liabilities	
Total reserves		+$ 9 million	Transactions deposits		+$90 million
Required reserves					
(+$9 million)					
Excess reserves					
(+$0)					
Loans & securities		$81 million			
Total:		+$90 million	Total:		+$90 million

Table 13-1 The Ultimate Effects Stemming from the Federal Reserve Bank of New York's $100 Million Security Transaction

Depository Institution	Increase in Required Reserves	Increase in Loans and Securities	Increase in Transactions Deposits
Boston	$ 10.0 million	$ 90.0 million	$ 100 million
Chicago	9.0 million	81.0 million	90 million
Minneapolis	8.1 million	72.9 million	81 million
All other depository institutions	72.9 million	656.1 million	729 million
All Depository Institutions Combined	**$100.0 million**	**$900.0 million**	**$1,000 million**

ultimate conclusion. Eventually, required reserves at *all* depository institutions will rise by $100 million. Loans and securities at *all* institutions will rise by $900 million. Total transactions deposits at *all* institutions ultimately will increase by $1,000 million, or $1 billion. (We shall explain shortly how we know that these total changes are correct; for the moment, take our word for these numbers.)

This example illustrates how a Federal Reserve Bank of New York transaction with a single securities dealer can cause transactions deposits across all depository institutions to expand by *more* than the amount of the transaction. In the example, a $100 million reserve injection via the purchase of securities by the New York Federal Reserve Bank has resulted in a tenfold increase in total transactions deposits, to $1,000 million.

1. How does a change in total depository institution reserves cause a multiple expansion of the deposit liabilities of these institutions? An increase in excess reserves induces the institution that receives the reserves to increase its lending or security holdings. The funds that it lends or uses to purchase securities typically are redeposited at other depository institutions, which can also expand their lending and security holdings. The result is a multiple expansion of deposits in the banking system.

THE FEDERAL RESERVE'S ROLE IN DEPOSIT EXPANSION The key to the multiple expansion of deposits that occurred in our example was the Federal Reserve's injection of $100 million in *new* reserves. What would have happened if, instead of the Federal Reserve Bank of New York, some other securities dealer had bought the securities from the dealer who had the account at the Boston depository institution? Then that other dealer would have transferred funds out of an account at some other depository institution. Deposits would again rise at the Boston depository institution, as in our previous example. But deposits would fall by an equal amount at another institution, which would then have to *reduce* its holdings of loans and securities. As a result, the initial $100 million increase in reserves at the Boston depository institution would be matched by a $100 million reduction in reserves at another depository institution. A simple *transfer* of funds *within* the banking system would occur, with no multiple expansion of deposits.

The Fed, Electronic Impulses, and Deposit Expansion

Why does the Federal Reserve's involvement in a transaction make such a difference? The reason is that the Federal Reserve is the single institution empowered to create depository institution reserves. When the Federal Reserve Bank of New York buys a security from a dealer, it produces reserves that previously had not existed in the banking system. This ultimately leads to the expansion of deposits summarized in Table 13-1.

Federal Reserve Open Market Operations

When the Federal Reserve buys or sells securities in the money or capital markets, it engages in **open market operations.** In the example above, in which the New York Federal Reserve Bank purchased $100 million in securities from a New York securities dealer, we considered the effects of an **open market purchase.** In contrast, if the transaction had involved an **open market sale,** the Federal Reserve Bank of New York would have sold U.S. government securities to the dealer.

HOW THE FED CONDUCTS AN OPEN MARKET PURCHASE   To better understand the mechanics of a Federal Reserve open market purchase, let's consider what must have occurred to initiate the first step of our example above. Figure 13-7 displays T-accounts for both the Federal Reserve and the Boston-based depository institution. When the New York Federal Reserve Bank purchases securities from a New York dealer with a transactions deposit account at the Boston institution, it typically makes a *wire transfer,* which is a transfer of funds—via computer—from the Fed directly to the Boston bank account of the dealer receiving the funds. The wire transfer, which in this case is known as a *book-entry security* transaction (see Chapter 15 for more details), digitally transfers ownership of the securities from the dealer to the Federal Reserve. Consequently, the Boston-based depository institution gains $100 million in reserve assets, while the Federal Reserve increases its reserve deposit liabilities by $100 million. But the Federal Reserve gains a matching $100 million in new assets—the securities that it has purchased from the New York dealer.

Thus, a Fed wire transfer of funds used to purchase securities is the action that causes the Boston institution's transactions deposits to rise by $100 million in the first place. Where do these funds come from? The answer is that the Fed creates them. Note that the Fed does not have to start a printing press to create the funds. It simply enters numbers into data files and then transmits the data to a receiving bank. The Fed effectively alters the quantity of money in circulation by transmitting *electronic impulses.*

OPEN MARKET SALES   What happens if the Federal Reserve *sells* $100 million in securities to a dealer with a transactions deposit account at the Boston depository institution? As shown in Figure 13-8 on the next page, the answer is that such an open market sale

Open market operations: Federal Reserve purchases or sales of securities.

Open market purchase: A Federal Reserve purchase of a security, which increases total reserves at depository institutions and thereby raises the size of the monetary base.

Open market sale: A Federal Reserve sale of a security, which reduces total reserves of depository institutions and thereby reduces the size of the monetary base.

On the Web
What open market operations has the Federal Reserve Bank of New York undertaken today? Go to **http://www.ny.frb.org/** and then click on "Open Market Operations."

FIGURE 13-7 T-Accounts for a Federal Reserve Open Market Purchase.	Open Market Purchase			
	Federal Reserve		**Boston Depository Institution**	
	Assets	**Liabilities**	**Assets**	**Liabilities**
	Securities +$100 million	Reserve deposits +$100 million	Reserve deposits +$100 million	Transactions deposits +$100 million

**FIGURE 13-8
T-Accounts for a Federal
Reserve Open Market Sale.**

Open Market Sale			
Federal Reserve		**Boston Depository Institution**	
Assets	**Liabilities**	**Assets**	**Liabilities**
Securities −$100 million	Reserve deposits −$100 million	Reserve deposits −$100 million	Transactions deposits −$100 million

of securities has exactly the opposite T-account effects as those stemming from an open market purchase. Whether the dealer pays the Federal Reserve for the securities by writing a check or transferring funds directly, the dealer's transactions deposits at the Boston institution decline by $100 million. This causes the Boston institution's reserve deposits with the Federal Reserve to fall by this amount.

At the Federal Reserve, the sale of securities causes its total assets to shrink by $100 million. Balancing this reduction in the Federal Reserve's assets is the decline in reserve deposits of depository institutions. Such an open market sale effectively *removes* reserves from the banking system.

> **2. What are Federal Reserve open market operations?** Open market operations are the purchases or sales of U.S. government securities by the Federal Reserve. Typically, the Fed purchases securities by wiring funds to the account of the dealer from whom the purchase is made. Open market purchases increase the total reserves of depository institutions. Open market sales reduce the total reserves of depository institutions.

How the Fed Expands and Contracts Total Deposits

We now have developed the key concepts that are needed to understand how the Federal Reserve influences the total quantity of deposits in the nation's banking system. Now let's see how to determine the *amounts* by which the Fed's actions can potentially expand, or contract, the total quantity of deposits at the country's depository institutions.

EXPANDING TOTAL DEPOSITS   Consider the example of an open market purchase of $100 million in securities by the Federal Reserve Bank of New York. The immediate effect of this purchase is an increase in total reserves in the banking system—specifically, at the Boston depository institution—of $100 million. Let's call a change in total reserves ΔTR, where the Greek letter delta (Δ) indicates a change in a variable. Then the direct effect of the open market purchase is a reserve increase equal to $\Delta TR = +\$100$ million.

Recall that we have assumed throughout our example that the legal required reserve ratio is equal to 10 percent, or 0.10. Let's denote this ratio as $rr_D = 0.10$. In addition, let's denote the change in deposits in the banking system by ΔD. This means that any change in required reserves *(RR)* in the banking system, ΔRR, is equal to $rr_D \times \Delta D$, because the level of required reserves equals $rr_D \times D$, where rr_D is the constant required reserve ratio.

Finally, remember that we assumed that the Boston-based depository institution and all other depository institutions desire to be fully loaned up, meaning that they prefer to hold no excess reserves. That means that the amount by which required reserves change matches the change in total reserves, or $\Delta RR = \Delta TR$.

Putting all this together tells us that

$$rr_D \times \Delta D = \Delta TR.$$

Now let's divide both sides of this equation by rr_D to get an expression for the change in deposits:

$$\frac{rr_D \times \Delta D}{rr_D} = \frac{\Delta TR}{rr_D}$$

or

$$\Delta D = (1/rr_D) \times \Delta TR.$$

This final expression tells us that the change in deposits equals a factor, $1/rr_D$, times a change in total reserves. In our example, $rr_D = 0.10$, so $1/rr_D = 10$. Hence, a change in reserves causes a tenfold increase in deposits. This explains our claim in Table 13-1 that a $100 million increase in total reserves caused by an open market purchase ultimately causes deposits at all depository institutions to expand by $1,000 million, or by ten times the amount of the reserve increase. We determine this amount simply by using the expression just developed:

$$\Delta D = (1/rr_D) \times \Delta TR = (10) \times (+\$100 \text{ million}) = +\$1,000 \text{ million}.$$

The factor $1/rr_D$ is called the **deposit expansion multiplier** because it tells us how much deposits in the banking system can rise or fall as a result of an increase or decrease of reserves by the Federal Reserve. In our example, the value of the deposit expansion multiplier is $1/rr_D = 1/(0.10) = 10$.

Deposit expansion multiplier: A number that tells how much aggregate transactions deposits at all depository institutions will change in response to a change in total reserves of these institutions.

CONTRACTING TOTAL DEPOSITS   An open market sale of U.S. government securities by the Fed would have the opposite effect on total deposits, as we can see by using the expression for deposit expansion. A $100 million sale of securities by the Federal Reserve causes reserves in the banking system to decline, so $\Delta TR = -\$100$ million in the case of an open market sale. Then, using our expression for ΔD, we have

$$\Delta D = (1/rr_D) \times \Delta TR = (10) \times (-\$100 \text{ million}) = -\$1,000 \text{ million}.$$

Whereas a Federal Reserve open market purchase induces a multiple expansion of deposits in the banking system, a Federal Reserve open market sale causes a multiple *contraction* of deposits.

Deposit Expansion and the Money Multiplier

As we discussed in Chapter 1, the amount of transactions deposits in the banking system is a key component of the *monetary aggregates,* or measures of the total quantity of money in circulation in the economy. This means that we have almost explained how the Federal Reserve can influence the nation's money stock.

We are not quite finished, however. Another key component of any monetary aggregate is the amount of *currency*—the government-produced paper money and coins that we use in simple hand-to-hand transactions. Currency typically constitutes more than 40 percent of the M1 measure of money. This is such a large portion that we cannot simply ignore it. Certainly, the Federal Reserve cannot ignore it because the Fed is the institution that supervises the distribution of this currency. If you have any dollar bills handy, take a look at one; you will see "Federal Reserve Note" printed prominently on the bill.

Depository Institution Reserves, the Monetary Base, and Money

As we discussed in Chapter 1, the narrowest monetary aggregate is the amount of money produced directly by the government, or the *monetary base*. The monetary base, *MB*, is the amount of currency, *C*, plus the total quantity of reserves in the banking system, *TR*, or

$$MB = C + TR.$$

We already know that if depository institutions hold no excess reserves, then $TR = RR = rr_D \times D$. Let's also assume that consumers and businesses desire to hold a fraction, *c*, of transactions deposits as currency. It then follows that $C = c \times D$, so that the expression for the monetary base, when we make these substitutions, can be written as

$$MB = (c \times D) + (rr_D \times D) = (c + rr_D) \times D.$$

Hence, we can express the monetary base as the sum of the desired currency ratio and the required reserve ratio multiplied times the amount of transactions deposits in the banking system.

A broader monetary aggregate, and the one on which we shall focus our attention, is M1. Recall from Chapter 1 that M1 is equal to the sum of currency and transactions deposits, or

$$M1 = C + D.$$

Because $C = c \times D$, we can rewrite the expression for M1 as

$$M1 = (c \times D) + D = (c + 1) \times D.$$

Now if we divide by *MB*, we get

$$\frac{M1}{MB} = \frac{(c + 1) \times D}{MB} = \frac{(c + 1) \times D}{(c + rr_D) \times D} = \frac{c + 1}{c + rr_D}.$$

If we multiply both sides of this equation by *MB*, we get

$$M1 = \frac{c + 1}{c + rr_D} \times MB,$$

which then is an expression for the quantity of money given the value of the monetary base and the ratios *c* and rr_D. This expression tells us that:

> **Once the Federal Reserve determines the size of the monetary base, the amount of the monetary aggregate M1 depends upon the required reserve ratio rr_D and the desired ratio of currency to transactions deposits for consumers and businesses given by *c*.**

The Money Multiplier

Now let's try to figure out how this algebra relates to the basic deposit expansion process. First, note that if *c* and rr_D are unchanged, then the above expression for the value of the M1 measure of money indicates that a change in the money stock is induced by a change in the monetary base, or

$$\Delta M1 = \frac{c + 1}{c + rr_D} \times \Delta MB.$$

Because rr_D is less than one, the factor multiplied by ΔMB in this new expression is greater than one. This means that a change in the monetary base has a *multiple* effect on the quantity of money. In fact, if we define a "money multiplier" m_M to be equal to the factor $(c + 1)/(c + rr_D)$, then we can write a final expression relating a change in the monetary base to a resulting change in the quantity of money:

$$\Delta M1 = m_M \times \Delta MB.$$

The **money multiplier,** m_M, is a number that tells us the size of the effect of a change in the monetary base on the quantity of money. To get an idea of roughly how large this multiplier might be, let's suppose that the desired ratio of currency holdings relative to deposits, c, equals 0.25. Then the value of the money multiplier would be $m_M = (c + 1)/(c + rr_D) = (0.25 + 1)/(0.25 + 0.10) = 1.25/0.35$, which is equal to approximately 3.6. Consequently, an increase in the monetary base would raise the total quantity of money by just over three and one-half times.

Recall that in our earlier example we came up with a deposit expansion multiplier that was equal to 10. Why is the money multiplier in this example only a third of that size? The reason is that the earlier example ignored the existence of currency. If securities dealers, businesses, and consumers desire to hold some cash in the form of currency, then each time a depository institution purchases new securities from dealers or makes new loans to businesses or consumers, some funds must leave the banking system in the form of currency holdings. At every step of the deposit expansion process, therefore, fewer funds are redeposited in depository institutions, leaving fewer funds for the institutions to use for security purchases or loans. As a result, the multiplier's value must be smaller when currency accounts for part of the quantity of money.

Money multiplier: A number that tells how much the quantity of money will change in response to a change in the monetary base.

Federal Reserve Policymaking and the Money Multiplier

Because of the deposit expansion process, the Federal Reserve cannot control monetary aggregates such as M1 directly. What it can do, however, is change the amount of reserves at depository institutions to influence such a monetary aggregate. Because the monetary base, *MB,* is the sum of currency, *C,* and total reserves, *TR,* it follows that the only way that the monetary base can change is if the Federal Reserve changes the quantity of currency, the amount of reserves, or both currency and reserves. Typically, the Federal Reserve does not use variations in the stock of currency to influence the total quantity of money. But it can, and does, conduct open market purchases to increase total reserves or open market sales to reduce total reserves. An open market purchase increases the monetary base and thereby causes a multiple increase in the quantity of money. An open market sale decreases the monetary base and thereby causes a multiple reduction in the quantity of money.

As we shall discuss in Chapter 17, the Federal Reserve does not have to rely on open market operations to influence the quantity of money through the money multiplier process. The Federal Reserve can also try to change total reserves at depository institutions by inducing depository institutions to borrow more or fewer reserves from Federal Reserve banks' discount windows. If depository institutions' discount window borrowings increase, then total reserves, the monetary base, and the quantity of money will also increase. If depository institutions' discount window borrowings decline, then total reserves, the monetary base, and the quantity of money will also decline.

The Federal Reserve could also choose to change the quantity of money by altering the required reserve ratio, rr_D. This would change the money multiplier and thereby cause the quantity of money to rise or fall even if total reserves in the banking system were to remain unchanged. The Federal Reserve rarely changes reserve requirements, however. Typically, it relies on daily open market operations coupled with intermittent changes in its discount window policies. (The U.S. reserve requirement of 10 percent for most balances in transactions accounts has not been changed since the 1990s, but central banks in some countries adjust reserve requirements more frequently; see the *Global Focus: Aiming Reserve Requirements at High-Risk Banks in China*.)

> **3. What is the money multiplier, and why is it important?**   The money multiplier is a number that determines the size of the effect on the quantity of money caused by a change in the monetary base. The money multiplier is important because the Federal Reserve can influence the quantity of money only by varying the size of the monetary base. Consequently, the money multiplier determines how Federal Reserve policy actions will affect the money stock.

Extended Money and Credit Multipliers

In light of the expressions that we have developed so far in this chapter, it might be tempting to think that the Fed can simply compute money multipliers and then determine precisely how to conduct monetary policies. Unfortunately for the Fed, things are not quite so simple.

The Time-Varying Money Multiplier

One problem that the Federal Reserve faces is that the money multiplier is not constant over time. Another is that M1 is not the only monetary aggregate. Indeed, for reasons we discuss in Chapter 19, the Fed has relied considerably more on the broader monetary aggregate M2 in recent years.

GLOBAL
Focus

Aiming Reserve Requirements at High-Risk Banks in China

Since the early 2000s, the Chinese central bank, the People's Bank of China, has adjusted its reserve requirements several times. For instance, it has increased the required reserve ratio for most deposits three times since early 2003. In making these changes, the central bank was trying to reduce the money multiplier and slow the growth of the money supply.

Recently, the People's Bank of China decided that it needed to do still more to rein in money supply growth, so it decided to boost reserve requirements once again. This time, however, it boosted required reserve ratios only for banks judged to be engaged in the riskiest lending activities. Thus, the central bank used a change in reserve requirements to try to achieve two goals simultaneously: (1) to cut back on the money supply, and (2) to induce the riskiest banks to allocate fewer funds to risky loans.

FOR CRITICAL ANALYSIS: How is the basic multiplier process of deposit expansion or contraction affected if some depository institutions face higher reserve requirements than other institutions?

Figure 13-9 shows estimates of the money multipliers for the M1 and M2 aggregates. The M1 multiplier is the ratio of M1 to the monetary base, while the M2 multiplier is the ratio of M2 to the monetary base. The M1 multiplier is always smaller than the M2 multiplier because M2 includes savings and time deposits that are subject to an expansion process following a change in the monetary base.

Why do money multipliers vary? One reason is that the desired ratio of currency to deposits, c, is not constant. Instead, this ratio typically changes with the extent to which currency is a favored means of undertaking some types of transactions in the economy. If you look back at the expression for the M1 money multiplier that we computed above, you will see that variations in this ratio will cause the multiplier to vary as well.

Excess Reserves and the Money Multiplier

Another important real-world factor that can cause variations in money multipliers is volatility in desired holdings of excess reserves by depository institutions. Up to this point we have assumed that depository institutions always desire to be fully loaned up. This has simplified our explanation of the basics of deposit expansion and the money multiplier process, but it is not very realistic. In fact, depository institutions usually *do* voluntarily hold some excess reserves.

REASONS THAT DEPOSITORY INSTITUTIONS HOLD EXCESS RESERVES   Why do depository institutions hold excess reserves, even though such reserves yield no explicit interest return? They do so because excess reserves yield an *implicit* return: if customers make unexpected deposit withdrawals, having excess reserves on hand saves depository institutions from having to bear the costs of calling in loans, selling securities, or borrowing reserve funds in order to meet their reserve requirements.

Another possible reason to hold some excess reserves is that doing so permits a depository institution to make speedy loans when good deals arise unexpectedly. If a long-standing customer with a credit line should need funds unexpectedly, it can be useful to have some on hand.

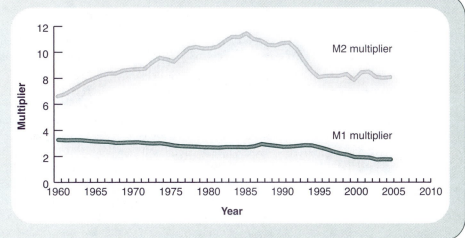

FIGURE 13-9
M1 and M2 Multipliers.

Because M2 includes a number of financial assets that are not included in M1, the M2 multiplier is significantly larger than the M1 multiplier. Both money multipliers vary over time.

SOURCE: Federal Reserve Bank of St. Louis, *Federal Reserve Economic Data,* various issues.

Of course, depository institutions incur an *opportunity cost* when they hold excess reserves. This is the interest return that the institutions forgo by holding cash instead of lending or purchasing securities. For this reason, depository institutions try to maintain their excess reserve holdings at levels that just cover the kinds of contingencies that they are likely to face in their own special circumstances. Nevertheless, depository institutions do hold positive, albeit small, amounts of excess reserves.

HOW EXCESS RESERVES CHANGE THE MONEY MULTIPLIER　　To see how excess reserves affect the money multiplier, let's take a last look at the money multiplier. Recall that the monetary base is $MB = C + TR$. If depository institutions hold excess reserves, then total reserves equal required reserves plus excess reserves, or $TR = RR + ER$, where ER denotes the amount of excess reserve holdings. Suppose that depository institutions desire to hold a fraction, e, of their transactions deposit liabilities as excess reserves. Then $ER = e \times D$, and $MB = C + TR = C + RR + ER$. Using the expressions that we have already developed, this means that the monetary base may be expressed as

$$MB = (c \times D) + (rr_D \times D) + (e \times D) = (rr_D + e + c) \times D.$$

This states that the monetary base is equal to the sum of the required reserve ratio, desired excess reserve ratio, and desired currency ratio multiplied times total transactions deposits.

Using the definitions for M1 and MB, we see that the money multiplier is equal to

$$\frac{\text{M1}}{MB} = \frac{C + D}{C + TR}.$$

Using the expressions that we have already developed, we can substitute for C and TR to rewrite the money multiplier as

$$\frac{\text{M1}}{MB} = \frac{(c + 1) \times D}{(rr_D + e + c) \times D}$$

$$= \frac{c + 1}{rr_D + e + c}.$$

The value of the multiplier now also depends on the desired ratio of excess reserve holdings to transactions deposits, e.

Note that the desired excess reserve ratio e appears in the denominator of the money multiplier. Consequently, if e increases, meaning that depository institutions desire to hold more excess reserves relative to their transactions deposit liabilities, the money multiplier gets smaller. This makes sense in the context of the deposit expansion process that underlies the multiplier. If depository institutions hold some excess reserves, then at each stage of the deposit expansion process they will make fewer loans or purchase fewer securities than they would if they did not hold excess reserves. This automatically reduces the extent to which deposits can expand in the banking system following a change in total reserves.

Excess reserve holdings of depository institutions typically are "small" relative to their total reserve holdings. In a given week, excess reserves rarely are much larger than around 1 percent of total depository institution reserve holdings. Yet excess reserve holdings also are highly variable. Figure 13-10 displays depository institutions' total holdings of excess reserves from May 2002 to May 2005. As you can see, there is significant volatility in excess reserves. This volatility contributes to variability in the money multiplier, thereby complicating the Federal Reserve's task in determining how its policies will affect monetary aggregates.

4. What factors influence the money multiplier? A key determinant of the size of the money multiplier is the amount of currency that consumers and businesses desire to hold relative to transactions deposits. Another important factor is the quantity of excess reserves that depository institutions wish to keep on hand in relation to transactions deposits. Both of these factors influence the amount of deposit expansion following changes in total reserves and, hence, the monetary base. For broader monetary aggregates such as M2, the deposit expansion process also affects savings and time deposits included in such aggregates. Therefore, desired consumer and business holdings of savings and time deposits relative to holdings of transactions deposits also affect the money multipliers for these broader monetary aggregates.

The Credit Multiplier

In recent years, the Federal Reserve has not focused its attention solely on monetary aggregates as indicators of the effects of its policies. Federal Reserve officials also look at other financial variables, such as market interest rates, prices of financial instruments, and prices of some commodities such as gold.

Another variable of interest to the Federal Reserve is the total amount of credit that depository institutions extend by lending or purchasing securities. As financial intermediaries, a key function that depository institutions perform is to issue such credit to help finance purchases of goods, services, and financial assets. Because multiple deposit expansion also entails multiple expansion of loans and security holdings at depository institutions, Federal Reserve policies can affect the volume of such purchases, and consequently economic activity, by influencing the aggregate amount of credit that depository institutions extend.

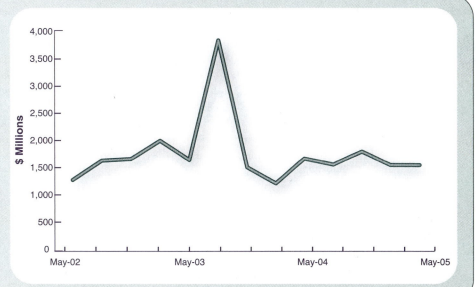

FIGURE 13-10
Excess Reserve Holdings of Depository Institutions.

Aggregate excess reserve balances can rise and fall considerably over time. This causes variability in the ratio of excess reserves to transactions deposits, which results in volatility in the money multiplier. Excess reserves increased considerably during the August 2003 power outage in the northeastern United States.

SOURCE: Board of Governors of the Federal Reserve System, H.3 (502) *Statistical Release.*

Figure 13-11 displays the conceptual T-account that would apply to all depository institutions that issue transactions deposits to finance lending, securities purchases, and holdings of required and excess reserve balances. The figure indicates that because assets and liabilities must balance, the sum of loans, securities, and required and excess reserves must equal the amount of deposits. If we let L denote the dollar amount of loans and S represent the dollar quantity of securities holdings, then this means that $L + S + RR + ER = D$.

TOTAL CREDIT   Now let's call the combined amount of loans and securities the *total credit* extended by depository institutions, or $L + S = TC$, where TC is the dollar amount of depository institution credit. Because the sum of loans, securities, and reserves equals deposits in the banking system (if we continue to simplify by ignoring other liabilities), then this tells us that $TC + RR + ER = D$. We can solve for total credit by subtracting RR and ER from both sides, to obtain

$$TC = D - RR - ER.$$

Hence, total credit is equal to transactions deposits minus required and excess reserves.

Because our T-account abstracts from reality by ignoring other kinds of deposits and other depository institution assets, let's look at changes in total credit resulting from changes in deposits or in required or excess reserves:

$$\Delta TC = \Delta D - \Delta RR - \Delta ER.$$

A BANK CREDIT MULTIPLIER   We leave it to you in problem 8 at the end of this chapter to show that after a couple of algebra steps this equation becomes

$$\Delta TC = \frac{1 - rr_D - e}{c + rr_D + e} \times \Delta MB.$$

Credit multiplier: A number that tells how much total loans and securities at depository institutions will change in response to a change in the monetary base.

Consequently, a change in the monetary base is multiplied by the factor $(1 - rr_D - e)/(c + rr_D + e)$ to cause a change in total credit. This factor is the **credit multiplier,** or a number that tells us the multiple expansion effect on total depository institution credit that a change in the monetary base induces. For instance, if $rr_D = 0.10$, $c = 0.25$, and $e = 0.01$, then the value of this multiplier is $(1 - 0.10 - 0.01)/(0.25 + 0.10 + 0.01) = 0.89/0.36$, or approximately 2.47. This would indicate that each \$1 increase in the monetary base would cause the amount of credit extended by depository institutions to rise by about \$2.47.

We can conclude that if the Federal Reserve conducts policies, such as open market operations, that alter the monetary base, then the result must be a change in the quantities of loans and securities at depository institutions. For instance, an open market purchase that increases the monetary base raises the combined amount of lending and security holdings of depository

---

FIGURE 13-11
A Consolidated T-Account for Depository Institutions.

Assets	Liabilities
Loans (*L*)	Transactions deposits (*D*)
Securities (*S*)	
Required reserves (*RR*)	
Excess reserves (*ER*)	

institutions. An open market sale, in contrast, reduces total loans and security holdings of these institutions. (In the presence of capital requirements, the effects of a change in the monetary base on the loan component of total bank credit may depend on the state of the economy and whether the monetary base increases or decreases; see *What Happens When Capital Requirements Meet Bank Credit Multipliers?*)

Note that the credit multiplier depends on the same basic factors as the money multiplier. These include the required reserve ratio, rr_D, the desired ratio of consumer and business holdings of currency to transactions deposits, c, and the desired ratio of depository institution holdings of excess reserves to transactions deposits, e. Consequently, variations in any of these factors cause the total credit multiplier to change, just as such variations cause movements in the money multiplier.

Changes in the monetary base exert multiplier effects on both the quantity of money and the total amount of depository institution credit. Which of these variables should the Federal Reserve actually *try* to influence? The answer to this question depends on whether money or credit relates more closely to the volume of economic activity, an issue that we shall consider more fully in Unit V. Before we can address this issue, however, you need to learn much more about the Federal Reserve, how it conducts its policies, and how those policies can affect the extent of economic activity.

MONEYXTRA!
Another Perspective

As you learned in Chapter 11, depository financial institutions face capital requirements. To consider how these requirements may affect the credit expansion process, go to the Chapter 13 reading, entitled "Does Bank Capital Matter for Monetary Transmission?" by Skander Van den Heuvel, from the Federal Reserve Bank of New York.
http://moneyxtra. swcollege.com

> **5. What is the credit multiplier?** The credit multiplier is a number that tells how much the combined amount of loans and security holdings of depository institutions will change as a result of a change in the monetary base. Because credit expansion accompanies deposit expansion at these institutions, the credit multiplier depends on the same basic factors that influence the money multiplier.

What Happens When... Capital Requirements Meet Bank Credit Multipliers?

As you learned in Chapter 11, central banks and depository institution regulators of many nations of the world now subject depository institutions to capital requirements. These requirements effectively limit the extent to which depository institutions can expand lending in relation to equity and other measures of capital.

Robert Bliss of the Federal Reserve Bank of Chicago and George Kaufman of Loyola University argue that the result can be quantitatively different effects of monetary policy on the lending component of bank credit. During an economic expansion, when the public's deposit holdings tend to increase, Fed efforts to curb growth in bank lending via a reduction in the monetary base will have the normal money multiplier effects. In times of economic contraction, however, two factors tend to reduce the Fed's ability to boost credit growth. First, an inflow of deposits generated by an expansion of the monetary base will not bring about a rise in lending at depository institutions that are bound by capital requirements. Second, during recessionary times, capital levels at depository institutions tend to decline in the face of increased loan defaults and greater needs to add to loan loss reserves. Thus, more depository institutions are likely to be constrained by capital requirements. Bliss and Kaufman conclude that in a recessionary period bank lending could be much less responsive to a given increase in the monetary base than it is to an equal-sized decrease during an economic expansion.

FOR CRITICAL ANALYSIS: Can capital requirements cause the overall bank credit multiplier discussed in this chapter to be smaller during recessions than during economic expansions? Why or why not?

Electronic Money and the Money Multiplier

As we have discussed in earlier chapters, and especially Chapter 2, several electronic money, or *e-money,* mechanisms are in use or under consideration at present. The use of stored-value cards is already widespread in several regions of the world. Furthermore, smart cards and online banking and payments techniques may engender growing use of *digital cash,* or funds contained in security-encrypted programs embedded in microchips or on hard drives.

How is digital cash likely to affect the process of determining the quantity of money in circulation? We can answer this question on two levels. The first focuses on the most immediate and straightforward effects of widespread adoption of digital cash, which are easier to assess. The second level leads to less clear-cut conclusions because it takes into account a number of indirect effects that the use of digital cash may have on the money supply process.

The Direct Effects of Digital Cash on the Money Supply Process

When assessing the implications of digital cash for the quantity of money in circulation, we must first recognize that the broad adoption of smart cards and other mechanisms for using digital cash will undoubtedly require a redefining of the monetary aggregates. Because digital cash will function as a medium of exchange, it ultimately will be included in the M1 definition of money. In turn, M1 is included within the broader monetary aggregates, so M2 and M3 will also include digital cash.

THE REVISED MONEY MULTIPLIER WITH DIGITAL CASH   We shall denote digital cash as DC. In the coming cyberworld with digital cash, the M1 definition of money will be the sum of government-issued currency, C, privately issued digital cash, DC, and privately issued transactions deposits, D. Thus, the expression for M1 will be

$$\text{M1} = C + DC + D.$$

Let's denote the public's desired holdings of digital cash relative to transactions deposits as dc, so $DC = dc \times D$. Recognizing again that $C = c \times D$, in a cyberworld with a significant volume of digital cash in circulation, we can write the expression for the M1 definition of money as

$$\text{M1} = (c + dc + 1) \times D.$$

Now we can determine an expression for the M1 money multiplier. We know that this multiplier is equal to M1/MB, where MB is the monetary base, or the amount of money issued directly by the government, which does not include privately issued digital cash. We know from our earlier discussion that we can express the monetary base as

$$MB = RR + ER + C = (rr_D + e + c) \times D.$$

Thus, in the presence of digital cash, the money multiplier is equal to

$$\frac{\text{M1}}{MB} = \frac{(c + dc + 1) \times D}{(rr_D + e + c) \times D}$$

$$= \frac{c + dc + 1}{rr_D + e + c}.$$

This expression indicates that, other things being equal, the widespread use of digital cash—the addition of the factor dc and an increase in its value as more and more people adopt digital cash—increases the money multiplier. The inclusion of *dc* in the money multiplier raises the value of the numerator, thereby pushing up the multiplier's value. Intuitively, the reason this occurs is that if people hold digital cash on smart cards, their personal computers, or other devices, then an increase in reserves in the banking system induces an expansion effect on the volume of transactions deposits, as well as on the volume of *digital cash.*

DIGITAL CASH IN THE DEPOSIT EXPANSION PROCESS   To see why this is so, imagine that the Fed in a cybereconomy of the not-so-distant future buys $1 million in government securities. Transactions deposits initially increase by $1 million, but the initial recipient of these funds allocates a portion of this amount to both government-issued currency *and* digital cash. The depository institution of the recipient can lend out the remaining deposits less an amount that it must hold to meet its reserve requirement. The institution's lending generates a deposit at another institution, and the depositor will also allocate some of these funds to government currency *and* to digital cash. Thus, at each stage of the deposit expansion process, there is an initial "leakage" of digital cash from transactions deposits, which by itself tends to push down the money multiplier. But funds held as digital cash are included in our revised definition of the quantity of money. Therefore, at every stage of the deposit expansion process, new digital cash is "created" as e-money included in M1. On net, therefore, the overall quantity of money increases with the addition of digital cash—again, under our assumption that all other things are equal—and the multiplier linking this measure of money to the monetary base must also rise in value.

It is important to recognize, however, that the expansion of digital cash occurs via the deposit expansion process generated by an increase in bank reserves. If the Fed injects more reserves into the banking system, then this generates a multiple increase in deposits, which in turn implies an increase in digital-cash holdings as individuals shift a desired portion of funds from deposit accounts to smart cards and other digital-cash storage devices. Unlike currency holdings, however, which together with reserves are constrained by the size of the monetary base created by the government, privately issued digital cash varies directly with the extent of transactions deposit expansion.

The Indirect Effects of Digital Cash on the Money Supply Process

The preceding discussion indicates that, *other things being equal,* the *immediate* effect of the broad adoption of digital cash will be an increase in the quantity of money and a rise in the value of the money multiplier. Over time, however, we would *not* expect that other things will *remain* equal. Consequently, in the long run we would anticipate that the money multiplier implications of digital cash are unlikely to be so clear-cut.

DIGITAL CASH AS A SUBSTITUTE FOR GOVERNMENT CURRENCY   To understand why, consider Table 13-2 on page 296, which lists the key characteristics of checks, government-issued currency, and digital cash. Clearly, people face a trade-off in deciding whether to hold currency or checks. Checks offer greater security: if a thief steals a woman's handbag containing cash and checks, she can tell her depository institution to halt payment on all checks in the handbag, but the thief can spend all the cash he has taken because cash payments are final at the point when a transaction is made. Currency requires face-to-face contact for purchases, whereas checks can be sent through the mail. Nevertheless, not everyone will accept a check in payment for a transaction, and a check payment is not final until the

Table 13-2 Features of Alternative Forms of Money

Feature	Checks	Currency	Digital Cash
Security	High	Low	High(?)
Cost per transfer	High	Medium	Low
Payment final, face-to-face	No	Yes	Yes
Payment final, non-face-to-face	No	No	Yes
Anonymity	No	Yes	Yes
Acceptability	Restricted	Wide	Uncertain at present

SOURCE: Aleksander Berentsen, "Monetary Policy Implications of Digital Money," *Kyklos* 51 (1998): 89–117.

check clears. Check transactions also are more expensive. In addition, currency transactions are anonymous, which may be desirable under some circumstances. After evaluating these features of currency and checks, people typically choose to hold *both* payment instruments.

Digital Cash versus Currency and Checks If people can also use digital cash, then they will compare its features with those currently offered by currency and checks. As Table 13-2 indicates, at present the extent of the acceptability of digital cash is uncertain. Nonetheless, we are contemplating a future in which digital cash will be nearly as acceptable as government-provided currency. As for security, digital cash held on smart cards without special security features such as personal identification numbers will be as susceptible to theft as government currency. Some digital cash, however, may be held on devices, such as laptop computers or even wristwatches (Swiss watch manufacturers have already developed watches with microchips for storing digital cash), requiring an access code before a microchip containing digital cash can be accessed. Overall, therefore, digital cash is likely to be somewhat more secure than government-provided currency, though not as secure as check transactions.

Finality and Anonymity Digital-cash transactions are likely to be less costly to undertake than those involving currency or checks. People will be able to access digital cash at home on their personal computers and will not have to go to depository institution branches or automated teller machines to obtain it (although they undoubtedly will be able to do this if they wish). In addition, they will be able to send digital cash from remote locations using the Internet, and digital-cash transactions will be instantaneously final. Unlike transactions using currency, therefore, digital-cash transactions need not be conducted on a face-to-face basis. Like currency transactions, however, most digital-cash transfers will be anonymous.

In most respects, therefore, digital cash looks like a "better" means of payment than government-provided currency. Certainly, for some time to come currency will be used to purchase a number of items—canned beverages and candy in vending machines, for example. Many economists, however, believe that widespread adoption of privately issued digital cash ultimately will tend to "crowd out" government-provided currency. Eventually, even vending machines are likely to have smart-card readers.

From the perspective of the money multiplier model of the money supply process, the ultimate displacement of a large portion of government-provided currency by digital cash will reduce the value of the desired ratio of government-provided currency to transactions deposits, thereby reducing the value of c in the money multiplier expression we derived on page 294. Although this would reduce the numerator of the money multiplier, it would also reduce the denominator, and the latter effect would dominate. Therefore, a decline in the use of government-provided currency as people switch to digital cash likely will also tend to increase the money multiplier somewhat.

OTHER EFFECTS OF DIGITAL CASH ON THE MONEY SUPPLY PROCESS   Table 13-2 also suggests that digital cash has some features that recommend its use relative to checks. For instance, in many circumstances making a digital-cash transaction over the Internet is likely to be more convenient and less costly than sending a check. Consequently, bank-issued digital cash may prove to be a substitute for some portion of transactions deposits. Any direct substitution of digital cash for transactions deposits, however, will affect only the composition of the quantity of money in circulation and will not directly influence the quantity of money.

In evaluating the effect of digital cash on the money supply process, we have defined the monetary base to include only government-issued money. Some economists argue that in the cybereconomy of the future, it will be more appropriate to include digital cash in the monetary base. Viewed from this perspective, the monetary base would include both government-issued and privately issued forms of money. In our discussion, however, we have followed the more traditional approach to defining the monetary base.

ONLINE BANKING AND THE MONEY SUPPLY PROCESS   What if online banking permits people to make payments directly from their checking accounts without having to write checks? Will this affect the money supply process?

By transferring funds electronically from their transactions deposit accounts via automated bill payment and other Internet-based online payment mechanisms, people simply avoid writing paper checks. Aside from possible resource-cost savings, the economic implications of the transactions are identical to those that arise if paper checks change hands, provided that the funds are redeposited in another depository institution. If normal redepositing occurs, then the only change is that the transactions that lie behind the normal deposit expansion process are mostly electronic in nature. Effects on balance sheets are unchanged. Thus, online transmission of checking funds has no fundamental effect on the money supply process.

This is true, however, only if all transactions deposits from which people can transmit funds online are maintained at depository institutions. If nondepository institutions find ways to issue transactions deposits via online mechanisms such as the Internet, then these deposits will also function as money, yet they will not be subject to reserve requirements. In this event, the money multiplier effectively will rise, potentially by a sizable amount. At present, any such activities are illegal; only traditional depository institutions have the power to issue transactions deposits accessible either by check or via the Internet. As we shall discuss in subsequent chapters, central banks around the globe are struggling to determine how to address efforts to get around this legal restriction. For you to understand why central banks struggle with this issue, however, we shall have to explain the nature of central banks. We turn to this subject in the next chapter.

> **MONEYXTRA!**
> **Online Case Study**
>
> To contemplate the monetary policy issues raised by variability in components of the M1 and M2 multipliers, go to the Chapter 13 Case Study, entitled "Sorting among the Multipliers." **http:// moneyxtra.swcollege.com**

> **6. How will electronic money affect the money supply process?**   The direct effect of adding privately supplied digital cash as a component of monetary aggregates will be an immediate increase in the size of the money multiplier linking the government-supplied monetary base to the quantity of money in circulation. This effect likely will be enhanced over time as people substitute digital cash for government-issued currency. The money multiplier will rise substantially if nondepository institutions find ways to issue transactions deposits via online banking mechanisms, but at this point such activities are illegal.

Chapter Summary

1. How a Change in Total Depository Institution Reserves Causes a Multiple Expansion of the Institutions' Deposits: An increase in total reserves at one depository institution induces it to expand its lending and its holdings of securities. The recipients of these funds deposit some or all of the funds in their transactions accounts at other depository institutions, which enables those institutions to increase their loans and security holdings as well. Hence, the initial increase in reserves causes a multiple expansion of transactions deposits throughout the banking system.

2. Federal Reserve Open Market Operations: These are Federal Reserve purchases or sales of securities. An open market purchase by the Fed increases total reserves of depository institutions. An open market sale by the Fed reduces total reserves of these institutions.

3. The Money Multiplier and Its Importance: The money multiplier is a number that sums up the total amount by which the quantity of money will change in response to a change in the monetary base. This number is important because Federal Reserve policies that alter the amount of total reserves in the banking system affect the size of the monetary base. Consequently, to know how much it should change total reserves to induce a given change in the quantity of money, the Federal Reserve needs to know the size of the money multiplier.

4. Factors That Influence the Money Multiplier: Any factor that affects the extent of the deposit expansion

process influences the size of the money multiplier. One important factor is the amount of currency that consumers and businesses wish to hold relative to their holdings of transactions deposits. Another is depository institutions' desired holdings of currency relative to transactions deposits. A third key factor is the required reserve ratio for transactions deposits that the Federal Reserve establishes. Finally, changes in banks' desired holdings of excess reserves influence the portion of new reserves that banks lend, thereby affecting the money multiplier.

5. The Credit Multiplier: This is a number that tells how much the total amount of credit that depository institutions extend by lending or buying securities will change in response to a change in the monetary base. Because credit expansion occurs alongside deposit expansion, the credit multiplier depends on the same basic factors that affect the money multiplier.

6. Electronic Money and the Money Supply Process: Including privately supplied digital cash as a component of monetary aggregates will have the direct effect of increasing the money multiplier relating the government-issued monetary base to the quantity of money in circulation. If people substitute digital cash for government-issued currency, this effect likely will tend to be enhanced over time. The money multiplier will rise considerably if nondepository institutions circumvent current legal restrictions on their ability to issue transactions deposits using online banking mechanisms.

Questions and Problems

(Answers to odd-numbered questions and problems may be found on the Web at **http://money.swcollege.com** under "Student Resources.")

1. Why is it that you cannot induce any net multiple deposit expansion in the banking system by buying a U.S. government security, yet the Federal Reserve can do so?

2. Suppose that the total liabilities of a depository institution are transactions deposits equal to $2,000 million. It has $1,650 million in loans and securities, and the required reserve ratio is 0.15. Does this institution hold any excess reserves? If so, how much?

3. A depository institution holds $150 million in required reserves and $10 million in excess reserves. Its remaining assets include $440 million in loans and $150 million in securities. If the institution's only liabilities are transactions deposits, what is the required reserve ratio?

4. Consider a world where there is no currency and depository institutions issue only transactions deposits and hold no excess reserves. The value of the money multiplier (for the M1 monetary aggregate) is equal to 4. What is the required reserve ratio? What is the total credit multiplier?

5. Explain in your own words why the money multiplier rises if consumers and businesses desire to hold less currency relative to their holdings of transactions deposits.

6. Explain why the money multiplier becomes larger if depository institutions wish to hold fewer excess reserves relative to transactions deposits that they issue.

7. Suppose that $c = 0.35$, $rr_D = 0.05$, and $e = 0.05$. In the absence of digital cash, and if banks issue only transactions deposits, what is the money multiplier for the M1 monetary aggregate? What is the total credit multiplier?

8. Show that the expression $\Delta TC = \Delta D - \Delta RR - \Delta ER$ can be rearranged into the total credit multiplier expression, $\Delta TC = [(1 - rr_D - e)/(c + rr_D + e)] \times \Delta MB$. [Hint: First write $\Delta TC = \Delta D - \Delta RR - \Delta ER = (1 - rr_D - e) \times \Delta D$. Then remember that the monetary base is $MB = C + TR = C + RR + ER = (c + rr_D + e) \times D$, so that a *change* in the monetary base is $\Delta MB = (c + rr_D + e) \times \Delta D$. Now solve this last equation for ΔD and substitute for ΔD in your expression for ΔTC.]

9. The money multiplier you encountered in this chapter relates most closely to the M1 definition of money. The M2 definition of money adds the total quantity of nontransactions, small-denomination savings and time deposits, N, to $M1 = C + D$, so $M2 = C + D + N$. Suppose that the public's desired holdings of nontransactions deposits, which are not subject to reserve requirements, are equal to n times their holdings of transactions deposits, so that $N = n \times D$. Under these assumptions, work out an expression for the money multiplier relating M2 to the monetary base.

10. Briefly review the ways increased use of smart cards and online accounts at financial institutions may affect the money supply process. Economists continue to evaluate whether digital cash is more likely to displace government-issued currency or bank-issued checking accounts. From the standpoint of controlling the total quantity of money in circulation, does it matter? Explain your reasoning.

11. Suppose that the required reserve ratio for transactions deposits is equal to 0.05. The public's desired ratio of government-issued currency to transactions deposits is equal to 0.4, and the public's desired ratio of digital cash to transactions deposits is equal to 0.1. The M1 definition of money includes digital cash. Depository institutions desire to hold no excess reserves. The Federal Reserve engages in a $2 million open market purchase of government securities from a dealer that has an account with a New York bank. Trace through the first three steps of the deposit expansion process that results, showing what happens to depository institution holdings of reserves and to the public's holdings of transactions deposits, government currency, and digital cash at each step. Based on your work, why does it make sense that the inclusion of digital cash increases the M1 money multiplier on net, even though at each stage of the deposit expansion process the public converts a portion of transactions deposits to digital cash outside the banking system? Explain your reasoning.

Before the Test

Test your understanding of the material covered in this chapter by taking the Chapter 13 interactive quiz at **http://money.swcollege.com**.

Online Application

In this chapter, you learned how monetary policy actions of the Federal Reserve induce changes in total deposits in the banking system. Now let's think about monetary policymaking in a world with online checking.

Internet URL: http://www.echeck.org/overview/what.html

Title: What Is the Echeck?

Navigation: First, go to the Echeck home page (**http://www.echeck.org**). Click on "Overview," and then click on "What Is Echeck?"

Application: Read the discussion, and then answer the following questions:

1. Are echecks substitutes for currency and coins, or are they substitutes for traditional paper checks? Does the answer to this question make a difference in how echecks are likely to feature in the money multiplier process?

2. Suppose that consumers and businesses widely adopt echeck technology. Would this affect the basic money multiplier model that we developed in this chapter? If so, how? If not, why not?

For Group Study and Analysis: Divide the class into groups. Have each group evaluate the likely effects of echeck adoption, as well as widespread adoption of other forms of electronic retail payment mechanisms, on both the money and credit multipliers. Re-form the class, and discuss the channels by which adoption of electronic moneys will potentially affect both multipliers.

Selected References and Further Reading

Berentsen, Aleksander. "Monetary Policy Implications of Digital Money." *Kyklos* 51 (1998): 89–117.

Bernkopf, Mark. "Electronic Cash and Monetary Policy." *FirstMonday* (Internet Journal at **http://www.firstmonday.dk**), 1996.

Bliss, Robert, and George Kaufman. "Bank Procyclicality, Credit Crunches, and Asymmetric Monetary Policy Effects: A Unifying Model." *Journal of Applied Finance,* Fall/Winter 2003, pp. 23–31.

Chami, Ralph, and Thomas Cosimano. "Monetary Policy with a Touch of Basel." Working Paper, International Monetary Fund and University of Notre Dame, 2003.

Humphrey, Thomas. "The Theory of Multiple Expansion of Deposits: What It Is and Whence It Came." Federal Reserve Bank of Richmond *Economic Review* 73 (March/April 1987): 3–11.

Kopecky, Kenneth, and David VanHoose. "Bank Capital Requirements and the Monetary Transmission Mechanism." *Journal of Macroeconomics* 26 (September 2004): 443–464.

McAndrews, James, and William Roberds. "The Economics of Check Float." Federal Reserve Bank of Atlanta *Economic Review,* Fourth Quarter 2000, pp. 17–27.

Osterberg, William, and James Thomson. "Bank Notes and Stored-Value Cards: Stepping Lightly into the Past." Federal Reserve Bank of Cleveland *Economic Commentary,* September 1, 1998.

Roberds, William. "What's Really New about the New Forms of Retail Payment?" Federal Reserve Bank of Atlanta *Economic Review,* First Quarter 1997, pp. 32–45.

Stevens, Ed. "Electronic Money and the Future of Central Banks." Federal Reserve Bank of Cleveland *Economic Commentary,* March 1, 2002.

Tanaka, Tatsuo. "Possible Economic Consequences of Digital Cash." *FirstMonday* (Internet Journal at **http://www.firstmonday.dk**), 1996.

Van den Heuvel, Skander. "Does Bank Capital Matter for Monetary Transmission?" Federal Reserve Bank of New York *Economic Policy Review,* May 2002, pp. 259–265.

MoneyXtra

Log on to the MoneyXtra Web site now (**http://moneyxtra.swcollege.com**) for additional learning resources such as practice quizzes, case studies, readings, and additional economic applications.

Central Banking and the Federal Reserve System

On August 14, 2003, cascading outages at power plants caused by a power-line failure in Ohio turned out lights from southern Michigan to parts of New York, including most of New York City. Suddenly, thousands of banks and other depository institutions faced a significant liquidity problem. In principle, these financial institutions had funds available to honor their obligations. Nevertheless, the collapse of the electricity grid had shut off power to thousands of bank branches, automated teller machines, and payment systems. With most of their computers unpowered and inoperable, depository institutions could not get access to funds, so they were unable to settle obligations to households, businesses, and other financial institutions across the nation.

The U.S. banking system did not grind to a complete stop, however. Financial gridlock was avoided in part because the Federal Reserve stood ready to serve as the banking system's lender of last resort. When depository institutions could not power up their computer systems to retrieve and transmit funds they owed to other parties on August 14 and 15, a number of them turned to the Federal Reserve for credit. Using emergency facilities provided by the Fed, the institutions arranged for Federal Reserve banks to transmit immediately borrowed funds—about twenty times more than usual—on their behalf. Once the institutions were able to access their systems and transfer funds electronically again, they repaid their loans to the Fed.

> ### Fundamental Issues
>
> 1. What were the first central banking institutions, and how did central banking initially develop in the United States?
>
> 2. Where did responsibilities for monetary and banking policies rest in the absence of a U.S. central bank in the nineteenth and early twentieth centuries?
>
> 3. What motivated Congress to establish the Federal Reserve System?
>
> 4. Why did Congress restructure the Federal Reserve in 1935?
>
> 5. Who makes the key policy decisions at the Federal Reserve?

The early-twentieth-century founders of the Federal Reserve could not have anticipated the financial ramifications of a power grid failure in the twenty-first century. Nevertheless, they did envision that situations might arise in which speedy policy reactions by a central banking institution could prevent financial collapse. In this chapter, you will learn more about this and other rationales for central banks in today's global economy.

The Central Banking Experience

The world's first central bank was the Swedish Sveriges Riksbank (known as the Risens Standers Bank until 1867), which was established in 1668. The Swedish parliament, the Riksdag, gave a special commission the responsibility of managing the Sveriges Riksbank,

On the Web

What induced Sweden to establish the world's first central bank? Learn more about the history of the Riksbank by going to its English-language home page at **http://www.riksbank.com**. Then click on "The Riksbank" and then click on "History."

which initially did not issue money. By 1701, however, the Riksbank had authority to issue "transfer notes" that basically functioned as a form of currency, and in 1789 the Riksdag established a National Debt Office that formally issued Swedish government currency. The Riksbank Act of 1897 made the Riksbank the only legal issuer of Swedish currency.

The second central bank was the Bank of England, which the English Parliament established in 1694. Parliament gave the Bank of England the power to issue currency notes redeemable in silver, and these notes circulated alongside notes issued by the government and private finance companies.

Expanding the Central Bank Population

As late as 1800, the Riksbank and the Bank of England were the only central banks. Indeed, the total number of central banks worldwide remained a single digit as late as 1873. Figure 14-1 shows that the number of central banks increased significantly, beginning in the late nineteenth century and especially during the latter part of the twentieth century. A portion of this growth stemmed from the establishment of central banks by former colonial states that achieved independence and developed their own currencies.

THE EUROPEAN SYSTEM OF CENTRAL BANKS In January 1999, the central banks of eleven European nations—Austria, Belgium, Finland, France, Germany, Ireland, Italy, Luxembourg, the Netherlands, Portugal, and Spain—formed the *European System of Central Banks.* Almost two years later, the Bank of Greece joined the system. The six-member executive board for this system is based at the *European Central Bank (ECB),* the hub of the European System of Central Banks located in Frankfurt, Germany. All final operating and policy decisions for the system, however, ultimately must be approved by an eighteen-member governing council composed of the executive board in Frankfurt and the governors of the twelve national central banks. Thus, each member nation plays a role in determining the policies of the European Central Bank.

This combination of centralized and decentralized decision making has its roots on the other side of the Atlantic Ocean, where another initially loose federation of states wrestled

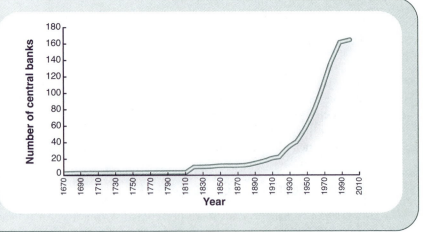

FIGURE 14-1
The Number of Central Banking Institutions, 1670 to the Present.

The twentieth century witnessed considerable growth in the number of central banks.

SOURCES: Forrest Capie, Charles Goodhart, and Norbert Schnadt, "The Development of Central Banking," in Capie et al., eds., *The Future of Central Banking: The Tercentenary Symposium of the Bank of England* (Cambridge: Cambridge University Press, 1994), pp. 1–231; and authors' estimates.

with money and banking problems for well over a century before settling on a unique central banking system. Ironically, this arrangement, the U.S. Federal Reserve System, was constructed in the early twentieth century following years of careful study of European central banking institutions. Hence, there is a circularity in the history of central banking institutions, with the early European experience forming the basis for U.S. central banking, which in turn has served as a model for today's European institutional structure.

The Origins of U.S. Central Banking, 1791–1836

Today, U.S. residents take for granted that the Federal Reserve is responsible for managing the nation's monetary affairs. Yet the Federal Reserve has been the U.S. central banking institution for only a little over a third of the nation's history. During nearly half of the U.S. republic's existence, there was no formal central bank. Consequently, you must first understand the historical background that led to the creation and development of the Fed.

Because the original thirteen states that composed the United States were settled mainly by English immigrants, their customs and legal precedents largely reflected those of England. These states, therefore, looked to British practices as a guide to developing banking institutions for the federal government that they initiated in 1791. The center of British arrangements was the Bank of England, which Parliament had established in 1694. This central bank was the main depository of the British government and also served as a key lender to the government, particularly during times of war. Ultimately, the Bank of England also became a central depository for other private banks of the British Empire. From this position the Bank of England effectively was able to establish and enforce policies that other banks felt obliged to follow.

THE BANK OF NORTH AMERICA   In 1781, when Robert Morris lobbied the Continental Congress to approve a **charter** (official banking license) for the Bank of North America, he and his supporters regarded the Bank of England as an example to emulate. Morris based many features of the charter of the Bank of North America on the original charter of the Bank of England. He and others who placed their funds in the Bank of North America also had high hopes that it might emerge as a central bank.

Charter: A governmental license to open and operate a bank.

Although the Bank of North America generally was conservatively managed and successful, it never rose to the stature of a central bank for several reasons. One was that the U.S. banking and financial systems were very small compared with those of the British Empire. Another was that U.S. financial markets were very decentralized. Finally, although the Continental Congress granted the Bank of North America a charter, it did not give the bank any special powers beyond those of the few other state-chartered banks of the time.

THE FIRST BANK OF THE UNITED STATES   When Alexander Hamilton, the new nation's first Treasury secretary, contemplated the establishment of the first U.S. central bank, he reviewed the history of the Bank of North America. Hamilton's ambition, however, was for the United States to have a central bank that would rival the Bank of England in power and influence. Toward this end, Hamilton convinced the U.S. Congress to establish a Bank of the United States modeled very much along the lines of the Bank of England.

In 1791, Congress granted the First Bank of the United States a twenty-year federal charter and authorized the U.S. Treasury to purchase a fixed amount of the First Bank's equity shares and to hold deposits at the First Bank. It also authorized the First Bank to open branches throughout the nation and to issue its own currency notes that the federal government would accept as payments for internal taxes, foreign tariffs, and fees for government services.

During its twenty years of existence, the First Bank generally was a stable and profitable institution. Nevertheless, Congress did not renew its charter in 1811, largely because of concerns that foreigners had acquired too many of its shares and that the First Bank might accumulate sufficient resources to influence the affairs of state banks. Indeed, by 1810 the directors of the First Bank had begun to recognize that they could reduce the overall volume of credit in the banking system by requesting that state banks redeem their notes with the gold reserves that backed those notes. In a sense this was the early-nineteenth-century equivalent of an open market sale by today's Fed, as discussed in Chapter 13. Although Hamilton had hoped that the First Bank would ultimately develop such financial power, Congress was unwilling to let the First Bank develop into a central banking institution capable of exercising such authority over the nation's banking and monetary affairs.

THE SECOND BANK OF THE UNITED STATES Just as the charter of the First Bank of the United States expired, the nation became embroiled in several disputes with Britain. During the resulting War of 1812, the U.S. Treasury found itself without an agent to assist it in raising funds to finance its wartime expenditures. The Treasury also lacked a central depository for the funds that it was able to raise. Furthermore, a significant period of inflation occurred after the conclusion of the war. These events together convinced President James Madison to recommend that Congress grant a federal charter to a Second Bank of the United States. Congress authorized a charter that would span the period 1816–1836. It also modeled the Second Bank closely upon the structure of the First Bank. The nation now seemed ready for a central banking institution.

By 1823, when Nicholas Biddle became the Second Bank's president, the bank was well on the way to becoming such an institution. In that year the Second Bank held almost half of all the specie (monetary gold and silver) in the nation. Like the First Bank, it had found that it could influence national credit conditions by choosing when and to what extent to redeem state bank notes for the specie that backed them. Under Biddle's direction, the Second Bank liked to think of itself as a benevolent institution, or in Biddle's own words, "the enemy of none, but the common friend of all."

Nevertheless, in 1836, the Second Bank officially closed its doors—political missteps by Biddle and the vehement opposition of President Andrew Jackson had led to its demise.

> **1. What were the first central banking institutions, and how did central banking initially develop in the United States?** The world's first central banks were in Sweden and England. Subsequently, other central banks were established in Europe, where today several nations have formed the European System of Central Banks. Although neither the First nor the Second Bank of the United States possessed the extensive monetary policy or bank regulatory powers of today's Federal Reserve, both in various respects represented the first central banking institutions of the United States. Both institutions had the capability to affect the rest of the U.S. banking system, and the Second Bank used this capability at various times.

Policy and Politics without a Central Bank, 1837–1912

Following the demise of the Second Bank of the United States, the U.S. Treasury again found itself without a central financial agent. It also was forced to find state-chartered banks with which to deposit its funds. The state banks that it chose became known as "pet banks," because banks that the Treasury did not select felt slighted.

THE FREE-BANKING PERIOD   Whether or not they were "pets," state banks faced neither federally chartered competition nor federal regulation for over two decades after the closure of the Second Bank. In a number of states, however, the degree of loan and deposit market rivalry among state-chartered banks actually increased with the advent of "free banking." As discussed in Chapter 2, the free-banking period lasted until the Civil War. During this interval, each state had its own banking rules, and many states permitted relatively open competition among banks.

What did the U.S. Treasury do during this period without the assistance of a central banking institution? Essentially, after several years of trial and error the Treasury figured out how to get along without a central bank. By 1846 an "Independent Treasury System" was in operation. Under this system, the Treasury Department issued notes that were close substitutes for money, and in 1847 it conducted the first open market operation in U.S. history when it repurchased outstanding securities that it had used to help finance the Mexican War (1846–1848). The Treasury made several more repurchases of outstanding securities during the next several years. Although the main justification was to reduce the size of the Treasury's outstanding debt, the Treasury tried to time several of its open market purchases during the late 1840s and early 1850s to stabilize national money and credit conditions.

In the autumn of 1857, however, a major banking panic occurred. Although this episode was muted and short-lived by the standards of some later financial crises, the Treasury's failure to offset the effects of the panic and the subsequent economic downturn had important political repercussions.

THE CIVIL WAR, GREENBACKS, AND NATIONAL BANKING   Most modern historians identify 1857 as the point at which the nation's steady drift toward sectionalism switched to a rushing current pushing toward violent hostility. In December 1860, South Carolina announced its secession from the United States, and within a few short months, other southern states had joined it in forming the Confederacy. By the middle of April 1861, Fort Sumter had fallen and the Civil War had begun. At this point, as we discussed in Chapter 2, the federal government issued an insignificant portion of the money in circulation.

The National Banking Act of 1863 encouraged most existing state banks to switch to new federal charters to qualify as depositories of Treasury funds. This legislation also established the first system of national reserve requirements. The 1865 amendment to the law adding a tax on the notes issued by state-chartered banks encouraged many state banks to switch to national charters and also induced a number of banks to offer more demand deposits instead of issuing notes. In these respects the National Banking Act laid the foundation for today's Federal Reserve System and transactions-deposit-based banking system even though the birth of the Federal Reserve was still a half-century in the future.

PANIC AND RESUMPTION OF THE GOLD STANDARD   By 1866, government-issued currency accounted for a third of the quantity of money in circulation in the United States. Yet the nation had no central banking institution to manage its monetary affairs. Again, it was up to the U.S. Treasury to do the job.

In 1873 a severe panic struck the nation's banking and financial markets. This event followed a precipitous decline in the quantities of money and credit that the Treasury made little effort to offset. The magnitude of the panic was significant and added fuel to a great national debate over what to do about the Greenbacks still in circulation. When Congress authorized the creation of Greenbacks—which were not backed by gold—during the Civil War (see Chapter 2), it had promised to remove them from circulation after the war ended. But to citizens of western and southern states, this would mean a further reduction in the amounts of money and credit available for their use. Many citizens of these states began a movement to keep the Greenbacks in circulation, and some even argued for increasing the number of Greenbacks.

Despite a loss at the polls in 1874 that stemmed in part from their stand in favor of redeeming the Greenbacks and returning to a full gold standard, an outgoing Republican congressional majority passed the *Resumption Act of 1875*. This law committed the federal government to return to a full gold standard by 1879. After the 1876 election returned the Republicans to power, the Greenback movement splintered.

Free silver: A late-nineteenth-century idea for unlimited coinage of silver to meet the monetary needs of a growing U.S. economy.

POPULISM, FREE SILVER, AND BIMETALISM   Although the Greenback movement had lost the battle, its members continued the fight to increase the quantity of money in circulation. A new political movement known as populism arose and ultimately led to the formation of the Populist Party in 1892. Many adherents to this movement adopted a new monetary proposal: **free silver,** or the unlimited coinage of silver as needed by the expanding U.S. economy. The idea was to allow the quantities of money and credit to grow through *bimetalism*. As discussed in Chapter 1, this is the simultaneous use of gold and silver as commodity standards.

According to the free silver proponents, Congress had committed the "Crime of 1873" by passing a law that ended the legal coinage of silver dollars. By 1890, the populist and free silver forces had made enough of an impression on Republican gold-standard adherents that the Republicans gave in and passed the *Sherman Silver Act,* which authorized the Treasury to purchase silver and to issue dollars backed by silver.

The timing turned out to be bad, however. In 1893 another banking panic occurred. Gold's value rose, and the market price of silver fell. To reaffirm its commitment to gold as the fundamental basis of the U.S. monetary system, Congress immediately repealed the Sherman Silver Act.

This set the stage for the final showdown over bimetalism. In a speech during the presidential campaign of 1896, Democratic candidate William Jennings Bryan accused William McKinley, the Republican candidate and a gold-standard proponent, of attempting to crush working people under the weight of the gold standard. In the most famous line from this speech, Bryan adopted a biblical allusion and declared, "You shall not press down upon the brow of labor this cross of thorns, you shall not crucify mankind upon a cross of gold." Nevertheless, Bryan lost this election, which was just one of his three failed attempts at the presidency.

> **2. Where did responsibilities for monetary and banking policies rest in the absence of a U.S. central bank in the nineteenth and early twentieth centuries?**   Until the Civil War, individual states determined their own banking policies. After the Civil War, the federal government established the national banking system and assumed a larger role in determining policies that affected banks. During this period with no central banking institution, the U.S. Treasury functioned as the nation's monetary policy institution.

PRELUDE TO THE FEDERAL RESERVE   After the Panic of 1893, which in many respects was even worse than the 1873 panic, even those who favored the gold standard began to believe that some type of monetary reform might be in order. This belief was reinforced in

1907 when yet another financial panic occurred. A conglomerate corporation known as Knickerbocker Trust attempted to corner stock in a company called United Copper. When its effort failed, Knickerbocker's own stock price collapsed. This convinced many stock traders on Wall Street that the stocks of other conglomerates would also plummet. In what economists call a *self-fulfilling* prophecy, the traders' simultaneous efforts to sell off shares in these companies *caused* the market prices of their stocks to fall.

Ultimately, Treasury Secretary George Cortelyou worked out a combined public and private "bailout" of several Wall Street banks and trusts. Cortelyou entrusted $25 million in public funds to the private use of J. P. Morgan, who made loans to rescue the most financially healthy institutions on Wall Street. Morgan also arranged for $25 million in private funds to be used for further lending to prop up these institutions, and the panic finally ended.

After the Panic of 1907 ended, President Theodore Roosevelt and members of Congress agreed that the nation should consider the creation of some type of central bank. The following year, Congress passed the *Aldrich-Vreeland Act,* which gave the Treasury secretary emergency powers to issue currency in the event of an emerging crisis that threatened to become a more widespread panic. The Aldrich-Vreeland Act also established a National Monetary Commission that was charged with developing a concrete plan for a U.S. central bank. Senator Nelson Aldrich led this commission, and the plan that it developed served as the basis for a bill that was pieced together in 1911 by Senators Carter Glass and Robert Owen. This bill became the *Federal Reserve Act of 1913.*

Origins and Evolution of the Fed

The Federal Reserve Act created the *Federal Reserve System* of central banking institutions. It called for this system to be supervised by a *Federal Reserve Board* composed of the Treasury secretary, the comptroller of the currency, and five additional members appointed by the president and confirmed by the Senate to ten-year terms. The Federal Reserve System, which today we often call the "Fed," was a kind of cooperative arrangement linking consumers, businesses, banks, and the federal government. At the heart of the system were twelve **Federal Reserve banks,** which were located in major cities in geographic regions called **Federal Reserve districts.** A private bank could opt to join the system by purchasing ownership shares in the Federal Reserve bank in its district. This would entitle it to some say in the selection of the board of directors of the Federal Reserve bank and to check-clearing services and other banking services that the district bank would provide.

To keep the Fed from being simply a "bankers' club," however, Congress required that the majority of each Federal Reserve bank's board of directors be composed of individuals representing interests of consumers and nonfinancial businesses. Furthermore, Congress placed the Federal Reserve Board in Washington, D.C, expressly to supervise the activities of the system of Federal Reserve banks.

Congress charged the Fed with three tasks:

1. To develop and supervise the distribution of a national currency, which the Fed was to stand ready to supply in quantities necessary to help avert budding financial panics.

2. To establish a nationally coordinated system of check-clearing and collection services.

3. To process the federal government's financial accounts and to serve as the central depository for government funds.

MONEYXTRA!
Another Perspective

To learn how the Federal Reserve assists the federal government in its financial affairs, go to the Chapter 14 reading, entitled "The Federal Reserve Banks as Fiscal Agents and Depositories of the United States," by Paula Hillery and Stephen Thompson of the Board of Governors of the Federal Reserve System. **http://moneyxtra.swcollege.com**

Federal Reserve banks: The twelve central banking institutions that oversee regional activities of the Federal Reserve System.

Federal Reserve districts: The twelve geographic regions of the Federal Reserve System.

> ### 3. What motivated Congress to establish the Federal Reserve System?
> The key reason that Congress created the Federal Reserve System was to ensure that a central bank would be available to provide monetary resources in sufficient amounts to avert potential banking and financial panics. Another congressional objective was to provide an institution that could centralize the clearing of payments across the nation. Congress also wanted the government to have a central depository for its funds.

The Early Fed, 1913–1935

As the Federal Reserve began its operations, it was constrained in two fundamental ways. First, the Federal Reserve Act seemed to be very specific about how the Fed could try to avert panics by lending to endangered institutions. The legislation required the Fed to lend funds through a specific mechanism called *rediscounting*. To borrow from a Federal Reserve bank, a private bank that was a Federal Reserve System member would have to post collateral in the form of discount bonds with low default risk. The Fed then would lend by purchasing these bonds at a further discount, hence "rediscounting" the bonds. The percentage of the additional discount was the Fed's **discount rate,** or the effective interest rate that the Fed would charge for its loan to the bank.

Discount rate: The rate of interest that the Federal Reserve charges to lend to a depository institution.

A second constraint stemmed from something important that the Federal Reserve Act *failed* to spell out in detail, namely, how powers were to be distributed *within* the Federal Reserve System. Although the legislation gave the Federal Reserve Board supervisory functions within the system, it did not give the Board the power to dictate policies to the individual Federal Reserve banks. The Board at best could try to muster systemwide coordination. Such efforts were not always successful, and much of the time the Federal Reserve banks conducted their own regional policies.

THE HESITANT FED   The outbreak of World War I in 1914 presented an immediate complication for the Fed. The war severely strained international flows of gold and currencies and threatened the stability of U.S. financial markets. Under the emergency provision of the Aldrich-Vreeland Act, Treasury Secretary William McAdoo, who was also a Federal Reserve Board member, arranged for the national and state banks to issue currency to help sustain the quantities of money and credit. McAdoo also insisted that the Federal Reserve purchase Treasury securities at very low yields. By the conclusion of hostilities in late 1918, the U.S. money stock had risen by about 70 percent. During the war other Federal Reserve Board members objected to McAdoo's policies, and he responded by threatening to invoke further emergency Treasury powers, including taking full control of all banking reserves. This gave the other Board members little choice but to acquiesce.

After the war the center of power within the Federal Reserve System shifted from the Treasury to the Federal Reserve bank presidents. This occurred largely through the efforts of Benjamin Strong, the president of the Federal Reserve Bank of New York. He had numerous political friends and important connections with J. P. Morgan and other financial leaders. Strong initiated the Fed's first open market operations, which led to conflicts with Board members who objected to this policy innovation. Nevertheless, Strong emerged as the dominant figure in the Federal Reserve System until he died in 1928. In October of the following year, the stock market crashed. In the midst of the continuing power vacuum created by Strong's death, no leading figure appeared at the Fed to coordinate a response to the crisis.

THE GREAT DEPRESSION AND REFORM OF THE FED   The Fed's initial response to the panic of late 1929 was to release more reserves into the banking system. As bank failures multiplied, however, Board members hesitated to bail out banks that they viewed as insolvent rather than simply illiquid. In retrospect, it is easy to see that they missed the point: the entire banking system had become illiquid, and only the Fed could have provided the liquidity that was necessary. In the end the Fed failed in this fundamental task that Congress had given it in 1913.

By 1933, a third of all the commercial banks in the United States had failed. Furthermore, the quantity of money had declined by about a third. The nation's banking and monetary system shrank, and the nation's economic activity shrank as well. The banking crisis reinforced the business downturn, and the economic decline reinforced the financial collapse. The nation had fallen into what we now call the *Great Depression* of the 1930s.

Restructuring the Fed   In the area of money and banking arrangements, Congress responded to the Great Depression in two ways. First, it passed the Glass-Steagall Act and other related banking legislation that we discussed in Chapter 11. Second, Congress passed the *Banking Act of 1935*. In many respects this legislation really amounted to a new "Federal Reserve Act," because it fundamentally restructured the Federal Reserve System.

A key provision of the Banking Act of 1935 was the centralization of internal Fed authority in Washington, D.C. But Congress no longer trusted the Federal Reserve Board as specified in the original Federal Reserve Act. Instead, Congress replaced that body with a new seven-member **Board of Governors of the Federal Reserve System.** Congress designated the Board of Governors as the key policymaking body within the Fed. To shield the Board from executive branch pressures, Congress excluded the Treasury secretary and the comptroller of the currency from Board governor positions. Instead, Congress required that the president appoint and that the Senate confirm all seven governors. It also specified that no more than four of the seven governors could belong to a single political party. Congress also lengthened the term of each governor to fourteen years and made the terms overlap so that the president would have the opportunity to appoint a new governor every two years.

New Lines of Authority   In a further effort to centralize internal Fed policymaking authority, the 1935 legislation created the offices of chair and vice chair of the Board of Governors. These offices would be held by governors appointed by the president to four-year renewable terms. The new law gave the chair, the vice chair, and the remainder of the Board of Governors the authority to determine reserve requirements within ranges established by the law. It also gave the Board of Governors the authority to approve the discount rates set by the Federal Reserve banks.

Finally, the Banking Act of 1935 established the **Federal Open Market Committee (FOMC),** which is composed of the seven governors and five of the twelve Federal Reserve bank presidents. Congress gave the FOMC the authority to determine the strategies and tactics of the Fed's open market operations. As we discuss later in this chapter, the FOMC is the key day-to-day policymaking authority within today's Federal Reserve System.

LESSONS FOR EUROPE?   Today's European System of Central Banks (ESCB) clearly regards the U.S. Federal Reserve System as something of a "role model." The ESCB's executive board of six individuals based in Frankfurt is analogous to the Fed's Board of Governors in Washington, and its governing council is analogous to the Fed's Federal Open Market Committee.

Nevertheless, in some respects the ESCB has more in common with the pre-1935 Federal Reserve System than with today's Fed. The twelve national central bank governors have a

Board of Governors of the Federal Reserve System: A group of seven individuals appointed by the president and confirmed by the Senate that, under the terms of the Banking Act of 1935, has key policymaking responsibilities within the Federal Reserve System.

Federal Open Market Committee (FOMC): A group composed of the seven governors and five of the twelve Federal Reserve bank presidents that determines how to conduct the Fed's open market operations.

On the Web

How is the European System of Central Banks structured? Learn more about this central banking system by going to the European Central Bank's home page at **http://www.ecb.int** and then clicking on "The European Central Bank."

majority in the ESCB's eighteen-member governing council, and a coalition of ten of these governors could potentially overrule the executive board, effectively dictating policy for the ESCB as a whole. Some observers worry that in the event of a major economic downturn, competing regional interests could lead to a policy paralysis at the ESCB analogous to the inaction of the Fed in the 1930s.

Like the pre-1935 Federal Reserve Board, the European Central Bank in Frankfurt also has no lender-of-last-resort authority. This power is held by the individual central banks or, in some instances, by national banking supervisors. Thus, a regional banking panic in Europe would have to be addressed by national authorities, and their actions might potentially be in conflict with the broader, Europe-wide goals of the European Central Bank.

For these reasons, a number of economists have contended that it is already time for the countries in the European Monetary Union to reform their central banking system. In their view, these nations have failed to take into account the hard lesson that the United States learned in the 1930s, which is that too much decentralization can be a mistake. (The European Monetary Union is also learning that efforts by its monetary policymakers to be secretive may not pay off; see the *Global Focus: The European Central Bank Tries to Get By with a Press Conference and a List.*)

4. Why did Congress restructure the Federal Reserve in 1935? A key defect of the original Federal Reserve Act of 1913 was that it did not spell out the lines of authority for Fed policymaking. This caused internal dissension within the Fed that complicated its ability to respond to crises such as the 1929 stock market crash and the subsequent financial panics. Congress also perceived that including Treasury officials on the Federal Reserve Board gave the executive branch of the federal government too much clout, so it sought to reduce the extent of the Treasury's influence on internal Fed policymaking.

GLOBAL

Focus

The European Central Bank Tries to Get By with a Press Conference and a List

The Federal Reserve releases information about major policy actions the same day that they are undertaken by Fed officials. The Fed also publishes detailed minutes of formal monetary policy deliberations within a few weeks after officials reach decisions on policy actions.

In contrast, the European Central Bank (ECB) *never* releases information about the substance of internal deliberations among its officials. Instead, the president of the ECB holds a press conference within an hour after ECB officials have reached decisions about policy actions, but typically the president is very vague about the rationales for policy actions. This lack of communication has complicated individuals' and businesses' efforts to better understand and predict monetary policy actions. Many economists have found evidence that uncertainty about the ECB's mone-

tary policies tends to make the demand for and supply of bonds more variable. As a consequence, interest rates and bond prices may be more volatile within the European Monetary Union than they would be if ECB officials were more open about their policymaking.

FOR CRITICAL ANALYSIS: Why do you suppose that the ECB recently began releasing a list of key policy decisions in advance of each press conference its president conducts?

The Evolution of the Modern Fed

In many respects the Banking Act of 1935 created a new institution. It created new offices with clearly defined responsibilities, and it centered the Fed's powers in the Board of Governors and its chair. But the legislation still left many points unaddressed, including the proper relationship between the Fed and the Treasury, the full extent of the chair's authority, and the ultimate economic goals that the Fed should pursue. Much of the Fed's history since 1935 reflects its efforts to deal with these issues.

THE FED'S FIGHT FOR INDEPENDENCE   The first leader of the new Federal Reserve System was a former Utah banker named Marriner Eccles. President Franklin Roosevelt appointed Eccles to the original Federal Reserve Board in 1934, and Eccles was instrumental in helping design and promote the reforms that Congress adopted in the Banking Act of 1935. He then served as chair of the Board of Governors until 1948. The original Federal Reserve Board building at 21st and C Streets in Washington, D.C., now bears his name because later Fed insiders credited Eccles with rescuing the Fed from "disgrace" following its performance between 1929 and 1933.

Working for the U.S. Treasury   During most of Eccles's time as chair, however, the Federal Reserve essentially functioned as an unofficial unit of the Treasury Department. This was particularly true during World War II, when the Fed's open market operations were geared toward maintaining high and stable prices for Treasury securities to assist the government's efforts to raise the funds needed to finance wartime expenditures. The Fed did this by buying and selling securities as needed to "peg" Treasury bill (T-bill) yields at relatively low levels.

The Fight for Fed Independence   After World War II ended, the Treasury pressured the Fed to continue this policy. The Fed, however, had become convinced that inflation, which had begun to heat up with the outbreak of the Korean conflict, would get out of control if it continued pegging T-bill yields. Behind the scenes, Fed officials successfully negotiated a settlement with the Treasury, which President Harry Truman grudgingly approved in 1951. This settlement is now called the **Federal Reserve–Treasury Accord,** or more simply "the Accord." The Accord was a joint agreement that the Fed could minimize the extent to which it "monetized" the public debt by purchasing securities as needed to keep market yields low.

Henceforth, the Fed has regarded itself as an *independent* institution *within* the government. Later presidents and Congresses would test the Fed's self-interpretation of its proper role "within the government."

Federal Reserve–Treasury Accord: A 1951 agreement that dissociated the Fed from a previous policy of pegging Treasury bill rates at artificially low levels.

"LEANING AGAINST THE WIND"   In 1953 William McChesney Martin, one of the chief negotiators of the Accord, was appointed Board chair—a position he would hold until 1970. Shortly after the beginning of his long tenure, Martin announced that the Fed's purpose "is to lean against the winds of deflation or inflation, whichever way they are blowing." Later he offered an alternative description of the Fed's job of containing inflationary pressures caused by short-term overexpansion of the economy: the Fed's role, he said, "is to take away the punch bowl just when the party gets going."

During much of Martin's time at the helm, the Fed sought to stabilize the level of **free reserves,** or the difference between the total amount of excess reserves and the total quantity of reserves borrowed from the Fed's discount window. The idea behind this policy was that if banks' holdings of excess reserves were high relative to their borrowings from the Fed, then it would be easier for them to lend. In contrast, if banks were short on excess reserves relative to

Free reserves: Total excess reserves at depository institutions minus the total amount of reserves that depository institutions have borrowed from the Fed.

reserves that they owed the Fed, their ability to extend new loans to consumers and businesses would be more contained. Hence, conducting open market operations with an aim to keeping the amount of free reserves relatively stable would ensure that credit conditions would be neither too loose nor too tight.

The growing U.S. involvement in the Vietnam conflict (1964–1973) complicated the Fed's policymaking through the end of the 1960s. When President Lyndon Johnson decided in 1965 to expand the U.S. commitment of ground forces to Vietnam without increasing taxes to pay the expenses, the Fed faced renewed pressures from the president and the Treasury to keep U.S. Treasury bond yields low. At one point President Johnson summoned Martin to his Texas ranch and lectured him on the dangers of raising interest rates.

By 1968, President Johnson had decided that additional taxes would be required to fund the military expenses that the government was incurring. But by then the inflation rate had reached 5 percent, which at that time in the United States was perceived as relatively high. In 1969, when Richard Nixon assumed the presidency, the inflation rate exceeded 6 percent.

THE TECHNOCRATIC FED   In 1970 President Nixon appointed a new Fed chair, Arthur Burns, a Columbia University economics professor and former adviser to President Dwight Eisenhower. Under Burns, the Federal Reserve attempted to take a more scientific approach to policymaking. The Board of Governors assigned a number of staff economists the task of developing reliable measures of monetary aggregates. Then it systematically began to frame its policymaking within the perspective of the likely effects on such aggregates as M1 and M2.

During Martin's term at the Fed, banks had begun to lend reserves in the federal funds market. By the time Burns became the Fed chief, the federal funds rate had become a widely recognized indicator of credit market conditions. A rise in the federal funds rate indicated a tightening of credit market conditions, while a fall in the federal funds rate signaled a loosening. Under Burns, however, the Fed began to use the federal funds rate as more than a policy indicator. Indeed, the Fed began to tailor its open market operations to move the federal funds rate to levels that it felt were consistent with its goals for magnitudes of the monetary aggregates. Although the Fed continued to pay close attention to the effects that its policies had on the spectrum of interest rates on other financial instruments, for the first time it also began to pay attention to the effects on the quantity of money.

Early in Burns's tenure at the Fed, the link between the dollar and gold was broken. In August 1971, President Nixon formally announced the end of the gold standard that had existed—at least officially—during most years since 1879. Although the United States had suspended its formal adherence to the gold standard during crises such as the Great Depression, this announcement finally severed entirely the tie between money and gold. Burns and other Fed officials now found themselves truly charged with anchoring the nation's currency system solely to confidence in the Fed's policymaking. This, to Burns and the Fed, was a key rationale for trying to aim Fed policies at stabilizing monetary aggregates as well as credit market conditions.

INFLATION AND MONETARY TARGETING   Despite Burns's effort to cultivate a reputation as an "inflation fighter" during his eight-year stint as Board chair, the inflation rate was higher, at 8 percent, when he completed his second term. In addition, suspicions mounted that during President Nixon's 1972 reelection campaign Burns might have conspired explicitly or implicitly to stimulate the economy through loosened Fed policies. This alleged effort to help Nixon's reelection prospects, critics charged, added further to inflationary pressures caused in large measure by sharp rises in oil prices that occurred during and after 1973.

In 1978 President Jimmy Carter appointed G. William Miller as the new chair of the Fed's Board of Governors. During Miller's brief tenure of seventeen months, the inflation rate rose into double digits. In July 1979, Miller became the Treasury secretary. President Carter then appointed Paul Volcker, a long-time Fed insider and then president of the Federal Reserve Bank of New York, as the new Fed chief.

Within three months after assuming the top job at the Fed, Volcker had agreed to a new approach to monetary policy. Under the new approach, the Fed would attempt to stabilize the growth of the monetary aggregates while de-emphasizing interest rate stability. The result, not surprisingly, was that interest rates became much more volatile. What was a surprise was that the monetary aggregates actually became more variable as well. Nevertheless, on net interest rates rose and money growth slowed. Inflation was contained.

In 1982 the Fed discontinued its experiment with trying to stabilize the monetary aggregates. Its rationale was that the relationship between the aggregates and economic activity had broken down. Indeed, as we shall discuss in Chapter 19, this did occur. Fed critics, however, charged that the Fed had never really made an honest effort to contain monetary variability. They viewed the abandonment of the new approach as further evidence that the Fed was not serious about controlling the monetary aggregates.

TODAY'S MIDDLE-OF-THE-ROAD FED Since 1987, the Fed has adopted yet another approach to conducting monetary policy: it attempts to stabilize the federal funds rate at a target value. In this respect, the policymaking of today's Fed is similar to the approach of the Fed under Arthur Burns. The Fed has been more successful in containing inflation in recent years, however. We shall examine recent experience with interest rate targeting in Chapter 21.

Since 1987 Alan Greenspan has been chair of the Fed's Board of Governors. To date, fewer complications have arisen during Greenspan's time in this position than occurred under several of his predecessors. Yet, within the Fed, there have been some significant changes in the way policies are formulated and implemented, which we shall also discuss in Chapter 21.

The Structure of the Fed

When Congress created the Federal Reserve in 1913 and revamped its structure in 1935, it was very mindful of traditional U.S. suspicions of the motives of central bankers and distrust of centralized authority. For this reason, Congress sought to construct a decentralized central banking institution that would be responsive to the concerns of U.S. citizens. At the same time, however, Congress recognized that a central bank should be operated by people who possess essential levels of competence in banking and finance. This meant that Congress needed to find a way to ensure that leaders of the Federal Reserve had banking and monetary policy experience. The somewhat convoluted structure of the Federal Reserve System reflects congressional efforts to trade off these conflicting objectives.

The Board of Governors

The seven Fed governors have several responsibilities. As noted above, the governors must authorize any discount rate change, and they also have the authority to set required reserve ratios within ranges established by law. In addition, the Board has oversight authority over the Federal Reserve district banks.

As noted in Chapter 11, the Fed is a key banking regulator charged with examining and supervising all state-chartered commercial banks that are members of the Federal Reserve

On the Web

What is going on at the Fed? Find a wealth of information about the Fed on the Internet, courtesy of the Fed itself. Following are Internet home page addresses for the Fed's Board of Governors and all twelve Federal Reserve banks:

Federal Reserve Source	Internet URL
Board of Governors	http://federalreserve.gov
Federal Reserve Bank of Atlanta	http://www.frbatlanta.org
Federal Reserve Bank of Boston	http://www.bos.frb.org
Federal Reserve Bank of Chicago	http://www.chicagofed.org
Federal Reserve Bank of Cleveland	http://www.clevelandfed.org
Federal Reserve Bank of Dallas	http://www.dallasfed.org
Federal Reserve Bank of Kansas City	http://www.kc.frb.org
Federal Reserve Bank of Minneapolis	http://minneapolisfed.org
Federal Reserve Bank of New York	http://www.ny.frb.org
Federal Reserve Bank of Philadelphia	http://www.phil.frb.org
Federal Reserve Bank of Richmond	http://www.richmondfed.org
Federal Reserve Bank of San Francisco	http://www.frbsf.org
Federal Reserve Bank of St. Louis	http://www.stlouisfed.org

System. The Fed also regulates the activities of financial holding companies and approves or disapproves proposed depository institution mergers, which invariably entail changes in the structure of a financial holding company.

The various consumer protection laws discussed in Chapter 12 also require enforcement actions by the Board of Governors. Consequently, the Board issues regulations intended to induce depository institutions to comply with the provisions of these laws.

All seven Board governors are automatic members of the twelve-member Federal Open Market Committee. The FOMC sets policy for the Fed's open market operations, so the numerical superiority of the Board relative to the other FOMC members gives the Board considerable authority over the day-to-day conduct of monetary policy. The FOMC also oversees Fed trading in foreign exchange markets, so the Board also has major influence over the Fed's international operations. (The Fed's Board of Governors incurs considerable expenses in performing its various functions; see the *Policy Focus: The Budget of the Fed's Board of Governors.*)

Because the Board of Governors has so many responsibilities, the various governors typically specialize in specific areas of policymaking. Normally, one governor will have key responsibilities in bank regulation, while another specializes in foreign exchange operations. The Board also has standing and *ad hoc* subcommittees in these and other areas of its responsibilities. These subcommittees consider policy issues and then make recommendations to the full Board.

The Federal Reserve Banks

Each Federal Reserve bank is a federally chartered corporation that has a sphere of influence largely confined to its own Federal Reserve district. Figure 14-3 shows the locations of the Federal Reserve district banks.

Figure 14-4 on page 316 illustrates the overall organizational structure of the Federal Reserve System. Member banks within each of the twelve districts own the equity shares of

The Budget of the Fed's Board of Governors

Each year, the Fed's Board of Governors spends more than half a billion dollars in performing its duties. About 70 percent of this amount is used for the wages and salaries of the Board's 1,900 employees. Figure 14-2 shows the functions to which the Board's total expenses are allocated. Together, two tasks—monetary policymaking and supervising and regulating depository institutions—account for more than three-fourths of the Board's total expenses.

FOR CRITICAL ANALYSIS: Why do you suppose that the seven members of the Fed's Board of Governors require so many employees?

FIGURE 14-2
Allocation of Federal Reserve Board Expenses.

Each year, the Fed's Board of Governors spends more than $500 million on monetary policymaking, supervision and regulation of depository institutions, and its various other duties.

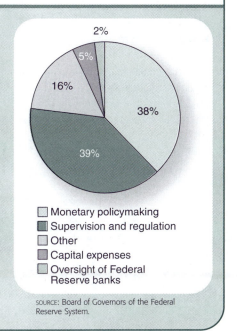

☐ Monetary policymaking
☐ Supervision and regulation
☐ Other
☐ Capital expenses
☐ Oversight of Federal Reserve banks

SOURCE: Board of Governors of the Federal Reserve System.

FIGURE 14-3
Federal Reserve District Banks.

This figure shows the locations of the twelve Federal Reserve banks and their geographic districts.

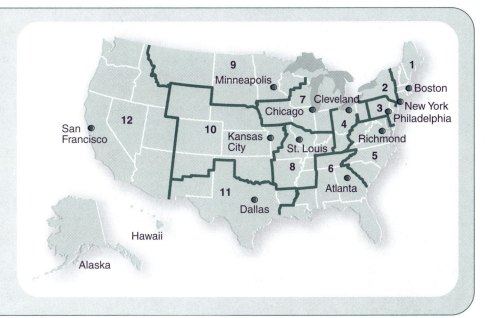

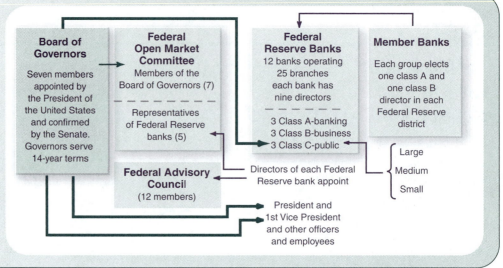

FIGURE 14-4
Organizational Structure of the Federal Reserve System.

The Federal Reserve's organizational structure reflects a mixture of centralized and decentralized policymaking.

SOURCE: Board of Governors of the Federal Reserve System.

the Federal Reserve bank of their district. Ownership of these shares entitles these member banks to elect six of the nine members of the board of directors of their Federal Reserve bank. Three of the six directors elected by member banks must be bankers from small, medium-sized, and large banks. The other three typically represent the interests of business or agriculture. The Board of Governors appoints the remaining three directors of each Federal Reserve bank. These directors cannot have banking connections, and the Board designates one member of this Board-appointed group as the chair of the board of directors of the Federal Reserve bank. Each Federal Reserve bank director serves for three years, and the terms are staggered so that a new director in each of the three categories is elected or appointed each year.

A key function of each Federal Reserve bank is to process electronic and nonelectronic clearings of payments. Together, then, the Federal Reserve banks and their twenty-five branches truly represent a "system" that routes payments from senders of funds to the ultimate receivers. (The Fed's role in clearing check payments is on the decline; see the *Cyber Focus: Will Image Processing Drive the Fed Out of the Check-Clearing Business?*)

Although we commonly speak of the "Fed's discount window," in fact each Federal Reserve bank operates its own lending facility. Furthermore, each has its own rules and regulations for discount window lending, although these are fairly similar across the twelve district banks. Since 2002, in all districts the discount rate has been set at 1 percentage point above the market federal funds rate.

Each Federal Reserve bank president is appointed by the bank's board of directors. The presidents are chief operating officers of the district banks. All twelve presidents also have input into deliberations of the FOMC, although only five presidents serve as voting members each year.

The Federal Open Market Committee

As noted earlier, the FOMC is composed of the seven Federal Reserve Board governors and five of the twelve district bank presidents. Because the Federal Reserve Bank of New York implements all the Fed's open market operations and foreign exchange trading, the president of this district bank is always a voting member in the FOMC. The remaining eleven district

CYBER
Focus

Will Image Processing Drive the Fed Out of the Check-Clearing Business?

The Federal Reserve banks are required by law to charge depository institutions fees for services that are sufficiently high to cover the Fed banks' costs in providing those services. Since 2003, however, the fees that Fed banks charge to clear physical checks have covered only 85 to 95 percent of the costs of check clearing. To meet its legal requirements, the Fed has been obliged to raise its check-clearing fees by 10 to 15 percent annually.

As you learned in Chapter 2, banks can now clear digital images of checks on the Internet. Private clearinghouses have found that they can perform this function at a lower per-unit cost than Federal Reserve banks. Consequently, these private institutions also charge less to clear digital images of checks than Fed banks—in fact, Fed banks currently charge more to process digital images of checks than to clear checks physically. As overall clearings of physical checks have declined with the rising use of debit cards, so has the Fed's share of the check-clearing business. In the mid-1990s, the Fed banks cleared about half of all checks in the United States. Today, they clear only slightly over one-fourth of all U.S. checks, and some observers have suggested that the Federal Reserve will exit the check-clearing business within the next decade.

FOR CRITICAL ANALYSIS: Why do you suppose that total employment at Federal Reserve banks has been stagnant during the 2000s?

bank presidents are separated into four groups, with a member of each group qualifying to vote in the FOMC each year on a rotating basis. The chair of the Board of Governors is automatically the FOMC chair.

The FOMC holds formal meetings eight to ten times per year. At these meetings, the voting members of the FOMC determine the wording of the **FOMC directive,** or the formal instructions to the operating officers at the Federal Reserve Bank of New York who supervise open market operations and foreign exchange trading. (During the last term of Fed chair Alan Greenspan, which ended in January 2006, some critics began to worry that his chairmanship of the FOMC failed to allow for sufficient policy debate; see *What Happens When the FOMC Begins to Behave Like a "GOMC"?*) The supervisor of open market operations is called the

FOMC directive: The official written instructions from the FOMC to the head of the Trading Desk at the Federal Reserve Bank of New York.

What Happens When... The FOMC Begins to Behave Like a "GOMC"?

Some years back, Susan Belden of Skidmore College examined dissenting FOMC votes—votes disagreeing with the Fed chair and the majority of the FOMC—between February 1970 and November 1987. She found that over this period, which preceded Alan Greenspan's appointment as Fed chair, about 9 percent of the votes of Federal Reserve bank presidents and Board governors were dissents.

During Greenspan's interval as chair, however, the percentage of FOMC dissenting votes dropped by nearly one-half. After 2001, the rate of dissent within the FOMC declined even further, to nearly 1 percent. There was so little disagreement with Greenspan's leadership that some critics began to complain that he had amassed too much power within the FOMC. The apparent lack of debate within the Fed, they contended, suggested that a more appropriate designation for the policymaking body was the "GOMC," or "Greenspan Open Market Committee."

FOR CRITICAL ANALYSIS: Why might other observers of the Greenspan Fed have regarded the lack of dissent within the FOMC as an indication of good leadership by the Fed chair?

Trading Desk: The Fed's term for the office at the Federal Reserve Bank of New York that conducts open market operations on the Fed's behalf.

head of the **Trading Desk** of the New York Federal Reserve Bank. The Trading Desk is a figurative term for the office at this district bank that engages in purchases and sales of securities on the Fed's account. The head of the Trading Desk functions as the FOMC's account manager and communicates daily with designated subcommittees of FOMC members.

> **5. Who makes the key policy decisions at the Federal Reserve?** Two key groups of individuals make the important policy decisions at the Fed. One of these groups is the Fed's Board of Governors, which is composed of seven people appointed by the president and approved by the Senate. The Board of Governors approves discount rate changes, sets reserve requirements, determines regulatory policies for state-chartered commercial banks that are Fed members, and regulates the activities of financial holding companies. The other main policymaking group is the Federal Open Market Committee (FOMC). The FOMC includes the Board of Governors and five of the twelve Federal Reserve bank presidents; it establishes the Fed's intentions concerning day-to-day conduct of monetary policy through open market operations. The Fed chair automatically serves as chair of the FOMC.

Chapter Summary

1. The First Central Banking Institutions, and How U.S. Central Banking Initially Developed: Sweden and England established the first central banks. Other European nations followed suit. Today, however, the European System of Central Banks is based in part on the U.S. experience. The first U.S. central banking institutions were the First and Second Banks of the United States, which operated from 1791 to 1811 and from 1816 to 1836. Although neither developed into a full central banking institution in the modern sense, each had the ability to influence the overall volume of money and credit in the U.S. economy.

2. Responsibilities for Monetary and Banking Policies without a Central Bank in the Nineteenth and Early Twentieth Centuries: From 1837 until the Civil War, the individual states established their own banking policies, but from the Civil War onward, both the states and the federal government formulated policies regarding depository institutions. Between 1837 and the founding of the Federal Reserve in 1913, the responsibility for monetary policy rested with the U.S. Treasury Department.

3. The Motivation for Congress to Establish the Federal Reserve System: Historical experiences with banking panics in 1857, 1873, 1893, and, finally, 1907 convinced national leaders that the United States needed a central banking institution that could help stem such panics by increasing the amounts of money and credit. Congress also desired for the federal government to have its own central depository for its funds, and it wished to provide a central banking institution to help coordinate the clearing of the growing volume of payments in the nation's large industrial economy.

4. The Rationale for the 1935 Congressional Restructuring of the Federal Reserve: The Fed's lack of success in reducing the ill effects of the 1929 stock market crash and subsequent bank failures and financial panics convinced Congress that the Fed needed clearly specified lines of authority and more independence from pressures from the president and the Treasury.

5. Those Who Make the Key Policy Decisions at the Federal Reserve: Decisions concerning the discount rate, reserve requirements, and regulation of Fed member banks and financial holding companies fall within the responsibilities of the Federal Reserve's seven-member Board of Governors. Day-to-day monetary policymaking via open market purchases and sales of securities is directed by the Federal Open Market Committee (FOMC), which is composed of the Board of Governors and five Federal Reserve bank presidents. The Board chair serves as chair of the FOMC.

Questions and Problems

(Answers to odd-numbered questions and problems may be found on the Web at **http://money.swcollege.com** under "Student Resources.")

1. What distinguishes a central bank from a purely private bank?

2. Based on the discussion in this chapter, does it appear to you that the First and Second Banks of the United States actively conducted monetary policies? In what way could they conduct such policies, whether or not they did so on an active basis? Explain.

3. Briefly outline the history of U.S. central banking from 1791 to 1836. In your view, what were the key central banking issues during this period?

4. Given that the U.S. Treasury Department functioned without a central bank from 1837 to 1913, do you think that a central bank such as the Fed is really necessary? Support your answer.

5. Before the creation of the Federal Reserve System, monetary issues often were themes of political campaigns. Since the Fed's founding, however, such issues rarely have been discussed in campaigns. Why might this be so?

6. In what fundamental ways did the Banking Act of 1935 truly "reform" the Fed? In what ways did it leave the institution unchanged?

7. In what respects is the Fed a "private" bank? In what respects is it a government agency?

8. In what ways is the European System of Central Banks (ESCB) like today's U.S. Federal Reserve System? In what ways is it different?

9. As discussed in this chapter, a series of severe banking crises ultimately led Congress to establish the Federal Reserve System as an institution that would help prevent such crises or deal with them if they did take place. In light of the structural differences between the Fed and the ESCB, do you think that the two institutions are equally capable of carrying out this responsibility?

10. The chair of the Board of Governors has considerable authority. What are the advantages and disadvantages of placing so much power with one individual?

Before the Test

Test your understanding of the material covered in this chapter by taking the Chapter 14 interactive quiz at **http://money.swcollege.com**.

Online Application

Internet URL: http://www.bis.org

Title: The Bank for International Settlements

Navigation: At the above home page address, click on "About BIS." Then, in the left margin, click on "Organisation/Government."

Application: Read the discussion, and answer the following questions:

1. Who owns the BIS, and what are its key functions?

2. In what ways is the BIS like a central bank? In what ways is it not a central bank?

For Group Study and Analysis: Go back to the BIS home page, and click on "Links to Central Banks." This facility provides links to a number of central banks around the world. Distribute countries (perhaps by geographic region) to groups of students to explore for information about the structure and functions of the central banks. Reconvene the entire class, and review the differences and similarities across this large set of central banks.

Selected References and Further Reading

Capie, Forrest, Charles Goodhart, Stanley Fischer, and Norbert Schnadt, eds. *The Future of Central Banking: The Tercentenary Symposium of the Bank of England.* Cambridge: Cambridge University Press, 1994.

Clarke, M. St. Clair, and D. A. Hall. *Legislative and Documentary History of the Bank of the United States.* New York: Augustus Kelley Publishers, 1967 (first published in 1832).

Federal Reserve Bank of San Francisco. "U.S. Monetary Policy: An Introduction, Part I: How Is the Fed Structured and What Are Its Policy Tools?" *FRBSF Economic Letter,* No. 2004-01, January 16, 2004.

Giuseppi, John. *The Bank of England.* London: Evands Brothers, 1966.

Goodhart, Charles. *The Evolution of Central Banks.* Cambridge, Mass.: MIT Press, 1988.

Grieder, William. *Secrets of the Temple: How the Federal Reserve Runs the Country.* New York: Simon & Schuster, 1987.

Hammond, Bray. *Banks and Politics in America.* Princeton: Princeton University Press, 1957 and 1985.

Havrilesky, Thomas. *The Pressures on American Monetary Policy.* Boston: Kluwer, 1993.

Landon-Lane, John, and Hugh Rockoff. "Monetary Policy and Regional Interest Rates in the United States, 1880–2002." National Bureau of Economic Research Working Paper No. 10924, November 2004.

Meltzer, Allan. *A History of the Federal Reserve System.* Chicago: University of Chicago Press, 2003.

Moen, Jon, and Ellis Tallman. "The Call Loan Market in the U.S. Financial System prior to the Federal Reserve System." Federal Reserve Bank of Atlanta Working Paper No. 2003-43, December 2003.

_____. "New York and the Politics of Central Banks, 1781 to the Federal Reserve Act." Federal Reserve Bank of Atlanta Working Paper No. 2003-42, December 2003.

Small, David, and James Clouse. "The Scope of Monetary Policy Actions Authorized under the Federal Reserve Act." Board of Governors of the Federal Reserve System, July 19, 2004.

Smith, Vera. *The Rationale of Central Banking.* Indianapolis: Liberty Press, 1990 (first published in 1936).

Timberlake, Richard. *Monetary Policy in the United States: An Intellectual and Institutional History.* Chicago: University of Chicago Press, 1993.

MoneyXtra

Log on to the MoneyXtra Web site now (**http://moneyxtra.swcollege.com**) for additional learning resources such as practice quizzes, case studies, readings, and additional economic applications.

The Federal Reserve and the Financial System

U.S. Central Credit Union (known as "U.S. Central") is a Kansas-based institution that serves as an automated clearinghouse providing computer-based clearing and payment services for more than 2,200 U.S. credit unions. On Monday, April 5, 2004, at about 2 A.M., U.S. Central employees began processing an unusually large number of weekend payment orders. Unbeknownst to them, the number of orders exceeded a limiting line of software code that the company's computers required to process payments. This event triggered a massive crash of U.S. Central's payment-clearing system. For four days, the company's employees and software providers worked feverishly to get the system working again. During that period, U.S. Central was unable to transmit more than 800,000 payments to credit unions and their members.

Who bears the risks associated with delays caused by breakdowns in payment systems? Why might central banking officials be concerned about such risks? This chapter focuses on these and other issues that central banks such as the Federal Reserve confront in today's financial system.

The Fed as a Central Bank

As you learned in Chapter 14, the Federal Reserve System is a complex public-policy institution. It is also a very large bank with twelve district "branches," twenty-five "sub-branches," and a "central office" in Washington, D.C. Before we get too wrapped up in the broader public-policy aspects of the Fed, let's begin by considering its banking operations.

The Fed's Balance Sheet

Each of the Federal Reserve banks has its own detailed balance sheet, as does the Board of Governors in Washington, D.C. The best way to gain a concrete understanding of the Fed's activities, however, is to examine the Fed's *consolidated balance sheet,* which is a T-account that displays the combined assets, liabilities, and equity capital for all units of the Federal Reserve System.

Fundamental Issues

1. What are the main assets and liabilities of the Fed?

2. In what ways is the Fed the government's bank?

3. What is the rationale for the Fed's role as a bank for private banks?

4. Why does the Fed play a supervisory role in the U.S. payment system?

5. In what ways do payment-system risks span national borders, and how do central banks seek to contain these risks?

THE FED'S ASSETS   Table 15-1 displays the Fed's consolidated balance sheet. The table displays both absolute dollar values and percentages relative to total assets and to total liabilities and net worth. You should concentrate on the percentages because dollar amounts change considerably over time, whereas the Fed's proportionate allocations of its assets and of its liabilities and equity capital tend to remain relatively stable.

1. **Treasury securities.** U.S. Treasury securities comprise the most important category of Fed assets. The 92.6 percent figure in Table 15-1 is a typical proportionate allocation of assets to government securities. About 80 percent of these government securities are Treasury bills and notes (maturities under ten years), and the remainder are Treasury bonds (maturities exceeding ten years).

2. **U.S. agency securities.**   In addition to securities issued by the U.S. Treasury, the Fed holds debt instruments issued by other U.S. government agencies. These securities account for a small and typically stable fraction of Fed assets.

3. **Discount window loans.**   The Federal Reserve also lends to private depository institutions via the discount window facilities of the Federal Reserve banks. As Table 15-1

Table 15-1 The Consolidated Balance Sheet of the Federal Reserve System ($ Millions, as of January 31, 2005)

Assets			Liabilities and Capital		
Asset	**Dollar Amount**	**Percentage of Total Assets**	**Liability**	**Dollar Amount**	**Percentage of Total Liabilities and Equity**
U.S. Treasury securities	$746,690	92.6%	Federal Reserve notes	$711,389	88.3%
Discount window loans	71	—	Bank reserve deposits	33,659	4.2%
Gold and SDR certificates	13,238	1.6%	U.S. Treasury deposits	4,971	0.6%
Foreign currency reserves	20,876	2.6%	Foreign official deposits	121	—
Cash items in process of collection	1,784	0.3%	Deferred credit items	1,942	0.2%
Other assets	23,395	2.9%	Other liabilities	29,921	3.7%
			Total liabilities	782,003	97.0%
			Equity capital	24,051	3.0%
Total assets	**$806,054**	**100.0%**	**Total liabilities and capital**	**$806,054**	**100.0%**

SOURCE: Board of Governors of the Federal Reserve System, *Federal Reserve Statistical Supplement,* April 2005.

indicates, the dollar amount of discount window lending and the proportionate asset allocation to such lending are very small. (Discount window borrowing remains low even though Fed officials have indicated in recent years that depository institutions should not feel stigmatized if they borrow reserves more often than in the past; see the *Policy Focus: A More Open Discount Window Fails to Generate Additional Borrowing.*)

4. **Gold certificates.** These assets remain on the Fed's balance sheet as a constant reminder of the nation's former adherence to a gold standard. When the gold standard was in operation, the Treasury Department sold gold to the Fed in exchange for money. The Treasury issued gold certificates to the Fed to indicate the Fed's ownership of the gold that the Treasury continued to hold in reserve. Hence, these certificates are Fed assets. As a share of total assets, however, they continue to decline over time as the absolute size of the Fed's assets increases with time.

5. **Special Drawing Right (SDR) certificates.** SDRs are assets issued by the International Monetary Fund (IMF), which is a financial institution owned and operated by over 180 countries. In the 1970s, the IMF issued SDRs as a type of international currency intended to compensate for the declining role of gold as a basis for the world's currency system. The United States is an IMF member nation, and the Treasury owns shares in the IMF via SDRs. The Treasury financed these SDR shares by issuing a fixed dollar amount of SDR certificates to the Fed. Consequently, SDR certificates, like gold certificates, constitute a Fed asset category that continues to decline in relative importance.

6. **Foreign currency reserves.** The Fed maintains a portfolio of assets denominated in the currencies of other nations. A key reason that the Fed holds these foreign-currency-denominated securities and deposits is so that it can trade them when it desires to try to

POLICY

Focus

A More Open Discount Window Fails to Generate Additional Borrowing

When the Fed began maintaining the discount rate exactly 1 percentage point above the federal funds rate in early 2003, it also announced that it would be more willing to lend than in the past. Fed officials expected that this announcement would encourage depository institutions to borrow larger amounts of reserves from the Fed and to borrow from the Fed more often.

Nevertheless, during the following six months, the amount and frequency of discount window borrowing barely changed. Consequently, in July 2003 the Fed, together with the Federal Deposit Insurance Corporation, the Office of the Comptroller of the Currency, the Office of Thrift Supervision, and the National Credit Union Administration, issued a press release stating that occasional use of the Fed's regular discount window facilities "should be viewed as appropriate and unexceptional."

Nevertheless, depository institutions have remained reluctant to borrow from the Fed. Some observers suggest that many still worry that outsiders may view heavier borrowing from the Fed as a possible sign of major liquidity problems. Others, however, think there is a more basic explanation for depository institutions' unwillingness to borrow very much or very often from the Fed: With the Fed's discount rate always set above the market federal funds rate, borrowing from the Fed simply isn't profitable.

FOR CRITICAL ANALYSIS: Under the current discount rate policy, what does the Fed have to gain from promoting more and larger discount window loans?

change the dollar's value in foreign exchange markets. We shall have more to say about this in Chapter 22.

7. **Cash items in the process of collection.** Finally, like any other bank (see Chapter 9), the Federal Reserve receives payments from other parties that it credits to its account although they have not yet "cleared" the payment system. Because such payments may be subject to cancellation until that time, the Fed lists them as *cash items in the process of collection.*

THE FED'S LIABILITIES AND EQUITY CAPITAL The Federal Reserve has several liabilities and its own special source of equity capital.

1. **Federal Reserve notes.** More than 88 percent of the Federal Reserve's total liabilities and equity capital is composed of *Federal Reserve notes.* These are the currency that the Fed issues and that we use to make most of our small purchases of goods and services. As a liability, Federal Reserve notes indicate that the Fed "owes" us something in exchange for these notes. Before the early 1930s, if you had sought to redeem a $1 Federal Reserve note at a Federal Reserve bank, you could have received gold in exchange. Now, however, you would receive a new $1 Federal Reserve note. So in what sense is this note really a liability? The answer is that if Congress were to close down the Federal Reserve System, the Fed would be liable to you for a dollar's worth of goods and services as of the time of its closure.

2. **Bank reserve deposits.** The second-largest liability of the Fed is reserve deposits of depository institutions. As we discussed in Chapter 13, depository institutions hold the bulk of these deposits to meet legal requirements established by the Fed. Depository institutions hold a small portion of these deposits as excess reserves, however. They often lend such reserves to one another in the federal funds market.

3. **U.S. Treasury deposits.** Another deposit liability of the Fed is composed of deposits of the U.S. Treasury. The Treasury draws on these funds to make payments such as purchases of goods and services or tax refunds.

4. **Foreign official deposits.** Foreign governments or official foreign financial institutions, including central banks such as the Bank of England or the Bank of Japan, hold dollar-denominated deposit accounts with the Fed. These are *foreign official deposits.* Many of these accounts are checking accounts, and foreign governments and central banks draw upon these accounts when they need to make dollar payments.

5. **Deferred availability cash items.** These are payments that the Fed has promised to another party or that it has made but that have yet to "clear."

6. **Equity capital.** The Fed's equity capital is composed of the ownership shares of banks that are members of the Federal Reserve System. At 3.0 percent, the Fed's equity capital is very low in relation to its assets.

1. What are the main assets and liabilities of the Fed? The primary assets of the Fed are U.S. government securities, including Treasury bills, notes, and bonds. The main liabilities are Federal Reserve notes, or currency, and reserve deposits of depository institutions.

The Fed as the Government's Bank

As we noted in Chapter 14, one original rationale for the creation of the Federal Reserve System in 1913 was the government's "need" for a central bank. As the main banking institution for the U.S. government, the Fed provides depository services to the Treasury. It also performs an important role as the Treasury's *fiscal agent* in financial markets.

GOVERNMENT DEPOSITORY   The U.S. Treasury holds deposits at each of the twelve Federal Reserve banks. As depositories of the Treasury, the Federal Reserve banks maintain the Treasury's accounts, clear checks drawn on those accounts, accept deposits of federal fees and taxes, and make electronic payments on the Treasury's behalf.

The Treasury also holds deposit accounts at private depository institutions. Many of these are **Treasury tax and loan (TT&L) accounts,** which are special checking accounts that the Treasury maintains with private institutions. Another key function of the Federal Reserve banks is to serve as TT&L account "go-betweens" on the Treasury's behalf. In this capacity, the Federal Reserve banks add to or draw from these TT&L accounts at other depository institutions on the Treasury's behalf to assist the Treasury in managing its cash.

> **Treasury tax and loan (TT&L) accounts:** U.S. Treasury checking accounts at private depository institutions.

Most Treasury payments to citizens and businesses flow from Federal Reserve bank deposits. The Federal Reserve banks handle payments that the Treasury disburses on a regular basis, such as Social Security benefits and salaries to federal employees, by making direct deposits into the recipients' accounts. Since 1991 the Treasury has made more payments by Fed-processed direct deposits than by checks.

FISCAL AGENT   The Federal Reserve functions as the key **fiscal agent** of the U.S. Treasury Department, meaning that it issues, services, and redeems debts on the Treasury's behalf. The Treasury issues debt instruments—bills, notes, and bonds—that the government uses to cover any shortfalls between its tax receipts and its expenditures on goods and services. The Treasury issues these securities at auctions. Although the Treasury announces the terms and conditions of the securities to be sold at the auctions, potential buyers submit bids for new securities to the Federal Reserve banks as well as to the Treasury's Bureau of the Public Debt. As the Treasury's fiscal agent, the Federal Reserve banks tabulate and summarize all bids and review them to ensure that they meet legal requirements. The Federal Reserve banks also issue the Treasury's securities to the purchasers and process the payments that the purchasers provide in exchange.

> **Fiscal agent:** A term describing the Federal Reserve's role as an agent of the U.S. Treasury Department, on whose behalf the Fed issues, services, and redeems debts.

To facilitate the transfer of securities, the Federal Reserve banks operate two *book-entry security systems.* These are computer systems through which the Fed maintains records of Treasury sales and interest and principal payments on its securities. Most financial institutions that purchase large volumes of Treasury securities do not actually hold paper securities; instead, they maintain computerized accounts with the Fed. The Fed provides holders of these accounts with regular statements and automatically transfers interest and principal into their accounts.

When an institution wishes to sell Treasury securities to which it has title, it typically does not send paper securities to the buyer. Instead, it instructs the Federal Reserve bank that maintains its book-entry security account to transfer its title of ownership from its account to the book-entry security account of the purchasing institution. The Fed then makes the transfer electronically. Large institutions typically initiate such transfers using direct computer links with Federal Reserve banks. Smaller institutions initiate transfers by telephone using computer modems and software that the Fed has developed for this purpose.

The Federal Reserve also sells and delivers *U.S. savings bonds* on the Treasury's behalf. These are low-denomination, nonmarketable Treasury securities that are popular instruments for many small savers. The Federal Reserve also credits interest on savings bonds when holders redeem them at authorized depository institutions.

> **2. In what ways is the Fed the government's bank?** The Fed is the main depository institution for the federal government. It also serves as the government's fiscal agent by operating the systems through which the Treasury sells new securities and makes interest and principal payments on outstanding securities.

THE FED'S INCOME AND EXPENSES One thorny issue for the Fed has been that the Treasury does not pay in full for the services that the Fed provides. Typically, the Treasury reimburses the Federal Reserve banks for only about a third of the costs that they incur in providing government depository services or acting as the Treasury's fiscal agent.

Where does the Fed get the funds to cover the unreimbursed expenses that it incurs on the Treasury's behalf? Recall that more than 90 percent of the Fed's assets are U.S. government securities. These yield a steady flow of interest to the Fed and constitute its primary source of income. The Fed uses much of this income to fund its operations.

The Fed's other main source of income is the fees that it charges depository institutions for services that it provides. Since 1981 this fee income has increased steadily as the Fed has continued to charge private depository institutions for the services that it offers as a "bank for bankers."

The Fed as the Bankers' Bank

Another justification that Congress provided for creating the Fed was a perceived need for a government-related institution that would centralize, oversee, and regulate the payment systems of the geographically dispersed U.S. economy. Congress also felt that such an institution was needed to function as a *lender of last resort* for depository institutions suffering temporary liquidity problems that might pose short-term threats to their individual solvency and to the broader stability of the financial system.

DO BANKS NEED A CENTRAL BANK? Congress answered "yes" to this question when it authorized the formation of the Fed. A common reason given for the Fed's role in the banking system is that private depository institutions *need* a central bank. The key rationale for such a "need" is the perception that financial markets are subject to **externalities,** or situations in which transactions between two parties can spill over to affect others. The classic externality is pollution, such as noise pollution. If you are *not* an enthusiast, say, of country-western or rap music, yet your neighbors on either side of your apartment or house enjoy purchasing and playing such music at loud volumes, then you likely suffer a **negative externality.** Even though the companies that produce and sell such music benefit from the sales and your neighbors benefit from consuming the music, you find yourself worse off as a result of the transactions between these parties.

Likewise, it is arguable that many financial transactions can generate externalities, many of which could be negative. For instance, suppose that an individual owes you money but cannot pay you until he completes a transaction with another party. If something goes awry in that other transaction, then you will be worse off even though you were not a direct party to the transaction. You experience a negative externality effect because the failure of that transaction to take place causes you to fail to get a payment that you had counted on receiving.

Externalities: Spillovers from the interactions of one set of individuals to others who otherwise are not involved in the transactions.

Negative externality: A reduction in the welfare of one individual caused by a transaction between other parties, even though the individual is not directly involved in the transaction.

A key justification for a central bank, therefore, is to supervise and regulate the processes and systems by which consumers, businesses, and financial institutions exchange payments. According to this view, financial institutions "need" a central bank to keep systems by which payments are exchanged operating smoothly on a day-to-day basis and to repair any breakdowns in these systems as they occur.

LENDER OF LAST RESORT　　The most dramatic sort of financial breakdown is a bank run, in which large numbers of depositors lose confidence in the ability of depository institutions to retain their asset values and seek to liquidate their accounts, thereby driving large numbers of institutions into insolvency (see Chapter 2). A key justification for the formation of the Federal Reserve System was that the Fed would prevent such runs from occurring by serving as the financial system's **lender of last resort.** This is a central banking institution that stands ready to lend to any temporarily illiquid but otherwise solvent institution to prevent its illiquidity from leading to a general loss of confidence that can set off a "run on the bank."

Under the provisions of the original Federal Reserve Act, a key duty of the Fed is to provide lender-of-last-resort assistance when needed. As amended by the Banking Act of 1935, the Federal Reserve Act authorizes the Fed to lend to *anyone* if it believes doing so is necessary to prevent a financial crisis. In practice, however, the Fed restricts itself to loans to depository financial institutions that find themselves caught in temporary "liquidity crunches." (Such a temporary "liquidity crunch" recently required prompt action by the Central Bank of Russia; see the *Global Focus: A Lender of Last Resort Forestalls a Russian Banking Crisis.*)

Lender of last resort: An institution that is willing and able to lend to any temporarily illiquid but otherwise solvent institution to prevent its illiquid position from leading to a general loss of confidence in that institution or in others.

GLOBAL
Focus

A Lender of Last Resort Forestalls a Russian Banking Crisis

In May 2004, the Central Bank of Russia revoked the license of a private bank called Sodbiznesbank after finding evidence that the bank's officers had engaged in illegal money laundering. During the next few days, rumors swirled throughout Russia that the central bank had found widespread illegal activities throughout the nation's private banking system. Soon lines began to form at branches of most of the country's largest private banks, as

depositors, fearing that the government would close the institutions, rushed to withdraw their funds.

In fact, none of the banks implicated by the rumors were under government suspicion. Nevertheless, widespread withdrawals by worried depositors created severe liquidity problems throughout the Russian banking system. The Central Bank of Russia first responded by slashing the required reserve ratio from 7 percent to 3.5 percent. This action failed to prevent the second-largest bank in the country, Guta Bank, from shutting its doors to long lines of customers waiting outside its branches. Soon lines also began to form at the nation's largest private bank, Alfa Bank.

After determining that Guta Bank was illiquid but solvent, the Russian central bank provided the bank with a large loan. The long lines of customers at both Guta Bank and Alfa Bank soon evaporated. In the end, even longtime critics of the Central Bank of Russia agreed that it had effectively prevented a full-scale banking crisis.

FOR CRITICAL ANALYSIS: Why might the Russian central bank's lowering of the reserve requirement have failed to generate sufficient liquidity to enable Guta Bank to meet depositors' requests for their funds?

> **3. What is the rationale for the Fed's role as a bank for private banks?**
> The key rationale is the possibility for negative externalities, or spillovers, that exists in the financial system. Because financial transactions among depository institutions and others are interconnected, there is a potential for bank runs and other crises. As a supervisory authority and lender of last resort, the Fed can potentially reduce the possibilities that such events might occur.

Cyberbanking, the Fed, and the U.S. Payment System

When an individual makes a transaction using currency, the transaction is final at the moment that the exchange of currency for a good, service, or asset takes place. In contrast, transactions with other means of payment, such as checks or wire transfers, are final only after depository institutions transfer funds from the account of the purchaser to the seller. Using these other means of payment, therefore, requires parties to a transaction to rely upon depository institutions as intermediaries in the nation's **payment system.** This is the institutional structure through which individuals, businesses, governments, and financial institutions make payments.

The Federal Reserve System is a significant part of the payment system of the United States. The Fed also monitors and regulates a significant portion of the payment system that it does not directly supervise and operate. Before we discuss the Fed's roles in the payment system, however, let's consider the current structure of the system.

Payment system: A term that refers broadly to the set of mechanisms by which consumers, businesses, governments, and financial institutions exchange payments.

Retail Payments

Today's payment system is a fascinating mix of old and new. As we discussed in Chapter 1, nonelectronic means of payment such as currency and checks account for about 92 percent of all transactions in the United States. At the same time, however, electronic payments account for approximately 90 percent of the *dollar value* of all transactions. This means that although U.S. residents continue to use currency and checks for the large number of low-value transactions that they make each day, they have adopted electronic payments as the primary means of conducting their less frequent but large-value transactions.

The U.S. payment system has two components. One consists of the various mechanisms for processing *retail payments,* which are funds transfers for transactions of relatively "small" value—tens of thousands of dollars or less. Consumer transactions with merchants using such media as currency, checks, and debit cards account for the bulk of retail payments. The other component of the payment system, which we shall discuss shortly, consists of the electronic delivery systems that process large-value transactions. (Recently, U.S. depository institutions have considered the costs and benefits of establishing a retail payment system for debit cards more like the system used in Canada; see *What Happens When U.S. Bankers Contemplate a Canadian-Style Debit-Card System?*)

NONELECTRONIC PAYMENTS In terms of number of transactions, the most popular means of retail payment in the United States are decidedly nonelectronic paper notes and coins. Such currency transactions alone make up over three-fourths of *all* U.S. transactions. Hence, the bulk of transactions in the U.S. economy remain very "low tech." Nevertheless,

What Happens When...   **U.S. Bankers Contemplate a Canadian-Style Debit-Card System?**

In the United States, when a consumer purchases $100 worth of goods and services from a retailer using a debit card, the retailer actually receives less than $100 from the depository institution that issued the consumer's debit card. This arrangement ensures that the institution receives income that compensates for the cost of processing the payment. The retailer is willing to pay this implicit fee in the belief that accepting debit cards generates more sales. In principle, retailers can also pass part of their share of debit-card processing costs along to consumers by charging higher prices, although most studies find little evidence that prices reflect all of retailers' debit-card costs.

In Canada, which has only a handful of banks and a single debit-card payment network, depository institutions cooperate in charging consumers fees that cover the bulk of the costs of processing debit-card payments. Estimates indicate that if such a system were adopted in the United States, consumers would have to pay an additional $4.3 billion to use debit cards. U.S. retailers would pay much less than they now do.

In the United States, there are thousands of depository institutions and more than thirty different networks. Linking the networks so that consumers could be charged debit-card fees for all transactions would be very costly. After commissioning a study of the costs and benefits of switching to a Canadian-style system, major U.S. depository institutions decided in the mid-2000s that they were unwilling to bear such costs. For the foreseeable future, U.S. consumers are unlikely to face debit-card fees as high as those now paid by Canadians.

FOR CRITICAL ANALYSIS: Why do you suppose that many economists suggest that even in a Canadian-style debit-card system, competition among U.S. depository institutions would lead to much lower debit-card fees for consumers? (Hint: Is the market power of depository institutions likely to be higher or lower in the United States than in Canada?)

---

currency transactions are quite small on average, so small that together they account for less than 0.5 percent of the total dollar value of all exchanges in the United States. Think of all the times you purchase such low-ticket items as candy bars or pens or pencils, and you will understand why this is the case.

Checks are the second most popular payment medium, accounting for a little under a sixth of all transactions and just below 12 percent of the total dollar value of all exchanges. Depository institutions clear millions of checks each day, for a total of more than 60 billion in a year. This is possible because nearly all checks have magnetic ink encryptions that special machines can read. This permits the machines to sort and distribute checks automatically. They can also process information for crediting and debiting accounts. This large-scale automation of check sorting, accounting, and distribution has kept the per check cost of clearing checks very low.

Other nonelectronic means of payment include money orders, traveler's checks, and credit cards. Together these make up less than 1 percent of both the total number of transactions and the dollar value of all transactions.

CONSUMER-ORIENTED ELECTRONIC PAYMENT SYSTEMS There now are several consumer-oriented electronic payment mechanisms. Most U.S. consumers have experience using *automated teller machine (ATM) networks,* which are depository institution computer terminals activated by magnetically encoded bank cards. There are more than 150,000 ATMs in the United States. On average, consumers perform about 100,000 transactions each year at a typical ATM, for an annual total of nearly 15 billion ATM transactions. Many consumers use ATM networks to make deposits, obtain cash from checking and savings accounts, and transfer funds among accounts. A growing number of consumers also pay some

MONEYXTRA!
Another Perspective

To consider how the wide use of checks in the United States poses an issue known as check float, go to the Chapter 15 reading, entitled "The Economics of Check Float," by James McAndrews and William Roberds, published by the Federal Reserve Bank of Atlanta. **http://moneyxtra. swcollege.com** of their bills using ATM networks. A recent innovation in ATM technology is the "Personal Touch" ATM, which offers visual contact with depository institution employees at another location. Using such ATM links, consumers now can apply for loans and mortgages, purchase mutual funds, and obtain information about loan and deposit terms and rates.

Automated clearinghouses (ACHs) are another type of consumer-oriented electronic payment mechanism. These are computer-based clearing and settlement facilities for the interchange of credits and debits via electronic messages instead of checks. ACHs, which facilitate about 12 billion transactions per year, process payments within one or two days after the request for a transfer of funds. Very common ACH transfers are automatic payroll deposits, in which businesses make wage and salary payments directly into employees' deposit accounts. The federal government also makes large use of ACH facilities. The Social Security Administration distributes many payments to Social Security beneficiaries via ACH direct-deposit mechanisms. In addition, the government disperses a growing portion of welfare and food stamp payments using an *electronic benefits transfer (EBT) system.* An EBT system functions like an ACH system but looks a lot like an ATM network to welfare and food stamp beneficiaries, because they receive their welfare funds or food stamps from special cash or food stamp disbursement machines. (Recently, ACHs have also become involved in electronic check clearing; see the *Cyber Focus: ARC Payments Take Off at Automated Clearinghouses.*)

Point-of-sale (POS) networks permit consumers to pay for purchases on the spot via direct deductions from their deposit accounts at depository institutions. The technology for POS networks has been available since the 1970s, and most large chains of department stores and other retail outlets use networks of cash-register terminals that are capable of processing all noncash transactions as POS payments. Nevertheless, POS networks have not developed as quickly as some observers expected. Only with the growing use of debit cards in the late 1990s and 2000s have limited POS systems become a reality. A deterrent to the growth of POS networks has been the uncertainty as to who would be willing to incur all the related costs of setting up the systems, which can be significant. Check-processing costs have remained so low that depository institutions have had little incentive to switch completely to POS networks, and many retailers still have little desire to incur the cost of installing the systems. POS networks are likely

On the Web

How do ACH systems function? Find out by visiting the Web site of the National Automated Clearing House Association at **http://www.nacha.org**, where you can click on "About Us" for a summary and "Resources" for links to many other informative Web sites.

Point-of-sale (POS) networks:
Systems in which consumers pay for retail purchases through direct deductions from their deposit accounts at depository institutions.

CYBER

Focus

ARC Payments Take Off at Automated Clearinghouses

To banks and their corporate customers, they are known as "accounts receivable conversions," or ARCs. To economists, however, these forms of payment, which are processed by automated clearinghouses, amount to electronic

check clearing. Instead of submitting checks received from their customers for either physical or digital clearing, companies send the checks to special "dropbox" locations at depository institutions. Accountants at these institutions then book the checks as ARCs and submit them for ACH clearing.

Most checks that are not converted to digital images for clearing are now processed as ARCs. The growing use of

ARCs to clear checks electronically has led to a dramatic increase in their share of all payments processed by ACHs—from less than 1 percent in 2002 to more than 15 percent today.

FOR CRITICAL ANALYSIS: Why might converting bundles of checks into ARCs for processing by automated clearinghouses sometimes be less expensive than scanning each check and clearing all the checks digitally via the Internet?

to become more widespread in the future only if consumers indicate a desire to use them—and to help pay for them either directly through fees to banks or indirectly through higher prices charged by retailers. Recent increases in consumer use of debit cards and online banking may gradually lead to greater consumer interest in POS networks.

IS THE UNITED STATES BEHIND THE "POWER CURVE"?   In Chapter 2 we discussed a number of ongoing cybertechnology developments in the U.S. financial system. In spite of these developments, however, U.S. consumers use paper-based, nonelectronic— mainly check—transactions much more than people in most other nations. As Table 15-2 indicates, the average U.S. resident made about 139 such transactions each year in the early 2000s—2 to 700 times more than residents of other nations.

Table 15-2 shows that residents of most other industrialized countries use electronic means of payment much more regularly than residents of the United States. Traditionally, *electronic giro* systems have been a popular retail payment mechanism in many European nations; in these systems, banks, post offices, and other payment intermediaries transfer funds via telephone lines or other forms of electronic communication. This eliminates the need for paper checks and for ACH networks. Europeans have also been more receptive to adopting stored-value cards, and a number of current smart-card projects are under way in European locales. (Banks in the European Union, or EU, are continuing to earn high fees from sending funds from one nation to another, even though European governments commonly claim that banking is now "borderless" within the EU; see on the next page the *Global Focus: European Banks Continue to Earn High Fees from Cross-Border Payments.*)

Wholesale Payments

Consumer-oriented electronic payment systems account for a growing portion of both the number and the dollar value of transactions. Yet, even though online banking, stored-value cards, and smart cards continue to make inroads, electronically processed retail payments make up small fractions of both classifications. Currently, most payments accomplished via

Table 15-2 Annual Noncash Transactions per Person in Selected Countries

Country	Number of Transactions per Person		Percentage of Electronic Payments
	Paper-Based	**Electronic**	
Belgium	2.8	135.8	98.0
Canada	48.2	144.4	75.0
France	68.3	108.8	61.4
Germany	1.8	91.1	98.1
Italy	9.3	32.9	78.0
Japan	1.5	28.4	95.0
Netherlands	—	147.2	100.0
Singapore	20.9	29.6	58.6
Sweden	0.2	114.8	99.8
Switzerland	0.6	111.0	99.5
United Kingdom	40.4	111.8	73.5
United States	138.7	129.8	48.3

SOURCE: Bank for International Settlements, 2005.

European Banks Continue to Earn High Fees from Cross-Border Payments

When the European Union, which now consists of twenty-five nations, was first established in 1990, one goal was to create a "single banking market," in which banks in all the EU member nations would operate as if no national borders existed. In January 2004, this goal finally became a reality, at least on paper. At that time, a new EU regulation went into effect requiring all EU banks to charge the same amount to process cross-border payments as they charge for funds transfers within their home countries.

There was a catch, however. Only someone making a "qualifying" cross-border payment can obtain services from a bank on the same terms as those requesting domestic funds transfers. To "qualify," the individual or firm requesting the cross-border payment must provide the bank with a number of precise details, including, among other things, the bank identification number and international bank identification code of the European bank that will receive the cross-border payment. EU banks themselves have ready access to such information, but most require the customer to provide it before a cross-border payment will qualify for equal treatment with domestic funds transfers.

So far, only about 1 percent of customers who have requested cross-border payments have provided sufficient information to meet these requirements. Thus, European banks have been able to continue charging their customers fees averaging about 17 percent of each cross-border payment to transfer funds to banks located in other EU nations.

FOR CRITICAL ANALYSIS: Why do you suppose that 99 percent of European residents who request cross-border payments to other EU banks have been willing to pay significant fees rather than collecting sufficient information to avoid the fees?

---

electronic delivery systems are *wholesale payments,* which are large-value transactions typically denominated in the hundreds of thousands or millions of dollars.

LARGE-VALUE ELECTRONIC PAYMENT SYSTEMS

The delivery systems for processing wholesale payments are **large-value wire transfer systems,** which are designed and operated specifically to manage electronic transfers of large sums. Large-value wire transfer systems transfer nearly 85 percent of the value of all payments initiated by consumers, businesses, governments, and financial institutions. Nevertheless, these systems handle less than 1 percent of the total number of transactions. Clearly, they truly specialize in transferring large transactions.

In the United States, there are two key large-value wire transfer systems. One is **Fedwire,** which is operated by the Federal Reserve System. All depository institutions that must hold reserves at Federal Reserve banks have access to Fedwire, although fewer than 2,000 institutions regularly use the system. Depository institutions pay fees for the wire transfer services that Fedwire provides, and they use Fedwire mainly for two specific kinds of transfer.

One of the main uses of Fedwire is for book-entry security transactions. As discussed above, the Fed operates book-entry security systems on behalf of the Treasury. Fedwire is the means by which depository institutions pay for the securities that they purchase using these systems. The second primary use of Fedwire is for funds transfers among the reserve deposit accounts that depository institutions maintain at Federal Reserve banks. When depository institutions extend or repay federal funds loans to other depository institutions, they send the funds on Fedwire. The average Fedwire payment is over $3 million, and the total average daily payment volume on the Fedwire system is nearly $1 trillion ($1,000,000,000,000).

Large-value wire transfer systems: Payment systems such as Fedwire and CHIPS that permit the electronic transmission of large dollar sums.

Fedwire: A large-value wire transfer system operated by the Federal Reserve that is open to all depository institutions that legally must maintain required reserves with the Fed.

The other major large-value wire transfer system in the United States is the **Clearing House Interbank Payment System (CHIPS).** This is a privately owned system operated by the New York Clearing House Association, which has about ninety member depository institutions. These institutions typically transfer funds for foreign exchange and Eurodollar transactions using CHIPS, and the average value of a CHIPS transaction is more than $6 million. The average daily payment volume on CHIPS is now about $1.5 trillion.

Table 15-3 lists the world's major large-value wire transfer systems and provides estimates of the annual number of transactions and flows of funds on these systems, which are similar in structure to Fedwire and CHIPS. For instance, the Bank of Japan's BOJ-NET system and the European Central Bank's TARGET system are analogous to Fedwire, and the European Banking Association's Euro-1 system and the British CHAPS system perform functions similar to those provided by CHIPS.

The Rationale for Fed Supervision: Payment-System Risks

Any financial transaction entails some degree of risk. When you accept a payment in currency, for instance, there is always a small chance that the bills that you receive might be counterfeit. Yet, unless you are in the habit of making large cash transactions, your risk of loss in a typical exchange where currency is the means of payment is fairly small. In the multimillion-dollar transactions on Fedwire and CHIPS, however, the dollar risks are much more significant. For this reason, the Federal Reserve is closely involved in monitoring and regulating CHIPS in addition to operating and supervising Fedwire.

Three types of risk arise in any payment system: *liquidity risk, credit risk,* and *systemic risk.* A key function of financial institutions and markets is to intermediate such risks. Nevertheless, as we discuss below, systemic risk may entail significant externalities for financial institutions and others who use large-value payment mechanisms. As we noted earlier, the existence of such externalities is a key rationale for the involvement of a central bank, such as the Fed, in a nation's financial system.

Clearing House Interbank Payment System (CHIPS): A large-value wire transfer system that links about ninety depository institutions and permits them to transmit large dollar sums relating primarily to foreign exchange and Eurodollar transactions.

On the Web

How many Fedwire transactions took place in the latest quarter? To track Fedwire data, go to the Federal Reserve's home page at **http://www.federalreserve.gov**, click on "Payment Systems," and then, under "Reserve Bank Payment Services," click on "Fedwire and Net Settlement Services."

Table 15-3 The World's Key Large-Value Wire Transfer Systems

Country/Payment System	Transactions (Millions)	Value ($ Trillions)
European Monetary Union		
TARGET	70.7	$590.3
Euro-1	39.2	55.6
Japan		
Zengin	5.4	104.6
BOJ-NET	18.5	614.4
United Kingdom		
CHAPS	30.3	87.6
United States		
Fedwire	127.3	501.2
CHIPS	68.1	343.4

SOURCES: Payment systems' statistical publications, various issues, 2005; authors' estimates.

Liquidity risk: The risk of loss that may occur if a payment is not received when due.

LIQUIDITY RISK

People do not always make payments on time. The risk of loss because payments may not be received when they are due is called **liquidity risk.** Losses arising from late payments may be in the form of opportunity costs, in that the late funds could have been used for other purposes. Sometimes the losses are more explicit. For instance, late receipt of a payment may complicate one's ability to honor another financial commitment.

The existence of liquidity risk accounts in large measure for the development of large-value wire transfer systems such as Fedwire and CHIPS. Before computer technology made such electronic mechanisms possible, depository institutions had to rely on hand delivery by courier or postal services. Sometimes delays occurred that generated significant implicit or explicit costs for these institutions. Wire transfers can be initiated within minutes. Once initiated, they are almost instantaneous.

CREDIT RISK

In many transactions, one party to the transaction makes good on her end of the deal before the other party reciprocates. This means that she has effectively extended credit to the other party, thereby exposing herself to **credit risk,** or the possibility that the other party will fail to honor fully the terms of the exchange.

Credit risk: The risk of loss that might occur if one party to an exchange fails to honor the terms under which the exchange was to take place.

One type of credit risk is *market risk,* which arises when one party to a financial exchange fails to honor the terms of the exchange because of some change in condition that makes fulfilling the bargain impossible. In such a situation, the two parties typically must get together and renegotiate the terms of the exchange, which causes the party that had honored its side of the bargain to incur a loss. Another form of credit risk is *delivery risk,* which is the possibility that one party in a financial transaction will fail entirely to honor the terms of the exchange. In such a situation, the other party to the transaction loses the entire value of the transfer.

Large-value wire transfer systems have elaborate rules intended to reduce participating institutions' exposures to both kinds of credit risk. These rules spell out the responsibilities of both parties to a wire transfer and the role of the system in adjudicating disputes concerning failure to settle a transaction in a timely fashion.

SYSTEMIC RISK

Participants in large-value wire transfer systems are interconnected, which can cause payment flows among depository institutions to be interdependent. For instance, a bank in San Francisco anticipating a wire transfer from a New York bank at 12:30 eastern standard time (EST) may agree to wire funds to a bank in Chicago at 12:45 EST. The Chicago bank, in turn, may have committed to wire funds to a Los Angeles bank at 1:00 EST, using the funds that it expects to receive from the San Francisco bank. Thus, if the New York bank fails to deliver the funds promised at 12:30 EST to the San Francisco bank, the latter bank may send funds to Chicago at 12:45 EST that it does not really have. Furthermore, if the New York bank finds that it is unable to send the funds at all, then an entire chain of payments may occur even though the institutions involved do not have sufficient funds to cover the payments.

Systemic risk: The risk that some depository institutions may not be able to meet the terms of their credit agreements because of failures by other institutions to settle transactions that otherwise are not related.

The risk that the New York bank will fail to settle its transaction with the bank in San Francisco is a liquidity or credit risk for the San Francisco bank. But for the Chicago and Los Angeles banks, it is **systemic risk.** This is a risk that some depository institutions, such as the Chicago and Los Angeles banks in our example, may be unable to honor credit agreements because of settlement failures in otherwise unrelated transactions. For these institutions, systemic risk is a negative externality that arises as a result of the interdependence of transactions in the payment system. It is the existence of such negative externalities that the Fed seeks to address via its supervisory role in the payment system. (Depository institutions are willing to take on liquidity, credit, and systemic risks because payments-related activities generate a large portion of their revenues; see the *Management Focus: The Payoff from Payment Intermediation.*)

MANAGEMENT
Focus

The Payoff from Payment Intermediation

As you learned in Chapter 2, a *payment intermediary* is an institution that assists the transmission of funds between a buyer and a seller. Even though payment intermediation has traditionally been a large part of the business of depository institutions, the amount that this aspect of their operations contributes to the bottom line has often been hard for economists to determine.

A study by Lawrence Radecki of the Federal Reserve Bank of New York attempted to determine banks' payoffs from providing payments-related services to their customers. Figure 15-1 displays his estimates of the sources of operating revenues for the twenty-five largest U.S. banking institutions. All told, Radecki estimated that revenues derived from payment intermediation—deposit account payments, credit-card processing, and securities processing—amounted to about 38 percent of the institutions' combined operating revenues.

FOR CRITICAL ANALYSIS: Why do banks function as both financial intermediaries and payment intermediaries?

FIGURE 15-1
Sources of Operating Revenues for the Top Twenty-Five U.S. Banking Institutions.

Revenues that banks earn from providing payments services account for a significant portion of their total revenues.

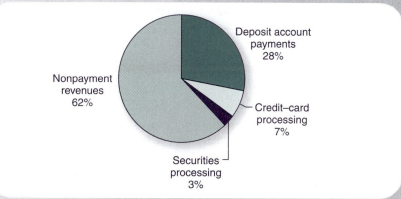

SOURCE: Lawrence Radecki, "Banks' Payment-Driven Revenues," Federal Reserve Bank of New York *Economic Policy Review* 5 (2, July 1999): 53–70.

---

4. Why does the Fed play a supervisory role in the U.S. payment system?

Although most transactions in the U.S. payment system involve cash or checks, the bulk of the dollar flows occur using large-value wire transfer systems. Because such systems link depository institutions in complex webs of payment flows, there is a potential for large negative externalities, or systemic risk. The Fed supervises these systems in an effort to reduce the extent of this risk.

Globally Linked Payments: Where Do Central Banks Fit In?

Systemic risk spans national borders. Thus, the Federal Reserve is not the only institution that frets over systemic risk in the payment system. Systemic risk is of concern to central banks throughout the world.

International Payment Risks

On June 26, 1974, Germany's Bankhaus I.D. Herstatt, at the time a major European banking institution, collapsed. German regulators closed the bank down at 3:30 P.M. Frankfurt time—after the bank had received foreign currency payments from banks based elsewhere in Europe but *before* the bank had made dollar payments that it owed to banks in the United States. Interbank settlements across the Atlantic were thrown into chaos. As word spread that a number of U.S. banks had failed to receive scheduled payments from Herstatt, other U.S. banks became reluctant to agree to payment transactions with banks suspected of trading with the German bank. Within a couple of hours, interbank payment flows among large U.S. depository institutions were nearly gridlocked.

Eventually, teams of accountants from private banks and central banks around the globe unraveled a complex web of interbank payment transactions. Within a few days, the flow of interbank payments returned to normal levels. Nevertheless, several U.S. banks determined that together they had lost as much as $200 million. The Herstatt episode unsettled U.S. financial markets, and several payment systems in other countries, including the United States, temporarily shut down.

Herstatt risk: The risk of any form of loss due to payment settlement failures that occur across national borders; named after a German bank that collapsed in 1974.

HERSTATT RISK Ever since this event, bankers and central bank officials have broadly referred to international payment-system risks as **Herstatt risk.** This term describes the risk of any form of loss due to payment settlement failures that occur across national boundaries.

Herstatt risk actually encompasses two forms of risk that arise primarily from payment processing relating to foreign currency transactions between payment intermediaries based in different countries. First, Herstatt risk refers in part to the direct liquidity and credit risks that payment intermediaries take on when they agree to receive payments from institutions located in other nations in different time zones. For the U.S. banks that had to wait for millions of dollars of payments or that experienced outright losses when Herstatt collapsed in 1974, these direct payment risks turned out to be significant.

Second, and more broadly, Herstatt risk refers to the systemic risks owing to global linkages among national payment systems. Because large payment intermediaries around the globe may be separated by significant time differences, these intermediaries face the potential that events occurring in one time zone, such as the German Herstatt failure, may have broader effects on the functioning of payment systems in another time zone. In this sense, Herstatt risk constitutes an *international externality* that arguably requires the cooperative supervisory and regulatory efforts of many central banks.

THE FOREIGN EXCHANGE MARKET, HERSTATT RISK, AND NETTING ARRANGEMENTS

Most cross-border payment transactions arise from trading in the world's foreign exchange markets. As a result of this trading, individual institutions experience considerable exposure to both liquidity and credit risk. Indeed, current estimates are that foreign exchange settlements account for 50 percent of the daily volume of the U.S., British, and European Monetary Union payment systems. When Herstatt failed in mid-1974, the average dollar value of a currency trade was $750,000. Today, the value of a typical currency exchange in the foreign exchange market exceeds $10 million. Undoubtedly, the upper limit on the systemic-risk exposure arising from foreign exchange transactions is only a fraction of the $4 trillion in aggregate daily currency trading in the world's foreign exchange markets, but even a small fraction of $4 trillion is a risk of considerable magnitude.

In recent years, central banks have advised bank managers to tighten and better police their systems for internal funds transfers, promote sound risk-management practices, and set up contingency plans for crisis management. In addition, they have called upon banks to establish *netting arrangements,* in which a bank tallies its trades with another bank during the course of a day and then makes (or receives) a single payment for the net amount of each currency it owes (or is owed by) that bank at the end of the day. Netting significantly reduces the amount of payment transactions among banks. Consequently, if one institution fails to deliver, its trading partners lose only the smaller, net amount owed, not the gross value of all trades with the failed bank.

Even before central banks began pushing for increased foreign exchange netting, banks had begun to respond to the growing liquidity and credit risks that they faced. During the 1990s and early 2000s, a number of banks established their own *bilateral netting* deals, which are one-to-one netting arrangements between banks. Some banks use netting services that supply proprietary computer software that keeps track of net flows of currency transactions. Accord, which is operated by the Society for Worldwide Interbank Financial Telecommunications (known as "Swift"), is an example of a bilateral netting system.

In addition, banks have set up *multilateral netting* arrangements, which extend netting deals to a number of institutions. For instance, the Exchange Clearing House, Ltd., operates a multilateral netting service for fifteen large European banks, and several large U.S. and Canadian banks operate a similar system called Multinet.

THE "FREE-RIDER PROBLEM"   Multilateral netting arrangements are used jointly by the participating institutions. Setup costs are a significant portion of the cost of a multilateral netting system. Once the system has been established, the day-to-day operating costs are relatively low.

As a result, multilateral netting systems often experience a **free-rider problem,** which occurs when some participants in a joint system such as multilateral currency netting take advantage of the fact that other participants have already shouldered the burden of establishing the arrangements. For instance, a few years ago, a banker was quoted as saying, "If somebody is going to go to all the trouble of setting up a clearing bank [for multilateral currency settlement] and you can join later, let him pay the expense."

The free-rider problem in foreign currency netting is a further justification offered for the involvement of central banks in the payment system. For profit-maximizing private banks, the free-rider problem reduces the incentive to incur the sizable costs of establishing a system that they know "free riders" will benefit from in the future. In the case of currency payment netting, however, which spans national boundaries, there is a rationale for central banks to *coordinate* their efforts. Thus, the free-rider problem in international payments processing has been a major incentive for central banks to work together to contain global payment-system risks. (In years past, banks using the Fed's Fedwire system have tried to free-ride on the Fed; see on page 338 the *Policy Focus: How the Fed Addresses the Fedwire Free-Rider Problem.*)

DEALING WITH THE FREE-RIDER PROBLEM   Taking the lead in this joint central bank effort has been the *Bank for International Settlements (BIS).* This institution, which is based in Basel, Switzerland, has functioned for several decades as a trustee for various international loan agreements and serves as an agent in miscellaneous foreign exchange markets for many of the world's central banks. Private U.S. banks, including Citibank and J.P. Morgan, participated with governments of the Group of Ten (G10) nations—Belgium, Canada, France, Germany, Italy, Japan, the Netherlands, Sweden, the United Kingdom, and the United States—in founding the BIS in 1930, and a number of private banks continue to own shares of ownership in the BIS. The original task of the BIS was to supervise the settlement of financial claims among European nations relating to World War I. After World War II, the BIS

Free-rider problem: A situation in which some individuals take advantage of the fact that others are willing to pay for a jointly utilized good, such as a system of multilateral netting of foreign exchange payments.

MONEYXTRA!
Online Case Study

To consider the issues raised by different means of settling payments, go to the Chapter 15 Case Study, entitled "Time to Eliminate Daylight Overdrafts on Fedwire?" **http://moneyxtra. swcollege.com**

How the Fed Addresses the Fedwire Free-Rider Problem

Final settlement on the Fed's Fedwire system does not occur until the end of each business day. Although depository institutions very rarely fail to settle their obligations on Fedwire, it is not uncommon for some to send wire transfer payments when they do not have funds in their reserve accounts with Fed banks to cover those payments. Thus, these institutions technically overdraw their reserve accounts. The Fed calls such Fedwire withdrawals of reserve deposit accounts *daylight overdrafts.* Panel (a) of Figure 15-2 displays a typical pattern of daylight overdrafts. Total overdrafts—negative reserve balances—reach their "peak" just before 2 P.M. As the afternoon progresses, an institution begins to receive funds transfers from others, and shortly before 4 P.M. its reserve account balance once again becomes positive.

Because the Fed would have to make good on any overdrafts by a bank that failed, daylight overdrafts on Fedwire have exposed the Fed to significant credit risks. In the late 1980s, peak daylight overdrafts amounted to nearly three times the size of the total reserves of all depository institutions, and it was not unusual for as many as a thousand institutions to overdraw their Fed deposit accounts within a given day. To solve its free-rider problem and give institutions an incentive to limit daylight overdrafts, in April 1994 the Fed began to charge an annual interest fee, based on a 360-day year and the 18-hour days that Fedwire is open. Since April

1995, this fee has been equal to 27 hundredths of 1 percent. As panel (b) of Figure 15-2 indicates, both average and peak overdrafts fell dramatically after the Fed began charging for them. Overdrafts have shown slight upward trends since then.

FIGURE 15-2
Daylight Overdrafts.

Panel (a) shows the typical pattern of daylight overdrafts for a large U.S. bank. Panel (b) displays the average and peak volumes of reserve account overdrafts by depository institutions at all twelve Federal Reserve banks.

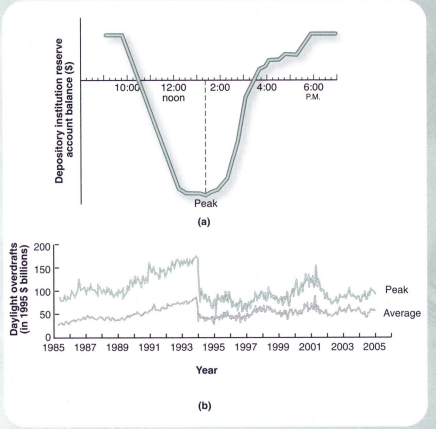

(a)

(b)

SOURCES: Board of Governors of the Federal Reserve System and Diana Hancock and James Wilcox, "Intraday Bank Reserve Management: The Effects of Caps and Fees on Daylight Overdrafts," *Journal of Money, Credit and Banking* 28 (2, November 1996): 870–908; Board of Governors of the Federal Reserve System.

FOR CRITICAL ANALYSIS: Given that daylight overdrafts on Fedwire expose the Fed to credit risk, why do you suppose that the Fed nonetheless permits positive daylight overdrafts for a fee instead of prohibiting daylight overdrafts altogether?

became a central agent for clearing payments among nations participating in the European Recovery Program, which was designed to rebuild European economies after the ravages of the war.

Ultimately, the BIS developed into a clearinghouse providing information to the central banks of the G10 nations plus the Bank of Switzerland, the Swiss central bank. Staff members of the BIS organize periodic briefings for top G10 central banking officials and coordinate conferences for staff economists of policymaking agencies of the G10 nations. As we discussed in Chapter 11, in 1988 central banks and other banking regulators of the G10 nations adopted the *Basel Agreement* establishing common risk-based bank capital standards under the auspices of the BIS. Today, the BIS also serves as a mechanism for coordinating central bank efforts to establish multilateral netting systems for international payment flows.

A recent result of these efforts is a currency payment settlement system called the *Continuous Linked Settlement (CLS) Bank,* which was established in 1997. Although the BIS and its member central banks helped initiate the formation of the CLS Bank, thereby absorbing some of its initial setup costs, the CLS Bank is a private institution. It is formally based in the United States, but the main site of its operations is London. The CLS Bank holds currency settlement accounts with G10 central banks and other central banks around the world, and it conducts continuous daily currency settlements on behalf of the largest banks in the world. The CLS Bank formally began its operations in 2000.

Common Payment-System Standards

In an international context, difficulties in payment-system settlements may arise because of different rules and legalities applying to transactions that cross from one nation's large-value wire transfer system to a system located in another country. For example, a U.S. payment intermediary may use CHIPS to transmit a payment to a Hong Kong bank that is a member of the British CHAPS system. These two large-value wire transfer systems may have slightly different rules about settling payments. In addition, the U.S., British, and Hong Kong legal systems may also have somewhat divergent perspectives on the duties and responsibilities of parties to an exchange of funds.

To address the possibility of problems arising from international cross-system payment transfers, the BIS has assisted in the development of a common set of rules called the *Lamfalussy standards.* These standards clarify the essential legal payment responsibilities of any payment intermediary that participates in a large-value wire transfer system operated within a G10 nation. Furthermore, all large-value wire transfer systems have agreed to operate within the framework of rules established under the Lamfalussy standards.

> **5. In what ways do payment-system risks span national borders, and how do central banks seek to contain these risks?** Payments relating to foreign-exchange-market transactions account for the bulk of international payment-system risks. Bankers and central bank officials refer to these specific risks collectively as Herstatt risk. Most efforts to contain Herstatt risk focus on limiting the magnitude of risk exposures through bilateral and multilateral netting of payments among banks that actively trade currencies in the foreign exchange market. Central banks and the Bank for International Settlements have assisted in establishing net settlement systems, and these institutions have also been at the forefront of developing common standards for international payment systems.

Chapter Summary

1. The Main Assets and Liabilities of the Fed: The Fed's holdings of government securities make up over 90 percent of its assets. An almost identical portion of its liabilities consists of the currency that it issues and reserve deposits of depository institutions, which together compose the monetary base.

2. Ways in Which the Fed Is the Government's Bank: The Treasury maintains large deposits with the Federal Reserve banks, which provide a number of depository services to the Treasury. In addition, the Fed issues securities on the Treasury's behalf, and it maintains book-entry security accounts through which the Treasury makes payments of interest and principal to large institutional holders of government securities.

3. The Rationale for the Fed's Role as a Bank for Private Banks: Because depository institutions are interconnected, breakdowns in transactions among a few institutions can spill over to create hardships for a large number of institutions. A key role for the Fed, therefore, is to contain the potential for such negative externalities in the financial system.

4. The Reason the Fed Plays a Supervisory Role in the U.S. Payment System: Most dollar flows in the U.S. payment system are large-value wire transfers on Fedwire and the Clearing House Interbank Payment System (CHIPS). These two systems together connect thousands of depository institutions. Although the systems increase the efficiency with which depository institutions can make transactions, they also expose the institutions to systemic risk, or the possibility of significant negative externalities arising from spillovers from a few institutions to many. The Fed monitors and supervises the payment system in an effort to contain these risks.

5. How Payment-System Risks Span National Borders, and How Central Banks Seek to Contain These Risks: Transfers of payments for foreign-exchange-market transactions generate the majority of international payment-system risks, which together are called Herstatt risk. Central banks, alone and together through the Bank for International Settlements (BIS), have promoted bilateral and multilateral netting of foreign-exchange-market payments as a key means of reducing banks' exposures to Herstatt risk. Central banks and the BIS have also pushed the development of common international standards for the world's major payment systems.

Questions and Problems

(Answers to odd-numbered questions and problems may be found on the Web at **http://money.swcollege.com** under "Student Resources.")

1. Explain in what sense currency is a liability of the Federal Reserve System.

2. What are the Fed's key roles as a central bank? In your view, what is the single most important role of a central bank? Could the Fed perform this role without performing its other roles? Explain your reasoning.

3. In your own words, define a negative externality. Explain how such externalities can arise in the financial system.

4. Any depository institution that is required to hold reserves with the Federal Reserve System has access to Fedwire. In contrast, the owners of CHIPS determine which institutions can join CHIPS and use its facilities; thus, the owners can require member institutions to provide information about their internal management procedures for handling risk. Some economists have speculated that these structural differences alone tend to make CHIPS a less risky large-value wire transfer system. Does this argument make sense to you? Why or why not? [Hint: Think back to the asymmetric-information problems of financial intermediation discussed in Chapter 8.]

5. Can you see any ways that the Federal Reserve's direct involvement in the U.S. payment system, via its operation of Fedwire and its own check-clearing and automated clearinghouse systems, assists it in its efforts to monitor and supervise the overall payment system? Explain.

6. Privately operated institutions that offer their own payment services often complain that the Fed has an "inherent competitive advantage." Sometimes they even claim that the Fed's business interest in its own payment systems can expose it to a conflict of interest in its role as a supervisor of the U.S. payment system. In your view, could these concerns have any merit? Why or why not?

7. Discuss the three basic ways that payment intermediaries are exposed to Herstatt risk arising from payments relating to foreign-exchange-market transactions. [Hint: Recall the three types of payment-system risks, and evaluate how these can arise in an international setting.]

8. Explain why net currency settlement helps reduce payment intermediaries' total exposures to Herstatt risk.

9. How can multilateral net settlement systems give rise to a free-rider problem?

10. In your view, is the free-rider problem likely to be sufficiently great to justify the involvement of central banks?

Before the Test

Test your understanding of the material covered in this chapter by taking the Chapter 15 interactive quiz at **http://money.swcollege.com**.

Online Application

Internet URL: http://www.chips.org

Title: The Clearing House Interbank Payment System

Navigation: Begin at the above Web site. In the left-hand margin of the CHIPS home page, click on "About Us."

Application: Read the discussion, and answer the following questions:

1. How does CHIPS limit credit risk?

2. What types of real-time settlement procedures does CHIPS use in an effort to contain settlement risks?

For Group Study and Analysis: Divide the class into four groups and assign each group a type of payment risk—liquidity, credit, systemic, or Herstatt. Have each group examine and summarize ways in which CHIPS has sought to address their assigned type of risk. In addition, ask each group to speculate about ways in which CHIPS still may experience problems in addressing their assigned type of risk.

Selected References and Further Reading

Berger, Allen, Diana Hancock, and Jeffrey Marquardt, eds. "Payment Systems Research and Public Policy: Risk, Efficiency, and Innovation." Federal Reserve Board Conference on Payment Systems Research and Public Policy, *Journal of Money, Credit, and Banking* 28 (Special Issue, November 1996).

Chakravorti, Sujit, and Timothy McHugh. "Why Do We Use So Many Checks?" Federal Reserve Bank of Chicago *Economic Perspectives,* Third Quarter 2002, pp. 44–59.

DeBrandt, Olivier, and Philipp Hartmann. "Systemic Risk: A Survey." European Central Bank Working Paper No. 5, November 2000.

DeCorleto, Donna, and Theresa Trimble. "Federal Reserve Banks as Fiscal Agents and Depositories of the United States in a Changing Financial Environment." *Federal Reserve Bulletin* 90 (Autumn 2004): 435–446.

Eisenbeis, Robert. "International Settlements: A New Source of Systemic Risk?" Federal Reserve Bank of Atlanta *Economic Review* 82 (Second Quarter 1997): 44–50.

Furfine, Craig, and Jeffrey Stehm. "Analyzing Alternative Daylight Credit Policies in Real-Time Gross Settlement Systems." *Journal of Money, Credit, and Banking* 30 (November 1998): 832–848.

Garbade, Kenneth, John Partlan, and Paul Santoro. "Recent Innovations in Treasury Cash Management." Federal Reserve Bank of New York *Current Issues in Economics and Finance* 10 (November 2004).

Gilbert, Adam, Dara Hunt, and Kenneth Winch. "Creating an Integrated Payment System: The Evolution of Fedwire." Federal Reserve Bank of New York *Economic Policy Review,* July 1997, pp. 1–7.

Green, Edward, and Richard Todd. "Thoughts on the Fed's Role in the Payment System." Federal Reserve Bank of Minneapolis *Quarterly Review* 25 (Winter 2001): 12–27.

Hancock, Diana, and David Humphrey. "Payment Transactions, Instruments, and Systems: A Survey." *Journal of Banking and Finance* 21 (December 1997): 1573–1624.

Kemppainen, Kari. "Competition and Regulation in European Retail Payment Systems." Bank of Finland Discussion Paper No. 16-2003, September 6, 2003.

McAndrews, James, and Samira Rajan. "The Timing and Funding of Fedwire Funds Transfers." Federal Reserve Bank of New York *Economic Policy Review,* July 2000, pp. 17–32.

VanHoose, David. "Bank Behavior, Interest Rate Determination, and Monetary Policy in a Financial System with an Intraday Fed-eral Funds Market." *Journal of Banking and Finance* 15 (April 1991): 343–365.

_____. "Central Bank Policymaking in Competing Payment Systems." *Atlantic Economic Journal* 28 (June 2000): 117–139.

MoneyXtra

Log on to the MoneyXtra Web site now (**http://moneyxtra.swcollege.com**) for additional learning resources such as practice quizzes, case studies, readings, and additional economic applications.

Unit V
Monetary Policy and the Economy

Contents

How Much Money Do People Want to Hold?—

The Demand for Money

How much money would you like to have on hand? The answer, of course, seems obvious: As much as possible! If this question is qualified, however, by adding the phrase "given your available income and wealth," then the answer is not so apparent. After all, you surely do not hold as much money as possible, because then you would have converted all your possessions to cash. Most of us choose to allocate only a fraction of our income or wealth to holding various forms of money, such as currency and checking deposits.

Economists have conducted hundreds of studies trying to identify the key factors that determine how much money residents of the United States and other nations desire to hold. So many studies have been conducted on this topic that economists sometimes refer to them as an "industry."

Most theories of the demand for money indicate that two key factors affecting how much money people wish to hold are the incomes that people earn and the interest rates on bonds and other financial instruments that they can hold instead of or alongside various forms of money. Nevertheless, economists have not reached a consensus about exactly how the public's total holdings of money respond to changes in incomes or interest rates. Some economists worry that it may never be possible to determine just how responsive total desired money holdings are to these key factors.

Why do so many economists study the determinants of the demand for money? Why are incomes and interest rates thought to be key factors affecting the public's desired money holdings? What aspects of the relationships between incomes and interest rates and the quantity of money demanded make it difficult for economists to agree on just how much influence these factors have on the amount of money people want to have on hand? These are the fundamental questions addressed in this chapter.

The Motives for Holding Money

When the subject of the demand for money comes up today, most economists think of the early-twentieth-century British economist John Maynard Keynes. Keynes tried to identify people's fundamental *motives* for holding coins, pieces of paper, and bank accounts that

Fundamental Issues

1. What is the Cambridge equation?

2. What are real money balances?

3. According to the inventory theory of the demand for money, what are the key factors influencing desired holdings of real money balances?

4. What do other transactions-related theories add to our understanding of the demand for money?

5. What theories explain the demand for real money balances based on money's function as a store of value?

6. What difficulties do economists face in trying to predict the overall demand for money?

offer little or no financial return. One of these he called the **transactions motive.** This is the incentive to hold non-interest-bearing currency and non- (or low-) interest-bearing transactions deposits for use as media of exchange in planned transactions, such as buying groceries each week and paying rent and utility bills each month.

In addition, Keynes proposed a *speculative motive* for holding real money balances. The more modern term for this incentive to hold money is the **portfolio motive,** which refers to the demand for money as one item in a broad portfolio of assets, based on expected relative rates of return. The portfolio motive, therefore, relates to money's role as a store of value. (A few people are *too* motivated to obtain cash; see *What Happens When Money Is Made More Colorful?*)

In this chapter we shall consider these motives and their implications for the overall demand for money in an economy. In addition, we shall consider how economists seek to measure total desired money holdings in an economy. We shall also evaluate the predictability of the overall demand for money. As you will learn in the next chapter, there are good reasons that economists—particularly those who work at the Federal Reserve—may wish to predict the demand for money.

The Transactions Demand for Money

Following earlier economic tradition, Keynes argued that total income is a key determinant of total desired money holdings. As income rises, Keynes concluded, so does the total quantity of money demanded to satisfy the transactions motive for holding money as a medium of exchange. Let's think about why this is likely to be the case and about whether we can be more specific in predicting *exactly* how much money a person is likely to hold relative to his or her income.

Transactions motive: The desire to hold currency and transactions deposits to use as media of exchange in planned transactions.

Portfolio motive: The desire to hold money as part of a strategy of balancing the expected rate of return on money with rates of return on other assets.

MONEYXTRA!
Another Perspective

Consider how the growing use of online payments may affect the demand for money by going to the Chapter 16 reading, entitled "Personal On-Line Payments," by Kenneth Kuttner and James McAndrews of the Federal Reserve Bank of Cleveland. **http://moneyxtra. swcollege.com**

What Happens When... **Money Is Made More Colorful?**

Once upon a time, U.S. currency was known as the "Greenback" because of the green hue of the background and the green ink on the back of the bills. Gradually, for the first time since 1905, the U.S. Bureau of Engraving and Printing has been introducing other colors of the rainbow. The latest version of the $20 bill, for instance, includes soft background colors. "TWENTY USA" is printed in blue, and tiny numeral 20s appear in yellow on the back of the bill. Within a peach background on the face of the bill, a blue eagle is positioned to the left of the presidential portrait, and a metallic green eagle and shield appear to the right. The bill also has a watermark, which is a faint image similar to the portrait that is visible when the bill is held up to light, and color-shifting ink that changes the numeral "20" in the lower-right corner on the face from copper to green.

New $50 bills have similar designs but also include a field of blue stars and three red stripes. Soon $100 and $10 bills will also have more colorful designs. The colorful makeovers are not due to the artistic fancies of those charged with engraving U.S. currency, but rather are intended to combat counterfeiting. At present, nearly one dollar out of every 12,400 in worldwide circulation is counterfeit. Bills with various hues and detailed features are very difficult to reproduce using old-fashioned printing-press technologies. They are also harder for modern counterfeiters to replicate, even using digital scanners and copiers.

FOR CRITICAL ANALYSIS: Why do you suppose that the Secret Service, which enforces the laws against counterfeiting, has been encouraging producers of scanners and copiers to incorporate software into their equipment that would automatically prevent scanning or copying U.S. currency?

The Demand for Money as a Medium of Exchange

Several components of common measures of money, such as currency and transactions deposits, either have no interest yields or pay interest at lower rates than alternative instruments. Why would anyone hold these money assets? The reason, as we discussed in Chapter 1, is that individuals and business firms use such money assets as media of exchange.

THE CAMBRIDGE EQUATION Because people use money assets to buy other goods and services, their demand for such assets as media of exchange depends on how many purchases they plan to make. This, of course, depends on their ability to spend, which in turn depends on their incomes.

A simple way to express this idea is through a relationship called the *Cambridge equation,* which is named for economists at Cambridge University in England who developed it at the beginning of the twentieth century. The Cambridge equation is

$$M^d = k \times Y,$$

in which M^d is the total nominal (current-dollar) quantity of money demanded for use as a medium of exchange, Y is the total current-dollar income of consumers and businesses, and k is a fraction that represents the portion of current-dollar income that consumers and businesses wish to hold as money.

For instance, suppose that the total income of all individuals and business firms is $10 trillion, which is roughly the size of total income in the United States. Then, if consumers and businesses desire to hold 20 percent of their income as money, the value of k is 0.2, and the total quantity of money demanded is equal to $k \times Y = 0.2 \times \$10$ trillion, or $2 trillion.

> **1. What is the Cambridge equation?** The Cambridge equation is a simple representation of the transactions theory of the demand for money. According to the Cambridge equation, people wish to hold a portion of their current-dollar income as money. Consequently, the quantity of money demanded varies directly with income.

THE DEMAND FOR REAL MONEY BALANCES In the form $M^d = k \times Y$, the Cambridge equation focuses on the demand for nominal, or current-dollar, money balances. When we decide how much cash to carry, however, what really matters to us is the purchasing power of the money we hold. Suppose, for instance, that you decide one morning to carry $15 in cash to cover the purchases that you intend to make that day—say, lunch for $10 and an afternoon snack for $5. After you leave home, however, the price level doubles. As a result, the lunch you had intended to purchase now costs $20, and your planned afternoon snack costs $10. Now your $15 will not even cover the complete lunch that you had planned, and you will have to forgo your afternoon snack. The purchasing power of your $15 in cash is half its previous value. To purchase the same lunch and snack, you will need to double your nominal money balances to $30. Thus, a doubling of prices requires a doubling of nominal money balances to maintain the required purchasing power for the day's expenses.

The upshot of this example is that the real purchasing power of nominal cash balances is the price-adjusted value of their money holdings, or $m = M/P$, where m denotes **real money balances**—the real purchasing power of the quantity of money in circulation—and P denotes an index of the overall prices of goods and services that people purchase using their real

Real money balances: The purchasing power of the quantity of money in circulation, measured as the nominal quantity of money divided by an index measure of the prices of goods and services.

incomes. It turns out that the Cambridge equation can tell us something about the total demand for real money balances. To see why, let's think about *real income,* which is the real value of all individuals' current-dollar income, which we shall denote as y. This is the price-adjusted value of total real income, or $y = Y/P$. By rearranging this relationship, we can express current-dollar income as $Y = y \times P$. Thus, another way to write the Cambridge equation is

$$M^d = k \times y \times P.$$

If we divide both sides of the Cambridge equation by P, we end up with

$$M^d/P = k \times y.$$

Of course, M^d/P is the demand for real money balances, or m^d. Consequently, the Cambridge equation tells us that the demand for real money balances is

$$m^d = k \times y,$$

which means that the *real* money balances that people wish to hold are a fraction, k, of their *real* incomes. The total real purchasing power of money holdings that people desire to maintain will depend on their total real income.

> **2. What are real money balances?** Real money balances are the purchasing power of the current-dollar value of the quantity of money that people hold. Economists measure real money balances by dividing the quantity of money in circulation by an index measure of the prices of goods and services. In the Cambridge equation, the quantity of real money balances demanded is equal to a desired fraction of real income.

The Inventory Approach to the Demand for Money

An obvious shortcoming of the basic Cambridge equation is that it fails to take into account the opportunity cost of holding money instead of other interest-bearing financial assets. Furthermore, the Cambridge equation does not allow for variations in the demand for money over time as a result of seasonal or other factors that are likely to affect individuals' spending patterns and, thus, their desired money holdings.

MONEY HOLDINGS AS AN INVENTORY One way to think about a change in desired money holdings that typically occurs during a seasonal spending period such as the Christmas season is to visualize it as an *inventory adjustment.* Just as a retailer that produces filters for air conditioners typically increases its available inventories of filters to sell during spring and summer, an individual increases his cash holdings during the weeks prior to the Christmas season. That is, the individual adjusts his desired *cash inventory* in recognition that he will need more cash on hand for the increased spending he will undertake before Christmas.

In the early 1950s, William Baumol of Princeton University and James Tobin of Yale University independently developed the idea of applying *inventory theory,* or the theory of how people determine the best inventory of a good to keep on hand, to achieve a better understanding of the transactions demand for money. Their theory came to be known as the **inventory theory of money demand.** What they both discovered was that while the Cambridge equation captures the "spirit" of the transactions motive, it likely overlooks some essential elements as well.

Inventory theory of money demand: A theory of the demand for money that focuses on how people determine the best inventory of money to keep on hand.

SIMPLIFYING ASSUMPTIONS OF THE CASH-INVENTORY THEORY   The basic theory of the transactions demand for money that Baumol and Tobin developed begins with some simplifying assumptions that capture the basic aspects of the inventory problem that people face when they try to determine how much money they should hold. One assumption is that all money holdings yield no interest return. This assumption rules out interest-bearing transactions deposits such as NOW accounts, but it is fairly straightforward to adjust the Baumol-Tobin approach to take into account interest-bearing forms of money.

A second key assumption is that people earn a fixed amount of real income, y, each period. Furthermore, people receive all income in the form of direct deposits into bond funds that yield an overall interest return equal to r. To hold money for use as a medium of exchange in planned purchases of goods and services, people must convert a portion of these bond holdings to real money balances. Making these conversions is not costless, however. Each conversion entails a fee equal to f.

Another assumption is that people buy goods and services at a constant rate. This is probably the hardest assumption to accept because it literally implies that a person is spending a fixed amount every second of every day. Although the theory can be modified to consider more realistic spending patterns, let's abstract from the "real world" to keep things as simple as possible. Figure 16-1 shows what the spending pattern of a recent college graduate with a real annual income of $36,000 looks like if she spends her entire annual income on her apartment rent, groceries, entertainment, and other goods and services at a constant rate during a year's time. She begins the year by receiving her $36,000 in real income as a direct deposit into her bond fund. Then she converts this amount into $36,000 in real money balances, which she spends at a constant rate during the year. At the end of the year, she has zero real money balances remaining.

Figure 16-1 illustrates a further simplifying assumption of the Baumol-Tobin inventory theory of the demand for money, which is that people use up all their real money balances before converting any more bonds into new cash balances. To continue spending during the next year, the person whose spending pattern is depicted in Figure 16-1 will have to convert more bonds into real money balances.

**FIGURE 16-1
An Annual Spending
Pattern with a Constant
Rate of Spending.**

This figure displays the spending pattern of an individual who receives her entire $36,000 annual real income payment at the beginning of the year and immediately converts it into real money balances. She then spends at a constant rate until she has no real money balances remaining at the conclusion of the year.

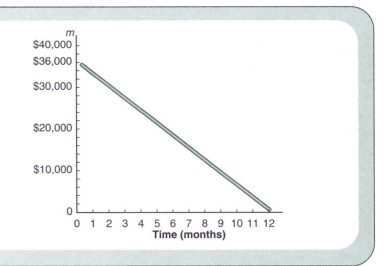

Most people, of course, do not start a year with a large cash balance that they stretch out over the entire twelve months. For instance, as shown in panel (a) of Figure 16-2, the individual whose spending pattern is depicted in Figure 16-1 might decide to finance her $36,000 in spending during the year with two $18,000 cash conversions. She could make one of these conversions at the beginning of the year and then spend at a constant rate until her money holdings are used up at the middle of the year. Then she could convert bonds into a new starting inventory of $18,000 in real money balances and spend them at a constant rate until year-end.

Panel (b) of Figure 16-2 illustrates yet another alternative. In this spending pattern, the individual chooses to make twelve (that is, monthly) cash conversions during the year. Because she knows that she will spend a total of $36,000 during the year, she converts $3,000 of bonds into real money balances at the beginning of a given month and spends at a constant rate until she needs to make a new cash conversion at the beginning of the next month.

The examples in Figure 16-2 illustrate a final assumption of the Baumol-Tobin inventory model of the demand for money: people make cash conversions in constant fractions of a year. In panel (a), for example, the individual makes a cash conversion from bonds to money every half-year. In panel (b), she makes cash conversions each twelfth of a year, or monthly.

THE AVERAGE REAL MONEY BALANCE OVER THE COURSE OF A YEAR An important implication of the spending patterns illustrated in Figures 16-1 and 16-2 is that a person's *average inventory* of real money balances depends on how often she makes cash conversions. As shown in Figure 16-1, a person who makes only one $36,000 cash conversion at the beginning of the year and then spends those funds at a constant rate throughout the year has an average real money balance of $18,000. Panel (a) of Figure 16-2 shows, however, that someone who makes two cash conversions of $18,000 at the beginning and middle of the year has an average real money balance of $9,000. For someone who makes monthly $3,000 cash conversions, the average money balance during the year is $1,500.

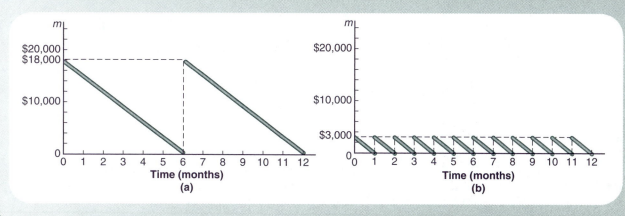

FIGURE 16-2
Alternative Spending Patterns.

An individual who spends a real amount of $36,000 at a constant rate during the year might, as in panel (a), make separate $18,000 cash conversions from her bond account at the beginning and middle of the year. Alternatively, as shown in panel (b), she might make monthly $3,000 conversions.

In each case, the individual's average real money balance depends on the number of cash conversions, n, that she makes during the year. In Figure 16-1, n is equal to 1, and the individual's average money balance is equal to $(y/1)/2 = \$36,000/2 = \$18,000$. In panel (a) of Figure 16-2, n is equal to 2, so her average money balance for the year is equal to $(y/2)/2 = (\$36,000/2)/2 = \$18,000/2 = \$9,000$. In panel (b) of Figure 16-2, n is equal to 12, so her average money balance equals $(y/12)/2 = (\$36,000/12)/2 = \$3,000/2 = \$1,500$. Clearly, this means that for any given number of cash conversions n, her average real money balance for the year is equal to $(y/n)/2$, or half the amount of each equally spaced cash conversion during the year.

DETERMINING THE OPTIMAL NUMBER OF CASH CONVERSIONS   Let's suppose that this individual is contemplating how many cash conversions she ought to make during the year. Should $n = 1$, as in Figure 16-1, so that she makes only one conversion and stretches out her available real cash balances for the entire year? Or should $n = 2$, as in panel (a) of Figure 16-2? Or should $n = 12$, as in panel (b) of Figure 16-2? Or should she select some other value for n, such as $n = 52$, which would mean weekly cash conversions?

Minimizing the Total Cost of Holding Money   The answer is that the individual should choose a number of conversions that minimizes her total cost of maintaining her inventory of real money balances over the course of the year. This cost has two components. One is the total conversion costs that she must incur during the year. Each conversion entails a fee equal to f, so her total cash-conversion cost is equal to this conversion fee, f, times the number of conversions, n, or $f \times n$. This is the upward-sloping line shown in Figure 16-3.

The other component of the individual's cost of holding money is the opportunity cost of holding real money balances during the year. This is equal to the forgone interest return, r, times the average money holding during the year, which we determined to equal $(y/n)/2 = y/(2 \times n)$. Thus, the total opportunity cost of holding money during the year is equal to $(r \times y)/(2 \times n)$. As Figure 16-3 shows, this cost steadily falls as the number of cash conver-

---

FIGURE 16-3
The Total Cost of Maintaining a Cash Inventory.

If each cash conversion that an individual makes entails a fee equal to f, and if she makes n conversions during a year, then her total cash-conversion costs for the year equal $f \times n$, which is the upward-sloping line in the figure. Her total opportunity cost of holding money during the year is equal to the forgone interest return, r, times her average money balance during the year, $y/(2 \times n)$, which is the downward-sloping curve. The total cost of holding real money balances

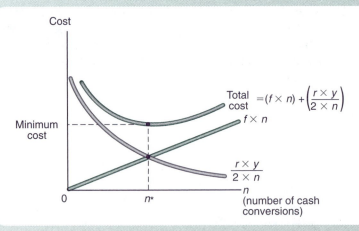

during the year is the sum of these two curves, which is the U-shaped curve. To minimize her total cost of

holding money, the individual chooses the number of cash conversions equal to n^*.

sions increases. [As n becomes larger, the denominator $2 \times n$ increases, so the total opportunity cost of holding money, $(r \times y)/(2 \times n)$, declines.]

Consequently, converting bonds to cash more often during the year has two effects on the total cost of maintaining a cash inventory. Increasing the number of cash conversions raises the explicit cost of paying fees to make conversions. At the same time, however, converting bonds to cash more often reduces the opportunity cost of holding money by reducing the average amount of real money balances that a person maintains.

The Cost-Minimizing Number of Conversions   The total cost of holding real money balances equals the sum of the explicit cash-conversion costs and the implicit opportunity cost of holding money. This is the vertical sum of both types of costs, which is the smooth U-shaped curve in Figure 16-3. For any given number of cash conversions, we can read up to a point on this curve and determine the total cost of holding real money balances. Naturally, an individual will choose to minimize this cost. Thus, she will choose the number of cash conversions that corresponds to the minimum point on the total cost curve. Problem 3 at the end of the chapter lets you work out an exact solution for the cost-minimizing number of conversions, which we denote as n^* in Figure 16-3.

Panel (a) of Figure 16-4 shows how a rise in the cash-conversion fee affects the number of cash conversions that minimizes the individual's total cost of maintaining her inventory of real money balances. A rise in the fee causes an upward rotation of the upward-sloping line giving the individual's explicit conversion costs. As a result, the total cost curve shifts upward and to the left. Hence, to minimize the costs of maintaining her money inventory, the individual should reduce her cash conversions from n^* to n^{**}.

FIGURE 16-4
Factors Influencing the Cost-Minimizing Number of Cash Conversions.

Panel (a) shows the effect of an increase in the conversion fee, f, on the cost-minimizing number of conversions during the year. A rise in this fee shifts the total cost curve upward and to the left. This causes the optimal number of cash conversions to decline. By way of contrast, an increase in the interest return on bonds, r, raises the opportunity cost of holding money during the year. As shown in panel (b), this causes the total cost curve to shift upward. Thus, a rise in the interest rate induces an increase in the cost-minimizing number of cash conversions during the year.

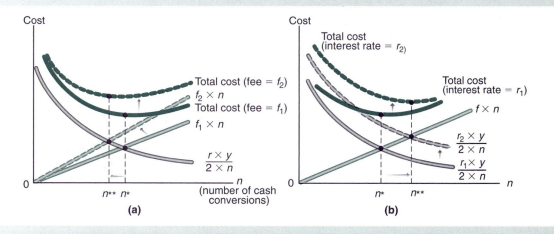

Panel (b) of Figure 16-4 shows what happens if there is an increase in r, the interest return on bonds. This increases the opportunity cost of real money balances, which shifts the total cost curve upward and to the right. Consequently, to minimize the total cost of holding money, the individual should increase the number of cash conversions, n^* to n^{**}.

THE OPTIMAL CASH BALANCE

We can now evaluate the key factors that the inventory approach predicts will influence the amount of real money balances that an individual wishes to hold. As we determined earlier, the theory indicates that the average money balance during the course of a year is equal to $(y/n)/2$, or $y/(2 \times n)$. Given the optimal number of conversions during the year, n^*, it follows that the quantity of money demanded is equal to $m^* = y/(2 \times n^*)$. This quantity clearly depends on real income. Furthermore, the optimal number of cash conversions depends on the interest rate and the cash-conversion fee, so the quantity of money demanded depends on these two factors as well.

Thus, the inventory theory of the demand for money implies that three key factors affect the amount of real money balances that an individual wishes to hold:

1. **Real income.** Although a rise in real income tends to increase the average opportunity cost of holding money and thereby raises the cost-minimizing number of conversions, the *direct* effect of an increase in real income is to raise the individual's average money balance during the year. As we ask you to show in problem 3 at the conclusion of the chapter, this direct effect dominates. A *rise in real income*, therefore, causes an *increase* in the quantity of money demanded.

2. **The interest rate.** As discussed, an increase in the interest rate on bonds raises the opportunity cost of holding an inventory of real money balances. The best way for an individual to respond to a rise in the interest rate, therefore, is to make more cash conversions and thereby reduce the average money inventory at any given point in time. Consequently, an *increase in the bond interest rate* induces a *reduction* in the quantity of money demanded.

3. **The cash-conversion fee.** As we noted earlier, an increase in the fee incurred in shifting funds from bond holdings to real money balances induces a cost-minimizing individual to cut back on the number of cash conversions. As a result, the average real money balance increases. Hence, an *increase in the cash-conversion fee* causes an *increase* in the quantity of money demanded.

As in the basic Cambridge equation approach, the inventory theory of the demand for money indicates that the quantity of money demanded depends directly on the real income people earn. In addition, however, the inventory theory also predicts that the quantity of real money balances that people wish to hold varies inversely with the nominal interest rate and directly with the explicit costs people face in shifting funds from bond holdings to cash inventories.

> **3. According to the inventory theory of the demand for money, what are the key factors influencing desired holdings of real money balances?**
> The inventory theory of money demand indicates that an increase in the opportunity cost of holding money caused by a rise in a market interest rate reduces the quantity of money demanded. It also implies that the quantity of money demanded depends positively on real income and cash-conversion fees.

Alternative Transaction-Based Theories of Money Demand

Although the Baumol-Tobin inventory theory is a half-century old, it has been a key starting point for many more elaborate and more recent theories of the demand for money by individuals and businesses. This does not mean, however, that economists are in agreement that the inventory theory is the best approach to understanding the determinants of desired holdings of real money balances.

THE SHOPPING-TIME THEORY   A common criticism of the inventory approach to the demand for money is that it takes for granted that people use money. Consequently, it fails to explain why money is what people use to buy goods and services. One possible way to remedy this perceived problem is to develop an alternative theory that sets out a clear motivation for using money in transactions. The **shopping-time theory of money demand** follows this approach by providing an explanation for why money has value as a medium of exchange. As its name implies, the shopping-time theory emphasizes money's role in reducing time spent shopping, thereby freeing up time for other activities.

The shopping-time theory is based on essential microeconomic principles that you learned in your first economics course. These are that people typically like to consume goods and services but also like to have leisure time. Nevertheless, every individual faces the constraint that there are only twenty-four hours in each day. In addition, to be able to consume, people must work to earn income, and they must spend time shopping for the goods and services that they consume. Time allocated to shopping is not available for leisure or work pursuits.

One way to obtain additional time for leisure or work is to reduce the amount of time spent shopping. In the shopping-time theory of money demand, this is the fundamental role of money. Other things being equal, having more real money balances available to spend tends to reduce the amount of time that an individual must devote to shopping. As in the inventory theory of money demand, holding real money balances entails an opportunity cost of forgone interest on bonds, so the quantity of money demanded depends negatively on the interest rate. In this respect, the shopping-time theory is similar to the inventory theory.

Because the shopping-time theory emphasizes money's role in facilitating the purchase of goods and services that people consume, however, the theory differs from the inventory theory in one fundamental prediction: *real consumption* replaces real income as a key determinant of the quantity of real money balances that people wish to hold. According to the shopping-time theory, as people increase their consumption of goods and services, they increase their holdings of real money balances in an effort to cut their shopping time. Consequently, the shopping-time theory predicts that an *increase in real consumption* generates an *increase* in the quantity of money demanded.

THE CASH-IN-ADVANCE APPROACH   A very different transaction-based approach to understanding the overall demand for money takes as "given" that money must be offered in exchange. This theory, called the **cash-in-advance approach** to money demand, starts with the assumption that people cannot buy most goods and services unless they have real money balances to spend. That is, they must have "cash in advance" of any purchases they wish to make.

Under the cash-in-advance approach to money demand, people naturally adjust the quantity of real money balances that they hold as they change the amount of time they devote to work and their resource allocations among consumption, investment in capital goods, and holdings of bonds and other financial assets. In other words, in the cash-in-advance theory the amount of money that people hold amounts to a *residual*—that is, a "leftover"—once they

Shopping-time theory of money demand: A theory of the demand for money that focuses on money's role in helping people reduce the amount of time they spend shopping, thereby freeing up more time for leisure or work.

Cash-in-advance approach: A theory of the demand for money based on the assumption that people must have real money balances in their possession before they can purchase any goods or services.

determine how much income they desire to earn given their talents and skills, how much they want to buy with that income, and how many financial assets they desire to hold.

This approach also indicates that the quantity of money demanded will depend positively on real income and negatively on the interest rate. In the cash-in-advance theory, however, real income itself depends on decisions about how much to work and choices concerning how to allocate one's earnings. As a result, the predictions about key determinants of the demand for money yielded by the cash-in-advance approach are less straightforward than those implied by the inventory and shopping-time theories. The predictions become even muddier in today's setting when people purchase many goods—called "credit goods" by those who developed the cash-in-advance approach—using credit cards or trade-credit invoicing systems. Nevertheless, many economists have found the cash-in-advance approach helpful as part of broader theories of the overall performance of an economy.

> **4. What do other transactions-related theories add to our understanding of the demand for money?** The shopping-time theory of money demand emphasizes the role that money plays in reducing the time an individual must spend shopping for goods and services; the theory indicates that the quantity of money demanded varies directly with real consumption. The cash-in-advance approach, which relies on the idea that people must offer money in exchange for goods, services, and assets, highlights how decisions about work effort can affect money holdings.

The Portfolio Demand for Money

The transactions motive focuses on money's role as a medium of exchange. At least since the ancient Greeks, philosophers had emphasized this factor in their thinking about money. When Keynes contemplated the demand for money in the 1920s and 1930s, however, he wished to take into account another important function of money: its role as a *store of value*.

As noted at the beginning of the chapter, this led Keynes to develop a theory of the *speculative motive* for holding money arising from the interplay between interest rates and the prices of financial assets such as bonds. The modern term for this rationale for holding money is the *portfolio motive*. The idea behind the portfolio motive is that money is just one of many financial assets among which individuals can allocate their wealth. Changes in relative returns on assets, which arise from interest rate changes and movements in bond prices, induce people to adjust their desired asset allocations, thereby causing changes in money holdings.

The Keynesian Portfolio Demand for Money

People can hold accumulated wealth in a number of ways. One is to hold nonfinancial assets, such as land, residential housing, or durable goods like automobiles. Another is to hold financial assets, such as bonds, stocks, and savings accounts. Keynes also viewed money as a key part of a person's financial wealth.

MONEY, BONDS, AND FINANCIAL WEALTH To keep things simple, let's assume that an individual's real financial wealth may be allocated only between real money holdings, m, and real holdings of another financial asset called "bonds," b. The factor that distinguishes money from bonds is that the nominal price of money is always equal to 1 unit of money (for instance, $1, 1 euro, 1 yen, etc.). In contrast, the nominal price of a bond can change over time. As a result, an individual who holds a bond earns a *capital gain* if the nominal price of the bond increases over a given interval in time or a *capital loss* if the nominal price of the bond falls during some other period. A $1 bill of U.S. currency or a $1 portion of a checking account at a bank has the same $1 *nominal* value over any given interval. Consequently, people cannot earn nominal capital gains or incur nominal capital losses if they hold all their financial wealth as currency or deposit forms of money. This makes the return on real money balances inherently more stable than the return on bond holdings. (During the mid-2000s, one particular type of bond was especially susceptible to capital losses; see the *Management Focus: Bond Investors Discover the Downside of Inflation Protection.*)

To think about how a person is likely to decide how to allocate real financial wealth between real money balances and bonds, let's suppose that at some given point in time, a person's nominal financial wealth is equal to some amount w. The individual can split this wealth between real money balances, m, which we shall assume are non-interest-bearing cash, and bond holdings, b, on which the individual earns an interest return, r. At the point in time we are considering, it must be true that the individual's financial wealth is equal to holdings of real money balances plus holdings of bonds:

$$w = m + b.$$

Because real financial wealth is constant at a point in time, it must be true that the sum of changes in money and bond holdings must equal zero, or $\Delta m + \Delta b = 0$. That is, any change in holdings of bonds, Δb, must be offset by an equal-sized change in money holdings in the opposite direction, $-\Delta m$. For example, suppose that a person who has $10,000 in real financial wealth holds $5,000 as real money balances and $5,000 as bonds. If this person wishes to

MANAGEMENT
Focus

Bond Investors Discover the Downside of Inflation Protection

As noted in Chapter 4, Treasury Inflation-Protected Securities (TIPS) have principal values that are adjusted for inflation each day using changes in the consumer price index as a benchmark. Thus, the principal for a TIPS grows at the rate of inflation and maintains its real value.

For the returns on ten-year TIPS to match those of other ten-year Treasury bonds, the inflation rate must remain roughly at least as high as the differential between the yield on the regular bonds and the inflation-protected bonds. In the bond market, this differential is called the "break-even inflation rate" required for TIPS to provide returns at least as high as those of regular bonds.

In the mid-2000s, the Federal Reserve embarked on a policy aimed at containing inflation by pushing up interest rates. Prices of TIPS, like those of other bonds, fall when interest rates increase, so the Fed's efforts to push up interest rates subjected owners of TIPS to capital losses. In addition, the Fed's success in holding down inflation kept the inflation rate just under the break-even inflation rate necessary for TIPS holders to do as well as they would have if they had held non-inflation-protected bonds instead. Thus, the Fed's anti-inflation policy subjected holders of TIPS to what Wall Street analysts called a "double whammy" capital loss.

FOR CRITICAL ANALYSIS: Under what circumstance could TIPS holders anticipate experiencing a "double whammy" capital gain? (Hint: Imagine a situation that is the exact opposite of the one that owners of TIPS faced in the mid-2000s.)

increase his bond holdings by $2,000, then he must reduce his money holdings by $2,000, leaving him with $3,000 in cash and $7,000 in bonds, so as to maintain the same total financial wealth of $10,000.

THE SPECULATIVE MOTIVE   Keynes recognized that allocating a fixed amount of real financial wealth between money and bonds implies a relationship between the demand for real money balances and the interest rate. Because bonds earn an explicit interest return, changes in the interest rate affect the market prices of bonds and an individual's desired bond holdings. But changing bond holdings requires altering money holdings. Consequently, interest rate variations typically will induce changes in desired holdings of money.

Interest Rate Expectations   Now let's consider how a person might adjust his money and bond holdings as part of a speculative strategy involving expected changes in interest rates. Because he understands that bond prices are inversely related to the market interest rate, he recognizes that his future capital losses or gains from bond holdings depend directly on whether interest rates rise or fall in the future. Consequently, the individual will adjust his portfolio of money and bonds in light of his *anticipation* of future movements in the interest rate.

Suppose that the market interest rate rises, in the present, to a level that the individual believes is rather high. As a result, he anticipates that the interest rate will decline in the future, and, therefore, bond prices will rise. Thus, he anticipates a future capital gain on bonds that he holds as part of his financial wealth. To further increase his anticipated capital gains from bond holdings, this individual will allocate more of his financial wealth to bonds in the present. To do this, however, he must reduce his holdings of money because his financial wealth is fixed in the present. Consequently, for this individual a current rise in the market interest rate causes him to reduce his desired money holdings. His demand for money depends negatively on the market interest rate.

Suppose instead that the market interest rate falls, in the present, to levels that the individual perceives to be rather low. Therefore, he anticipates that the market interest rate will rise in the future, causing bond prices to fall and causing him to incur capital losses on his existing bond holdings. To avoid some of these anticipated future losses, he will sell bonds in the present, thereby allocating more of his fixed financial wealth to holdings of money. Hence, a current fall in the market interest rate induces him to increase the amount of money demanded. Again, the individual's demand for money is inversely related to the market interest rate.

Money Demand and the Interest Rate   From this line of reasoning, Keynes concluded that the portfolio motive for holding money implies that real income is not the only determinant of money holdings. The demand for money should also depend on the nominal interest rate. Furthermore, *there should be a negative relationship between the quantity of money demanded and the interest rate.*

The modern approach to Keynes's speculative motive for holding money builds on concepts borrowed from the theory of portfolio choice discussed in Chapter 7. Indeed, the theory of portfolio choice itself began with research on the demand for money by James Tobin of Yale University in the 1950s. Tobin later won the Nobel Prize for his early work on the modern portfolio theory of money demand and its larger contribution to the modern theory of finance. This theory focuses on an individual's determination of how much money to hold in light of potential average portfolio returns and risks. In addition to Keynes's prediction that the quantity of money demanded is inversely related to the interest rate, the modern portfolio theory also predicts that the *variability* of the interest rate plays a role.

Money as a Social Store of Value: The Overlapping-Generations Approach to the Demand for Money

Keynes's speculative theory and the modern portfolio theory focus on an individual's portfolio allocation. A more recent theory emphasizing money's store-of-value property is the **overlapping-generations approach,** whose proponents view money as a means of storing and transferring wealth across time.

Overlapping-generations approach: A theory of money demand that emphasizes how societies use money as a way to store and transfer wealth across time.

A BASIC OVERLAPPING-GENERATIONS ECONOMY Figure 16-5 depicts the essential foundations of the overlapping-generations approach. The figure illustrates successive generations of people who have two-period lifetimes. In the first period of their lives, "youth," people work and save for their retirement in the "old-age" period. People do not work in the retirement period. At the beginning of the old-age period of one generation, another generation emerges and lives through its period of youth. Thus, in each period the economy's population includes both young and old people. Generations overlap—hence, the name of this approach to understanding the demand for money.

Let's suppose that the economy's productive capacity expands at a constant rate each period. Let's further suppose that there initially is no money in this economy. In this situation, people will have to store goods to consume when they reach retirement. The total amount of goods that they can consume during their lifetime is limited to the amount that they produce in their youth, so they must allocate these goods across their youthful and old-age periods of life. This is so even though the economy is growing, so that the youth who are working during a given generation's old-age period produce a larger amount of goods and services than the generation that preceded them was capable of producing.

MONEY IN THE OVERLAPPING-GENERATIONS ECONOMY Now let's add money to this overlapping-generations economy. During their youth, people know that they will be able to use money to purchase goods and services during their retirement years from the youthful people who will be producing these goods and services. Because the economy is growing each period, they also know that more goods and services will be available for each person to consume during his or her retirement.

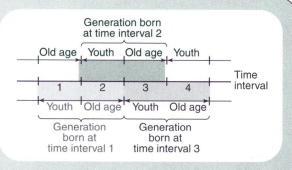

**FIGURE 16-5
A Basic Overlapping-Generations Economy.**

This figure shows the fundamental setup of the overlapping-generations approach to the demand for money. There are successive generations of people with two-period lifetimes. While one gen-

eration is in its "youth," the other is experiencing "old age." Thus, generations overlap.

As long as money is acceptable in exchange each period, people will be able to use money to buy goods and services in any period. Consequently, old-age individuals will be able to use money balances that they accumulated in their youth to purchase some of the goods and services produced by those who are currently young. Money, therefore, enables the current old-age individuals to consume a portion of the goods and services *currently produced* by youthful individuals. (In addition, of course, older individuals may wish to make transfers to the younger generation in the form of gifts, and recent innovations by depository institutions are making such transfers easier to arrange; see the *Cyber Focus: Student to Parent, "Instead of a Check, How about an Online Transfer?"*) It turns out that in a growing economy this ability to hold and use money over time permits each generation to consume more goods and services than the generations could have consumed within their lifetimes if money did not exist.

Thus, the overlapping-generations approach to money demand emphasizes money's role as a welfare-increasing "social compact." When the foundations of the approach are expanded to include a role for financial markets, it turns out that the combined aggregate money holdings of an economy's young and old individuals depend negatively on market interest rates. In addition, money holdings depend positively on income or, in some versions of the approach, on consumption (as in the shopping-time theory discussed earlier).

Although these implications of the overlapping-generations approach replicate those of other theories, adherents of the overlapping-generations approach prefer it to others for one fundamental reason: the approach gives an explanation for the existence of money at the same time that it explains total money holdings within an economy. In addition, the approach offers a theory of why people may wish to trade goods, services, and financial assets, namely, that relative differences in the wealth positions of successive generations induce trade among generations.

CYBER
Focus

Student to Parent, "Instead of a Check, How about an Online Transfer?"

Online banking once was limited to basic Web-based services such as arranging automatic bill payments or shifting funds between the customer's own accounts. Now, in an effort to further cut the use of paper checks and associated processing costs, many depository institutions are expanding the services available through online banking by allowing a customer to transfer funds to the accounts of another customer. For instance, parents who wish to send funds to their child at college can use a home personal computer and Web connection to shift the funds from their account to the student's account at the same institution.

Banks such as Citibank and Bank of America have taken this form of Internet-based funds transfer a step further. They are now allowing customers to make Web transfers of funds from their accounts directly to the accounts held by individuals at *other* depository institutions. To make such cross-institutional account transfers, the customers simply need to have the numbers of the accounts to which they wish to transmit the funds.

FOR CRITICAL ANALYSIS: What advantages do online funds transfers have over transmitting payments using such instruments as checks and debit cards?

> **5. What theories explain the demand for real money balances based on money's function as a store of value?** There are two basic store-of-value theories of money demand. The modern portfolio theory views an individual's choice of what portion of wealth to hold as money as dependent primarily on the average portfolio return and the variability of that return. The overlapping-generations approach to money demand emphasizes money's role as a mechanism for storing and shifting wealth over time.

The Money Demand Schedule

Each of the theories of the demand for money emphasizes different aspects of money's role in the economy. As a result, there are some differences in the theories' predictions concerning factors that are likely to determine the demand for money. According to the inventory theory, for example, costs of converting bonds to money influence the timing of conversions and thereby affect average money holdings. In addition, the modern portfolio theory of money demand indicates that the variability of bond returns should also influence desired holdings of real money balances. These two factors do not emerge directly in the other theories.

Nevertheless, all the theories share two essential predictions:

1. An increase in the *opportunity cost* of holding money, measured as a bond rate or an average return on a bond portfolio, causes people to reduce their holdings of real money balances.

2. An increase in the size of a *scale factor* such as income, consumption, or financial wealth raises people's desired money holdings.

Because so many approaches to the demand for money agree that these factors should be important, they are the focus of most efforts to assess the real-world determinants of total desired money holdings. (There is now considerable evidence about the real-world importance of income and the interest rate as determinants of the demand for money; see on page 362 the *Global Focus: How Responsive Is the Demand for Money to Income and the Interest Rate?*)

The Basic Money Demand Schedule

We can capture the predicted money demand relationships using a simple diagram of a *money demand schedule,* which is a graphical depiction of the relationship between the quantity of money demanded and the nominal interest rate. A typical money demand schedule is shown in panel (a) of Figure 16-6 on page 360. Its downward slope reflects the inverse relationship between the quantity of real money balances demanded and the nominal interest rate that the various money demand theories agree should exist. In addition, we label the schedule $m^d(y_1)$ to indicate that the *position* of the money demand schedule depends, according to several of the theories, on the current level of real income, such as a real income level equal to y_1.

Panel (b) of Figure 16-6 illustrates the effect of an increase in real income, from y_1 to a larger amount y_2. At any given nominal interest rate, people demand more real money balances as a result, so the money demand schedule would shift rightward, as shown in panel (b) by the shift from $m^d(y_1)$ to $m^d(y_2)$.

FIGURE 16-6
A Money
Demand Schedule.

Panel (a) depicts a typical money demand schedule. Because the quantity of money demanded depends inversely on a market interest rate, the money demand schedule slopes downward. Its position depends on a scale variable such as the real income level, y_1. Panel (b) illustrates the effect of an increase in real income to y_2, which is a rightward shift of the money demand schedule.

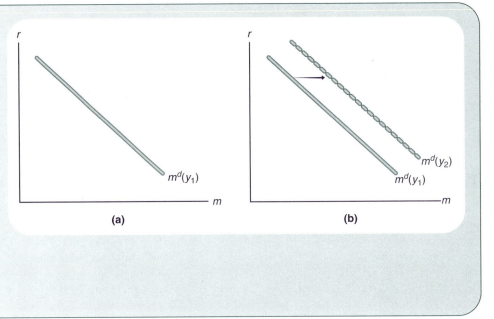

The Identification and Simultaneity Problems

To gauge the extent to which factors such as interest rates or income affect desired money holdings in the real world, economists examine actual data. To measure real money balances that people in an economy actually hold at any given time, they divide the nominal quantity of money in circulation by an index measure of the overall level of prices (see Chapter 17 for more on price indexes). Then they use statistical techniques to assess the degree to which factors such as observed interest rates and real income, consumption, and/or wealth levels help to explain observed variations in real money holdings.

Identification problem: The problem that economists face in evaluating whether real-world data are consistent with the downward-sloping money demand schedule that money demand theories predict, given the fact that both money demand and money supply vary over time.

THE IDENTIFICATION PROBLEM   Figure 16-7 illustrates one problem that economists face in accomplishing this task. This is called the **identification problem** in money demand estimation, or the difficulty in assessing whether real-world data actually trace out a money demand schedule consistent with theory. Panel (a) shows the best possible situation for someone who wishes to "identify" a real-world money demand schedule. As we discussed in Chapter 13, we can envision the nominal quantity of money *supplied* by the Federal Reserve as equal to the product of a money multiplier times the monetary base. Let's use M^s to denote this nominal quantity of money supplied. If the aggregate price level is equal to P, then the quantity of real money balances supplied by the Fed equals M^s/P. Panel (a) of Figure 16-7 shows what happens if the Fed varies the supply of money over time (assuming no appreciable change in the price level, real income, or any other factor). As you can see, this causes a change in the equilibrium interest rate in the *market for real money balances*. The result is a movement along the money demand schedule and a neat "tracing out" of the schedule. If real-world data arose solely from changes in the supply of money, then economists would have an easy time identifying a real-world money demand schedule.

FIGURE 16-7
The Identification Problem.

Panel (a) indicates that if the money demand schedule is stationary, but the money supply schedule shifts rightward over time, then real-world data for interest rates and corresponding levels of real money balances trace out the money demand schedule. The identification problem arises, however, when a scale factor such as real income rises, say, from y_1 to y_2, or declines, say, from y_2 to y_3, thereby causing the rightward and leftward shifts in the money demand schedule shown in panel (b). Using real-world data for interest rates and quantities of real money balances then would identify the money supply schedule instead of the money demand schedule. An even more complicated situation is depicted in panel (c), where both the money demand schedule and the money supply schedule shift over time, so that neither schedule is identified.

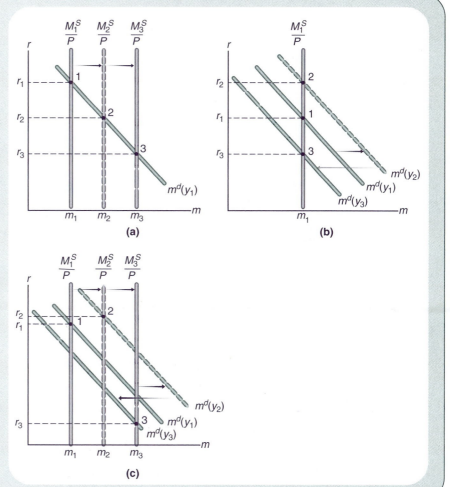

In fact, the situation depicted in panel (a) is likely to be extremely rare. One reason for this is that real income (or alternative scale factors such as consumption or wealth) can rise or fall over time, thereby causing the money demand schedule to shift to the right or left, as shown in panel (b). If an economist collected data on interest rates and real money balances alone and made a plot of these data for a period that happened to coincide with the situation depicted in panel (b), then she would actually identify the money supply schedule instead of the money demand schedule. Panel (c) depicts an even more complicated situation, in which the positions of *both* the money demand schedule *and* the money supply schedule vary over time.

The best way to account for the potential shifts in money demand and supply is for economists to take into account changes in various scale factors, such as real income, consumption, or financial wealth, when trying to identify a real-world money demand schedule. As long as at least one of these factors has no significant effect on the position of the money supply schedule, then statistical techniques should permit economists to identify a money demand relationship.

How Responsive Is the Demand for Money to Income and the Interest Rate?

To measure the responsiveness of the quantity of an item demanded to a particular factor influencing the demand for that item, economists estimate *elasticities of demand.* For instance, to gauge how responsive the demand for money is to income, economists consider the *income elasticity of the demand for money,* which is the percentage change in the quantity of real money balances demanded resulting from a percentage change in real income, or $\%\Delta m^d/\%\Delta y$, where "$\%\Delta$" denotes the percentage change.

According to the Cambridge equation, $m^d = k \times y$, the percentage change in the quantity of real money balances equals the percentage change in the portion of income that people allocate to real money holdings plus the percentage change in real income, or $\%\Delta m^d = \%\Delta k + \%\Delta y$. The key assumption of the Cambridge equation is that the fraction k is constant, so $\%\Delta k = 0$. This means that it should be true that $\%\Delta m^d = \%\Delta y$, or $\%\Delta m^d/\%\Delta y = 1$. According to the Cambridge equation, therefore, the income elasticity of the demand for money should equal 1. Other transactions theories tend to predict a smaller value for the income elasticity of money demand, but all theories agree that the value of the income elasticity, $\%\Delta m^d/\%\Delta y$, should be positive. The quantity of money demanded should respond directly to an increase in real income.

Subramanian Sriram, an economist at the International Monetary Fund, reviewed the evidence from sixty-six studies of money demand in different countries to see if they reached any common conclusions about the determinants of the demand for money on a global basis. Panel (a) of Figure 16-8 shows how many income elasticity estimates fell within various ranges. As you can see, most of the estimates are clustered in the ranges between 0.75 and 1.25. Panel (b) of the figure shows the average and median (values halfway between highest and lowest) estimates of income elasticities of the demand for money from panel (a). In fact, all the estimates are very close to a value of 1. This may indicate that the Cambridge equation, the simplest possible approach, is not such a bad approximation to the real-world demand for money.

Among the studies that Sriram reviewed, estimates of the *interest elasticity of the demand for money,* $\%\Delta m^d/\%\Delta r$, ranged all the way from -0.02, indicating that a 1 percent rise in the interest rate would cause only a 0.02 percent decline in the quantity of money demanded, to -9, which implies that money holdings would fall by 9 percent in response to a 1 percent increase in the interest rate. The main conclusion so far is that the interest sensitivity of money demand likely varies considerably both from country

---

Simultaneity problem: The problem of accounting for the possibility that factors influencing the quantity of money demanded are themselves affected by how many real money balances people hold, which can complicate assessments of how well real-world observations square with theories of money demand.

THE SIMULTANEITY PROBLEM A potentially significant problem in using real-world data to assess the key determinants of the demand for money is the **simultaneity problem,** or the possibility that factors that influence the quantity of money demanded are themselves affected by how many real money balances people hold. For example, as we shall discuss in Chapters 17 and 18, conditions in the market for real money balances ultimately affect equilibrium real national income. Thus, aggregate money holdings, interest rates, and real income actually are determined *simultaneously* in the real world. This means that statistical tests that assume that data on a scale factor such as real income are independent from observed money holdings will not yield trustworthy answers.

To deal with the simultaneity problem, economists typically use "two-stage" statistical estimation procedures. They locate data on variables that they know are likely to affect real income but are highly unlikely to be related to desired holdings of real money balances. Incorporating these data into their statistical analysis of money demand permits economists to take into account any feedback effects from desired money holdings to real income. Then, at least in principle, economists can determine the net effect the changes in real income directly exert on desired holdings of real money balances.

GLOBAL
Focus

to country and over time within individual countries.

FOR CRITICAL ANALYSIS: If the interest elasticity of the demand for money really is as low as −0.02, what would that imply about the relative real-world importance of the speculative motive for holding money?

FIGURE 16-8
Estimated Income Elasticities of Money Demand.

Panel (a) displays the distribution of the estimated income elasticities of demand for components of M1, M1 itself, and M2 from sixty-six studies covering a number of different nations. Panel (b) displays the average and median values of the income elasticity estimates from these studies.

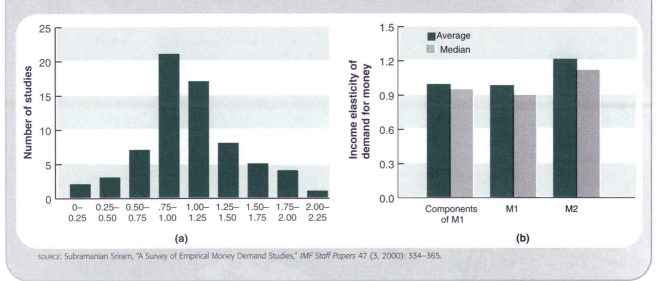

(a)

(b)

SOURCE: Subramanian Sriram, "A Survey of Empirical Money Demand Studies," *IMF Staff Papers* 47 (3, 2000): 334–365.

6. What difficulties do economists face in trying to predict the overall demand for money?   Most theories of money demand agree that the quantity of money demanded should depend negatively on the interest rate and positively on income. Hence, the money demand schedule should slope downward in a graph with the interest rate measured along the vertical axis and the quantity of real money balances measured along the horizontal axis, and an increase in income should shift the schedule rightward. Attempting to estimate the position and shape of the money demand schedule with real-world data is complicated by the identification problem, which arises from the fact that variations in both money demand and money supply typically take place. Another difficulty is the simultaneity problem: changes in the demand for money can affect real income and, in turn, the interest rate, complicating the process of disentangling the independent effects of income and the interest rate on the demand for money.

MONEYXTRA!
Online Case Study

Gain an understanding of how difficulties in predicting money can cause real-world policy problems by going to the Chapter 16 Case Study, entitled "Wrestling with Money Demand Prediction Problems at the Fed." **http:// moneyxtra.swcollege.com**

Chapter Summary

1. The Cambridge Equation: This equation represents the most basic transactions theory of the demand for money. It indicates that people desire to hold a portion of their current-dollar income as money. Therefore, the quantity of money demanded varies directly with income.

2. Real Money Balances: Real money balances are the purchasing power of the total nominal quantity of money, which economists measure by dividing the quantity of money in circulation by an index measure of the prices of goods and services. According to the Cambridge equation, the quantity of real money balances that people desire to hold is equal to a desired fraction of their real income.

3. Key Factors Influencing Desired Holdings of Real Money Balances in the Inventory Theory of Money Demand: According to the inventory theory of the demand for money, people hold inventories of real money balances to use as a medium of exchange. They adjust their inventories by converting interest-bearing assets into cash. The theory predicts that an increase in market interest rates raises the opportunity cost of holding money, thereby inducing a reduction in the quantity of money demanded. The theory also indicates that the quantity of money demanded depends positively on real income and cash-conversion fees.

4. What Other Transactions-Related Theories Add to Our Understanding of the Demand for Money: According to the shopping-time theory of money demand, which focuses on how using money helps reduce the amount of time that an individual devotes to shopping for goods and services, the quantity of money demanded depends positively on real consumption. In the cash-in-advance approach to money demand, real income remains the key scale variable, but other factors such as an individual's allocation of time between work and leisure also influence the demand for money.

5. Theories That Explain Money Demand through Money's Store-of-Value Function: The modern portfolio theory focuses on choices that people must make when they allocate their financial wealth in light of the average portfolio return and the variability of that return. The overlapping-generations approach to the theory of money demand emphasizes money's social role in allowing people to store and allocate wealth across time.

6. Difficulties Economists Face in Trying to Predict the Overall Demand for Money: Money demand theories agree that there is a negative relationship between the quantity of real money balances demanded and the interest rate; thus, the money demand schedule should slope downward in a graph with the interest rate measured along the vertical axis and the quantity of real money balances measured along the horizontal axis. Most theories also indicate that money demand is positively related to income, so a rise in income should shift the schedule rightward. The fact that both the money demand and the money supply schedules vary over time creates an identification problem that complicates efforts by economists to use real-world data to estimate the position and slope of the money demand schedule. The simultaneity problem, or the fact that changes in the demand for money can affect real income and, in turn, the interest rate, further complicates the effort to determine the separate effects of income and the interest rate on money demand.

Questions and Problems

(Answers to odd-numbered questions and problems may be found on the Web at **http://money.swcollege.com** under "Student Resources.")

1. Suppose that economists determine that M2 is the monetary aggregate most useful for guiding monetary policy and also determine that people desire to hold one-fourth of their current-dollar incomes in the form of money. At present, total holdings of assets included in M2 amount to $2.4 trillion. According to the Cambridge equation, what is the current-dollar level of national income? Show your work.

2. In question 1, suppose that the current value of an index of the overall prices of goods and services in the economy is equal to 1.067. What is real national income? What is the value of the level of real money balances? Show your work, and round to the nearest hundredth of a trillion dollars (that is, round to the nearest 10 billion dollars).

3. Use the inventory theory of the demand for money to work out an exact expression for the cost-minimizing number of conversions. Then use this solution in the expression for the average cash balance to determine the optimal cash balance that an individual will hold, in terms of the cash-conversion fee, the interest rate, and real income. [Hint: Note in Figure 16-3 that the number of conversions that minimizes total cost happens to correspond to the point where the upward-sloping cash-conversion cost line and the downward-sloping implicit opportunity cost curve cross. Therefore, at this point that they share in common, it must be true that $f \times n = (r \times y)/(2 \times n)$. You can solve this equation for n. Then use this solution for n in the expression for the average real money balance to solve for the individual's optimal holdings of money.]

4. Suppose that greater competition among mutual funds and depository institutions leads to a reduction in the market fee that mutual funds and depository institutions charge to convert funds from bond accounts to real money balances. Use the inventory theory of the demand for money to reason out the likely effect on total desired holdings of real money balances throughout the economy. Explain your answer.

5. The inventory theory of the demand for real money balances indicates that the level of real income is the key scale factor influencing desired money holdings. The shopping-time theory, however, indicates that *real consumption* is the appropriate scale factor. Even though they possess a lot of data on income and consumption, however, economists have had trouble determining which of these scale factors actually has the greater *independent* influence on money demand in the real world. Why do you suppose this is so? Explain.

6. Early versions of the cash-in-advance approach to the demand for money, which were developed in the 1960s, assumed that people have to use money to obtain all goods and services. By the 1980s, however, most economists using this approach felt that this assumption was unreasonable in a world with credit cards and other revolving-credit arrangements. Do you agree? How might you modify the cash-in-advance approach to make it more applicable to today's world? Explain.

7. Critics of the overlapping-generations approach to the demand for money often claim that it may help explain why money exists but does a poor job of helping economists understand the quantity of money that people currently hold. Proponents of the theory respond that it is not possible to understand present money holdings unless economists also take into account underlying reasons for the existence of money. Evaluate these positions.

8. Suppose that the money supply schedule is stationary but the money demand schedule shifts rightward and leftward over time because of variations in the public's use of technologies for making exchanges. How would this affect economists' efforts to determine the slope and position of the money demand schedule?

9. Suppose that the United States experiences a period during which the economy's money demand schedule tends to shift leftward over time. At the same time, the Federal Reserve's goal is to keep interest rates from changing, so it varies the position of the money supply schedule as required to attain this objective. Would this pose an identification problem or a simultaneity problem for a researcher interested in evaluating the demand for money using data collected during this period? Explain, using a diagram to assist.

10. Suppose that there is widespread adoption of cybertechnologies that enable people to economize on their holdings of real money balances. Use a diagram of the market for real money balances to show the effect of this development on the position of the economy's money demand schedule and on the market interest rate. Suppose, in addition, that the economy's level of real income tends to be inversely related to market interest rates. Would this pose an identification problem or a simultaneity problem for a researcher interested in evaluating the demand for money using data collected during this period? Explain, using a diagram to assist.

Before the Test

Test your understanding of the material covered in this chapter by taking the Chapter 16 interactive quiz at **http://money.swcollege.com**.

Online Application

Internet URL: http://research.stlouisfed.org/fred2

Title: Federal Reserve Economic Data (FRED)

Navigation: Go to the Web page of the Federal Reserve Bank of St. Louis (**http://www.stlouisfed.org**). Under "Economic Research," click on "Economic Data—FRED."

Application: Follow the instructions below, and answer the questions:

1. Click on "Monetary Aggregates," and then click on "M2 Money Stock" (M, NSA). Print the M2 data so that you can have them by your side as you continue. Now go back to the "Economic Data—FRED" page, and click on "Interest Rates," followed by "Treasury Constant Maturity" and then "6-Month Treasury Constant Maturity Rate" (M). According to theories of the demand for money, the quantity of money demanded varies inversely with market interest rates. Reviewing the M2 and six-month Treasury security rates since 1982, does this relationship appear in the data? Based on the discussion in this chapter, can you offer some reasons for why the relationship may not be apparent in the data?

2. Go back to "Monetary Aggregates" and click on "M2 Own Rate." Explain what these data measure. How would you expect this factor to influence the relationship between other market interest rates and the quantity of money (M2) demanded?

For Group Study and Analysis: FRED contains numerous financial data series. Break the class up into three groups assigned to examine data for M1, M2, and M3. Have each group take a look at the rest of the FRED database and determine what data might be helpful in trying to estimate the demand for the assigned monetary aggregate.

Selected References and Further Reading

Duca, John, and David VanHoose. "Recent Developments in Understanding the Demand for Money." *Journal of Economics and Business* 56 (July/August 2004): 247–272.

Dutkowsky, Donald, and H. Sonmez Atesoglu. "The Demand for Money: A Structural Econometric Investigation." *Southern Economic Journal* 68 (July 2001): 92–106.

Elyasiani, Elyas, and Alireza Nasseh. "The Appropriate Scale Variable in the U.S. Money Demand: An Application of Nonnested Tests of Consumption versus Income Measures." *Journal of Business and Economic Statistics* 12 (January 1994): 47–55.

Goldfeld, Stephen. "Demand for Money: Empirical Studies." In *The New Palgrave: Money,* ed. John Eatwell, Murray Milgate, and Peter Newman, pp. 131–143. New York: W. W. Norton, 1989.

Laidler, David. *The Demand for Money: Theories, Evidence, and Problems,* 4th ed. New York: HarperCollins, 1993.

Marquis, Milton. *Monetary Theory and Policy.* Minneapolis–St. Paul: West Publishing Company, 1996.

McCallum, Bennett, and Marvin Goodfriend. "Demand for Money: Theoretical Studies." In *The New Palgrave: Money,* ed. John Eatwell, Murray Milgate, and Peter Newman, pp. 117–130. New York: W. W. Norton, 1989.

Serletis, Apostolos. *The Demand for Money: Theoretical and Empirical Approaches.* Boston: Kluwer, 2001.

Sriram, Subramanian. "A Survey of Empirical Money Demand Studies." *IMF Staff Papers* 47 (3, 2000): 334–365.

Thompson, Neil. *Portfolio Theory and the Demand for Money.* New York: St. Martin's Press, 1993.

MoneyXtra

Log on to the MoneyXtra Web site now (**http://moneyxtra.swcollege.com**) for additional learning resources such as practice quizzes, case studies, readings, and additional economic applications.

Monetary Policy, Interest Rates, and the Economy

For years, the Federal Reserve has kept a close eye on business inventory investment—goods that firms have produced but have not yet sold. The Fed has found that during business downturns, businesses cut prices to sell off previously unsold goods. Firms also cut back on production of new goods. As a consequence, total inventory investment declines. Indeed, during the typical business downturn between 1952 and 1982, reductions in inventory investment accounted for an annual decline in economic activity of about 1.4 percent on average. During the 1990–1991 business downturn, however, declining inventory investment accounted for a decline in economic activity only about half as large. The 2001 economic downturn witnessed an even smaller effect from declining inventory investment.

What changed during the 1990s and 2000s, the Fed determined, was that businesses adopted new information technologies. Growing use of telecommunications devices, computers, and the Internet allowed businesses to keep inventory levels lower and to adjust their inventory investment more smoothly in response to changes in economic activity. As a consequence, economic downturns now generate smaller declines in inventory investment, which in turn tends to reduce the overall severity of downturns.

In this chapter, you will learn that overall business investment spending, which includes inventory investment as well as purchases of new items such as equipment and computer software, is an important determinant of an economy's overall productive performance. You will also learn that the effects that monetary policy actions exert on business investment expenditures are a key aspect of the mechanism by which these actions can ultimately influence the economy's performance. First, however, you must learn about how we gauge a nation's overall production of goods and services.

> ## *Fundamental Issues*
>
> 1. How do economists measure a nation's aggregate production of goods and services and its price level?
>
> 2. How does a change in the market interest rate affect real GDP?
>
> 3. How can monetary policy influence the market interest rate?
>
> 4. What is the transmission mechanism by which monetary policy exerts effects on real GDP?
>
> 5. What factors determine the magnitude of the effect of a monetary policy action on real GDP?

Gross Domestic Product and Price Deflators

To determine how monetary policies that the Federal Reserve or other central banks conduct influence a nation's overall economic performance, economists must first have a reliable measure of "economic activity." The most widely used measure is *gross domestic product*, or *GDP*.

Measuring Economic Activity: GDP

The primary measure of economic activity during a given interval is the total value, computed using current market prices, of *final* goods and services produced by businesses during that period. This is called the economy's **gross domestic product (GDP).** (When policymakers at institutions such as the World Bank or the International Monetary Fund try to measure the world's GDP, they must decide which market prices are appropriate for valuing all the goods and services produced; see the *Global Focus: Is World GDP Understated?*)

Businesses earn revenues on the output that they sell to consumers, other businesses, and the government. These revenues flow to the individuals who provide *factors of production* to businesses, which the businesses use to produce the goods and services that they sell. Factors of production include labor, land, capital, and entrepreneurship. The earnings of the individuals who supply these factors of production are wages and salaries, rents, interest and dividends, and profits. Adding together all these receipts for all individuals in the economy yields the total income earnings of all individuals. Ultimately, the total value of output that businesses produced becomes the combined earnings of all individuals. This means that for all intents and purposes, GDP is also a good measure of the total income receipts of all individuals.

The Components of GDP

Although GDP can be tabulated by adding up all the earnings of all factors of production, a more straightforward approach is to add together all expenditures on final goods and services produced during a particular year. Essentially, they determine the magnitude of the flow of total spending in product markets.

Panel (a) of Figure 17-1 shows the four fundamental forms of spending on final goods and services since 1996. One is **consumption spending** by households. Another is **investment spending,** which includes business spending on new capital goods. Investment spending also encompasses net accumulations of inventories of newly produced goods, as well as spending on construction—houses and apartment buildings—by households and businesses. *Gross private domestic investment* includes all investment spending during a year. Some investment expenditures, however, are allocated toward replacement of worn-out capital, or depreciation.

GLOBAL

Focus

Is World GDP Understated?

To measure global GDP, economists commonly begin by converting the value of each nation's GDP into U.S. dollars. They do this by multiplying a nation's GDP by the exchange rate of the dollar for that nation's currency unit. Then the economists add up the dollar values of the GDPs of all nations to obtain a dollar value of global GDP. Using this method, current world GDP is less than $40 trillion per year, or just below 3.5 times U.S. GDP.

A problem with using exchange rates to convert other nations' GDPs into dollar values is that prices tend to be lower in less developed nations than in the United States and other developed countries. Thus, a U.S. dollar can often purchase more goods and services in those nations than it can in developed nations. When the calculation of global GDP is adjusted to take this fact into account, the U.S. dollar value of world GDP jumps to well over $50 trillion.

FOR CRITICAL ANALYSIS: How might understating GDP bias estimates of the growth of the income of an average resident of planet Earth?

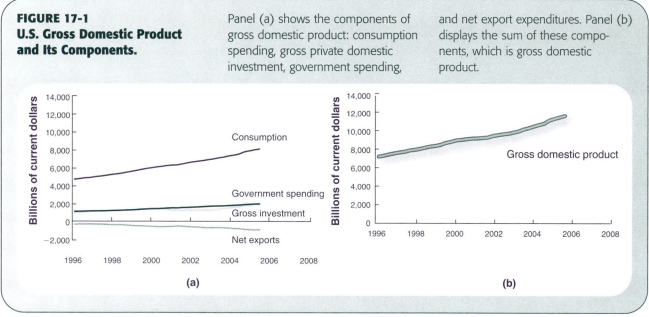

FIGURE 17-1
U.S. Gross Domestic Product and Its Components.

Panel (a) shows the components of gross domestic product: consumption spending, gross private domestic investment, government spending, and net export expenditures. Panel (b) displays the sum of these components, which is gross domestic product.

SOURCES: *Economic Indicators*, various issues; authors' estimates.

Thus, *net private domestic investment* is equal to gross private domestic investment minus depreciation. Economists typically regard net investment as a better indicator of how much an economy's stock of capital goods grows during a year. Nonetheless, gross investment measures total spending on such items. For this reason, gross investment is included in GDP.

The third component of GDP is **government spending.** This is the aggregate amount of spending on goods and services by state, local, and federal governments.

The fourth type of expenditures on final goods and services produced in an economy is **net export spending,** which is equal to total expenditures on domestically produced goods and services by residents of other nations, less spending on foreign-produced goods and services by domestic residents that does not constitute spending on domestic production. Since the early 1980s, net export spending has been negative. This means that expenditures by U.S. residents on foreign goods and services have exceeded foreign spending on U.S.-produced goods and services.

For any given year, the sum of all four types of expenditures on domestically produced final goods and services equals GDP for that year. These totals for years since 1996 are displayed in panel (b) of Figure 17-1. (More often than not, volatility in investment expenditures contributes to variations in GDP; see on the next page *What Happens When Businesses Suddenly Stop Buying Computers and Software?*)

Real versus Nominal GDP

As shown in Figure 17-1, U.S. GDP has persistently increased over time. It has done so for two reasons. One reason is that the economy has grown, meaning that businesses have expanded their resources and found ways to increase their production of goods and services. Another reason, however, is that prices have risen over time. Such overall price

Government spending: Total state, local, and federal government expenditures on goods and services.

Net export spending: The difference between spending on domestically produced goods and services by residents of other countries and spending on foreign-produced goods and services by residents of the home country.

MONEYXTRA!
Another Perspective

To learn about how a mismatch of federal government spending and tax revenues has pushed the federal budget into deficit since the early 2000s, use the Chapter 17 reading, "The Federal Budget: What a Difference a Year Makes," by Alan Viard of the Federal Reserve Bank of Dallas. **http:// moneyxtra.swcollege.com**

What Happens When... **Businesses Suddenly Stop Purchasing Computers and Software?**

Most people link the recession that began in early 2001 to the terrorist attacks on New York and Washington, D.C., that took place in September of that year. The climate of uncertainty created by those attacks undoubtedly contributed to the economic downturn. Nevertheless, economists at the National Bureau of Economic Research (NBER) formally dated the onset of the recession to March 2001, six months before the attacks.

Economists did not have to look far to see a key factor that likely contributed to a falloff in spending. As you can see in Figure 17-2, at the beginning of 2001 business investment in equipment, including computers and telecommunications devices, and in software began to drop off. This investment decline accelerated in early 2001 and accounted for the bulk of the overall drop in investment spending that most economists agree ultimately was most responsible for bringing about the recession.

FOR CRITICAL ANALYSIS: Looking back at the components of aggregate spending on U.S. goods and services depicted in Figure 17-1, which typically exhibits the most variation over time?

FIGURE 17-2
U.S. Business Investment Spending on Equipment and Software.

Total business investment spending on equipment and software rose steadily until 2000. Then it abruptly declined until 2002 when it began to recover again.

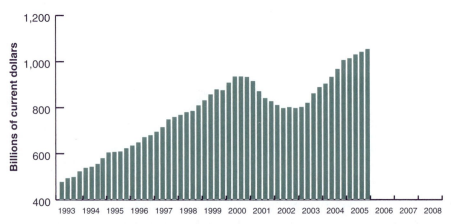

SOURCES: Bureau of Economic Analysis; authors' estimates.

Real gross domestic product (real GDP): A price-adjusted measure of aggregate output, or nominal GDP divided by the GDP price deflator.

increases, or inflation, have increased the *measured value* of all produced goods and services. This means that you cannot necessarily look at panel (b) of Figure 17-1 and conclude that the actual production of goods and services has consistently increased in the United States. Some portion of the general rise in GDP shown in the figure occurred simply because prices rose over time as well. Consequently, using GDP as a measure of actual productive activity in the economy would lead to an overstatement of the true volume of such activity when inflation occurs.

To see why a distinction must be made, suppose that your employer doubles the wages that you receive for providing labor services. Thus, your measured income has increased. But if the overall prices that you have to pay to purchase goods and services also double, then you really are no better off. Likewise, if total income as measured by GDP doubles simply because prices have increased by a factor of two, then the total volume of economic activity really has not changed.

To avoid this problem, economists use an adjusted measure of GDP, called **real gross domestic product.** This measure of the total production of final output accounts for the effects of price changes and thereby more accurately reflects the economy's true volume of productive activity. Because the flow of final product ultimately makes its way to individuals as a flow of total earnings, real GDP is also a measure of the true aggregate income that individuals receive net of artificial increases resulting from inflation.

To distinguish real GDP from the unadjusted GDP measure, economists refer to unadjusted GDP as **nominal gross domestic product,** or GDP "in name only," because it has been measured in current-dollar terms with no adjustment for effects of price changes.

The Price Level

Because real GDP measures the economy's true volume of production, multiplying real GDP by a measure of the overall price level will yield the value of real GDP measured in current prices, which is nominal GDP. That is, if y denotes real GDP and P is a measure of the overall price level, then total nominal GDP, denoted Y, is equal to $Y = y \times P$.

The factor P in this expression is called the **GDP price deflator,** or simply the "GDP deflator." It is called a "deflator" because the expression for nominal GDP, $Y = y \times P$, can be rearranged to obtain $y = Y/P$. That is, real GDP, y, is equal to nominal GDP, Y, adjusted by dividing, or "deflating," by the factor P. Economists establish P by defining a base year in which nominal GDP equals real GDP ($Y = y$), so that the value of the GDP deflator is one ($P = 1$). Then the base year is used as a reference point. Thus, a value of 3 for the GDP deflator for a given year would mean that the overall level of prices has tripled since the base year. For instance, suppose that nominal GDP, Y, is equal to \$12 trillion and the value of the GDP deflator, P, is equal to 2. Then real GDP can be calculated by deflating the \$12 trillion figure for nominal GDP by a factor of one-half. Dividing \$12 trillion by 2 yields real GDP of \$6 trillion. Panel (a) of Figure 17-3 depicts the GDP deflator for the United States since 1959.

Nominal gross domestic product (nominal GDP): The value of production of final goods and services calculated in current-dollar terms with no adjustment for the effects of price changes.

GDP price deflator: A measure of the overall price level; equal to nominal GDP divided by real GDP.

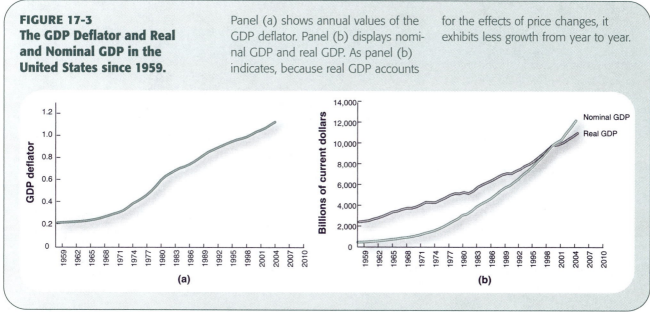

FIGURE 17-3
The GDP Deflator and Real and Nominal GDP in the United States since 1959.

Panel (a) shows annual values of the GDP deflator. Panel (b) displays nominal GDP and real GDP. As panel (b) indicates, because real GDP accounts for the effects of price changes, it exhibits less growth from year to year.

SOURCES: *Economic Report of the President,* 2005; *Economic Indicators,* various issues.

Panel (b) of Figure 17-3 plots both real and nominal GDP. Note that in 2000 nominal and real GDP are equal because 2000 is the base year in which $P = 1$, so $Y = y$. Clearly, adjusting for price changes has a significant effect on how GDP figures are interpreted. This is why it is so important to use the GDP deflator to convert nominal GDP into real GDP. Only the latter measure can really provide information about the actual volume of economic activity. (The overall price level can be measured in various ways; see the *Policy Focus: The Alphabet Soup of Price Indexes*)

---

1. How do economists measure a nation's aggregate production of goods and services and its price level? Economists measure a country's total production using gross domestic product (GDP), which is the market value of all final goods and services produced during a given period. Nominal GDP is the total value of newly produced goods and services computed using the prices at which they sold during the year they were produced. In contrast, real GDP is the value of final goods and services after adjusting for the effects of year-to-year price changes. The basic approach to calculating real GDP is to divide nominal GDP by the GDP deflator, which is a key measure of the level of prices relative to prices for a base year.

POLICY

Focus

The Alphabet Soup of Price Indexes

There are three basic alternatives to the GDP deflator as measures of the overall level of prices. Best known is the *consumer price index (CPI)*, which is a weighted average of prices of a full set of goods and services that the Bureau of Labor Statistics (BLS) in the U.S. Department of Labor determines a typical U.S. consumer purchases each year. The second key measure of the price level is the *producer price index (PPI)*, which is a weighted average of prices of goods that the BLS determines a typical business charges for the goods and services it sells. The third price-level measure is the *personal consumption expenditure (PCE)* price index, which the Bureau of Economic Analysis (BEA) in the U.S. Department of Commerce

calculates as an average of two different fixed-weight price indexes based on shifting baskets of goods and services purchased by consumers each year.

One problem with the CPI and PPI is that relative prices of goods change over time, so people substitute among goods, changing their spending allocations. This means that the fixed weights that the BLS assigns to a "typical" consumer or producer when computing the CPI and PPI are *artificially* fixed. For any truly representative consumer or producer, the weights surely must change somewhat from year to year. Using the PCE helps address this problem by calculating year-to-year price changes based on averages of weights in the two years.

In addition, in calculating the CPI and PPI, the BLS uses *list* prices, which are the prices that businesses formally print in catalogues, price lists, and so

on. During times of heated competition for business, however, consumers often can get bargain prices below those in the formal price lists available to the BLS. The proliferation of discount retailers since the 1980s may have worsened this measurement problem for the CPI and PPI. Nevertheless, data collection problems for the PCE may be even more severe because the BEA estimates consumer spending on goods and services by subtracting sales to businesses and governments from total sales. Thus, the BEA measures consumer spending only indirectly for purposes of constructing index weights.

FOR CRITICAL ANALYSIS: Why do you suppose that policymakers typically choose to track all four measures of the price level—the GDP deflator, the CPI, the PPI, and the PCE—instead of focusing on only one measure?

Aggregate Expenditures, Interest Rates, and Economic Activity

What factors will determine your decisions about how much to contribute to the nation's total spending on goods and services during the coming year? As a consumer, one factor that undoubtedly comes to your mind is the prices of the various goods and services that you might decide to purchase. Another factor is the amount of income that you will earn during the year. In addition, if you happen to be a businessperson contemplating equipment purchases financed by borrowing, then the market interest rate will also play a role.

In fact, these three factors—the price level, income, and the interest rate—are the fundamental variables of concern to a central bank such as the Federal Reserve System when it contemplates how its policies will affect economic activity. We shall consider the price level in considerable detail in Chapter 18. In this chapter, we focus on the role of income and the interest rate as key factors affecting the total real expenditures of consumers and businesses and, consequently, equilibrium real GDP.

Real GDP and Real Consumption Expenditures

When consumers' real income increases, they can allocate the additional real income in two ways. They can save it by purchasing the financial assets discussed in Unit II, or they can spend it on goods and services. Typically, consumers allocate their real income to both activities. Consequently, aggregate income earnings directly influence aggregate consumption expenditures.

As discussed above, aggregate earnings sum to real GDP. A rise in real GDP, therefore, pushes up consumers' real income, which in turn boosts consumption spending. Of course, consumption spending is itself a key component of real GDP. This implies that, at least up to a point, any other rise in real GDP—say, additional spending by the government, businesses, or foreign residents—will tend to push real GDP up even further.

Given sufficient information about the size of the direct effect of an increase in real GDP on real income and on consumption spending, it is possible to determine how much more real GDP will rise in response to greater government, business, or foreign spending. Suppose, for instance, that individuals typically allocate $0.80 of each additional $1 in real income they receive to purchases of goods and services. In this situation, the **marginal propensity to consume *(MPC)*,** or the additional consumption spending generated by an increase in real income, is equal to $0.80/$1.00, or 0.80.

Suppose that a business spends $20 million to build a new computer network. This spending is part of real gross private domestic investment, so real GDP increases by $20 million. This immediate effect on real GDP is shown in the first line of Table 17-1 on page 374.

In addition, however, the $20 million that the business pays companies to construct the computer network generates a $20 million increase in the real incomes of the owners and employees of these companies. As shown in line 2 of Table 17-1, because the marginal propensity to consume is 0.80, these individuals respond by increasing their consumption spending by 0.80 × $20 million, or by $16 million. Of course, this consumption spending generates $16 million more in real income for other business owners and workers. As shown in line 3 of Table 17-1, this causes consumption spending to rise once more, by 0.80 × $16 million = 0.80 × 0.80 × $20 million, or by an additional $12.8 million.

If we continued the mathematics, we would find that these and additional rounds of induced real consumption spending sum to $100 million. Thus, the $20 million increase in desired

Marginal propensity to consume *(MPC)*: The amount of additional real consumption spending induced by an increase in real income.

Table 17-1 The Response of Real GDP to a $20 Million Increase in Investment Spending

1	Increase in investment spending =	$20.000 million
2	Induced rise in consumption spending = 0.80 × $20.000 million =	$16.000 million
3	Induced rise in consumption spending = 0.80 × $16.000 million =	$12.800 million
4	Induced rise in consumption spending = 0.80 × $12.800 million =	$10.240 million
5	Induced rise in consumption spending = 0.80 × $10.240 million =	$ 8.192 million
.	.	
.	.	
.	.	
Total	Overall increase in real GDP = [1/(1 − *MPC*)] × $20 million =	$100.000 million

When a business increases its desired investment in a computing network by $20 million (line 1), this expenditure causes the real incomes of the owners and employees of the firms that construct the network to rise by $20 million. If the marginal propensity to consume is 0.80, then the consumption spending by these individuals rises by 0.80 × $20 million, or $16 million (line 2). This $16 million in consumption spending generates a $16 million increase in incomes for other households, so their consumption spending increases by 0.80 × $16 million, or $12.8 million (line 3). Ultimately, the increase in total expenditures brought about by the $20 million increase in desired investment equals $20 million × [1/(1 − 0.80)] = $20 million × 5, or $100 million.

investment causes *all* real expenditures *including* real consumption spending to increase by an amount that is a *multiple*—in this case, 5—of the investment increase. It turns out that, in general, the mathematical value of the multiple effect on real GDP equals $1/(1 - MPC)$. In this particular example, in which the *MPC* equals 0.80, the value of $1/(1 - MPC)$ is $1/(1 - 0.80) = 5$. This is why the ultimate effect of a $20 million increase in business investment on real GDP is 5 times higher, or $100 million.

In our example, we assumed that a rise in desired business investment accounted for the $20 million increase in desired expenditures. It is important to recognize that a $20 million increase in spending by the government or a $20 million rise in foreign spending on domestic exports would result in the same outcome. The multiple effect of real investment spending on real GDP that operates through induced increases in consumption spending turns out to be particularly important for monetary policy, however. The reason, which we consider next, is that the amount of real investment expenditures that businesses desire to undertake depends on the market interest rate. (Sometimes businesses decide to engage in more investment at the same time that they sell more products abroad, leading to nothing but good news for the economy; see the *Management Focus: How a Two-Pronged Multiplier Effect Unexpectedly Benefited the U.S. Economy.*)

The Market Interest Rate, Real Investment Spending, and Real GDP

When a business considers making a real investment, such as the purchase of a new computer network, it does so because it anticipates that the investment will yield a future stream of earnings. You learned in Chapter 4 that the discounted present value of funds to be received in the

How a Two-Pronged Multiplier Effect Unexpectedly Benefited the U.S. Economy

During the year following the 2001 recession, U.S. real GDP increased by only 2.2 percent. This increase in real GDP was at least one percentage point lower than the real GDP growth the U.S. economy had experienced immediately after most previous recessions.

Economic forecasters decided that they had been overly optimistic in predicting real GDP growth for 2003 and reduced their forecast for that year by an average of one percentage point, to 2.5 percent.

Then two things happened during the second half of 2003: both business investment spending and net exports suddenly increased. These two events each had predictable multiplier effects on real GDP. As a consequence, during the last six months of 2003, real GDP growth exceeded 6 percent. This sudden burst pushed the rate of

growth of real GDP for the entire year above 4 percent. Instead of having been too optimistic in their predictions for 2003, economic forecasters turned out to have been much too pessimistic because they failed to predict the multiplier effects generated by higher investment expenditures and net export spending.

FOR CRITICAL ANALYSIS: Why is the multiplier effect of each additional dollar of investment spending the same as the multiplier effect of an additional dollar of net export spending?

future depends inversely on the market interest rate. Thus, the discounted present value of the stream of future earnings from investment spending that a business might undertake today also depends inversely on the market interest rate.

It follows that an decrease in the market interest rate raises the discounted present value of the stream of future earnings that firms anticipate receiving if they engage in a particular level of real investment spending. Firms will be inclined, therefore, to respond to a decrease in the market interest rate by increasing their desired amount of investment expenditures. As discussed above, the rise in real investment spending generated by a decrease in the market interest rate directly boosts real GDP. In addition, the induced changes in real consumption spending generate a multiple effect on real GDP.

In contrast, an increase in the market interest rate results in a decrease in the discounted present value of anticipated returns from investment spending. A rise in the market interest rate, therefore, tends to bring about a decrease in desired real investment spending, which in turn must ultimately reduce real GDP by a multiple amount.

2. How does a change in the market interest rate affect real GDP? Key determinants of aggregate expenditures on goods and services are total real income, which affects real consumption spending, and the interest rate, which influences investment spending. A decrease in the market interest rate generates an increase in real investment spending. The resulting rise in real GDP generates additional real income. This rise in real income induces increases in real consumption spending that ultimately generate a rise in real GDP that is a multiple of the increase in investment spending. In contrast, an increase in the market interest rate causes real investment spending to fall, which eventually brings about declines in real consumption spending and a fall in real GDP that is a multiple of the reduction in investment expenditures.

Monetary Policy and the Equilibrium Interest Rate

In Chapter 16, you learned that several theories of the demand for money emphasize the motivation for people to hold money for future use in transactions. According to these theories, individuals desire to have liquidity available to be able to purchase goods and services when they wish to do so. Nevertheless, basic theories of money demand also suggest that people hold money as an alternative to holding other financial assets. There is a relatively low risk to holding money, but most forms of money pay zero or very low interest rates. Hence, by holding money, individuals incur an opportunity cost equal to the market interest rate that they could have earned by holding a financial asset such as a Treasury security.

Consequently, people typically choose to hold less money as the market interest rate increases or to hold more money as the interest rate declines. This conclusion suggests that the market interest rate must adjust as necessary to make people willing to hold the quantity of money placed in circulation through the actions of a central bank, such as the Federal Reserve. When people are satisfied holding the amount of money outstanding, then the interest rate is at its *equilibrium* level. Let's now consider how this equilibrium interest rate is determined and how monetary policy actions can cause it to change.

The Markets for Money and Bonds

You learned about the market for money in Chapter 16. Panel (a) of Figure 17-4 depicts this market. The vertical schedule depicts the economy's *money supply schedule.* The central bank influences the nominal money supply, M^s, by varying the monetary base or by changing the required reserve ratio. The central bank cannot determine the price level, however. We shall consider how the price level is determined in Chapter 18. For now, as a simplification, we assume that the current year is the base year, so the GDP deflator, P, is equal to 1; hence, the M^s schedule is also the

FIGURE 17-4
The Equilibrium Interest Rate.

Panel (a) shows the money supply schedule (M^s), which the central bank can influence by altering the monetary base or the required reserve ratio, and the money demand schedule (M^d). All individuals in the economy are satisfied holding the nominal quantity of money supplied by the central bank at the nominal interest rate r_1, which is the equilibrium interest rate. Panel (b) displays the supply of bonds available to the public and depository institutions (B^s) and the overall demand for bonds (B^d). The quantity of bonds demanded decreases as the price of

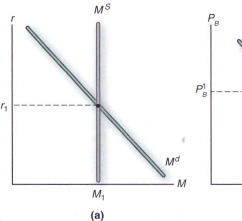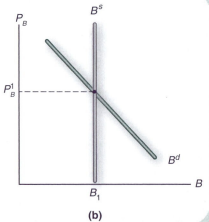

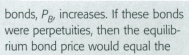

bonds, P_B, increases. If these bonds were perpetuities, then the equilibrium bond price would equal the

annual coupon return, C, divided by the equilibrium interest rate, r_1.

supply of real money balances. The schedule depicting the demand for money, M^d, slopes downward because as the interest rate rises, the opportunity cost of holding money that pays low or no rates of interest increases, inducing people to cut back on money holdings.

The crossing point of the two schedules in panel (a) depicts a situation in which all individuals in the economy are satisfied holding the nominal money stock supplied by the central bank. Consequently, at this single point the quantity of money demanded by the public is equal to the quantity of money supplied via the efforts of the central bank. Therefore, the interest rate adjusts to achieve this equilibrium point, and r_1 is the *equilibrium* interest rate. This is the single interest rate at which people are satisfied holding the quantity of money supplied.

As in Chapter 16, suppose that all financial wealth is divided between money and bonds, whose prices, as you learned in Chapter 4, are inversely related to the interest rate. In panel (b), therefore, the equilibrium interest rate, r_1, corresponds to an equilibrium bond price in the market for bonds. This bond price, denoted P_B^1, occurs at the point at which the economy-wide demand for bonds, B^d, crosses the supply of bonds available to both the public and depository institutions, B^s. As a specific example, suppose that all bonds traded in the bond market depicted in panel (b) of Figure 17-4 are perpetuities paying an annual coupon return equal to C. As discussed in Chapter 4, in the absence of risk and transactions costs, the price of these perpetuities is C/r. Thus, in this special situation, the equilibrium bond price P_B^1 in panel (b) would be equal to C/r_1.

We can conclude from Figure 17-4 that the market interest rate is attained when the public is satisfied holding the quantity of money supplied by the central bank. In addition, the equilibrium bond price, at which the quantity of bonds demanded throughout the economy equals the quantity of bonds supplied, must be consistent with the equilibrium interest rate. Thus:

> **At the market interest rate, both the market for money and the bond market must simultaneously be in equilibrium.**

In other words, at the equilibrium rate of interest, people are satisfied holding *both* the quantity of money and the quantity of bonds supplied.

Open Market Operations and the Market Interest Rate

To consider how monetary policy affects the market interest rate, let's suppose that the central bank engages in an open market purchase. This policy action has effects in both the money and bond markets. These effects are illustrated in Figure 17-5 on page 378.

When the Fed purchases bonds, it reduces the supply of bonds available to the public and to depository institutions. Hence, the bond supply schedule shifts leftward in panel (b) of Figure 17-5, from B_1^s to B_2^s. As you learned in Chapter 13, another effect of an open market purchase is an increase in bank reserves and the monetary base. The resulting money multiplier effect on the quantity of money in circulation generates an increase in the money supply, from M_1^s to M_2^s, which is shown in panel (a).

At the initial market interest rate r_1 in panel (a), there is an excess quantity of money supplied following the open market purchase. Consequently, the interest rate must adjust to a new, *lower* equilibrium level, r_2, at which the public is satisfied holding the larger quantity of money supplied. At the same time, at the corresponding initial bond price P_B^1 in panel (b), there is an excess quantity of bonds demanded after the open market purchase has been completed. The bond price, therefore, must adjust to a new, *higher* equilibrium level, P_B^2.

The decline in the market interest rate induced by the Fed's open market purchase, given an unchanged price level, constitutes the **liquidity effect** of monetary policy. It is called a

Liquidity effect: A fall in the equilibrium nominal interest rate resulting from an increase in the money supply, holding the price level unchanged.

**FIGURE 17-5
Effects of an Open
Market Purchase in
the Money and Bond Markets.**

A purchase of bonds by the Fed
reduces the supply of bonds to the
public and depository institutions in
panel (b) and increases the monetary base and hence the money supply in panel (a). There is an excess
quantity of money supplied at the initial equilibrium interest rate r_1, which
corresponds to an excess quantity of
bonds demanded at the initial equilibrium bond price P_B^1. Thus, in panel
(a), there is a movement from point
E_1 to point E_2, and the equilibrium
interest rate declines to r_2. In panel

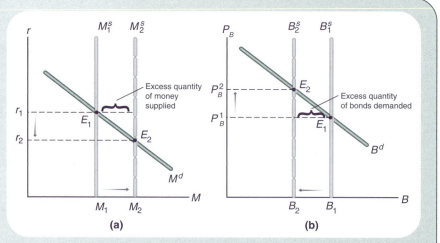

(b), the equilibrium bond price rises
to P_B^2 as a result of the movement
from point E_1 to point E_2. The decline
in the interest rate resulting from the

Fed's open market purchase is the liquidity effect of monetary policy.

liquidity effect because the open market purchase raises the overall liquidity in the economy.
The public will be satisfied with the higher level of liquidity that results only if the market
interest rate declines. The rise in the equilibrium bond price corresponding to the decline in
the market interest rate discourages individuals from buying additional bonds because of their
concern that future bond price decreases will yield capital losses. Thus, as long as the market
interest rate declines and the equilibrium bond price increases, people will be willing to hold
the larger quantity of money in circulation that results from the open market purchase.

The Discount Rate, the Required Reserve
Ratio, and the Market Interest Rate

In contrast to the effects depicted in Figure 17-5, changes in either the discount rate or the
required reserve ratio do not affect the outstanding supply of bonds available to the public and
depository institutions. Nevertheless, actions involving these potential tools of monetary policy can also generate liquidity effects on the market interest rate.

To see how a central bank such as the Federal Reserve can induce a liquidity effect without engaging in open market operations, consider Figure 17-6. A decrease in the discount rate
causes the monetary base to increase by inducing depository institutions to borrow more
reserves from Federal Reserve banks, and a decrease in the required reserve ratio increases the
money multiplier. Either policy action, therefore, induces an increase in the money supply in
panel (a), from M_1^s to M_2^s. As a result, the market interest rate declines, from r_1 to r_2.

In panel (b) of Figure 17-6, the supply of bonds available to individuals and depository
institutions remains unchanged because the Fed has not bought or sold bonds. In the case of
either a discount rate cut or a decrease in the required reserve ratio, however, depository institutions have more reserves available to purchase interest-bearing bonds. Thus, either Fed pol-

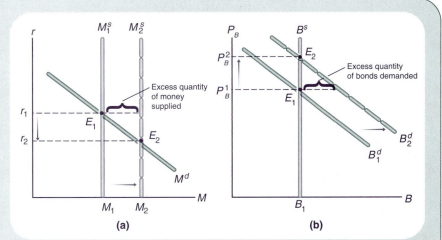

FIGURE 17-6
Effects of a Decrease in the Discount Rate or the Required Reserve Ratio in the Money and Bond Markets.

A reduction in the Fed's discount rate or a decrease in the required reserve ratio causes the money supply to increase in panel (a). Because depository institutions have more reserves available, the demand for bonds increases in panel (b). There is an excess quantity of money supplied at the initial equilibrium interest rate r_1, which corresponds to an excess quantity of bonds demanded at the initial equilibrium bond price P_B^1. Thus, in panel (a) there is a movement from point E_1 to point E_2, and the equilibrium interest rate declines to r_2. In panel (b) the equilibrium bond price rises to P_B^2 as a con- sequence of the movement from point E_1 to point E_2.

icy action brings about an increase in the demand for bonds by depository institutions. This, in turn, causes the economy-wide demand for bonds to rise, from B_1^d to B_2^d. Consequently, the equilibrium bond price increases, from P_B^1 to P_B^2.

As in the case of a Fed open market purchase, either a reduction in the discount rate or a decrease in the required reserve ratio generates a liquidity effect. The market interest rate declines, and there is a corresponding increase in the equilibrium bond price.

3. How can monetary policy influence the market interest rate? The market interest rate is the rate of interest at which people are satisfied holding the quantity of money supplied through policies of the central bank. A central bank action that increases the quantity of money raises the amount of total liquidity in the economy, thereby generating a reduction in the market interest rate called the liquidity effect of monetary policy. A corresponding rise in the equilibrium bond price gives people an incentive not to purchase more bonds because of the potential for future capital losses. The simultaneous decline in the market interest rate and increase in the equilibrium bond price thereby ensure that people will be willing to hold the larger quantity of money in circulation.

The Transmission of Monetary Policy

Thus far in this chapter, we have seen that monetary policy can affect the market interest rate and that changes in the market interest rate affect real investment spending, which in turn influences real GDP. This line of causation from monetary policy actions to real GDP traces out a "mechanism" by which the policies of central banks such as the Federal Reserve can exert effects on economic activity.

The Monetary Policy Transmission Mechanism

Figure 17-7 illustrates the linkage from monetary policy actions to interest rates, investment spending, and real GDP, which is the traditional *monetary policy transmission mechanism.* Our discussion, which assumes that other factors in the economy, such as inflation, are unchanged, indicates that this transmission takes place through two linkages. First, an open market purchase that increases the quantity of money in circulation brings about a liquidity effect that reduces the market interest rate. Second, the resulting decline in the market interest rate causes desired investment expenditures to rise. In the end, therefore, as summarized in Figure 17-7, an expansionary monetary policy induces a rise in real GDP.

Of course, a decrease in the discount rate or the required reserve ratio could also induce the same outcomes as those summarized in Figure 17-7. In addition, an open market sale or an increase in the discount rate or the required reserve ratio would generate opposite effects: an increase in the market interest rate, a reduction in real investment, and a decline in real GDP. (It is important to keep in mind that the basic monetary transmission mechanism depicted in Figure 17-7 assumes that factors other than the interest rate are unchanged; see the *Global Focus: The People's Bank of China Learns That the Real Interest Rate Is What Matters.*)

4. What is the transmission mechanism by which monetary policy exerts effects on real GDP? The monetary policy transmission mechanism sums up the linkages through which a monetary policy action ultimately brings about a change in real GDP. An open market operation or a change in the discount rate or required reserve ratio generates a change in the money supply and the supply of or demand for bonds. The result is a liquidity effect on the market interest rate that, in turn, brings about a response in desired real investment spending. Finally, this change in investment expenditures induces both a direct change in real GDP and a multiple effect on real GDP via the induced change in consumption spending.

FIGURE 17-7
The Transmission Mechanism of Monetary Policy.

An expansionary monetary policy action, such as a series of open market purchases, induces a liquidity-effect reduction in the equilibrium interest rate. This in turn generates an increase in desired investment spending, which brings about an increase in equilibrium real GDP.

GLOBAL
Focus

The People's Bank of China Learns That the Real Interest Rate Is What Matters

In October 2004, the People's Bank of China, the country's central bank, engaged in a monetary policy action that pushed up market interest rates, very slightly, for the first time in nine years. The objective of the interest rate increase was to try to reduce China's annual rate of growth of real GDP, which exceeded 7.5 percent in the early 2000s. In spite of the policy-induced boost in interest rates, investment spending, which accounts for more than 40 percent of GDP in China, actually *increased.* As a consequence, real GDP growth *rose* in the mid-2000s.

Something else also occurred in 2004: China began to experience inflation instead of deflation. Accompanying the shift to an inflationary environment was a rise in inflation expectations. Recall from Chapter 4 that the real interest rate equals the nominal interest rate minus the expected inflation rate. Even though the People's Bank of China pushed up the nominal interest rate slightly, the rise in the expected inflation rate was greater, so the real interest rate actually declined. This is why investment spending and real GDP rose even faster in the mid-2000s even though China's central bank pushed up market interest rates.

FOR CRITICAL ANALYSIS: Why do you think that critics of the People's Bank of China argued that it should have acted more than once in nine years to push up nominal interest rates if it was serious about reducing the nation's GDP growth?

Factors Influencing the Size of Monetary Policy's Effects on Real GDP

According to this proposed mechanism for monetary policy effects, the amount of the effect of a monetary policy action on real GDP depends on three key factors: the size of the liquidity effect on the market interest rate, the responsiveness of real investment expenditures to a change in the market interest rate, and the impact of a change in investment spending on real GDP. Let's consider each of these factors in turn.

1. **The interest elasticity of the demand for money.** If the liquidity effect is large, then the ultimate effect of a monetary policy action on real GDP is more likely to be sizable. If the liquidity effect is small, then the ultimate effect on real GDP is more likely to be negligible.

    The size of the liquidity effect, in turn, depends on how sensitive the demands for money and bonds are to changes in the market interest rate. To see that this is so, consider Figure 17-8 on the next page. Panels (a) and (b) depict money and bond demands that exhibit little interest rate sensitivity. In this situation, the Keynesian portfolio demand for money discussed in Chapter 16 plays a limited role in influencing individuals' holdings of money. Hence, the demands for money and bonds depicted in panels (a) and (b) are relatively *inelastic.* That is, a given proportionate decrease in the interest rate generates relatively small proportionate increases in the quantities of money and bonds demanded.

    In contrast, panels (c) and (d) of Figure 17-8 depict relatively *elastic* money and bond demands, implying that the portfolio demand for money has a significant effect on the public's desired holdings of money. Compared with the money and bond demand schedules in panels (a) and (b), those in panels (c) and (d) are relatively *elastic,* meaning that a given proportionate decrease in the interest rate generates relatively *large* proportionate increases in the quantities of money and bonds demanded.

Both pairs of panels in the figure show the effects of an open market purchase, which expands the supply of money while reducing the supply of bonds available to the public and to depository institutions. In the case of relatively inelastic money and bond demands depicted in panels (a) and (b), individuals' money and bond holdings are relatively unresponsive in the face of a decrease in the market interest rate. Thus, the downward pressure on the market interest rate caused by the resulting rise in the money supply and fall in the bond supply produces relatively little response in the quantities of money and bonds demanded. The market interest rate, therefore, declines by a relatively large amount.

FIGURE 17-8
Money and Bond Demand Elasticities and Policy-Induced Interest Rate Changes.

In panels (a) and (b), the demands for money and bonds are relatively inelastic, so the quantities of money and bonds demanded are relatively insensitive to changes in the interest rate and the price of bonds. An open market purchase of bonds by the Fed reduces the supply of bonds to the public and depository institutions in panel (b) and increases the money supply in panel (a). In panel (a), there is a relatively large liquidity-effect reduction of the equilibrium interest rate, from r_1 at point E_1 to r_2 at point E_2, and in panel (b) there is a relatively large increase in the equilibrium bond price, from P_B^1 at point E_1 to P_B^2 at point E_2. Panels (c) and (d) show the effects of an open market purchase when money and bond demands are relatively elastic. In panel (c), there is a relatively small liquidity-effect decrease in the equilibrium interest rate, from r_1, at point E_1 to r_2 at point E_2, and in panel (d) there is a relatively small rise in the equilibrium bond price, from P_B^1 at point E_1 to P_B^2 at point E_2.

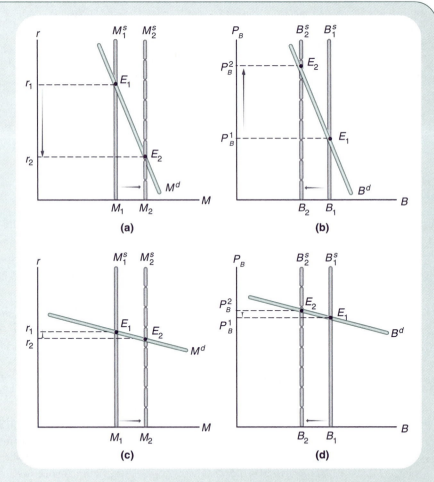

In panels (c) and (d) the public's desired money and bond holdings are very sensitive to a change in the market interest rate. The decline in the market interest rate in response to the increase in the money supply and the decrease in the bond supply caused by the open market purchase induces large portfolio adjustments by the public. The large proportionate increase in the quantity of money demanded and the significant proportionate decrease in the quantity of bonds demanded relieve pressure for any additional adjustment in the market interest rate. Thus, the market interest rate declines by a relatively small amount.

2. **The interest elasticity of desired investment spending.** For any given change in the market interest rate induced by a monetary policy action, the magnitude of the policy's ultimate effect on economic activity depends on the interest elasticity of desired investment spending. Suppose, for instance, that a proportionate change in the market interest rate has a small proportionate effect on businesses' real investment expenditures; that is, investment spending is relatively *inelastic*. In this case, even a relatively large liquidity effect on the market interest rate cannot have a significant effect on real investment expenditures and, consequently, on real GDP.

    In contrast, if desired investment spending is relatively *elastic,* a given proportionate change in the nominal interest rate induces a relatively large proportionate change in real investment expenditures. Hence, a change in the market interest rate has a larger effect on real investment expenditures. Thus, monetary policy has a greater impact on real GDP when desired investment spending is relatively elastic.

3. **The marginal propensity to consume.** Once a change in the market interest rate brought about by a monetary policy action alters real investment expenditures, real GDP increases by the amount of the rise in gross domestic investment. In addition, however, consumers respond to the resulting rise in their incomes by increasing their consumption spending, thereby producing an additional effect on real GDP that is a multiple of the change in real investment spending.

    How much consumption responds to a change in real GDP initially generated by a change in real investment spending depends on the marginal propensity to consume. If the marginal propensity to consume is relatively small, then the multiple effect of a change in real investment spending on real GDP is also relatively small. In this instance, any given change in investment spending induced by a monetary policy action is somewhat muted.

    In contrast, if the marginal propensity to consume is relatively large, then the multiple effect of a change in real investment spending on real GDP is also relatively large. A given change in real investment expenditures brought about by a monetary policy action is thereby enhanced.

Table 17-2 on the next page summarizes the three key factors that determine the magnitude of the ultimate effect of a change in the quantity of money supplied on real GDP. As the table indicates, the monetary policy transmission mechanism tends to be weakened by a relatively large interest elasticity of demand for money, a relatively small interest elasticity of desired investment, and a relatively small marginal propensity to consume. The transmission mechanism is strengthened by a relatively small interest elasticity of money demand, a relatively large interest elasticity of desired investment, and a relatively large marginal propensity to consume.

Table 17-2 Factors Affecting the Monetary Policy Transmission Mechanism

	Factors That Weaken the Transmission Mechanism	Factors That Strengthen the Transmission Mechanism
Interest elasticity of the demand for money	Relatively large; hence, a relatively small liquidity effect on interest rate	Relatively small; hence, a relatively large liquidity effect on interest rate
Interest elasticity of desired investment	Relatively small; hence, a relatively small change in real investment spending	Relatively large; hence, a relatively large change in real investment spending
Marginal propensity to consume	Relatively small; hence, a relatively small multiple effect on consumption	Relatively large; hence, a relatively large multiple effect on consumption

5. What factors determine the magnitude of the effect of a monetary policy action on real GDP? The interest elasticity of the demand for money influences the size of the liquidity effect of monetary policy. If the demand for money is relatively interest-inelastic, then a change in the quantity of money has a relatively large effect on the market interest rate. The interest elasticity of desired investment expenditures then determines how responsive investment spending is to a change in the interest rate. If desired real investment spending is relatively interest-elastic, then a change in the market interest rate has a relatively large effect on real investment expenditures. Finally, the multiple effect of the change in investment on real GDP depends on how much consumption spending rises in response to the resulting rise in incomes. If the marginal propensity to consume is relatively large, then the multiple effect of investment on real GDP is relatively large.

Chapter Summary

1. How Economists Measure a Nation's Aggregate Production of Goods and Services and Its Price Level: The key measure of a country's total production is gross domestic product (GDP), which is the market value of all final goods and services produced within the country's borders during a given period. The total value of newly produced goods and services computed using the prices at which they sold during the year they were produced is known as nominal GDP. The value of final goods and services in terms of base-year prices is real GDP, which equals nominal GDP divided by the GDP deflator, which is a measure of the overall level of prices.

2. How a Change in the Market Interest Rate Affects Real GDP: Total real income, which influences real consumption spending, and the interest rate, which affects investment spending, are key determinants of

aggregate expenditures on goods and services. An increase in the market interest rate brings about a decrease in real investment spending, and the resulting fall in real GDP reduces real income. This decline in real income induces decreases in real consumption spending that eventually generate a fall in real GDP that is a multiple of the decrease in investment spending. In contrast, a decrease in the market interest rate causes real investment spending to rise, which ultimately generates increases in real consumption spending and an increase in real GDP that is a multiple of the rise in investment expenditures.

3. How Monetary Policy Can Influence the Market Interest Rate: The market interest rate is the rate of interest at which people are satisfied holding the quantity of money in circulation. A policy action by a central bank that increases the quantity of money raises the amount of total liquidity in the economy. The resulting reduction in the market interest rate is called the liquidity effect of monetary policy. A related increase in the equilibrium bond price reduces the incentive to hold bonds so as to avoid potential future capital losses. The decline in the market interest rate and increase in the equilibrium bond price thereby ensure that people will be satisfied holding the larger quantity of money supplied by the central bank.

4. The Transmission Mechanism by Which Monetary Policy Exerts Effects on Real GDP:
The set of linkages by which a monetary policy action ultimately brings about a change in real GDP is called the monetary policy transmission mechanism. An open market operation or a change in the discount rate or required reserve ratio causes the money supply and the supply of or demand for bonds to change. Consequently, there is a liquidity effect on the market interest rate. This interest rate variation generates a change in desired real investment expenditures that brings about both a direct change in real GDP and a multiple effect on real GDP through an induced change in consumption spending.

5. Factors That Determine the Magnitude of the Effect of a Monetary Policy Action on Real GDP:
The magnitude of the liquidity effect of monetary policy depends on the interest elasticity of the demand for money. If money demand is relatively interest-elastic, then a change in the quantity of money has a relatively small effect on the market interest rate. The responsiveness of investment expenditures to a change in the interest rate depends on the interest elasticity of desired investment spending. If desired real investment expenditures are relatively interest-elastic, then a change in the market interest rate has a relatively large effect on real investment spending. The multiple effect of the change in investment on real GDP depends on the extent to which consumption spending rises in response to the resulting increase in incomes. The multiple effect on real GDP is relatively large when the marginal propensity to consume is relatively large.

Questions and Problems

(Answers to odd-numbered questions and problems may be found on the Web at **http://money.swcollege.com** under "Student Resources.")

1. In your own words, define GDP.

2. Consider the following data ($ billions) for a given year:

Consumption spending	$8,000	Wages and salaries	$7,300
Interest income	600	Depreciation	1,400
Rental income	300	Government spending	2,200
Investment spending	2,300	Net export spending:	−450
Profits	1,900		

Calculate gross domestic product.

3. Explain the distinction between nominal GDP and real GDP.

4. Consider a two-good economy. In 2006, firms in this economy produced 25 units of good X, which sold at a market price of $4 per unit, and 15 units of good Y, which sold at a market price of $4 per unit. In 2007, the economy produced the same amounts of both X and Y, but the price of good X rose to $6 per unit, and the price of good Y increased to $5 per unit. What were the values of nominal GDP in 2006 and 2007?

5. In question 4, if 2006 is the base year, what were the values of real GDP in 2006 and 2007?

6. Using your answers from questions 4 and 5 and assuming again that 2006 is the base year, what is the value of the GDP price deflator for 2006? What is the approximate value (rounded to the nearest hundredth) of the GDP price deflator for 2007? What is the approximate value (rounded to the nearest percentage point) of inflation between 2006 and 2007?

7. Suppose that the GDP deflator for the year considered in question 2 has a value of 1.42. Based on your answer to question 2, what is real GDP for this year?

8. Suppose that the demands for money and bonds are very interest-inelastic. The Federal Reserve engages in an open market sale. Use appropriate diagrams of the markets for money and bonds to determine the effects of this policy action on the equilibrium interest rate and the equilibrium bond price.

9. What difference does it make to your answer to question 8 if the demands for money and bonds are instead very interest-elastic? Use appropriate diagrams to assist in your explanation.

10. Suppose that the demands for money and bonds are very interest-inelastic. The Federal Reserve increases the required reserve ratio. Use appropriate diagrams of the markets for money and bonds to determine the effects of this policy action on the equilibrium interest rate and the equilibrium bond price.

11. What difference does it make to your answer to question 10 if the demands for money and bonds are instead very interest-elastic? Use appropriate diagrams to assist in your explanation.

Before the Test

Test your understanding of the material covered in this chapter by taking the Chapter 17 interactive quiz at **http://money.swcollege.com**.

Online Application

To view the most current information concerning the consumer price index (CPI), take a look at the home page of the Bureau of Labor Statistics. As noted in this chapter, the CPI is a fixed-weight index measure of the U.S. price level.

Internet URL: http://stats.bls.gov/eag/eag.us.htm

Title: Bureau of Labor Statistics: Economy at a Glance

Navigation: Begin at the home page of the Bureau of Labor Statistics (**http://stats.bls.gov**).

Application: Perform the indicated operations, and answer the following questions:

1. On the Bureau of Labor Statistics home page, under the heading "At a Glance Tables," click on "U.S. Economy at a Glance," and then click on "Consumer Price Index." Scan down that page, and under the heading "CPI Fact Sheets," click on "How to Use the Consumer Price Index for Escalation." Read the material at this location. Based on this discussion, what exactly does the CPI measure?

2. Back up to "U.S. Economy at a Glance." Click on the graph box and take a look at the chart. How much does the CPI appear to vary from year to year? Has it varied much within the most recent year?

Selected References and Further Reading

Clayton, Gary E., and Martin Gerhard Giesbrecht. *A Guide to Everyday Economic Statistics.* New York: McGraw-Hill, 1995.

Council of Economic Advisers. *Economic Indicators.* Washington, D.C.: U.S. Government Printing Office, various issues.

_____. *Economic Report of the President.* Washington, D.C.: U.S. Government Printing Office, February 2005.

International Monetary Fund. *World Economic Outlook.* Washington, D.C., October 1996.

U.S. Department of Commerce. *Survey of Current Business.* Washington, D.C., various issues.

MoneyXtra

Log on to the MoneyXtra Web site now (**http://moneyxtra.swcollege.com**) for additional learning resources such as practice quizzes, case studies, readings, and additional economic applications.

Money, Business Cycles, and Inflation

You may have heard your parents, grandparents, and perhaps even great-grandparents complain that a dollar just does not buy what it did in years past. If so, they were certainly correct. Consider a great-grandparent who was born around 1900. By the time that individual was your age, a rising price level had eroded the dollar's value to the point that it could be used to buy only what 40 cents would have purchased in 1900. Within another 20 years, however, a decline in the price level had pushed the dollar's value back up somewhat, so by 1938 a dollar would buy an amount of goods and services that 60 cents could have purchased in 1900. From that year onward, the price level steadily increased. If your great-grandparent set aside any dollars to give to one of your parents in the 1970s, each of those dollars could purchase only an amount of goods and services equal to what 25 cents could have bought in 1900. If your parent held onto those dollars to give to you today, each would allow you to buy an amount of goods and services equivalent to what a nickel would have enabled your great-grandparent to purchase in 1900.

What factors cause the price level to decrease and the purchasing power of the dollar to rise, as occurred between 1918 and the 1930s? What factors cause the price level to increase and the purchasing power of the dollar to fall, as has happened in the years since the 1930s? In this chapter, you will learn the answers to these questions.

Cycles in Economic Activity

Variations in real GDP relative to its long-run growth path are known as **business cycles.** Figure 18-1 on the next page illustrates some key concepts associated with a complete business cycle. The dashed line in the figure shows a hypothetical growth path for **natural GDP,** which is what economists call the level of real GDP along the long-run growth path that the economy otherwise would follow in the absence of cyclical fluctuations. The solid curve is a hypothetical growth path for *actual* GDP, which may fluctuate.

Recessions and Expansions

When actual real GDP declines, economists say that the economy experiences a phase in the business cycle called a **recession.** The National Bureau of Economic Research normally defines a recession as a recurring period of decline in total output, income,

Fundamental Issues

1. What are business cycles, and what are their key features?

2. What is aggregate demand, and how do monetary policy actions affect aggregate demand?

3. What are the long-run implications of monetary policy actions for real GDP and the price level?

4. How can monetary policy actions simultaneously affect real GDP and the price level in the short run?

5. How can the public's expectations influence the short-run effects of monetary policy?

FIGURE 18-1
A Hypothetical Business Cycle.

At a business-cycle trough, actual real GDP is at its lowest point relative to the long-run growth path of natural GDP, so the vertical distance between actual and natural GDP levels reaches its maximum size for the cycle. The period in which real GDP declines toward this trough is a recession. Beyond the trough of the business cycle, actual real GDP rises back toward and beyond its long-run growth path until it reaches its peak for the cycle. This period is called a

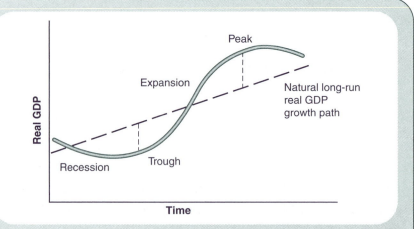

business-cycle expansion. At the point at which the expansion peaks, the vertical distance between the actual real GDP growth path and the natural GDP growth path reaches its maximum size.

Business cycles: Variations in real GDP around its long-run growth path.

Natural GDP: The level of real GDP that is consistent with the economy's natural rate of growth.

Recession: A decline in real GDP lasting at least two consecutive quarters, which can cause real GDP to fall below its long-run, natural level.

Trough: The point along a business cycle at which real GDP is at its lowest level relative to the long-run natural GDP level.

Depression: An especially severe recession.

Expansion: A point along a business cycle at which actual GDP begins to rise, perhaps even above its natural, long-run level.

Peak: The point along a business cycle at which real GDP is at its highest level relative to the long-run, natural GDP level.

employment, and trade that lasts at least six months to a year and affects many sectors of the economy.

When a recession reaches its low point, actual real GDP is at its lowest point relative to its natural path. At this point, therefore, the vertical distance between the natural GDP growth path and the actual growth path reaches its maximum size for the cycle. This point is the **trough** of the business cycle; at the trough, business activity is at its lowest level over the course of the entire business cycle. If the recession is severe, then actual real GDP may be well below the economy's natural level. Furthermore, if a severe recession lasts a particularly long time, then economists say that an economy experiences a **depression.** Economists often disagree about when recessions are sufficiently severe for this term to apply, but all agree that a depression occurred in the United States during the 1930s.

When actual real GDP begins to rise again, the economy enters the **expansion** phase of the business cycle. At the point where actual real GDP rises to its highest point relative to natural GDP, the business cycle is at its **peak.** The cycle then continues.

Actual business cycles are not as simple as the one illustrated in Figure 18-1. During various periods in the past, the actual path of real GDP has been much less smooth than the hypothetical path shown in the figure. Furthermore, the durations of expansions and recessions have rarely been of equal length. Table 18-1 displays the durations between troughs and peaks of the twenty-two business cycles that the United States has experienced since 1899. As the table indicates, the lengths of the expansion and recession phases of business cycles have varied considerably.

Unemployment and the Business Cycle

Business cycles entail movements in aggregate GDP that affect us all. For some of us, the effects of business-cycle recessions can hit especially hard when they generate job losses. By way of contrast, expansions can pave the way to brighter futures for many families as they bring about overall reductions in unemployment.

Table 18-1 Business-Cycle Expansions and Contractions in the United States

Peak	Trough	Peak	Duration in Months* Recession	Expansion	Cycle
June 1899	December 1900	September 1902	18	21	39
September 1902	August 1904	May 1907	23	33	56
May 1907	June 1908	January 1910	13	19	32
January 1910	January 1912	January 1913	24	12	36
January 1913	December 1914	August 1918	23	44	67
August 1918	March 1919	January 1920	7	10	17
January 1920	July 1921	May 1923	18	22	40
May 1923	July 1924	October 1926	14	27	41
October 1926	November 1927	August 1929	13	21	34
August 1929	March 1933	May 1937	43	50	93
May 1937	June 1938	February 1945	13	80	93
February 1945	October 1945	November 1948	8	37	45
November 1948	October 1949	July 1953	11	45	56
July 1953	May 1954	August 1957	10	39	49
August 1957	April 1958	April 1960	8	24	32
April 1960	February 1961	December 1969	10	106	116
December 1969	November 1970	November l973	11	36	47
November 1973	March 1975	January 1980	16	58	74
January 1980	July 1980	July 1981	6	12	18
July 1981	November 1982	July 1990	16	92	108
July 1990	March 1991	March 2001	8	120	128
March 2001	November 2001		8	—	—

*Cycles are measured from peak to peak.

SOURCES: National Bureau of Economic Research; *Survey of Current Business;* authors' estimates.

On the Web
Where can you find out when the National Bureau of Economic Research has determined that a recession is under way? The answer is to visit the NBER's home page at **http://www.nber.org**, where you can click on "NBER Publications and Data" in the right-hand margin, then "Business Cycle Dates."

THE UNEMPLOYMENT RATE To determine the extent of total unemployment in the U.S. economy, the government tabulates the **unemployment rate,** which is simply the percentage of the civilian labor force that is unemployed. Terminology is crucial. The civilian labor force consists of all individuals sixteen years of age to retirement who are not in the military or confined to an institution such as a hospital and who either have a job or are actively seeking a job. The number of people in the civilian labor force who are unemployed includes all who are not working yet are available for and actively seeking a job. This means that people who are not employed but who also are not actively looking for work are not included in either the civilian labor force or the ranks of the unemployed. Such *discouraged workers* are not counted in calculations of the unemployment rate.

It also is important to understand that the official unemployment rate is an *estimate.* The government does not calculate the entire labor force. On behalf of the Bureau of Labor Statistics, the Bureau of the Census conducts a monthly *Current Population Survey* covering 60,000 households in about 2,000 counties and cities across the fifty states and the District of Columbia. The BLS then uses the information from this monthly survey to calculate its estimates of the size of the labor force and the number of people in the labor force who are unemployed. It then uses these estimates to calculate the unemployment rate.

Unemployment rate: The percentage of the civilian labor force that is unemployed.

MONEYXTRA!
Economic Applications

Do technological advances result in higher unemployment? To review alternative perspectives on this debate and make your own judgment, go to EconDebate Online. **http://moneyxtra. swcollege.com**

BUSINESS CYCLES AND THE UNEMPLOYMENT RATE The unemployment rate varies systematically across business cycles, as Figure 18-2 shows. Recessions, the shaded periods in the figure, are accompanied by higher unemployment rates. During business-cycle expansions, in contrast, unemployment rates tend to decline.

Economists classify three components of the unemployed portion of the nation's civilian labor force. One is **frictional unemployment,** which describes the portion of the labor force consisting of people who are qualified for gainful employment but are temporarily out of work. They may be in this situation because they recently quit a job and have accepted another job that they will begin in a few weeks.

Another component of unemployment is **structural unemployment.** This refers to the portion of the civilian labor force made up of people who would like to be gainfully employed but who lack skills and other attributes necessary to obtain a job. The duration of unemployment for such individuals can stretch into months or perhaps even years.

Most economists define the ratio of those who are frictionally and structurally unemployed to the civilian labor force as the **natural rate of unemployment,** or the unemployment rate that would arise if the economy could stay on its long-run growth path. The variations in the overall unemployment rate shown in Figure 18-2 thereby would arise from changes in the third category of unemployment, called **cyclical unemployment.** This is the portion of the civilian labor force composed of those who lose their jobs because of business-cycle fluctuations.

A key issue of concern to economists inside and outside the Federal Reserve is whether the Fed can undertake policies that can influence the economy's rate of growth or smooth cyclical fluctuations in economic activity.

Frictional unemployment: The portion of total unemployment arising from the fact that a number of workers are between jobs at any given time.

Structural unemployment: The portion of total unemployment resulting from a poor match of workers' abilities and skills with current needs of employers.

Natural rate of unemployment: The portion of the unemployment rate that is accounted for by frictional and structural unemployment.

Cyclical unemployment: The portion of total unemployment resulting from business-cycle fluctuations.

FIGURE 18-2
Unemployment Rates and Phases of the Business Cycle.

The cyclical component of the unemployment rate increases during business-cycle downturns. As a result, the overall unemployment rate typically rises during recessions.

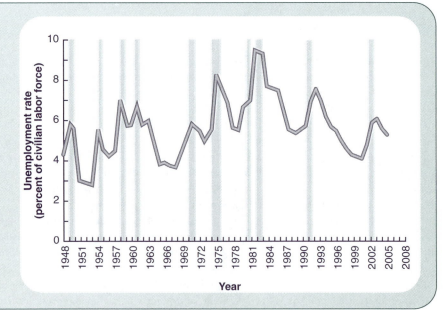

SOURCES: *Economic Report of the President,* 2005; National Bureau of Economic Research, *Economic Indicators.*

> **1. What are business cycles, and what are their key features?** Business cycles are fluctuations in real GDP above or below the level that is consistent with the economy's long-run growth. Recessions occur when real GDP falls below its long-run level, and expansions take place when real GDP rises back to or even above its long-run level. Although the existence of frictional and structural unemployment implies that there is a natural unemployment rate, the overall unemployment rate has a cyclical component that rises during recessions and falls during expansions.

Aggregate Demand and Monetary Policy

How might central banks go about smoothing business cycles to prevent major swings in real GDP and the unemployment rate? To answer this question, we must consider the possible channels by which monetary policy actions may influence real GDP and the price level. A key channel is *aggregate demand,* or a relationship between the price level and total planned expenditures on goods and services.

Money, the Quantity Equation, and Aggregate Demand

The most basic approach to aggregate demand is based on the **quantity theory of money,** which proposes that people hold money primarily for its use as a medium of exchange.

THE QUANTITY THEORY OF MONEY   Economists have long realized that money serves as a store of value, unit of account, and standard of deferred payment. Nevertheless, they originally viewed the medium-of-exchange property of money as the basis for explaining how much money people desire to hold. Consequently, the quantity theory of money focuses on money's role as a medium of exchange. To understand how much money people desire to hold, the quantity theory concentrates on explaining the demand for money for purchases of newly produced goods and services.

The starting point for the quantity theory of money is the **equation of exchange:**

$$M \times V \equiv P \times y.$$

In the equation of exchange, M is the nominal quantity of money, or the current-dollar value of currency and checking deposits held by the nonbank public. The term V represents the **income velocity of money,** or the average number of times people spend each unit of money on final goods and services per unit of time. Consequently, the left-hand side of the equation of exchange is the value of current-dollar monetary payments for final goods and services. On the right-hand side of the equation, the price level for final goods and services is multiplied by real GDP. This quantity is also the current-dollar value of monetary payments for final goods and services. Therefore, both sides of the equation of exchange must be identical. The equation of exchange is thus an accounting definition, or identity. It states that the product of the nominal quantity of money times the average number of times that people use money to buy goods and services ($M \times V$) must equal the market value of the goods and services that they use the money to purchase ($P \times y$).

An economic identity is a truism. It is not a theory of how people make decisions. The foundation of the quantity *theory* of money is the *Cambridge equation,* which you learned about in Chapter 16. Recall that the Cambridge equation is

$$M^d = k \times Y,$$

Quantity theory of money: The theory that people hold money primarily for transactions purposes; ultimately yields a relationship between the price level and desired real expenditures on final goods and services.

Equation of exchange: An accounting identity that states that the nominal value of all monetary transactions for final goods and services is identically equal to the nominal value of the output of goods and services purchased.

Income velocity of money: The average number of times a unit of money is used to purchase final goods and services within an interval.

where M^d denotes the total nominal quantity of money all people in the economy wish to hold and k is a fraction $(0 < k < 1)$. The Cambridge equation, therefore, says that people desire to hold some fraction of their nominal income as money. As we discussed in Chapter 17, the current-dollar value of production, $P \times y$, corresponds to the total level of nominal GDP, Y. Thus, the Cambridge equation may also be written as

$$M^d = k \times P \times y.$$

Thus, if $k = 0.2$, then people wish to hold 20 percent, or one-fifth, of their nominal income as money.

THE AGGREGATE DEMAND SCHEDULE   We now have the essential building blocks that we need to understand how aggregate demand and the price level are determined in the quantity theory of money. Suppose that the amount of nominal money balances supplied through the actions of a central bank is equal to an amount M_1. In equilibrium, all individuals in the economy desire to hold this quantity of money balances, so

$$M^d = M_1.$$

The Cambridge equation then indicates that

$$M_1 = k \times P \times y.$$

If we divide both sides of this equation by $k \times P$, we obtain

$$M_1/(k \times P) = y.$$

Reversing the two sides of this equation then leaves us with

$$y^d = M_1/(k \times P).$$

Aggregate demand schedule (y^d): The combinations of various price levels and levels of real GDP at which individuals are satisfied with their consumption of output and their holdings of money.

This is an equation for the economy's **aggregate demand schedule.** The aggregate demand schedule is all combinations of real GDP and price levels at which households are satisfied holding the available quantity of nominal money balances (M_1 in this example), given their average desired ratio of money holdings, k.

Figure 18-3 depicts the aggregate demand schedule. As the equation for the aggregate demand schedule indicates, the quantity of real goods and services that people wish to purchase declines as the price level rises. An increase in the price level raises nominal income and thereby induces people to raise their holdings of nominal money balances. Thus, when the price level rises from P_1 to P_2, people reduce their expenditures, and the aggregate real value of the amount of goods and services demanded falls from y_1 to y_2. This is a leftward *movement along* the aggregate demand schedule.

SHIFTS IN THE AGGREGATE DEMAND SCHEDULE   Two factors can cause the aggregate demand schedule's position to change. One is a change in the quantity of money supplied by the government or by a central bank. As you can see by referring to the equation for the schedule, $y^d = M_1/(k \times P)$, a rise in the quantity of money to an amount larger than M_1 increases the right-hand side of the equation. As a result, the nominal purchasing power available to all individuals in the economy is higher at any given price level, and so people desire to purchase more real goods and services at any given price level. The aggregate demand schedule shifts to the right. Thus, aggregate demand *rises.* In contrast, a decline in the quantity of money shifts the aggregate demand schedule to the left, and aggregate demand *falls.*

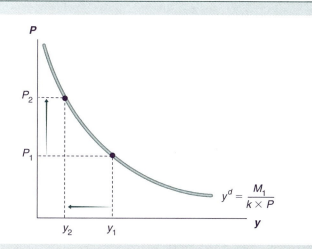

FIGURE 18-3
The Aggregate Demand Schedule
of the Quantity Theory of Money.

The aggregate demand schedule
stems from the Cambridge equation.
It is negatively sloped, indicating that
at higher price levels, with the nominal
quantity of money and the Cambridge
k unchanged, the aggregate real value
of goods and services demanded
declines.

The other factor that can influence the position of the aggregate demand schedule is a change in the value of k in the Cambridge equation. For instance, suppose that a technological change, such as the widespread use of debit cards and automated teller machines at banks, reduces people's desire to keep ready cash on hand. Then the value of k declines, as people hold fewer money balances relative to their nominal income, $Y = P \times y$. Referring once more to the equation for the aggregate demand schedule, $y^d = M_1/(k \times P)$, you can see that a decline in k, because it reduces the denominator of the right-hand side of the equation, increases the total purchasing power available to individuals in the economy. Just as an increase in the quantity of money supplied causes a rise, or rightward shift outward, in the aggregate demand schedule, so does a decline in the demand for money by individuals. In contrast, a rise in money demand will induce a reduction in aggregate demand and a leftward shift in the aggregate demand schedule.

Monetary Policy, the Interest Rate, and Aggregate Demand

As you learned in Chapter 16, most theories, and considerable evidence, indicate that another factor affecting money demand is the interest rate. Thus, as discussed in Chapter 17, the interest rate plays a fundamental role in the traditional view of the monetary policy transmission mechanism.

THE CAMBRIDGE EQUATION REVISITED   An interest-rate-based linkage from monetary policy to aggregate demand is absent from the Cambridge equation approach to aggregate demand. For any given level of real GDP, y, the equation of exchange identity tells us that $M \times V \equiv P \times y$. If the aggregate demand equation is satisfied, it is also true that at a given level of real GDP, $y = M/(k \times P)$. If we substitute this value for real GDP into the equation of exchange identity, we see that

$$M \times V \equiv P \times [M/(k \times P)] = M/k.$$

Now, if we divide both sides of this equation by M, we get

$$V = 1/k.$$

This says that a key assumption behind the Cambridge equation approach to aggregate demand is that the income velocity of money is equal to the reciprocal of the k factor of proportionality in the Cambridge equation.

Because the Cambridge equation assumes that k is constant, this tells us that the Cambridge equation implicitly assumes that the income velocity of money is constant. Is this a reasonable assumption? Figure 18-4 shows the U.S. income velocity of money, which clearly has changed over time.

What causes the income velocity of money to vary? Recall that the income velocity of money is the average number of times that the quantity of money is used in exchange for real goods and services. How much money people desire to hold for use in purchasing goods and services, of course, depends on their demand for real money balances, which in turn depends in part on the interest rate. Consequently, we should expect the interest rate to influence the income velocity of money and, as a result, to play a role in the linkage from monetary policy to aggregate demand. (The quantity theory of money indicates, however, that changes in the money stock can influence aggregate demand even in the absence of an interest rate linkage; see the *Global Focus: The Bank of Japan Confronts the Quantity Theory of Money.*)

THE INTEREST RATE, THE REAL BALANCE EFFECT, AND AGGREGATE DEMAND   To evaluate the role of the interest rate as a factor linking monetary policy and aggregate demand, consider Figure 18-5 on page 396, which displays the effects in the market for real money balances of a rise in the price level, from P_1 to P_2. As shown in panel (a), at a higher price level, the real value of the nominal quantity of money in circulation is lower. Consequently, other things being equal, the real supply of money declines, from M^s/P_1 to M^s/P_2, and the market interest rate increases, from r_1 to r_2. Economists call this increase in market interest rates the **real balance effect** because it results from a change in the real value of the nominal quantity of money in circulation generated by a change in the price level.

As you learned in Chapter 17, a rise in the market interest rate causes desired real investment expenditures to decline. In conjunction with a multiple effect on consumption spend-

Real balance effect: An increase in the nominal rate of interest that results from an increase in the price level, holding total depository institution reserves unchanged.

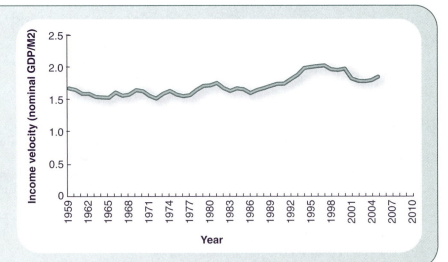

FIGURE 18-4
The Income Velocity of Money in the United States.

The U.S. income velocity of money using the Federal Reserve's M2 measure of money has remained within a relatively narrow range since the late 1950s. Nevertheless, its value has exhibited year-to-year variability.

The Bank of Japan Confronts the Quantity Theory of Money

From the late 1990s through the mid-2000s, nominal interest rates in Japan were very close to zero. During the same period, the nation's price level fell. According to officials at the Bank of Japan, the Japanese central bank, the inability to push interest rates any lower meant that monetary policy could do little to raise aggregate demand. Thus, the officials argued, the Bank of Japan could not prevent Japan's deflation.

Aside from a four-month period in early 2002, the M2 measure of the quantity of money in circulation in Japan declined from the late 1990s through the mid-2000s. Of course, the quantity theory of money implies that a negative rate of growth of the money supply will produce negative growth in the price level, or deflation. Application of the quantity theory of money, therefore, suggests that the Bank of Japan actually had a lot to do with Japan's deflationary situation. It also indicates that raising the rate of money growth in Japan could ultimately have brought the deflationary experience to an end.

FOR CRITICAL ANALYSIS: If the Bank of Japan had actually increased the money supply between the late 1990s and mid-2000s, why might the Japanese price level have increased even if the nominal interest rate had remained close to zero?

---

ing, this decrease in real investment spending brings about a reduction in total spending on newly produced goods and services. Hence, as shown in panel (b) of Figure 18-5, this implies an inverse relationship between the price level and real GDP, or a downward-sloping aggregate demand schedule.

The aggregate demand schedule depicted in Figure 18-5 has the same basic shape when the quantity of money in circulation influences the market interest rate. As Figure 18-6 on page 397 indicates, the interest-rate-based monetary policy transmission mechanism likewise implies that changes in the nominal money supply can influence aggregate demand. This occurs in a different way than in the quantity theory's approach, however. In panel (a), at the current price level P_1, a rise in the nominal money supply causes the supply of real money balances to increase, from M_1^s/P_1 to M_2^s/P_1. This generates a liquidity effect on the market interest rate, which declines. The resulting increase in investment expenditures and the associated multiple effect on consumption spending cause total aggregate spending on final goods and services to increase at the price level P_1. Aggregate demand rises, as shown in panel (b).

Thus, the quantity theory's approach to aggregate demand and the approach of the traditional interest-rate-based transmission mechanism both yield downward-sloping aggregate demand schedules that shift rightward in response to an increase in the quantity of money. Nevertheless, the quantity theory's approach does not provide an explanation for why central banks, such as the Federal Reserve, commonly formulate policy in terms of interest rates. In contrast, the interest-rate-based transmission mechanism includes a fundamental role for the interest rate. For this reason, we shall emphasize this latter approach to explaining how monetary policy affects aggregate demand. Realistically, however, both the direct effects of money on spending implied by the quantity theory's approach and the interest-rate-based spending effects implied by the traditional monetary policy transmission mechanism are likely to prove important.

FIGURE 18-5
The Market for Real Money Balances, the Interest Rate, and Aggregate Demand.

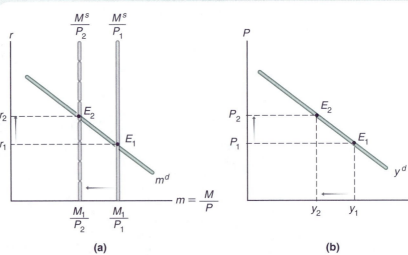

(a)   **(b)**

An increase in the price level reduces the real value of the nominal quantity of money in circulation and thereby shifts the supply of real money balances leftward in panel (a). This generates a movement along the demand schedule for real money balances, m^d, from point E_1 to point E_2. The result in panel (a) is the real balance effect: the nominal interest rate increases in response to a rise in the price level. An increase in the interest rate brings about a reduction in desired investment spending, so total expenditures on final goods and services decline, resulting in a movement from point E_1 to point E_2 in panel (b). These two points in panel (b) lie along a downward-sloping aggregate demand schedule.

2. What is aggregate demand, and how do monetary policy actions affect aggregate demand? Aggregate demand is a relationship between the price level and total planned expenditures on goods and services. The quantity theory of money indicates that people split their income between money holdings and spending on goods and services. Consequently, a rise in the price level reduces the real value of money holdings and thereby induces people to reduce real expenditures, so the aggregate demand schedule slopes downward. When we take into account that the demand for money varies inversely with the interest rate, a decline in real money balances also causes the market interest rate to rise. This increase in the interest rate generates a decline in desired real investment and a reduction in total planned expenditures, thereby also yielding a downward-sloping aggregate demand schedule. An increase in the quantity of money in circulation boosts total planned expenditures at any given price level and thereby shifts the aggregate demand schedule rightward.

Monetary Policy, Real GDP, and the Price Level in the Long Run

How do monetary policy actions ultimately influence real GDP and the price level? Most economists agree that a key factor determining the answer to this question is the speed at which prices of factors of production adjust to changes in the level of prices of goods and services.

FIGURE 18-6
The Interest-Rate-Based Transmission Mechanism and Aggregate Demand.

With the price level unchanged, an increase in the quantity of money in circulation causes the supply of real money balances to rise in panel (a), thereby generating a liquidity-effect reduction in the nominal interest rate, from r_1 at point E_1 to r_2 at point E_2. This decrease in the interest rate induces a rise in desired investment expenditures, which in turn generates a multiple effect on consumption spending on final goods

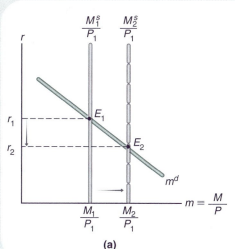
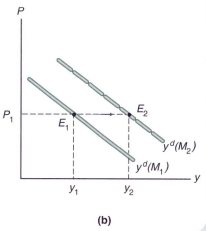

(a) (b)

and services. The result in panel (b) is a rightward shift in the aggregate

demand schedule given by the distance from point E_1 to point E_2.

Long-Run Aggregate Supply, Real GDP, and the Price Level

In the **long run,** prices of factors of production have sufficient time to adjust in equal proportion to changes in the prices of goods and services. Consider, for instance, the long-run adjustment to a price-level increase in the market for labor. When the price level increases, the real value of the current nominal wage rate that firms pay workers to provide labor services declines. Firms respond by increasing the quantity of labor demanded. From the perspective of workers, however, a rise in the price level reduces the real value of the current nominal wage rate, which induces workers to reduce the quantity of labor they desire to supply. The rise in the quantity of labor demanded and the decline in the quantity of labor supplied create a shortage of labor at the current nominal wage rate. Firms respond by bidding up the nominal wage rate until the real wage returns to the level it was at before the rise in the price level occurred. This adjustment requires the nominal wage rate to rise by exactly the same proportionate increase as the initial rise in the price level. In addition, once equilibrium is attained again in the labor market, employment returns to its original level.

Consequently, if nominal wage rates have sufficient time to adjust, labor employment will remain unchanged in the face of an increase in the price level. The same basic reasoning applies to the employment of other factors of production, including capital, land, and entrepreneurship. Given sufficient time, the nominal prices of these factors of production will adjust in direct and equal proportion to a change in the level of prices of goods and services. Furthermore, the equilibrium quantities of the factors of production employed will be unaffected by a change in the price level.

Of course, if an increase in the price level leaves the quantities of all factors of production unchanged, then, other things being equal, total production of final goods and services will also

Long run: A period sufficiently long that nominal wages and other input prices adjust in equal proportion to a change in the price level.

On the Web
How fast are nominal wages rising in the United States? Take a look at U.S. employment cost trends by going to the home page of the Bureau of Labor Statistics at **http://stats.bls.gov**. Under "Wages, Earnings, and Benefits," click on "Employment Costs," and click on "Employment Cost Index." Choose desired intervals to display percentage changes in "Civilian Workers, Wages and Salaries," and select "All Years."

Long-run aggregate supply schedule: The relationship between the production of real GDP and the price level when there is sufficient time for nominal wages and other input prices to adjust in equal proportion to a change in the price level.

remain unchanged. It follows that, as shown in Figure 18-7, the **long-run aggregate supply schedule,** denoted y_{LR}^s and depicting the long-run relationship between the production of real GDP and the price level, must be vertical. In the figure, therefore, the long-run aggregate supply schedule is vertical at a level of real GDP given by y_1, which is the long-run equilibrium level of real GDP.

Also shown in Figure 18-7 is a downward-sloping aggregate demand schedule. At the point at which the two schedules cross, the nation's price level has adjusted to ensure that total desired spending on domestic output of goods and services equals aggregate real GDP produced by all firms. In the figure, this condition is satisfied at the price level P_1, which is the long-run equilibrium price level.

Long-Run Determinants of Real GDP and the Price Level

The position of the long-run aggregate supply schedule is determined by the technology available to firms and by the quantities of factors of production that firms choose to employ given that technology. A technological improvement or a rise in the employment of an input such as labor or capital brings about a long-run increase in real GDP. The result, as shown in panel (a) of Figure 18-8, is a rightward shift in the long-run aggregate supply schedule. The long-run equilibrium level of real GDP increases. With aggregate demand unchanged, there is an associated decline in the equilibrium price level, or **deflation.** Such aggregate-supply-induced deflation often occurs during periods of rapid economic growth. For instance, the U.S. price level declined as a result of the considerable economic growth that occurred between 1870 and 1895. (Today, sustained periods of growth-induced deflation are under way in other parts of the world, but deflation is not always a result of economic growth; see *What Happens When Deflation Occurs as a Result of Falling Aggregate Demand rather than Increasing Aggregate Supply?*)

Panel (b) of Figure 18-8 illustrates how monetary policymakers could prevent the price level from declining. The appropriate monetary policy is to increase the money supply at a

Deflation: A decline in the price level during a period of time.

FIGURE 18-7
Equilibrium Real GDP and the Equilibrium Price Level in the Long Run.

When nominal wages and other input prices have sufficient time to adjust equiproportionately to changes in the price level, a change in the price level leaves the production of final goods and services unaffected. Thus, the long-run aggregate supply schedule, y_{LR}^s, is vertical. The equilibrium price level, P_1, equates total real desired expenditures on final goods and services with the production of real GDP, y_1.

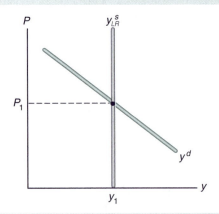

FIGURE 18-8
Deflation versus Long-Run Price Stability in a Growing Economy.

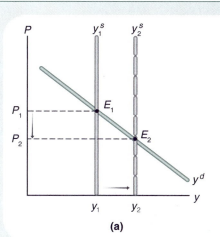 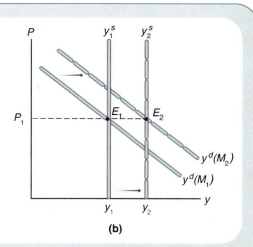

(a)   (b)

As shown in panel (a), an increase in long-run aggregate supply, from y_1^s to y_2^s, results in a movement along the aggregate demand schedule from point E_1 to point E_2. Real GDP increases from y_1 to y_2. The equilibrium price level declines, from P_1 to P_2, so deflation occurs. Panel (b) shows how monetary policymaking could prevent deflation from taking place in a growing economy. Appropriate increases in the quantity of money in circulation, from M_1 to M_2, can increase aggregate demand as required to maintain the same equilibrium price level at both point E_1 and point E_2, thereby achieving price stability.

rate consistent with shifting the aggregate demand schedule rightward at the same pace as the rise in aggregate supply. As a consequence, the equilibrium price level remains unchanged in the long run, even as real GDP rises with the growth in long-run aggregate supply.

What Happens When... **Deflation Occurs as a Result of Falling Aggregate Demand rather than Increasing Aggregate Supply?**

Between 2001 and 2005, the average annual rate of change in the price level in China was very slightly below zero, implying slight deflation on average, but the average annual rate of growth in China's real GDP exceeded 7.5 percent. In Japan, the average annual rate of growth of real GDP was significantly lower, at about 1.3 percent, but the rate of deflation was higher, at nearly 1.7 percent. Thus, during these years, real GDP increased in both China and Japan, but the price level decreased. This implies that in both nations, the long-run aggregate supply schedule shifted rightward at a faster pace than aggregate demand.

Compare this recent experience of China and Japan to that of another country in a different five-year period: the United States between 1930 and 1934. During this period, the rate of deflation averaged almost 5 percent per year, yet U.S. real GDP *declined* by more than 9 percent per year. Analyzing this situation in terms of long-run aggregate supply and aggregate demand implies that only

the occurrence of two events can explain the U.S. deflation of the early 1930s. For real GDP to have declined, one of these events must have been a *decrease* in long-run aggregate supply. But if U.S. aggregate demand had increased or even remained unchanged, this decline in long-run aggregate supply would have generated an increase in the price level. Thus, the other event that must have occurred in the United States between 1930 and 1934 was a *decrease* in aggregate demand. Clearly, the contrasting experiences of China and Japan in recent years and that of the United States in the 1930s demonstrate that sustained deflation can result either from economic growth or from a persistent decline in aggregate demand.

FOR CRITICAL ANALYSIS: How might the fact that the U.S. money supply fell by about a third between 1930 and 1934 help explain the deflationary episode that the nation experienced during this period?

MONEYXTRA!
Another Perspective

To understand how economists try to measure the long-term trend of inflation in the United States, go to the Chapter 18 reading, entitled "Comparing Measures of Core Inflation," by Todd Clark of the Federal Reserve Bank of Kansas City.
**http://moneyxtra.
swcollege.com**

3. What are the long-run implications of monetary policy actions for real GDP and the price level? In the long run, when the level of product prices increases, wages and the prices of other factors of production adjust in equal proportion. As a consequence, firms' employment of labor and utilization of other factors remain unchanged. This implies that firms' production of goods and services remains the same following an increase in the price level, so the long-run aggregate supply schedule is vertical. A monetary policy action that expands the quantity of money and induces a rise in aggregate demand causes the equilibrium price level to increase but leaves equilibrium real GDP unaffected.

Monetary Policy, Real GDP, and the Price Level in the Short Run

Business cycles occur when real GDP departs from its long-run equilibrium level. Such cyclical movements in real GDP take place in the **short run,** a period of time sufficiently brief that input prices fail to adjust fully to changes in product prices.

Short-Run Aggregate Supply, Real GDP, and the Price Level

Short run: A period sufficiently brief that nominal wages and other input prices do not adjust in equal proportion to a change in the price level.

To consider the determination of real GDP and the price level in the short run, think about what happens if the prices that firms receive for the sale of their products increase while the wage rate remains unchanged at a contractually negotiated level, W^c. Firms' revenues per unit increase when prices increase, but per-unit production costs remain the same. Consequently, firms can profit from expanding their production of goods and services in response to higher product prices.

In the short run, therefore, a rise in the price level generates an increase in real GDP. As shown in Figure 18-9, this means that the **short-run aggregate supply schedule,** denoted $y^s(W^c)$ to reflect that it is explained by contracts that fix wages during the short run, slopes upward.

Short-run aggregate supply schedule: The relationship between the production of real GDP and the price level when there is not enough time for nominal wages and other input prices to adjust in equal proportion to a change in the price level.

An aggregate demand schedule is also depicted in Figure 18-9. At the point at which the short-run aggregate supply schedule and the aggregate demand schedule cross, a short-run equilibrium exists. During a period of time short enough that wages fail to adjust fully to price-level movements, the nation's price level adjusts to equate aggregate desired spending on domestic output of goods and services with real GDP produced by all firms. In the figure, this condition is satisfied at the price level P_1, which is the short-run equilibrium price level.

Short-Run Determinants of Real GDP and the Price Level

Because the short-run aggregate supply schedule in Figure 18-9 depends on the existence of contracts that prevent wages from adjusting fully to price changes, changes in contracted wages alter the position of the aggregate supply schedule. For instance, panel (a) of Figure 18-10 on page 402 illustrates the effects of a general increase in the level of wages contracted by workers and firms, from W_1^c to W_2^c. At any given price level, a wage increase results in

FIGURE 18-9
Equilibrium Real GDP and the Equilibrium Price Level in the Short Run.

Nominal wages set by contracts at the level W^c do not adjust in equal proportion to changes in the level of product prices, so an increase in the price level induces an increase in production of final goods and services. Thus, real GDP increases when the price level rises, and the short-run aggregate supply schedule, $y^s(W^c)$, slopes upward. The equilibrium price level, P_1, equates total real

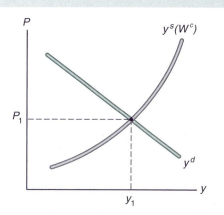

desired expenditures on final goods and services with the short-run

amount of real GDP produced at this price level, y_1.

higher per-unit production costs for firms even though the firms' per-unit revenues are unchanged. Naturally, firms respond by reducing their output of final goods and services. Other things being equal, real GDP declines at any given price level, so the short-run aggregate supply schedule shifts leftward in response to the rise in contracted wages. There is an upward movement along the aggregate demand schedule, and the equilibrium price level increases, from P_1 to P_2. As the price level increases, firms become more willing to increase production somewhat. Equilibrium real GDP declines, from y_1 to y_2, but it does not fall as much as it would have in the absence of the price-level change.

In addition to wage increases, sudden rises in the costs of any key factors of production, such as higher prices of oil or natural gas used to produce energy, could cause the short-run supply schedule to shift leftward. Such events are commonly known as **aggregate supply shocks,** and they all yield the effects shown in panel (a) of Figure 18-10: a short-run reduction in real GDP and a simultaneous increase in the price level, or inflation. (The extent to which the aggregate supply schedule shifts leftward in response to a given increase in the price of oil may have diminished in recent years; see on page 403 the *Management Focus: A Retooled U.S. Economy Becomes More Insulated from Oil Price Shocks.*)

Panel (b) of Figure 18-10 illustrates another way that inflation can occur in the short run. An increase in aggregate demand, perhaps brought about by an increase in the quantity of money in circulation and the associated reduction in interest rates, generates an upward movement along the short-run aggregate supply schedule. The equilibrium price level increases, from P_1 to P_2. Thus, one short-run effect of the expansion in aggregate demand is inflation. As the price level increases, firms' per-unit revenues increase. With wages unchanged in the short run, firms' per-unit costs remain the same. This induces firms to increase production, and real GDP increases in the short run.

Aggregate supply shocks:
Events, such as a sudden rise in the level of nominal wages or an increase in energy prices, that generate shifts in the position of the short-run aggregate supply schedule.

FIGURE 18-10
Alternative Causes of
Inflation in the Short Run.

As shown in panel (a), one
possible cause of inflation in
the short run is an aggregate
supply shock, such as a leftward shift in the short-run
aggregate supply schedule
induced by an increase in the
contract wage, from $y^s(W_1^c)$ to
$y^s(W_2^c)$. This generates a
movement back along the
aggregate demand schedule,
from point E_1 to point E_2. Equilibrium real GDP declines in the short
run, from y_1 to y_2, and the equilibrium
price level rises from P_1 to P_2. Panel
(b) illustrates another possible cause
of inflation in the short run. An

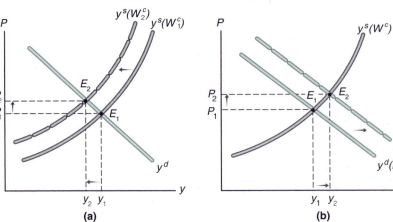

increase in aggregate demand, perhaps as a result of an increase in the
nominal money stock from M_1 to M_2,
brings about a movement up along
the short-run aggregate supply sched-

ule, from point E_1 to point E_2. In this
case, equilibrium real GDP increases,
and the equilibrium price level rises,
from P_1 to P_2.

Reconciling the Short-Run and
Long-Run Effects of Monetary Policy

How will the price level and real GDP respond over time if the Federal Reserve engages in an
expansionary monetary policy action, such as a series of open market purchases? Figure 18-11
provides the answer to this question by tracing out such a policy action's short-run and long-
run effects.

The initial short-run equilibrium point in Figure 18-11—and the long-run equilibrium point
as well—is point E_1. An expansionary monetary policy action that increases the money stock from
M_1 to M_2 causes the aggregate demand schedule to shift rightward. In the short run, with the initially contracted level of wages, this induces an upward movement along the short-run aggregate
supply schedule, $y^s(W_1^c)$. The result is an initial increase in the equilibrium price level, from P_1
to P', which in turn generates a short-run increase in real GDP, from y_1 to y', at point E_2.

In the long run, however, workers renegotiate their wage contracts with firms so that wages
fully adjust to the rising level of product prices. The contracted wage rises from W_1^c to W_2^c.
This wage boost causes the short-run aggregate supply schedule to shift leftward and brings
about a further increase in the price level, to P_2 at point E_3. The resulting movement back and
to the left along the new aggregate demand schedule, $y^d(M_2)$, causes equilibrium real GDP to
decline to its original level, y_1, which is the long-run equilibrium level of real GDP.

In this way, monetary policy actions can influence both the equilibrium price level and
equilibrium real GDP in the short run. In the long run, however, monetary policy actions
affect only the price level and leave the long-run level of real GDP unaffected.

MANAGEMENT
Focus

A Retooled U.S. Economy Becomes More Insulated from Oil Price Shocks

In 1973, 1980, and 1990, significant increases in the price of oil generated aggregate supply shocks, which contributed to recessions during those years. Oil prices also rose during the early and mid-2000s. Although the inflation-adjusted price remained below the 1980 level of $93 per barrel (in 2006 dollars), the price increases during the 2000s were sharp and persistent, so many economists worried that the experiences of 1973, 1980, and 1990 might be repeated.

In fact, estimates indicate that the oil price increases may have reduced the average annual rate of growth of real GDP during the early and mid-2000s by an average of one-half of a percentage point. The estimated effects of higher oil prices on aggregate supply during the 2000s were much smaller than those in previous years because U.S. industries now use fossil fuels less extensively.

In the early 1970s, nearly one and a half barrels of oil were required to produce a typical set of final goods and services valued at $1,000. Since the 1970s, U.S. industries have adopted numerous fuel-saving techniques. As a result, producing $1,000 worth of final goods and services now requires only about two-thirds of a bar-

rel of oil. When the price of oil shoots up, therefore, the reduction in the capability of firms to produce goods and services is much more muted today than in years past. For this reason, an equal-sized surge in inflation-adjusted oil prices generates smaller aggregate supply shocks now than it did before.

FOR CRITICAL ANALYSIS: Under what circumstance could the short-run aggregate supply schedule shift rightward even during times when prices of oil and other fossil fuels are rising? (Hint: Wages and prices of inputs other than fossil fuels also affect the position of the short-run aggregate supply schedule.)

FIGURE 18-11
Short-Run and Long-Run Effects of an Expansionary Monetary Policy Action.

In the short run, an increase in aggregate demand caused by an expansion of the quantity of money in circulation, form M_1 to M_2, brings about a movement from point E_1 to point E_2 along the short-run aggregate supply schedule, $y^s(W_1^c)$. Equilibrium real GDP initially increases, from y_1 to y', and the equilibrium price level rises, from P_1 to P'. In the long run, however, workers have sufficient time to renegotiate the contract wage at a higher level, which causes the short-run aggregate supply schedule to shift leftward, to

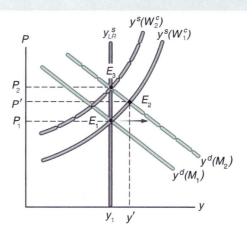

$y^s(W_2^c)$. This generates a movement back along the aggregate demand schedule, from point E_2 to point E_3. Equilibrium real GDP falls to its long-

run equilibrium level, and the equilibrium price level rises further, to P_2.

> **4. How can monetary policy actions simultaneously affect real GDP and the price level in the short run?** In the short run, contractual agreements can prevent wages from adjusting in equal proportion to changes in the price level. Increases in product prices thereby cause firms' per-unit revenues to rise without per-unit costs rising as rapidly, which encourages firms to increase their production of goods and services. Thus, an increase in the price level generates an increase in real GDP. The short-run aggregate supply schedule slopes upward, so an increase in aggregate demand induced by an increase in the money stock pushes up both the price level and real GDP in the short run. In the long run, wages and other input prices ultimately rise in response to the higher price level generated by the increase in the quantity of money. Short-run aggregate supply decreases, so the price level rises further in the long run, and real GDP returns to its long-run equilibrium level.

Expectations and Monetary Policy

At what point does the short run end and the long run begin? In other words, by what process does the economy make the transition from a short-run equilibrium in which monetary policy can influence real GDP to a long-run equilibrium in which it cannot?

The essential answer is that the long run is an interval whose length is determined by the availability of information to workers and firms when they negotiate wages. In the absence of full information, wage contracts reflect imperfect information about the future movements of the price level. Thus, wages will fail to adjust completely to price changes, and equilibrium real GDP will vary with changes in the price level induced by monetary policy actions.

Exactly what information is really available to people in the short run, and how do they use this information to develop price-level forecasts to use in determining wages? Economists have adopted two basic types of expectation hypotheses to address this question. One is the hypothesis of *adaptive expectations*. The other is the *rational expectations hypothesis*.

Adaptive Expectations

Many of the choices that we make each day depend on our anticipations of future events. Should you register for a course for the coming term with a professor with a reputation as an average-quality instructor, or should you wait until the course is taught the following term by a better instructor, yet at a potentially higher tuition rate? Should you buy a sweater at a department store today, or do you expect that it might be available at a sale price in a couple of weeks? Should you take a job at the salary you have been offered for the coming year, or would you be better off searching for a position at a higher salary, given that you expect the price level to rise during the coming year?

Clearly, to make any decisions that have future consequences, you must act on forecasts that you make based on whatever information you currently possess. Such information includes the prices of goods and services that you buy each day in your own town or city, prices of items that you see advertised in local and national media, and information that you glean from reports in regional and national news media.

How do you use such information to infer the current aggregate inflation rate for the United States? How do you forecast future inflation? Most likely, you would have trouble providing a detailed, scientific answer to either of these questions. Certainly, it is unlikely that you engage in any formal statistical analysis or use a computer to make such a forecast. You probably just do the best that you can, given the information available to you, and you make your "best guess."

But what is a person's best guess of inflation? Simply saying that an individual does the best that he or she can with limited information is not a very specific statement. Economists must be more specific about their assumptions when they evaluate the short- and long-run effects of monetary policy on real GDP and the price level. For this reason, they have developed precise conceptions about alternative processes by which people form expectations.

ADAPTIVE EXPECTATIONS PROCESSES   One way to make an inference about the aggregate price level or to forecast the future inflation rate is to do so "adaptively." The easiest way to understand what this means is to consider an example. Imagine that a friend, or perhaps even a pollster, asks you for your forecast of the U.S. inflation rate for next year. How would you come up with an answer?

One approach might be to collect data on inflation rates for the past twenty or twenty-five years. You then could plot these on a chart and make a rough drawing of the "trend line" along these points and beyond. The next point on your trend line would then give your forecast of next year's inflation rate.

If you have taken a statistics course, you might use a more sophisticated method. You could use statistical techniques to determine the specific equation for the trend line that best fits the inflation data that you have collected. This equation would enable you to give a predicted value, or forecast, of the inflation rate for a given year, including next year.

Either of these forecasting methods would require you to expend time and effort to collect and analyze many years worth of inflation data. If you do not wish to incur this opportunity cost to make a sophisticated inflation forecast, then you could choose a simpler method. For instance, you might just guess that next year's inflation rate will turn out to be an average of the inflation rates over the past three years. Even simpler, you might guess that next year's inflation rate will turn out to be similar to the inflation rate during the past year.

Each of the above forecasting methods is an example of an **adaptive expectations** process, because each method entails using only past information. Drawing a rough trend line, using statistical techniques to calculate an exact trend line, computing a three-year average, and just extrapolating from the current inflation rate share the common feature that past data formed the sole basis for the inflation forecast.

Adaptive expectations: Expectations that are based only on information from the past up to the present.

IMPLICATIONS OF ADAPTIVE EXPECTATIONS   The upward slope of the short-run aggregate supply schedule depends on the assumption that workers agree to wages based on imperfectly informed forecasts of the price level and inflation rate. If the workers' forecasts turn out to be incorrect, then wages will not keep pace with changes in the price level, and there will be a movement along the aggregate supply schedule and a change in real GDP when the price level changes.

The production of real GDP requires the passage of time, however. Consequently, short-run real GDP cannot occur unless an interval passes before workers realize that their price-level forecasts were wrong. During this interval, which is a period that corresponds to the short run, workers can fail to realize that a rise in the nominal wage may stem solely from an increase in the price level. As a result, when the nominal wage rises, for a time workers can misperceive this increase as a rise in their real wage, leading them to supply more labor services. This permits firms to produce more final goods and services, so real GDP increases.

The hypothesis that workers use adaptive expectations processes is consistent with the short-run aggregate supply schedule. If workers make their price-level forecasts adaptively, then they must always wait for new information about the price level before changing their expectations. Consequently, over some intervals policy actions that boost the price level will always cause workers to misperceive their true real wages, at least for a short time. Thus, such policies can have short-run effects on real GDP.

DRAWBACKS OF ADAPTIVE EXPECTATIONS   Just because an expectations hypothesis happens to fit a theory does not mean that it is a reasonable hypothesis. Indeed, many economists reject the idea of adaptive expectations. One reason for this negative judgment is that if people really used adaptive expectations processes, then they would often make forecasts that they realize in advance should turn out to be wrong. Suppose, for instance, that a person's adaptive method for forecasting next year's inflation rate is to calculate an average of the inflation rates for the past three years. If this average is equal to 2 percent, then that would be the individual's forecast of the inflation rate for next year.

Now suppose that the person reads in the newspaper that a new majority on the Federal Reserve have decided to increase money growth significantly, as compared with previous years. A person who would stick with the three-year-averaging procedure to forecast the inflation rate would consciously ignore this new information, even though the individual reasonably should recognize that higher money growth would push up next year's inflation rate. This means that monetary policy analysis based on the hypothesis of adaptive expectations would yield forecasts of the inflation rate that were consistently less than the actual rate of inflation. Thus, any theory based on adaptive expectations will be internally inconsistent because the people whose behavior the policy analysis attempts to mimic would behave inconsistently.

Another troublesome aspect of the hypothesis of adaptive expectations is that there is no way to say, in advance, what adaptive expectations process is "best." For example, one individual might use twenty-five years of past annual inflation data to plot a rough trend line to guide her forecasts of the inflation rate, another person might use the same technique using data from the previous forty years, and yet another might use fifty years of data. Someone else might calculate a weighted average of inflation over the past five years. Indeed, the number of possible adaptive expectations schemes is infinite. Which one should we include when analyzing the short-run and long-run effects of monetary policy? There is no good way to answer this question.

Rational Expectations

Rational expectations hypothesis: The idea that individuals form expectations based on all available past and current information and on an essential understanding of factors that affect the price level.

An alternative to the adaptive expectations approach to monetary policy analysis is called the **rational expectations hypothesis.** According to this hypothesis, an individual makes the best possible forecast of the price level and inflation rate using all available past *and current* information *and* drawing on an understanding of what factors affect product prices. In contrast to an adaptive forecast, which only looks backward because it is based on past information, a rational forecast also looks forward while taking into account past information as well.

Consider, for instance, the earlier example, in which someone initially made a forecast of inflation using an average of the past three years' inflation rates but then learned that the Federal Reserve intended to increase the money growth rate substantially. If the individual's goal is to do her best to predict inflation so that she can make her best possible choices for the coming year, then sticking with her original, adaptive forecast clearly would not be in her own best interest. The *rational* way for the individual to respond to the new information would be to use her own understanding concerning how a higher money growth rate will influence the price level and the inflation rate. Then the individual would update her inflation rate forecast accordingly.

Hence, the difference between adaptive and rational expectations can be summarized as follows:

> An *adaptive* expectation is based only on past information. In contrast, a *rational* expectation takes into account both past and current information, plus an understanding of how the economy functions.

ADVANTAGES OF THE RATIONAL EXPECTATIONS HYPOTHESIS Because the rational expectations hypothesis does not impose artificial constraints on how people use information, it is a more general theory of expectations formation than the hypothesis of adaptive expectations. Whereas an adaptive expectations process uses only past information, the rational expectations hypothesis states that if an individual can improve on an adaptive forecast, then that is what the individual will do.

This does not deny that a person's rationally formed expectation may sometimes look like an adaptive expectation. If a person has only past information and no special insight into how the economy functions, then an adaptive forecast may be the best that person can do. In this circumstance, an adaptive expectation will be the individual's rational expectation.

It seems likely, nevertheless, that people would use all available current information plus all conceptions about the economy's workings when they try to infer the price level and forecast the inflation rate. Consequently, a rationally formed expectation should, under most circumstances, differ from a purely adaptive expectation. Specifically, in contrast to most adaptive expectations, a rational expectation is an *unbiased forecast,* meaning that on average a rationally formed expectation is correct. In contrast, adaptive forecasts are typically biased, so adaptive expectations are usually systematically incorrect on average.

Even though rational expectations generally will be better than adaptive expectations, forecasts based on all current information and an understanding of how the economy works still will not always be correct. For instance, the widespread adoption of Doppler radar by the National Weather Service has improved the ability of weather forecasters to predict locations where tornadoes may form. This only means that tornado forecasts are better than before. It does not mean that such forecasts always are on the mark. Likewise, rationally formed forecasts of the price level and inflation rate are closer to the mark, on average, than adaptive forecasts. But the actual price level and inflation rate can still turn out to be different than people rationally predicted.

IMPLICATIONS OF THE RATIONAL EXPECTATIONS HYPOTHESIS FOR MONETARY POLICY How do the economic effects of monetary policy depend on the public's expectations? Figure 18-12 on the next page explains what happens if the public is able to correctly anticipate an increase in the money supply engineered by Fed policy actions. The rise in the quantity of money in circulation, of course, brings about an increase in aggregate demand. If the public correctly anticipates the monetary expansion, however, then the public will also expect the resulting increase in the price level. Workers will bargain for higher wages, so wages will adjust fully to the increase in the price level. Consequently, even as the aggregate demand schedule shifts rightward, the aggregate supply schedule will shift leftward. In the short run, the expansionary monetary policy results only in an increase in the equilibrium price level and generates no change in equilibrium real GDP.

What happens if the public fails to anticipate the Fed's expansionary policy actions in the short run? In that event, policy effects are exactly as depicted in Figure 18-11 on page 403: In the short run, the expansionary monetary policy actions boost real GDP, but they leave real

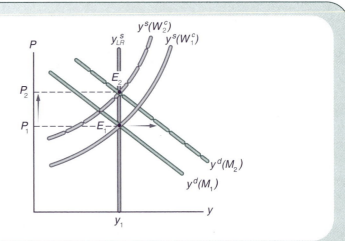

FIGURE 18-12
The Short-Run Effects of a Fully Anticipated Expansionary Monetary Policy Action.

In the short run, a fully anticipated increase in the quantity of money in circulation, from M_1 to M_2, causes the aggregate demand schedule to shift rightward. At the same time, because workers expect that the price level will rise due to the monetary expansion, they immediately bargain for higher wages, which causes the short-run aggregate supply schedule to shift leftward, from $y^s(W_1^c)$ to $y^s(W_2^c)$. There is a short-run movement from point E_1 to point E_2 along the long-run aggregate supply schedule. There is no deviation of real GDP from its long-run equilibrium level. The price level rises in the short run, from P_1 to P_2.

GDP unaltered in the long run. The price level increases somewhat in the short run but rises further in the long run.

As already noted, the rational expectations hypothesis does not imply that the public correctly anticipates future events such as expansionary monetary policy actions. Thus, to the extent that Fed policy actions are not fully anticipated, they can still have short-run effects on real GDP. To the extent that policy actions *are* anticipated, however, responses such as renegotiated wage contracts will shift the short-run aggregate supply schedule leftward, thereby muting somewhat the short-run real GDP effects of monetary policy. Because rational expectations are unbiased forecasts, on average policy actions are anticipated. Thus, short-run policy effects on real GDP are more likely to be relatively fleeting if the public's expectations are rationally formed.

5. How can the public's expectations influence the short-run effects of monetary policy? An adaptive expectation is formed using only past information. Consequently, an adaptive expectation is typically a biased forecast. A rationally formed expectation is based on past and current information and on an understanding of how macroeconomic variables are determined. Hence, a rational expectation is an unbiased forecast. To the extent that the public's expectations are rationally formed, the public is more likely, on average, to correctly anticipate policy actions. More fully anticipated policy actions have more muted short-run effects on real GDP, so rationally formed expectations by the public imply that monetary policy actions are less likely to influence real GDP, even in the short run.

Chapter Summary

1. Business Cycles and Their Characteristics: Business cycles are variations in real GDP around its long-run growth path. Recessions are periods when real GDP declines below its long-run level, and expansions occur when real GDP increases to levels that for a time can exceed its long-run level. Frictional and structural unemployment exist even without business cycles, but the overall unemployment rate has a cyclical component that tends to rise during recessions and to decline during expansions.

2. Aggregate Demand and How It Is Affected by Monetary Policy Actions: The aggregate demand schedule displays total planned expenditures on goods and services at each possible price level. According to the quantity theory of money, individuals divide their income between money holdings and spending on goods and services. An increase in the price level decreases the real value of their money holdings and induces them to cut back on real expenditures. Consequently, the aggregate demand schedule is downward sloping. Alternatively, when the quantity of money demanded depends negatively on the interest rate, a decline in real money balances generates an increase in the interest rate through the real balance effect. Thus, desired real investment declines, as do total desired real expenditures, so that the aggregate demand schedule slopes downward. A rise in the nominal money stock increases total desired real expenditures at each possible price level, which shifts the aggregate demand schedule to the right.

3. The Long-Run Implications of Monetary Policy Actions for Real GDP and the Price Level: In the long run, nominal wages and other input prices adjust equiproportionately to an increase in the level of product prices. Thus, the employment of labor and the utilization of other inputs by firms remain unchanged when the price level rises, so real GDP is unchanged, and the long-run aggregate supply schedule is vertical. An expansion in the nominal money stock brings about an increase in aggregate demand that pushes up the equilibrium price level but has no effect on equilibrium real GDP.

4. How Monetary Policy Actions Can Simultaneously Affect Real GDP and the Price Level in the Short Run: In the short run, nominal wages set by contracts can fail to adjust fully to variations in the price level. Higher product prices push up per-unit revenues for firms, but firms' per-unit costs do not increase as speedily, thereby inducing firms to increase production. Thus, a rise in the price level brings about a short-run increase in real GDP, so the short-run aggregate supply schedule is upward sloping. An increase in the quantity of money in circulation that raises aggregate demand boosts both the price level and real GDP in the short run. Ultimately, wages and prices of other factors of production rise in the long run in response to the higher price level, which causes short-run aggregate supply to fall. In response, there is an additional long-run rise in the price level, and real GDP falls back to its long-run equilibrium level.

5. How the Public's Expectations Can Influence the Short-Run Effects of Monetary Policy: Because an adaptive expectation is based only on past information, it is usually biased. In contrast, a rational expectation is typically an unbiased forecast because it is formed using past and current information and an understanding of the key determinants of the price level. If the public's expectations are rational, then on average the public is more likely to correctly anticipate policy actions, and short-run policy effects on real GDP will be reduced. Thus, even in the short run, monetary policy actions are less likely to influence real GDP when expectations are formed rationally.

Questions and Problems

Answers to odd-numbered questions and problems may be found on the Web at **http://money.swcollege.com** under "Student Resources.")

1. In the long run, what specific factors might play a part in influencing the rate of growth in a nation's real GDP? Explain.

2. Suppose that economic growth occurs during the next ten years, but the money stock remains unchanged during that period. Predict the effects that this would have on equilibrium real GDP and the equilibrium price level.

3. Suppose that a nation experiences a severe earthquake that reduces the long-run level of real GDP. Predict the effects that this would have on equilibrium real GDP and the equilibrium price level.

4. Suppose that the increasing use of the Internet to make transactions with credit cards causes the income velocity of money to decline substantially. Predict what, if any, long-run effects this would have on the price level and real GDP.

5. Suppose that the Cambridge k is equal to 0.20. Real GDP is equal to 5 trillion base-year dollars, and the price level is equal to 1.2 current-year dollars per base-year dollar. What is the current-dollar value of the quantity of money in circulation?

Before the Test

Test your understanding of the material covered in this chapter by taking the Chapter 18 interactive quiz at **http://money.swcollege.com**.

Online Application

According to the aggregate demand–aggregate supply model, in the short run real GDP, and hence labor employment, should rise when the price level inceases. Thus, in the short run, the unemployment rate should be inversely related to changes in the inflation rate, other things being equal. This application allows you to take a direct look at unemployment and inflation data to judge for yourself whether the two variables appear to be related.

Internet URL: http://stats.bls.gov

Title: Bureau of Labor Statistics: Economy at a Glance

Navigation: Begin at the home page of the Bureau of Labor Statistics (**http://stats.bls.gov**). Under "At a Glance Tables," click on "U.S. Economy at a Glance."

Application: Perform the indicated operations, and answer the following questions:

1. Click on "U.S. Economy at a Glance." Then click on "Consumer Price Index." Take a look at the solid line showing inflation in the graph box. How much has the inflation rate varied in recent years? Compare this behavior with previous years, especially the mid-1970s to the mid-1980s.

2. Back up to "Economy at a Glance," and now click on "Unemployment Rate." Take a look at the graph box. During what recent years was the unemployment rate approaching and at its peak value? Do you see any appearance of an inverse relationship between the unemployment rate and the inflation rate (question 1 above)?

For Group Study and Analysis: Divide the class into groups, and have each group search through the "Economy at a Glance" site to develop an explanation for the key factors accounting for the recent behavior of the unemployment rate. Have each group report back with its explanation. Is there any one factor that best explains the recent behavior of the unemployment rate?

Selected References and Further Reading

Clark, Todd. "Comparing Measures of Core Inflation." Federal Reserve Bank of Kansas City *Economic Review*, Second Quarter 2001, pp. 6–31.

Espinoza-Vega, Marco, and Jang-Ting Guo. "On Business Cycles and Countercyclical Policies." Federal Reserve Bank of Atlanta *Economic Review*, Fourth Quarter 2001, pp. 1–11.

Federal Reserve Bank of Kansas City. *Policies for Long-Run Economic Growth*. 1992.

Gould, David, and Roy Ruffin. "What Determines Economic Growth?" Federal Reserve Bank of Dallas *Economic Review*, Second Quarter 1993, pp. 25–40.

Miller, Roger, and David VanHoose. *Macroeconomics: Theories, Policies, and International Applications*, 3d ed. Cincinnati: ITP–South-Western, 2004.

MoneyXtra

Log on to the MoneyXtra Web site now (**http://moneyxtra.swcollege.com**) for additional learning resources such as practice quizzes, case studies, readings, and additional economic applications.

Unit VI
The Conduct of Monetary Policy

Contents

Day-to-Day Monetary Policy—

Fed Operating Procedures

Since the European Monetary Union (EMU) was formed in 1999, economists at the EMU's monetary policymaking institution, the European Central Bank (ECB), have paid close attention to the "Euro area interbank rate." Over the years, this interest rate, which is the average rate of interest at which European depository institutions are willing to lend funds, has exhibited a number of sudden jumps and declines.

The Euro area interbank rate is regarded as an important monetary indicator, so ECB economists have been working hard to improve their understanding of what factors have caused it to fluctuate. Toward this end, they have been seeking to better understand the key factors determining both the demand for reserves by EMU depository institutions and the supply of reserves by the ECB. As a guide for their efforts, the ECB economists have carefully studied how Fed economists in the United States estimate the demand for and supply of reserves in the U.S. federal funds market. The Euro area interbank rate, ECB economists have determined, fluctuates in ways that are very similar to the responses of the federal funds rate to changes in the demand for and supply of reserves in the United States.

Fundamental Issues

1. What are the key instruments of monetary policy?

2. What key factors affect the demand for reserves by depository institutions?

3. How do Federal Reserve policies influence the supply of reserves to depository institutions and the federal funds rate?

4. How is the federal funds rate related to other market interest rates?

5. How do Federal Reserve policies affect the quantity of money?

6. What are Federal Reserve operating procedures, and what operating procedures has the Federal Reserve used in recent years?

Why are the demand for and supply of reserves held by U.S. depository institutions the fundamental determinants of the U.S. federal funds rate? How can the Federal Reserve influence the amount of reserves supplied, the quantity of reserves that depository institutions choose to hold, and the market value of the federal funds rate? How do induced changes in the federal funds rate ultimately affect other market interest rates and the quantity of money in circulation? In this chapter, you will learn the answers to all these important questions.

The Instruments of Monetary Policy

In its role as monetary policymaker, the Fed can influence the monetary base, monetary aggregates, credit flows, and, ultimately, other economic variables such as interest rates, real GDP, and the rate of inflation. It does so using its available monetary policy *instruments,* which are factors that the Fed can determine, at least in principle, on a day-to-day basis.

Open Market Operations

Open market operations are the key means by which the Fed conducts monetary policy each day. As we discussed in Chapter 14, the voting members of the Federal Open Market Committee (FOMC)—the seven Federal Reserve Board governors and five Federal Reserve bank presidents—determine the general strategy of open market operations at meetings that take place every six to eight weeks. They outline this strategy in the FOMC directive, which lays out the FOMC's general objectives, mandates short-term federal funds rate objectives, and establishes specific target ranges for monetary aggregates. After each meeting, the FOMC issues a brief statement to the media, which then run stories about the Fed's action or inaction and what it is likely to mean for the economy. Typically, these stories appear under headlines such as "Fed Cuts Key Interest Rate," "Fed Acts to Push Up Interest Rates," or "Fed Decides to Leave Interest Rates Alone."

The FOMC leaves it to the Federal Reserve Bank of New York's Trading Desk to implement the directive from day to day during the weeks between FOMC meetings. The media spend little time considering how the Trading Desk conducts its policies, taking it for granted that the Fed can implement the policy action that it says it plans to undertake. In this chapter, you will learn what happens behind the scenes.

THE MECHANICS OF OPEN MARKET OPERATIONS   The Trading Desk's open market operations typically are confined to a one-hour interval each weekday morning. The New York Fed's Trading Desk conducts two types of open market operations. One type, called an *outright transaction,* is an open market purchase or sale in which the Fed is not obliged to resell or repurchase securities at a later date. The other kind of operation is a *repurchase-agreement transaction.* As discussed in Chapters 1 and 3, repurchase agreements are contracts that commit the seller of a security to repurchase the security at a later date. The Trading Desk often buys securities from dealers under agreements for the dealers to repurchase them at a later date. The Trading Desk also commonly uses *reverse repurchase agreements* when conducting open market sales. These are agreements for the Fed to repurchase the securities from dealers at a later time.

Table 19-1 summarizes the Fed's open market transactions during a typical year. The Trading Desk often uses outright purchases or sales when it wishes to change the aggregate level of depository institution reserves. In contrast, it normally uses repurchase agreements when its main goal is simply to stabilize the current level of reserves. Nevertheless, the Trading

Table 19-1 Fed Open Market Transactions during 2005 ($ Millions)

Outright transactions:	
Purchases	$ 49,250
Sales and redemptions	1,525
Repurchase agreements and matched transactions:	
Purchases	2,110,000
Sales	2,142,605
Net change in Federal Reserve System open market account	15,120

SOURCES: Board of Governors of the Federal Reserve System, *Federal Reserve Bulletin Statistical Supplement,* April 2005; authors' estimates.

Desk can substitute repurchase-agreement transactions for outright purchases or sales to change the overall reserve level by appropriately mismatching repurchase-agreement transactions on a continuous basis.

A MULTIPLIER VIEW OF THE EFFECTS OF OPEN MARKET OPERATIONS

As you learned in Chapter 13, open market operations that change the total amount of reserves at depository institutions cause the monetary base to change. A variation in the size of the monetary base, in turn, alters the quantities of money and credit.

Recall from Chapter 13 that a change in the quantity of money, M, induced by a change in the monetary base, MB, is equal to the money multiplier times the amount of the change in the monetary base, or

$$\Delta M = m_M \times \Delta MB,$$

where m_M is the money multiplier. In Chapter 13, we found that the value of this multiplier for M1 is $m_M = (c + 1)/(rr_D + e + c)$, where c is the public's desired holdings of currency relative to transactions deposits, rr_D is the required reserve ratio for transactions deposits, and e is the desired ratio of excess reserve holdings to transactions deposits for depository institutions. Likewise, if m_{TC} denotes the value of the credit multiplier, then the amount by which all depository institutions change total credit, TC, by lending and acquiring securities, in response to a change in the monetary base is equal to

$$\Delta TC = m_{TC} \times \Delta MB.$$

In Chapter 13, we determined that the value of the total credit multiplier is $m_{TC} = (1 - rr_D - e)/(c + rr_D + e)$.

Recall that the monetary base is equal to the sum of currency, C, and total reserves, TR. But we can think of total reserves at depository institutions as arising from one of two sources. One way that depository institutions can obtain reserves from the Fed is to borrow reserves directly from the Fed's discount window. Such reserves are *borrowed reserves*, denoted BR. The primary way that depository institutions get reserves from the Fed, however, is through open market operations. These reserves, called *nonborrowed reserves*, denoted NBR, are the amount of total reserves not borrowed from the Fed. Total reserves then are the sum of borrowed reserves and nonborrowed reserves, or $TR = BR + NBR$.

Hence, open market operations cause a change in nonborrowed reserves and thereby change total reserves and the monetary base. As a result, changes in nonborrowed reserves caused by open market operations have direct multiplier effects on the quantities of money and credit. From our relationships above, the amounts of these effects on money and credit could be computed using the following equations:

$$\Delta M = m_M \times \Delta NBR$$

and

$$\Delta TC = m_{TC} \times \Delta NBR.$$

For instance, suppose that the money multiplier is equal to $m_M = 2.5$ and the credit multiplier is equal to $m_{TC} = 3$. In this instance, a $10 million open market purchase by the Fed increases the quantity of money by $25 million and the total amount of loans and securities held by depository institutions by $30 million. This helps us to see why the Fed uses open market operations as its key means of conducting monetary policy, given that it can conduct such operations any day that it wishes, thereby producing desired changes in the amounts of money and credit.

The Discount Window

In principle, another way that the Fed can influence the quantities of money and credit is by inducing changes in depository institution borrowing at the discount window. The Fed can do this by altering the terms under which it stands willing to lend to depository institutions.

DISCOUNT WINDOW POLICY   Earlier in the Fed's history, depository institutions borrowed from the Fed via a process called "discounting." A depository institution would post U.S. government securities at a Federal Reserve bank, which would increase the institution's reserve account balance by an amount smaller than the value of the securities. When the discount arrangement expired, the depository institution would repurchase the securities at their true value. The Federal Reserve bank would keep the difference as a "discount rate," or effective interest charge for the loan.

Today, most discount window loans are actually *advances*. The Fed simply increases the balance in the borrowing institution's reserve account and has an officer of the institution sign a promissory note. The term *discount window borrowing* remains with us, however. And the interest rate that the Fed charges for advances continues to be known as the *discount rate*, even though it is really just a lending rate.

THE DISCOUNT RATE, MONEY, AND CREDIT IN THE MULTIPLIER MODEL   A depository institution's main alternative to borrowing new reserves from the Fed is to borrow existing reserves from other depository institutions in the federal funds market. This means that a key determinant of total discount window borrowing is the difference, or *spread,* between the federal funds rate and the discount rate. As the amount by which the federal funds rate exceeds the discount rate rises or the amount by which the discount rate exceeds the federal funds rate declines, discount window borrowing becomes relatively more attractive to depository institutions.

Suppose that the Fed decides to use discount window policy as a means of increasing the quantity of money and credit. This requires reducing the discount rate relative to the federal funds rate. This causes borrowed reserves to rise by some amount, ΔBR, which results in an increase in total reserves and in the monetary base, thereby generating a multiplier effect on the quantity of money:

$$\Delta M = m_M \times \Delta BR.$$

That is, the quantity of money rises by the induced rise in borrowed reserves times the money multiplier. Likewise, the increase in borrowed reserves induces a multiplier effect on the amount of credit extended by depository institutions:

$$\Delta TC = m_{TC} \times \Delta BR.$$

This says that the total amount of loans and securities at depository institutions rises by the induced increase in borrowed reserves multiplied by the credit multiplier.

An Indirect Policy Approach   Note that once the Fed induces a given change in discount window borrowing, the multiplier effects on money and credit are analogous to those generated by open market operations. Nevertheless, the effects of discount window policy are much less direct because the Fed must be able to cause the difference between the discount rate and the federal funds rate to change by just the right amount to induce the desired change in borrowing.

For almost eighty years, the Fed tended to keep the discount rate unchanged for weeks at a time, and it typically set the discount rate slightly below the federal funds rate. In 2002, however, the Fed altered the way it lends to depository institutions. It now sets the discount rate *above* the federal funds rate. This discourages depository institutions from seeking loans unless they truly face significant liquidity problems. At present, the Fed keeps the discount rate 1 percentage point higher than the market-determined federal funds rate. Thus, if the market federal funds rate is 3 percent, the discount rate is 4 percent. If the federal funds rate increases to 3.5 percent, the Fed automatically raises the discount rate to 4.5 percent.

Theory, Not Fact   In principle, the Fed could continue to use the discount rate as an instrument of monetary policy by changing the amount by which the discount rate exceeds the federal funds rate. For instance, if the Fed reduced the differential from 1 percentage point to 0.05 percentage point, this would greatly reduce depository institutions' disincentive to borrow from the Fed. As Fed lending increased in response, borrowed reserves would rise. The Fed has indicated that it does not plan to conduct monetary policy in this way, however.

Reserve Requirements

As we discussed in Chapter 11, the Depository Institutions Deregulation and Monetary Control Act of 1980 empowered the Fed to impose uniform reserve requirements on all federally insured depository institutions. Since that time the Fed has mandated that all such institutions hold reserves as fractions of their transactions deposit balances. These reserve requirements are the final key tool that the Fed has at its disposal to influence monetary and credit aggregates.

COMPUTATION OF RESERVE REQUIREMENTS   Today, the Fed's reserve requirements are fairly simple. For the first $50 million or so in transactions deposits, any depository institution must hold 3 percent as required reserves. For deposits in excess of this amount, depository institutions must hold 10 percent as reserves. Because most transactions deposits in the United States are at the largest institutions, this means that the bulk of transactions deposits are subject to the 10 percent requirement. From 1984 to 1998, depository institutions computed their required reserves by averaging their transactions deposits over a two-week *computation period*. Then they applied the Fed's required reserve ratios to this average amount of deposits and maintained an average reserve level consistent with their reserve requirement during a two-week reserve *maintenance period*. The maintenance period and computation period largely overlapped, so depository institutions' required reserves were very closely related to their current deposits.

In 1998, however, the Fed decided to return to the procedure that it had used for calculating required reserves before 1984. Under this procedure, the *computation period* precedes the *maintenance period* by several days. As a result, depository institutions have more time to determine the amounts of reserves that they will have to hold each week to meet their reserve requirements.

HOW RESERVE REQUIREMENT CHANGES AFFECT MONEY AND CREDIT   To see how reserve requirements themselves might be changed to influence the amounts of money and credit, recall that the basic money multiplier is $m_M = (c + 1)/(rr_D + e + c)$ and the basic credit multiplier is $m_{TC} = (1 - rr_D - e)/(c + rr_D + e)$. A reduction in the required reserve ratio, rr_D, increases the values of both multipliers. This makes sense because if reserve requirements are lower, then depository institutions can lend more reserves at every stage of the process of deposit and credit expansion. In contrast, an increase in the required reserve ratio reduces the multipliers.

This means that changes in reserve requirements can alter the quantities of money and credit by increasing or reducing the multipliers that link money and credit to the monetary base. In principle, therefore, the Fed could try to influence the amounts of money and credit by varying its required reserve ratios. The Fed, however, rarely does this. Every change in reserve requirements necessitates alterations in planning and management by both the Fed and depository institutions. Therefore, the Fed usually changes reserve requirements as rarely as possible. Indeed, the Fed has changed reserve requirement ratios only three times since 1980, and none of these changes was for the purpose of influencing the quantities of money or credit. Furthermore, if anything, the Fed's stance on reserve requirements since the mid-1990s has further *reduced* their significance. (Indeed, the use of "sweep accounts" by depository institutions has allowed them to reduce their required reserves considerably since the mid-1990s; see *What Happens When Banks Can "Sweep" Deposits to Accounts Not Subject to Reserve Requirements?*)

1. What are the key instruments of monetary policy? The Fed's key tool for conducting monetary policy on a day-to-day basis is open market operations, which change the amount of nonborrowed reserves and thereby affect the monetary base and the quantities of money and credit. A secondary policy tool is discount window policy. By changing the terms by which it makes discount window loans available, the Fed can influence the amount of reserves that depository institutions borrow, which also ultimately affects the amounts of money and credit. A third, but seldom-used, tool is required reserve ratios. Changes in these ratios alter the money and credit multipliers, thereby causing variations in monetary and credit aggregates.

MONEYXTRA!
Another Perspective

To learn about all the various factors affecting bank reserve holdings in recent years, go to the Chapter 19 reading, entitled "Are U.S. Reserve Requirements Still Binding?" by Paul Bennett and Stavros Peristiani of the Federal Reserve Bank of New York.
**http://moneyxtra.
swcollege.com**

What Happens When... **Banks Can "Sweep" Deposits to Accounts Not Subject to Reserve Requirements?**

In the 1970s, U.S. depository institutions began to offer automatic-transfer-service accounts. These accounts allow the institutions to shift funds automatically from savings deposits to checking accounts whenever a customer's checking balance falls to zero. In 1993, a few large banks realized that there was no legal rule against *reversing* the flow of funds between checking and savings accounts. To the extent allowed under the law, the banks began to shift, or "sweep," funds from checking accounts subject to reserve requirements to savings deposits not subject to such requirements.

Within a short time, other depository institutions realized that the use of such "sweep accounts" could allow them to greatly reduce their effective reserve requirements. Since late 1995, required reserves that U.S. depository institutions hold at Federal Reserve banks have fallen by more than 50 percent as funds in sweep accounts at depository institutions have increased from less than $10 billion to nearly

$700 billion. Of course, funds "swept" away from checking accounts to savings accounts are not included in M1 but remain part of M2. This explains why the growth of M1 suddenly halted in the 1990s even as M2 growth continued unabated.

Indeed, today most economists have given up on using M1 as a monetary policy indicator. Because M2 includes both checking deposits and the savings deposits that are part of sweep programs, this monetary aggregate has remained untarnished by the explosion of sweep accounts. Few economists, including those at the Fed, pay much attention to M1 anymore because it is so distorted by sweep programs.

FOR CRITICAL ANALYSIS: How do you think that sweep accounts have likely affected the rate of growth of the monetary base since the mid-1990s?

The Demand for Depository Institution Reserves

The money multiplier approach is useful for assessing the essential effects of changes in the Federal Reserve's monetary policy instruments. Nevertheless, it does not address several questions: How does Federal Reserve policymaking influence interest yields? How do changes in interest rates affect money holdings of consumers and businesses? To answer these questions, you must understand the factors that determine how many reserves depository institutions wish to hold.

The Federal Funds Rate and Excess Reserves

Recall from Chapter 13 that, because of the money multiplier process, depository institutions play a key role in determining the quantity of money. From the day-to-day perspective of depository institutions, the key interest rate is the federal funds rate because this is the rate at which these institutions can lend or borrow reserves from day to day to meet reserve requirements or to fund their extensions of credit through lending or purchases of securities.

THE OPPORTUNITY COST OF HOLDING EXCESS RESERVES
As we discussed in Chapter 13, depository institutions usually maintain some holdings of reserves over and above the amounts that they must hold to meet the Fed's reserve requirements. These reserves are *excess reserves*. Normally, depository institutions hold excess reserves as a contingency against a need for cash arising, perhaps, from unanticipated deposit withdrawals or unexpected opportunities for profitable loans or security purchases.

Holding reserves as vault cash or as reserve deposits with Federal Reserve banks yields no interest return to depository institutions, however. Instead of holding such excess reserves, depository institutions can easily lend them to other institutions that wish to borrow such reserves in the federal funds market. In so doing, the lending institutions convert non-interest-bearing excess reserves into short-term loans that generate revenues and enhance profitability.

This means that the federal funds rate—the rate of interest at which depository institutions borrow from and lend to one another in the federal funds market—is the best measure of the opportunity cost of holding excess reserves. If the federal funds rate is relatively low, then the opportunity cost that depository institutions incur by holding excess reserves is relatively small, and they will be more likely to hold relatively large amounts of excess reserves. But if the federal funds rate rises significantly, the opportunity cost of holding excess reserves will increase, and depository institutions will be more likely to lend these reserves to other institutions in the federal funds market.

THE INVERSE RELATIONSHIP BETWEEN THE FEDERAL FUNDS RATE AND EXCESS RESERVES
This reasoning implies that the demand for excess reserves by depository institutions should be *inversely related* to the federal funds rate. If the federal funds rate rises, then depository institutions will desire to hold fewer excess reserves. In contrast, if the federal funds rate falls, then depository institutions will be more willing to maintain larger balances of excess reserves.

In principle, therefore, the Federal Reserve can influence how many reserves depository institutions desire to hold even without any reserve requirements. It can do this by enacting policies that alter the federal funds rate. We shall return to this point shortly, when we discuss how the Fed supplies reserves to depository institutions.

Transactions Deposits and Required Reserves

As you learned in Chapter 13, however, required reserves constitute the predominant component of depository institution reserve holdings. As we already noted, the Fed assesses two required reserve ratios: a 3 percent ratio for just over the first $50 million in transactions deposits (the Fed adjusts this threshold upward from time to time) at each depository institution and a 10 percent ratio for all transactions deposits above this level. The 10 percent ratio applies to the bulk of transactions deposits, so we can approximate the total amount of reserves that depository institutions desire to hold to meet reserve requirements by

$$RR = rr_D \times D,$$

where RR denotes required reserves, rr_D is the required reserve ratio, and D represents the total amount of transactions deposits at depository institutions.

Suppose that the amount of transactions deposits in the banking system is equal to $430 billion. Then, with a required reserve ratio of $rr_D = 0.10$, the amount of reserves that depository institutions demand equals $RR = rr_D \times D = 0.10 \times \$430$ billion $= \$43$ billion. (Typically, banks' holdings of excess reserves in relation to required reserves are relatively low, but in recent years excess reserves have been very high relative to required reserves at Japanese banks; see the *Global Focus: Why Japanese Banks Hold So Many Excess Reserves.*)

Depository Institutions' Total Reserve Demand

The total reserves that depository institutions desire to hold is the sum of their desired holdings of excess reserves and the amount of reserves that they demand to meet reserve requirements established by the Fed. Because depository institutions must hold sufficient reserves to

GLOBAL

Focus

Why Japanese Banks Hold So Many Excess Reserves

In the United States, total holdings of excess reserves rarely amount to more than 5 percent of the banks' required reserves. Until the 2000s, this was also true of Japanese banks. Beginning in late 2000, though, excess reserves of Japanese banks started rising rapidly. By the end of 2001, total excess reserve holdings at Japanese banks had reached 100 percent of the banks' required reserves. A year later, excess reserves were 200 percent greater than required reserves. By the

mid-2000s, excess reserves at Japanese banks were hovering at levels between 400 and 500 percent of their required reserves.

What generated such a rapid escalation of excess reserve holdings in Japan? Two factors played a role. First, market interest rates on Japanese bonds began to drop significantly in the late 1990s and reached levels close to 0 percent in the early 2000s. Thus, the opportunity cost that Japanese banks incurred by holding excess reserves was very low. Second, during the early 2000s, many Japanese banks experienced serious financial problems. Fearing that a number of banks might fail, Japanese depositors with-

drew funds from their bank deposit accounts at an increased rate, which in turn induced banks to hold more excess reserves. Only when Japanese market interest rates began to rise somewhat and the likelihood of insolvencies began to decline did banks' excess reserve holdings begin to drop as a percentage of required reserves beginning in the mid-2000s.

FOR CRITICAL ANALYSIS: How might the very subdued demand for business loans in Japan during the early 2000s have contributed to the upswing in Japanese banks' excess reserve holdings?

meet their reserve requirements, the *minimum* amount of reserves that they demand is equal to their required reserves. In Figure 19-1, this is shown as the $43 billion amount computed above based on a required reserve ratio of $rr_D = 0.10$ and a level of transactions deposits of $430 billion.

In addition, however, depository institutions usually hold some amount of excess reserves. As we discussed above, the amount of funds that these institutions allocate to excess reserves depends on the opportunity cost of these funds, as measured by the federal funds rate, denoted r_f in Figure 19-1. If the federal funds rate is sufficiently high, such as $r_f = 10$ percent, then the opportunity cost may be high enough that depository institutions choose to hold zero excess reserves. In this situation, their desired total reserve holdings will be equal to the minimum amount that they must hold to meet reserve requirements, or $43 billion. This is the uppermost point of the reserve demand schedule shown in Figure 19-1.

But if the federal funds rate is lower, such as $r_f = 5$ percent, then depository institutions will perceive a reduced opportunity cost of holding excess reserves. Consequently, they will be more willing to hold such reserves as a contingency against deposit withdrawals or the possibility that profitable loan or security opportunities might arise. Figure 19-1 indicates a situation in which depository institutions are willing to hold an amount of excess reserves equal to $ER = $2 billion at this lower federal funds rate. At this rate, therefore, the total reserves demanded by depository institutions equal the sum of the $43 billion that they must hold to meet their reserve requirements and the $2 billion in excess reserves that they are willing to hold at the federal funds rate of $r_f = 5$ percent, or $TR = RR + ER = $43 billion + $2 billion = $45 billion.

This analysis indicates that there is an *inverse relationship* between the federal funds rate and total reserves demanded by depository institutions. The **reserve demand schedule** in Figure 19-1 depicts this inverse relationship. This schedule, which we denote TR^D, shows how total reserves desired by depository institutions vary with changes in the federal funds

Reserve demand schedule: A graphical depiction of the inverse relationship between the total amount of reserves demanded by depository institutions and the federal funds rate.

FIGURE 19-1
The Demand for and Supply of Total Depository Institution Reserves.

The minimum amount of reserves that depository institutions demand is the amount that they must hold to meet their reserve requirements. With a required reserve ratio of 10 percent and total transactions deposits of $430 billion, this amount is $43 billion. At a market federal funds rate of 5 percent, depository institutions hold $2 billion in excess reserves, so the total quantity of reserves demanded equals $45 billion. If the Fed supplies $45 billion in reserves, then the mar-

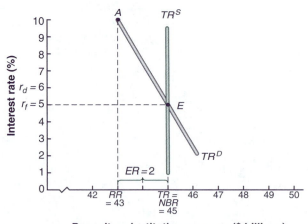

ket federal funds rate is 5 percent at point *E*, and the quantity of reserves

supplied equals $45 billion.

rate. Along this schedule, a rise in the federal funds rate induces depository institutions to demand fewer reserves until they reach the minimum amount needed to meet their reserve requirements. A decline in the federal funds rate, in contrast, induces depository institutions to accumulate increasingly large amounts of reserves at levels above the minimum required amount. Hence, the reserve demand schedule slopes downward.

> **2. What key factors affect the demand for reserves by depository institutions?** Depository institutions desire to hold reserves to meet reserve requirements and as a contingency against unexpected cash needs. Consequently, the main factors affecting their desired reserve holdings are the required reserve ratio, the quantity of transactions deposits in the banking system, and the opportunity cost of holding reserves in excess of those required. The opportunity cost of holding excess reserves is the federal funds rate that institutions could earn by lending excess reserves in the federal funds market.

The Supply of Depository Institution Reserves

When Congress enacted the Federal Reserve Act of 1913, it gave the Federal Reserve System the authority to lend to depository institutions. Then, in the Banking Act of 1935, it granted the Fed the authority to conduct open market operations. Hence, these congressional actions authorized the Fed to supply reserves to the nation's depository institutions. If we want to understand the supply side of the reserves market, we must turn our attention back to the Fed.

The Discount Window and Borrowed Reserves

As we discussed earlier, one way that the Federal Reserve supplies reserves to depository institutions is through direct discount window loans to individual institutions. In principle, the Fed can alter the total volume of this lending by changing the terms under which it makes reserves available, but in actuality, the Fed rarely changes the basic rules under which it lends.

Since the Fed's 2002 policy change that places the discount rate exactly 1 percentage point above the market federal funds rate, depository institutions have had little incentive to borrow reserves from the Fed at all. This means that the amount of borrowed reserves supplied by the Fed from its discount window is typically at or very close to zero at any given time.

Open Market Operations and Nonborrowed Reserves

The key means by which the Fed supplies new reserves to depository institutions is through open market purchases of government securities. The quantity of reserves that it supplies in this way are *nonborrowed reserves, NBR.*

You will see shortly that the Federal Reserve Bank of New York's Trading Desk can influence interest rates by conducting open market operations that *change* the amount of nonborrowed reserves in the banking system. In the absence of any open market purchases or sales, however, the amount of nonborrowed reserves is a constant amount. Furthermore, this amount of nonborrowed reserves places a *lower bound* on the amount of reserves in the nation's banking system at a given point in time. These reserves can circulate among depository institutions, but the aggregate volume of reserves cannot fall below this level in the absence of open market operations by the New York Fed's Trading Desk.

The Fed's Supply of Total Depository Institution Reserves

On the Web

What is the current distribution of depository institution reserves? Find out the split of total reserves between borrowed and nonborrowed reserves and between required and excess reserves by viewing the Federal Reserve's H.3 *Statistical Release* at **http://www.federalreserve.gov/releases/**.

Figure 19-1 on page 420 also depicts the supply schedule for total depository institution reserves. As we have discussed, the base level of reserves supplied by the Fed is the quantity of nonborrowed reserves, NBR, which the Fed has supplied through past open market purchases. Thus, the total amount of reserves supplied by the Fed cannot fall below this quantity, which in Figure 19-1 is equal to $NBR = \$45$ billion.

In the past, whenever the federal funds rate exceeded the discount rate, depository institutions borrowed additional reserves from the Fed's discount window. Suppose that at some time before 2002, the discount rate was equal to $r_d = 4.5$ percent. In that case, if the federal funds rate was less than 4.5 percent, depository institutions had no incentive to borrow reserves from the Fed. Under such circumstances, the amount of reserves supplied by the Fed was the amount of nonborrowed reserves, NBR. But if the federal funds rate was higher than the discount rate, as it usually was, then depository institutions would borrow additional reserves directly from the Fed. For instance, suppose that the federal funds rate, r_f, was 5 percent. The 0.5 percentage point spread between the federal funds rate and the discount rate might have induced institutions to *borrow* \$1 billion from the Fed's discount window. Then the amount of borrowed reserves would have been equal to $BR = \$1$ billion, and the total quantity of reserves supplied by the Fed would have been the sum of the \$44 billion in nonborrowed reserves and the \$1 billion in borrowed reserves, or $TR = NBR + BR = \$44$ billion $+ \$1$ billion $= \$45$ billion.

In Figure 19-1, however, we assume that with the discount rate set above the market federal funds rate at $r_d = 6$ percent, which is how the Fed now sets the discount rate, the quantity of reserves that depository institutions borrow from the Fed is approximately \$0 billion. Therefore, the **reserve supply schedule** in Figure 19-1, which is labeled TR^S, is vertical at the level of nonborrowed reserves of $NBR = \$45$ billion. This schedule shows that the amount of reserves that the Fed supplies to depository institutions does not vary with the federal funds rate.

Reserve supply schedule: A graphical depiction of the relationship between the total amount of reserves supplied by the Fed and the federal funds rate.

Determining the Equilibrium Federal Funds Rate

The market for total depository institution reserves attains an equilibrium when the total quantity of reserves that depository institutions demand from the Federal Reserve is just equal to the total quantity of reserves that the Fed supplies through open market operations and discount window loans. When this state of balance occurs, there are no pressures for the federal funds rate to rise or to fall. The resulting federal funds rate is the *equilibrium federal funds rate*.

Figure 19-1 depicts such an equilibrium situation. The total depository institution reserve demand schedule slopes downward to the right of the minimum amount of reserves that depository institutions desire to hold to meet their reserve requirements, $RR = \$43$ billion. The total reserve supply schedule is vertical at the quantity of nonborrowed reserves $NBR = \$45$ billion. At the point where the two schedules cross, the quantity of reserves demanded by depository institutions is equal to the quantity of reserves supplied to these institutions by the Fed, at \$45 billion.

The equilibrium federal funds rate in Figure 19-1 is equal to $r_f = 5$ percent. At this federal funds rate, the total amount of reserves demanded by depository institutions just matches the total quantity of reserves that the Fed supplies. Hence, there are no pressures for the federal funds rate to rise or to fall. The reason is that depository institutions are satisfied holding the amount of reserves that the Fed has supplied as long as the federal funds rate is equal to 5 percent.

Figure 19-2 summarizes the factors that determine the quantities of reserves supplied and demanded. The Fed's open market operations determine the quantity of nonborrowed reserves (NBR = $45 billion in our example). The required reserve ratio and total deposits determine the amount of required reserves (RR = $43 billion in our example). The federal funds rate determines the opportunity cost of holding excess reserves and, consequently, the amount of excess reserve holdings of depository institutions (ER = $2 billion). Therefore, reserve requirements, total deposits in the banking system, and the federal funds rate all influence the total amount of reserves demanded by depository institutions.

At the equilibrium federal funds rate, the total amount of reserves supplied by the Fed is equal to the total amount of reserves demanded by depository institutions. That is, the federal funds rate adjusts so that these quantities just balance. In our example, the amounts of reserves demanded and supplied are equal (TR = $45 billion) at an equilibrium federal funds rate of r_f = 5 percent.

**FIGURE 19-2
Factors That Determine the Equilibrium Federal Funds Rate.**

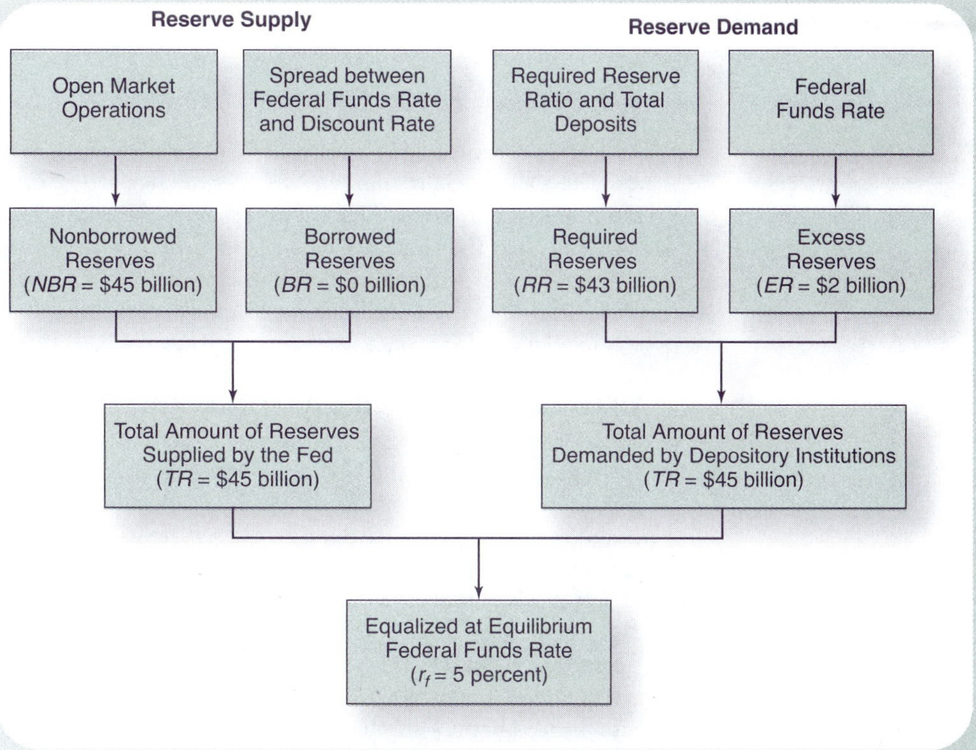

The Fed supplies non-borrowed reserves via its open market operations. In Figure 19-1 on page 420, with the discount rate always set above the federal funds rate, no depository institutions borrow reserves from the Fed. Depository institutions hold most reserves to meet reserve requirements, and their excess reserve holdings vary with the opportunity cost of excess reserves, which is the federal funds rate. In Figure 19-1, these factors together yield $43 billion in required reserves and $2 billion in excess reserves. The federal funds rate adjusts to equalize the quantity of reserves supplied by the Fed and the quantity of reserves demanded by depository institutions.

Reserve Supply

| Open Market Operations | Spread between Federal Funds Rate and Discount Rate |
| Nonborrowed Reserves (NBR = $45 billion) | Borrowed Reserves (BR = $0 billion) |

Total Amount of Reserves Supplied by the Fed (TR = $45 billion)

Reserve Demand

| Required Reserve Ratio and Total Deposits | Federal Funds Rate |
| Required Reserves (RR = $43 billion) | Excess Reserves (ER = $2 billion) |

Total Amount of Reserves Demanded by Depository Institutions (TR = $45 billion)

Equalized at Equilibrium Federal Funds Rate (r_f = 5 percent)

> **3. How do Federal Reserve policies influence the supply of reserves to depository institutions and the federal funds rate?** The Fed controls the supply of reserves by determining the amount of nonborrowed reserves through open market purchases or by influencing the amount of reserves that depository institutions borrow through changes in its discount window policies. Because the equilibrium federal funds rate arises from the balancing of the quantity of reserves demanded by depository institutions with the quantity of reserves supplied by the Fed, the Fed's open market operations and discount window policies ultimately determine the value of the federal funds rate.

The Market for Reserves, Interest Rates, and the Quantity of Money

As we discussed in Chapter 4, the federal funds rate is only one of many interest yields that are determined in the money and capital markets. And yet media reports often indicate that the Fed has decided to change the *overall level* of interest rates in the economy. Let's consider how Fed actions that affect the equilibrium federal funds rate can spill over to influence other interest yields.

The Federal Funds Rate and the Treasury Security Yield Curve

Recall from Chapter 4 that interest rates on different financial instruments are related in two respects. One relationship is the *risk structure of interest rates:* financial instruments with identical terms to maturity will have different market yields as a result of different degrees of risk. The other relationship is the *term structure of interest rates:* financial instruments with similar risk features will have different market yields if they have different terms to maturity. To understand how the federal funds rate relates to the Treasury bill rate, we must take into account both of these concepts.

YIELD CURVES FOR FEDERAL FUNDS AND TREASURY SECURITIES As we discussed in Chapter 4, we can construct a *yield curve* for Treasury securities by plotting the yields that correspond to the securities' various terms of maturity, such as three months, six months, twelve months, and so on. Such a yield curve relates the interest rates on Treasury securities alone, because Treasury securities all have the same low risk. The existence of a term premium typically causes the Treasury securities yield curve to slope upward even in circumstances in which traders in financial markets do not expect interest rates to change.

We can also construct a yield curve for federal funds loans. As we noted in Chapter 3, most federal funds loans have one-day maturities, but some are *term federal funds loans* with maturities of one or more weeks. Typically, the yields on such term federal funds loans increase with the term of the loan. Consequently, the federal funds yield curve also slopes upward.

Federal funds loans, however, are riskier than Treasury securities. The government stands behind the Treasury securities that it issues with the full taxing power that it possesses. This makes defaults on such securities extremely unlikely. In contrast, most federal funds loans are unsecured transactions backed only by the ability of a borrowing depository institution to repay the loan when its one-day or multiday term ends. Although federal funds loan defaults are fairly rare, they do occur from time to time. In addition, on rare occasions parties to a federal funds transaction have disagreed on how to interpret the terms that they negotiated, and the result has been costly delays in the final settlement on the transaction.

DETERMINING THE TREASURY BILL RATE   Because federal funds loans are riskier financial instruments than Treasury securities, there is a *risk premium* for any federal funds loans with maturities that match those of Treasury securities. This means that the federal funds yield curve will lie *above* the Treasury securities yield curve, as in Figure 19-3. At any term to maturity, the vertical distance between the two yield curves represents the risk premium.

Note that the actual terms to maturity on term federal funds loans are never as lengthy as the shortest terms of Treasury bills (T-bills). Nevertheless, we can *infer* these dashed portions of both yield curves in Figure 19-3 by calculating the federal funds yields that would emerge from successively renewing federal funds loans from week to week and by examining the prices of Treasury securities that are within days of final maturity.

Once we have constructed yield curves for federal funds loans and Treasury securities, we can determine the equilibrium interest yield on a six-month T-bill, as depicted in Figure 19-3. Given an equilibrium one-day term federal funds rate of $r_f = 5$ percent, the six-month Treasury security rate consistent with the risk and term structures of interest rates must be equal to $r = 4$ percent. Because a six-month T-bill is nearly risk-free, it typically has a lower yield than a one-day federal funds loan even though the six-month T-bill has a much longer 182-day term to maturity. In the real world, however, the difference between the federal funds rate and the six-month T-bill rate normally is about 0.25 to 0.50 percentage point, rather than the 1 percentage point differential that we have chosen as a round number for our example in Figure 19-3.

FIGURE 19-3
Determining the Treasury Bill Rate.

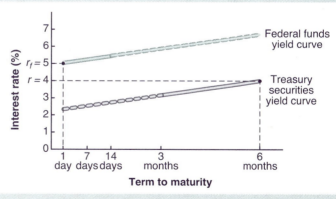

The Treasury securities yield curve typically slopes upward. Though market yields on very short Treasury maturities do not exist, they can be inferred from prices of Treasury securities that are within days of maturity—hence, the dashed portion of the Treasury securities yield curve. Likewise, the federal funds yield curve also slopes upward over maturities that range from a day to several weeks. Longer-term federal funds rates may be extrapolated from actual market rates on short-maturity federal funds loans—hence, the dashed portion of the federal funds yield curve. Federal funds are riskier than Treasury securities, so the federal funds rate typically exceeds the Treasury security rate that applies to a given maturity. Consequently, the Treasury security yield curve lies below the federal funds yield curve. If the equilibrium federal funds rate for a one-day maturity is 5 percent, then the six-month Treasury bill rate consistent with the term and risk structures of interest rates is 4 percent.

> ### 4. How is the federal funds rate related to other market interest rates?
> Federal Reserve policies determine the supply of reserves to depository institutions and thereby influence the equilibrium federal funds rate. The risk and term structures of interest rates link the federal funds rate to other market interest rates, including Treasury security rates.

The Equilibrium Quantity of Money

Now we are in a position to evaluate all aspects of the linkage from Fed policymaking to the quantity of money. Figure 19-4 depicts this linkage from the Fed's primary policy tools to the determination of total aggregate money holdings in the economy. In panel (a), the Fed's choice of a discount rate one percentage point above the federal funds rate and of a level of nonborrowed reserves equal to $NBR = \$45$ billion determines the supply of total reserves to depository institutions. Given the demand for reserves by those institutions, the equilibrium

---

FIGURE 19-4
Determining the Equilibrium Quantity of Money.

In the market for reserves, the federal funds rate adjusts to equilibrate the quantity of reserves demanded by depository institutions with the quantity of reserves supplied by the Fed at a level of $45 billion. Given an equilibrium federal funds rate of $r_f = 5$ percent, the term and risk structures of interest rates reflected by the positions and shapes of the Treasury security and federal funds yield curves determine the equilibrium interest rate on a six-month Treasury bill, $r = 4$ percent. This interest rate is the opportunity cost of holding money. At this rate, and given their current total income, consumers and businesses choose to hold money balances of $1,000 billion ($1 trillion). In this instance, this is the equilibrium quantity of money.

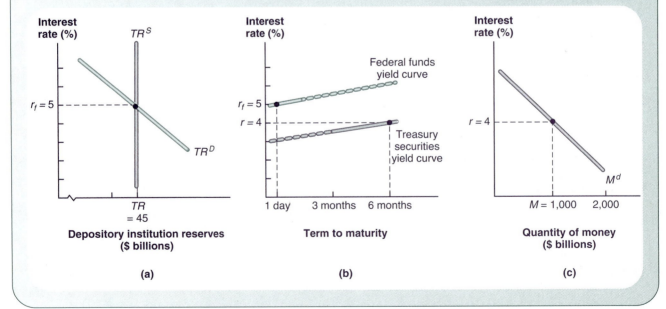

federal funds rate that maintains equilibrium in the reserves market, at a total reserve level of $45 billion, is equal to $r_f = 5$ percent.

Panel (b) of Figure 19-4 then shows the determination of the six-month T-bill rate. The interest yield on six-month T-bills that is consistent with the risk and term structures of interest rates depicted by the federal funds and Treasury security yield curves in panel (b) is equal to $r = 4$ percent. This interest yield is the opportunity cost of holding money. Panel (c) then shows the determination of the equilibrium quantity of money. From the money demand schedule, we can see that the total amount of desired money holdings at a 4 percent interest yield on six-month Treasury securities is $1,000 billion ($1 trillion). This, in our example, is the equilibrium quantity of money.

Of course, this is just an example. Values of the Fed's policy tools, total reserves, the federal funds rate, Treasury security rates, and the quantity of money vary from week to week and even from day to day. But Figure 19-4 shows the essential mechanics by which the Fed's policy choices relate to the final determination of the amount of money in the economy. Understanding the linkages depicted in Figure 19-4 is necessary for understanding how the Fed has conducted monetary policy in the past and how it conducts monetary policy today.

LINKING FED POLICIES IN THE MARKET FOR RESERVES TO THE QUANTITY OF MONEY   Figure 19-5 uses solid arrows to chart the full policy connections that our example illustrates. Through open market operations and discount window policy, the Fed can control the total supply of reserves to depository institutions. The interaction of the Fed's

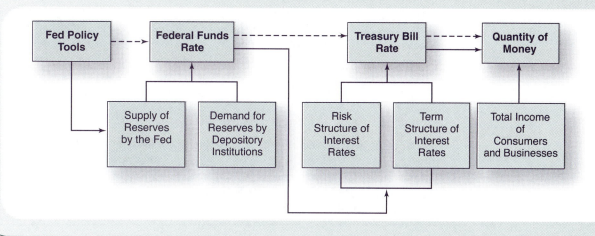

FIGURE 19-5
Linking Fed Policy Tools to the Quantity of Money.

This figure summarizes how Fed policy tools relate to the determination of the equilibrium quantity of money. Changes in a Fed policy instrument affect the supply of reserves and influence the equilibrium federal funds rate. Via the term and risk structures of interest rates, this induces a change in the Treasury bill rate, which alters the opportunity cost of holding money and thereby gives people the incentive to change their desired money holdings. The indirect, interest rate channel of monetary policy is indicated by the dashed arrows: Fed policy tools affect the federal funds rate, which influences the Treasury bill rate, which, in turn, affects the equilibrium quantity of money.

supply of reserves with depository institutions' demand for reserves then determines the federal funds rate. Then the risk and term structures of interest rates, as reflected by the shapes and positions of the federal funds and Treasury security yield curves, determine the equilibrium T-bill rate that measures the opportunity cost of money holdings by consumers and businesses. Given their incomes, individuals and businesses then take into account this opportunity cost and determine the total amount of money that they desire to hold. This is the equilibrium quantity of money.

The *dashed arrows* in Figure 19-5 depict basic connections from the Fed to the quantity of money. Fed policy tools directly influence the federal funds rate, which, in turn, affects the T-bill rate. Then, given the total income of households and businesses, the T-bill rate influences their total money holdings. Consequently, the dashed arrows capture the essential *interest rate channel* through which Fed policy tools affect the quantity of money.

HOW FED POLICY ACTIONS CHANGE THE QUANTITY OF MONEY   Because the Fed changes reserve requirements very infrequently and varies the discount rate automatically with the federal funds rate, open market operations are the primary means by which the Fed makes tactical monetary policy adjustments from day to day and week to week. This policy tool exerts its effects by changing the total amount of reserves that the Fed supplies to depository institutions. Such variations in the supply of total depository institution reserves cause changes in the equilibrium federal funds and T-bill rates and alterations in the quantity of money that consumers and businesses desire to hold.

To understand how the Fed can cause such changes, let's think about how a change in the supply of reserves affects interest rates and the quantity of money. Figure 19-6 illustrates the effects of an open market purchase, which increases the total quantity of reserves supplied at the current equilibrium federal funds rate. Hence, the open market purchase generates an imbalance in the market for depository institution reserves: the quantity of reserves supplied by the Fed exceeds the quantity of reserves demanded by depository institutions. Depository institutions increase their excess reserve holdings only if the federal funds rate falls, causing the opportunity cost of holding excess reserves to decline. Thus, the second effect of the open market purchase is a reduction in the equilibrium federal funds rate.

The fall in the federal funds rate leads to an expected decline in the federal funds rate for future days as well. This means that expected interest rates across the term and risk structures of interest rates decrease. At a six-month term to maturity, the interest yield on a Treasury security falls. The final effect stems from the fact that this reduction in the six-month T-bill rate causes the opportunity cost of holding money to decline. As a result, individuals and businesses increase their money holdings. The open market purchase thereby causes the quantity of money to increase. (Although a monetary policy action often generates nearly equal shifts of the Treasury and federal funds yield curves, as in Figure 19-6, sometimes one curve may become steeper or shallower than the other; see on page 430 the *Management Focus: For a While, a "Curve-Flattening" Strategy Paid Off for Investors.*)

> **5. How do Federal Reserve policies affect the quantity of money?**   Open market operations alter the supply of reserves to depository institutions, thereby changing the federal funds rate. Via the risk and term structures of interest rates, such variations in the federal funds rate induce movements in the Treasury bill rate and alter the opportunity cost of holding money. This causes individuals and businesses to change the amount of money that they hold.

FIGURE 19-6
Inducing an Increase in the Quantity of Money.

A Fed open market purchase increases the amount of reserves, from TR to TR', and thereby induces a decline in the equilibrium federal funds rate, from r_f to r_f'. People then expect that future federal funds rates will be lower, and so the federal funds yield curve shifts downward. Other things being equal, the risk premium between a Treasury security and a federal funds loan will remain the same at any term to maturity, so the Treasury security yield curve shifts downward, and the six-month Treasury bill rate falls from r to r'. This reduction in the opportunity cost of holding money will induce people to increase their holdings of money, so the equilibrium quantity of money rises from M to M'.

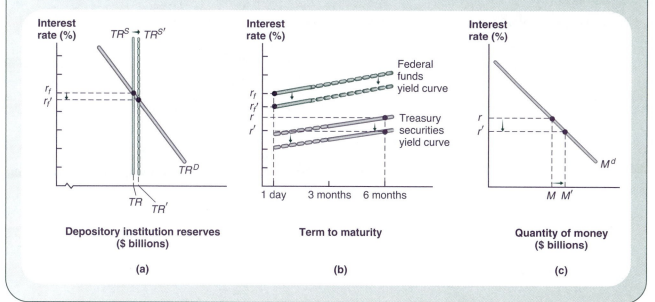

(a) Depository institution reserves ($ billions)

(b) Term to maturity

(c) Quantity of money ($ billions)

Federal Reserve Operating Procedures

Once a battle begins, military leaders must make a number of tactical decisions. They have to decide how to deploy and maneuver their land, air, and naval forces in a manner that is consistent with their overall strategic plan. Likewise, Fed officials often must vary their policy tools each day or week as they try to follow the broad strategy that they have established for a period encompassing many weeks or months. Like military officers, Fed officials must develop tactics, or day-to-day and week-to-week policy actions that are consistent with their broader strategy for monetary policy.

Monetary Policy Operating Procedures

As human beings, Fed officials sometimes make mistakes; their short-term policy decisions turn out to be inconsistent with their broader strategy for monetary policy. If the Fed makes a tactical policy mistake one day or week, it can attempt to compensate for its error the following day or week. Nevertheless, to achieve its strategic goals over many weeks or months, the Fed must follow appropriate daily and weekly tactics in its conduct of monetary policy. Indeed, a policy strategy can be defined as a *set of tactics*. For this reason, let's begin by

MANAGEMENT
Focus

For a While, a "Curve-Flattening" Strategy Paid Off for Investors

In 2004 and 2005, contractionary monetary policy actions by the Fed pushed up the one-day federal funds rate and term federal funds rates by more than 1 percentage point. Consequently, the federal funds yield curve shifted upward over its entire range. Interest yields on U.S. Treasury bills with one-, three-, and six-month maturities also rose by more than 1 percentage point during 2004 and 2005. During the same period, however, yields on five-year Treasury notes increased by just a little more than 0.5 percentage point, and yields on twenty-year Treasury bonds experi-

enced only a tiny increase. Thus, the Treasury securities yield curve shifted upward mainly at the lowest maturities and barely budged at the highest maturities. As a result, it became shallower.

A key factor contributing to a shallower Treasury securities yield curve was a bond-trading strategy employed by investors. The Fed was gradually pushing up the federal funds rate in 2004 and 2005 in an effort to contain aggregate demand and reduce inflation. Many investors became convinced that the Fed's policies would ultimately succeed and that the Fed would be able to push interest rates back down in later years. Thus, they anticipated that long-term bond rates would remain nearly unchanged and, hence, that prices of long-term bonds would not appreciably decline.

Acting on this anticipation, investors engaged in what became known as a "curve-flattening" strategy. They responded to the Fed's policy actions during 2004 and 2005 by trading Treasury notes of, say, two- and five-year maturities for ten- and twenty-year Treasury bonds. As investors continued to supply funds to the market for long-term bonds, of course, market interest rates on these bonds remained nearly level. Thus, investors' expectations that longer-term Treasury bond rates would not rise actually helped restrain increases in interest rates on these bonds, thereby making the Treasury securities yield curve shallower.

FOR CRITICAL ANALYSIS: What types of Fed policy actions could have generated the upward shift in the federal funds yield curve that occurred during 2004 and 2005?

---

discussing how the Fed can make tactical policy changes using its available policy tools. Once we understand how the Fed can conduct policy on a daily or weekly basis, we can then consider how it pursues broader strategies by adopting particular operating procedures for monetary policy.

Sometimes critics contend that the Fed makes too many policy decisions "by the seat of its pants." Yet the Fed typically follows predetermined *strategies* in its conduct of monetary policy. In military thinking, a strategy is the formation of broad plans for achieving an overall objective through an intended set of battlefield movements. Likewise, for the Fed, a *monetary policy strategy* is a general plan for achieving some set of economic objectives. The Fed normally tries to implement such a strategy by following an **operating procedure,** which is a self-imposed guideline for conducting monetary policy over a horizon stretching across several weeks or months. During the past thirty-five years, the Fed has experimented with a variety of operating procedures.

Operating procedure: A guideline for conducting monetary policy over several weeks or months.

Alternative Operating Procedures for Monetary Policy

The Fed may adopt two basic types of *strategies* over periods of many weeks, months, or even years. One strategy involves focusing on target levels for depository institutions' reserves. The other strategy entails targeting an interest rate.

A RESERVES-TARGETING PROCEDURE   A possible approach to a reserves-targeting strategy is for the Fed to establish a target value for total reserves. Then it can conduct open market operations as needed to keep the level of total reserves at this target level.

To understand the tactical approach that the Fed needs to follow from day to day if it pursues a reserves-targeting strategy, consider panel (a) of Figure 19-7. To keep the equilibrium level of reserves at a targeted level, the Fed must determine the likely position of total reserve demand. If the Fed forecasts that reserve demand will be TR_1^D, then to achieve a target level of total reserves denoted TR^*, it must adjust the amount of nonborrowed reserves to a level that places the reserve supply schedule at the location given by TR_1^S. If banks increase their demand for excess reserves, causing the reserve demand schedule to shift to the right, to TR_2^D, then to maintain its total reserve target the Fed must maintain the supply of reserves at TR_1^S.

Why might the Fed use such an operating procedure? One reason is that if the Fed's objective is to target the quantity of money, and if the money multiplier is relatively insensitive to interest rate changes, then keeping total reserves stable will help to stabilize the monetary base and the total quantity of money. Furthermore, such an operating procedure will automatically keep variability in interest rates from influencing the amount of reserves at

FIGURE 19-7
Reserve- versus Interest-Rate-Oriented Operating Procedures.

If a central bank targets bank reserves, then, as shown in panel (a), an increase in total reserve demand resulting from a rise in desired excess reserve holdings by banks requires keeping the reserve supply schedule

in position to maintain the target reserve level, denoted TR^*. Hence, with a reserve-oriented operating procedure, stabilizing the level of bank reserves often entails greater variability in interest rates. Panel (b) illustrates an interest-rate-oriented operating procedure, in which the central bank sets a federal funds rate target of r_f^*. In the face of an increase in reserve

demand, keeping the interbank funds rate at this target level will require an increase in the supply of reserves, which the central bank can bring about by conducting open market purchases and increasing nonborrowed reserves, thereby causing the level of bank reserves to rise from TR_1 to TR_2.

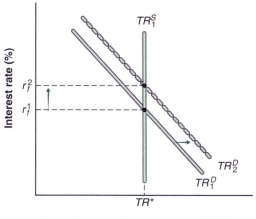

Depository institution reserves ($ billions)

(a)

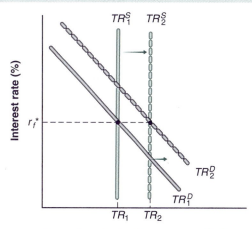

Depository institution reserves ($ billions)

(b)

depository institutions, thereby preventing volatility in the monetary base that such interest rate volatility could otherwise produce.

Note, however, that a Fed operating procedure that stabilizes total reserves tends to make interest rates more variable. In our example, for instance, we observed that the Fed had to let the federal funds rate increase to keep total reserves stabilized at the target level. As discussed in Chapter 17, however, induced increases in Treasury security yields and other interest rates could cause reductions in spending flows in the economy. Consequently, a potentially negative aspect of a reserves-targeting operating procedure is that it can lead to significant interest rate volatility that translates into more variability in economic activity.

A FEDERAL-FUNDS-RATE-TARGETING PROCEDURE   An alternative Fed operating procedure focuses on reducing or eliminating such interest rate volatility. Panel (b) of Figure 19-7 depicts a *federal-funds-rate-targeting operating procedure*. Here, the Fed establishes a target for the federal funds rate, denoted r_f^*. If the Fed anticipates that the total reserve demand schedule will be at the position given by TR_1^D, then achieving this target for the federal funds rate requires setting the level of reserves at TR_1. Under this operating procedure, if a rise in banks' demand for excess reserves causes reserve demand to shift rightward to TR_2^D, then the Fed must *increase* the supply of reserves. It can do so by engaging in open market purchases that raise nonborrowed reserves. Hence, this operating procedure of targeting the federal funds rate achieves more stable interest rates but can produce larger variations in bank reserves.

Why might the Fed choose to target the federal funds rate? The main reason is that doing so eliminates any perceived adverse effects that interest rate variability might have on the economy. As long as the risk and term structures of interest rates are stable, targeting the federal funds rate also keeps Treasury security rates from changing, thereby stabilizing the opportunity cost of holding money. This can contribute to greater stability of the equilibrium quantity of money demanded.

Targeting the federal funds rate can have a potentially significant drawback, however. Suppose that there is variability in the demand for money by consumers and businesses arising from factors other than the opportunity cost of money, such as variations in their incomes. Because a federal-funds-rate-targeting procedure stabilizes the opportunity cost of holding money, such variations in the total demand for money translate into the maximum possible changes in the amount of money that consumers and businesses choose to hold. By stabilizing interest rates, the Fed keeps the opportunity cost of money from changing so as to help offset such swings in desired money holdings. This can make the equilibrium quantity of money demanded more volatile than it otherwise would be. If controlling the amount of money is a Fed objective, then this negative aspect of targeting the federal funds rate can make it a less desirable operating procedure. In addition, as you learned in Chapter 18, to the extent that the quantity of money influences aggregate spending and aggregate demand, such variability in the quantity of money could also lead to greater short-run volatility in real GDP.

Past and Current Federal Reserve Operating Procedures

In light of the trade-offs associated with both reserves- and interest-rate-based operating procedures, what strategies has the Fed actually used in past years? How have they worked out? The Fed has been around since 1913, but let's confine ourselves to the most recent three and a half decades as we consider these questions.

FEDERAL FUNDS RATE TARGETING, 1970–1979   As we discussed briefly in Chapter 14, the Fed first began to think about its policy strategies more "scientifically" at the beginning of the 1970s. At that time, it chose to target the federal funds rate. Technically, the Fed established a "target range" for the federal funds rate, but typically its policy tactics entailed keeping the federal funds rate very close to the middle of this target range.

The Fed adopted federal funds rate targeting in an effort to achieve greater stability in the quantity of money and in economic activity. As our discussion above pointed out, however, targeting the federal funds rate poses problems in attaining these objectives if money demand becomes more variable. Unfortunately for the Fed, this is exactly what happened after the early 1970s. The Fed began to miss its monetary targets by wide margins, and the nation's income, spending, and inflation rate became more volatile. By 1979, the Fed was searching for a new operating procedure.

NONBORROWED RESERVES TARGETING, 1979–1982   During the 1970s, Fed critics argued that it should switch to targeting total reserves and permit the federal funds rate to vary in the marketplace. In the fall of 1979, the Fed decided to experiment with a slightly different type of reserves-based operating procedure. The Fed would try to predict how many reserves depository institutions would borrow during the coming months, and then it would determine the amount of nonborrowed reserves necessary to keep total reserves stable in light of its prediction. The Fed then treated this level of *nonborrowed reserves* as its policy target.

By aiming for a nonborrowed reserves objective, the Fed ended up allowing some variability in total reserves. This offset somewhat the negative aspect of a reserves-based procedure that we discussed above: interest rate variability. Nevertheless, interest rates were much more volatile after the Fed switched to nonborrowed reserves targeting in late 1979. Furthermore, by allowing total reserves to vary somewhat, the Fed also ended up permitting the quantity of money to vary from its target level. In the end, targeting nonborrowed reserves led to significant variations in *both* interest rates and the quantity of money.

BORROWED RESERVES TARGETING, 1982–1987   In 1982, the Fed tried an operating procedure that "split the difference" between targeting reserves and targeting the federal funds rate. It began to target the level of *borrowed reserves*. This was not really a novel policy, however. Recall from Chapter 14 that during the 1950s and 1960s the Fed tried to stabilize *free reserves,* or the difference between excess reserves and borrowed reserves. By targeting borrowed reserves, the Fed tended to stabilize free reserves, so this 1980s procedure looked a lot like a return to old-style policymaking.

In a sense it also looked like federal funds rate targeting. At this time, the Fed set the discount rate *below* the federal funds rate, and the key determinant of the amount of discount window borrowing by depository institutions was the difference between the federal funds rate and the discount rate. The way the Fed attempted to stabilize borrowed reserves was by keeping this difference stable, which, in turn, required a stable federal funds rate. And so targeting borrowed reserves also entailed keeping the federal funds rate from being excessively volatile.

Indeed, some critics of the Fed argued that the borrowed reserves procedure was really a "cover" for a return to federal funds rate targeting. A few even contended that the Fed never seriously targeted nonborrowed reserves but implicitly stabilized the federal funds rate instead. Nevertheless, a study by Thomas Cosimano and Richard Sheehan of the University of Notre Dame found strong evidence that the Fed really did use the three separate operating

On the Web

What is the Federal Reserve's current policy stance regarding open market operations and the federal funds rate? Find out by going to the Federal Open Market Committee's Web site at **http://www.federalreserve.gov/fomc** and clicking on "Meeting calendar, statements, and minutes" and then "Minutes" for the most recent month.

procedures. Their study involved sophisticated statistical analysis, but you can get a flavor for why they reached this conclusion by considering Figure 19-8, which is taken from a 1990 study by Carl Walsh of the University of California at Santa Cruz. Panel (a) shows how the equilibrium federal funds rate moved in response to Fed announcements of the size of M1. Because the Fed kept the funds rate near its target before 1979, such announcements typically had little effect on the federal funds rate. But when the Fed targeted nonborrowed reserves between 1979 and 1982, the federal funds rate varied considerably. During the period after 1982, when the Fed switched to borrowed reserves targeting, the federal funds rate varied more than it did during the period of federal funds rate targeting but less than it did during the interval of nonborrowed reserves targeting.

Panel (b) of Figure 19-8 displays the monthly growth rates for M1 between 1970 and 1987. As noted above, variability in the growth of M1 actually *increased* during the 1979–1982 interval when the Fed targeted nonborrowed reserves, as compared with the 1970s when the Fed used a federal-funds-rate-targeting procedure. During the period from 1982 to 1987, the variability of M1 growth declined slightly but was still much greater than during the 1970s. Consequently, both panels in Figure 19-8 indicate that the Fed really did use three distinctive operating procedures during the 1970s and 1980s.

FIGURE 19-8
Variability of the Federal Funds Rate and M1 Growth under Different Operating Procedures.

As shown in panel (a), federal funds rate variability rose considerably when the Fed switched from targeting the federal funds rate to targeting nonborrowed reserves in 1979 and then fell significantly when the Fed switched to targeting borrowed reserves in 1982. Panel (b) shows that the variability of money growth likewise rose after 1979 and then declined somewhat after 1982.

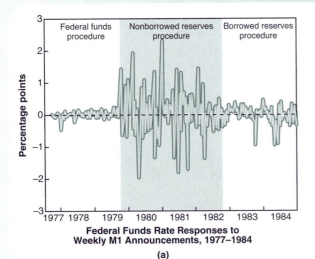

(a)

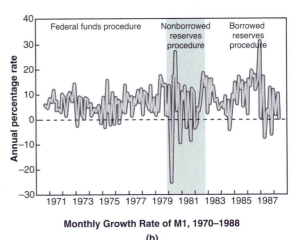

(b)

SOURCE: Carl E. Walsh, "Issues in the Choice of Monetary Policy Operating Procedures," in *Monetary Policy for a Changing Financial Environment,* ed. William Haraf and Phillip Cagan (Washington, D.C.: AEI Press, 1990), pp. 8–37.

RENEWED TARGETING OF THE FEDERAL FUNDS RATE, 1988 TO THE PRESENT

In October 1987, stock prices plummeted, as many stocks lost over a third of their values in a single day. To help prevent a broader financial crisis, the Fed announced that it stood ready to provide as much liquidity as needed. It also decided to keep interest rates stable to prevent further volatility in the prices of financial instruments. To do this, it switched to a federal funds rate target once again.

From 1988 until the present, the Fed has continued to use the federal funds rate as its strategic variable of monetary policy. Its tactics, however, have differed from the approach of the 1970s. In contrast to the Fed of the 1970s, today's Fed has been much more willing to *adjust* the target value of the federal funds rate when conditions have warranted. This increased flexibility has helped offset some of the otherwise undesirable features of this policy procedure. Even former critics of the Fed have given it high marks for its willingness to change its federal funds rate target to stabilize economic activity. Only the future will tell, however, if the Fed will be able to maintain such a flexible approach to this operating procedure. We shall explore this issue in more detail in Chapter 21.

> **6. What are Federal Reserve operating procedures, and what operating procedures has the Federal Reserve used in recent years?** Operating procedures are strategies that the Fed adopts to guide its open market operations and discount window policies over the course of many weeks, months, or even years. The Fed basically can choose between operating procedures that target reserves and procedures that focus on the federal funds rate. Since the 1970s, the Fed has used operating procedures that have targeted the federal funds rate, nonborrowed reserves, and borrowed reserves. Currently, the Fed targets the federal funds rate.

Chapter Summary

1. The Primary Tools through Which the Fed Conducts Monetary Policy: The Fed's fundamental day-to-day monetary policy instrument is open market operations. Fed purchases and sales of securities change the amount of nonborrowed reserves and thereby alter the monetary base and the quantities of money and credit. In addition, by changing the terms by which it lends reserves through the discount window, the Fed can influence the amount of reserves that depository institutions borrow, which also ultimately affects the amounts of money and credit. A third, though infrequently used, instrument is reserve requirements. Changes in the required reserve ratios alter the money and credit multipliers, thereby generating variations in monetary and credit aggregates.

2. Key Factors That Affect the Demand for Reserves by Depository Institutions: There are three determinants of depository institutions' demand for reserves. Two of these are the required reserve ratio set by the Fed and the total quantity of transactions deposits in the banking system, which together determine the amount of required reserves. The third factor is the opportunity cost to banks of holding excess reserves, which is the federal funds rate.

3. How Federal Reserve Policies Influence the Supply of Reserves to Depository Institutions and the Federal Funds Rate: The Fed's open market operations determine the amount of nonborrowed reserves in the banking system, and its discount window policies influence the amount of borrowed reserves. Consequently, through open market purchases and sales or alterations in the terms at which depository institutions may borrow from the discount window, the Fed can change the supply of reserves and affect the equilibrium federal funds rate.

4. The Linkage between the Federal Funds Rate and Other Market Interest Rates: The risk and term structures of interest rates link Treasury security rates and other interest yields to the federal funds rate, which the Fed can influence with its policy tools. Consequently, Fed policy actions that alter the federal funds rate ultimately cause other market interest rates to move in the same direction as the federal funds rate.

5. How Federal Reserve Policies Affect the Quantity of Money: Open market operations vary the supply of reserves to depository institutions, thereby inducing changes in the equilibrium federal funds rate. Changes in the federal funds rate induce movements in the Treasury bill rate through the risk and term structures of interest rates. This alters the opportunity cost of holding money, thereby inducing people to adjust the amount of money that they hold.

6. Types of Federal Reserve Operating Procedures, and Operating Procedures That the Federal Reserve Has Used in Recent Years: Operating procedures are the guidelines by which the Fed pursues its broader economic goals. The Fed typically must choose between operating procedures that entail targeting reserve measures and a procedure of stabilizing or targeting the federal funds rate. In recent decades, the Fed has experimented with targeting the federal funds rate, nonborrowed reserves, and borrowed reserves. Since the late 1980s, the Fed has targeted the federal funds rate but has adjusted its target for this rate more often than when it used a similar operating procedure in the 1970s.

Questions and Problems

(Answers to odd-numbered questions and problems may be found on the Web at **http://money.swcollege.com** under "Student Resources.")

1. Explain why an open market sale causes a change in the quantity of money by inducing a change in the monetary base instead of a change in the money multiplier.

2. What practical constraints make it impracticable for the Federal Reserve to vary reserve requirements on a weekly basis, so as to use this policy instrument as a frequent tool of monetary policy? In light of these constraints, can you think of any rationale for reserve requirements? Explain.

3. Explain why the demand schedule for depository institution reserves slopes downward.

4. Suppose that most of the nation's banks apply a new computerized inventory-tracking system to manage their excess reserves, thereby enabling them to reduce their excess reserves to minimal levels. Assuming no response by the Federal Reserve, what effect will this have on the equilibrium federal funds rate?

5. The Federal Reserve wishes to reduce the quantity of money but does not wish to do so by conducting open market operations. Use appropriate diagrams to explain how the Fed can accomplish its goal.

6. As we discussed, the Fed's current operating procedure is to target the federal funds rate. If the Fed wishes to reduce reserve requirements for some reason unrelated to monetary policy needs, should it buy or sell securities to keep the federal funds rate at its target level? Explain your reasoning.

7. Why is the six-month Treasury bill rate typically lower than the one-day federal funds rate even though the federal funds yield curve lies above the Treasury security yield curve?

8. Draw appropriate diagrams, and show how the Fed can push up market interest rates via an open market operation.

9. Suppose that the Fed is targeting the federal funds rate and there is an increase in the demand for money because of a rapid expansion in the economy's level of nominal GDP, perhaps because of rapid inflation. Keeping in mind that part of the total quantity of money is deposits subject to reserve requirements (and assuming that not all such deposits are part of sweep account programs), reason out the effect on the reserve demand schedule. Outline a policy action that will enable the Fed to keep the federal funds rate at its target value in the face of this event. Use diagrams to assist in explaining your answer.

10. As an extension to question 9, suppose that the Fed wishes to keep the quantity of money unchanged at its original level following the rise in the demand for money. Can the Fed maintain its current target for the federal funds rate? Explain.

11. The Fed currently uses an operating procedure in which it targets the federal funds rate, but it changes its target more often than in the 1970s, when it used a similar procedure. In light of the drawbacks associated with this procedure, is there any potential gain from the Fed's greater flexibility in setting the federal funds rate target? Explain your reasoning. [Hint: Think about how this approach can help "split the difference" between the gains and losses of interest rate targeting versus reserves targeting.]

Before the Test

Test your understanding of the material covered in this chapter by taking the Chapter 19 interactive quiz at **http://money.swcollege.com**.

Online Application

Internet URLs: http://www.stlouisfed.org and **http://www.bis.org**

Titles: Federal Reserve Board Data on OCD Sweep Account Programs and Bank for International Settlements

Navigation: Go to the first URL above. Click on "Economic Research." In the top menu, on the right, select "Monetary Aggregates." Then click on "Data: Federal Reserve Board Data on OCD Sweep Account Programs."

Application: Read the discussion, and answer the following questions:

1. What are the two types of sweep account programs? What constraints do banks face on their ability to shift funds from checkable deposits into deposits not subject to reserve requirements?

2. Click on "Monthly Sweeps Data" to observe data on the amounts most recently "swept" by U.S. banks. Based on the discussion in the article, is it correct to adjust the M1 measure of money by directly subtracting these amounts?

For Group Study and Analysis: Assign groups to various regions of the world (e.g., North America, South America, Western Europe, Eastern Europe, Asia, and Africa). Have each group go to the home page of the Bank for International Settlements (**http://www.bis.org**) and click on "Links to Central Banks." From there, they can navigate to the Web sites of central banks worldwide. Ask each group to examine each Web site for information about reserve requirement policies and operating procedures of other central banks. Regroup, and compare notes. How forthcoming are central banks concerning their policies regarding reserve requirements and operating procedures? For those whose operating procedures can be deduced, do reserve requirements appear to be an important element?

Selected References and Further Reading

Anderson, Richard, and Robert Rasche. "Retail Sweep Programs and Bank Reserves." Federal Reserve Bank of St. Louis *Review* 83 (January/February 2001): 51–72.

Bennett, Paul, and Spence Hilton. "Falling Reserve Balances and the Federal Funds Rate." Federal Reserve Bank of New York *Current Issues in Economics and Finance* 3 (April 1997).

Cosimano, Thomas, and Richard Sheehan. "The Federal Reserve Operating Procedure, 1984–1990: An Empirical Analysis." *Journal of Macroeconomics* 16 (Summer 1994): 573–588.

Demiralp, Selva, and Dennis Farley. "Declining Required Reserves, Funds Rate Volatility, and Open Market Operations." *Journal of Banking and Finance* 29 (May 2005): 1131–1152.

Krainer, John. "Retail Sweeps and Reserves." Federal Reserve Bank of San Francisco *Economic Letter*, No. 2001-02, January 26, 2001.

Moschitz, Julius. "The Determinants of the Overnight Interest Rate in the Euro Area." European Central Bank Working Paper No. 393, September 2004.

Ogawa, Kazuo. "Why Commercial Banks Hold Excess Reserves: The Japanese Experience." Institute of Social and Economic Research Discussion Paper No. 625, Osaka University, December 2004.

Prati, Alessandro, Leonardo Bartolini, and Giuseppe Bertola. "The Overnight Interbank Market: Evidence from the G-7 and the Euro Zone." *Journal of Banking and Finance* 27 (October 2003): 2045–2083.

Sellon, Gordon, Jr., and Stuart Weiner. "Monetary Policy without Reserve Requirements: Analytical Issues." Federal Reserve Bank of Kansas City *Economic Review* 81 (Fourth Quarter 1997): 5–24.

VanHoose, David, and David Humphrey. "Sweep Accounts, Reserve Management, and Interest Rate Volatility." *Journal of Economics and Business* 53 (July/August 2001): 387–404.

Walsh, Carl, E. "Issues in the Choice of Monetary Policy Operating Procedures." In *Monetary Policy for a Changing Financial Environment,* ed. William Haraf and Phillip Cagan. Washington, D.C.: AEI Press, 1990.

MoneyXtra

Log on to the MoneyXtra Web site now (**http://moneyxtra.swcollege.com**) for additional learning resources such as practice quizzes, case studies, readings, and additional economic applications.

What Should the Fed Do?—

Objectives and Targets of Monetary Policy

Fundamental Issues

1. What are the ultimate goals of monetary policy?

2. Why might a central bank use an intermediate monetary policy target?

3. What are policy time lags, and how might they cause well-meaning monetary policymakers to destabilize the economy?

4. Why is monetary policy credibility a crucial factor in maintaining low inflation?

5. How might monetary policy credibility be achieved?

6. Do countries necessarily gain from making their central banks more independent?

In a very unusual public setting, two members of the Federal Reserve's Board of Governors openly disagreed about monetary policy. During a conference panel discussion, one governor, Ben Bernanke, made a case for the Fed to proclaim and pursue a target rate of inflation, such as 2 percent per year. The other governor, Donald Kohn, argued strenuously against Bernanke's proposal. Aiming for an inflation target, Kohn contended, would excessively constrain Fed policymakers.

A few months later, out of the public spotlight, the Board of Governors brought together officials and economists from across the Federal Reserve System to discuss the relative merits of changing Fed policymaking to target the inflation rate versus maintaining the status quo. Following two days of discussion, the Fed issued a formal statement saying that it would "defer" further consideration of inflation targets to a later date. In the meantime, Fed economists would subject the idea to "further study."

In this chapter, you will learn about goals and targets of monetary policy. You will also learn about theories suggesting that an inherent "inflation bias" of monetary policy might be reduced if the Fed would commit itself to a policy of low inflation—perhaps via the use of explicit inflation targets.

Internal and External Objectives of Monetary Policy

Up to now, you have learned about how monetary policy actions may influence real GDP, employment, and prices. What goals should the Federal Reserve and other central banks seek to achieve? How should they go about pursuing those goals? In this chapter, you will learn that even when there happens to be widespread agreement concerning the appropriate *objectives* of monetary policy, the best way to *implement* monetary policy still may not be apparent.

In this chapter, we shall begin by examining the factors that determine the **ultimate goals,** or final economic objectives, of monetary policy. Then we shall devote the bulk of the remainder of the chapter to contemplating how the Fed might go about pursuing these goals.

Internal Goals of Monetary Policy

In Chapters 17 and 18, you learned how monetary policy actions can alter interest rates, desired investment expenditures, and equilibrium real GDP, thereby influencing aggregate demand and the price level. Because monetary policy actions can affect the nation's economic performance, the Fed can contemplate adopting policy strategies with an explicit intention of achieving specific national economic goals.

One aim of central banks and governments might be to achieve *internal goals,* or purely domestic policy objectives. Although the Fed might seek to achieve a number of internal goals, most economists focus on three sets of internal goals that monetary policymakers might pursue.

INFLATION GOALS   As Table 20-1 shows, a number of social costs are potentially associated with inflation and inflation variability. In light of these costs, there is a good justification for the Fed to try to maintain low (or even no) inflation. In addition, there is a strong rationale for limiting year-to-year variability in inflation rates. (The social costs associated with inflation are not borne equally across all members of society; see on the next page the *Policy Focus: How Pervasive Is "Inflation Inequality" in the United States?*)

OUTPUT GOALS   Another potential ultimate goal of economic policy might be to prevent sharp swings in real GDP relative to its long-run level. Pursuing this policy goal could, according to some of the economic theories we have discussed, limit business cycles.

EMPLOYMENT GOALS   Labor is a key factor of production, and in a democratic republic workers also account for the bulk of voters. Consequently, policymakers are likely to feel pressures to pursue policies that aim to prevent significant variability in worker unemployment rates and that might spur greater growth in real GDP and employment.

Legislated Internal Goals

Can the Fed pursue inflation, real GDP, and employment goals simultaneously? Certainly, stabilizing real GDP will often be consistent with an objective of stable employment and a low unemployment rate. Nonetheless, as you learned in Chapter 18, attempting to push up real GDP can also boost the equilibrium price level, so there may be conflicts among these objectives.

MONEYXTRA!
Another Perspective

To learn more about nations' experiences with inflation targeting, go to the Chapter 20 reading, entitled "Inflation Target Design: Changing Inflation Performance and Persistence in Industrial Countries," written by Pierre Siklos and published by the Federal Reserve Bank of Atlanta. **http://moneyxtra. swcollege.com**

Ultimate goals: The final objectives of economic policies.

MONEYXTRA!
Economic Applications

Should the Federal Reserve aim at a zero inflation policy? To review alternative perspectives on this debate and make your own judgment, go to EconDebate Online. **http://moneyxtra. swcollege.com**

Table 20-1 The Costs of Inflation and Inflation Variability

Type of Cost	Cause
Resources expended to economize on money holdings (more trips to banks, etc.)	Rising prices associated with inflation
Costs of changing price lists and printing menus and catalogues	Individual product/service price increases associated with inflation
Redistribution of real incomes from individuals to the government	Inflation that pushes people into higher, nonindexed nominal tax brackets
Reductions in investment, capital accumulation, and economic growth	Inflation variability that complicates business planning
Slowed pace of introduction of new and better products	Volatile price changes that reduce the efficiency of private markets
Redistribution of resources from creditors to debtors	Unexpected inflation that reduces the real values of debts

POLICY

Focus

How Pervasive Is "Inflation Inequality" in the United States?

Rates of changes in price indexes such as the GDP deflator and the consumer price index (CPI) provide an indication of the inflation experienced by the "average" household. But every household's spending undoubtedly departs from the average in some way. Recently, Federal Reserve Bank of New York economists Bart Hobijn and David Lagakos investigated just how much "inflation inequality" exists in the United States.

Hobijn and Lagakos found evidence of substantial disparities in household-specific inflation rates, resulting mainly from differing levels of consumption of three categories of goods: education, health care, and gasoline. As a student, you will not be surprised that households with children enrolled in college tend to experience higher inflation than many other households. So do households with more elderly members. These households consume more health care, and prices of health care have often risen faster than prices of other goods and services. In addition, households whose members commute relatively long distances in automobiles naturally consume more gasoline, and the price of this commodity has risen faster than other prices in recent years.

Nevertheless, Hobijn and Lagakos found that, in general, a household that faces generally higher inflation than others typically does so only for a relatively short time. Consequently, deviations of household-specific inflation from the inflation experienced by an "average" household do not last for much more than a year. To the extent that inflation inequality exists, it is neither pervasive nor persistent. This implies that aggregate inflation measures really are reasonable measures of the inflation experienced by a typical household.

FOR CRITICAL ANALYSIS: How might the central bank of a particular nation modify its inflation goals if it determined that inflation inequality across households in that nation was both pervasive and persistent?

On the Web

What was the substance of the most recent statements to Congress by the chair of the Fed's Board of Governors? You can review the chair's testimony and report by going to the Fed's Web site at **http://federalreserve. gov**, where you can click on "Monetary Policy" and then on "Monetary Report to the Congress."

For this reason, nations sometimes choose to make economic goals explicit. In the United States, two laws lay out a course for economic policymakers. One is the *Employment Act of 1946*, which legally commits all agencies of the federal government to the objectives of "maximum employment, production, and purchasing power." Thus, the 1946 act officially seeks the highest possible employment and real GDP levels as well as low inflation. This legislation is silent, however, about exactly how the U.S. government should address potential trade-offs among these goals.

In 1978, Congress established more concrete objectives when it passed the *Full Employment and Balanced Growth Act*, more commonly known as the *Humphrey-Hawkins Act*. This legislation set goals for 1983 of an unemployment rate of 3 percent and an inflation rate of 0 percent. When 1983 arrived, however, the problems with trying to legislate explicit objectives became apparent: in that year, the actual unemployment rate exceeded 9 percent, and actual inflation was about 5 percent. By the early 2000s, however, the unemployment rate had fallen to 4 percent, and the inflation rate hovered between 1 and 3 percent, both of which were closer to the 1978 targets. Nevertheless, most economists are doubtful that the natural rate of unemployment is as low as 3 percent in the United States.

External Goals of Monetary Policy

In addition to purely domestic, internal goals, a nation's central bank may also be concerned about international payment flows. Thus, policymakers at the Fed or other central banks may desire to achieve *external goals*, or objectives for international flows of goods, services, income, and assets or for the relative values of their national currencies.

Why would a nation's residents want central bank policymakers to pursue external objectives? One reason is that international factors help determine domestic outcomes in an open economy, in which residents of the nation engage in significant volumes of trade with other nations. In an open economy, international considerations may affect the nation's ability to achieve its real GDP, employment, and inflation objectives. Consequently, internal and external objectives may go hand in hand. Another reason, however, is that a number of a nation's citizens may have immediate interests in the international sectors of their nation's economy. They may perceive that international variables themselves—such as the nation's trade balance—should be ultimate policy goals.

INTERNATIONAL OBJECTIVES AND DOMESTIC GOALS   Two factors that play a role in determining a country's aggregate expenditures are export expenditures on the nation's output of goods and services by residents of other nations and import spending by its own residents on foreign-produced goods and services. An increase in export expenditures increases aggregate expenditures, whereas a rise in import spending reduces the fraction of disposable income available for consumption of domestically produced output. Therefore, both of these international factors influence the equilibrium level of real GDP.

It follows that a central bank such as the Federal Reserve must consider the volumes of export and import expenditures when contemplating appropriate policy strategies. At a minimum, a central bank must account for the real GDP effects of trade-related expenditures that are unrelated to purely domestic influences. More broadly, however, a central bank may reach the conclusion that achieving its internal goals requires careful attention to international factors. For example, a central bank may seek to achieve balanced international trade as part of a general strategy intended to achieve its domestic real GDP, employment, and inflation objectives.

EXTERNAL BALANCE FOR ITS OWN SAKE   Central banks in most countries, however, typically regard external objectives as being separable from internal objectives. Workers and business owners in industries that export large portions of their output often push their governments to enact policies that promote exports. At the same time, workers and business owners in industries that rely on domestic sales of their output may pressure government and central bank officials to pursue policies that restrain imports. Persistent efforts by both of these interest groups could induce a nation's policymakers to seek trade balance *surpluses*—exports over and above imports—as external-balance objectives.

History is replete with examples of nations that have sought to achieve persistent trade surpluses. In the seventeenth and eighteenth centuries, for example, successive generations of British citizens advocated a national policy of **mercantilism.** This school of thought holds that inflows of payments relating to international commerce and trade are a primary source of a nation's wealth. During this period, therefore, British mercantilists advocated policy actions designed to promote exports and to hinder imports. A fundamental difficulty with mercantilist thought, of course, is that if *all* countries simultaneously try to attain trade surpluses through import limits, international commerce will likely be stymied. Realization of this self-defeating aspect of mercantilism led to its decline in the nineteenth century. Mercantilist thought supports the goals of special interest groups in any open economy, however, so these groups still use mercantilist arguments today in an effort to pressure policymakers to maintain balanced trade, if not trade surpluses.

The interests of exporters and importers may also make exchange rate objectives part of the mix of external-balance goals. On the one hand, a reduction in the exchange value of a nation's currency effectively makes domestically produced goods less expensive to foreign residents.

Mercantilism: The idea that a primary determinant of a nation's wealth is international trade and commerce, so a nation can gain by enacting policies that spur exports while limiting imports.

Thus, if export industries comprise an important political interest group, a country's central bank may face pressures to reduce the value of its currency. On the other hand, an increase in a currency's exchange value reduces the effective price that domestic residents pay for foreign-produced goods. Consequently, if importers have considerable political clout, a central bank may be lobbied to push up the value of the nation's currency.

In the face of potentially conflicting ultimate goals and generally vague guidance from legislators, how should central bank officials conduct monetary policies? What near-term goals should they pursue in an effort to achieve broader, ultimate economic policy objectives? These are the issues that we shall address in the remainder of this chapter and in the chapters that follow.

> **1. What are the ultimate goals of monetary policy?** The ultimate goals of the Federal Reserve and other central banks are the final objectives of monetary policy strategies and actions. Central banks often pursue two categories of economic goals. One consists of internal objectives, which are ultimate goals for national real GDP, employment, and inflation. Under the terms of 1946 and 1978 legislation, the formal goals of the U.S. government and the Federal Reserve System include low and stable inflation rates, high and stable GDP growth, and a high and stable employment level. The other category of potential ultimate goals for a nation's monetary policy consists of external-balance objectives, which are objectives for the trade balance, or exports relative to imports.

Intermediate Targets of Monetary Policy

As you have learned in previous chapters, monetary policy actions can potentially have short-term or even longer-term effects on real GDP and employment. Monetary policy actions certainly can influence the price level.

Hence, central banks clearly perform important tasks. Indeed, some observers have called the chair of the Fed's Board of Governors the second-most-important person in the United States, after the president.

Intermediate Monetary Policy Targets

Although the Fed cannot control the total quantity of deposits in the banking system directly, it clearly can influence this amount by conducting open market operations—buying or selling U.S. government securities. In addition, by varying reserve requirements, the Fed can affect the size of the money multiplier linking a change in reserves caused by its open market operations to the total amount of money in circulation. Finally, the Fed can influence the total amount of reserves held by private banks by changing the discount rate that it charges such institutions, thereby inducing them either to increase or to reduce the amounts of reserves that they borrow from the Federal Reserve banks.

Thus, even though the Federal Reserve and other central banks of the world cannot directly "control" the quantity of money in circulation, they could use their policy instruments—in the case of the Fed, open market operations, the discount rate, and reserve requirements—to try to vary the quantity of money in a precise effort to achieve their inflation, real GDP, and employment objectives. Nevertheless, rather than taking such a direct approach, most central banks typically have sought to achieve **intermediate targets** of monetary policy. An intermediate target is an economic variable whose value a central bank tries to control because it feels that doing so is consistent with its ultimate objectives. Such a variable is distinguishable from the central bank's ultimate policy goals but is sufficiently closely related that it can serve as a "stand-in" or "proxy" for the ultimate objectives, as indicated in Figure 20-1.

Intermediate target: An economic variable that a central bank seeks to control because it determines that doing so is consistent with its ultimate objectives.

The Rationales for Intermediate Targeting

There are two rationales for using an intermediate target in monetary policy. One is that central bank officials often have difficulty reaching agreement about the ways in which monetary policy affects inflation, real GDP, and employment in the short and long run. The other rationale is that even if central bank policymakers could unanimously agree on how their policy actions influence economic activity, they typically possess limited information about the economy.

PROBLEMS WITH DIRECTLY PURSUING ULTIMATE POLICY GOALS As you have learned, monetary policy actions can affect inflation, real GDP, and employment. In any central bank, however, different officials often subscribe to distinctly different views about how monetary policy can affect the economy, making it difficult for central bank policymakers to reach a consensus concerning the best means of attaining ultimate policy objectives.

Consequently, the policymakers may *compromise* by seeking to achieve an intermediate monetary policy target. For example, as we shall discuss in more detail shortly, in the past several central banks have used the quantity of money as an intermediate target variable. Not all economic theories agree that monetary policy actions affect real GDP and employment, but all theories indicate that a sustained change in depository institution reserves should cause monetary aggregates and the price level to move in the same direction, if not in exactly the same proportion. Lacking agreement on any other aspect of how the monetary policy process works, central bank officials might compromise by trying to aim for a monetary objective.

CONDUCTING MONETARY POLICY WITH LIMITED INFORMATION Even if all policymakers could agree on one "true" economic theory, they would still have a strong economic justification for using an intermediate monetary policy target. The reason is that central bank officials must conduct monetary policy in the absence of perfect information. Some economic variables, such as interest rates and the quantities of money or credit, can be measured day-to-day or week-to-week. Other variables, such as nominal GDP, can be estimated weekly but generally are known only on a monthly basis. Still others, particularly the price

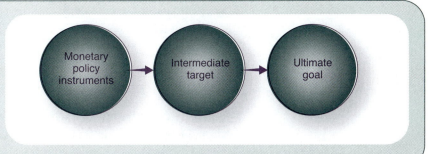

FIGURE 20-1
The Intermediate Targeting Strategy for Monetary Policy.

An intermediate target is a macroeconomic variable that a central bank seeks to influence as a stand-in for its ultimate goals, which are more difficult to observe or influence in the near term.

level, real GDP, and employment, can at best be tracked (or, in the case of real GDP, estimated) only from month to month. Even then, central bank and government statisticians often revise their calculations of these variables in the weeks following their initial release.

Consequently, current information about the central bank's ultimate policy goals—inflation, real GDP, and employment—typically is the least readily available. In contrast, interest rate, money, and credit data are more likely to be available for observation and use at any given moment. Nominal GDP, data are not forthcoming as quickly as these financial data, but still generally appear more frequently than information about ultimate policy goal variables.

The notion of using an economic variable as an intermediate target follows naturally from the fact that information about other variables is more readily available than information about ultimate objectives. By aiming for an intermediate target, a central bank can more quickly discern whether it is on the way to achieving the basic intent of its policies. Otherwise, monetary policymakers might have to wait much longer to make this assessment.

Choosing an Intermediate Target Variable

A central bank that decides to use an intermediate targeting approach to conducting monetary policy must then choose an appropriate target variable. In selecting its intermediate target variable, a central bank considers several criteria.

CHARACTERISTICS OF INTERMEDIATE TARGETS   To be useful, an intermediate target variable should exhibit four key attributes:

1. **Frequently observable.** Because information timing is a fundamental rationale for using an intermediate targeting approach, an intermediate target variable should be observable more frequently than ultimate goal variables. As we discussed above, the price level, real GDP, and employment are at best observable on a monthly basis. Consequently, the central bank is likely to choose an intermediate target variable that it can observe from week to week or even from day to day.

2. **Consistency with ultimate goals.** Achieving a target value for an intermediate variable should be consistent with achieving the central bank's ultimate objectives. If a central bank were to hit its chosen intermediate target successfully only to discover that it had widely missed its goals for inflation, real GDP, and employment, then its policy strategy would have been counterproductive.

3. **Definable and measurable.** Defining and measuring an intermediate target variable should be a straightforward task. If a potential intermediate target variable is susceptible to redefinition because of intermittent regulatory or technological changes, then a central bank would have trouble settling on a consistent way to measure the target variable and evaluate its relationship to ultimate policy goals.

4. **Controllable.** The central bank should be able to readily influence the value of the intermediate target variable. Otherwise, it would be futile for the central bank to try to achieve its ultimate policy objectives by attaining its intermediate target.

THE MENU OF POTENTIAL INTERMEDIATE TARGET VARIABLES   Several alternative categories of economic variables might qualify as intermediate monetary policy targets. Consequently, central banks around the globe have adopted a number of different intermediate targeting procedures over the years.

Monetary Aggregates Many nations, including Germany, the United Kingdom, and Japan, have experimented with procedures that use *monetary aggregates,* or alternative measures of the nominal quantity of money in circulation, as intermediate target variables. In the United States, the Federal Reserve in the past has targeted M1 and M2.

The basic rationale for targeting a monetary aggregate has been that various economic theories indicate that the quantity of money should help determine aggregate demand, thereby influencing the price level and, possibly, real GDP and employment. Thus, central bank policymakers have believed that a relationship should exist between monetary aggregates and their inflation, real GDP, and employment objectives. Furthermore, values of monetary aggregates typically are known weekly. Finally, central banks clearly have the ability to influence monetary aggregates.

Nevertheless, central banks have had some difficulties using intermediate monetary targeting approaches. One problem has been that regulatory and technological changes have blurred the lines among various financial assets that function as money. In the United States, for instance, the Federal Reserve has redefined M1 or M2 every few years as new forms of money-like assets have emerged. The existence of more than one monetary aggregate is itself indicative of the problems in defining "money." Another problem that was particularly bothersome in the 1980s and early 1990s was a breakdown in the previously consistent relationship between the basic M1 and M2 aggregates and GDP. Furthermore, as we noted in Chapter 19, the advent of sweep accounts since the mid-1990s has significantly degraded the usefulness of the M1 aggregate.

Credit Aggregates Another quantitative financial target, which central banks in China and Russia have emphasized, is a *credit aggregate* target, which is a measure of the volume of lending. One type of credit aggregate is *aggregate credit,* or the total amount of all lending in an economy. A narrower credit aggregate is *total bank credit,* or total lending and securities holdings by banks. As you learned in Chapter 13, central banks can influence such measures of credit, because the expansion of bank lending accompanies the multiple expansion of bank deposit money. Thus, Fed policy instruments can affect total credit as well as the total quantity of money in circulation. Additionally, credit aggregates usually are straightforward to define and to measure, and credit data usually are observable weekly.

Credit aggregates, however, suffer from problems similar to those that monetary aggregates entail. In particular, relationships between credit measures and ultimate goals generally have been *at least* as tenuous as relationships between monetary aggregates and ultimate goals.

Interest Rates The most commonly used intermediate monetary policy target is the *price of credit,* or the nominal interest rate. Central banks can observe interest rates daily and often by the minute. In addition, central banks' policy actions can have clear-cut effects on nominal interest rates.

Interest rates and economic activity are not always closely related, however. While lower interest rates can spur capital investment and economic activity, increased income raises the demand for credit and pushes nominal interest rates upward. Hence, the relationship between nominal interest rates and real GDP is not always predictable. In addition, there are many interest rates that central banks could consider targeting, including interest rates on financial instruments with short and long maturities.

Nominal GDP In recent years many economists have proposed that *nominal gross domestic product (GDP)* be used as a target, even though nominal GDP data are not available much more frequently than observations of real GDP and the price level. The essential argument favoring targeting nominal GDP hinges on the fact that nominal GDP by definition is equal to real GDP times the GDP price deflator. There are a number of competing theories about how monetary policy influences the price level and real GDP, but this definitional relationship indicates that if a central bank wishes to stabilize real GDP and prices, then minimizing variations in the growth rate of nominal GDP would help contain volatility in either of these ultimate goal variables.

Exchange Rates   A number of central banks have used exchange rates as intermediate targets of monetary policy. This policy procedure has been particularly common in small economies open to cross-border trade and financial flows.

The rationale for exchange rate targeting is that in small countries buffeted by international events beyond their control, real GDP, employment, and inflation often depend on the exchange value of a nation's currency. Thus, central banks in these nations often conclude that their main task should be to keep the exchange rate at a level consistent with ultimate economic goals. As we shall discuss in Chapter 22, key issues then become how to determine the appropriate target for the exchange rate and what procedure to follow to keep the exchange rate close to this target level.

> **2. Why might a central bank use an intermediate monetary policy target?**
> Because of limitations on the availability of data on ultimate objectives and different interpretations of how monetary policy actions influence ultimate policy goals, central banks such as the Federal Reserve sometimes adopt an intermediate target. Such an intermediate target variable should be observable with greater frequency than ultimate goal variables, easy to measure, subject to influence through monetary policy actions, and closely related to ultimate policy objectives. Possible intermediate target variables include money and credit aggregates, interest rates, nominal GDP, and exchange rates.

Time Lags in Monetary Policy and the Case for Rules

As explained in the preceding section, the existence of information lags can be an important hindrance to a central bank's successful attainment of its ultimate policy goals. A related problem is the time that it takes central bank officials themselves to adjust their policies in response to changing circumstances. This forces policymakers to make a crucial decision that can have significant consequences: Should they alter their policies in response to each short-term change in the economy, or should they stand firm on a policy approach that they feel has the best chance of achieving their long-term goals? A key goal of the remainder of this chapter is to evaluate the trade-offs that central banks face when deciding which approach to adopt.

Policy time lags: The time intervals between the need for a counter-cyclical monetary policy action and the ultimate effects of that action on an economic variable.

A fundamental problem faced by any policymaker, whether it is a public utility, a college's board of trustees, or the Fed's Federal Open Market Committee, is the existence of **policy time lags.** These are the intervals between the need for a policy action and the ultimate effects of that action on an economic variable. Any policymaker faces three types of constraints on its ability to make the best policy choices that it can as quickly as such choices should be made:

1. In the presence of time lags, at any given point in time policymakers have limited information about current events.

2. Policymakers are fallible human beings who face constraints on their abilities to recognize and respond appropriately to changing circumstances, particularly in light of lags in their recognition of varying circumstances.

3. Policymakers are constrained by their lack of certainty about the timing and size of the effects of their policy actions.

Together, these constraints can slow policymakers' responses to episodes or incidents that may require speedy attention if policymakers are to attain their goals.

Time Lags in Monetary Policy

There are three types of time lags in monetary policymaking: the *recognition lag,* the *response lag,* and the *transmission lag.* Let's discuss each in turn before considering their broader consequences.

THE RECOGNITION LAG   As we have seen, a key problem central banks such as the Fed confront as they pursue their ultimate inflation, real GDP, employment, and external-balance objectives is limited current information. Not only are data on many economic variables available only on a monthly basis, but government statisticians often must revise these monthly computations as they discover measurement or calculation errors. Thus, Fed policymakers cannot always be certain that initially reported values for ultimate-goal variables are accurate. On some occasions, government statisticians have had to correct their computations of annualized GDP growth rates for given quarters by more than 50 percent!

Such data uncertainties complicate the lives of policymakers. To understand why, suppose that a nation's inflation rate increases significantly because of an unexpected rise in aggregate demand. If all other factors are unchanged, an appropriate central bank response is to cut back open market purchases, thereby reducing the growth of the supply of reserves to depository institutions. This policy action offsets the rise in aggregate demand and stems upward pressures on the price level. Given the data limitations that they face, however, central bank officials may not realize that inflation has begun to rise until a number of weeks have passed.

The time between the need for a monetary policy action and the recognition of that need is known as the **recognition lag.** As in this example, the recognition may be only a few weeks, but it can easily stretch to a few months. For instance, even if central bank officials notice the rise in the inflation rate, they may take some time to determine its causes. Some officials might speculate that temporary factors that have pushed up business costs are responsible, leading them to argue that the central bank should not take any action. Misleading signals such as this could hold up central bank action to contain aggregate-demand-induced inflation for several additional weeks.

Recognition lag: The interval that passes between the need for a countercyclical policy action and the recognition of this need by a policymaker.

THE RESPONSE LAG   Even after policymakers conclude that altered economic circumstances call for a policy change, they may take some time to decide on the appropriate action. The **response lag** is the time between the recognition of the need for a change in monetary policy and the actual implementation of a policy action.

In the United States, the response lag for monetary policy should not exceed six to eight weeks, which is the typical period between formal meetings of Federal Reserve policymakers. Indeed, the response lag could be even shorter, because Fed officials across the nation communicate each day. Nevertheless, a longer response lag is also possible if Fed officials are unable to reach a consensus about the best policy action to undertake. For instance, some Fed

Response lag: The interval between the recognition of a need for a countercyclical policy action and the actual implementation of the policy action.

officials might argue for a speedy and sizable response to a perceived increase in the inflation rate, while other officials argue for a more gradual, measured response. Such disagreements among Fed officials could delay policy actions, thereby significantly lengthening the monetary policy response lag.

Transmission lag: The interval that elapses between the implementation of an intended countercyclical policy and its ultimate effects on an economic variable.

THE TRANSMISSION LAG   Once implemented, a monetary policy action takes time to transmit its effects to overall economic activity. The time that passes before an implemented monetary policy exerts its effects on economic activity is the **transmission lag.** In earlier chapters, we have shifted schedules and discussed the effects of policy actions on real GDP or the price level without regard for the time it takes for such effects to occur. In fact, months may pass before the full effects of monetary policy actions are transmitted to ultimate policy goal variables. According to current estimates, the average length of the monetary policy transmission lag is roughly twelve months. Thus, as a result of the combined recognition, response, and transmission lags, well over a year may elapse between the initial need for a monetary policy action and that action's final effects on the economy.

Time Lags and the Case for Monetary Policy Rules

Time lags can pose a real problem for central banks. To see why, consider Figure 20-2. The curve labeled y^a in panel (a) shows the path that real GDP would follow in the *absence* of any policy actions. For simplicity, we assume that the anticipated path of real GDP is a relatively smooth business cycle. The curve labeled y^p depicts the central bank's *planned* path for the contributions of its policy actions to real GDP in light of its anticipation that real GDP in the absence of its policies will follow the path y^a.

SUCCESSFUL COUNTERCYCLICAL MONETARY POLICY   We assume that the central bank officials plan to pursue a *countercyclical* policy strategy by increasing their contributions to real GDP when they anticipate that real GDP will decline and reducing their contributions to real GDP when they expect it to rise.

At any given time, the actual level of real GDP in the presence of policy actions, denoted y, is the sum of y^a and y^p. Note that the figure assumes that monetary policymaking can add to total real GDP, at least in the short run. As we discussed in Chapter 18, the extent to which this occurs depends on the degree to which the public correctly anticipates policy actions. We shall assume, however, for purposes of an illustrative example that policy can make some contribution, and other diagrams in this chapter will mirror this assumption.

If the central bank successfully pursues its countercyclical policy strategy, the result is an actual path of real GDP, y, that is smoother than the anticipated real GDP path in the absence of policy actions, y^a. Thus, the central bank successfully dampens the business cycle.

HOW TIME LAGS CAN MAKE MONETARY POLICY DESTABILIZING   The same curves shown in panel (a) of Figure 20-2 appear as dashed curves in panel (b). The solid curves, however, depict actual paths that might arise in the presence of policy time lags if the central bank reacts to unexpected departures of real GDP from the path that it had anticipated. Panel (b) shows a temporary change in the path of real GDP in the absence of policy effects, denoted y^{a*}. We assume in this example that real GDP drops below the level that the central bank had anticipated beginning at a point in time denoted t_1. The path of real GDP without any policy effects then stays below its anticipated path until the time t_4, when it again returns to the anticipated path.

FIGURE 20-2
How Policy Time Lags Can Make Well-Intentioned Policy Destabilizing.

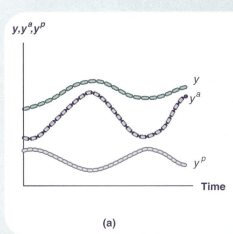

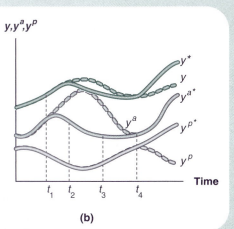

(a)   (b)

Panel (a) illustrates a possible situation in which policy actions help to stabilize real GDP over time. The path labeled y^a illustrates a hypothetical anticipated path for real GDP in the absence of policy actions. The path labeled y^p shows a planned countercyclical path for real GDP contributions of monetary policy, in which a policymaker reduces its contribution to real GDP as real GDP in the absence of policy is rising and increases its contribution to real GDP as real GDP in the absence of policy is declining. As a result, the path of total real GDP, y, is smoother than it would otherwise have been. Panel (b) shows the potential result of policy time lags. Here, the path of actual real GDP in the absence of policy, y^{a*}, falls below the path anticipated by the policymaker, y^a, beginning at time t_1. Because of the recognition lag, however, the policymaker fails to discover this has occurred until time t_2. The response lag slows the policymaker's response to this change until time t_3, and the transmission lag holds up the actual effects of the policy action until time t_4. By this time, however, real GDP in the absence of policy has returned to its predicted path once again, so the new policy contributions to real GDP are procyclical and destabilizing.

Visualizing the Effects of Time Lags   The time that passes between t_1 and t_2 is the time interval that elapses before the central bank realizes that the actual path of real GDP has fallen below the anticipated path. Thus, this period is the *recognition lag*. At time t_2, central bank officials have no way of knowing that in the absence of their policy contributions, real GDP will eventually return to the anticipated path at time t_4. Thus, in their effort to engage in countercyclical monetary policy, at time t_3 the officials decide to implement a policy action that increases the central bank's contribution to real GDP. The time that passes between t_2 and t_3 is the interval between the central bank's recognition of the need for a countercyclical policy change and the implementation of this intended change, or the *response lag*.

Finally, it takes time for the policy change to have an effect. In panel (b), by time t_4, the policy change finally begins to take effect following a *transmission lag* between t_3 and t_4. As a result, the contribution of monetary policy to real GDP increases. The actual path of policy contributions to real GDP, denoted y^{p*}, turns upward, whereas the central bank's *original* plan would have called for a reduction in policy contributions to real GDP to commence at time t_4. Yet t_4 is the point in time at which real GDP in the absence of policy's contribution has already *returned* to its anticipated path. In the end, the policy-influenced real GDP path, denoted $y*$, is the sum of the y^{a*} and y^{p*} curves. As you can see, in this example the well-meaning effort of the central bank to stabilize real GDP actually ends up yielding a path of real GDP that is *more variable* than it would have been if the central bank had not reacted to the temporary fall in real GDP.

Thus, in this example, even though the central bank's effort to conduct a countercyclical policy is well intended,

Time lags in recognition, response, and transmission can end up producing a *procyclical* monetary policy.

The central bank would have come closer to its objective of smoothing the business cycle if it had stuck to its original planned policy path, y^p.

Discretion versus Rules   Nobel Prize–winning economist Milton Friedman argued a half-century ago that situations such as the one illustrated in panel (b) of Figure 20-2 can be relatively common. He argued that despite their good intentions in conducting countercyclical policies, central banks nevertheless may *add* to cyclical real GDP fluctuations via their well-meaning attempts to dampen natural cycles. This, Friedman contended, is a basic defect of **discretionary policymaking,** or undertaking monetary policy responses on an *ad hoc* basis. In the presence of lengthy and variable policy time lags, Friedman concluded, discretionary policymaking can more often than not end up destabilizing economic activity.

For this reason, Friedman suggested that central banks adopt **policy rules.** These are policy strategies to which central banks *commit* themselves. Friedman recommended that central banks should pursue these strategies no matter what events occur. In his view, standing by a policy rule will, on average, prevent unintentional destabilizing actions by central banks themselves. With the simplest type of policy rule, a central bank neither adds to nor subtracts from its contributions to real GDP. For instance, the central bank would strive to maintain a constant growth rate of depository institution reserves, the monetary base, or a monetary aggregate. (Some economists argue that the Fed should use a mix of rules and discretion, and the Fed's statements often appear to support the view that it already uses this policymaking approach; see *What Happens When What the Fed Says Is Almost As Important As What It Does?*)

Discretionary policymaking: The act of responding to economic events as they occur, rather than in ways the policymaker might previously have planned in the absence of those events.

Policy rule: A commitment to a fixed strategy no matter what happens to other economic variables.

What Happens When...   **What the Fed Says Is Almost As Important As What It Does?**

In January 2002, the Fed made the broad announcement that its monetary policymaking would, until stated otherwise, be intended to be "accommodative." In August 2003, the Fed amended this statement to say that monetary policymaking would be accommodative for a "considerable period." By January 2004, the Fed indicated that it could be "patient" in deciding whether to continue to be accommodative. Finally, in May 2004, the Fed said that it planned to end its accommodative monetary policy approach at a "measured" pace.

Throughout this period, the Fed's chosen words such as *accommodative, considerable period, patient,* and *measured* were featured in headlines of media stories about its monetary policies. When the Fed first used the term *accommodative* in 2002, a swift decrease in U.S. market interest rates was in progress. Thus, it became apparent to all that the Fed intended this word to imply a commitment to relatively high money growth and low interest rates. Then, in 2003 the use of the qualifier *considerable period* indicated that the Fed planned to maintain a commitment to its "accommodative" policy approach.

Nevertheless, by using the word *patient* in early 2004, the Fed signaled that its commitment to high money growth and low interest rates might be nearing an end. At its discretion, the Fed decided a few months later to gradually embark on a new commitment to more constrained money growth and higher interest rates. Hence, it used the word *measured* to describe the pace at which it intended to push up market interest rates.

FOR CRITICAL ANALYSIS: What do you suppose the Fed anticipated that it would gain, in the short run, from its efforts between 2002 and 2004 to convince households and firms that interest rates would remain low for a "considerable period"? (Hint: How do consumers and businesses respond to low interest rates, and why might the Fed have regarded such a response as desirable in a period when real GDP growth was sluggish?)

3. What are policy time lags, and how might they cause well-meaning monetary policymakers to destabilize the economy? There are three types of policy time lags: (1) the recognition lag, which is the time between the need for a monetary policy action and a central bank's realization of that need; (2) the response lag, which is the interval between the recognition of the need for an action and the actual implementation of a policy change; and (3) the transmission lag, which is the time between the implementation of a policy action and the action's ultimate effects on the economy. All told, these lags can sum to well over a year in duration. They can also lead a central bank that responds to events as they occur to enact a policy change that is procyclical, thereby destabilizing the economy. This is one argument in favor of monetary policy rules, or fixed commitments to specific monetary policy strategies.

Discretionary Monetary Policy and Inflation

In addition to an argument based on policy time lags, another argument against policy discretion has been developed by Robert Barro of Harvard University and David Gordon of Clemson University. It focuses on the likely tendency of a discretionary monetary policymaker to enact policies that are inflationary.

A Monetary Policy Game and a Theory of Inflation

In recent years, economists have applied *game theory*—the theory of strategic interactions among individuals or institutions—to issues relating to central banking. Barro and Gordon have applied game theory to the problem of rules versus discretion in monetary policymaking. You need not have studied game theory to understand their essential argument, however. All you need to understand are concepts that we have already discussed in earlier chapters.

EQUILIBRIUM REAL GDP AND THE PRICE LEVEL AND ULTIMATE GOALS OF MONETARY POLICY Figure 20-3 on the next page illustrates the situation that Barro and Gordon consider. Nominal wages are contracted at the level W_1^c. Once the nominal wage is fixed, then the short-run aggregate supply schedule, $y^s(W_1^c)$, slopes upward, as we discussed in Chapter 18.

In the long run, when workers and firms are fully informed, nominal wages adjust equiproportionately with price changes. Thus, the long-run aggregate supply schedule, y_{LR}^s, is vertical at the economy's current long-run level of real GDP, denoted y_1.

Finally, the aggregate demand schedule, y_1^d, slopes downward. A possible equilibrium is point *A*, where all three schedules cross at the equilibrium price level P_1. Hence, point *A* depicts a situation in which the short-run equilibrium and the long-run equilibrium coincide; here the contract wage workers and firms have negotiated happens to match the nominal wage that would have arisen if the labor market had equilibrated the demand for labor with the supply of labor.

In addition, Figure 20-3 also includes a level of real GDP denoted y^*. This is the ultimate real GDP objective of the nation's central bank. A key assumption is that this target level of real GDP is *greater* than the long-run level of real GDP, y_1. The reason is that y^* is the **capacity output** for the economy, or the real GDP that firms could produce if labor and other productive factors were employed to their utmost. One factor that can cause the long-run level of real

Capacity output: The real GDP that the economy could produce if all resources were employed to their utmost.

FIGURE 20-3
Equilibrium Real GDP and the Price Level and Policy Goals.

A full long-run equilibrium in the market for real GDP arises at the point where the aggregate demand, short-run aggregate supply, and long-run aggregate supply schedules cross. At this point, denoted point A, the long-run level of real GDP is equal to y_1, and the equilibrium price level is equal to P_1. The capacity output level is y^*. This is a level of real GDP that workers and firms could produce but do not at the present time because

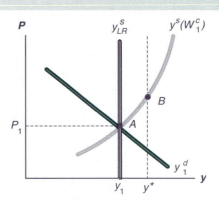

other factors, such as income taxes and costs of regulation, reduce the long-run level of real GDP below the capacity level. The basic theory of

inflationary policy proposes that policymakers would like to raise real GDP toward capacity output but would also prefer not to increase the price level.

GDP to lie below its full-capacity level is income taxes. By assessing marginal tax rates on workers' incomes, governments induce workers to supply fewer labor services than they would otherwise have desired. As a result, firms produce less real output of final goods and services than they would otherwise have planned to produce in the absence of income taxes.

Another reason that the long-run level of real GDP usually is below the capacity output level is the presence of government regulations. For instance, governments commonly institute licensing requirements that restrict entry into various industries, thereby restraining their production of goods and services. Consequently, government regulations can reduce real GDP relative to what it would have been in the absence of regulations.

In addition to the capacity output goal y^*, the central bank has one other ultimate objective: to minimize the inflation rate. Because the primary way a central bank can influence real GDP in the short run is through monetary policy actions that change the position of the aggregate demand schedule, however, the central bank faces a trade-off between its two goals. An increase in aggregate demand from point A in Figure 20-3 would cause a rightward movement along the short-run aggregate supply schedule, thereby raising real GDP toward the target y^* at point B. Yet a rise in aggregate demand would also cause the price level to rise, resulting in higher inflation; hence, remaining at the current equilibrium point A would be more desirable from the standpoint of the central bank's inflation objective. Consequently, a central bank that cares about both real GDP and inflation goals typically would desire for aggregate demand to rise somewhat from point A, so as to increase real GDP. How much the central bank will be willing to expand aggregate demand will depend on the relative weights that the central bank assigns to its two objectives.

MONETARY POLICY DISCRETION AND INFLATION   Figure 20-3 describes a situation in which there are two sets of "players" in the monetary policy game. On the one hand, to determine the setting for the contract wage W^c, workers and firms must make their best rational forecast of the price level given their understanding of the policy goals of the central bank and the economic situation that the central bank confronts. On the other hand, the central bank must decide what action it should take to alter aggregate demand given its understanding of how workers and firms determine the contract wage.

Figure 20-4 depicts four *potential* outcomes that might arise from the interaction between workers and firm managers, who set the contract wage and thereby determine the position of the aggregate supply schedule, and the central bank, which chooses a monetary policy action that determines the position of the aggregate demand schedule. The four potential outcomes of this interaction are points A, B, C, and D. Let's consider each in turn.

Point A is the same initial equilibrium point that we discussed in Figure 20-3. Because it is a long-run equilibrium point, the contract wage W_1^c reflects a correct expectation by workers and firms that the price level will be equal to P_1. Hence, at this initial point workers and firms produce the long-run level of real GDP.

The Incentive to Raise Aggregate Demand   Nevertheless, the central bank wishes to raise real GDP above the long-run level, y_1, toward the capacity level, y^*. Thus, the central bank has an incentive to embark on a monetary policy action to raise aggregate demand from y_1^d to y_2^d in an effort to induce a short-run rise in real GDP, at point B. As noted earlier, a central bank would not try to push real GDP all the way to y^*, because this would entail greater inflation. Point B, therefore, represents a compromise outcome for the central bank in light of the trade-off it faces: real GDP would rise *toward* the capacity target at the cost of *some* inflation.

Because we assume that workers and firms know the central bank's goals, however, they will not let the point B outcome occur. At point B, the price level would be higher than workers and firms anticipated when setting the contract wage W_1^c. Hence, the real wage that workers would earn at point B would be lower than they had bargained for, and real GDP would exceed the long-run level that firms desire to produce. Point B, therefore, cannot be an equilibrium point that could arise in the monetary policy game. It would be inconsistent with the contracting strategy of workers and firms.

FIGURE 20-4
Potential and Equilibrium Outcomes of a Monetary Policy Game.

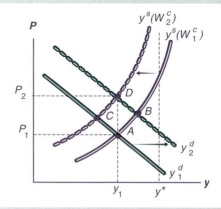

If the current equilibrium for the economy is point A and the central bank's goals are to raise real GDP toward the capacity output level y^* but to keep inflation low, then splitting the difference between these conflicting objectives requires inducing a rise in aggregate demand, to point B. But if workers realize that prices will rise, they will bargain for higher contract wages, which shifts the aggregate supply schedule leftward. This means that if the central bank were to ignore the temptation to raise aggregate demand, the result would be higher prices and lower real GDP at point C. To avoid this, the central bank feels pressure to raise aggregate demand as workers expect. Therefore, the final equilibrium is at point D, with unchanged real GDP but a higher price level.

The Public's Response   Instead, workers and firms will recognize that the central bank has an incentive to shift the aggregate demand schedule from y_1^d to y_2^d, and they respond by raising their price expectation and negotiating a higher contract wage, W_2^c. This would cause the aggregate supply schedule to shift leftward, from $y^s(W_1^c)$ to $y^s(W_2^c)$. The result is point D in Figure 20-4. Point D is consistent with the contracting strategy of workers and firms, because at this point they have chosen the contract wage optimally, taking into account the behavior they expect from the central bank. In addition, point D is consistent with the central bank's strategy, which is to raise aggregate demand in an attempt to increase real GDP while keeping inflation low (even though, after the fact, the central bank would not succeed in its effort). Consequently, in contrast to point B, point D *could* be a possible equilibrium in the monetary policy game.

Given that the central bank will fail to expand real GDP toward the capacity goal, it might seem logical to suppose that the central bank would recognize its inability to raise real GDP and commit itself to leaving the aggregate demand schedule at the position y_1^d. Such a commitment would constitute a policy *rule* in that the central bank would avoid responding to its incentive to try to raise real GDP in the short run. If workers and firms do *not* believe that the central bank would follow through on this commitment, however, then they would still raise their price expectation and negotiate an increase in the contract wage. This would cause the aggregate supply schedule to shift from $y^s(W_1^c)$ to $y^s(W_2^c)$. Thus, if the central bank followed through with a commitment to leave aggregate demand at y_1^d, point C would result. Point C, however, would be inconsistent with the central bank's strategy, because at this point inflation occurs and real GDP falls even *further* below the capacity objective. Therefore, point C could not be an equilibrium point in the monetary policy game.

Under a special circumstance, one other equilibrium point could arise in the monetary policy game. This is point A. *If* the central bank would commit to maintaining the aggregate demand schedule at y_1^d, and *if* workers and firms could be induced to believe that the central bank would honor that commitment, then point A would be maintained as the final equilibrium point. There would be no inflation, the central bank would accept its inability to raise real GDP toward the capacity level, and workers and firms would be satisfied at the long-run level of real GDP.

The Problem of Central Bank Credibility

Figure 20-5 is another version of Figure 20-4 that displays only the two possible equilibrium points of the monetary policy game, points A and D, so that we can focus our attention solely on these two potential outcomes. Point A would result from a commitment to a monetary policy rule, so it denotes a *commitment policy equilibrium*. Point D, in contrast, arises from an inability or unwillingness by the central bank to make such a commitment. Point D, in other words, is a point of *discretionary policy equilibrium*. Thus, these two points constitute the alternative outcomes that would result from following a policy rule or pursuing discretionary policymaking.

Policy credibility: The believability of a commitment by a central bank or governmental authority to follow specific policy rules.

CREDIBILITY   The key determinant of which equilibrium point actually occurs is **policy credibility,** or the believability of the central bank's willingness and ability to commit to a monetary rule. If a central bank is willing and able to follow through on such a commitment, then workers and firms can believe that it will stick to its rule. The initial point A will remain the equilibrium of the policy game, and the economy will remain at the long-run level of real

FIGURE 20-5
The Inflation Bias of Discretionary Monetary Policy.

Point A represents a noninflationary equilibrium point of the monetary policy game that arises only if the central bank can make a credible commitment to zero inflation. In the absence of a credible zero-inflation commitment, point D is the equilibrium point that arises from the monetary policy game, as discussed in Figure 20-4. Hence, the increase in the price level resulting from a movement from point A to point D is an *inflation bias* resulting from discretionary monetary policy.

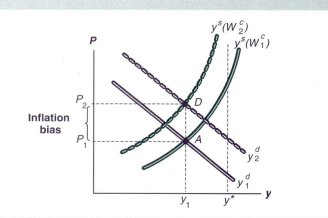

GDP without experiencing inflation. But if workers and firms doubt the central bank's willingness to honor its commitment, or if they feel that the central bank is willing but unable to do so, then this lack of policy credibility will lead to an equilibrium at point D.

Policy credibility is difficult to achieve in the setting that we have described because of the **time-inconsistency problem** that exists in our example. This problem is that although commitment to a policy rule yields zero inflation, as at point A in Figure 20-5, this commitment is inconsistent with the strategies of workers and firms if the central bank can alter its policy strategy at a later time. In our example, after workers and firms have committed to a contract wage, the central bank could attempt to expand aggregate demand, which would benefit the central bank but not the workers and firms themselves (point B in Figure 20-4). To protect themselves against such an alteration in policy, workers and firms increase the contract wage, thereby forcing even a central bank that might otherwise prefer to stick to a rule to expand aggregate demand to avoid a decline in real GDP (point C in Figure 20-4). These interactions between workers and firms and the central bank result in an equilibrium at point D in Figure 20-5.

Time-inconsistency problem: The policy problem that can result if a policymaker has the ability, at a future time, to alter its strategy in a way that is inconsistent both with the desires and strategies of private individuals and with its own initially announced intentions.

THE INFLATION BIAS   The result of the time-inconsistency problem and the lack of policy credibility is a higher price level at point D as compared with point A. Economists call the difference between the new price level, P_2, at point D and the initial price level, P_1, at point A the **inflation bias** arising from discretionary monetary policy. This is a bias toward inflation that exists from the ability of a central bank to determine its policies in a discretionary manner when there is a time-inconsistency problem and a lack of policy credibility. The inflation bias of discretionary policy is a second reason—along with the potential for discretionary policy to be destabilizing in the presence of time lags—that many economists argue that society should find ways to dissuade central banks from using discretionary policies by making monetary policy rules credible. How society might accomplish this is our next topic.

Inflation bias: The tendency for the economy to experience continuing inflation as a result of the time-inconsistency problem of discretionary monetary policy.

4. Why is monetary policy credibility a crucial factor in maintaining low inflation?   If people establish nominal contracts, then a monetary policymaker has an incentive to enact policies that will raise aggregate demand in an effort to expand real GDP toward its capacity level. Consequently, workers and firms negotiating wage contracts will be unlikely to believe a central bank's stated intention to limit inflation, which would reduce the purchasing power of workers' wages. As a result, workers and firms will negotiate higher wages, thereby reducing aggregate supply and causing real GDP to fall in the absence of higher aggregate demand. This pressures the central bank into raising aggregate demand and thereby creating an inflation bias. The only way for a central bank to avoid this inflation bias would be for its commitment to low inflation to be credible to workers and firms.

Making Monetary Policy Rules Credible

It is one thing to argue that potential gains can be obtained from sticking with a monetary policy rule. It is another thing altogether to establish a mechanism for attaining such an outcome in the face of a time-inconsistency problem.

As you have learned in earlier chapters, money growth is a key determinant of the inflation rate. Consequently, this is the natural starting point for most discussions of how to reduce the inflation bias arising from discretionary policy. Such discussions focus on finding a way to induce a central bank to follow a policy rule and to make such a rule credible.

Constitutional Limits on Monetary Policy

Some economists, such as Milton Friedman of the Hoover Institution at Stanford University, have suggested that one way to eliminate the inflation bias would be to constrain central banks directly. This might be accomplished in the United States by amending the U.S. Constitution to require a constant annual growth rate for the quantity of money. Thus, this approach would seek to establish the credibility of a monetary policy rule by legally *requiring* the Federal Reserve, or more broadly the U.S. government, to pursue the rule.

A key problem with the constitutional amendment idea is determining the appropriate numerical rule for money growth. After all, the U.S. economy's real GDP growth has varied from decade to decade. Whereas a *3* percent money growth rule might have been consistent with zero inflation in the 1960s, a 2 percent money growth rule might be preferable for the current decade.

Achieving Monetary Policy Credibility by Establishing a Reputation

In the absence of such radical institutional changes, how could a central bank act on its own to make its commitments to low inflation more credible? One approach might be to establish and maintain a reputation as a "tough inflation fighter." To understand how this could enable a central bank to reduce inflation, refer back to Figure 20-4 on page 453. Recall that if the central bank honors a commitment not to raise aggregate demand in pursuit of short-term gains in real GDP but is not believed by workers and firms, then the result will be higher inflation and reduced real GDP, which is shown in Figure 20-4 by a movement from point *A* to point

C. If the central bank cares only about today's outcome, it will never want point *C* to occur. But if the central bank wishes to establish its reputation as an inflation fighter, then it might be willing to let the economy experience lower real GDP at point *C* in Figure 20-4. Henceforth, its promises not to increase aggregate demand might then be credible to workers and firms.

A number of economists argue that this was what the Fed did in 1979 following the significant rise in inflation that Figure 20-6 shows took place during the preceding years. According to these economists, in 1979 and 1980 the Fed held firm to a commitment to keep aggregate demand from increasing. At first, workers and firms did not find this commitment to be credible. A sharp recession then occurred in 1980 and 1981, as a steady rise in nominal wages pushed up business costs and resulted in a reduction in real GDP—just as the movement from point *A* to point *C* depicts in Figure 20-4. As a result, in the years that followed, the Fed's commitment to lower inflation was credible, and actual inflation rates fell, as shown in Figure 20-6.

Appointing a "Conservative" Central Banker

It is easier for a central bank official to establish a reputation for being "tough" in the fight against inflation if it is well known that the official truly dislikes inflation. Some observers of the Fed's fight against inflation in the 1980s have concluded that one reason that the anti-inflation effort was so successful was President Carter's 1979 appointment of Paul Volcker, a Fed official whose dislike for inflation was well known, as the chair of the Fed's Board of Governors. The Fed's inflation-fighting reputation then was maintained, these observers argue, when President Reagan appointed Alan Greenspan, another known hawk on inflation, to that position.

The theory of the discretionary inflation bias illustrated in Figure 20-5 on page 455 indicates that appointing anti-inflation central bank officials may indeed be a way to reduce the inflation bias. A key factor influencing the size of the inflation bias is how much central bank officials dislike inflation relative to how much they desire to try to raise real GDP toward its capacity level. Thus, appointing a **conservative central banker,** or an individual who dislikes inflation more than the average member of society, is one way to reduce the size of the inflation bias. Such an individual would choose to expand aggregate demand by a small amount, because a rise in aggregate demand is inflationary.

Conservative central banker: A central bank official who dislikes inflation more than the average citizen in society and who therefore is less willing to induce discretionary increases in the quantity of money in an effort to achieve short-run increases in real GDP.

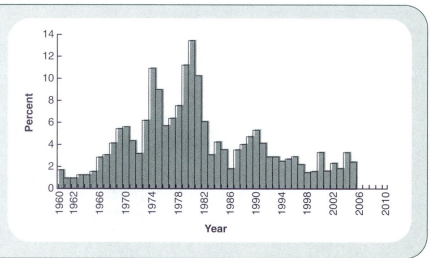

FIGURE 20-6
Annual Inflation Rates in the United States.

This figure plots annual rates of change in the consumer price index. Although average inflation has been lower since the 1980s, as compared with the end of the 1960s and the 1970s, inflation nonetheless has occurred in every single year.

SOURCES: *Economic Report of the President,* 2005; *Economic Indicators* (various issues); authors' estimates.

Central Banker Contracts

Central banker contract: A legally binding agreement between a government and a central bank official that holds the official responsible for the nation's inflation performance.

In recent years, several economists, including Carl Walsh of the University of California at Santa Cruz, have proposed establishing explicit **central banker contracts.** These are legally binding agreements between a government and central bank officials that provide for the officials to be punished and/or rewarded based on the central bank's inflation performance. Research by Walsh and others has indicated that such contracts could nearly eliminate the inflation bias of discretionary monetary policy.

In principle, a central banker contract could also reward an official with a bonus or a higher salary for maintaining low and stable prices. Although some think it is unseemly to pay central bank officials bonuses for doing the job that they are supposed to be doing in the first place, proponents of such schemes argue that this might be a small cost for society to incur in exchange for reduced inflation.

Central Bank Independence

The idea behind establishing central banker contracts is that they would make central bank officials more *accountable* for their performances. Using the contracts would not, however, rule out granting central bank officials considerable *independence* to conduct monetary policy as they see fit, while continuing to hold them responsible if inflation gets out of hand.

Indeed, many economists argue that central bank independence may be the key to maintaining low inflation rates. After all, a conservative central banker cannot establish a reputation as a tough inflation fighter if he or she is hamstrung by legal requirements to try to achieve other objectives as well, such as a low unemployment rate or a high growth rate for real GDP. Furthermore, even if a central banker contract holds an official accountable for a nation's inflation performance, achieving the required performance may be difficult unless the official has sufficient independence to pursue this objective in the most efficient manner.

Central bank independence has two dimensions: *political independence,* or the ability to reach decisions free of influence by the government and other outside individuals or groups, and *economic independence,* or the ability to control its own budget or to resist efforts by the government to induce the central bank to make loans to the government or to provide other forms of direct support to government policies. Hence, we can reach the following conclusion:

> **A truly independent central bank would be both politically and economically independent. Political independence would permit the central bank to conduct the policies that it believes to be best in the long run, without the influence of short-term political pressures. Economic independence would give the central bank the budgetary freedom to conduct these policies.**

5. How might monetary policy credibility be achieved? One possible approach to achieving credibility would be to make it illegal for central banks to allow inflation to exceed a specified rate. Alternatively, central bank officials could be signed to contracts that condition their employment or salaries on their inflation performance. To help ensure that central banks would be less likely to institute inflationary policies, governments could appoint conservative central bankers who are known to have a distaste for inflation. Finally, central bankers can gain credibility by permitting real GDP to fall in the near term as a way to convince workers of their commitment to low future inflation. This would require granting central banks sufficient independence.

Central Bank Independence: International Evidence

To evaluate the real-world effects of granting greater independence to central banks, economists have developed measures of the extent of central bank independence that take into account both its economic and its political dimensions. Then they have looked for relationships between these measures and other economic variables.

Any one nation's historical experience with central banking typically is limited. After all, each nation has only one central bank, and many countries have not changed the structures of their central banks in decades. Consequently, economists have evaluated the experiences of many countries.

Evidence Favoring Central Bank Independence

The basic theory of monetary policy discretion indicates that the degree of central bank independence might be related to a nation's inflation performance. Thus, initial studies of the economic effects of central bank independence began by examining its potential role in affecting the behavior of inflation.

CENTRAL BANK INDEPENDENCE AND INFLATION   International evidence that central bank independence is related to good inflation performance has been provided by economists Alberto Alesina and Lawrence Summers, both of Harvard University. This evidence is summarized in panels (a) and (b) of Figure 20-7. In each panel, an index of central bank independence is measured along the horizontal axis of the diagram. An increase in this index indicates that a nation's central bank is more politically and/or economically independent. In the diagram in panel (a), average annual inflation rates between the mid-1950s and the late 1980s are measured along the vertical axis. The result is an *inverse relationship* between

FIGURE 20-7
Central Bank Independence, Average Inflation, and Inflation Variability in Major Developed Nations.

As shown in panel (a), nations with more independent central banks, such as Germany, Switzerland, and the United States, have experienced lower average inflation rates as compared with countries with less independent central banks. Panel

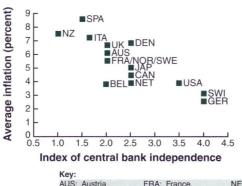

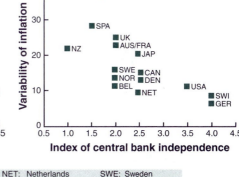

Key:

AUS: Austria	FRA: France	NET: Netherlands	SWE: Sweden
BEL: Belgium	GER: Germany	NOR: Norway	SWI: Switzerland
CAN: Canada	ITA: Italy	NZ: New Zealand	UK: United Kingdom
DEN: Denmark	JAP: Japan	SPA: Spain	USA: United States

(b) shows that nations with more independent central banks also have experienced less variable rates of inflation.

SOURCE: Alberto Alesina and Lawrence Summers, "Central Bank Independence and Macroeconomic Performance," *Journal of Money, Credit, and Banking* (May 1993): 151–162.

central bank independence and average inflation, meaning that countries with more independent central banks tend to experience lower average inflation. Note that the two nations with the most independent central banks during this period, Germany and Switzerland, had average inflation rates of around 3 percent. The two nations with the least independent central banks, in contrast, which were New Zealand (which since has opted for a more independent central bank) and Spain (which since has joined the European Monetary Union), experienced average inflation rates that were more than twice as high.

Panel (b) of Figure 20-7 measures the variance of inflation along the vertical axis. Again there is an inverse relationship: countries with more independent central banks tend to experience less inflation volatility. Thus, increased central bank independence tends to yield more price stability as well as lower average inflation.

DOES CENTRAL BANK INDEPENDENCE AFFECT REAL GDP? Some critics of granting central banks considerable independence have argued that the result could be worsened economic performance. If central banks concentrate too much attention on inflation, the critics argue, they will fail to smooth out business cycles. As a result, real GDP growth might be reduced.

Figure 20-8 provides some evidence about this issue. It plots average real GDP growth rates and the variability of these growth rates relative to an index of central bank independence for sixty countries. There is no apparent effect of central bank independence on either average GDP growth or its variability.

Some Potential Problems with Central Bank Independence

An implication of Figures 20-7 and 20-8 is that central bank independence might be a "no-lose proposition." That is, it appears to be possible to reduce the average level and variability of inflation without any apparent effects on the average level or variability of real GDP growth. These implications of the data convinced a number of countries to grant more independence

On the Web

Is it possible to keep track of what is going on at most of the world's central banks? You can do this by going to the home page of the Bank for International Settlements (**http://www.bis.org**) and clicking on "Links to Central Banks." Here, you will find links to the Web sites of many central banks.

FIGURE 20-8
Central Bank Independence, Average GDP Growth, and Variability of GDP Growth.

This figure shows that average real GDP growth and the standard deviation of real GDP growth for a large number of countries do not appear to be systematically related to an index of central bank independence.

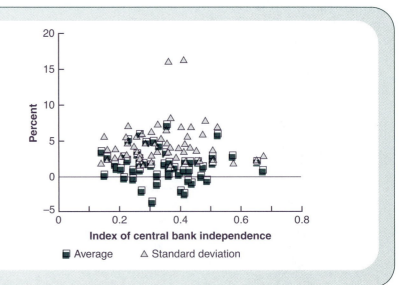

SOURCE: Carl Walsh, "Is There a Cost to Having an Independent Central Bank?" Federal Reserve Bank of San Francisco *Weekly Letter,* No. 94-05, February 4, 1994.

to their central banks. Recent examples include Japan, Mexico, and Pakistan. The evidence also induced the nations that joined the European Monetary Union in 1999 to grant considerable independence to the European Central Bank.

It remains to be seen, however, whether central bank independence is a cure-all for high and variable inflation. In spite of the apparent positive effects that greater central bank independence appears to have had in some parts of the world, there are good reasons to take a cautious view on the idea that it is a remedy for the world's inflationary ills.

CENTRAL BANK INDEPENDENCE ISN'T REALLY A "FREE LUNCH"   One of the first things you learn in an economics principles course is that there is no such thing as a "free lunch." To obtain an item, people typically must give up something in exchange. There is growing evidence that the same is true of central bank independence.

As Figure 20-9 illustrates, a possible by-product of central bank independence is that a given reduction in the inflation rate may cause a greater proportionate decline in the real GDP of a country with a relatively more independent central bank. There are two possible reasons for this effect. One is that because the inflation rate tends to be lower in countries with more independent central banks, the general level of prices naturally rises less rapidly in response to an increase in real GDP. This means that the short-run aggregate supply schedule is likely to be shallower in a nation with a more independent central bank. As a result, any given decline in inflation induces a larger short-run reduction in real GDP, holding all other factors unchanged.

In addition, because inflation variability is lower in nations with more independent central banks, people have less incentive to alter the terms of their employment contracts as often. Thus, to the extent that such contracts exist, they will keep nominal wages unchanged for longer periods. This also contributes to the shallower short-run aggregate supply schedule for a nation with an independent central bank.

Consequently, the positive effects that may result from greater central bank independence—lower and less variable inflation—may have spillover effects that can influence the

---

FIGURE 20-9
Central Bank Independence and the Inflation-Output Trade-off.

Estimates of the extent to which real GDP varies with inflation are plotted along the vertical axis of this figure. There appears to be a positive relationship between these estimates and the degree of central bank independence. This implies that a given reduction in the inflation rate may induce a greater proportionate decline in real GDP for a country that has a relatively more independent central bank.

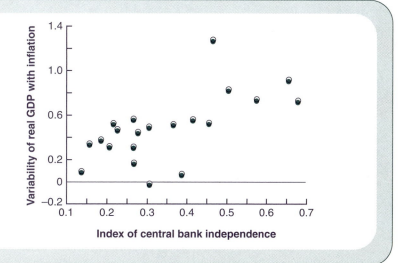

SOURCE: Carl Walsh, "Output-Inflation Tradeoffs and Central Bank Independence," Federal Reserve Bank of San Francisco *Weekly Letter*, No. 95-31, September 22, 1995.

extent to which real GDP responds to changes in the inflation rate. A fall in inflation could induce a larger decrease in real GDP in a nation that has granted its central bank greater independence than in a nation with a less independent central bank. As a result, a relatively independent central bank may nonetheless face a problem in trying to reduce inflation: a relatively larger decrease in real GDP.

Of course, this potential effect works in reverse as well. With a shallower aggregate supply curve, higher inflation causes a greater relative increase in real GDP. For this reason, greater central bank independence has the interesting effect of increasing the short-term benefit of raising inflation. Thus, an independent central bank operated by officials who care about real GDP actually could face a greater temptation to push up the inflation rate in an effort to induce an increase in real GDP. This might make households and firms worry about whether even an independent central bank will hold inflation down. At least in theory, therefore, central bank independence does not necessarily make central banks more credible.

GREATER CENTRAL BANK INDEPENDENCE MAY NOT BENEFIT ALL COUNTRIES   Following the initial publication of the evidence, summarized in Figures 20-7 and 20-8, that increased central bank independence can have inflation benefits without affecting real GDP, other economists conducted more studies. In particular, some economists examined larger sets of countries including less developed and emerging economies not examined in the earlier research.

As Figure 20-10 indicates, when less developed and emerging economies are included, the implications of central bank independence become less clear-cut. Average inflation does not necessarily appear to be lower as central banks in these nations are granted greater independence. Indeed, some studies have found hints of a *positive* relationship between central bank independence and inflation in less developed and emerging economies.

Such studies have led a number of economists to conclude that there is more to the story than central bank independence alone. It may be that greater central bank independence can have beneficial inflation effects only if certain preconditions are already satisfied. These may

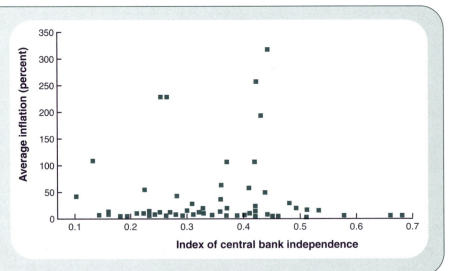

FIGURE 20-10
Central Bank Independence and Average Inflation for a Large Set of Countries.

When less developed and emerging economies are included in studies of central bank independence and inflation, it becomes less certain that there is a relationship between these variables.

include having in place a system of well-defined property rights, bankruptcy rules, judicial adjudication, and the like, so that the ill effects of inflation are apparent to all owners of capital and other productive resources. Many less developed and emerging economies lack these characteristics, which are commonplace in developed nations. This may help to explain why the inflation-reduction gains that developed nations experience from increased central bank independence do not appear to be shared by other countries. (The fact that many less developed nations have less independent central banks may help to explain why greater openness to imports and exports may reduce inflation more in these nations than in highly developed countries; see the *Global Focus: Are Openness to International Trade and Central Bank Independence Substitutes for Reducing Inflation?*)

CAN ECONOMISTS REALLY MEASURE CENTRAL BANK INDEPENDENCE?

Economists construct indexes of central bank independence, such as those used in Figures 20-7 through 20-10, by assigning numerical weights to such factors as the degree of independence that central banks have to buy and sell bonds; to lend to banks, the government, or others; and to regulate their nation's banking system. Many studies also factor in whether central bank officials are politically appointed, the lengths of their terms of office, and so on. Typically, the numerical weight assigned to a factor such as the length of an official's term of office is arbitrary, as are the cutoff points for weighting these terms. For instance, one study

GLOBAL
Focus

Are Openness to International Trade and Central Bank Independence Substitutes for Reducing Inflation?

Economists have recognized for some time that nations that are more open to international trade tend to have lower inflation rates. They have come up with a number of hypotheses that might explain why this is so. For instance, greater ability to import and export factors of production might help input prices adjust more nearly equally to movements in output prices. This might make the short-run aggregate supply schedule less shallow, reduce a central bank's ability to try to boost real GDP in the short run, and thereby

reduce the inflation bias of discretionary monetary policy. In addition, greater openness to international trade might also promote increased competition in domestic markets that restrains the ability of domestic firms to raise prices as rapidly as they would if they were protected from foreign rivals.

Since the late 1980s, however, the inverse relationship between openness to international trade and inflation rates has become less apparent for the most developed countries, even though it still seems to exist for less developed nations. Recent research by Joseph Daniels and Farrokh Nourzad, both of Marquette University, and one of the authors of this text suggests one possible explanation for this observation. The most developed nations, including most recently New Zealand, the United Kingdom, and nations in the European Monetary Union, have

granted their central banks considerable independence. The greater central bank independence in these countries has accounted for much of the reduction in their inflation rates, leaving less potential for inflation-reducing gains from greater openness to international trade. In contrast, central bank independence is not as common in less developed nations. Thus, these countries have much more to gain, in terms of inflation reductions, from opening their borders to more international trade.

FOR CRITICAL ANALYSIS: Why might nations whose residents and governments desire to *eliminate* inflation regard central bank independence and openness to international trade as *complementary* ways of attaining this inflation goal?

might say that a term of more than ten years deserves a relatively high independence weight, while another might give a similar weight to terms in excess of eight years.

Economists may even disagree about what factors really make a central bank more independent. To some, considerable independence in regulating private banks counts as a positive factor. Others take the opposite view, seeing this as a way that a central bank might be exposed to pressures to avoid contractions that could be harmful to the national banking system.

James Forder of Balliol College in England has found that studies of the effects of central bank independence may be highly influenced by these subjective choices. Thus, the conclusions of many of these studies may not be very robust—that is, they may be very sensitive to slight changes in the ways that economists have chosen to measure central bank independence.

For the moment, however, most economists remain convinced that greater central bank independence has the beneficial effect of lowering average inflation and reducing the variability of inflation. The future experience of countries that have made their central banks more independent in recent years may provide some stronger evidence one way or the other concerning the pros and cons of central bank independence.

> **6. Do countries necessarily gain from making their central banks more independent?** Most studies indicate that developed countries with more independent central banks tend to experience lower and less variable inflation without adverse effects on real GDP. Nevertheless, less developed and emerging economies with more independent central banks do not appear to experience the same reductions in average inflation and inflation variability that developed nations experience. It is not as clear, therefore, whether less developed and emerging economies gain from granting more independence to central banks. In addition, there is some evidence that increased central bank independence makes the aggregate supply curve shallower. Economists do not entirely agree about how to measure central bank independence, which calls into question some of the evidence in favor of the idea.

Chapter Summary

1. The Ultimate Goals of Monetary Policy: These are the final aims of the policy strategies and actions conducted by a central bank such as the Federal Reserve. In the United States, the 1946 Employment Act and the 1978 Humphrey-Hawkins Act established low and stable inflation, high and stable GDP growth, and high and stable employment as formal ultimate objectives of monetary policy. These are examples of internal objectives, which are purely domestic goals. A nation's central bank may also aim to achieve external-balance objectives, which are goals for the country's trade balance, or exports relative to imports.

2. Why a Central Bank Might Use an Intermediate Monetary Policy Target: A central bank such as the Federal Reserve typically adopts an intermediate target

because it faces limitations on the availability of data on its ultimate objectives and because its officials have different interpretations of how monetary policy actions influence these ultimate policy goals. Any intermediate target for monetary policy should be an economic variable that can be observed more frequently than ultimate goal variables. In addition, it should be straightforward to measure, controllable via monetary policy actions, and closely related to ultimate policy objectives. The menu of possible intermediate target variables includes money and credit aggregates, interest rates, nominal GDP, and exchange rates.

3. Policy Time Lags, and How They Might Cause Well-Meaning Monetary Policymakers to Destabilize the Economy: Policy time lags are the intervals separating a need for a policy action and the action's eventual effects on the economy. The recognition lag is the time between the need for a Fed policy action and the Fed's realization of the need, and the response lag is the interval between the recognition of the need for an action and the actual implementation of a policy change. Finally, the transmission lag is the time between the implementation of a policy action and the action's ultimate effects on the economy. Together, these three policy time lags can amount to an interval in excess of a year. They can also cause a discretionary policymaker that reacts to changing circumstances to undertake a policy action that is procyclical, despite the policymaker's intention to enact a countercyclical policy. This potential for policy to destabilize the economy is a key argument favoring the adoption of policy rules, or fixed commitments to specific policy strategies.

4. Why Policy Credibility Is a Crucial Factor in Maintaining Low Inflation:
When nominal contracts exist, a monetary policymaker can push real GDP toward its capacity level by increasing aggregate demand. Consequently, workers and firms that establish wage contracts will doubt the sincerity of the policymaker's commitment to restrain inflation, and they will negotiate higher wages. This will reduce aggregate supply and cause real GDP to decline in the absence of higher aggregate demand. To avoid this outcome, the policymaker must raise aggregate demand and create an inflation bias. To avoid this inflation bias, the policymaker would have to find a way to make the low-inflation commitment credible.

5. How Monetary Policy Credibility Might Be Achieved:
A direct approach would be to make it unlawful for central banks to permit inflation in excess of a certain rate. Another approach would be to sign central bank officials to contracts that base their continued employment or their salaries on a nation's inflation outcomes. To reduce the likelihood that central banks would pursue inflationary policies, governments could appoint central banking officials who are known to dislike inflation. Finally, a central bank can gain credibility by permitting real GDP to decline in the short run in the face of people's doubts about its commitments to policy rules. To be able to demonstrate its commitment in this way, however, the central bank would have to be sufficiently independent from political influences.

6. Whether Countries Necessarily Gain from Making Their Central Banks More Independent:
Most studies examining developed nations that have granted various degrees of independence to their central banks find that increasing the degree of independence tends to reduce inflation rates and to make inflation rates less variable without reducing the average growth of real GDP or making real GDP growth more variable. There is no clear evidence, however, that less developed and emerging economies experience reductions in average inflation and inflation variability when they grant greater independence to their central banks. Furthermore, some studies indicate that increased central bank independence tends to make the aggregate supply curve shallower, so efforts to reduce inflation may require greater short-term reductions in real GDP in nations with more independent central banks. Finally, economists do not agree on the best way to measure central bank independence. This fact makes it harder to judge the strength of the evidence on this issue.

Questions and Problems

(Answers to odd-numbered questions and problems may be found on the Web at **http://money.swcollege.com** under "Student Resources.")

1. In your view, what should be the most important ultimate goal of monetary policy? Take a stand, and support your answer.

2. Briefly discuss the rationales for a central bank's adoption of an intermediate target. Which seems to you to be most important? Explain your reasoning.

3. List the key criteria for choosing among alternative intermediate targets of monetary policy. Does any of these seem to you to be more important than the others? Why?

4. List and define the three types of policy time lags.

5. Which of the policy time lags discussed in question 4 is likely to be least problematical for monetary policy? Explain your reasoning.

6. Which of the policy time lags discussed in question 4 is likely to pose the most significant problem for monetary policy? Explain your reasoning.

7. Why can the time-inconsistency problem lead to an inflation bias when workers and firms set nominal wages in employment contracts?

8. Explain, in your own words, why a constitutional prohibition against inflation may not be a viable solution to the time-inconsistency problem.

9. Evaluate the following statement: "A real strength of performance contracts for central bankers is that they give central bankers policy discretion while subjecting them to a societal rule."

10. Explain the distinction between political and economic independence of central banks. Are both necessary for central banks to have the independence required to conduct anti-inflationary monetary policies? Why or why not?

11. In 1997, just before the European Central Bank (ECB) was established, German and French leaders argued about whether the ECB should be overseen by a committee of political leaders. French leaders supported the establishment of such a group, saying that it would ensure that political leaders could steer the ECB toward policies consistent with higher economic growth for Europe. German leaders opposed the idea, which they argued would lead to higher European inflation. In light of what you have learned in this chapter, which country's leaders do you think were correct? Explain your reasoning.

12. How can increased central bank independence make a country's aggregate supply curve shallower? Why can this actually reduce the credibility of a central bank?

13. Evaluate the following statement: "According to the basic game-theoretic view of discretionary monetary policy and inflation, central bank independence alone will not necessarily restrain a central bank from pursuing inflationary policies. Thus, it should be no surprise to economists that there is no apparent relationship between the degree of central bank independence and inflation outside of the world's developed nations."

Before the Test

Test your understanding of the material covered in this chapter by taking the Chapter 20 interactive quiz at **http://money.swcollege.com**.

Online Application

Internet URL: http://federalreserve.gov/

Title: Minutes of the Federal Open Market Committee

Navigation: Go to the above URL, the home page of the Fed's Board of Governors. Click on "Monetary Policy," click on "Federal Open Market Committee," and then click on "Meetings calendar, statements, and minutes" for the most recent data.

Application: Read the minutes for the most recent date, and answer the following questions:

1. Based on the FOMC minutes, what are the Fed's key internal objectives of monetary policy?

2. Did external objectives appear to play a role in the FOMC's most recent deliberations? If so, which external objective appeared to receive greatest weight?

For Group Study and Analysis: Have two or three separate groups of students look at FOMC minutes for different dates, with at least one of the groups looking farther back in time. Do the answers to the questions above appear to change over time? Does the Fed appear to have used an intermediate monetary policy target over the course of the last several FOMC meeting cycles? If so, what is it?

Selected References and Further Reading

Barro, Robert J. *Monetary Policy*. Cambridge, Mass.: Harvard University Press, 1990.

Cukierman, Alex. *Central Bank Strategy, Credibility, and Independence*. Cambridge, Mass.: MIT Press, 1992.

Daniels, Joseph, Farrokh Nourzad, and David VanHoose. "Openness, Central Bank Independence, and the Sacrifice Ratio." *Journal of Money, Credit, and Banking* 37 (April 2005): 371–379.

_____. "Openness, Centralized Wage Bargaining and Inflation." Marquette University and Baylor University, April 2005.

Dwyer, Gerald, Jr. "Rules and Discretion in Monetary Policy." Federal Reserve Bank of St. Louis *Review* 75 (May/June 1993): 3–14.

Forder, James. "The Case for an Independent European Central Bank: A Reassessment of Evidence and Sources." *European Journal of Political Economy* 14 (February 1998): 53–71.

Friedman, Milton. "The Effects of a Full–Employment Policy on Economic Stability: A Formal Analysis." In *Essays in Positive Economics*. Chicago: University of Chicago Press, 1953.

Hobijn, Bart, and David Lagakos. "Inflation Inequality in the United States." Federal Reserve Bank of New York Staff Report No. 173, October 2003.

Waller, Christopher. "Performance Contracts for Central Bankers." Federal Reserve Bank of St. Louis *Review* 77 (September/October 1995): 3–14.

Walsh, Carl. "Optimal Contracts for Central Bankers." *American Economic Review* 85 (March 1995): 150–167.

MoneyXtra

Log on to the MoneyXtra Web site now (**http://moneyxtra.swcollege.com**) for additional learning resources such as practice quizzes, case studies, readings, and additional economic applications.

What the Fed Does—

Interest Rate Targeting and Economic Activity

During a nearly four-year interval ending in early 2004, the Federal Reserve's target for the federal funds rate steadily declined, from just above 6 percent to 1 percent. Then, starting in January 2004, the Fed's target for the federal funds rate began to increase steadily, mainly through a series of quarter-percentage-point boosts implemented at roughly eight-week intervals.

Throughout this period, the Fed was searching for a value of the federal funds rate that it has come to call the "neutral federal funds rate." At the neutral federal funds rate, the rate of growth of actual real GDP is neither speeded up nor slowed relative to the rate of growth of potential real GDP. Potential real GDP, in turn, is the level of real GDP estimated to be consistent with resource use at the maximum sustainable level. If the actual market federal funds rate is below the neutral level, therefore, actual real GDP is increasing at a faster pace than potential GDP. This would indicate that aggregate demand is rising too fast relative to aggregate supply, which would tend to put upward pressure on inflation. In contrast, if the actual value of the federal funds rate is above the neutral level, actual real GDP is rising at a slower rate than potential GDP, thereby implying sluggish growth in aggregate demand relative to aggregate supply and decelerating inflationary tendencies.

The Federal Reserve faces a fundamental problem in identifying the neutral federal funds rate: its value varies over time. The neutral federal funds rate changes whenever there are variations in the trend rate of growth of potential output. Shifts in the term and risk structures of interest rates also alter the neutral federal funds rate. Thus, the Fed must aim at a moving target.

Why does the Federal Reserve use a federal funds rate target as its primary tool of monetary policy, and what are the implications of its choice? When you have completed this chapter, you will be able to answer this question.

Interest Rate Targeting—A Global Phenomenon

When the media report on monetary policy actions undertaken by the Federal Reserve System, the European Central Bank (ECB), the Bank of Japan, or any other central bank, they rarely include an in-depth discussion of the central bank's recent operations in financial markets. Certainly, reports in the financial press typically do not talk in terms of nonborrowed reserves, the supply of or demand for reserves, or money multipliers. Even though you have learned that these concepts are part of the nuts and bolts of how monetary policy actions work, media commentators typically focus on interest rates: Will the Fed boost interest rates? Will the ECB respond in kind? Will the Bank of Japan cut rates?

Interest Rate Targeting around the Globe

The media focus on interest rates because the world's central banks have oriented their policies around interest rates. As Table 21-1 indicates, central banks frequently intervene in their nation's financial markets. They normally use open market operations or some kind of central bank lending facility to maintain a market interest rate at a target level.

Thus, *interest rate targeting* is the primary means by which the bulk of the world's central banks—and certainly those in the most developed nations—conduct monetary policy. On a daily or weekly basis, each central bank varies the supply of reserves to its nation's banking system with the intention of keeping an interest rate at or very near a target level. In turn, a central bank seeks to establish interest rate targets that are consistent with its broader objectives for its nation's economy.

Rationales for Interest Rate Targeting

Why have so many central banks decided to target interest rates? One traditional rationale for this approach emphasizes its potential to be consistent with attaining economic stability. A more recent explanation is that interest rate targeting may be a more credible anti-inflation policy than alternative approaches to monetary policymaking.

Table 21-1 The Frequency of Central Bank Operations and Their Policy Targets

	Frequency of Policy Operations	Central Bank Operating Target
Australia	Daily	Overnight rate
Canada	Daily	Overnight rate
European Monetary Union*	Daily	Overnight rate
Japan	At least weekly	Overnight rate
Sweden	Weekly	Overnight rate
United Kingdom	At least weekly	1- to 3-month rate
United States	Daily	Overnight rate

*Austria, Belgium, Finland, France, Germany, Greece, Ireland, Italy, Luxembourg, the Netherlands, Portugal, and Spain.

SOURCE: Claudio E. V. Borio, "The Implementation of Monetary Policy in Industrial Countries: A Survey," *Bank for International Settlements Economics Papers*, No. 47, July 1997.

On the Web

How have the world's central banks conducted interest-rate-oriented policies in recent years? For excellent overviews of monetary policy procedures of central banks, go to the home page of the Bank for International Settlements (**http://www. bis.org**). To learn more about central bank policies in developed nations, click on "Publications and Statistics," then on "Working Papers," and scroll down to No. 40, by Claudio Borio. To find out more about central bank policymaking in emerging economies, go back to "Publications and Statistics" and click on "BIS Papers." Then click on "All Policy Papers" and scroll down to No. 5.

THE TRADITIONAL RATIONALE FOR INTEREST RATE TARGETING   The traditional argument supporting interest rate targeting suggests that this approach is more likely to be consistent with an ultimate real GDP objective if the main sources of variability in the economy are volatility in the demand for money and in the demand for depository institution reserves. Shifts in the money demand schedule or in reserve demand cause market interest rates to change, thereby inducing variations in desired investment spending. These changes in investment expenditures then cause equilibrium real GDP to deviate from the central bank's target level.

By targeting an interest rate, a central bank automatically offsets these sources of variability in equilibrium real GDP. Of course, interest rate targeting exposes equilibrium real GDP to other sources of variability. For instance, unexpected changes in aggregate expenditures, such as a decline in consumption or in spending by foreign residents on domestic exports, can cause equilibrium real GDP to differ from the central bank's objective. Likewise, variability in aggregate supply can cause price-level movements that also can cause real GDP and the price level to vary from the central bank's goals. These sources of economic variability would normally require changes in interest rates to induce compensating adjustments in investment spending. Targeting the interest rate prevents these compensating adjustments from taking place. Consequently, according to this traditional rationale, interest rate targeting appears to be a good approach to monetary policy only when variations in aggregate expenditures or in aggregate supply are small and uncommon.

If this traditional perspective were the entire story, we would have to conclude that for most economies fluctuations in the demand for money and in depository institutions' reserve demands are the overriding source of volatility and that most of the world's nations rarely experience variability in either aggregate expenditures or aggregate supply. In fact, however, all countries do experience unexpected changes in aggregate expenditures from time to time. They also encounter unanticipated variations in aggregate supply, which often result from variations in the prices of important factors of production, such as oil and other commodities. Indeed, the large run-ups in oil prices during the 1970s, the significant declines in oil and commodity prices in the 1980s and 1990s, and the oil-price increases in the 2000s were important sources of economic variability in developed and emerging economies.

Consequently, the traditional argument in favor of interest rate targeting must at best be only part of the story. There must be another rationale for why so many central banks target interest rates.

THE PROBLEM OF ASYMMETRIC INFORMATION IN MONETARY POLICYMAK-ING   As we discussed in Chapter 20, another problem central banks face when conducting monetary policy is that people may not believe their commitment to low-inflation policies. When people know that a central bank would like real GDP to be near the economy's capacity level, they anticipate that the central bank will attempt to expand aggregate demand in the short run, thereby inducing inflation. This gives workers an incentive to bargain for higher wages than they would otherwise have been willing to accept. Such wage increases, in turn, tend to shift the aggregate supply schedule upward and to the left (see Figure 20-5 on page 455). To prevent the short-run reduction in real GDP that would occur, the central bank engages in exactly the aggregate demand expansion that people had anticipated. Thus, this interaction between the public and the central bank leads to an *inflation bias* in monetary policy.

Why are people so often unwilling to believe a central bank's commitment to fighting inflation? For one thing, just as seeing is believing, "not seeing" can be "not believing." During his tenure as Fed chair, Alan Greenspan hardly ever passed up an opportunity to preach the virtues of price stability. Nevertheless, the price level rose in every single year of his time as chair.

Another reason a central bank's commitment to price stability may be doubted is that firms and households have incomplete knowledge of the objectives of central bank officials and, as a result, may misinterpret their policy actions. Households and firms also are imperfectly informed about the behind-the-scenes political infighting that sometimes occurs at central banks. Behind closed doors, the president, prime minister, or legislators may subject central bank officials to various types of pressures, such as threats to cut their budget or reduce their independence, unless they conduct monetary policy as the government desires. Similarly, unannounced changes in the composition of central bank governing boards or even in advisory groups may have effects that outsiders cannot observe. For all these reasons, it can be hard to discern the actual goals of central bank officials.

Even when the officials attempt to make their objectives clear, they may not succeed. As we discussed in Chapter 20, policy time lags can complicate a central bank's efforts to recognize the need for countercyclical policy actions, implement those actions, and observe their effect on economic activity. In the meantime, the public may misperceive the central bank's slow response, implementation, and transmission and policy actions as an indication of a lack of interest in countering cycles in economic activity. Furthermore, there may be an unexpected slippage in the monetary policy transmission mechanism. Thus, a central bank could enact a policy that fails to have the intended effects. Households and firms may misinterpret this policy failure as a lack of central bank commitment to stated objectives.

Thus, there is an *asymmetric-information* problem in monetary policymaking. Only central bank officials themselves really know their true aims, the political pressures they face, and the difficulties they encounter in implementing policies intended to achieve their true aims. All that people outside the central bank see is the actual policy actions and the effects of those actions.

On the Web
What are the Fed's latest announcements? Go to the home page of the Fed's Board of Governors (**http://federalreserve.gov**) and click on "News and Events." Under "Press Releases," you can view the latest announcements of changes in the Fed's discount rate, alterations in procedures for calculating bank reserve requirements, and other policy actions.

CREDIBILITY AND THE SIGNAL-EXTRACTION PROBLEM

It follows that central bank policy actions and their effects provide **monetary policy signals,** or informational messages to the public about the goals of central bank officials. Because of the asymmetric-information problem that people outside central banks face, however, the information these signals provide is not *complete*.

Suppose, for example, that the Federal Reserve decides to use a monetary aggregate, such as the monetary base or M1, as its intermediate monetary policy target. The Fed announces that each quarter (every three months), it plans for the monetary aggregate to grow at an annualized rate of no more than 5 percent and no less than 3 percent. Nevertheless, during the following quarter, data indicate that the monetary aggregate grew at a rate of 8 percent. The central bank issues statements indicating that the cause was unexpected changes in the demand for money. People know that this could be true. They also know that there could be other explanations: Fed officials may wish to push up aggregate demand unexpectedly to raise real GDP, or perhaps they have given in to pressures from the president or Congress to enact this policy.

Thus, policy actions are *imperfect signals* of the true intentions of central bank officials. Economists call the difficulties that people face in trying to read the true aims of policymakers from these imperfect policy signals a **signal-extraction problem.** Economic theory indicates that the best solution to the signal-extraction problem is people's best guess—which economists call their *subjective expectation*—of the true objectives that the policy signal reveals. People form this subjective expectation given their knowledge of the backgrounds of central bank officials and their understanding of the kinds of on-the-job pressures the officials are likely to face.

Monetary policy signal: An occurrence that provides information about the objectives of central bank officials.

Signal-extraction problem: The problem of trying to infer a policymaker's true goals from the imperfect signal transmitted by the policymaker's actions.

DOES INTEREST RATE TARGETING IMPROVE CENTRAL BANK CREDIBILITY?

Now let's contemplate what factors can make policy actions better signals of central bank officials' true intentions. We can learn about the background of a central bank official such as Alan Greenspan by reading biographical sketches and following news of his activities and statements. We can keep tabs on press reports concerning interactions between central bank and government officials, such as Greenspan's traditional weekly breakfasts with the Treasury secretary. Because of the asymmetric-information problem we face, however, there is a limit to how much more information we can gather about a central bank official's activities and aims.

Something else we can do, however, is to evaluate factors that can cause a central bank to succeed or fail in attaining its stated objectives. One of these is the central bank's ability to achieve its intermediate policy goals. Recall from Chapter 20 that to be useful, an intermediate target variable should be consistent with the central bank's ultimate policy goals, frequently observable, definable and measurable, and controllable. Although limited data on monetary aggregates are available daily, central banks typically have complete information about monetary aggregates only on a weekly basis. Financial innovations and regulatory changes, such as the growth of sweep accounts since the mid-1990s, complicate the ability of central banks to define and measure monetary aggregates. Furthermore, the controllability of a monetary aggregate depends on a number of factors, such as the stability and interest elasticity of the demand for money.

By way of contrast, central banks typically have minute-by-minute access to information about market interest rates. Financial markets accurately define and precisely measure interest rates, often within hundredths of a basis point (that is, within a ten-thousandth of a percent). In addition, central banks normally have considerable ability to influence interest rates via open market operations.

Thus, by adopting an interest rate as an intermediate policy target, a central bank can make the public's signal-extraction problem less complicated. People have an easier time inferring the central bank's true objectives from its monetary policy actions. For instance, suppose that the Fed uses a monetary aggregate as its intermediate target, as it did in the late 1970s. If the monetary aggregate grows at a faster rate than people anticipated, then they must try to figure out if this resulted from unintentional policy errors by the Fed arising from slippage in monetary control or from intentional efforts to expand aggregate demand. Given all the linkages among day-to-day policy actions, interest rates, economic activity, and money demand, reaching a conclusion about this issue is not easy. Now suppose that the Fed uses an interest rate as its intermediate policy objective. If there is a decline in this interest rate that the Fed does not reverse, then it is very unlikely that the decline was unintentional. In this way, an interest rate target provides a much clearer signal than a monetary target. (Some economists suggest that the Fed could send the clearest possible interest rate signal if it relied on a computer instead of human policymakers to determine monetary policy; see the *Cyber Focus: Why Not Use the "Taylor Rule" to Determine Monetary Policy with a Computer?*)

As a result, interest rate targeting can make a central bank's monetary policy stance more credible than it would be otherwise. As you learned in Chapter 20, enhanced credibility improves the likelihood that a central bank can limit the inflation bias of discretionary monetary policy. Thus, even though consistency with ultimate targets is an important consideration in choosing an intermediate target, a central bank may achieve significant credibility gains from adopting an interest rate target. A number of economists believe that this is the primary reason most of the world's central banks implement monetary policies using interest rate targets. Others, however, worry that targeting an interest rate may be fundamentally inconsistent with price stability, because when a central bank targets an interest rate, it may permit the quantity of money in circulation to drift over time. We next turn our attention to this issue.

MONEYXTRA!
Another Perspective

To further investigate the evidence concerning Taylor rules, go to the Chapter 21 reading, entitled "How Useful Are Taylor Rules for Monetary Policy?" by Sharon Kozicki of the Federal Reserve Bank of Kansas City.
**http://moneyxtra.
swcollege.com**

CYBER
Focus

Why Not Use the "Taylor Rule" to Determine Monetary Policy with a Computer?

Must the Fed rely on people to make monetary policy decisions, or in today's world of interest rate targeting, could a computer be used to perform this task? In the 1990s, John Taylor of Stanford University suggested a relatively simple equation that the Fed might use to determine the appropriate interest rate target. This equation entailed setting the interest rate target based on an estimated long-run real interest rate, the current deviation of the actual inflation rate from the Fed's inflation objective, and the gap between actual real GDP and a measure of potential GDP. Taylor and other economists applied his equa-

tion, which has become known as the "Taylor rule," to actual Fed policy choices and found that it came very close to predicting the interest rate targets that the Fed has actually selected over time.

The Federal Reserve Bank of St. Louis now regularly tracks target levels for the federal funds rate predicted by a basic Taylor-rule equation. Figure 21-1 displays paths of both the actual federal funds rate and alternative Taylor-rule predictions under different assumptions about the Fed's inflation objective (goals of 0, 1, 2, 3, or 4 percent inflation). As you can see, the actual federal funds rate has remained close to the Taylor-rule predictions over time. To some economists, Figure 21-1 implies an alternative to having numerous Fed officials and economists devote untold hours of labor to deciding on a federal funds rate target. Instead, they suggest, a computer could be programmed to conduct the minimal open market oper-

ations required to vary the supply of reserves to the banking system as needed to attain a federal funds rate consistent with the Taylor rule.

Statements by Fed officials and writings by Fed economists tend to agree that the Taylor rule provides useful "guideposts" for determining values for its interest rate target. Nevertheless, Fed policymakers commonly rule out taking the human touch out of the monetary policy process. As one example, they point to the 1995–1998 interval, when the Fed adopted a generally more contractionary policy than the Taylor rule specified. As another, they identify the post-2002 period, when the Fed implemented a more expansionary policy than a computer would have delivered.

FOR CRITICAL ANALYSIS: Why does the Taylor rule specify lower federal funds rates for higher Fed inflation objectives?

FIGURE 21-1
Actual Federal Funds Rates and Values Predicted by a Taylor-Rule Equation.

This figure displays both the actual path of the federal funds rate since 1996 and the target paths specified by a Taylor-rule equation for alternative

annual inflation objectives of 0, 1, 2, 3, and 4 percent.

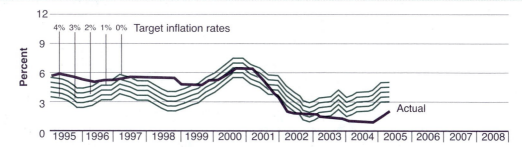

SOURCE: Federal Reserve Bank of St. Louis *Monetary Trends,* various issues.

> **1. Why do most of the world's central banks target nominal interest rates?** One possible reason is the traditional rationale, which is that interest rate targeting may be the intermediate-targeting procedure most consistent with attaining economic stability. Another rationale arises from the fact that interest rates are so visible to the public and are relatively easy for central banks to influence. As a result, interest rates are especially clear signals of central banks' monetary policy intentions. Thus, interest rate targeting may improve the credibility of monetary policymaking for many central banks.

Interest Rate Targeting, Base Drift, and the Price Level

Shortly after the Fed unofficially ended its experiment with monetary targeting in the early 1980s, Milton Friedman had the following to say about Fed policymaking:

> There is an old story about a farmer who used his barn door for target shooting. A visitor was astounded to find that each of the numerous targets on the door had a bullet hole precisely in the center of the bull's-eye. He later discovered the secret of such remarkable accuracy. Unobserved, he saw the farmer first shoot at the door and then paint the target.
>
> That is the precise counterpart of the way in which the Federal Reserve System hits its monetary bull's-eye. It simply repaints its target. ("The Fed Hasn't Changed Its Ways," *Wall Street Journal*, August 20, 1985)

Today, we know that when Friedman complained about "target repainting," the Fed was in the midst of a transition to its current interest-rate-targeting procedure. Nevertheless, the basic phenomenon that Friedman described, known as *base drift*, remains an issue today.

Base Drift and "Price-Level Nonstationarity"

Base drift: The tendency of a measure of total depository institution reserves or a monetary aggregate to fail to adjust to a level consistent with fixed long-run average growth.

Panel (a) of Figure 21-2 illustrates the phenomenon of **base drift.** This is a tendency for a reserve measure or a monetary aggregate—nonborrowed reserves, the monetary base, M1, and the like—to vary over time without necessarily returning to a level consistent with a single long-run average growth rate. As a result, there is no fixed trend growth rate of reserve measures or monetary aggregates. Essentially, Fed policies produce meandering growth of reserves and monetary aggregates.

Panel (a) of Figure 21-2 shows the actual drift of the M1 aggregate during the late 1970s and early 1980s, when the Fed claimed to be engaged in monetary targeting. Panel (b) illustrates how the base drift in panel (a) can take place. Suppose that at point *A* in panel (b) the Fed announces a desired growth rate for M1 of no less than 4 percent and no greater than 8 percent. The midrange of these two growth rates is its announced *target* growth rate of 6 percent. During the following weeks, the Fed permits money growth to drift toward the upper part of its target growth range. Now suppose that at the next Federal Open Market Committee meeting, which occurs at the time indicated by point *B*, Fed officials reaffirm their commitment to the same target growth rate and range of permitted deviations from this target. The result, however, is *upward drift* of M1. Base drift occurs.

FIGURE 21-2
Base Drift.

Panel (a) shows the actual drift of the M1 monetary aggregate during the late 1970s and early 1980s, a period when the Fed claimed that its goal was to target this aggregate. Panel (b) shows how this phenomenon of base drift can occur. If the Fed permits a monetary aggregate to drift toward the upper part of its target growth range in the fourth quarter (Q) of one year and then resets its target growth ranges at the beginning of the second year, the result is base drift.

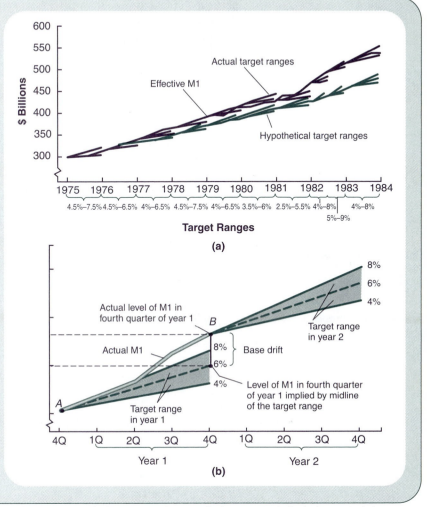

SOURCE: Alfred Broaddus and Marvin Goodfriend, "Base Drift and the Longer Run Growth of M1: Experience from a Decade of Monetary Targeting," Federal Reserve Bank of Richmond *Economic Review* 70 (November/December 1984): 3–14.

The phenomenon of base drift is not limited to the United States. Other central banks have followed the Fed's example in permitting drift in reserve and monetary aggregates. The drift in these aggregates has important implications for the behavior of aggregate prices in nations around the world.

As you learned in previous chapters, all the theories of the link between monetary policy and economic activity indicate that increases in reserves and monetary aggregates induce increases in aggregate demand. The resulting outward shifts in the aggregate demand schedule cause the equilibrium price level to rise.

Hence, the base drift illustrated in Figure 21-2 should invariably lead to drift in the price level as well. Indeed, base drift is associated with **price-level nonstationarity.** This term refers to a pattern of price-level changes over time in which the price level never settles down to a long-run average, or stationary, level. Instead, the price level, like depository institution reserves and monetary aggregates, drifts over time. Consistent with the pattern of M1 growth

Price-level nonstationarity: Failure of the price level to adjust to a constant long-run average level; upward (or downward) drift of the price level over time.

illustrated in Figure 21-2, during the past several decades the general pattern of price-level drift has been *upward*.

This leads to an important conclusion. Base drift can cause the price level to drift; that is, base drift can lead to nonstationarity of the price level, so that the price level never settles at a long-run average value. Because the general tendency has been for the price level to drift upward, inflation has occurred.

Is Base Drift Unavoidable?

Over the years, many observers have criticized the Fed and other central banks for allowing base drift to occur. Halting base drift, they argue, is the key to eliminating inflation. For this reason, a number of economists have sought to understand why the Fed and other central banks tolerate drift of depository institution reserves and monetary aggregates.

BASE DRIFT AS A BY-PRODUCT OF INTEREST RATE SMOOTHING
One potential source of base drift that economists have emphasized is the Fed's efforts to reduce interest rate variability. Economists refer to such efforts as **interest rate smoothing.**

Interest rate smoothing: Central bank efforts to attain an ultimate objective of interest rate stability.

Higher Real GDP and Base Drift
To see how interest rate smoothing can cause base drift, take a look at Figure 21-3. Panel (a) shows the effects of increases in the demand for reserves by depository institutions when the Fed's goal is to keep the federal funds rate from changing. Suppose that a rise in real GDP induces people to hold more real money balances, so required reserves increase. Thus, money reserve demand rises from TR_1^d to TR_2^d. To maintain the federal funds rate at its initial equilibrium value of r_f^1, the Fed must increase the reserve supply, and hence the money stock, to eliminate upward pressure on the federal funds rate. Likewise, if reserve demand increases again a few weeks later, to TR_3^d, the Fed again must bring about an additional increase in the reserve supply.

Panel (b) shows how total depository reserves adjust over time as a result of the Fed's actions to smooth interest rates. As you can see, in this example total nominal reserves *(TR)* of depository institutions drift upward. Consequently, the monetary base (total reserves plus currency) and the quantity of money in circulation are likely to drift as well.

A Drifting Price Level
Panel (c) illustrates a possible reason for the rises in real GDP that induced the increases in reserve demand shown in panel (a). The reason is successive increases in aggregate demand, possibly generated by a sudden increase in consumption or in spending by foreign residents on domestic exports. If the Fed had not smoothed interest rates, higher interest rates would have reduced investment spending, which would have dampened these increases in aggregate demand. Because of the Fed's interest-rate-smoothing efforts, however, aggregate demand shifts out fully in panel (c). As shown in panel (d), the result is upward drift in the price level. The price level is nonstationary because the Fed's efforts to smooth interest rates reinforce increases in aggregate demand.

This example illustrates the essential feature of an argument made by Marvin Goodfriend, a research economist at the Federal Reserve Bank of Richmond: interest rate smoothing can potentially result in base drift and price-level nonstationarity. Does this argument imply that the Fed's current practice of interest rate targeting necessarily causes base drift? For Goodfriend and others, the answer to this question is definitely yes if the Fed becomes so caught up in interest rate smoothing that this objective begins to dominate its efforts. In this case, interest rate smoothing may effectively become an *ultimate* goal of Fed policy, rather than part of its intermediate-targeting procedure. When interest rate smoothing becomes a final goal of monetary policy, base

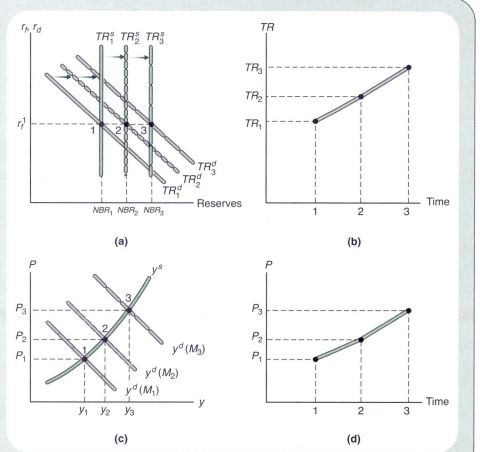

FIGURE 21-3
Interest Rate Smoothing, Base Drift, and Price-Level Nonstationarity.

Panel (a) depicts how the Fed must adjust nonborrowed reserves *(NBR)* and the position of the reserve supply schedule to keep the federal funds rate unchanged in the face of back-to-back increases in reserve demand in period 2 and period 3. The result, as shown in panel (b), is upward drift in total depository institution reserves. Panel (c) shows how the Fed's policy actions in panel (a) will, in the absence of any other changes, cause the money stock and aggregate demand to increase. The result, as depicted in panel (d), is upward drift of the price level, which is called price-level nonstationarity.

drift and price-level nonstationarity result. Thus, as we shall discuss in more detail later in this chapter, a key issue when the Fed targets an interest rate is how often it should adjust its target. According to Goodfriend, failure to adjust the interest rate target in the face of changing economic conditions helps to explain base drift and nonstationary prices.

ALTERNATIVE RATIONALES FOR BASE DRIFT   Does real-world experience with base drift and price-level nonstationarity imply that the Fed devotes excessive attention to limiting variability of interest rates? Some Fed critics take this position, and they may be correct. There are, however, other possible explanations of base drift that do not require central bank overattention to smoothing interest rates.

1. **Monetary targeting.** Base drift can also occur when a central bank is overzealous in seeking to target a monetary aggregate period by period. Suppose, for example, that in the current period the adoption of a payment-system innovation induces a significant fall in the demand for money. To achieve a monetary target, the Fed must induce a reduction in market interest rates by expanding depository institution reserves. This fall in interest rates, in turn, spurs desired investment spending, which induces an increase in aggregate demand

and upward pressure on the price level. Of course, the rise in real GDP tends to push the demand for money back up somewhat, thereby assisting the Fed's effort to maintain its monetary target and contain the expansion in aggregate demand. Nevertheless, on net the Fed's effort to achieve its monetary target during the current period typically will push up reserves and the price level somewhat. If payment-system innovations or other unexpected events affecting money demand take place with the passage of time, then efforts to achieve a monetary target within each period can result in price-level nonstationarity.

2. **Exchange rate smoothing.** Base drift and price-level nonstationarity can also occur because of international factors. For example, consider a small nation that is completely open to international flows of funds. Recall from Chapter 5 that in this situation the *uncovered interest parity* condition should hold. Thus, the interest rate on a financial instrument issued in the small nation, r, will equal the interest rate on an instrument with the same risks and maturity issued in another country, r^*, plus the expected rate of depreciation of the small nation's currency relative to the currency of the other country, denoted s^e. Thus, uncovered interest parity implies that $r = r^* + s^e$ or, equivalently, that $r - r^* = s^e$, so that the differential in the two nations' interest rates equals the expected rate of currency depreciation.

   Now suppose that one of the key goals of the small nation's central bank is to engage in *exchange rate smoothing* by limiting variability of the exchange rate. To be successful in this task, the central bank must conduct open market operations to try to minimize expected depreciation, s^e. But keeping s^e as small as possible requires ensuring that the interest rate differential, $r - r^*$, remains very small. Hence, to smooth the exchange rate the central bank essentially must engage in interest rate smoothing. As we noted earlier, this can result in base drift and nonstationarity of the price level.

3. **International interdependence.** In principle, international factors can lead to base drift even when central banks do not overtly seek to smooth exchange rates. Widespread international trade causes economies to be *interdependent,* meaning that changes in prices or real GDP in one country can influence prices or real GDP in another nation. As a result, efforts to achieve domestic objectives can implicitly require exchange rate smoothing. For example, if the people in a nation import a large portion of the goods they consume from another country, then that nation's consumer prices depend on both the other country's price level and the rate of exchange of the nation's currency for the currency of the other country. Thus, reducing variability of consumer prices ultimately requires the nation's central bank to smooth exchange rates. Again, the result can be base drift and a nonstationary home price level.

Thus, there are several competing explanations for why central banks such as the Federal Reserve permit base drift and price-level nonstationarity. Too much attention to smoothing interest rates, targeting monetary aggregates, or smoothing exchange rates can lead a central bank to permit depository institution reserves, the monetary base, monetary aggregates, and the price level to wander over time.

This means that using an interest rate target to conduct monetary policy does not necessarily cause base drift and nonstationary prices. Indeed, a properly formulated interest-rate-targeting policy should limit the potential for base drift and price-level nonstationarity to occur. After all, a policy of reducing upward drift of reserves, monetary aggregates, and the price level is consistent with attaining the highest degree of central bank credibility—a key argument for targeting an interest rate in the first place.

To help reduce the potential for the price level to be nonstationary, many economists have suggested that central banks should set their interest rate targets with the explicit aim of achieving a target inflation rate. This policy of *inflation targeting* has been explicitly or implicitly pursued in several countries including Canada, New Zealand, the United Kingdom, and Sweden. Some observers believe that the Fed has implicitly pursued a type of inflation-targeting approach in recent years. Inflation targeting still permits the price level to drift upward over time, however. After all, inflation is by definition a rise in the price level over time. Completely eliminating price-level nonstationarity would require a policy of aiming for a fixed price level (at least on average) using an interest-rate-targeting approach. So far none of the world's central banks has pursued such a policy.

> **2. What are base drift and price-level nonstationarity, and what accounts for these phenomena?** Base drift is the tendency for reserve and monetary aggregates to vary over time without ever settling down to levels consistent with a fixed long-run average growth rate. Price-level nonstationarity is the failure of the price level to adjust to a constant long-run average level. Both phenomena can result when interest rate smoothing is an ultimate goal of central banks. Period-by-period targeting of monetary aggregates can also cause price-level nonstationarity, however, as can exchange rate smoothing and other factors arising from the interdependence of nations' economies. Thus, interest rate targeting may or may not be responsible for base drift and price-level nonstationarity.

Interest Rate Targeting and the Term Structure

In Chapter 19, we discussed how the Fed influences market interest rates. Day to day the Fed focuses on the market for bank reserves. Equilibrium in this market determines the federal funds rate, or the rate on interbank loans with daily maturities. Changes in the market federal funds rate induced by the Fed's open market operations can influence interest rates on other financial instruments with different risk characteristics and longer terms to maturity, such as Treasury securities.

An interesting issue is how the Fed's interest-rate-targeting policy influences the relationship among interest rates at various terms to maturity. It turns out that in some respects day-to-day Fed policymaking using the federal funds rate can have important effects on this relationship. In other ways, however, the federal funds rate is less important than you might expect it to be.

Monetary Policy and Interest Rates

Recall from Chapter 4 that the modern theory of the term structure combines the expectations theory with the preferred habitat theory. Under the expectations theory, a longer-term interest rate is an average of current and expected future short-term interest rates. If people expect that short-term interest rates are equally likely to rise and fall, then the *yield curve*—a curve plotting interest rates at various terms to maturity—should be horizontal. But, in actual experience, yield curves typically slope upward. Thus, as indicated by the preferred habitat theory, economists typically add a *term premium* to the average of current and expected short-term rates to compute longer-term interest rates. Term premiums on longer-term instruments stem from savers' preference to hold bonds with shorter maturities. That is, savers must earn a somewhat higher return to induce them to hold longer-term instruments instead.

THE FEDERAL FUNDS RATE AS THE "ANCHOR" OF THE TERM STRUCTURE

Most federal funds loans have a maturity of twenty-four hours. Consequently, the federal funds rate is at the lowest end of the maturity spectrum.

The Fed uses the federal funds rate as its day-to-day target for monetary policy. It follows from the basic theory of the term and risk structures of interest rates that the federal funds rate "pins down"—or, as economists like to put it, *anchors*—the shortest-maturity rates for yield curves of various types of financial instruments.

As you have learned, sustained open market operations that alter the targeted value of the federal funds rate change both the current twenty-four-hour term rate on federal funds and expected future values of this rate. According to the expectations theory, therefore, such Fed policy actions shift the federal funds yield curve. If risk premiums remain unchanged, this ultimately causes other yield curves, such as the Treasury securities yield curve, to shift in the same direction. In a manner of speaking, changing the target federal funds rate alters the position of the anchor for other interest rates.

Indeed, the daily federal funds rate is a very good predictor of market rates at the shorter (one- to three-month maturities) end of the maturity spectrum. A study by Glenn Rudebusch of the Federal Reserve Bank of San Francisco has credited this relationship to the Federal Reserve's policy of allowing relatively large daily deviations of the federal funds rate from the Fed's target for that rate but offsetting such deviations the following day via open market operations. As a result, financial market traders usually consider daily deviations of the federal funds rate from the target rate to be temporary. For instance, if today's funds rate appears abnormally high relative to the Fed's target rate, then traders anticipate that future daily rates will return to the target rate.

POLICY ANNOUNCEMENTS AND INTEREST RATE VARIABILITY   Given the federal funds rate's role as an anchor for other interest rates, people pay close attention to Fed policies regarding its day-to-day federal funds rate target. Before February 1994, however, the Fed did not publicly announce its target. At the time of each Federal Open Market Committee (FOMC) meeting, it would make available to the public a summary of the FOMC's deliberations from the *prior* meeting several weeks earlier. Otherwise, everyone outside the Fed had to infer the target value of the federal funds rate from the Fed's actions in the market for reserves.

Naturally, when the Fed made no move to alter its federal funds rate over a lengthy period, it was relatively easy to guess the target. During times of turbulence in financial markets, however, inferring the target could be more difficult. From time to time during the 1980s, Fed officials unexpectedly altered the federal funds rate target following conference calls that took place *between* FOMC meetings. As a result, traders sometimes interpreted very short-term swings in the market for reserves as possible signs of Fed moves to change its target, when in fact the variations arose from unexpected shifts in reserve demand.

Thus, traders had to make uncertain guesses about the Fed's intentions. As a result, there was some "slippage" in the relationship between the federal funds rate "anchor" and other longer-term interest rates. Short-term fluctuations in the daily federal funds rate could thereby induce significantly larger variations in market interest rates for other financial instruments.

Since February 1994, however, the Fed has announced its federal funds rate target immediately after the FOMC has deliberated. Because traders now know for certain what the target is, they can feel more assured that any rise in funds rate variability does not represent a change in monetary policy.

Efficient Markets and Indicators of Fed Policy

In light of the key role that the federal funds rate plays in influencing the general level of market interest rates, people have traditionally regarded it as an especially important signal of Fed policy. Indeed, in studies of the effects of monetary policy on the economy, many researchers have assumed that the federal funds rate is a key **monetary policy indicator,** that is, an economic variable that provides a particularly important signal of the intended effects of Fed monetary policy.

In recent years this idea has been questioned by other researchers. For instance, Michelle Garfinkel of the University of California at Irvine and Daniel Thornton of the Federal Reserve Bank of St. Louis have applied the theory of efficient markets (see Chapter 7) to this issue. They find that even though Fed open market operations directly influence the reserves market in which the federal funds rate is determined, these operations also exert speedy influences in markets for other financial instruments with longer maturities. Even before the Fed began publicly announcing its policy target, for instance, it rarely took longer than a day for other interest rates to adjust to changes in the federal funds rate.

Indeed, Garfinkel and Thornton conclude that open market operations also affect conditions in the market for one-day Treasury security *repurchase agreements.* As we discussed in Chapter 1, these are financial contracts to sell Treasury securities with a promise to repurchase them the next day. Because financial markets are so efficient, the resulting changes in interest yields on Treasury security repurchase agreements quickly influence interest rates on Treasury securities. Consequently, Treasury security rates and other shorter-term interest rates respond to Fed open market operations just as quickly as the federal funds rate does. For this reason, Garfinkel and Thornton argue that the federal funds rate is not a better monetary policy indicator than any other market interest rate.

Monetary policy indicator: An economic variable that gives the public an especially clear signal of the intended effects of monetary policy actions.

> **3. How does interest rate targeting influence the term structure of interest rates?** The Fed's daily target for the federal funds rate pins down, or anchors, the low-maturity end of the term structure of interest rates. Given term and risk premiums, market forces then determine other interest rates. Since 1994 the Fed has helped reduce slippage between the federal funds rate and other market rates by publicly announcing its target for the federal funds rate. Nevertheless, because U.S. financial markets are highly efficient, the federal funds rate is not necessarily a better indicator of Fed policy intentions than most other interest rates.

On the Web
What do the latest federal funds futures prices indicate about the market's expectation of future federal funds rates? Find out by going to the home page of the Chicago Board of Trade at **http://cbot.com.** Click on "Interest Rate" and then on "Fed Funds."

Interest Rate Targeting and the Economy

Economists generally agree that in today's highly efficient financial markets, the Fed's current policy of establishing a day-to-day target for the federal funds rate permits it to target the general level of interest rates. Nevertheless, at any given time there is rarely a consensus among economists as to what the general level of interest rates should be. In any given week, some commentators may contend that the Fed has set interest rates too high, while others argue that interest rates are too low, and still others say that interest rates are fine where they are.

How does the Fed determine its interest rate target? How does it decide the time has come to raise or lower its target? Why is this sometimes a difficult decision to make? These are the next issues we must consider.

The Fed's Balancing Act: The Liquidity Effect versus the Real Balance Effect

To have the best chance of achieving its ultimate policy goals, a central bank must establish credibility. People must believe that it is committed to those ultimate objectives. To establish a credible interest-rate-targeting policy, however, a central bank must make clear to everyone that it stands ready to change its interest rate target as needed to attain its ultimate goals. If it holds too fast to a goal of attaining a fixed interest rate objective, then the central bank ends up smoothing interest rates. As you learned earlier, the result is drift of reserves, money, and prices. Typically, another outcome is inflation. If so, this further damages the central bank's credibility, making the pursuit of anti-inflationary policies even more difficult in the future.

This need to establish credibility may explain why you so often hear Federal Reserve officials claiming that they are on guard and ready to react to events that could lead to an upsurge in inflation. If Fed officials really desire to keep inflation very low, then it makes sense that they will wish to adjust interest rates to help maintain the credibility of their commitment to their ultimate goals.

Naturally, an issue that often arises when the Fed uses an interest rate target is what direction it should move interest rates in response to a given set of economic events. For instance, suppose that you are a member of the Fed's Board of Governors confronted with the following situation: The U.S. economy has been expanding for several years, but recent signs of weakness have led many forecasters to conclude that a recession could be just around the corner. Nevertheless, the unemployment rate is at its lowest level in more than thirty years. A recent uptick in the rate of growth of the price level could signal an upsurge in inflation. At the next FOMC meeting, should you argue for pushing up the Fed's interest rate target, for reducing it, or for taking a wait-and-see approach and leaving it unchanged?

This fictitious situation parallels the real-world situation that the Fed faced in 1999 and 2000 before it became clear in 2001 that economic activity was shrinking. To see why the situation is a potentially difficult one, recall what you learned in Chapters 17 and 18 about the liquidity effect and the real balance effect of monetary policy. Remember that the *liquidity effect* is a decline in the equilibrium nominal interest rate resulting from sustained open market purchases, given an unchanged price level. If you, as a Fed governor, wish to forestall a pending recession via a liquidity-effect reduction in interest rates that would spur investment spending and aggregate demand, then you might argue for reducing the Fed's interest rate target. But you face a problem in recommending this course of action. The ensuing rise in aggregate demand would tend to push up the price level, thereby reducing the real supply of depository institution reserves and placing upward pressure on interest rates. Keeping the interest rate target low in the face of this *real balance effect* then would require further open market purchases that ultimately would fuel further price increases. At some point in the future, therefore, the Fed would surely have to reverse itself and raise its interest rate target again.

By way of contrast, suppose that you choose to argue for raising the interest rate target. In the short run, this would induce a drop in desired investment spending, reduce aggregate demand, and stem inflationary pressures. The short-term cost, however, could be the hastening of a recession—and potentially a deeper recession. (Pushing up the interest rate target can also induce a rapid and negative effect on the level of stock prices; see *What Happens When Monetary Policy Actions Affect the Stock Market?*)

Interest Rate Targeting and Expected Inflation

Clearly, the Fed can find itself walking a tightrope when it targets a nominal interest rate. To see why, remember from Chapter 4 that the *real interest rate* is equal to $r^r = r - \pi^e$, where r^r is the real rate of interest and π^e is the expected inflation rate. Now suppose that the Fed's interest rate target is equal to $\hat{r}$. This means that when the Fed achieves its interest rate target, the targeted nominal interest rate must be equal to the sum of the real interest rate and the expected inflation rate, or $\hat{r} = r^r + \pi^e$.

From this perspective, it is clear that the Fed can keep a nominal interest rate at the target level only if it can somehow bring about a level of the real interest rate or of the expected inflation rate that is consistent with its interest rate target. So what nominal interest rate target should the Fed aim to achieve?

Recall that in the long run, monetary policy actions have meager effects on real variables. These include real GDP *and* the real rate of interest. Thus, beyond a short-term horizon, targeting a nominal interest rate ultimately entails aiming for a specific overall inflation expectation on the part of households and firms. That is, if the real interest rate is determined independently of monetary policy, then achieving an interest rate target equal to $\hat{r} = r^r + \pi^e$ requires inducing people to form an inflation expectation equal to the Fed's nominal interest rate target minus the real rate of interest, or $\pi^e = \hat{r} - r^r$.

This tells us something very important about a Fed policy of interest rate targeting. In the long run, the interest rate target that the Fed chooses should be consistent with attaining a specific expected inflation rate. Remember that the basic theories of monetary policy's effects on economic activity that we surveyed in Chapters 17 and 18 often include consideration of the rational expectations hypothesis. According to this hypothesis, on average people form inflation expectations consistent with the true inflation rate. Furthermore, in the long run the actual inflation rate is the average inflation rate. Consequently, we are led to an inescapable conclusion: if people form rational expectations, then in the long run the Fed's interest rate target should be consistent with the current expected inflation rate, which in turn should ultimately be consistent with the path of actual inflation.

What Happens When... **Monetary Policy Actions Affect the Stock Market?**

Fed policymakers commonly deny that they pay much attention to how their interest rate policies affect stock prices. Nevertheless, they are certainly aware that stock prices quickly fall when interest rates rise and that stock prices increase when interest rates decline.

A higher Fed interest rate target has two effects that cause stock prices to decline. First, a higher interest rate target may reduce firms' net worth and hence the value of the collateral they use to obtain loans. Consequently, firms have to cut back on production. This reduces their anticipated future cash flows, causing a decrease in the demand for stocks and a fall in stock prices. Second, a higher target interest rate boosts the risk-free rate of return available to investors,

which raises the rate at which investors discount the future. Consequently, the discounted present value of the stream of (already reduced) anticipated future cash flows that firms' operations will generate declines. Investors' demand for stocks declines further, and so do stock prices.

FOR CRITICAL ANALYSIS: Why do you suppose that stock prices also typically fall when investors merely *anticipate* that the Fed is about to increase its target interest rate? (Hint: What happens to the demand for bonds in the present when investors expect that bond prices will decline in the future?)

A Credible Interest Rate Target

For instance, suppose that the real interest rate is at a long-run level of 3 percent and the current expected inflation rate is 3 percent. A nominal interest rate target value of 4 percent will be unsustainable. Indeed, people will know that trying to maintain a nominal interest rate below 6 percent will entail further expansion of aggregate demand, which will bring about further inflationary pressures. A nominal interest rate target of 5 percent, therefore, will send a clear signal to households and firms that the Fed has embarked on an inflationary policy. This low interest rate target will *reduce* the Fed's policy credibility. Only a target interest rate of 6 percent will signal to households and firms that the Fed's current policy stance is credible.

Now that you are armed with this long-run perspective, put yourself back in the place of a member of the Fed's Board of Governors facing the situation of recent solid real growth but perhaps an impending recession, a historically low unemployment rate, and a recent uptick in the inflation rate. If you care about the Fed's long-term anti-inflation credibility, then the key issue you face in determining the appropriate interest rate target is what direction the inflation rate is truly headed. If the inflation rate is really about to rise, then it is time to raise the target for the nominal interest rate. If not, then holding firm at the current interest rate target may be the appropriate policy. Only if you have firm outside indications that the recent inflation uptick is temporary and that actual inflation will turn downward in the future should you argue for a reduction in the Fed's target for the nominal interest rate.

> **4. Why are accurate inflation forecasts necessary for successful implementation of the Fed's interest-rate-targeting procedure?** The Fed and other central banks target nominal interest rates. A targeted nominal interest rate, therefore, is equal to the sum of the real interest rate and the expected inflation rate. In the long run, the real interest rate is not influenced by monetary policy. If the interest rate target is set too low in light of current expected inflation, then the Fed will lose anti-inflation credibility. Thus, the Fed's interest-rate-targeting policy must be consistent with current inflation expectations, which, if people form rational expectations, reflect the average path that inflation will actually follow.

Implications of Interest Rate Targeting for the World Economy

As Table 21-1 on page 469 indicates, many central banks target a market interest rate. As you learned in Chapter 5, however, international financial markets are very open today, which means that the international interest parity conditions discussed in Chapter 5 are more likely to hold today than in years past. One of these, the *uncovered interest parity* condition that we referred to earlier in this chapter, has some important implications for central banks' interest-rate-targeting policies.

Interest Rate Targeting, International Interest Parity, and Exchange Rates

As we noted earlier, under uncovered interest parity, the following is true:

$$r - r^* = s^e,$$

where r^* is a foreign interest rate and s^e is the expected rate of depreciation of the domestic currency. Thus, when capital flows freely and uncovered interest parity holds, the differential between the home interest rate and the foreign interest rate equals the expected rate of home currency depreciation.

Now suppose that your home country is Mexico. You are an official at the Bank of Mexico. The foreign nation is the United States, so r^* is determined via the Federal Reserve's interest-rate-targeting procedure. Because Mexico has a small economy, the Bank of Mexico cannot influence the Fed's interest rate target. U.S. and Mexican financial markets are very open to cross-border flows of financial assets, so the condition of uncovered interest parity approximately holds.

When confronted with open and efficient international financial markets, therefore, the Bank of Mexico faces a choice. One option is to set its own target in light of Mexican economic conditions and allow the actual and expected peso-dollar exchange rate to adjust until the expected currency depreciation equals the resulting interest differential. Another is to try to smooth the exchange rate and thereby keep expected currency depreciation close to zero. This approach, however, essentially takes away the Bank of Mexico's freedom to independently set its own interest rate target. As we have noted in this chapter, it can also lead to upward drift in prices and a loss of policy credibility.

Indeed, during the several years leading up to 1994, the Bank of Mexico sought to maintain a steady rate of exchange rate depreciation. In a sense, this made Mexican central banking a straightforward proposition: all the Bank of Mexico had to do was to set its own interest rate target so that it maintained a nearly constant interest differential vis-à-vis U.S. interest rates. Ultimately, however, this policy of maintaining a relatively fixed interest differential became out of step with underlying conditions in the Mexican economy and financial system. In 1994, therefore, the Bank of Mexico raised its interest rate target and allowed the peso's value to adjust in foreign exchange markets. As predicted by the uncovered interest parity condition, rapid expected and actual depreciation of the peso occurred.

Is the Fed Becoming a Multinational Central Bank?

Later in the 1990s other nations—Thailand, Indonesia, Malaysia, and Brazil—had similar experiences. In an effort to avoid sharing the same fate, however, Argentina had already adopted a **currency board** arrangement. A currency board is an institution that issues a national currency at a strictly fixed rate of exchange with respect to the currency of another country. The first currency boards were established by nations that were members of the British Commonwealth, such as Hong Kong, the Cayman Islands, the Falkland Islands, and Gibraltar, which issued currency based on reserves of the British currency, the pound sterling. Singapore also has a currency board system.

Currency board: An institution that issues currency at a fixed rate of exchange with respect to another nation's currency.

In Argentina's case, its own peso was backed 100 percent by U.S. dollars. By truly fixing a one-for-one exchange rate in 1991, Argentina sought to link its financial markets to the more stable markets in the United States. When Brazil, Argentina's key trading partner, let its currency, the *real,* float in 1998, Brazilian interest rates shot up considerably. In Argentina, however, only some short-term interest rate instability occurred. Most observers believed the reason for the instability was fear that Argentina might abandon its currency board as it in fact did in 2002.

DOLLARIZATION: THE FED AS A MULTINATIONAL CENTRAL BANK   By 1999, Argentina had begun to contemplate an even more radical change in its monetary arrangements. It was considering **dollarization,** or the abandonment of its own currency in favor of direct use of the U.S. dollar as a medium of exchange, unit of account, store of value, and

Dollarization: A country's adoption of the U.S. dollar as its sole medium of exchange, unit of account, store of value, and standard of deferred payment.

standard of deferred payment. If it had implemented dollarization, Argentina would have had to import sufficient U.S. currency for people to use in hand-to-hand transactions. It would also have had to convert all Argentine financial accounts and contracts to dollars at the prevailing fixed rate of exchange.

When Argentina eliminated its currency board in 2002, the idea of an Argentinian dollarization was scuttled. Nevertheless, several Latin American nations began to consider dollarization. In 2000 Ecuador followed Panama's earlier example by dollarizing its economy. For the United States, both pros and cons are associated with the dollarization of part of Latin America. Dollarization would make it easier for U.S. companies to do business with Latin America, which accounts for about a fifth of U.S. trade.

In addition, increased use of the dollar outside the United States could create a financial windfall for the U.S. government. As we discussed in Chapter 1, governments earn *seigniorage,* the difference between the market value of money and the cost of its production, from producing money. When a country such as Ecuador dollarizes, it pays for the stock of U.S. dollars it needs for hand-to-hand trade by its residents by giving the U.S. government interest-bearing securities. The U.S. government then earns the interest on those securities, but as usual it does not pay interest on its currency. Worldwide seigniorage is now worth more than $15 billion a year to the U.S. Treasury. Dollarization by other Latin American countries undoubtedly would increase U.S. seigniorage considerably. At the same time, Fed and U.S. Treasury officials have expressed concerns about dollarization. If the Fed were to raise interest rates, say, in an effort to contain U.S. inflation, its action might be inappropriate for a dollarized Latin American economy. Thus, such a Fed action could have negative consequences outside the United States, fostering resentment and encouraging policymakers in dollarized countries to deflect blame for their economic problems onto U.S. policymakers. This could give governments of dollarized countries political cover for dodging tough decisions on appropriate economic policies within their own countries.

A FUTURE BIPOLAR OR TRIPOLAR MONETARY SYSTEM?   Emerging economies in eastern Europe have extended the idea of dollarization to the European Monetary Union's euro. Bulgaria, for instance, announced in 1999 that it might begin using the euro as its official currency. Other eastern European nations are considering the idea as well.

Some commentators have suggested that Russia should contemplate either "euro-izing" or dollarizing its economy. Dollarization might be easier to implement quickly, given that so many Russians already hold dollars. A key argument favoring adoption of the euro, however, is that Russia has relatively large trade flows with western European nations.

At present, these proposals are no more than ideas that various nations have explored. Nevertheless, in a world of interest rate targeting and internationally open financial markets, the idea of dollarization (or "euro-ization") has been one reaction to the reduced scope for relatively small countries to credibly conduct independent monetary policies.

Smaller, developing nations may or may not ultimately follow through on their dollarization ideas. Nevertheless, central banks in many of these nations gradually have sought to link their interest rate targets to those of the Fed, the European Central Bank, and, to a lesser extent in recent years, the Bank of Japan. In this way, world monetary policy interactions may become increasingly bipolar, or even tripolar, in the future. For this reason, monetary policy interactions among these three central banks have become a key focus of those interested in understanding Fed policymaking. We shall turn to this issue in the next chapter.

5. What are the international implications of interest rate targeting? In a world of very open financial markets, the uncovered interest parity condition is likely to be nearly satisfied. As a result, expected currency depreciation is approximately equal to the difference between national interest rates. This presents central banks that target interest rates in small, emerging economies with a choice. One is to target their interest rates in an effort to achieve ultimate goals at home, thereby permitting foreign exchange markets to determine how much their currencies depreciate or appreciate. The other is to try to smooth exchange rates and adjust their interest rate targets as needed, relative to those of large economies. The latter option constrains the ability to conduct independent monetary policies, so some nations have opted for currency board arrangements, in which they issue currencies that are strictly related to the currency of another major nation. Some nations have contemplated replacing their currency with another nation's currency.

Chapter Summary

1. Rationales for Interest Rate Targeting by Most of the World's Central Banks: A traditional rationale for interest rate targeting is that an interest rate may be the intermediate target that is most consistent with economic stabilization. Another rationale is that interest rate targeting may help central banks maintain their anti-inflation credibility. Because interest rates are readily observable and easy for central banks to influence, they may be particularly clear signals of the objectives of monetary policy. Thus, using interest rate targets could enhance the credibility of central banks.

2. Base Drift and Price-Level Nonstationarity and Their Possible Causes: Base drift takes place whenever measures of depository institution reserves or monetary aggregates fail to adjust to levels consistent with a fixed long-run average rate of growth. Price-level nonstationarity occurs when a nation's price level drifts upward (or downward) over time without converging to a long-run average level. Central bank efforts to engage in excessive interest rate smoothing can cause base drift and price-level nonstationarity. Monetary targeting, exchange rate smoothing, and international economic interdependence can also cause base drift and price-level nonstationarity, however. For this reason, interest-rate-targeting policies are not necessarily responsible for these phenomena.

3. Interest Rate Targeting and the Term Structure of Interest Rates: The target that the Fed establishes for

the twenty-four-hour federal funds rate pins down, or anchors, the low-maturity end of the term structure of interest rates. Financial markets then determine other market interest rates in light of existing term and risk premiums. Before 1994, Fed did not openly divulge its daily target for the federal funds rate, which increased uncertainty about future daily interest rates and thereby weakened somewhat the relationship between the federal funds rate and other market rates. Since 1994, the Fed has announced its target, and this has tightened the relationship. Nonetheless, U.S. financial markets are so efficient that the federal funds rate probably is not a better indicator of Fed policy objectives than most other market rates.

4. The Importance of Accurate Inflation Forecasts for Successful Implementation of Interest Rate Targeting: Any nominal interest rate that a central bank might target is equal to the sum of the real interest rate and the expected inflation rate. Because the real interest rate is not affected by monetary policy in the long run, the Fed's interest rate target must be consistent with current inflation expectations. The Fed will lose anti-inflation credibility if it sets the interest rate target too low in light of current expected inflation. In turn, if people form expectations rationally, then the expected inflation rate indicates the true average path of inflation.

5. International Implications of Interest Rate Targeting: Interest rate targeting in a world environment with very open flows of funds among national financial markets makes it more likely that the uncovered interest parity condition will be nearly satisfied. Consequently, expected currency depreciation is approximately equal to the difference between national interest rates. This limits the options of central banks in small, emerging economies. They can target interest rates to try to attain ultimate objectives and allow foreign exchange markets to determine how much their currencies depreciate or appreciate. Alternatively, they can attempt to smooth exchange rates and

vary their interest rate targets relative to those of larger economies, which sharply limits their ability to conduct independent monetary policies. Given this constraint, a few nations have established currency board arrangements, in which they issue currencies at a set rate of exchange relative to the currency of another major nation. Some nations have considered dollarization, in which they replace their currency with the U.S. dollar, and others have recently contemplated replacing their currency with the European Monetary Union's euro.

Questions and Problems

(Answers to odd-numbered questions and problems may be found on the Web at **http://money.swcollege.com** under "Student Resources.")

1. Suppose that the money multipliers relating the monetary base to M1 and M2 are highly variable, reflecting various sources of slippage from the reserves market through the term structure of interest rates to the equilibrium quantity of money. Would these conditions tend to favor targeting a monetary aggregate or an interest rate as an intermediate monetary policy target? Could money-multiplier variability tend to favor either approach from the standpoint of monetary policy credibility? Explain your reasoning for both answers.

2. Explain the basic argument for why interest rate targeting has the potential to make a Fed commitment to an anti-inflationary monetary policy more credible to the public.

3. Explain the basic concepts of base drift and price-level nonstationarity.

4. Most economists agree that price-level nonstationarity need not always accompany base drift. Explain verbally, or using graphs if they are helpful, how this could happen. Explain your reasoning. [Hint: Think about the kind of situation in which trying to make the price level stationary over time might require drift of a reserve aggregate, such as nonborrowed reserves.]

5. Under what circumstances is interest rate targeting most likely to be associated with base drift and price-level nonstationarity?

6. When is interest rate targeting least likely to induce base drift and price-level nonstationarity?

7. Suppose that a change in the twenty-year Treasury bond rate provides a signal of Fed policy intentions that is as clear as an accompanying change in the federal funds rate. What might you be able to infer about U.S. financial markets and about the relative usefulness of the federal funds rate as a key monetary policy indicator? Why?

8. In the short run, higher nominal interest rates can induce a contraction of aggregate demand and a decline in equilibrium real GDP. In the long run, however, higher nominal interest rates are associated with higher actual and expected inflation. Explain why this complicates the Fed's interest-rate-targeting procedure.

9. Why does the Fed depend on inflation forecasts to help it determine its interest rate targets?

10. Suppose that you are the chief of a central bank in a small developing country, and you use interest rate targeting to implement monetary policy. Large flows of financial assets and traded goods move across your borders with a large nation, and the large nation's central bank also uses an interest rate target. One of your key policy goals is to limit actual and expected changes in the rate of exchange of your currency for the currency of the large nation. Can you conduct your own monetary policy independent of the policy of the other nation's central bank? Why or why not?

Before the Test

Test your understanding of the material covered in this chapter by taking the Chapter 21 interactive quiz at **http://money.swcollege.com**.

Online Application

Internet URL: **http://users.erols.com/kurrency/**

Title: Currency Boards

Navigation: Open the above Web site. Then, under the heading "Currency Boards," click on "Introduction to Currency Boards."

Application: Read the article, and then answer the following questions:

1. What are the key features of an "orthodox" currency board?

2. In what ways has Bulgaria's currency board differed from an orthodox currency board?

For Group Study and Analysis: The article lists a number of countries that have used currency boards in the past and present. Set up groups to examine nations with currency boards in specific regions of the world. Have each group develop a list of nations in its region that have had good or poor experience with currency boards. What factors appear to influence how well a currency board works?

Selected References and Further Reading

Bernanke, Ben, Thomas Laubach, Frederic Mishkin, and Adam Posen, eds. *Inflation Targeting: Lessons from the International Experience.* Princeton, N.J.: Princeton University Press, 1999.

Carlstrom, Charles, and Timothy Fuerst. "The Taylor Rule: A Guidepost for Monetary Policy?" Federal Reserve Bank of Cleveland *Economic Commentary,* July 2003.

Cover, James, and David VanHoose. "Political Pressures, Credibility, and the Choice of the Optimal Monetary Policy Instrument." *Journal of Economics and Business* 52 (July/August 2000): 325–341.

Daniels, Joseph, and David VanHoose. "The Nonstationarity of Money and Prices in Interdependent Economies." *Review of International Economics* 7 (February 1999): 87–101.

Garfinkel, Michelle, and Daniel Thornton. "The Information Content of the Federal Funds Rate: Is It Unique?" *Journal of Money, Credit, and Banking* 27 (August 1995): 838–847.

Goodfriend, Marvin. "Interest Rates and the Conduct of Monetary Policy." *Carnegie-Rochester Series on Public Policy* 34 (1991): 7–30.

Rudebusch, Glenn. "Federal Funds Interest Rate Targeting, Rational Expectations, and the Term Structure." *Journal of Monetary Economics* 35 (April 1995): 245–274.

Svensson, Lars. "Price-Level Targeting versus Inflation Targeting: A Free Lunch?" *Journal of Money, Credit, and Banking* 31 (August 1999): 277–295.

Swanson, Eric. "Federal Reserve Transparency and Financial Market Forecasts of Short-Term Interest Rates." Board of Governors of the Federal Reserve System, February 2004.

Thornton, Daniel. "The Fed and Short-Term Interest Rates: Is It Open Market Operations, Open Mouth Operations, or Interest Rate Smoothing?" *Journal of Banking and Finance* 28 (March 2004): 475–498.

Walsh, Carl. "Interest Rates and Monetary Policy." Chapter 10 in *Monetary Theory and Policy.* Cambridge, Mass.: MIT Press, 1998.

Yeyati, Levy, and Federico Sturzenegger, eds. *Dollarization: Debates and Policy Alternatives.* Cambridge, Mass.: MIT Press, 2003.

MoneyXtra

Log on to the MoneyXtra Web site now (**http://moneyxtra.swcollege.com**) for additional learning resources such as practice quizzes, case studies, readings, and additional economic applications.

Policymaking in the World Economy—

International Dimensions of Monetary Policy

Fundamental Issues

1. What are the pros and cons of fixed versus floating exchange rates?

2. What is the monetary approach to exchange rate determination?

3. What is the portfolio approach to exchange rate determination?

4. How effective are foreign-exchange-market interventions?

At the beginning of the twentieth century, Argentina was one of the most prosperous nations in the world. Even after decades of economic decline during that century, many of Argentina's residents liked to think of themselves as "South American Europeans" and began to look down on their Brazilian neighbors. Nevertheless, Argentina worked together with Brazil, Paraguay, and Uruguay to form the Mercosur customs union, and trade between Argentina and Brazil expanded by 400 percent between Mercosur's founding in 1991 and the end of 1998. A new spirit of cooperation had emerged between the nations.

By the early 2000s, however, groups of unemployed Argentine workers trooped up and down the streets of Buenos Aires, the capital city of Argentina, carrying signs stating "Made in Brazil—No!" as part of a "Buy Argentine" campaign. Guests appearing on a public affairs program nearly came to blows after business leaders on the program complained that Brazil's investment climate was better than Argentina's. Talk-show hosts began branding Argentine consultants working with Brazilian companies as "traitors."

What happened? Brazil devalued its currency and then allowed it to float— albeit not entirely freely—in foreign exchange markets. In the meantime, Argentina kept its currency at parity with the U.S. dollar, as it had done consistently since 1991. Between late 1999 and early 2001, wages and other business costs in Brazil fell nearly 30 percent below those of Argentina. Multinational firms such as Philips Electronics and Goodyear and a number of Argentine companies started shifting production from Argentina to Brazil, taking thousands of jobs along with them. By 2002, Argentina had abandoned its system for maintaining parity with the U.S. dollar.

Clearly, it can make a big difference whether a nation fixes its exchange rate or allows the value of its currency to float. Under what circumstances is it desirable to peg the exchange value of a nation's currency? What are the advantages and disadvantages of a floating exchange rate for monetary policymaking? Should the world's central banks work together to aim for stable output and prices, or should they at least fix exchange rates in an effort to maintain mutually stable rates of worldwide inflation or deflation? Can central banks fix exchange rates? These are questions of real-world significance. They also are questions that we shall address in this chapter, which considers the international aspects of monetary policy.

Fixed versus Floating Exchange Rates

As discussed in Chapter 21, some countries have abandoned central-banking arrangements in favor of currency boards. Unlike a central bank, a currency board does not have a discount window. It does not impose reserve requirements, nor does it regulate private banks. The single duty of a currency board is to issue a national currency at a fixed rate of exchange relative to the currency of another nation.

In years past, many central banks, including the Federal Reserve, sought to maintain fixed exchange rates. Since the 1970s, however, the United States and a number of other nations have permitted their exchange rates to float, meaning that global market forces determine their values.

What factors should a country take into account when choosing between fixed and floating exchange rates? We begin our exploration of the international dimensions of monetary policy by contemplating this important question.

An Argument for Fixed Exchange Rates

In a system of floating exchange rates, variations in the demand for or supply of foreign exchange cause the exchange rate to fluctuate. As we noted in Chapter 5, changes in the exchange rate can affect the market values of incomes and of financial assets that are denominated in foreign currencies. This can increase the foreign exchange risks that a nation's residents face, thereby inducing them to incur costs to avoid these risks.

HEDGING AGAINST FOREIGN EXCHANGE RISK As you learned in Chapter 6, a country's residents are not defenseless in the face of foreign exchange risk. They can *hedge* against such risks, meaning that they can adopt strategies intended to offset the risk arising from exchange rate variations.

For instance, as discussed in Chapter 6, households, firms, and financial institutions can hedge against foreign exchange risks by using derivatives such as forward currency contracts, currency futures, currency options, and currency swaps. They can use forward or futures contracts to ensure that they will receive the current market forward exchange rate on the future delivery of a sum of currency. They can also use options and swaps to try to protect flows of foreign-currency-denominated earnings from fluctuations arising from exchange rate swings.

THE COSTS OF HEDGING Hedging against foreign exchange risks is not costless, however. Often, businesses and financial institutions that wish to hedge must pay for the time and talents of experts in the use of hedging strategies. Individuals must pay these experts fees and commissions. In addition, the hedging strategies themselves can sometimes entail taking potentially risky positions that expose holders of derivatives to other kinds of risk if market conditions change unexpectedly.

One common rationale for fixing exchange rates is that this policy can reduce or perhaps even eliminate hedging costs. If exchange rates are fixed, the argument goes, then the potential for exchange rate variability is greatly diminished, and households and businesses will not have to incur the costs of hedging against foreign exchange risks. (One proposal for trying to reduce exchange rate volatility while permitting exchange rates to float is to implement a "Tobin tax"; see the *Policy Focus: Would Imposing a "Tobin Tax" Reduce Exchange Rate Volatility?*)

Exchange Rates as Shock Absorbers

Proponents of fixed exchange rates argue that the world's people would be better off if their governments adopted a system of completely rigid exchange rates. Indeed, taken to its logical extreme, this argument implies that we would be better off with a *single world currency*. If we all were to adopt the same currency, after all, all foreign exchange risks would be eliminated. Furthermore, people would no longer have to incur the costs of converting one currency into another. For example, today a U.S. tourist traveling from San Francisco to China must pay a fee to convert U.S. dollars to Chinese renminbi. Such fees would no longer exist if U.S. and Chinese residents all used the same currency.

Nevertheless, if a system of rigid exchange rates would be so advantageous, then why do most developed nations allow their exchange rates to be market determined? If people could gain from using a common currency, why are there so many separate currencies? Presumably, there must be potentially significant disadvantages from fixing exchange rates or from adopting a single currency. There must be a solid rationale for why so many nations have their own currencies and several countries allow their exchange rates to float.

POLICY

Focus

Would Imposing a "Tobin Tax" Reduce Exchange Rate Volatility?

The late Nobel laureate James Tobin once suggested that imposing a special tax—now known as a *Tobin tax*—on foreign exchange transactions might weaken the incentive for traders to engage in purely speculative exchanges. Today's proponents of a Tobin tax argue that there is "excessive" trading in foreign exchange markets because of so-called noise traders. These are traders who engage in foreign exchange trans-

actions as each new scrap of data—even ultimately irrelevant data—arrives. Their trading activities add to volatility in the demand for and supply of foreign exchange.

Imposing a Tobin tax, proponents suggest, would discourage noise trading, thereby lessening exchange rate variability, reducing hedging expenses, and making a system of floating exchange rates more efficient. One problem with this idea is that such a tax could reduce global exchange rate volatility only if it is applied in every foreign exchange market. Otherwise, traders could simply respond to a Tobin tax in their home market by moving their operations to other locales.

Another problem is that when faced with a Tobin tax, other traders who do not simply respond to foreign-exchange-market noise would have less incentive to engage in transactions that correct the currency mis-pricings created by noise traders. Thus, it is not completely certain that even coordinated efforts by all the world's nations to impose and enforce a Tobin tax would actually reduce exchange rate volatility.

FOR CRITICAL ANALYSIS: Why might governments in search of revenues to fund their expenditures be attracted to the idea of the Tobin tax even if its implementation did not reduce exchange rate volatility?

A RATIONALE FOR SEPARATE CURRENCIES AND FLOATING EXCHANGE
RATES   The theory of *optimal currency areas,* which was developed by Robert Mundell of Columbia University, offers an explanation for why different nations might wish to issue separate currencies. It also explains under what circumstances people in different geographic regions, such as Colorado and Michigan, can benefit from adopting a common currency unit.

A Two-Region Example   To understand the fundamental idea of an optimal currency area, consider an imaginary situation. Suppose that there is a large island whose residents have divided into two groups inhabiting separate regions of nearly identical size: region *A* and region *B*. Residents of each region specialize in producing different goods and services. Firms in region *A* manufacture garden equipment, and firms in region *B* produce digital television sets. Wages and other prices of factors of production in each region are sticky in the short run.

Households and firms in the two regions trade their goods and services across the border separating the regions, but barriers prevent the flow of people and their possessions between the regions. For instance, perhaps the residents of the regions speak different languages or have cultural, religious, or political differences that have led them to erect these barriers. In any event, these obstacles to cross-border movements prevent people in the two regions from exchanging labor or other factor services. All they can do is take their final goods and services to the border to trade.

Each region has its own government. Each government, in turn, issues its own "national" currency. Therefore, to trade goods and services across the border separating the regions, people must convert their currencies at the prevailing exchange rate between the two currencies.

Adjusting to Changes in the Relative Demands for Regional Products   Now envision the following event: A best-selling book on the joys of gardening induces couch potatoes across the island to turn off their televisions and begin planting. As a result, people in both regions reduce their demand for digital televisions produced in region *B* and increase their demand for the garden equipment produced in region *A*. This causes the firms in region *B* to reduce their demands for labor and other factors of production. Consequently, real GDP in region *B* begins to decline. Because wages are sticky, unemployment begins to rise in region *B*. Simultaneously, firms in region *A* raise their production in the face of the increased demand for garden equipment across the island. As a result, region *A* begins to run a trade surplus, and its real GDP and employment rise.

If the rate of exchange between the regions' currencies is fixed, then the assumed short-run stickiness of wages and prices causes unemployment to persist for some time in region *B* following the changes in consumers' tastes. In the long run, of course, the price of the garden equipment manufactured in region *A* will increase, and the price of the digital televisions made in region *B* will decline, leading to a rebalancing of trade between the two regions. Until this long-run adjustment occurs, however, region *B* can experience a significant unemployment problem.

If the exchange rate is flexible, however, then the trade surplus in region *A* and the accompanying trade deficit in region *B* induce a rapid depreciation in the value of region *B*'s currency relative to the currency of region *A*. This causes an immediate fall in the effective price of region *B*'s digital televisions as perceived by residents of region *A*. At the same time, there is a quick rise in the effective price of region *A*'s garden equipment faced by residents of region *B*. As a result, trade between the two nations is balanced much more rapidly with a floating exchange rate. Furthermore, region *B*'s unemployment problem is more short lived.

In this example, the two regions benefit from using separate currencies with a floating rate of exchange. Fixing the exchange rate—or taking the further step of adopting a single currency—would eliminate the ability of the exchange rate to adjust to changes in relative demands for the regions' goods. This would expose the regions to the possibility of chronic payments imbalances and unemployment problems.

Of course, residents of regions with separate currencies and a market-determined exchange rate face foreign exchange risks and costs of converting currency. Nevertheless, adopting individual currencies and a floating exchange rate protects the regions from unemployment dangers that arise from language, cultural, or legal barriers to worker migration.

OPTIMAL CURRENCY AREAS   Now suppose that the conditions that led to the restrictions on cross-border migration or commuting break down. Consequently, residents of region A can move freely to region B to work, and vice versa. Let's further suppose that shortly after this development, once again the demand for region A's garden equipment rises and the demand for region B's digital televisions declines.

Again the immediate results are a trade surplus, higher real GDP, and higher employment in region A and a trade deficit, lower output, and lower employment in region B. As a result, some residents of region B find themselves without work. Now, however, these unemployed region B residents can migrate—or perhaps commute—to newly available jobs in region A. Unemployment in region B, therefore, is at worst a temporary phenomenon. Indeed, unemployment in both regions together is minimized in the face of such changes in the relative demands for their products.

In this example, there is no reason that the exchange rate should not be fixed, thereby permitting residents of both regions to avoid foreign exchange risks and the costs of hedging against these risks. Indeed, economists would conclude that the two regions together constitute an **optimal currency area**—a geographic area within which fixed exchange rates can be maintained without slowing regional adjustments to changing regional conditions. Furthermore, within such an optimal currency area, separate regions find it beneficial to adopt a *common currency* if the cost of converting currencies for regional trade exceeds any perceived gain from having separate currencies. Thus, if the residents of regions A and B continue to perceive sizable benefits from using separate currencies even though no barriers otherwise separate their regions, they may be willing to continue to incur the currency conversion costs that arise when they trade goods. If, however, the currency conversion costs are sufficiently large relative to the potential benefits of maintaining separate currencies, the residents of the two regions may gain, on net, from adopting a single, common currency.

RATIONALES FOR SEPARATE CURRENCIES   What benefits might residents of two regions with few or no barriers to labor mobility perceive that would justify maintaining separate currencies? One might be a widespread perception that loss of a region's unique currency would entail a sacrifice of political sovereignty. If the region is a nation-state with its own cultural history that its residents associate with its currency—for instance, the United Kingdom's pound sterling and the memories it evokes of a former global empire—then convincing the residents to give up their currency could prove difficult.

LACK OF FISCAL INTEGRATION   Nationalist feelings are not the only reason why a country might choose not to join others in using a single currency. National governments maintain their own budgets with their own sources of revenues and distributions of expenditures. The key source of any government's revenues is taxes. As we discussed in Chapter 1, one type of taxation is *seigniorage,* or central bank profits earned from producing money whose market value exceeds its cost of production.

Optimal currency area: A region within which fixed exchange rates can be maintained without inhibiting prompt internal adjustments of employment and real GDP to changes in international market conditions.

Table 22-1 provides estimates of average annual rates of seigniorage relative to GDP and to government spending for selected nations between the early 1970s and the 1990s. As you can see, in several countries seigniorage has comprised less than 1 percent of GDP and less than 2 percent of government expenditures. In others, however, seigniorage has been a significant revenue source. In these nations, the government might have to undertake the politically painful task of increasing other taxes if it were to lose seigniorage following adoption of a common currency. Thus, these nations may value having a separate currency more than others.

For example, suppose that our hypothetical regions *A* and *B* together constitute an optimal currency area. Consequently, the two regions can maintain a fixed exchange rate without experiencing long-term trade imbalances or unemployment. Nonetheless, if the government of region *A* depends to a much larger extent upon seigniorage as a revenue source than the government of region *B,* then region *A* may be unwilling to adopt a common currency. Thus, the two regions might keep their exchange rate fixed yet continue to use separate currencies.

THE ADVANTAGE OF COMPETING CURRENCIES   Another rationale for retaining separate currencies is the potential economic benefits of *currency competition.* This idea was first put forward by Frederick Hayek, a prominent economist of the mid-twentieth century.

Table 22-1 Average Annual Rates of Seigniorage Relative to Gross Domestic Product and Government Expenditures

Country	Seigniorage as a Percentage of GDP	Seigniorage as a Percentage of Government Spending
New Zealand	0.38	1.04
Denmark	0.39	1.05
United States	0.43	1.96
Kuwait	0.46	2.01
United Kingdom	0.47	1.28
France	0.55	1.39
Germany	0.69	2.35
Japan	0.96	5.62
Kenya	0.98	4.00
Sri Lanka	1.52	4.97
Korea	1.57	9.70
India	1.72	11.82
Spain	2.03	7.76
Colombia	2.32	17.57
Uganda	2.38	21.65
Brazil	3.04	13.71
Costa Rica	3.33	15.09
Mexico	3.72	18.97
Bolivia	3.81	19.76
Iran	4.66	15.09
Nicaragua	7.86	23.70
Yugoslavia	11.87	148.95
Israel	14.84	22.28

SOURCE: Reid Click, "Seigniorage in a Cross-Section of Countries," *Journal of Money, Credit, and Banking* 30 (May 1998): 154–171.

Hayek argued that a central bank may be hesitant to place too much currency in circulation if it knows that such an action will reduce the exchange value of its nation's currency relative to those of other nations, thereby inducing people to hold less of its currency and reducing its seigniorage. Competition with currencies issued by other central banks, therefore, could lead a country's central bank to hold back on inflationary money growth.

Thus, Hayek argued, having many national currencies effectively in competition with each other can be advantageous to the residents of all nations. Indeed, Hayek concluded that people ultimately could lose if governments adopted a common currency. This, he felt, would reduce the extent of currency competition and thereby remove an important check on inflation in the regions that adopted the common currency. (The euro's emergence as a major world currency may also provide a check on U.S. seigniorage earnings; see *What Happens When the Euro Rivals the Dollar as a "Vehicle Currency"?*)

Does the European Monetary Union Make Economic Sense?

MONEYXTRA!
Online Case Study

Contemplate the issues that a nation faces when it chooses between fixed and floating exchange rates by going to the Chapter 22 Case Study, entitled "Time for a Fixed Exchange Rate?" **http://moneyxtra. swcollege.com**

The theory of optimal currency areas explains why nations might wish to use different currencies and let their exchange rates float. If nations use immigration restrictions, capital controls, and the like to restrain the flow of people and other productive factors *across* their borders, then it makes sense to use their own currencies *within* their borders. Allowing the exchange rate to adjust to variations in international demand and supply conditions then permits speedier price-level, real GDP, and employment adjustments to such variations. This helps to explain why residents of Argentina and Brazil, nations with somewhat different languages and cultures and hence with relatively limited cross-border movements of people and productive factors, might prefer to have their own separate currencies and to let their exchange rate vary.

What Happens When... **The Euro Rivals the Dollar as a "Vehicle Currency"?**

Since the end of World War II, the U.S. dollar has been the world's main *vehicle currency,* which, as you learned in Chapter 3, is a currency commonly used outside the country of origin to conduct international transactions. The world's major banks denominate most assets and liabilities used in cross-border transactions in dollars. In addition, most financial instruments issued in international money and capital markets have also been denominated in dollars. Many of these dollar holdings outside the United States, of course, generate seigniorage revenues for the U.S. Federal Reserve. After all, the Fed can use dollar-denominated currency and bank reserves to fund its own holdings of interest-bearing securities, thereby generating seigniorage.

Nevertheless, during the past few years more and more international transactions have involved euros instead of dollars. Although nearly 57 percent of banks' assets and liabilities allocated for use in international transactions are still denominated in dollars, the euro's share of transactions in international money and capital markets now rivals or surpasses the share going to the dollar. Indeed, the euro is now used to denominate about half of international money market instruments, compared with the dollar's 28 percent share.

As the dollar's use as a vehicle currency has declined, there has been a general worldwide substitution away from holdings of dollars in favor of the euro. Consequently, the Fed's seigniorage revenues have dropped off somewhat, and the seigniorage earnings of the European Central Bank have been rising.

FOR CRITICAL ANALYSIS: Why does widespread international acceptance of dollars and euros enable both to function as vehicle currencies in international markets for goods, services, and financial assets?

REDUCING HEDGING AND CONVERSION COSTS   The theory also helps to explain why residents of both Colorado and Michigan might wish to use dollars, even though they are separated by over a thousand miles. Because there is such easy mobility of labor and capital within the United States, relatively little social cost is associated with fixing a one-for-one exchange rate and adopting a common currency in the two U.S. states, as well as in the other forty-eight. By using a common currency, residents of the states also save the costs of hedging to avoid foreign exchange risks. In addition, when a Michigan resident visits relatives in Denver or when a Colorado resident buys a good listed on the Web site of a Detroit-based retailer, neither has to worry about costs of converting currencies.

INCREASED MOBILITY   Finally, the theory helps to explain why nations within the European Monetary Union (EMU) adopted the euro as a common accounting unit beginning in 1999 and introduced a common currency in 2002. These nations are closely linked by trade in goods, services, and financial assets. In addition, in recent years they have somewhat reduced obstacles to flows of people and productive factors. For these reasons, adopting a common currency in EMU nations entailed fewer drawbacks than it would have just a decade or two before.

A few western European nations, such as the United Kingdom and Denmark, for now have forgone joining the EMU. There are at least two reasons for their hesitancy. Undoubtedly, one concern in the United Kingdom is the loss of the pound sterling and its historical role as a symbol of British sovereignty. Another reason is uncertainty about whether all of western Europe really constitutes an optimal currency area. Typically, comparisons of labor mobility in western Europe with those of other countries with single currencies, such as the United States and Canada, indicate that labor is much less mobile in western Europe. This implies that this portion of the world was not a strong candidate for an optimal currency area at the time the EMU was formed.

Nonetheless, for twelve nations—Austria, Belgium, Finland, France, Germany, Ireland, Italy, Luxembourg, the Netherlands, Portugal, and Spain in 1999 and Greece in 2001—the EMU has become a reality. These and other potential EMU members have embarked on a fascinating real-world experiment in which nations are adopting a common currency even though they fail to fully satisfy the classic criteria for an optimal currency area.

---

1. What are the pros and cons of fixed versus floating exchange rates?
A key drawback of floating exchange rates is the potential for foreign exchange risks generated by exchange rate variability. Fixing the exchange rate reduces the foreign exchange risks. A key problem with a fixed exchange rate, however, is that this policy eliminates the exchange rate's ability to serve as a shock absorber in the event of changing international market conditions. This is particularly true for nations with barriers to mobility of labor and other real productive factors. Such nations can benefit from adopting their own currencies and allowing exchange rates to change with evolving market forces. Furthermore, even countries within an optimal currency area may resist joining a monetary union if (1) their residents are sufficiently averse to giving up sovereignty, (2) their national governments would lose seigniorage revenues that they could not recoup via other sources of taxation, or (3) the countries fear that the loss of currency competition could remove restraints on inflationary policymaking.

Can Central Banks Peg Exchange Rates?

Even though nations continue to have their own separate currencies, a number of countries still aim to maintain fixed rates of currency exchange. These nations have determined that the costs of hedging against foreign exchange risks are greater than the costs generated by the lack of shock-absorbing adjustments in the exchange rate.

How do central banks go about trying to fix exchange rates? Can they maintain fixed rates of currency exchange? Let's try to answer these questions using the fundamental concepts that we have developed in earlier chapters.

Foreign-Exchange-Market Interventions and Exchange Rates

We must begin by developing an understanding of how central banks can attempt to influence exchange rates. To do so, central banks must become active participants in foreign exchange markets.

FOREIGN-EXCHANGE-MARKET INTERVENTION

Recall from Chapter 5 that we can envision the equilibrium spot exchange rate, S, as determined by the intersection of currency demand and supply schedules. Consider point A in Figure 22-1, at which the equilibrium exchange rate for Thailand, measured in Thai *baht* per U.S. dollar, is $S_1 = 45$ baht per dollar. At this market exchange rate, the equilibrium quantity of dollars traded for baht within a given time period is equal to Q^e.

Now suppose that the Bank of Thailand, the Thai central bank, decides that an exchange rate equal to $\bar{S} = 40$ baht per dollar is preferable in light of its objectives for internal and external balance. Clearly, this preferred exchange rate is below the market exchange rate. At $\bar{S}$, therefore, the quantity of dollars demanded in exchange for baht by currency traders, $\bar{Q}^d$, is greater than the quantity supplied, $\bar{Q}^s$. There will an excess quantity of dollars demanded by

**FIGURE 22-1
Intervening in the
Foreign Exchange Market
to Peg the Exchange Rate.**

The free-market equilibrium exchange rate arises at point A in the diagram. This exchange rate is $S_1 = 45$ Thai baht per U.S. dollar. If the Bank of Thailand desires to peg the exchange rate at $\bar{S} = 40$ baht per dollar, then it must provide the excess quantity of dollars demanded, $\bar{Q}^d - \bar{Q}^s$, by selling dollar-denominated assets in exchange for baht, to yield a total quantity of baht traded for dollars within the given time interval at point

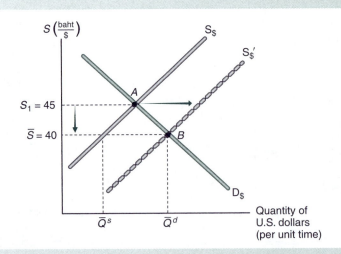

B. Hence, the Bank of Thailand must reduce its foreign exchange reserves to peg the baht's value relative to the dollar.

private individuals, companies, and financial institutions in the foreign exchange market at the Bank of Thailand's desired exchange rate, $\bar{S}$.

Thus, for the Bank of Thailand to be able to peg the exchange rate at $\bar{S}$, within the given period of time it must be willing and able to supply the excess quantity of dollars, which is equal to $\bar{Q}^d - \bar{Q}^s$. The Bank of Thailand therefore must sell this quantity of dollars in exchange for baht. Thus, it must use dollar-denominated assets, such as cash and securities, that it has on hand to purchase baht-denominated assets.

Let's suppose that the Bank of Thailand decides to try to peg the exchange rate at $\bar{S}$ in Figure 22-1. By selling $\bar{Q}^d - \bar{Q}^s$ in dollar-denominated assets, the Bank of Thailand conducts a **foreign-exchange-market intervention.** That is, it conducts official foreign exchange transactions, using some of its existing foreign-currency reserves—in this case, dollar-denominated assets—with an intention to alter the value of its currency. The effect of the Bank of Thailand's intervention is to shift the dollar supply schedule to the right. By purchasing baht with some of its existing reserves of dollar-denominated assets, the Bank of Thailand can thereby push the exchange rate downward, from $S_1 = 45$ baht per dollar at point A to $\bar{S} = 40$ baht per dollar at point B. It can peg the exchange rate at the desired value.

Keep in mind, however, that Figure 22-1 applies to a particular period of foreign-exchange-market trading, such as a given week in the month of February. If market conditions remain unchanged during the following week, then point A will again be the natural free-market equilibrium point, and S_1 will be the market exchange rate in the absence of actions by the Bank of Thailand. In this circumstance, the Bank of Thailand will have to repeat its intervention during this following week to keep the baht-dollar exchange rate fixed at $\bar{S}$. If the market conditions illustrated in Figure 22-1 prevail week after week, the Bank of Thailand will have to continue to draw upon its initial quantity of dollar-denominated assets. It will be able to *maintain* the exchange rate peg of $\bar{S}$ only as long as its reserves of dollar assets hold out.

Foreign-exchange-market intervention: A central bank purchase or sale of foreign-currency reserves in an effort to alter the value of its nation's currency.

FOREIGN-EXCHANGE-MARKET INTERVENTION AND THE MONETARY BASE

Recall from Chapter 15 that the key liabilities of a central bank such as the Federal Reserve or the Bank of Thailand are the currency it issues and the reserve deposits of depository institutions. Together, currency and depository institution reserves comprise the nation's *monetary base*. Thus, if the quantity of currency is equal to C and the total quantity of depository institution reserves is equal to TR, then the nation's monetary base is equal to $MB = C + TR$.

The key assets of central banks are their holdings of bonds and other securities. As you learned in Chapter 15, the bulk of these holdings are domestic securities. International economists refer to a central bank's domestic security holdings as **domestic credit,** which we denote as DC. The other securities are part of a central bank's foreign exchange reserves, denoted FER.

Domestic credit: A central bank's holdings of domestic securities.

To keep things simple, let's suppose that, as shown in Figure 22-2 on page 500, domestic and foreign securities are the only assets of a central bank and that currency and depository institution reserves are its only liabilities. (Indeed, these assets and liabilities comprise 80 to 90 percent of the balance sheets of most central banks.) We know that the sum of the central bank's liabilities equals the monetary base. Because the central bank's assets must equal its liabilities, it follows that the sum of domestic credit and foreign exchange reserves must equal the sum of currency and total reserves of depository institutions, or the monetary base. That is, $DC + FER = C + TR = MB$. Thus, we can think of the monetary base in two ways. From the perspective of the central bank's liabilities, the monetary base is equal to currency plus total reserves of depository institutions. Viewed from the asset side of the central bank's balance sheet, the monetary base is composed of domestic credit and foreign exchange reserves.

FIGURE 22-2
A Simplified Central Bank Balance Sheet.

Assets	Liabilities
Domestic credit (DC)	Currency (C)
Foreign exchange reserves (FER)	Total reserves (TR)
Monetary base (MB)	Monetary base (MB)

The main assets of a central bank are domestic credit, such as domestic government securities, and foreign exchange reserves, which include holdings of foreign currencies and foreign-currency-denominated bonds. The key liabilities of a central bank are the domestic currency that it issues and the reserves of depository institutions. Viewed from either the asset side or the liability side of the balance sheet, these sum to the nation's monetary base.

STERILIZED VERSUS NONSTERILIZED FOREIGN-EXCHANGE-MARKET INTERVENTIONS The fact that the sum of domestic credit and foreign exchange reserves is a nation's monetary base has an important implication. Foreign-exchange-market interventions that change the quantity of foreign exchange reserves, *FER*, can cause the nation's monetary base to change.

For example, suppose that, as in the example illustrated in Figure 22-1 on page 498, the Bank of Thailand wishes to push the baht-dollar exchange rate below its private-market level. To do so, it must sell dollar-denominated foreign exchange reserves. Thus, *FER* declines. Because the monetary base is $MB = DC + FER$, then as long as domestic credit, *DC*, does not change, the Thai monetary base must also fall. Of course, the monetary base is also equal to $MB = C + TR$. If the Bank of Thailand keeps the stock of currency unchanged, then its sale of foreign exchange reserves also entails a reduction in total depository institutions reserves. This means that a sale of foreign exchange reserves has essentially the same immediate effect as a domestic open market sale. It reduces total reserves of depository institutions and causes the monetary base to decline.

A central bank does not have to allow interventions to affect depository institution reserves and the monetary base, however. In our example, the Bank of Thailand could engage in **sterilization** by preventing the foreign-exchange-market intervention from affecting the monetary base. In the case of a sale of foreign exchange reserves, the Bank of Thailand can do this by simultaneously purchasing an amount of domestic securities equal to the amount of foreign-currency-denominated assets it sells. As a result, when *FER* declines, *DC* rises by an equal amount, so the Thai monetary base is unchanged.

By way of contrast, a *nonsterilized* foreign-exchange-market sale entails a reduction in foreign exchange reserves with no matching increase in domestic credit. Consequently, a nonsterilized intervention leads to a change in the monetary base.

Sterilization: A central bank action to prevent variations in its foreign exchange reserves from affecting the monetary base.

The Monetary Approach to Evaluating the Effects of Foreign-Exchange-Market Interventions

One key perspective on the ultimate effects of foreign-exchange-market interventions on exchange rates is the **monetary approach** to exchange rate determination. It indicates that the key determinant of the equilibrium exchange rate is the quantity of money supplied by a central bank.

Monetary approach: A theory of exchange rate determination that predicts that the fundamental determination of a nation's exchange rate is the quantity of money supplied by its central bank.

THE MONETARY APPROACH TO EXCHANGE RATE DETERMINATION The monetary approach to exchange rate determination has its roots in the quantity theory of money discussed in Chapter 18. Suppose that purchasing power parity (see Chapter 5) holds, so that

$$P = S \times P^*.$$

That is, the domestic price level, P, equals the spot exchange rate times the foreign price level, P^*. In the case of Thailand, therefore, if purchasing power parity holds, then the price level in Thailand equals the baht-dollar exchange rate times the U.S. price level.

Recall that the money-multiplier process discussed in Chapter 13 indicates that

$$M = m_M \times MB,$$

so that the quantity of money in circulation is equal to a money multiplier times the monetary base. The monetary base is $MB = DC + FER$, so we can rewrite the money-multiplier expression for the quantity of money as

$$M = m_M \times (DC + FER).$$

Finally, recall that according to the quantity theory of money, the quantity of money demanded is determined by the Cambridge equation:

$$M^d = k \times P \times y,$$

where k is a fraction that indicates the portion of nominal GDP that people desire to hold as money and $P \times y$ is nominal GDP, with y denoting real GDP.

In equilibrium, the quantity of money demanded is equal to the quantity of money supplied, so $M^d = M$, or

$$k \times P \times y = m_M \times (DC + FER).$$

Under purchasing power parity, however, $P = S \times P^*$. Thus, we can substitute $S \times P^*$ for P to get

$$k \times S \times P^* \times y = m_M \times (DC + FER).$$

Finally, we can solve this equation for S:

$$S = \frac{m_M \times (DC + FER)}{k \times P^* \times y}.$$

According to the monetary approach to exchange rate determination, the equilibrium exchange rate equals the money multiplier times the sum of domestic credit and foreign exchange reserves divided by the product of the Cambridge k, the foreign price level, and domestic real GDP. Thus, the monetary approach predicts that the equilibrium exchange rate will rise (the domestic currency will depreciate) if (1) the money multiplier rises, (2) the central bank increases domestic credit, (3) the central bank increases its foreign exchange reserves, (4) the Cambridge k decreases, so that the domestic demand for money falls, (5) the foreign price level decreases, or (6) domestic real GDP falls. (Consistent with the monetary approach to exchange rate determination, during the 2000s the Swiss exchange rate increased following foreign-exchange-market interventions that boosted the Swiss monetary base; see on the next page the *Global Focus: A Swiss Monetary Policy Based on Foreign-Exchange-Market Interventions.*)

A Swiss Monetary Policy Based on Foreign-Exchange-Market Interventions

In early 2003, nominal interest rates in Switzerland fell very close to zero percent per year, and market interest rates remained near zero for the next couple of years. During this period, the nation found itself mired in its second recession of the 2000s, but the Swiss National Bank could not push *market* interest rates any lower.

Consequently, the Swiss National Bank switched from interest rate changes to foreign-exchange-market interventions as its main instrument of monetary policy. Purchases of foreign exchange reserves and the resulting increases in the Swiss monetary base caused the Swiss franc to depreciate relative to the currencies of most other nations. Swiss exports, which account for 45 percent of Switzerland's GDP, thereby became less expensive for residents of the nation's trading partners. Net exports in Switzerland rose, bringing about a rise in aggregate demand and a short-run increase in real GDP.

FOR CRITICAL ANALYSIS: Were Swiss *real* interest rates necessarily close to zero during 2003 and the following years?

EVALUATING NONSTERILIZED VERSUS STERILIZED FOREIGN-EXCHANGE-MARKET INTERVENTIONS USING THE MONETARY APPROACH   According to the monetary approach, the exchange rate effects of foreign-exchange-market interventions depend crucially on whether or not a central bank sterilizes the interventions. In the case of a nonsterilized intervention, such as a sale of dollar-denominated assets by the Bank of Thailand, foreign exchange reserves fall without an offsetting increase in domestic credit. As a result, *FER* declines, and the equilibrium spot exchange rate, *S*, decreases. This is consistent with the foreign-exchange-market adjustment depicted in Figure 22-1 on page 498.

By way of contrast, the monetary approach implies that sterilized foreign-exchange-market interventions will not influence the equilibrium exchange rate. In the solution for *S* above, note that if *DC* increases by the same amount that *FER* declines, then on net the numerator remains unaltered, and the equilibrium exchange rate does not change. Thus, if the central bank engages in an open market purchase that expands domestic credit by the same amount as the reduction in its foreign exchange reserves caused by a sale of foreign-currency-denominated assets, the net effect of its actions is an unaltered exchange rate.

This means that according to the monetary approach, Figure 22-1 depicts only the effect of a nonsterilized foreign-exchange-market intervention. Thus, the monetary approach indicates that Figure 22-1 is incomplete.

Figure 22-3 depicts the modification that the monetary approach implies is necessary when the Bank of Thailand sells dollar-denominated assets to increase the supply of dollars in the foreign exchange market. This intervention tends to push the exchange rate toward $\bar{S}$ at point *B*. Under the monetary approach interpretation, the decline in foreign exchange reserves at the Bank of Thailand reduces the Thai money supply and thereby reduces the Thai price level. Under purchasing power parity, therefore, the exchange rate must fall to $\bar{S}$. In the absence of sterilization, this would be the end of the story.

If the Bank of Thailand purchases domestic securities to sterilize its foreign-exchange-market sale, however, point *B* cannot be the final equilibrium. The reason is that the resulting increase in domestic credit pushes the Thai money supply back up. At the exchange rate $\bar{S}$, Thai residents do not wish to hold the additional baht that the Bank of Thailand supplies via domestic open market operations and the resulting multiple increase in deposits within the

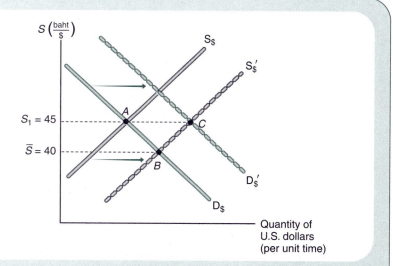

FIGURE 22-3
Effects of a Sterilized Foreign-Exchange-Market Intervention under the Monetary Approach to Exchange Rate Determination.

As in Figure 22-1, the sale of foreign exchange reserves by the Bank of Thailand initially reduces the Thai monetary base and money supply and shifts the dollar supply schedule rightward. If the Bank of Thailand sterilizes this intervention by purchasing domestic securities, then the Thai monetary base and money supply rise to their original levels. The monetary approach to exchange rate determination indicates that at the exchange rate $\overline{S} = 40$ baht per dollar, Thai residents will not wish to hold this amount of Thai money, so they enter the foreign exchange market seeking to purchase dollars with baht. This causes the dollar demand schedule to shift to the right, and the exchange rate returns to its original level of $S_1 = 45$ baht per dollar. Thus, according to the monetary approach, a sterilized intervention cannot influence the exchange rate.

Thai banking system. Thai residents enter the foreign exchange market seeking to exchange unwanted baht for dollars, which causes the dollar demand schedule to shift rightward in Figure 22-3. The exchange rate returns to its initial equilibrium value of S_1 at point C. Because the Thai money supply on net is unchanged, the Thai price level also does not change. Consequently, under purchasing power parity the exchange rate remains unaltered. A sterilized foreign-exchange-market sale leaves the equilibrium exchange rate unchanged.

2. What is the monetary approach to exchange rate determination?
According to the monetary approach to exchange rate determination, nonsterilized foreign-exchange-market interventions influence exchange rates by changing the monetary base. As a result, nonsterilized interventions alter the quantity of money supplied relative to the quantity demanded, inducing an exchange rate adjustment. Sterilized foreign-exchange-market interventions, however, leave the monetary base and the money supply unchanged. Consequently, the monetary approach indicates that sterilized interventions cannot influence exchange rates.

The Portfolio Approach to Evaluating the Effects of Foreign-Exchange-Market Interventions

The monetary approach to exchange rate determination focuses exclusively on the exchange rate's role in bringing about an equalization of the quantity of money demanded with the quantity of money supplied. The **portfolio approach** to exchange rate determination, by way

Portfolio approach: A theory of exchange rate determination that predicts that a nation's exchange rate adjusts to ensure that its residents are satisfied with their allocation of wealth among holdings of domestic money, domestic bonds, and foreign bonds.

of contrast, proposes a broader role for the exchange rate. According to this approach, the exchange rate adjusts to permit residents of a nation to achieve a desired allocation of *all* financial assets, including domestic and foreign bonds as well as holdings of domestic money.

THE PORTFOLIO APPROACH TO EXCHANGE RATE DETERMINATION   To illustrate the basic foundation of the portfolio approach to exchange rate determination, let's suppose that all financial wealth within a nation is split among holdings of domestic money, M, domestic bonds, B, and foreign bonds, B^*. Thus, if we use the spot exchange rate, S, to value foreign bonds in terms of the domestic currency, the domestic-currency value of financial wealth, W, is

$$W \equiv M + B + (S \times B^*).$$

Thus, financial wealth by definition is equal to holdings of domestic money and bonds plus the domestic-currency value of holdings of foreign bonds. Under the portfolio approach to exchange rate determination, the exchange rate adjusts until people are satisfied with their allocation of current financial wealth among these three financial assets.

This means that as in the monetary approach to exchange rate determination, the exchange rate ultimately must settle at a level that is consistent with the equalization of the quantity of money demanded with the quantity of money supplied. In addition, however, the exchange rate must adjust to ensure that the quantity of domestic bonds demanded equals the quantity of domestic bonds supplied and that the quantity of foreign bonds demanded equals the quantity of foreign bonds supplied.

THE PORTFOLIO-BALANCE EFFECT   Now let's reconsider the effect of a foreign-exchange-market intervention in which the Bank of Thailand sells foreign exchange reserves in an effort to achieve a desired exchange rate $\overline{S}$ that is below the free-market exchange rate S_1. As you have seen, according to the monetary approach, the Bank of Thailand can peg the exchange rate at the below-free-market value of $\overline{S}$ only if it conducts a nonsterilized sale of dollar-denominated assets that reduces the money supply. In contrast, a sterilized intervention leaves the money supply unchanged, so the exchange rate remains unaltered at its free-market equilibrium value of S_1.

Under the portfolio approach, this is not the final effect of a sterilized intervention, however. If the Bank of Thailand sterilizes its sale of foreign exchange reserves by conducting open market purchases of bonds that keep the Thai monetary base unchanged, then its purchases of domestic bonds reduce the quantity of domestic bonds available for private exchange. At the same time, its sale of foreign exchange reserves includes sales of U.S. bonds. Hence, a sterilized foreign-exchange-market intervention is, in effect, an exchange of U.S. bonds for Thai bonds. This means that the Bank of Thailand's sterilized intervention results in a net reduction in the demand for U.S. assets in favor of holdings of Thai assets. Obtaining the baht required to accomplish this net portfolio reshuffling of domestic and foreign bonds entails supplying dollars in the foreign exchange market. As a result, the dollar supply schedule shifts rightward as originally shown in Figure 22-1 on page 498. The exchange rate thereby declines from S_1 to $\overline{S}$ even though sterilization leaves the Thai money supply unchanged.

Hence, the portfolio approach indicates that sterilized foreign-exchange-market interventions have an exchange rate effect that is absent from the monetary approach. Economists call this a **portfolio-balance effect.** Because the portfolio approach views the exchange rate as the relative price of imperfectly substitutable bonds, changes in government or central bank holdings of bonds denominated in various currencies influence exchange rates by affecting the

Portfolio-balance effect: A fundamental prediction of the portfolio approach to exchange rate determination, in which changes in central bank holdings of domestic and foreign bonds alter the equilibrium prices at which traders are willing to hold these bonds, inducing a change in the exchange rate.

equilibrium prices at which traders are willing to hold these assets. For instance, in our example above, the Bank of Thailand's intervention alters the quantity of domestic assets relative to the quantity of foreign assets held by individuals and firms. As a result, the expected return on domestic assets falls to induce individuals and firms to readjust their portfolios in favor of domestic assets. This readjustment, in turn, requires an appreciation of the domestic currency. Thus, the portfolio-balance effect enables a central bank to induce an increase in the value of its currency by purchasing domestic bonds and selling foreign bonds.

THE ANNOUNCEMENT EFFECT   The portfolio approach also indicates the possibility that an intervention can have an **announcement effect.** This effect occurs when foreign-exchange-market interventions provide currency traders with previously unknown information that alters their willingness to demand or supply currencies in the foreign exchange markets. The announcement effect can exist if a central bank's intervention clearly reveals some kind of "inside information" that traders did not have previously. Thus, a foreign-exchange-market intervention intended to induce a reduction in the exchange rate, such as the Bank of Thailand's intervention in our example, can send a signal to currency traders that the baht will appreciate relative to the dollar in the future. If currency traders believe that this appreciation will take place, then they will increase their holdings of the domestic currency, which in our example is the baht. This concerted action by currency traders then causes an actual currency appreciation. Hence, the announcement effect, like the portfolio-balance effect, induces a rise in the value of the domestic currency.

Announcement effect: A change in the exchange rate resulting from an anticipation of near-term changes in foreign-exchange-market conditions signaled by an intervention by a central bank.

> **3. What is the portfolio approach to exchange rate determination?** Under the portfolio approach to exchange rates, both nonsterilized and sterilized interventions can affect exchange rates. Sterilized interventions leave the monetary base and money supply unchanged, but they change portfolio allocations between domestic and foreign financial assets. Exchange rates must change for individuals, firms, and financial institutions to be satisfied with their portfolio reallocations. Thus, sterilized interventions have portfolio-balance effects on exchange rates. Furthermore, the portfolio approach indicates that sterilized interventions can alter exchange rates through announcement effects.

Evidence on the Effects of Foreign-Exchange-Market Interventions

To be able to fix exchange rates, central banks must have the capability to peg exchange rates at values that differ from their free-market values. Thus, central banks can successfully fix exchange rates only if foreign-exchange-market interventions have independent short- and long-term effects on market exchange rates.

SHORT-RUN EFFECTS OF INTERVENTIONS   As you have seen, theories of the effects of foreign-exchange-market interventions have mixed implications. On the one hand, the monetary approach indicates that only nonsterilized interventions can have even near-term effects on exchange rates. On the other hand, the portfolio approach predicts that sterilized interventions can induce portfolio-balance and announcement effects that cause exchange rates to adjust in response.

For this reason, economists have sought to evaluate the theories by examining data from real-world foreign-exchange-market interventions. Kathryn Dominguez of Harvard University and Jeffrey Frankel of the University of California at Berkeley conducted an exhaustive study of foreign-exchange-market interventions during the 1980s and 1990s. They found evidence that both the portfolio-balance effect and the announcement effect were important during these years, especially in the late 1980s, a period when many of the world's governments conducted sizable interventions. A number of these interventions were *coordinated* actions, in which central banks cooperated in their efforts to influence exchange rates. Consequently, foreign-exchange-market interventions had their greatest potential to influence exchange rates during this period.

Dominguez and Frankel found considerable evidence that these interventions actually did affect exchange rates. Interestingly, Dominguez and Frankel found that the *announcements* of the interventions had larger effects on exchange rates than the actual magnitudes of the interventions themselves. This, they believe, provides strong evidence of announcement effects in interventions. Thus, they conclude that the data from this period provide support for the predictions of the portfolio approach, at least in the short run.

THE BIG FOREIGN-EXCHANGE-MARKET INTERVENTIONS OF THE 1980S

The most significant recent episode of coordinated currency interventions took place beginning in September 1985. At the Plaza Hotel in New York, the finance ministers and central bankers of the so-called G5 nations—France, Germany, Japan, the United Kingdom, and the United States—announced that "in view of the present and prospective change in fundamentals, some orderly appreciation of the main non-dollar currencies against the dollar is desirable. We stand ready to cooperate more closely to encourage this when to do so would be helpful."

This pact among central banks became known as the Plaza Agreement. In 1987, the G5 nations reaffirmed this agreement at the Louvre Palace by adopting the Louvre Accord to continue their efforts to manage exchange rates. The official rhetoric that followed the adoption of these policy agreements and the policy actions they brought about indicated that the G5 nations believed they had largely accomplished their objective of stabilizing exchange rates at "desired" levels.

THE LONGER-TERM EFFECTS OF INTERVENTIONS

Some economists, however, doubt that the central banks really achieved their objectives for more than a fleeting time. Among these doubters are Michael Bordo of Rutgers University and Anna Schwartz of the National Bureau of Economic Research. Bordo and Schwartz conducted a study in which they tabulated data on the foreign exchange interventions coordinated by the United States, Germany, and Japan between early 1985 and late 1989. Figure 22-4 displays their estimates of the combined dollar amounts of interventions by central banks and finance ministries during that period.

Based on their study of these interventions, Bordo and Schwartz reached three conclusions. First, the interventions were sporadic and highly variable. Consequently, the interventions may have *added to*, instead of reducing, foreign-exchange-market volatility and uncertainty. The result was that individuals and firms experienced unexpected changes in their wealth, as wealth was effectively transferred from some individuals and firms to others. The increased risk arising from such wealth transfers probably induced many financial market traders to increase their hedging activities. Effectively, the foreign-exchange-market interventions forced private traders to incur extra costs of hedging against the risks of unexpected central bank interventions.

FIGURE 22-4
Combined U.S., German, and Japanese Interventions, February 1985–August 1989.

The total dollar amount of the foreign exchange interventions by the United States, Germany, and Japan during the late 1980s varied considerably from month to month.

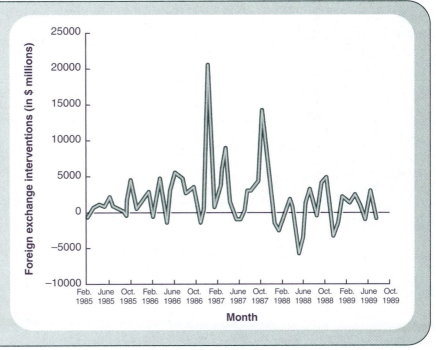

SOURCE: Michael Bordo and Anna Schwartz, "What Has Foreign Exchange Market Intervention since the Plaza Agreement Accomplished?" *Open Economies Review* 2 (1991): 39–64.

Second, Bordo and Schwartz found that foreign-exchange-market interventions during the late 1980s were very small in size relative to total trading in the markets. For instance, in April 1989 total foreign exchange trading amounted to $129 *billion* per day, yet the Fed purchased only $100 *million* in marks and yen in that entire month—on a single day. Indeed, Fed purchases of marks and yen for all of 1989 amounted to about $17.7 billion, or the equivalent of less than 14 percent of foreign-exchange-market trading for an average *day* in April of that year. Given that a coalition of the world's largest central banks was able to generate only a relatively tiny volume of foreign-exchange-market trading activity during the 1985–1989 period, Bordo and Schwartz question the likelihood that central bank interventions can really have *long-lasting* effects on exchange rates.

Third, Bordo and Schwartz found that while the Federal Reserve and the Treasury together accounted for over $1 billion in realized gains from foreign exchange transactions in 1985 through 1989, the Netherlands lost 600 million Dutch guilders on dollar interventions in 1986 and 1987, and Germany reportedly lost 9 billion deutschemarks in the fourth quarter of 1987 alone. Bordo and Schwartz question the wisdom of central bank and finance ministry gambles with such large stakes, given their limited abilities to achieve exchange rate goals. In Bordo and Schwartz's view, central banks that participated in the coordinated effort to reduce the dollar's value exposed their governments, and hence their taxpaying citizens, to risks of sizable foreign exchange losses.

Nevertheless, many economists join Dominguez and Frankel in arguing that foreign exchange interventions can and do influence exchange rates from time to time. The coordinated interventions of the late 1980s, they point out, were unambiguously associated with an interval in which the value of the dollar declined. This decline, they note, continued beyond the period of active interventions, potentially implying longer-term effects.

THE POSSIBLE EFFECT OF COUNTRY SIZE   In spite of this view, efforts to manipulate exchange rates by central banks in developed nations, whose currencies trade actively in foreign exchange markets, have been muted since the early 1990s. Economists who doubt the ability of these central banks to influence their exchange rates, such as Bordo and Schwartz, believe that the central banks have recognized their inability to bring about long-lasting changes in exchange rates by intervening in foreign exchange markets that experience huge daily trading volumes. They note that today most efforts to peg exchange rates are undertaken by central banks in smaller, emerging economies, whose currencies trade in foreign exchange markets with low volumes of trading. Interventions in these thinner markets, they argue, are more likely to move exchange rates in directions that central banks desire.

Table 22-2 displays the exchange rate arrangements adopted by most of the world's nations. As you can see, the most developed nations have floating-exchange-rate systems. The countries that try to fix their exchange rate typically are among the world's smallest economies.

Table 22-2 Exchange Rate Arrangements around the Globe

Pegged to a Single Currency or Composite Currency Unit	Aruba, Bahamas, Bahrain, Bangladesh, Barbardos, Belize, Bhutan, Botswana, Burundi, Cape Verde, China, Comoros, Cyprus, Denmark, Egypt, El Salvador, Fiji, Iceland, Iran, Iraq, Jordan, Kuwait, Latvia, Lebanon, Lesotho, Libya, Macedonia, Malaysia, Maldives, Malta, Morocco, Myanmar, Namibia, Nepal, Netherlands Antilles, Oman, Qatar, Samoa, Saudi Arabia, Seychelles, Solomon Islands, Swaziland, Syria, Trinidad, Turkmenistan, Ukraine, United Arab Emirates, Vietnam
Crawling Peg or Crawling Bands	Bolivia, Costa Rica, Honduras, Hungary, Israel, Nicaragua, Poland, Sri Lanka, Tunisia, Turkey, Uruguay, Venezuela
Managed Float	Algeria, Argentina, Azerbaijan, Belarus, Cambodia, Croatia, Czech Republic, Dominican Republic, Ethiopia, Guatemala, India, Jamaica, Kenya, Kyrgyz Republic, Malawi, Nigeria, Norway, Pakistan, Paraguay, Romania, Singapore, Slovak Republic, Slovenia, Suriname, Tajikistan, Uzbekistan
Independent Float	Afghanistan, Albania, Angola, Armenia, Australia, Brazil, Canada, Chile, Colombia, Congo, Eritrea, Gambia, Ghana, Guinea, Guyana, Haiti, Indonesia, Japan, Kazakhstan, Korea, Liberia, Madagascar, Mauritius, Mexico, Moldova, Mongolia, Mozambique, New Zealand, Papua New Guinea, Peru, Philippines, Russian Federation, Rwanda, Sierra Leone, Somalia, South Africa, Sudan, Sweden, Switzerland, Tanzania, Thailand, Uganda, United Kingdom, United States, Yemen, Zambia, Zimbabwe
Exchange Arrangements with a Shared Currency	Antigua & Barbuda, Austria, Belgium, Benin, Burkina Faso, Cameroon, Central African Republic, Chad, Cote d'Ivoire, Dominica, Ecuador, Equatorial Guinea, Finland, France, Gabon, Germany, Greece, Grenada, Guinea-Bissau, Ireland, Italy, Kiribati, Luxembourg, Mali, Marshall Islands, Micronesia, Netherlands, Niger, Palau, Panama, Portugal, St. Kitts & Nevis, St. Lucia, St. Vincent & the Grenadines, San Marino, Senegal, Spain, Togo
Currency Board	Bosnia & Herzegovina, Brunei Darussalam, Bulgaria, Djibouti, Estonia, Hong Kong (China), Lithuania

SOURCE: International Monetary Fund.

4. How effective are foreign-exchange-market interventions? There is some evidence that portfolio-balance and announcement effects have had short-run effects on exchange rates. This was particularly true during the period of widespread foreign exchange interventions in the 1980s. Data from this same period also indicate, however, that even coordinated central bank interventions had relatively small and fleeting effects on exchange rates. These interventions may also have added to exchange rate volatility, and they may have caused taxpayer losses owing to greater currency risks incurred by governments and central banks.

Chapter Summary

1. The Pros and Cons of Fixed versus Floating Exchange Rates: The main argument against floating exchange rates is that exchange rate volatility caused by changing market forces can increase foreign exchange risks. Adopting a fixed exchange rate reduces the potential for such risks to arise, thereby saving people from having to incur costs to hedge against those risks. An important argument against fixed exchange rates is that in nations whose workers and other factors of production are relatively immobile, pegging the exchange rate removes a key source of immediate flexibility in relative prices, thereby eliminating a key means by which the nations' employment and real GDP levels can automatically adjust to changes in international market conditions.

2. The Monetary Approach to Exchange Rate Determination: This theory of the exchange rate effects of central bank policy actions indicates that nonsterilized foreign-exchange-market interventions can affect exchange rates via changes in the monetary base. Nonsterilized interventions cause the quantity of money supplied to change relative to the quantity of money demanded, which causes the exchange rate to adjust to reattain money market equilibrium. The monetary approach indicates that sterilized foreign-exchange-market interventions cannot affect exchange rates, because sterilized interventions have no effect on the monetary base and the money supply.

3. The Portfolio Approach to Exchange Rate Determination: This theory of the exchange rate effects of foreign-exchange-market interventions predicts that both nonsterilized and sterilized interventions can influence exchange rates. According to the portfolio approach, both types of interventions alter portfolio allocations between domestic and foreign financial assets. A portfolio-balance effect thereby occurs, because the exchange rate must adjust to induce a nation's residents to be satisfied with their portfolio reallocations. In addition, the portfolio approach predicts that announcement effects can influence exchange rates as traders reallocate their portfolios in response to the signal provided by the central bank's interventions.

4. The Effectiveness of Foreign-Exchange-Market Interventions: Studies of central bank interventions in foreign exchange markets indicate that interventions exert effects on exchange rates, especially when the central banks coordinate interventions, as occurred in the 1980s. Nevertheless, there is also evidence that these effects may have been relatively small and short lived. Foreign-exchange-market interventions may also increase the variability of exchange rates, and they may expose taxpayers to losses stemming from increased currency risks incurred by governments and central banks.

Questions and Problems

(Answers to odd-numbered questions and problems may be found on the Web at **http://money.swcollege.com** under "Student Resources.")

1. Suppose that the residents of a particular country speak a language that most others around the world do not know. There also are legal and natural impediments to movements of other factors of production across the nation's borders. The nation's central bank maintains a fixed exchange rate. Recently, there has been a worldwide fall in the demand for the nation's primary products. Could this nation gain from letting its exchange rate float? Explain your reasoning.

2. Why might Europe benefit more fully from its adoption of a single currency if all of its residents shared at least one common language? Explain.

3. Suppose that the Bank of Thailand wishes to peg the exchange value of the baht relative to the dollar at a level above the market exchange rate. Draw a diagram of the demand for and the supply of dollars in the foreign exchange market, and explain what actions the Bank of Thailand would have to undertake to peg the baht's value.

4. Suppose that the Bank of Thailand has succeeded in pegging the baht-per-dollar exchange rate above the market exchange rate. Now the central bank decides to peg the exchange rate at a higher value. How will the Bank of Thailand do this?

5. Write out an equation for the monetary approach to the determination of the exchange rate. Suppose that domestic credit equals $400 million, foreign exchange reserves equal $200 million, the money multiplier is 2, the fraction of nominal GDP that individuals desire to hold as money is 20 percent, the foreign price level is 1.2, and domestic real GDP is $5 billion.

   a. What is the quantity of domestic money in circulation?

   b. What is the equilibrium exchange rate?

6. Suppose that the central bank facing the situation described in question 5, in which the monetary approach to exchange rate deter-

mination applies, conducts an unsterilized foreign-exchange-market intervention and increases foreign exchange reserves by $50 million.

   a. What is the equilibrium exchange rate?

   b. Does the domestic currency appreciate or depreciate?

7. Suppose that the central bank facing the situation described in question 5, in which the monetary approach to exchange rate determination applies, conducts a sterilized foreign-exchange-market intervention and reduces foreign exchange reserves by $100 million.

   a. What is the equilibrium exchange rate?

   b. Does the domestic currency appreciate or depreciate?

8. According to the monetary approach to exchange rate determination, why should a sterilized foreign-exchange-market intervention fail to influence the value of a nation's currency?

9. In the portfolio approach to exchange rate determination, what is the difference between the portfolio-balance effect and the announcement effect?

10. Why does the portfolio approach to exchange rate determination predict that a sterilized foreign-exchange-market intervention can influence the value of a nation's currency?

Before the Test

Test your understanding of the material covered in this chapter by taking the Chapter 22 interactive quiz at **http://money.swcollege.com**.

Online Application

Internet URL: http://www.ecb.int and **http://www.bis.org**

Title: About the European Central Bank

Navigation: Begin at the home page of the European Central Bank (**http://www.ecb.int**), and click on "The European Central Bank."

Application: Perform the indicated operations, and answer the accompanying questions:

   1. Click on "History" and read the article. In what ways is policymaking within the European System of Central Banks different from policymaking under the old European Monetary System?

2. Back up to the opening page of the ECB's site, and under "About the organization," click on "ECB, ESCB, and the Eurosystem." Finally, click on "Organizational Principles of the Eurosystem." Read the article. What aspects of the ESCB's structure promote policy credibility?

For Group Study and Analysis: Divide the class into groups. Go to **http://www.bis.org**, and then click on "Link to Central Banks." Have each group explore Web sites of the central banks that are currently in the ESCB. What are the roles of the individual national central banks within the ESCB? Within their domestic economic and financial systems?

Selected References and Further Reading

Bonser-Neal, Catherine. "Does Central Bank Intervention Stabilize Exchange Rates?" Federal Reserve Bank of Kansas City *Economic Review* 81 (First Quarter, 1996): 43–57.

Bordo, Michael, and Anna Schwartz. "What Has Foreign Exchange Market Intervention since the Plaza Agreement Accomplished?" *Open Economies Review* 2 (1991): 39–64.

Cavallo, Michele. "To Float or Not to Float? Exchange Rate Regimes and Shocks." Federal Reserve Bank of San Francisco *Economic Letter* No. 2005-01, January 2005.

Dominguez, Kathryn, and Jeffrey Frankel. *Does Foreign Exchange Intervention Work?* Washington, D.C.: Institute for International Economics, 1993.

Ghosh, Atish, Ann-Marie Gulde, and Holger Wolf. *Exchange Rate Regimes: Choices and Consequences.* Cambridge, Mass.: MIT Press, 2002.

Lewis, Karen. "Are Foreign Exchange Intervention and Monetary Policy Related, and Does It Matter?" *Journal of Business* 68 (1995): 185–214.

_____. "On Occasional Monetary Policy Coordinations That Fix the Exchange Rate." *Journal of International Economics* 26 (1989): 139–155.

Mundell, Robert. "A Theory of Optimal Currency Areas." *American Economic Review* 51 (1961): 657–665.

MoneyXtra

Log on to the MoneyXtra Web site now (**http://moneyxtra.swcollege.com**) for additional learning resources such as practice quizzes, case studies, readings, and additional economic applications.

GLOSSARY

Actuary: An individual who specializes in using mathematical and statistical principles to calculate insurance premiums and to estimate an insurance company's net worth.

Adaptive expectations: Expectations that are based only on information from the past up to the present.

Adverse selection: The problem that those who desire to issue financial instruments are most likely to use the funds they receive for unworthy, high-risk projects.

Aggregate demand schedule (y^d): The combinations of various price levels and levels of real GDP at which individuals are satisfied with their consumption of output and their holdings of money.

Aggregate supply shocks: Events, such as a sudden rise in the level of nominal wages or an increase in energy prices, that generate shifts in the position of the short-run aggregate supply schedule.

American option: An option that allows the holder to buy or sell a security at any time before or including the date at which the contract expires.

Announcement effect: A change in the exchange rate resulting from an anticipation of near-term changes in foreign-exchange-market conditions signaled by an intervention by a central bank.

Annuities: Financial instruments that guarantee the holder fixed or variable payments at some future date.

Anticipated-income approach: A depository institution management philosophy that calls for depository institutions to make loans more liquid by issuing them as installment loans that generate income in the form of periodic payments of interest and principal.

Appreciation: A rise in the value of one currency relative to another.

Arbitrage: Purchasing an asset at the current price in one market and profiting by selling it at a higher price in another market.

Asset: Anything owned by a person or business that has a market value.

Asset-liability management approach: A depository institution management philosophy that emphasizes the simultaneous determination of both the asset and the liability sides of the institution's balance sheet.

Asymmetric information: Information possessed by one party to a financial transaction but not by the other party.

Automated bill payment: Direct payment of bills by depository institutions on behalf of their customers.

Automated clearinghouses: Institutions that process payments electronically on behalf of senders and receivers of those payments.

Automated-transfer-system (ATS) account: A combined interest-bearing savings account and non-interest-bearing checking account in which the former is drawn on automatically when the latter is overdrawn.

Bank Insurance Fund (BIF): The FDIC's fund that covers insured deposits of commercial banks.

Bank run: An unexpected series of cash withdrawals at a depository institution that can induce its failure.

Banker's acceptance: A bank loan typically used by a company to finance storage or shipment of goods.

Banknotes: Privately issued paper currency.

Barter: The direct exchange of goods, services, and financial assets.

Base drift: The tendency of a measure of total depository institution reserves or a monetary aggregate to fail to adjust to a level consistent with fixed long-run average growth.

Best efforts deal: An investment banking arrangement in which the investment bank has an option to buy a portion of the issuing firm's securities but is not required to do so.

Beta: A measure of the sensitivity of a financial instrument's expected return to changes in the value of all financial instruments in a market portfolio; calculated as the percentage change in the value of a financial instrument resulting from a 1 percent change in the value of all financial instruments in the portfolio.

Bimetallic standard: A monetary system in which the value of money depends on the values of two precious metals, such as gold and silver.

Board of Governors of the Federal Reserve System: A group of seven individuals appointed by the president and confirmed by the Senate that, under the terms of the Banking Act of 1935, has key policy-making responsibilities within the Federal Reserve System.

Branch banking: A depository institution organizational structure in which institutions operate offices at a number of geographic locations.

Brokers: Institutions that specialize in matching buyers and sellers of financial instruments in secondary markets.

Bullion: Uncoined gold or silver used as money.

Business cycles: Variations in real GDP around its long-run growth path.

Business finance companies: Finance companies that typically specialize in making loans to small businesses.

Call option: An option contract giving the owner the right to purchase a financial instrument at a specific price.

Capacity output: The real GDP that the economy could produce if all resources were employed to their utmost.

Capital controls: Legal restrictions on the ability of a nation's residents to hold and trade assets denominated in foreign currencies.

Capital gain: An increase in the value of a financial instrument at the time it is sold as compared with its market value at the date it was purchased.

Capital goods: Goods that may be used to produce other goods or services in the future.

Capital loss: A decline in the market value of a financial instrument at the time it is sold as compared with its market value at the time it was purchased.

Capital markets: Markets for financial instruments with maturities of one year or more.

Capital mobility: The extent to which savers can move funds across national borders for the purpose of buying financial instruments issued in other countries.

Capital requirements: Minimum equity capital standards that regulators impose upon depository institutions.

Cash assets: Depository institution assets that function as media of exchange.

Cash items in process of collection: Checks deposited with a bank for immediate credit but not yet cleared for final payment to the bank; usually referred to simply as "cash items."

Cash-in-advance approach: A theory of the demand for money based on the assumption that people must have real money balances in their possession before they can purchase any goods or services.

Central banker contract: A legally binding agreement between a government and a central bank official that holds the official responsible for the nation's inflation performance.

Certificates of deposit (CDs): Time deposits issued by banks and other depository institutions. Many CDs are negotiable instruments that are traded in secondary markets.

Charter: A governmental license to open and operate a bank.

Clearing House Interbank Payment System (CHIPS): A large-value wire transfer system that links about ninety depository institutions and permits them to transmit large dollar sums relating primarily to foreign exchange and Eurodollar transactions.

Closed stored-value system: An e-money system in which consumers use cards containing prestored funds to buy specific goods and services offered by a single issuer of the cards.

Closed-end funds: Mutual funds that sell nonredeemable shares whose market values vary with the market values of the underlying mix of financial instruments held by the mutual funds.

Coinsurance: An insurance policy feature that requires a policyholder to pay a fixed percentage of a loss above a deductible.

Collateral: Assets that a borrower pledges as security in case it should fail to repay the principal or interest on a loan.

Commercial and industrial (C&I) loans: Loans that commercial banks and other depository institutions make to businesses.

Commercial banks: Depository financial institutions that issue checking deposits and specialize in making commercial loans.

Commercial loans: Long-term loans made by banks to businesses.

Commercial paper: A short-term debt instrument issued by businesses in lieu of borrowing from banks.

Commodity money: A good with a non-monetary value that is also used as money.

Commodity standard: A money unit whose value is fully or partially backed by the value of some other physical good such as gold or silver.

Common stock: Shares of corporate ownership that entitle the owner to vote on management issues but offer no guarantees of dividends or of market value in the event of corporate bankruptcy.

Confirmed credit lines: Depository institution commitments to provide an individual or a business with a fixed amount of credit upon demand within some short-term interval.

Conservative central banker: A central bank official who dislikes inflation more than the average citizen in society and who therefore is less willing to induce discretionary increases in the quantity of money in an effort to achieve short-run increases in real GDP.

Consumer finance companies: Finance companies that specialize in making loans to individuals for the purchase of durable goods or for home improvements.

Consumer loans: Long-term loans made by banks and other institutions to individuals.

Consumption spending: Total purchases of goods and services by households.

Contributory pensions: Pensions funded by both employer and employee contributions.

Controllable liabilities: Liabilities whose dollar amounts banks can directly manage.

Conversion-of-funds approach: A depository institution management philosophy under which managers try to fund assets of specific maturities by issuing liabilities with like maturities.

Core capital: Defined by current capital requirements as shareholders' equity plus retained earnings.

Corporate bonds: Long-term debt instruments of corporations.

Correspondent balances: Deposit accounts that banks hold with other banks.

Country risk: The potential for returns on international financial instruments to vary because of uncertainties concerning possible changes in political and economic conditions within a nation.

Coupon return: A fixed interest return that a bond yields each year.

Coupon yield equivalent: An annualized T-bill rate that can be compared with annual yields on other financial instruments.

Covered interest parity: A prediction that the interest rate on one nation's financial instrument should approximately equal the interest rate on a similar instrument in another nation plus the forward premium, or the difference between the forward exchange rate and the spot exchange rate divided by the spot exchange rate.

Credit derivatives: Financial instruments that have returns based on loan credit risks.

Credit multiplier: A number that tells how much total loans and securities at depository institutions will change in response to a change in the monetary base.

Credit risk: The risk of loss that might occur if one party to an exchange fails to honor the terms under which the exchange was to take place.

Credit union: A type of depository institution that accepts deposits from and makes loans to only a group of individuals who are eligible for membership.

Currency: Coins and paper money.

Currency board: An institution that issues currency at a fixed rate of exchange with respect to another nation's currency.

Currency future: An agreement to deliver to another a standardized quantity of a specific nation's currency at a designated future date.

Currency option: A contract granting the holder the right to buy or sell a given amount of a nation's currency at a certain price within a specific period of time.

Currency swap: An exchange of payment flows denominated in different currencies.

Current yield: The coupon return on a bond divided by the bond's market price.

Cybertechnologies: Technologies that connect savers, investors, traders, producers, and governments via computer linkages.

Cyclical unemployment: The portion of total unemployment resulting from business-cycle fluctuations.

Debasement: A reduction in the amount of precious metal in a coin that the government issues as money.

Debit card: A plastic card that allows the bearer to transfer funds to a merchant's account, provided that the bearer authorizes the transfer by providing personal identification.

Deductible: A fixed amount of an insured loss that a policyholder must pay before the insurer is obliged to make payments.

Default risk: The chance that an individual or a firm that issues a financial instrument may be unable to honor its obligations to repay the principal and/or to make interest payments.

Default swap: A credit derivative that requires the seller to assume the face value of a debt in the event of default.

Deflation: A decline in the price level during a period of time.

Demand deposits: Non-interest-bearing checking accounts.

Deposit expansion multiplier: A number that tells how much aggregate transactions deposits at all depository institutions will change in response to a change in total reserves of these institutions.

Deposit insurance premium: The price that depository institutions pay to the FDIC's insurance fund in exchange for a guarantee of federal insurance of covered deposits that they issue.

Depository financial institutions: Financial institutions that issue checking and savings deposits that are included in measures of money and that legally must hold reserves on deposit with Federal Reserve banks or in their vaults.

Depreciation: A decline in the value of one currency relative to another.

Depression: An especially severe recession.

Derivative credit risk: Risk stemming from the potential default by a party in a derivative contract or from unexpected changes in credit exposure because of changes in the market yields of instruments on which derivative yields depend.

Derivative market risk: Risk arising from unanticipated changes in derivatives market liquidity or from failures in payments systems.

Derivative operating risk: Risk owing to a lack of adequate management controls or from managerial inexperience with derivative securities.

Derivative securities: Financial instruments whose returns depend on the returns of other financial instruments.

Digital cash: Funds contained on computer software, in the form of secure algorithms, that is stored on microchips and other computer devices.

Discount rate: The rate of interest that the Federal Reserve charges to lend to a depository institution.

Discounted present value: The value today of a payment to be received at a future date.

Discretionary policymaking: The act of responding to economic events as they occur, rather than in ways the policymaker might previously have planned in the absence of those events.

Disintermediation: A situation in which customers of depository institutions withdraw funds from their deposit accounts and use these funds to purchase financial instruments directly.

Diversification: Holding a mix of financial instruments with returns that normally do not move together.

Dividends: Periodic payments to holders of corporate equities.

Dollarization: A country's adoption of the U.S. dollar as its sole medium of exchange, unit of account, store of value, and standard of deferred payment.

Domestic credit: A central bank's holdings of domestic securities.

Double coincidence of wants: The situation when two individuals are simultaneously willing and able to make a trade; a requirement for barter.

Dual banking system: A regulatory structure in which either states or the federal government can grant bank charters.

Duration: A measure of the average time during which all payments of principal and interest on a financial instrument are made.

Duration gap: The average duration of a depository institution's assets minus the average duration of its liabilities.

Economic risk: A foreign exchange risk that stems from the possibility that exchange rate movements can affect the discounted present value of future streams of income.

Economies of scale: The reduction in the average cost of fund management that can be achieved by pooling savings together and spreading management costs across many people.

Economies of scope: The ability to produce a mix of products at a lower cost than the overall cost of producing each product separately.

Efficient structure theory: A theory of depository institution market structure in which greater market concentration and higher depository institution profits arise from the fact that a few depository institutions can operate more efficiently in loan and deposit markets than a large number of institutions.

Efficient-markets hypothesis: A theory that states that equilibrium prices of and returns on financial instruments should reflect all past and current information plus traders' understanding of how market prices and returns are determined.

Electronic money (e-money): Money that people can transfer directly via electronic impulses.

Equation of exchange: An accounting identity that states that the nominal value of all monetary transactions for final goods and services is identically equal to the nominal value of the output of goods and services purchased.

Equities: Shares of ownership, such as corporate stock, issued by business firms.

Equity capital: The excess of assets over liabilities, or net worth.

Eurobonds: Long-term debt instruments issued in a currency other than that of the country where the instruments are issued.

Eurocommercial paper: A short-term debt instrument issued by a firm and denominated in a currency other than that of the country where the firm is located.

Eurocurrency deposits: Bank deposits denominated in the currency of one nation but located in a different nation.

Eurocurrency markets: Markets for bonds, loans, and deposits denominated in the currency of a given nation but held and traded outside that nation's borders.

Eurodollars: Dollar-denominated deposits located outside the United States.

Euronotes: Medium-term debt instruments issued in a currency other than that of the country where the instruments are issued.

European option: An option that allows the holder to buy or sell a financial instrument only on the day that the contract expires.

Excess reserves: Depository institutions' cash balances at Federal Reserve banks or in the institutions' vaults that exceed the amount that they must hold to meet legal requirements.

Exchange rate: The price of one nation's currency in terms of the currency of another country.

Exercise price: The price at which the holder of an option has the right to buy or sell a financial instrument; also known as the *strike price*.

Expansion: A point along a business cycle at which actual GDP begins to rise, perhaps even above its natural, long-run level.

Expectations theory: A theory of the term structure of interest rates that views bonds with differing maturities as perfect substitutes, so their yields differ only because short-term interest rates are expected to rise or fall.

Externalities: Spillovers from the interactions of one set of individuals to others who otherwise are not involved in the transactions.

Federal funds market: The money market in which banks borrow from and lend to each other deposits that they hold at Federal Reserve banks.

Federal funds rate: A short-term (usually overnight) interest rate on interbank loans in the United States.

Federal Open Market Committee (FOMC): A group composed of the seven governors and five of the twelve Federal Reserve bank presidents that determines how to conduct the Fed's open market operations.

Federal Reserve banks: The twelve central banking institutions that oversee regional activities of the Federal Reserve System.

Federal Reserve districts: The twelve geographic regions of the Federal Reserve System.

Federal Reserve–Treasury Accord: A 1951 agreement that dissociated the Fed from a previous policy of pegging Treasury bill rates at artificially low levels.

Fedwire: A large-value wire transfer system operated by the Federal Reserve that is open to all depository institutions that legally must maintain required reserves with the Fed.

Fiat money: A token that has value only because it is accepted as money.

Finance company: A financial institution that specializes in making loans to relatively high-risk individuals and businesses.

Financial instruments: Claims that those who lend their savings have on the future incomes of the borrowers who use those funds for investment.

Financial intermediation: Indirect finance through the services of an institutional "middleman" that channels funds from savers to those who ultimately make capital investments.

Firm commitment underwriting: An investment banking arrangement in which the investment bank purchases and distributes to dealers and other purchasers all securities offered by a business.

Fiscal agent: A term describing the Federal Reserve's role as an agent of the U.S. Treasury Department, on whose behalf the Fed issues, services, and redeems debts.

Fisher equation: An equation stating that the nominal interest rate equals the sum of the real interest rate and the expected inflation rate.

Fixed annuity: A financial instrument, typically issued by an insurance company, that pays regular, constant installments to the owner beginning at a specific future date.

FOMC directive: The official written instructions from the FOMC to the head of the Trading Desk at the Federal Reserve Bank of New York.

Foreign exchange: Exchange of currencies issued by different countries.

Foreign exchange market: A system of private banks, foreign exchange brokers and dealers, and central banks through which households, businesses, and governments purchase and sell currencies of various nations.

Foreign exchange market efficiency: A situation in which the equilibrium spot and forward exchange rates adjust to reflect all available information, in which case the forward premium is equal to the expected rate of currency depreciation plus any risk premium. This, in turn, implies that the forward exchange rate on average predicts the expected future spot exchange rate.

Foreign-exchange-market intervention: A central bank purchase or sale of foreign-currency reserves in an effort to alter the value of its nation's currency.

Foreign exchange risk: The potential for the value of a foreign-currency-denominated financial instrument to vary because of exchange rate fluctuations.

Forward contract: A contract requiring delivery of a financial instrument at a specified price on a certain date.

Forward currency contract: A forward contract calling for delivery of foreign currency, or financial instruments denominated in a foreign currency, at a specific exchange rate on a certain date.

Fractional-reserve banking: A system in which banks hold reserves equal to less than the amount of total deposits.

Free-banking laws: Laws in force in many U.S. states between 1837 and 1861 that allowed anyone to obtain a charter authorizing banking operations.

Free reserves: Total excess reserves at depository institutions minus the total amount of reserves that depository institutions have borrowed from the Fed.

Free-rider problem: A situation in which some individuals take advantage of the fact that others are willing to pay for a jointly utilized good, such as a system of multilateral netting of foreign exchange payments.

Free silver: A late-nineteenth-century idea for unlimited coinage of silver to meet the monetary needs of a growing U.S. economy.

Frictional unemployment: The portion of total unemployment arising from the fact that a number of workers are between jobs at any given time.

Futures contract: An agreement to deliver to another a given amount of a standardized commodity or financial instrument at a designated future date.

Futures options: Options to buy or sell futures contracts.

Gap management: A technique of depository institution asset-liability management that focuses on the difference ("gap") between the quantity of assets subject to significant interest rate risk and the amount of liabilities subject to such risk.

GDP price deflator: A measure of the overall price level; equal to nominal GDP divided by real GDP.

Gold bullion: Within a gold standard, the amount of gold used as money.

Gold standard: A monetary system in which the value of money is linked to the value of gold.

Government spending: Total state, local, and federal government expenditures on goods and services.

Gross domestic product (GDP): The value, tabulated using market prices, of all final goods and services produced within a nation's borders during a given period.

Hedge: A financial strategy that reduces the risk of capital losses arising from interest rate or currency risks.

Hedge funds: Limited partnerships that, like mutual funds, manage portfolios of assets on behalf of savers, but with very limited governmental oversight as compared with mutual funds.

Herstatt risk: The risk of any form of loss due to payment settlement failures that occur across national borders; named after a German bank that collapsed in 1974.

Historical value accounting: A traditional accounting procedure in which a depository institution's assets are always valued at their original values.

Identification problem: The problem that economists face in evaluating whether real-world data are consistent with the downward-sloping money demand schedule that money demand theories predict, given the fact that both money demand and money supply vary over time.

Idiosyncratic risk: Risk that is unique to a particular financial instrument; also known as *nonsystematic risk*.

Illiquidity: A situation in which a banking institution lacks the cash assets required to meet requests for depositor withdrawals.

Income velocity of money: The average number of times a unit of money is used to purchase final goods and services within an interval.

Inflation bias: The tendency for the economy to experience continuing inflation as a result of the time-inconsistency problem of discretionary monetary policy.

Insider information: Information that is not available to the public.

Insolvency: A situation in which the value of a bank's assets falls below the value of its liabilities.

Installment credit: Loans to individual consumers that entail periodic repayments of principal and interest.

Interest: The payment, or yield, received in exchange for extending credit by holding any financial instrument.

Interest expense: The portion of depository institution costs incurred through payments of interest to holders of the institutions' liabilities.

Interest income: Interest revenues that depository institutions derive from their holdings of loans and securities.

Interest rate: The percentage return, or percentage yield, earned by the holder of a financial instrument.

Interest-rate forward contract: A contract committing the issuer to sell a financial instrument at a given interest rate as of a specific date.

Interest rate future: A contract to buy or sell a standardized denomination of a specific financial instrument at a given price at a certain date in the future.

Interest rate risk: The possibility that the market value of a financial instrument will change as interest rates vary.

Interest rate smoothing: Central bank efforts to attain an ultimate objective of interest rate stability.

Interest rate swap: A contractual exchange of one set of interest payments for another.

Intermediate target: An economic variable that a central bank seeks to control because it determines that doing so is consistent with its ultimate objectives.

Intermediate-term maturity: Maturity between one year and ten years.

International capital markets: Markets for cross-border exchange of financial instruments that have maturities of a year or more.

International money markets: Markets for cross-border exchange of financial instruments with maturities of less than one year.

Interstate branching: The operation of banking offices in more than one state.

Intrastate branching: The operation of banking offices anywhere within a state.

Inventory theory of money demand: A theory of the demand for money that focuses on how people determine the best inventory of money to keep on hand.

Inverted yield curve: A downward-sloping yield curve.

Investment: Additions to the stock of capital goods.

Investment banks: Institutions that specialize in marketing and underwriting sales of firm ownership shares.

Investment-grade securities: Bonds with relatively low default risk.

Investment spending: The sum of purchases of new capital goods, spending on new residential construction, and inventory investment.

Junk bonds: Bonds with relatively high default risk.

Large-denomination time deposits: Deposits with set maturities and denominations greater than or equal to $100,000.

Large-value wire transfer systems: Payment systems such as Fedwire and CHIPS that permit the electronic transmission of large dollar sums.

Lender of last resort: An institution that is willing and able to lend to any temporarily illiquid but otherwise solvent institution to prevent its illiquid position from leading to a general loss of confidence in that institution or in others.

Level premium policy: A whole life insurance policy under which an insurance company charges fixed premium payments throughout the life of the insured individual.

Liability: A legally enforceable claim on the assets of a business or individual.

Limit orders: Instructions from other stock exchange members to specialists to execute stock trades at specific prices.

Limited payment policy: A whole life insurance policy under which an insured individual pays premiums only for a fixed number of years and is insured during and after the payment period.

Liquidity: The ease with which an asset can be sold or redeemed for a known amount of cash at short notice and at low risk of loss of nominal value.

Liquidity effect: A fall in the equilibrium nominal interest rate resulting from an increase in the money supply, holding the price level unchanged.

Liquidity risk: The risk of loss that may occur if a payment is not received when due.

Load funds: Mutual funds marketed by brokers who receive commissions based on the return of the funds.

Loan commitment: A lending arrangement in which a depository institution promises to extend credit up to some predetermined limit at a contracted interest rate and within a given period of time.

Loan loss provisions: An expense that depository institutions incur when they allocate funds to loan loss reserves.

Loan loss reserves: An amount of cash assets that depository institutions hold as liquidity that they expect to be depleted as a result of loan defaults.

London Interbank Offer Rate (LIBOR): The interest rate on interbank loans traded among six large London banks.

Long position: An obligation to purchase a financial instrument at a given price and at a specific time.

Long run: A period sufficiently long that nominal wages and other input prices adjust in equal proportion to a change in the price level.

Long-run aggregate supply schedule: The relationship between the production of real GDP and the price level when there is sufficient time for nominal wages and other input prices to adjust in equal proportion to a change in the price level.

Long-term maturity: Maturity of more than ten years.

Luxury asset: An asset with a wealth elasticity of demand greater than 1, which indicates that an individual raises holdings of the asset more than proportionately in response to a given proportionate increase in wealth.

M1: Currency plus transactions deposits.

M2: M1 plus savings and small-denomination time deposits and balances of individual and broker-dealer money market mutual funds.

M3: M2 plus large-denomination time deposits, Eurodollars and repurchase agreements, and institution-only money market mutual funds.

Marginal propensity to consume *(MPC)*: The amount of additional real consumption spending induced by an increase in real income.

Market-based regulation: Regulation that uses observable measures of depository institution risk as guidelines for supervisory enforcement.

Market concentration: The degree to which the few largest depository institutions dominate loan and deposit markets.

Market power: The ability of one or a few depository institutions to dominate loan and deposit markets sufficiently to set higher loan rates and lower deposit rates as compared with purely competitive market interest rates.

Market risk: Risk that is common to all financial assets within a portfolio; also called *systematic risk.*

Market structure: The organization of the loan and deposit markets in which depository institutions interact.

Market value accounting: An accounting procedure in which a depository institution (or its regulator) values its assets in terms of the approximate market prices at which those assets would sell at present in secondary markets.

Maturity: The time until final principal and interest payments are due to the holders of a financial instrument.

Medium of exchange: An attribute of money that permits it to be used as a means of payment.

Mercantilism: The idea that a primary determinant of a nation's wealth is international trade and commerce, so a nation can

gain by enacting policies that spur exports while limiting imports.

Monetary aggregate: A grouping of assets sufficiently liquid to be defined as a measure of money.

Monetary approach: A theory of exchange rate determination that predicts that the fundamental determination of a nation's exchange rate is the quantity of money supplied by its central bank.

Monetary base: A "base" amount of money that serves as the foundation for a nation's monetary system. Under a gold standard, the amount of gold bullion; in today's fiat money system, the sum of currency in circulation plus reserves of banks and other depository institutions.

Monetary policy indicator: An economic variable that gives the public an especially clear signal of the intended effects of monetary policy actions.

Monetary policy signal: An occurrence that provides information about the objectives of central bank officials.

Money: Anything that functions as a medium of exchange, store of value, unit of account, and standard of deferred payment.

Money markets: Markets for financial instruments with maturities of less than one year.

Money market deposit accounts: Savings accounts with limited checking privileges.

Money market mutual funds: Pools of funds from savers that managing firms use to purchase short-term financial assets such as Treasury bills and commercial paper.

Money multiplier: A number that tells how much the quantity of money will change in response to a change in the monetary base.

Moral hazard: The possibility that a borrower may engage in more risky behavior after a loan has been made.

Mortgage-backed securities: Financial instruments whose return is based on the underlying returns on mortgage loans.

Mortgage loans: Long-term loans to individual homeowners or to businesses for purchases of land and buildings.

Multi-employer pensions: Pensions whose accumulations and benefit rights may be transferred from one employer to another.

Municipal bonds: Long-term debt instruments issued by state and local governments.

Mutual fund: A mix of financial instruments managed on behalf of shareholders by investment companies that charge fees for their services.

Mutual ownership: A depository institution organizational structure in which depositors own the institution.

National Association of Securities Dealers Automated Quotation (Nasdaq): The electronic network over which most over-the-counter stocks are traded.

Natural GDP: The level of real GDP that is consistent with the economy's natural rate of growth.

Natural rate of unemployment: The portion of the unemployment rate that is accounted for by frictional and structural unemployment.

Necessity asset: An asset with a wealth elasticity of demand less than 1, which implies that an individual increases holdings of the asset less than proportionately in response to a given proportionate increase in wealth.

Negative externality: A reduction in the welfare of one individual caused by a transaction between other parties, even though the individual is not directly involved in the transaction.

Negotiable-order-of-withdrawal (NOW) accounts: Interest-bearing checking deposits.

Net export spending: The difference between spending on domestically produced goods and services by residents of other countries and spending on foreign-produced goods and services by residents of the home country.

Net interest margin: The difference between a depository institution's interest income and interest expenses as a percentage of total assets.

Net worth: The excess of assets over liabilities, or equity capital.

No-load funds: Mutual funds that investment companies market directly to the public and that charge management fees instead of brokerage commissions.

Nominal exchange rate: An exchange rate that is unadjusted for changes in the two nations' price levels.

Nominal gross domestic product (nominal GDP): The value of production of final goods and services calculated in current-dollar terms with no adjustment for the effects of price changes.

Nominal interest rate: A rate of return in current-dollar terms that does not reflect anticipated inflation.

Nominal yield: The coupon return on a bond divided by the bond's face value.

Noncontributory pensions: Pensions funded solely by employers.

Noncontrollable liabilities: Liabilities whose dollar amounts bank customers largely determine once banks have issued the liabilities to them.

Noninterest income: Revenues that depository institutions earn from sources other than interest income, such as trading profits or fees that they charge for services that they provide their customers.

Normal profit: A profit level just sufficient to compensate depository institution owners for holding equity shares in the depository institution instead of purchasing ownership shares of other enterprises.

Off-balance-sheet banking: Bank activities that earn income without expanding the assets and liabilities that the banks report on their balance sheets.

Open-end funds: Mutual funds whose shares are redeemable at any time at prices based on the market values of the mix of financial instruments held by such funds.

Open market operations: Federal Reserve purchases or sales of securities.

Open market purchase: A Federal Reserve purchase of a security, which increases total reserves at depository institutions and thereby raises the size of the monetary base.

Open market sale: A Federal Reserve sale of a security, which reduces total reserves of depository institutions and thereby reduces the size of the monetary base.

Open smart-card system: An e-money system in which consumers use smart cards with embedded microprocessors, which may be issued by a number of institutions, to purchase goods and services offered by multiple retailers.

Open stored-value system: An e-money system in which consumers buy goods and services using cards containing prestored funds that are offered by multiple card issuers and accepted by multiple retailers.

Operating procedure: A guideline for conducting monetary policy over several weeks or months.

Optimal currency area: A region within which fixed exchange rates can be maintained without inhibiting prompt internal adjustments of employment and real GDP to changes in international market conditions.

Option: A financial contract giving the owner the right to buy or sell an underlying financial instrument at a certain price within a specific period of time.

Overlapping-generations approach: A theory of money demand that emphasizes how societies use money as a way to store and transfer wealth across time.

Over-the-counter (OTC) broker-dealer: A broker-dealer that trades shares of stock that are not listed on organized stock exchanges.

Over-the-counter (OTC) stocks: Equity shares offered by companies that do not meet listing requirements for major stock exchanges, or choose not to be listed there, and instead are traded in decentralized markets.

Overvalued currency: A currency whose present market-determined value is higher than the value predicted by an economic theory or model.

Pay-as-you-go pensions: Pensions that are not fully funded when employees retire.

Payment intermediary: An institution that facilitates the transfer of funds between buyer and seller during the course of any purchase of goods, services, or financial assets.

Payment system: A term that refers broadly to the set of mechanisms by which consumers, businesses, governments, and financial institutions exchange payments.

Peak: The point along a business cycle at which real GDP is at its highest level relative to the long-run, natural GDP level.

Pension funds: Institutions that specialize in managing funds that individuals save for retirement.

Perfect competition: A market structure in which no single depository institution can influence loan or deposit interest rates. Hence, rivalry among institutions yields market loan and deposit interest rates that just cover the costs that the institutions incur in making loans and issuing and servicing deposits.

Perpetuity: A bond with an infinite term to maturity.

Point-of-sale (POS) networks: Systems in which consumers pay for retail purchases through direct deductions from their deposit accounts at depository institutions.

Point-of-sale (POS) transfer: Electronic transfer of funds from a buyer's account to the firm from which a good or service is purchased at the time the sale is made.

Policy credibility: The believability of a commitment by a central bank or governmental authority to follow specific policy rules.

Policy rule: A commitment to a fixed strategy no matter what happens to other economic variables.

Policy time lags: The time intervals between the need for a countercyclical monetary policy action and the ultimate effects of that action on an economic variable.

Portfolio: The group of financial instruments held by an individual, which together make up the individual's financial wealth.

Portfolio approach: A theory of exchange rate determination that predicts that a nation's exchange rate adjusts to ensure that its residents are satisfied with their allocation of wealth among holdings of domestic money, domestic bonds, and foreign bonds.

Portfolio motive: The desire to hold money as part of a strategy of balancing the expected rate of return on money with rates of return on other assets.

Portfolio-balance effect: A fundamental prediction of the portfolio approach to exchange rate determination, in which changes in central bank holdings of domestic and foreign bonds alter the equilibrium prices at which traders are willing to hold these bonds, inducing a change in the exchange rate.

Preferred habitat theory: A theory of the term structure of interest rates that views bonds as imperfectly substitutable, so yields on longer-term bonds must be greater than those on shorter-term bonds even if short-term interest rates are not expected to rise or fall.

Preferred stock: Shares of corporate ownership that entail no voting rights but entitle the owner to dividends if any are paid by the corporation and to any residual value of the corporation after other creditors have been paid.

Price-level nonstationarity: Failure of the price level to adjust to a constant long-run average level; upward (or downward) drift of the price level over time.

Primary market: A financial market in which newly issued financial instruments are purchased and sold.

Primary reserves: Cash assets.

Prime rate: The interest rate that U.S. banks charge on loans to the most credit-worthy business borrowers.

Principal: The amount of credit extended when one makes a loan or purchases a bond.

Prospectus: A formal written offer to sell securities.

Purchased funds: Very short-term bank borrowings in the money market.

Purchasing power of money: The value of money in terms of the amount of real goods and services it buys.

Purchasing power parity (PPP): A condition that states that if international arbitrage is unhindered, the price of a good or service in one nation should be the same as the exchange-rate-adjusted price of the same good or service in another nation.

Pure monopoly: The dominance of a loan or deposit market by a single depository institution or by a small group of institutions that work together to maximize their profits.

Put option: An option contract giving the owner the right to sell a financial instrument at a specific price.

Quantity theory of money: The theory that people hold money primarily for transactions purposes; ultimately yields a relationship between the price level and desired real expenditures on final goods and services.

Rational expectations hypothesis: The idea that individuals form expectations based on all available past and current information and on an essential understanding of factors that affect the price level.

Real balance effect: An increase in the nominal rate of interest that results from an increase in the price level, holding total depository institution reserves unchanged.

Real bills doctrine: A bank management philosophy that calls for lending primarily to borrowers who will use the funds to finance production or shipping of physical goods, thereby ensuring speedy repayment of the loans.

Real exchange rate: An exchange rate that has been adjusted for differences between two nations' price levels, thereby yielding the implied rate of exchange of goods and services between those nations.

Real gross domestic product (real GDP): A price-adjusted measure of aggregate output, or nominal GDP divided by the GDP price deflator.

Real interest parity: An equality between two nations' real interest rates that arises if both uncovered interest parity and relative purchasing power parity are satisfied.

Real interest rate: The anticipated rate of return from holding a financial instrument after taking into account the extent to which inflation is expected to reduce the amount of goods and services that this return could be used to buy.

Real money balances: The purchasing power of the quantity of money in circulation, measured as the nominal quantity of money divided by an index measure of the prices of goods and services.

Recession: A decline in real GDP lasting at least two consecutive quarters, which can cause real GDP to fall below its long-run, natural level.

Recognition lag: The interval that passes between the need for a countercyclical policy action and the recognition of this need by a policymaker.

Redlining: A practice under which some depository institution managers allegedly have refused to lend to individuals or businesses located in particular geographic areas.

Regulatory arbitrage: The act of trying to avoid regulations imposed by banking authorities in one's home country by moving offices and funds to countries with less constraining regulations.

Reinvestment risk: The possibility that available yields on short-term financial instruments may decline, in which case holdings of longer-term instruments might be preferable.

Repurchase agreement: A contract to sell financial assets with a promise to repurchase them at a later time.

Required reserves: Legally mandated reserve holdings at depository institutions, which are proportional to the dollar amounts of transactions accounts.

Required reserve ratios: Fractions of transactions deposit balances that the Federal Reserve mandates that depository institutions maintain either as deposits with Federal Reserve banks or as vault cash.

Reserves: Cash held by depository institutions in their vaults or on deposit with the Federal Reserve System.

Reserve demand schedule: A graphical depiction of the inverse relationship between the total amount of reserves demanded by depository institutions and the federal funds rate.

Reserve deposits: Deposit accounts that depository institutions maintain at Federal Reserve banks.

Reserve supply schedule: A graphical depiction of the relationship between the total amount of reserves supplied by the Fed and the federal funds rate.

Response lag: The interval between the recognition of a need for a countercyclical policy action and the actual implementation of the policy action.

Return on assets: A depository institution's profit as a percentage of its total assets.

Return on equity: A depository institution's profit as a percentage of its equity capital.

Revolving credit: Loans to individuals that permit them to borrow automatically up to specified limits and to repay the balance of the loan at any time.

Revolving credit commitments: Loan commitments that permit borrowers to borrow and repay as often as they wish within an interval in which the commitment is binding on a depository institution.

Risk aversion: The preference, other things being equal, to hold assets whose returns exhibit less variability.

Risk premium: The amount by which one instrument's yield exceeds the yield of another instrument as a result of the first instrument being riskier and less liquid than the second.

Risk structure of interest rates: The relationship among yields on financial instruments that have the same maturity but differ because of variations in default risk, liquidity, and tax rates.

Risk-adjusted assets: A weighted average of bank assets that regulators compute to account for risk differences across types of assets.

Risk-based capital requirements: Regulatory capital standards that account for risk factors that distinguish different depository institutions.

Risk-based deposit insurance premiums: Premiums that depository institutions pay the FDIC based on the varying degrees to which they are capitalized and on the differing risk factors that they exhibit.

Sales finance companies: Finance companies that specialize in making loans to individuals for the purchase of items from specific retailers or manufacturers.

Saving: Forgone consumption.

Savings and loan association: A type of depository institution that has traditionally specialized in mortgage lending.

Savings Association Insurance Fund (SAIF): The FDIC's fund that covers insured deposits of savings institutions.

Savings bank: Another type of depository institution that has specialized in mortgage lending.

Savings deposits: Interest-bearing savings accounts without set maturities.

Secondary market: A financial market in which financial instruments issued in the past are traded.

Secondary reserves: Securities that depository institutions can easily convert to cash in the event that such a need arises.

Securities: Financial instruments.

Securities and Exchange Commission (SEC): A group of five presidentially appointed members whose mandate is to enforce rules governing securities trading.

Securities underwriting: A guarantee by an investment bank that a firm that issues new stocks or bonds will receive a specified minimum price per share of stock or per bond.

Securitization: The process of pooling loans with similar risk characteristics and selling the loan pool in the form of a tradable financial instrument.

Segmented markets theory: A theory of the term structure of interest rates that views bonds with differing maturities as nonsubstitutable, so their yields differ because they are determined in separate markets.

Seigniorage: The difference between the market value of money and the cost of its production, which is gained by the government that produces and issues the money.

Shiftability theory: A management approach in which depository institutions hold a mix of illiquid loans and more liquid securities that act as a secondary reserve held as a contingency against potential liquidity problems.

Shopping-time theory of money demand: A theory of the demand for money that focuses on money's role in helping people reduce the amount of time they spend shopping, thereby freeing up more time for leisure or work.

Short position: An obligation to sell a financial instrument at a given price and at a specific time.

Short run: A period sufficiently brief that nominal wages and other input prices do not adjust in equal proportion to a change in the price level.

Short-run aggregate supply schedule: The relationship between the production of real GDP and the price level when there is not enough time for nominal wages and other input prices to adjust in equal proportion to a change in the price level.

Short-term maturity: Maturity of less than one year.

Signal-extraction problem: The problem of trying to infer a policymaker's true goals from the imperfect signal transmitted by the policymaker's actions.

Simultaneity problem: The problem of accounting for the possibility that factors influencing the quantity of money demanded are themselves affected by how many real money balances people hold, which can complicate assessments of how well real-world observations square with theories of money demand.

Single-employer pensions: Pensions that are established by an employer only for its own employees and are nontransferable to other employers.

Small-denomination time deposits: Deposits with set maturities and denominations of less than $100,000.

Smart card: A card containing a microprocessor that permits storage of funds via security programming, that can communicate with other computers, and that does not require online authorization for funds transfer to occur.

Specialists: Stock exchange members that are charged with trading on their own accounts to prevent dramatic movements in stock prices.

Spot exchange rate: The spot-market price of a currency indicating how much of one country's currency must be given up in immediate exchange for a unit of another nation's currency.

Spot market: A market for contracts requiring the immediate sale or purchase of an asset.

Standard of deferred payment: An attribute of money that permits it to be used as a means of valuing future receipts in loan contracts.

Standby commitment underwriting: An investment banking arrangement in which the investment bank earns commissions for helping the issuing firm sell its securities under the guarantee that the investment bank will purchase for resale any initially unsold securities.

Sterilization: A central bank action to prevent variations in its foreign exchange reserves from affecting the monetary base.

Stock exchanges: Organized marketplaces for corporate equities and bonds.

Stock index future: An agreement to deliver, on a specified date, a portfolio of stocks represented by a stock price index.

Stock options: Options to buy or sell firm equity shares.

Store of value: An attribute of money that allows it to be held for future use without loss of value in the meantime.

Structural unemployment: The portion of total unemployment resulting from a poor match of workers' abilities and skills with current needs of employers.

Structure-conduct-performance (SCP) model: A theory of depository institution market structure in which the structure of loan and deposit markets influences the behavior (conduct) of depository institutions in those markets, thereby affecting their performance.

Structured early intervention and resolution (SEIR): A regulatory system, established by the FDIC Improvement Act of 1991, that authorizes the FDIC to intervene quickly in the management of a depository institution that threatens to cause losses for the federal deposit insurance funds.

Subordinated notes and debentures: Capital market instruments with maturities in excess of one year that banks issue with the provision that depositors have primary claim to bank assets in the event of failure.

Supplementary capital: Under current standards used to calculate required capital, a measure that includes certain preferred stock and most subordinated debt.

Supranormal profits: Levels of profit above those required to induce depository institution owners to hold shares of ownership in those institutions instead of shares of other businesses.

Swap: A contract entailing an exchange of payment flows between two parties.

Syndicated loan: A loan arranged by one or two banks but funded by these and other banks.

Systemic risk: The risk that some depository institutions may not be able to meet the terms of their credit agreements because of failures by other institutions to settle transactions that otherwise are not related.

T-account: A side-by-side listing of the assets and liabilities of a business such as a depository institution.

Term federal funds: Interbank loans with maturities exceeding one day.

Term life policy: A life insurance policy under which an individual is insured only during a limited period that the policy is in effect.

Term premium: An amount by which the yield on a long-term bond must exceed the yield on a short-term bond to make individuals willing to hold either bond if they expect short-term bond yields to remain unchanged.

Term structure of interest rates: The relationship among yields on financial instruments with identical risk, liquidity, and tax characteristics but differing terms to maturity.

Terminally funded pensions: Pensions that must be fully funded by the date that an employee retires.

Time-inconsistency problem: The policy problem that can result if a policymaker has the ability, at a future time, to alter its strategy in a way that is inconsistent both with the desires and strategies of private individuals and with its own initially announced intentions.

Too-big-to-fail policy: A regulatory policy that protects the largest depository institutions from failure solely because regulators believe that such failure could undermine the public's confidence in the financial system.

Total capital: Under current bank capital requirements, the sum of core capital and supplementary capital.

Total reserves: The total balances that depository institutions hold on deposit with Federal Reserve banks or as vault cash.

Trading Desk: The Fed's term for the office at the Federal Reserve Bank of New York that conducts open market operations on the Fed's behalf.

Transaction risk: A foreign exchange risk arising from the possibility that the proceeds from trading a financial instrument may change as a result of exchange rate variations.

Transactions deposits: Checking accounts.

Transactions motive: The desire to hold currency and transactions deposits to use as media of exchange in planned transactions.

Translation risk: A foreign exchange risk resulting from altered home-currency values of foreign-currency-denominated financial instruments caused by fluctuations in exchange rates.

Transmission lag: The interval that elapses between the implementation of an intended countercyclical policy and its ultimate effects on an economic variable.

Treasury bills (T-bills): Short-term debt obligations of the federal government issued with maturities of three, six, or twelve months.

Treasury bonds: Treasury securities with maturities of ten years or more.

Treasury notes: Treasury securities with maturities ranging from one to ten years.

Treasury tax and loan (TT&L) accounts: U.S. Treasury checking accounts at private depository institutions.

Trough: The point along a business cycle at which real GDP is at its lowest level relative to the long-run natural GDP level.

Ultimate goals: The final objectives of economic policies.

Uncovered interest parity: A relationship between interest rates on bonds that are similar in all respects other than that they are denominated in different nations' currencies. According to this condition, the yield on the bond denominated in the currency that holders anticipate will depreciate must exceed the yield on the other bond by the rate at which the currency is expected to depreciate.

Undervalued currency: A currency whose present market-determined value is lower than that predicted by an economic theory or model.

Unemployment rate: The percentage of the civilian labor force that is unemployed.

Unit of account: An attribute of money that permits it to be used as a measure of the value of goods, services, and financial assets.

Universal banking: A banking environment in which banks face few, if any, restrictions on their powers to offer a full range of financial services and to own shares of stock in corporations.

Value-at-risk model: A statistical framework for evaluating how changes in interest rates and financial instrument prices are likely to affect the overall value of a portfolio of financial assets.

Variable annuity: A financial instrument, typically issued by an insurance company, that beginning on a specific future date pays the owner a stream of returns that depends on the value of an underlying portfolio of assets.

Vault cash: Currency that a depository institution holds on location to honor cash withdrawals by depositors.

Vehicle currency: A commonly accepted currency that is used to denominate a transaction that does not take place in the nation that issues the currency.

Wealth: An individual's total resources.

Wealth elasticity of demand: The percentage change in the quantity of an asset demanded by an individual divided by a given percentage change in the individual's wealth.

Whole life policy: A life insurance policy whose benefits are payable to a beneficiary whenever the insured person's death occurs and that accumulates a cash value that the policyholder may acquire prior to his or her death.

Wire transfers: Payments made via telephone lines or through fiber-optic cables.

Yield curve: A chart depicting the relationship among yields on bonds that differ only in their terms to maturity.

Yield to maturity: The rate of return on a bond if it is held until it matures, which reflects the market price of the bond, the bond's coupon return, and any capital gain from holding the bond to maturity.

Zero-coupon bonds: Bonds that pay lump-sum amounts at maturity.

Index